PAUL
the
Missionary

---

*Realities, Strategies
and Methods*

ECKHARD J.
SCHNABEL

IVP Academic
An imprint of InterVarsity Press
Downers Grove, Illinois

Apollos
Nottingham, England

InterVarsity Press, USA
P.O. Box 1400, Downers Grove, IL 60515-1426, USA
World Wide Web: www.ivpress.com
Email: email@ivpress.com

APOLLOS (an imprint of Inter-Varsity Press, England)
Norton Street, Nottingham NG7 3HR, England
Website: www.ivpbooks.com
Email: ivp@ivpbooks.com

InterVarsity Press®, USA, is the book-publishing division of InterVarsity Christian Fellowship/USA®, a student movement active on campus at hundreds of universities, colleges and schools of nursing in the United States of America, and a member movement of the International Fellowship of Evangelical Students. For information about local and regional activities, write Public Relations Dept., InterVarsity Christian Fellowship/USA, 6400 Schroeder Rd., P.O. Box 7895, Madison, WI 53707-7895, or visit the IVCF website at <www.intervarsity.org>.

Inter-Varsity Press, England, is closely linked with the Universities and Colleges Christian Fellowship, a student movement connecting Christian Unions throughout Great Britain, and a member movement of the International Fellowship of Evangelical Students. Website: www.uccf.org.uk

Design: Cindy Kiple

Images: Scala/Art Resource, NY

USA ISBN 978-0-8308-2887-6

UK ISBN 978-1-84474-349-0

Printed in the United States of America ∞

InterVarsity Press is committed to protecting the environment and to the responsible use of natural resources. As a member of Green Press Initiative we use recycled paper whenever possible. To learn more about the Green Press Initiative, visit <www.greenpressinitiative.org>.

Library of Congress Cataloging-in-Publication Data

Schnabel, Eckhard J.
  Paul, the missionary: realities, strategies, and methods / Eckhard
J. Schnabel.
    p. cm.
  Includes bibliographical references and indexes.
  ISBN 978-0-8308-2887-6 (pbk.: alk. paper)
  1. Paul, the Apostle, Saint. 2. Missionaries—Biography. 3.
Missions—Biblical teaching. 4. Bible. N.T. Epistles of
Paul—Criticism, interpretation, etc. 5. Apostles—Biography. I.
Title.
BS2506.3.S35 2008
225.9'2—dc22
[B]

                                                          2008022665

P	21	20	19	18	17	16	15	14	13	12	11	10	9	8	7	6	5	4	3	2	1
Y	26	25	24	23	22	21	20	19	18	17	16	15	14	13	12	11	10		09		08	

For Peter T. O'Brien

Missionary, Theologian, Pastor and Friend

Contents

Preface 11

Abbreviations 17

List of Figures and Tables 20

Introduction 21

   1   Missionary Strategies and Methods: *Defining Terms* 22

   2   The Task of Missionary Work: *Describing Goals* 32

   3   Missionary Methods as a Problem: *Finding Solutions* 34

   4   Descriptive and Normative Readings:
      Hermeneutical Clarifications 37

1 The Missionary Work of the Apostle Paul 39

   1.1 Paul, Apostle to Jews and Gentiles: *Conversion and Call* . . . 40

   1.2 Paul and Jerusalem 47

   1.3 Paul in Arabia, Jerusalem, Cilicia and Syria 58

   1.4 Paul on Cyprus and in Galatia 74

   1.5 Paul in Macedonia and Achaia 89

   1.6 Paul in the Province of Asia 107

1.7 Paul in Illyricum, Caesarea, Rome, Spain,
     Crete and Rome 111

2 **The Missionary Task According to Paul's Letters** 123

2.1 The Letter to the Galatian Christians. 124

2.2 The Letters to the Christians in Macedonia:
     Thessalonians and Philippians. 126

2.3 The Letters to the Christians in Achaia: *Corinthians* 130

2.4 The Letter to the Christians in the City of Rome. 139

2.5 The Letters to the Christians in Asia:
     Colossians and Ephesians 143

2.6 The Letters to Coworkers: *Timothy and Titus.* 149

2.7 The Apostle as Missionary, Pastor and Theologian 151

3 **The Missionary Message of the Apostle Paul** 155

3.1 Preaching Before Jewish Audiences 156

3.2 Preaching Before Gentile Audiences 162

3.3 Explaining the Gospel in Civic Settings 168

3.4 Ideological Confrontation:
     The Proclamation of Jesus Messiah and Kyrios 183

3.5 Cultural Confrontation: *The Explication of the Gospel.* 189

3.6 Pastoral Consolidation:
     Encouragement for the Followers of Jesus 196

3.7 Apologetic Confrontation: *The Defense of the Gospel* 200

4 **The Missionary Goals of the Apostle Paul** 209

4.1 Preaching the Gospel 210

4.2 Preaching the Gospel to Jews and to Gentiles. 215

4.3 Geographical Movement 221

4.4 Conversion of Individuals 225

4.5 Establishing Communities of Followers of Jesus 231

4.6 Teaching New Converts 236

4.7 Training New Missionaries 248

5 The Missionary Methods of the Apostle Paul 256

5.1 Cities, Regions and Provinces 258

5.2 Synagogues, Marketplaces, Lecture Halls, Workshops
and Private Houses 287

5.3 Ethnic Identity, Class and Culture 306

5.4 Establishing Contact as a Public Speaker 334

5.5 The Persuasiveness of the Message: *The Problem of Rhetoric* . 341

5.6 The Credibility of the Messenger 354

5.7 Explanations for Missionary Success 356

6 The Task of Missionary Work in the Twenty-First Century . 374

6.1 The Calling and Sending of Missionaries 382

6.2 The Content of Missionary Proclamation 394

6.3 The Proclamation of the Gospel and Church Planting . . . 400

6.4 The Teaching of the Followers of Jesus 419

6.5 The Purpose and the Work of the Local Church 422

6.6 The Challenge of Culture 445

6.7 The Power of God 451

Bibliography 459

Author Index 493

Subject Index 497

Scripture Index 510

Preface

IT HAS BEEN NEARLY ONE HUNDRED YEARS that Roland Allen wrote a book titled *Missionary Methods: St. Paul's or Ours? A Study of the Church in the Four Provinces*, published in the series Library of Historic Theology by Robert Scott Roxburghe House in London in 1912. Born in 1868, Allen had trained as an Anglican priest and served in northern China with the Society for the Propagation of the Gospel from 1895 until 1903. During the Boxer Rebellion in 1900, he was the chaplain to the British Legation in Beijing. After he had to return to England due to ill health, he served as a vicar in the Church of England, resigning in 1907 because he found himself unable to perform solemn religious ceremonies for undeserving persons "who habitually neglect their religious duties, or openly deny the truth of the Creeds, or by the immorality of their lives openly defy the laws of God." While helping various missionary societies with deputation work, he read the works of Adolf von Harnack (*The Mission and Expansion of Christianity in the First Three Centuries*. 2nd ed. London: Williams & Norgate, 1908) and William M. Ramsay (*St. Paul the Traveller and the Roman Citizen*. London: Hodder & Stoughton, 1896), processing his own experiences in China and (in 1910/1911) in India. While many were enthusiastic about the World Missionary Conference in Edinburgh (1910), others regarded it as "the apotheosis of missionary triumphalism"; for Allen, the conference epitomized his worst misgivings about the current attitudes of Western missionaries. His growing convictions about the nature of authentic missionary work prompted him to write *Missionary Methods: St. Paul's or Ours?*[1]

In part one Allen examines the political, geographical, moral and social conditions of the world in which Paul operated as a missionary, concluding that he enjoyed no peculiar advantages in proclaiming the gospel. Paul had no preconceived strategy as regards his geographical movements: he went where God's Spirit led him, he sought open doors, he aimed at converting men and women to faith in Jesus Christ. The second part studies Paul's presentation of the gospel, including the significance of miracles and the role of financial support. Part three focuses on Paul's training of the new converts: Paul planted churches that quickly became self-supporting and self-governing, as the apostle did not rely on Christian workers paid from foreign sources. As regards his teaching, Paul did not provide the new churches with elaborate and extensive doctrinal teaching, but limited himself to establish simple and strong foundations. Paul left the newly planted churches after a few months, trusting in the power of the Holy Spirit to guide the new communities of believers. In part four Allen examines the realities of authority and discipline in the new churches, arguing that Paul did not strive to formulate a law and enforce an external authority; rather than making clear-cut legal demands that must be obeyed to the letter, Paul suggests principles and trusts the Holy Spirit, who dwells in the church, to apply these principles to specific problems as they arise. For Paul the unity of the church is not based on organization but on the power of the Holy Spirit and on the life that the Spirit inspires. In the concluding part five Allen laments that on the mission field of his day, the churches established by missionaries have not become indigenous: they continued to be dependent on the West, and they did not display any new forms of Christian life. He identifies the causes of this failure in racial and religious pride, in lack of faith that has created fear and distrust of "native" independence. Allen believes that two fundamental principles that guided Paul's missionary work have universal relevance. First, Paul preached the gospel, not a law. Second, since Paul

---

[1]See Hubert J. B. Allen, *Roland Allen: Pioneer, Priest, and Prophet* (Cincinnati: Forward Movement Publications; Grand Rapids: Eerdmans, 1995). See the narrative of Hubert Allen, Roland Allen's grandson, in <www.ocms.ac.uk/pdf/roland_allen.pdf>.

trusted in the Holy Spirit, he believed in his converts, willing to "retire" from newly established churches so that they might learn to exercise the powers which they possessed in Jesus Christ.

Henry Whitehead, bishop of Madras, writes in his introduction to the first edition of 1912 that he is grateful to Mr. Allen "for this effort to bring our missionary methods to the test of apostolic precedent." He laments the fact that there exists

> a very wide and marked difference between the methods and principles of St. Paul and the methods and principles of modern missions. We neglect the open doors and then spend time and money largely in preaching to people who show no willingness to accept the faith. We found Churches and keep them in leading strings for a hundred years, and even then are not within measurable distance of giving them independence. We transplant to the mission field the elaborate system of teaching and organization with which we are familiar at home. We impose discipline upon our converts as an external law and authority.

Whitehead ends his introduction by affirming that "the fact remains that, where St. Paul conspicuously succeeded, we have conspicuously failed. May it not be because we have worked upon widely different principles?"[2]

The reprints of Allen's *Missionary Methods* since the 1950s include a foreword by Bishop Lesslie Newbigin, which ends with a "warning" for the reader: "Once he has started reading Allen, he will be compelled to go on. He will find that this quiet voice has a strange relevance and immediacy to the problems of the Church in our day. And I shall be surprised if he does not find before long that many of his accustomed ideas are being questioned by a voice more searching than the word of man."[3] If Allen had agreed with this sentiment, he would have pointed out that this voice is the voice of God, the Lord of the mission of the church, who continues to speak to the church through the example of the apostle Paul. By no means outdated, Allen's work deserves to be read in the twenty-first century.

---

[2] Henry Whitehead, in Roland Allen, *Missionary Methods: St. Paul's or Ours? A Study of the Church in the Four Provinces*, Library of Historic Theology (London: Robert Scott Roxburghe, 1912), pp. vii-ix.

[3] Lesslie Newbigin, in Roland Allen, *Missionary Methods: St. Paul's or Ours?* (Reprint; Grand Rapids: Eerdmans, 2001), pp. i-iii.

This book is not an attempt to update Allen's work in all respects. It is an invitation to read the relevant New Testament texts more closely and to take note of the realities of the Greco-Roman world which impacted Paul's missionary work more accurately. Our knowledge of the Greco-Roman world and of Second Temple Judaism has increased; New Testament scholarship has progressed. In our own Christian context today, the church has become truly global: there are more practicing Christians in the Majority World, formerly called the Third World, than in Europe and North America. The churches in Africa, Asia and Latin America have become truly independent, sending more missionaries than the churches in Europe and North America.

Allen wrote as a former missionary in China and as a priest in the Church of England who had become frustrated with the structures and with some of the entrenched traditions of both his church and of missionary societies. I write as a New Testament scholar who has taught theological students in the Philippines, Germany and the United States of America. Allen wrote about Paul with a view to challenge mission societies and missionaries to change their methods, indeed their behavior. I write about Paul with a view to challenge pastors and missionaries, students and practitioners to read Paul again, more closely than before, and to evaluate the goals and the methods of their pastoral and missionary ministry in the light of the missionary work of the apostle. This focus explains, among other matters, that I do not explore the theme of the kingdom of God which some contemporary missiologists regard as a fundamental theological concept that encompasses everything that the church does. While Paul uses the phrase *kingdom of God* several times, clearly assuming that his readers know what he is talking about, it is not a central category for his theology as we encounter it in his letters. The focus on Paul means that this book is a historical study—mostly, since chapter six explores several basic matters, related to questions of missionary practice and church growth, seeking to help the reader to move from the New Testament to biblical evaluations of current practices and to practical applications of the missionary mandate. Still, readers should not look for a discussion of topics such as globalization, tribalization, poverty, megacities, social and economic injustice, environmental issues such as global warning, terrorism, digital communication, local and national Christian movements, indigenous churches in the majority world, and countless missionary initiatives and church growth methods—all important matters that directly affect missionary work today.

A more technical treatment of Paul's missionary vision, work and methods can be found in chapters twenty-four through twenty-eight of my *Early Christian Mission* (InterVarsity Press 2004, pp. 923-1485). There the reader will find a fuller treatment of many of the matters discussed in the present book. Some material has been adapted from several published essays: "Contextualizing Paul in Athens: The Proclamation of the Gospel Before Pagan Audiences in the Graeco-Roman World," *Religion & Theology* 12 (2005): 172-90; "The Objectives of Change, Factors of Transformation, and the Causes of Results: The Evidence of Paul's Corinthian Correspondence," *Trinity Journal* 12 (2005): 179-204; "Other Religions: Saving or Secular," in *The Gospel for All Nations: A Response to Inclusivism*, edited by Chris Morgan and Robert Peterson (Downers Grove, Ill.: InterVarsity Press, 2008), pp. 98-122; as well as from my commentary on Paul's first letter to the Corinthians (*Der erste Brief des Paulus an die Korinther. Historisch-Theologische Auslegung*. Wuppertal: R. Brockhaus, 2006). The information in the notes provides basic documentation for primary and secondary sources and for views held by various authors. For fuller documentation the reader is directed to *Early Christian Mission*.

Various parts of this book have been presented in lecture form in various academic settings, including the conferences of the German Evangelical Theological Society in Bad Blankenburg, Germany (2001); the Evangelical Theological Society in Toronto, Canada (2002); the German Evangelical Missiological Society in Korntal, Germany (2005); and the New Testament colloquium at the University of South Africa in Pretoria, South Africa (2005); the Mid-West Regional Conference of the Evangelical Missiological Society in Deerfield, Illinois (2005); the Gheens Lectures at Southern Baptist Theological Seminary in Louisville, Kentucky (2006); the Drumwright Lectures at Southwestern Baptist Theological Seminary in Fort Worth, Texas (2007); and lectures at Cincinnati Christian University and Colombo Theological Seminary, Sri Lanka (2007). It was a special privilege to speak before missionaries who have been serving courageously and faithfully in the Republic of Chad in situations that are at least as challenging as those in which the apostle Paul found himself. I am grateful to the organizers and hosts of these conferences and lectureships and to the faculty and students who listened and discussed matters pertaining to the missionary work of the early church. I have immensely benefited from the many thoughtful responses and the critical interaction, which have helped me to sharpen my thinking.

Special thanks are due to several colleagues who have read the manuscript in whole or in part and who have made valuable suggestions: Richard Cook, Craig Ott, James Plueddemann, Elizabeth Yao-Hwa Sung and How Chuang Chua. David Luy, my teaching assistant, has carefully read the manuscript and noted, among many other helpful suggestions, complex sentences that could benefit from more intelligible restatement. Benjamin Schnabel, competent as always, helped with the maps. Finally, I thank Daniel Reid from InterVarsity Press for his continued interest in the early Christian mission and for suggesting this project.

Eckhard J. Schnabel

Abbreviations

AGAJU	Arbeiten zur Geschichte des antiken Judentums und des Urchristentums
AncB	Anchor Bible
AThANT	Abhandlungen zur Theologie des Alten und Neuen Testaments
BBR	*Bulletin for Biblical Research*
BDAG	W. Bauer, F. W. Danker, W. F. Arndt, F. W. Gingrich. *A Greek-English Lexicon of the New Testament and Other Early Christian Literature*. 3rd ed.
BECNT	Baker Exegetical Commentary on the New Testament
BNTC	Black's New Testament Commentaries
BNP	*Brill's New Pauly*
BZ	*Biblische Zeitschrift*
BZNW	Beihefte zur Zeitschrift für die neutestamentliche Wissenschaft
CBQ	*Catholic Biblical Quarterly*
DLNTD	*Dictionary of the Later New Testament and Its Developments*. Edited by P. H. Davids and R. P. Martin
DPL	*Dictionary of Paul and His Letters*. Edited by G. F. Hawthorne, R. P. Martin and D. G. Reid
EDNT	*Exegetical Dictionary of the New Testament*. Edited by H. Balz and G. Schneider

EDWM	*Evangelical Dictionary of World Missions.* Edited by A. S. Moreau
EKK	Evangelisch-Katholischer Kommentar
EMQ	*Evangelical Missions Quarterly*
EpComm	Epworth Commentary
EPRO	Études préliminaires aux religions orientales dans l'empire romain
ETAM	Ergänzungsbände zu den Tituli Asiae Minoris
FRLANT	Forschungen zur Religion und Literatur des Alten und Neuen Testaments
HThR	*Harvard Theological Review*
HTS	Harvard Theological Studies
ICC	International Critical Commentary
IG	Inscriptiones Graecae. Edited by O. Kern
IGR	*Inscriptiones Graecae ad res Romanas pertinentes.* Edited by E. Leroux
IRM	*International Review of Mission*
IThS	Innsbrucker theologische Studien
JBL	*Journal of Biblical Literature*
JETS	*Journal of the Evangelical Theological Society*
JPTSup	Journal of Pentecostal Theology Supplement Series
JRA	*Journal of Roman Archaeology*
JRASup	Journal of Roman Archaeology Supplement Series
JSNT	*Journal for the Study of the New Testament*
JSNTSup	Journal for the Study of the New Testament Supplement Series
JSOT	*Journal for the Study of the Old Testament*
JTS	*Journal of Theological Studies*
KEK	Kritisch-exegetischer Kommentar über das Neue Testament
MAMA	Monumenta Asiae Minoris Antiqua
Neot	*Neotestamentica*
NICNT	New International Commentary on the New Testament
NICOT	New International Commentary on the Old Testament
NIDNTT	*The New International Dictionary of New Testament Theology.* Edited by C. Brown
NIGTC	New International Greek Testament Commentary

NSBT	New Studies in Biblical Theology
NTS	*New Testament Studies*
NTTS	New Testament Tools and Studies
NTSup	Novum Testamentum Supplement Series
OCD	*The Oxford Classical Dictionary.* 3rd edition. Edited by S. Hornblower and A. Spawforth
OED	*Oxford English Dictionary*
OGIS	*Orientis graeci inscriptiones selectae.* Edited by W. Dittenberger
PNTC	Pillar New Testament Commentary
PTMS	Pittsburgh Theological Monograph Series
SEG	*Supplementum epigraphicum graecum*
SNTSMS	Society of New Testament Studies Monograph Series
StUNT	Studien zur Umwelt des Neuen Testaments
TDNT	*Theological Dictionary of the New Testament.* Edited by G. Kittel and G. Friedrich
TRE	*Theologische Realenzyklopädie.* Edited by G. Krause and G. Müller
TSAJ	Texte und Studien zum Antiken Judentum
TynB	*Tyndale Bulletin*
WBC	Word Biblical Commentary
WMANT	Wissenschaftliche Monographien zum Alten und Neuen Testament
WUNT	Wissenschaftliche Untersuchungen zum Neuen Testament
ZBK	*Zürcher Bibelkommentare*
ZPE	*Zeitschrift für Papyrologie und Epigraphik*
ZThK	*Zeitchrift für Theologie und Kirche*

List of Figures and Tables

FIGURES

1.1 Nabatea. 62

1.2 The province of Syria (North) 68

1.3 Cilicia 70

1.4 Cyprus 76

1.5 Lycia-Pamphylia 78

1.6 The province of Galatia (South) 80

1.7 The province of Asia 90

1.8 Bithynia-Pontus 91

1.9 Macedonia 93

1.10 Macedonia and Achaia. 95

1.11 Achaia 99

1.12 Illyricum 114

1.13 Spain 119

1.14 Crete 120

5.1 The synagogue in Ostia 291

5.2 The forum in Corinth 296

5.3 Workshop in the Casa del Fabbra in Pompeii 299

5.4 Private house (Terrace House 2) in Ephesus 302

TABLES

1.1 Paul's Visits to Jerusalem 58

1.2 Paul's Travels 122

Introduction

WHEN ROLAND ALLEN WROTE ABOUT Paul's missionary methods, he did not have to define terms. He could begin with a paragraph—often quoted by missionaries and missiologists—that summarizes the apostle's missionary work:

> In little more than ten years St Paul established the Church in four provinces of the Empire, Galatia, Macedonia, Achaia and Asia. Before AD 47 there were no churches in these provinces; in AD 57 St Paul could speak as if his work there was done, and could plan extensive tours into the far west without anxiety lest the churches which he had founded might perish in his absence for want of his guidance and support.[1]

Nearly a hundred years later, it is no longer self-evident what the term *mission* should not imply.

Some Christians operate with a very broad understanding of *mission*, describing all activities of the church as "missional," that is, characterized by mission insofar as they participate in "God's mission" *(missio Dei).*[2] Thus social work, projects supporting racial reconciliation, charitable giving, drama groups and much more constitutes mission. Some reject the traditional notion that mission has anything to do with "inducing people

---

[1]Roland Allen, *Missionary Methods: St. Paul's or Ours?* Library of Historic Theology (London: Robert Scott Roxburghe, 1912), p. 3.
[2]See recently Christopher J. H. Wright, *The Mission of God: Unlocking the Bible's Grand Narrative* (Downers Grove, Ill.: InterVarsity Press, 2006), pp. 48-74.

of non-Christian faiths or of other Christian denominations to convert to one's own church."[3] Some distinguish "mission" and "missions": the former describes God's comprehensive purposes for the world, purposes in whose realization God's people participate, while the latter describes the activity of missionaries and evangelists, church planters and laypeople who reach unbelievers with the gospel of Jesus Christ. The following paragraphs define the term *mission* and examine the meaning and the relevance of the terms *strategy* and *method* as applied to the missionary work of the apostle Paul.

1. Missionary Strategies and Methods: Defining Terms

Before explaining what I mean when I speak of missionary strategies and methods, I need to define what the term *mission* means. In the context of historical and sociological studies of Christianity and also of other religions, the following definition of *mission* (or *missions* in terms of "missionary work") includes both general criteria and particular activities. *The term "mission" or "missions" refers to the activity of a community of faith that distinguishes itself from its environment in terms of both religious belief (theology) and social behavior (ethics), that is convinced of the truth claims of its faith, and that actively works to win other people to the content of faith and the way of life of whose truth and necessity the members of that community are convinced.*[4] When I define the word *mission* for a study that examines the missionary work of the apostle Paul and its relevance for doing missionary work today, three factors need to be noted.

Intentionality and movement. First, since the English term *mission* is derived from the Latin words *missio* ("sending") and *mittere* ("to send"), it seems obvious that intentionality and movement should be integral parts

---

[3]Wolfgang Reinbold, *Propaganda und Mission im ältesten Christentum. Eine Untersuchung zu den Modalitäten der Ausbreitung der frühen Kirche*, FRLANT 188 (Göttingen: Vandenhoeck & Ruprecht, 2000), p. 7, with quotations from J. Wietzke, J. Moltmann and V. Fedorov.

[4]Eckhard J. Schnabel, *Early Christian Mission* (Downers Grove, Ill.: InterVarsity Press, 2004), 1:11. Cf. Eric J. Sharpe, "Mission," in *A Dictionary of Comparative Religion*, ed. S. G. F. Brandon (London: Weidenfeld & Nicolson, 1970), p. 444; Francis M. DuBose, *God Who Sends: A Fresh Quest for Biblical Mission* (Nashville: Broadman, 1983); Martin Goodman, *Mission and Conversion: Proselytizing in the Religious History of the Roman Empire* (Oxford: Clarendon, 1994), pp. 2-7; Reidar Hvalvik, *The Struggle for Scripture and Covenant: The Purpose of the Epistle of Barnabas and Jewish-Christian Competition in the Second Century*, WUNT 2/82 (Tübingen: Mohr Siebeck, 1996), pp. 270-71.

in the definition of *mission* if we continue to use this term. Mission proceeds from an authority that sends envoys and a message to other people
and to other places.[5] There is no reason to abandon either intentionality or
geographical movement in the definition of *mission*. Intentionality refers
to the purpose of the mission as designed by the initiator or sender of the
messenger as well as to the purpose of the mission as understood by the
messenger. Geographical movement is movement from point A to point
B. The distance between these two points depends on the mission. In the
Greek world the envoys that one city sends to another may have to travel
(by foot) only a day or two before they reach the community that they
have been tasked to reach with a particular message. Envoys sent by the
Roman emperor may have to travel for several weeks before they reach,
for example, the ruler of Armenia, with whom the emperor seeks to communicate. Mission thus understood has nothing to do with traveling to
"foreign" countries or with crossing cultures.

The two features of intentionality and movement are present in Jesus'
mission. As God sent Jesus Christ into the world, both intentionality and
movement from one place to another is involved. John's Gospel makes this
point most explicitly. Without using "sending" language, the prologue of
the Fourth Gospel[6] begins with a statement about the existence and the
identity of "the Word," which is Jesus "in the beginning" (i.e., before the
creation of the world):

> In the beginning was the Word, and the Word was with God, and the
> Word was God. *He was in the beginning with God.* All things came into
> being through him, and without him not one thing came into being. (Jn
> 1:1-3a, emphasis added)

The text continues to explain the nature of "the Word" and thus the

---

[5]See DuBose, *God Who Sends.*
[6]On Jesus' mission as described and explained in the Gospel of John see Andreas J. Köstenberger,
*The Missions of Jesus and the Disciples According to the Fourth Gospel. With Implications for the Fourth
Gospel's Purpose and the Mission of the Contemporary Church* (Grand Rapids: Eerdmans, 1998); on
the element of "movement from one place to another" see ibid., pp. 28-30. Köstenberger defines
mission in the Fourth Gospel in the following manner: "Mission is the specific *task* or purpose
which a person or group seeks to accomplish, *involving various modes of movement*, be it sending
or being sent, coming and going, ascending and descending, gathering by calling others to follow,
or following" (41).

nature of Jesus' mission with the metaphor of light: "What has come into being in him was life, and the life was *the light of all people. The light shines in the darkness*, and the darkness did not overcome it" (Jn 1:3b-5).

An integral feature of light is movement from the source of light to areas that are dark but are illuminated once the light reaches them. A few verses later John describes more specifically the movement of Jesus, who came after God had sent John the Baptist (Jn 1:6-9), from God's eternal world of light into humankind's world of darkness:

> The true light, which enlightens everyone, *was coming into the world*. He was in the world, and the world came into being through him; yet the world did not know him. *He came to what was his own*, and his own people did not accept him. But to all who received him, who believed in his name, he gave power to become children of God, who were born, not of blood or of the will of the flesh or of the will of man, but of God. And *the Word became flesh* and *lived among us*, and we have seen his glory, the glory as of a father's only son, full of grace and truth. (Jn 1:9-14)

This introductory statement speaks not only about the movement of the incarnate Word from the world of God into the world of human beings, but also describes the intention of the coming of "the Word" as "the true light": Jesus came to enlighten human beings (v. 11), he came to enable people to become members of God's family (v. 12), and he came to bring God's grace and truth (v. 14). In a classical formulation concerning God's love and Jesus' coming into the world, John speaks of God's giving (movement) and God's intentions in the mission of Jesus, his Son:

> God so loved the world that *he gave his only Son, so that everyone* who believes in him may not perish but *may have eternal life*. Indeed, God did not *send the Son into the world* to condemn the world, but *in order that the world might be saved through him*. (Jn 3:16-17)

Jesus describes his mission in the Fourth Gospel in the following terms, combining movement and intentionality:

> I have come down from heaven, not to do my own will, but to do the will of him who sent me. (Jn 6:38)

> Those who speak on their own seek their own glory; but *the one who seeks the glory of him who sent him* is true, and there is nothing false in him. (Jn 7:18)

The one who sent me is with me; he has not left me alone, for *I always do what is pleasing to him.* (Jn 8:29)

I have not spoken on my own, but the Father who sent me has himself given me a commandment about what to say and what to speak. (Jn 12:49)

Jesus' missionary commission in the Gospel of John charges his disciples to engage in the same type of mission which he had been given by God: "Peace be with you. As the Father has sent me, so I send you" (Jn 20:21).

According to the Gospel of Luke, Jesus described his self-understanding and his mission in his first public appearance in the synagogue in Nazareth. A central aspect of Jesus' self-understanding is connected with his quotation of an Old Testament text that describes the ministry of the Servant of the Lord:

The Spirit of the Lord is upon me, because he has anointed me *to bring good news to the poor. He has sent me to proclaim* release to the captives and recovery of sight to the blind, to let the oppressed go free, to proclaim the year of the Lord's favor." (Lk 4:18-19, quoting Is 61:1-2; cf. Is 58:6)

Jesus asserts that he has been sent by the Lord God to the Jewish people (movement) in order to bring good news (intention). When on one occasion the citizens of Capernaum insist that Jesus stay in town, Jesus asserts, "I must proclaim the good news of the kingdom of God to the other cities also; for I was sent for this purpose" (Lk 4:43).

Here the movement is not from God to the Jewish people but from one city to another city. Again, movement is linked with a statement about the intention of Jesus' mission. He states emphatically (Gk *dei*) that the purpose (Gk *epi touto*) of his being sent is the proclamation of the news of God's kingdom. Jesus proclaims the good news that God was now fulfilling the promises given to the prophets concerning his return to his people. He proclaims that the arrival of God's sovereign rule promised for the "last days" has become a reality in and through his own ministry. As Jesus teaches and heals, as he reaches out to the sinners, and as he drives out demons, the kingdom of God has become a present reality—a reality, however, that still awaits consummation.[7]

Several passages describe the mission of the disciples in similar terms, highlighting both movement[8] and intention:

> Ask the Lord of the harvest *to send out* (Gk *ekhalē*) laborers into his harvest. (Mt 9:38, emphasis added)

> *These twelve Jesus sent out with the following instructions*: "Go nowhere among the Gentiles, and enter no town of the Samaritans." (Mt 10:5)

> See, *I am sending you out* like sheep into the midst of wolves; so be wise as serpents and innocent as doves. (Mt 10:16)

> And he appointed twelve, whom he also named apostles, to be with him, and *to be sent out to proclaim the message*. (Mk 3:14)

> He called the twelve and began to *send them out* two by two, and *gave them authority over the unclean spirits*. (Mk 6:7)

> And he sent them out to proclaim the kingdom of God and to heal. (Lk 9:2)

> After this the Lord appointed seventy others and *sent them on ahead of him* in pairs *to every town and place* where he himself intended to go. (Lk 10:1)

> He said to them, "The harvest is plentiful, but the laborers are few; therefore ask the Lord of the harvest to *send out laborers into his harvest*." (Lk 10:2)

Paul describes the mission of Jesus also in terms of movement from God into the world and in terms of the intentionality of Jesus' mission: "But when the fullness of time had come, *God sent his Son, born of a woman*, born under the law, *in order to redeem* those who were under the law, *so that we might receive adoption as children*" (Gal 4:4-5).

Paul describes his own mission in terms of movement (sent to the Gentiles) and in terms of intentionality (to proclaim Jesus Christ):

> Paul an apostle—*sent* neither by human commission nor from human authorities, but *through Jesus Christ and God the Father*, who raised him from the dead. . . . But when God, who had set me apart before I was born and

---

[7]See Chrys C. Caragounis, "Kingdom of God," *DPL*, pp. 415-30; George R. Beasley-Murray, *Jesus and the Kingdom of God* (Grand Rapids: Eerdmans, 1986); I. Howard Marshall, *New Testament Theology: Many Witnesses, One Gospel* (Downers Grove, Ill.: InterVarsity Press, 2004), pp. 78-81, 121-25, 145-52.

[8]Geographical movement is sometimes underlined with the Greek prefix *ek-/ex-* meaning "out"; the RSV often translates *apostellein* ("to send") with the phrase "to send out" despite the missing prefix *ek-*, interpreting (correctly) the meaning of *apostellein*.

called me through his grace, was pleased to reveal his Son to me, *so that I might proclaim him among the Gentiles.*" (Gal 1:1, 15-16)

Thus, *when we define* missionary work, *intentionality and geographical movement are legitimate elements of such a definition.*

Uneasiness concerning this emphasis is often linked with the suspicion that such an understanding of mission implies imperialist notions of the superiority of the sending church or the missionary, notions of the inferiority of the recipients of the mission, and not least the concept of "authority."[9] While the evils of imperialism do not need to be documented here, it remains an existentialist (and thoroughly Western!) illusion to posit that a world without authority is possible or even desirable.[10] Parents, whose cultural and social mission is to raise their children to become adults, have what one may call a "superior authority," as they have the means and the knowledge to help their children become responsible members of society. They are "imperialist" only when they are abusive, which is unfortunately not a rare situation, but certainly not the norm. Teachers who are "sent" by a school board or a ministry of culture to train children in reading and writing, in mathematics and in history, in the sciences and in the arts know more than their students and thus exercise authority in the classroom—which does not mean that they treat their students as inferior dimwits. A car mechanic who advises a customer that his or her car needs new brakes has superior knowledge: the customer who ignores the authoritative advice of the expert does so at his or her own peril.

The nature of missionary work in the early church. Second, if a contemporary definition of *mission* is to have any connection with the New Testament, the nature of the early Christian mission needs to be considered. The argument that the word *mission* does not occur in the New Testament is incorrect. The Latin verb *mittere* corresponds to the Greek verb *apostellein*, which occurs 136 times in the New Testament (97 times in the Gospels, used both for Jesus having been "sent" by God and for the

---

[9]On Protestant missionary work and imperialism see Brian Stanley, *The Bible and the Flag: Protestant Missions and Imperialism in the Nineteenth and Twentieth Centuries* (Leicester, U.K.: InterVarsity Press, 1990).

[10]For a philosophical rehabilitation of authority see Hans-Georg Gadamer, *Truth and Method* (London: Sheed & Ward, 1975), pp. 245-53.

Twelve being "sent" by Jesus). The noun *apostolē* ("sending, apostleship") is used in Romans 1:5 to describe Paul's missionary calling, in 1 Corinthians 9:2 for Paul's "missionary" or "apostolic" work, in Galatians 2:8 for the missionary calling of Paul and Peter, and in Acts 1:25 in the technical sense of "apostolic" office.

The Twelve were *called* by Jesus to become "fishers of people" (Mk 1:17; cf. Mt 10:1), and they were *sent out* to proclaim the good news of the kingdom of God and to heal the sick and drive out demons (Mt 10:5-8; cf. Lk 9:1-5). After Jesus' resurrection, they were commissioned to "go and make disciples of all nations" (Mt 28:19; cf. Acts 1:8).

Similarly Paul was *called* by the risen Lord to preach the gospel *among the Gentiles* (Gal 1:15-16; Rom 1:5; Acts 9:15; 26:16-18).

The threefold reality of missionary work. Third, when we base our definition of *mission* on the model of the work of the apostles in the early church, we describe a threefold reality.

1. Missionaries *communicate the news of Jesus the Messiah and Savior* to people who have not heard or accepted this news. Jews need to believe that Jesus of Nazareth is the promised Messiah whose death has atoned for sins. Gentiles need to believe that the God of Abraham is the only true God who created the world and humankind, and that Jesus, the Jewish preacher who was active in the villages of northern Judea and who was executed by crucifixion, is the Savior of the world, voiding all alternative religious commitments.

2. Missionaries communicate *a new way of life* that replaces, at least partially, the social norms and the behavioral patterns of the society in which the new believers have been converted. For Gentiles this means, for example, that they no longer visit pagan temples. They no longer frequent prostitutes or sleep with their slave girls. Members of the upper class who have become Christians abandon their customary dislike for the socially "inferior."

3. Missionaries integrate the new believers into *a new community*. The new converts become disciples. Being a follower of Jesus Christ is not a private philosophy or an individual ethic. It is a transforming reality that connects all believers as "children of God" in a community where they worship God and Jesus Christ. They learn from God and Jesus Christ by studying the Scriptures of Israel and the words of Jesus. And they learn to

care for one another.

Thus, *missionaries establish contact with non-Christians, they proclaim the news of Jesus the Messiah and Savior (proclamation, preaching, teaching, instruction), they lead people to faith in Jesus Christ (conversion, baptism), and they integrate the new believers into the local community of the followers of Jesus (Lord's Supper, transformation of social and moral behavior, charity).*

In order to gain a first-hand understanding of Paul's missionary activities, we will survey the apostle's missionary work as described in the book of Acts in part one. Before I specifically discuss the strategy and the methods of his missionary work, it will be important to comprehend Paul's understanding of his missionary task as described in his letters; this will be the subject of part two. Because Paul's missionary methods cannot be separated from the message that he preached as a missionary, his proclamation before Jewish and Gentile audiences will be studied in part three.

***Definitions of* strategy *and* method**. The *Oxford English Dictionary* defines *strategy* as the art of a commander-in-chief in terms of "the art of projecting and directing the larger military movements and operations of a campaign," usually distinguished from tactics, which is "the art of handling forces in battle or in the immediate presence of the enemy." More generally, as defined for example in a business context or in politics, *strategy* is "a plan for successful action based on the rationality and interdependence of the moves of the opposing participants." As far as Paul's missionary work is concerned, these larger issues of goals and "action plans" will be discussed in part four.

Method, or in military terms "tactics," is defined as "a procedure for attaining an object," or more generally as "a way of doing anything, especially according to a defined and regular plan; a mode of procedure in any activity, business, etc." Paul's missionary methods will be the focus of our discussion in part five.

Did Paul have a missionary strategy? A final answer can only be given after a review of the exegetical evidence in his letters and in the book of Acts. As an initial answer, the judicious words of J. Herbert Kane deserve to be repeated:

Much depends on the definition of strategy. If by strategy is meant a deliberate, well-formulated, duly executed plan of action based on human observation and experience, then Paul had little or no strategy; but if we take the word to mean a flexible *modus operandi* developed under the guidance of the Holy Spirit and subject to His direction and control, then Paul did have a strategy.[11]

According to Kane, the problem of today's experts in mission and evangelism is the fact that

> we live in an anthropocentric age. We imagine that nothing of consequence can be accomplished in the Lord's work without a good deal of ecclesiastical machinery—committees, conferences, workshops, seminars; whereas the early Christians depended less on human wisdom and expertise, more on divine initiative and guidance. It is obvious that they didn't do too badly. What the modern missionary movement needs above everything else is to get back to the missionary methods of the early church.[12]

This is my goal in this book: *to provide a close reading of the relevant New Testament texts that help us understand Paul's missionary work— proclaiming the good news of Jesus Christ and establishing communities of believers—in terms of the goals that he had and in terms of the methods that he used.*

Since our primary sources are fragmentary it is not possible to write a complete history of Paul's missionary work. Of Paul's literary writings, we have a relatively sparse amount that takes up 154 pages in the Nestle-Aland edition of the Greek New Testament, containing about 32,000 words—the content of three or four one-hour lectures! Luke's account in the book of Acts is fragmentary as well. He introduces the twelve apostles in Acts 1, but then focuses on Peter (Acts 2—12) for the years A.D. 30-41, whom he "abandons" in the year A.D. 41/42 when Peter leaves Jerusalem even though he presumably continued to engage

---

[11]J. Herbert Kane, *Christian Missions in Biblical Perspective* (Grand Rapids: Baker, 1976), p. 73. See Wilbert R. Shenk, "Mission Strategies," in *Toward the Twenty-First Century in Christian Mission: Essays in Honor of Gerald H. Anderson*, ed. J. M. Phillips and R. T. Coote (Grand Rapids: Eerdmans, 1993), pp. 218-34, who suggests the *missio Dei*—God's purposes in and for the world—as the basic theological framework for thinking about mission strategies.

[12]Kane, *Christian Missions*, p. 73. David J. Hesselgrave, *Planting Churches Cross-Culturally*, 2nd ed. (Grand Rapids: Baker, 2000), pp. 43-44, agrees.

in missionary work until his death around A.D. 67. Luke then turns to Paul's missionary work (Acts 13—28) for the years A.D. 42-62, omitting the earlier phase of his ministry from A.D. 31/32 until his arrival in Syrian Antioch in A.D. 42. Luke mentions followers of Jesus in Damascus (Acts 9:1-2, 10), in the Italian city of Puteoli (Acts 28:13-14) and in the city of Rome (Acts 28:14-15), without informing his readers who had established the Christian communities in these cities (presumably because his readers knew this already).[13]

We do not know whether Paul used a different approach to missionary preaching in his early years compared with his *modus operandi* in his later years. Apart from Paul's ministry in Pisidian Antioch (A.D. 46/47), Corinth (A.D. 50-51), and Ephesus (A.D. 52-55), for which we have more extensive evidence in the book of Acts, we know very little about his work in other cities. And we know next to nothing about his early missionary work in Arabia and in Syria and Cilicia in the twelve years between A.D. 32/33-45. By the time we have more evidence for Paul's missionary methods for the ten years from A.D. 46-55, Paul had already twelve years of missionary experience.

Thus the assertion that Paul "had comparatively little opportunity to base his strategy on observation and experience"[14] when he engaged in missionary work in Galatia, Macedonia, Achaia and Asia is unwarranted. Such verdicts are based on the available evidence for the later phase of Paul's missionary work between A.D. 46-55, ignoring that fact that Paul had engaged in missionary work in Arabia between A.D. 33-34 and in Syria and Cilicia between A.D. 38-45. Wouldn't Paul have used the experience during these twelve years in Arabia, Syria and Cilicia in order to modify his methods in view of new and specific circumstances? Moreover, as J. H. Kane observed, despite two thousand years of missions history, missionaries still do not operate on the basis of "a deliberate, well-formulated, duly

---

[13]It is a common mistake to think that what Luke does not report in the book of Acts did not happen, concluding, for example, that "God passed over the twelve apostles to choose the apostle Paul. A decade had gone by without the apostles following through on the commission to evangelize the Gentiles" (C. Gordon Olson, *What in the World Is God Doing? The Essentials of Global Missions: An Introductory Guide*, 5th ed. [Cedar Knolls, N.J.: Global Gospel Publishers, 2003], p. 55). On the missionary work of the Twelve see Schnabel, *Early Christian Mission*, 1:389-910.

[14]Hesselgrave, *Planting Churches Cross-Culturally*, p. 44.

executed plan of action based on human observation and experience"[15] which guarantees success in every instance.

2. The Task of Missionary Work: Describing Goals

The goals of Paul's missionary work can be described as follows. First, Paul knew himself to be called to preach the message of Jesus Christ. He introduces himself to the Christians in the city of Rome with these words: "Paul, a servant of Jesus Christ, called to be an apostle, set apart for the gospel of God" (Rom 1:1). In 1 Corinthians 2:2 he specifies that as a pioneer missionary he focuses his preaching on "Jesus Christ, and him crucified."

Second, Paul knew himself particularly called to preach the gospel of Jesus Christ to Gentiles, that is, to polytheists who worshiped other gods. He reminds the Roman Christians of the fact that he is "a debtor both to Greeks and to barbarians, both to the wise and to the foolish" (Rom 1:14). Yet Paul also preached before Jewish audiences. He reminds the Corinthian Christians that his proclamation of Jesus as the crucified Messiah, Savior and Lord is "a stumbling block to Jews and foolishness to Gentiles" (1 Cor 1:23). Paul asserts that he is "not ashamed of the gospel; it is the power of God for salvation to everyone who has faith, to the Jew first and also to the Greek" (Rom 1:16).

Third, Paul's goal was to reach as many people as possible. He wants to preach "to Greeks and to barbarians, both to the wise and to the foolish" (Rom 1:14). He proclaimed the good news of Jesus Christ "from Jerusalem and as far around as Illyricum" (Rom 15:19). He engaged in missionary work in Judea and in Arabia. He moved north to preach in Syria and Cilicia. He then moved west to preach on Cyprus, in the provinces of Galatia and Pamphylia in central and southern Asia Minor. When his plans to preach in the Province of Asia, the westernmost province in Asia Minor, could not be carried out, he moved further west to Europe and preached in Macedonia and in Achaia. Then he moved east again to preach the gospel in the province of Asia, reaching a goal that had been out of reach earlier. Because he has now "no further place for me in these regions," Paul

---

[15]Kane, *Christian Missions*, p. 73, conceding that Paul had little or no missionary strategy if the latter is defined in this manner.

planned to visit the city of Rome and from there to reach Spain (Rom 15:23-24). His geographical travels describe an upper half circle from Jerusalem via Syria, Asia Minor, Europe and Rome to Spain.

Fourth, Paul seeks to lead individual people to believe in the one true God and in Jesus Christ, the Messiah, Savior and Lord. This means that Jews would have to acknowledge that Jesus, the crucified preacher from Nazareth, was indeed the promised Messiah, that his death is God's climactic answer to the problem of human sin that neither God's covenant with Abraham nor the Mosaic law could completely solve, and that he was raised from the dead as vindication of his mission and preaching. Gentiles would have to turn from their traditional deities to the God of Israel, abandoning the pagan temples with their rituals to serve the one true and living God, to believe in Jesus who rescues sinners from the wrath of God, to accept the atoning significance of Jesus' death on the cross, to have their lives shaped by the Jewish Scriptures and by Jesus' and the apostles' teaching, and to wait for Jesus Christ's return (1 Thess 1:9-10; 1 Cor 1:18—2:5).

Fifth, Paul established new churches, communities of followers of Jesus Christ—both Jews and Gentiles, men and women, free and slaves—and teaches the new believers the Word of God, the teachings of Jesus, the significance of the gospel for everyday living. Paul describes this aspect of his missionary work as follows:

> I became its servant according to God's commission that was given to me for you, to make the word of God fully known, the mystery that has been hidden throughout the ages and generations but has now been revealed to his saints. To them God chose to make known how great among the Gentiles are the riches of the glory of this mystery, which is Christ in you, the hope of glory. It is he whom we proclaim, warning everyone and teaching everyone in all wisdom, so that we may present everyone mature in Christ. For this I toil and struggle with all the energy that he powerfully inspires within me. (Col 1:25-29)

Apart from promoting sound Christian doctrine, Paul insisted on the evaluation of the teaching in local churches on the basis of the truth of the gospel (Gal 1:6-9) and on the basis of apostolic teaching (1 Cor 15:1-5), an evaluation that on occasion necessitates the rejection of false teachings.

These matters will be more fully developed in chapter four when we study in greater detail the missionary goals of the apostle Paul. Since Paul's goals are in many respects the direct result of the message of a crucified Savior, Paul's missionary message will be described in part three.

3. MISSIONARY METHODS AS A PROBLEM: FINDING SOLUTIONS

The conviction of the early church that the news of Jesus the Messiah and Savior is the news of God's climactic saving intervention results quite naturally in a basic missionary method.

First, people need to hear the message about Jesus Christ, a message for which the early followers of Jesus used the term *euangelion* or "gospel" as a short-hand summary. This means that both Jews and pagans need to be introduced to the gospel in personal conversations or in more formal settings, whether planned or spontaneous. In a fundamentally oral culture the verbal communication of the gospel to individuals and groups is the only manner in which a message can be communicated to people who are not connected with the sender of the message in an established network (such as in a family, in which members who live at a distance can be informed about matters deemed important through a letter). *The oral proclamation of the gospel was a fundamental element of the missionary work of the early church.*

Second, the people who need to hear the news of Jesus live in cities, towns and villages. In the ancient world, many people traveled, both by land and by sea.[16] However, as the vast majority of people were poor, most travel was local. In order for people of different cities and regions to hear the gospel, missionaries need to travel and visit cities and the villages controlled by cities in the various regions of the Mediterranean world. *Geographical movement from city to city, from region to region, and from province to province was a principal element of missionary work in the first century.*

Third, for people to hear the gospel, they will have to be sought out in places in which they are willing to listen and to engage in conversations. For Jews, the natural place for religious discourse and discussion was the

---

[16]See Lionel Casson, *Travel in the Ancient World* (1974; reprint, Baltimore: Johns Hopkins University Press, 1994).

synagogue. Because the Jews were allowed by the Roman emperors and provincial governors to meet weekly,[17] Paul had regular opportunities to preach and teach the members of local Jewish communities. For pagans, the city centers were spaces in which people were accustomed to hearing speeches. In Greek cities this took place in the *agora* or "marketplace" in the city center, in Roman cities in the *forum*, the civic center of the city. On occasion Paul was able to use lecture halls. Workshops in private houses and meetings in private homes provided further opportunities for Paul to reach people with the message of Jesus Christ. When Paul was invited by the city council of Athens to explain his teaching, he was willing and prepared to give an account of his message in an official setting. When his ministry in Ephesus provoked a major uproar in the city, Paul was willing to go to the theater, which seated twenty-four thousand people, in order to speak to the crowds—a plan that fellow Christians and provincial authorities advised him not to carry out (Acts 19:30-31). *Since the goal of missionary work is to reach as many people as possible with the gospel, Paul went to any locale in which people would be willing to listen to the message of Jesus Christ.*

There seems to have been only one type of location where Paul was evidently unwilling to preach the gospel. Paul did not proclaim the news of Jesus in the temples of the various deities that were worshiped in a particular city. Paul exhorted the Corinthian Christians not to dine in pagan temples (1 Cor 10). While this exhortation does not preclude the possibility that Paul would enter the precinct of a temple in order to preach the gospel there to the worshipers of Zeus, Apollo or Isis, this is not very likely. The closest that Paul seems to have come to preaching on the premises of a local temple was the Lystra incident (Acts 14). When excited crowds surmise that Paul and Barnabas are visiting deities, and when the priest of Zeus makes preparations for sacrifices in the temple of Zeus located outside of the city, Paul gives an evangelistic speech, presumably near the gates that are mentioned in Acts 14:13, which are either the gates of the temple or the gates of the city. No New Testament text mentions Paul or any of the other apostles preaching on the premises of a pagan temple. As

---

[17]See Miriam Pucci Ben Zeev, *Jewish Rights in the Roman World: The Greek and Roman Documents Quoted by Josephus Flavius*, TSAJ 74 (Tübingen: Mohr Siebeck, 1998).

Paul's preaching in the local synagogues repeatedly led to charges before Roman officials that he undermines the traditions of the city and engages in illegal activities (Acts 17:5-7; 18:12-13), preaching the gospel inside a pagan temple would have been an ill-advised risk that would probably have landed him in even more serious trouble.

Fourth, Paul proclaimed the news of Jesus to Jews and to Greeks, to the rich and to the poor, to the tiny minority of the educated and to the masses of the uneducated, to men and to women. Paul excluded no one from hearing the message of Jesus Christ: he describes himself as a "a debtor both to Greeks and to barbarians, both to the wise and to the foolish" (Rom 1:14). Paul's missionary method was not predicated on the question of who would respond more readily to the gospel. Paul was convinced that "all have sinned and fall short of the glory of God" (Rom 3:23). Thus all people need to hear the message of Jesus the Messiah and the Savior. *Since Paul wanted to reach all people in a given location, matters of ethnic identity, class, culture or gender did not control his missionary focus.*

Fifth, as people in antiquity were accustomed to encountering and listening to traveling orators, *the expectations and the procedures that are triggered in such encounters had to be considered.* These expectations, based on contemporary models of itinerant philosophers, were both positive and negative, helpful and obstructive. In 1 Thessalonians 2:3-8 Paul disassociates himself from the deception, cunning and cajolery that characterized itinerant philosophers in contemporary society. In 1 Corinthians 2:1-5 Paul gives an autobiographical account of his arrival in the city of Corinth and of the methods of his proclamation. He emphasizes that he dispensed intentionally with the art of contemporary rhetoric when he preached the gospel: he had no interest in being the center of attention or being praised by others; he needed no suggestions for a subject on which to speak, providing him with the opportunity to demonstrate his superior rhetorical skills. His message of Jesus, the crucified Messiah and Lord, could not be rendered convincing since this message was bound to be unavoidably offensive to Jewish audiences and nonsensical to pagan audiences.

The *modus operandi* of Paul's missionary work is characterized by a high degree of flexibility. Some of the constant features—for example, reaching Jews in local synagogues or organizing the new converts in groups which regularly met in private houses—were less the result of a specific "method" but the quite natural result of basic convictions (Jews need to hear and accept the good news of Jesus the Messiah) or of historical-political realities (when it became impossible to regularly teach in the local synagogue, private houses were the "default" location as there were no other viable alternatives). The word *method* in the title of part five is thus somewhat subversive: Paul did not follow a "defined and regular plan" which might guarantee the success of his missionary preaching.

4. Descriptive and Normative Readings: Hermeneutical Clarifications

Once I have described Paul's missionary method, the crucial question arises whether we can take the basic elements of Paul's missionary work and condense them into a "method."

David Hesselgrave offers the following arguments why missionaries today should look to Paul's missionary methods for guidance in their own work.[18] (1) The Greco-Roman world of the first century is remarkably similar to our world today. This is particularly true with regard to multiculturalism, the "intercultural flow of peoples of different races and backgrounds." (2) Because Paul was a "master builder" of the church (1 Cor 3:10), his approach to missionary work is at least instructive. (3) While it was his message that Paul regarded as normative, he also believed that his Christian living was an example of what followers of Jesus should be and do. (4) The broad parameters of Paul's missionary work have not changed: missionaries go where people live, they preach the gospel, they gain converts, they gather new believers into churches, they instruct new believers in the faith, and they appoint leaders. (5) Just as Paul's missionary methods took into account local circumstances, missionaries today will naturally adapt specific aspects of Paul's *modus operandi*.

While this evaluation of the applicability of Paul's missionary methods is balanced and fair, the question of whether and how to apply Paul's missionary methods today remains a difficult one. Whenever we move from Scripture to our own time, seeking to let Scripture shape the life of

---

[18]Hesselgrave, *Planting Churches Cross-Culturally*, pp. 44-46.

the church, we face the dichotomy of a historical past and contemporary present.

Richard Hays, in his important book on New Testament ethics, divides this task into four overlapping operations.[19] (1) The *descriptive* task entails a careful exegesis of the New Testament texts, noting distinctive themes and emphases without prematurely harmonizing them. (2) The *synthetic* task, based on the conviction that there is coherence among the various New Testament texts and authors, proceeds to describe the unity of ethical perspective within the diversity of the canon. (3) The *hermeneutical* task seeks to bridge the difference between the past of the historical Paul and the present of the contemporary church, appropriating the message of the New Testament as a word of God addressed to us. (4) The *pragmatic* task applies the careful exegesis, the consideration of the unity of the New Testament texts and the imaginative work of correlating the world of the New Testament with our own world to individual persons and to Christian communities. The last two tasks can be combined under the heading of *application:* "The hermeneutical task is the cognitive or conceptual application of the New Testament's message to our situation, and the pragmatic task is the enacted application of the New Testament's message in our situation."[20]

This program of applying the paradigms and the imperatives of New Testament ethics to the contemporary church is relevant also for the application of Paul's missionary methods to contemporary missions. The emphasis of this book is on the first two tasks: chapters one, two and three are descriptive; chapters four and five are synthetic; and chapter six is hermeneutical and pragmatic.

---

[19]Richard B. Hays, *The Moral Vision of the New Testament: Community, Cross, New Creation: A Contemporary Introduction to New Testament Ethics* (New York: HarperCollins, 1996), pp. 3-7; cf. Richard B. Hays, "Scripture-Shaped Community: The Problem of Method in New Testament Ethics," *Interpretation* 44 (1990): 42-55.

[20]Hays, *Moral Vision*, p. 7; see ibid., pp. 7-10 regarding objections to this program of doing New Testament ethics.

1

The Missionary Work
of the Apostle Paul

In Christ Jesus, then, I have reason to boast of my work for God. For I will
not venture to speak of anything except what Christ has accomplished
through me to win obedience from the Gentiles, by word and deed, by
the power of signs and wonders, by the power of the Spirit of God, so that
from Jerusalem and as far around as Illyricum I have fully proclaimed the
good news of Christ. Thus I make it my ambition to proclaim the good
news, not where Christ has already been named, so that I do not build
on someone else's foundation, but as it is written, "Those who have never
been told of him shall see, and those who have never heard of him shall
understand."

This is the reason that I have so often been hindered from coming to you.
But now, with no further place for me in these regions, I desire, as I have
for many years, to come to you when I go to Spain. For I do hope to see you
on my journey and to be sent on by you, once I have enjoyed your company
for a little while.

ROM 15:17-24

MOST OF THE MORE DETAILED INFORMATION that we have about
Paul's missionary work comes from Luke's account in the book of Acts.[1]

---

[1] For a discussion of the historical reliability of the book of Acts see Colin J. Hemer, *The Book of Acts
in the Setting of Hellenistic History*, ed. C. H. Gempf, WUNT 49 (Tübingen: Mohr Siebeck, 1989);

It has been customary to describe Paul's mission in terms of three distinct "journeys," as the headings in many Bible translations as well as the legends of the maps in Bibles and in Bible atlases demonstrate: the "first missionary journey" covers Paul's ministry on Cyprus and in Galatia (Acts 13—14). The "second missionary journey" takes Paul via Asia Minor to Europe, where he preaches in the provinces of Macedonia and Achaia (Acts 15:36—18:22). The "third missionary journey" focuses on Paul's ministry in Ephesus, which concludes with a journey to Macedonia and Achaia (Acts 18:23—21:16). This description assumes that Paul's missionary ministry began, essentially, in A.D. 45, when he and Barnabas set out from Antioch in Syria to preach the gospel on the island of Cyprus. Since Paul was converted perhaps as early as A.D. 31/32, this would mean that he waited for nearly fifteen years before obeying Jesus' call to preach the gospel to Gentiles (Gal 1:15-16). This is rather unlikely. Paul himself asserts that he engaged in missionary work in Arabia right after his conversion (Gal 1:16-17; cf. 2 Cor 11:32), before preaching the gospel in Syria and Cilicia (Gal 1:21-24). As the following discussion will demonstrate, we can more profitably distinguish fifteen phases or locations of Paul's missionary work in the thirty-five years between his conversion in A.D. 31/32 on the road to Damascus and his death in Rome around A.D. 67.

Before we survey Paul's missionary work, it will be helpful to survey the available information about Paul's family background, his education, his conversion to faith in Jesus the Messiah and Savior, and his call to missionary ministry. At the end of this chapter I will describe the complex relationship that Paul had with the church in Jerusalem and its leaders.

1.1 PAUL, APOSTLE TO JEWS AND GENTILES: CONVERSION AND CALL

Paul was born in Tarsus (Acts 21:39; 22:3), the metropolis of Cilicia, which was administered by the Roman governor of the Province of Syria throughout much of the first century.

Ben Witherington, *New Testament History: A Narrative Account* (Grand Rapids: Baker, 2001), pp. 174-78; Eckhard J. Schnabel, *Early Christian Mission* (Downers Grove, Ill.: InterVarsity Press, 2004), 1:20-35.

The history of Cilicia in the first century B.C. and A.D. is complicated.[2] When the Romans organized the province of Asia in 133 B.C., the western region of Cilicia Tracheia, together with Pamphylia and Pisidia, was annexed to Cappadocia. When Pompey reorganized the East in 68 B.C. and stopped the activities of pirates in Rugged Cilicia, the two Cilician regions were united with Lycia, Pamphylia and Pisidia and organized as the Provincia Cilicia, with Tarsus as the capital; at this time the province consisted of five administrative districts: Lycaonia, Pamphylia, Isauria, Cilicia and Cyprus. After Augustus reorganized this region in 29 or 25 B.C., Cilicia Tracheia was again annexed to Cappadocia. When Tiberius elevated Cappadocia to the status of an imperial province in A.D. 17, significant territorial changes took place: the eastern part of the province of Cilician was divided between Galatia and Syria, while the western region of Cilicia Tracheia was placed under the control of client rulers. When Vespasian reorganized the East in A.D. 72, Tarsus became again the capital of the reestablished province of Cilicia. The unusually large number of towns and villages during the Roman period suggests that eastern and southern Cilicia had a much higher population density than other regions in Asia Minor during this time.[3]

Paul came from a devout Jewish family that belonged to the Pharisaic movement.[4] He was, in his own words, "circumcised on the eighth day, a member of the people of Israel, of the tribe of Benjamin, a Hebrew born of Hebrews; as to the law, a Pharisee" (Phil 3:5; cf. Gal 1:14). His family was evidently able to trace their lineage to the tribe of Benjamin. The statement that he is "a Hebrew born of Hebrews" suggests that his parents brought him up speaking Hebrew and Aramaic, and that the family strictly adhered to the Jewish way of life regulated by the stipulations of the law, avoiding as much as possible any assimilation to Gentile customs and maintaining contact with the Jewish community in Palestine.[5]

---

[2]See Claude Mutafian, *La Cilicie au carrefour des empires* (Paris: Belles Lettres, 1988).

[3]Friedrich Hild and Hansgerd Hellenkemper, *Kilikien und Isaurien*, Tabula Imperii Byzantini 5 (Wien: Österreichische Akademie der Wissenschaften, 1990), pp. 23, 99.

[4]Gal 1:13-14; Phil 3:5-6; 2 Cor 11:22-23; Rom 11:1; Acts 9:11.30; 21:39; 22:3. On Paul before his conversion see Jerome Murphy-O'Connor, *Paul: A Critical Life* (Oxford: Oxford University Press, 1996), pp. 32-70; Martin Hengel and Anna Maria Schwemer, *Paul Between Damascus and Antioch: The Unknown Years* (London: SCM; Louisville: Westminster John Knox, 1997).

[5]See Peter T. O'Brien, *The Epistle to the Philippians. A Commentary on the Greek Text*, NIGTC

His Hebrew name was Saul (Heb *Šaʾul;* Gk *Saulos*). His Roman (or Greek) name was *Paulos*. Roman citizens had three official names *(tria nomina):* (1) the *praenomen*, older names for individuals such as Marcus or Gaius;[6] (2) the *nomen* or *gentilicium*, the family name passed from the father to the children, retained after marriage; (3) the *cognomen*, the name of the individual.[7] In official documents two further elements could be added: (4) the *filiatio*, the name of the father;[8] and (5) the *tribus*, that is, the indication of the Roman voting "tribe" to which the citizen belonged.[9] The name Paulos or "Paul" was either the cognomen of his family, that is, the official element of his name as a Roman citizen, which his family received after manumission from the Roman owner who had released an ancestor (his father?) from slavery. Or "Paul" was the *signum* or *supernomen*, that is, the Roman, Latin-sounding surname that the family used. Since we have no information about the history of Paul's family, there is no certainty in this matter. It is possible, however, that Paul's father received Roman citizenship through manumission. Several church fathers claim to know that Paul's father, living in Gischala in Galilee, had been sold as a slave as a prisoner of war, perhaps in connection with Pompey's conquest of Palestine in 63 B.C.[10] Roman citizenship did not mean Roman ethnicity, of course, nor does it not prove competency in the use of the Latin language. In the provinces of the empire, Roman citizenship was a source of pride for some individuals, for example by the proud display of the *tria nomina*, and the source

---

(Grand Rapids: Eerdmans, 1991), pp. 371-72.

[6]The *praenomen* was often abbreviated (*M.* for Marcus, *C.* for Gaius). People could choose from eleven praenomina, members of the aristocracy from six praenomina. Cf. H. Solin, *OCD*, pp. 1024-26.

[7]Initially the cognomen supplemented the praenomen, later it replaced the praenomen. The cognomen could be a Latin, Greek or "barbaric" name. The cognomen sometimes indicated personal characteristics, sometimes it was derived from the names of the traditional gods.

[8]The *filiatio* was the father's praenomen or cognomen; it was noted in the genitive case before *filius* ("son") or before *filia* ("daughter").

[9]The name of Cicero, the famous lawyer and politician of the last decades of the Roman Republic may serve as an illustration. His official name was M. Tullius M. f. Cor. Cicero: M(arcus) is the praenomen; Tullius is the nomen (or gentilicium); M. f. = M(arci) f(ilius) ("son of Marcus) is the filiation, the praenomen of his father; Cor. = Cor(nelia tribu) ("of the tribus Cornelia") is the voting tribe; Cicero is the cognomen.

[10]Jerome *Commentarium . . . ad Philemonem* 23; *De viris illustribus* 3.5; Photius, *Quaestiones Amphilocium* 116. Cf. Rainer Riesner, *Paul's Early Period: Chronology, Mission Strategy, Theology* (Grand Rapids: Eerdmans, 1998), pp. 151-53.

of increased social prestige in the community. Other individuals down-played their Roman identity.[11]

We do not know when Paul moved from Tarsus to Jerusalem. Some scholars have suggested that this move occurred when he was still a child, which would mean that he spent his formative years in the Jewish capital. Willem C. van Unnik bases his arguments for this view on the three Greek participles that describe the main phases of Paul's biography in Acts 22:3, suggesting that Luke takes up a traditional literary scheme which itemizes three stages of development: the birth in Tarsus in Cilicia *(gegennēmenos)*, childhood and education in the parental home before reaching school age *(anatethrammenos)*, education by teachers *(pepaideumenos)*. The reference to "this city" *(en tē polei tautē)*, that is to Jerusalem, is linked with *anatethrammenos*, which means that Paul left Tarsus before he reached school age.[12] The assumption that Luke adopted a familiar literary scheme that allows us to pinpoint Paul's move from Tarsus to Jerusalem cannot be cannot be proven, however. Paul's excellent Greek and his sovereign use of the Greek translation of the Hebrew Bible indicates that his upbringing in Tarsus must have played a major role in his education, even though it must take "second place after Jerusalem in Paul's biography."[13]

The fact that young Saul/Paul came to Jerusalem to study indicates that his parents were well-to-do. Paul certainly had access to the elites in the Greek and Roman cities in which he preached the gospel, as his contact with Sergius Paullus, the governor of Cyprus (Acts 13:4-12) demonstrates. The high social status of Paul provides the easiest explanation for Paul's friendship with the asiarchs in Ephesus.[14] His native language

---

[11]George Williamson, "Aspects of Identity," in *Coinage and Identity in the Roman Provinces*, ed. C. Howgego et al. (Oxford: Oxford University Press, 2004), p. 25.

[12]Willem C. van Unnik, "Tarsus or Jerusalem: The City of Paul's Youth," in *Sparsa Collecta*, NT-Sup 29 (1952; reprint, Leiden: Brill, 1973), pp. 259-320; cf. Joseph A. Fitzmyer, *The Acts of the Apostles*, AncB 31 (New York: Doubleday, 1998), p. 704; C. K. Barrett, *The Acts of the Apostles*, ICC (Edinburgh: T & T Clark, 1994-1998), 2:1035; Ben Witherington, *The Acts of the Apostles: A Socio-Rhetorical Commentary* (Grand Rapids: Eerdmans, 1998), pp. 668-69.

[13]Martin Hengel, "Der vorchristliche Paulus," in *Paulus und das antike Judentum*, Tübingen-Durham-Symposium im Gedenken an den 50. Todestag Adolf Schlatters, ed. M. Hengel and U. Heckel, WUNT 58 (Tübingen: Mohr Siebeck, 1991), p. 238.

[14]Steven M. Baugh, "Paul and Ephesus: The Apostle Among his Contemporaries" (Ph.D. diss., University of California, Irvine, 1990), p. 153.

was probably Greek, due to his early years living in Tarsus. He would have spoken fluent Aramaic and Hebrew, due to his upbringing in a devout and conservative Jewish family and his rabbinic studies. Growing up in Cilicia, he may even have understood the indigenous Cilician dialect. And there is the possibility that he may have spoken some Latin, although his status as a Roman citizen does not prove this.[15] His letters and the book of Acts indicate that Paul studied the Torah from a Pharisaic perspective under rabbi Gamaliel and that he received a basic (Greek) rhetorical education in a Jewish-Hellenistic school in Jerusalem.

Paul the persecutor. Saul/Paul persecuted the followers of Jesus in Jerusalem (Acts 8:3) and probably in other locations throughout Judea (Gal 1:22-23), and he planned to arrest Christians in Damascus, a city in Syria (Acts 9:2-3; 22:5; 26:12). Luke mentions Saul for the first time in connection with the stoning of Stephen in Jerusalem. When Paul asserts that he wanted to "destroy" the church, he probably means that he wanted to make it impossible for followers of Jesus to exist within the institution of the synagogue. "Paul may have attempted to deny this right by all means, whether with the help of learned rabbinic discussion or by organizing disciplinary measures of the synagogues against the Christians, or by spontaneous eruptions of bodily force."[16] In his later years Paul himself was subjected to the synagogue punishment of "forty lashes minus one" (2 Cor 11:24-25).

Why did Saul/Paul persecute the followers of Jesus? The most plausible answer to this question is the recognition that the proclamation of the earliest followers of Jesus was regarded as so utterly despicable and mistaken that Paul became convinced that aggressive measures needed to be taken in order to stop the activities of these people. Jews who rejected the claims of the Jewish believers in Jesus[17] were convinced that faith in Jesus as Mes-

---

[15]See Fergus Millar, *The Roman Empire and Its Neighbours*, 2nd ed. (1981; reprint, London: Duckworth, 1996), p. 197, on the survival of Cilician throughout the Roman period. On Paul's knowledge of Latin cf. Hengel and Schwemer, *Paul Between Damascus and Antioch*, p. 119.

[16]Karl-Wilhelm Niebuhr, *Heidenapostel aus Israel. Die jüdische Identität des Paulus nach ihrer Darstellung in seinen Briefen*, WUNT 62 (Tübingen: Mohr Siebeck, 1992), pp. 60-61.

[17]I adopt the definition of "Jewish believers in Jesus" as "Jews by birth or conversion who in one way or another believed Jesus was their savior," while "Jewish Christians" (used as a noun) describes "ethnic Jews who, as believers in Jesus, still practiced a Jewish way of life"; cf. Oskar Skarsaune, "Jewish Believers in Jesus in Antiquity—Problems of Definition, Method, and Sources," in *Jewish*

siah and in the atoning efficacy of his death on the cross was an attack on the foundations of Torah obedience as the basis of Israel's salvation that Yahweh had revealed to Moses.

Paul's conversion. As Saul/Paul traveled from Jerusalem to Damascus, the old Syrian capital where he wanted to arrest believers in Jesus, he had an encounter with Jesus.[18] Paul describes this encounter as "seeing the Lord" (1 Cor 9:1), as an "appearance" of the risen Christ (1 Cor 15:8). Luke describes a "light from heaven" (Acts 9:3; 22:6; 26:13). Paul describes the "seeing" of the Lord Jesus as "a real, 'objective' seeing of a supernatural reality in divine splendor of light, which makes itself known as the 'Lord' and is recognized by him as such."[19] Paul fell to the ground[20] and was addressed by the voice of Jesus the Lord who has been exalted at the right hand of God.

After Paul arrived in Damascus—blinded as a result of the brightness of the light in which Jesus had revealed himself—a local Christian with the name of Ananias conveyed to him a word from Jesus. He informed Paul that Jesus had commissioned him to proclaim his name to all the world (Acts 9:15-16; 22:14-15).

> A certain Ananias, who was a devout man according to the law and well spoken of by all the Jews living there, came to me; and standing beside me, he said, "Brother Saul, regain your sight!" In that very hour I regained my sight and saw him. Then he said, "The God of our ancestors has chosen you to know his will, to see the Righteous One and to hear his own voice; for you will be his witness to all the world of what you have seen and heard. And now why do you delay? Get up, be baptized, and have your sins

---

Believers in Jesus: The Early Centuries, ed. O. Skarsaune and R. Hvalvik (Peabody, Mass.: Hendrickson, 2007), pp. 3, 9.

[18]Gal 1:11-17; Phil 3:3-17; 1 Tim 1:12-16; Acts 9:1-21; 22:6-21; 26:12-18. On Paul's conversion and the consequences for his theology see Dean S. Gilliland, *Pauline Theology and Mission Practice* (Grand Rapids: Baker, 1983), pp. 71-117; Seyoon Kim, *The Origin of Paul's Gospel*, 2nd ed., WUNT 2/4 (Tübingen: Mohr Siebeck, 1984); Alan F. Segal, *Paul the Convert: The Apostolate and Apostasy of Saul the Pharisee* (New Haven, Conn.: Yale University Press, 1990); Richard N. Longenecker, ed., *The Road from Damascus: The Impact of Paul's Conversion on His Life, Thought, and Ministry* (Grand Rapids: Eerdmans, 1997); Hengel and Schwemer, *Paul Between Damascus and Antioch*, pp. 24-61.

[19]Hengel and Schwemer, *Paul Between Damascus and Antioch*, p. 39.

[20]Acts 9:4; 22:7; 26:14. The horse that is sometimes mentioned in this context is a later embellishment, reflected in Christian art and in children's Bibles.

washed away, calling on his name." (Acts 22:12-16)

Paul himself asserts later that he is an apostle because he has seen the Lord after his death and resurrection, just as the Twelve had seen Jesus (1 Cor 15:5-11).[21]

> Last of all, as to one untimely born, he appeared also to me. For I am the least of the apostles, unfit to be called an apostle, because I persecuted the church of God. But by the grace of God I am what I am, and his grace toward me has not been in vain. On the contrary, I worked harder than any of them—though it was not I, but the grace of God that is with me. Whether then it was I or they, so we proclaim and so you have come to believe. (1 Cor 15:8-11)

The phrase "one untimely born" (Gk *ektrōma*) designates in Greek literature "untimely birth," "miscarriage," "abortion" (sometimes induced). The terms refers "to untimely birth, whether the child lives or not. The decisive feature is the abnormal time of birth and the unfinished form of the one thus born."[22] The meaning is not "late birth" (Paul being the last of the apostles to be called) but "unexpected birth." Some interpret the term as making the point that Paul was converted to faith in Jesus Christ not in the course of a natural development but unexpectedly, without being psychologically or theologically prepared for this event.[23] Some assume the meaning "stillbirth," arguing that Paul describes his life before his conversion as a state of death, that is, when he encountered Jesus he was spiritually dead.[24] Others see allusions to Genesis 35:16-20, Numbers 12:12, Isaiah 49:4 or Hosea 13:13,[25] which, however, would not have been

---

[21]It is difficult to provide a historically cogent answer to the question of how the audio-vision of Paul—he heard a voice and he saw Jesus in the splendor of a bright light—compared with the bodily appearance of the risen Jesus among the disciples after Easter.

[22]J. Schneider, *TDNT* 2:465. BDAG, p. 311, gives "miscarriage" as the basic meaning (with reference to Num 12:12; Job 3:16; Eccles 6:3; Philo *Leg. All.* 1, 76), providing the following definition: "a birth that violates the normal period of gestation (whether induced as abortion, or natural premature birth or miscarriage, *untimely birth*."

[23]See James D. G. Dunn, *The Theology of Paul the Apostle* (Grand Rapids: Eerdmans, 1998), p. 311.

[24]Philipp Bachmann, *Der erste Brief des Paulus an die Korinther*, 4th ed., KNT 7 (Leipzig: Deichert, 1936), pp. 433-34; Gerhard Sellin, *Der Streit um die Auferstehung der Toten. Eine religionsgeschichtliche und exegetische Untersuchung von 1 Korinther 15*, FRLANT 138 (Göttingen: Vandenhoeck & Ruprecht, 1986), pp. 242-51.

[25]See e.g., George W. E. Nickelsburg, "An ἔκτρωμα, Though Appointed from the Womb: Paul's Apostolic Self-Description in 1 Cor 15 and Galatians 1," *HThR* 79 (1986): 198-205; N. Thomas

immediately intelligible to the Corinthian Christians. The most plausible interpretation relates the focus of the term not to the mode of Paul's conversion but to the state of affairs of Paul's situation before his conversion: Paul uses a term that describes a human being in a desolate, bleak, dismal state. He describes himself as a miscarriage (v. 8) in order to underline the fact that he was not worthy to encounter the risen Lord Jesus Christ, since he had persecuted the followers of Jesus (v. 9). Having persecuted Christians, Paul regarded himself as a miserable, pitiful, pathetic human being who did not deserve to be pardoned, called and commissioned by Jesus Christ.[26]

1.2 PAUL AND JERUSALEM

Before I describe Paul's missionary work, it will be helpful to survey Paul's relationship with the church in Jerusalem, a relationship that was not without conflict.[27]

Paul's visit in A.D. 33/34. When Paul visited Jerusalem in A.D. 33/34 for the first time after his conversion (Acts 9:27-30; Gal 1:18-19), he was introduced to the apostles by Barnabas. Paul acknowledged the authority of the Jerusalem apostles, but he had preached the message of Jesus Christ immediately after his conversion both in Arabia and in Damascus without consulting them (Gal 1:16). During his visit Paul "went in and out among them in Jerusalem" and preached the gospel "boldly" (Acts 9:28) among the Jews, as he had done in Damascus (Acts 9:27). Paul was not only a guest of the apostles: he participated in their missionary activities in Jerusalem.

The famine relief visit and consultation with Peter (A.D. 44). Paul's second visit to Jerusalem after his conversion is connected with the famine relief visit in A.D. 44. Paul and Barnabas visit Jerusalem before embarking on the missionary outreach to Cyprus and to Galatia, bringing gifts

---

Wright, *The Resurrection of the Son of God*, Christian Origins and the Question of God 3 (London: SPCK; Minneapolis: Fortress, 2003), pp. 328-29.

[26]P. von der Osten-Sacken, *EDNT*, 1:423; Harm W. Hollander and Gijsbert E. van der Hout, "The Apostle Paul Calling Himself an Abortion: 1 Cor. 15:8 Within the Context of 1 Cor. 15:8-10," *NT* 38 (1996): 224-36; David E. Garland, *1 Corinthians*, BECNT (Grand Rapids: Baker, 2003), p. 693.

[27]See Schnabel, *Early Christian Mission*, 2:983-1030, for details.

from the church in Antioch on account of a severe famine in Judea (Acts 11:27-30). This visit is to be identified with Paul's visit to Jerusalem that he mentions in Galatians 2:1-10 when he was accompanied not only by Barnabas but also by Titus, an uncircumcised Gentile Christian.[28]

There had been a change of leadership in the Jerusalem church around A.D. 41/42. The Twelve left Jerusalem, presumably as the result of the persecution initiated by king Herod Agrippa I, who targeted the leaders of the church (Acts 12:1-4). It was during this time that the leadership of the Jerusalem church was transferred to a group of Jewish believers who are described as "elders" (Acts 11:30; 15:2, 4, 6, 22, 23; 16:4; 21:18). The famine relief visit of Paul and Barnabas was paid to these elders who had replaced the apostles; that is, it evidently took place after the departure of the apostles in A.D. 41/42. This reconstruction does not exclude the presence of Peter in Jerusalem at this point in time: he appears, together with the other apostles, in Jerusalem again in Acts 15:2 on the occasion of the Apostles' Council. Peter might have been active in the relative vicinity of Jerusalem and Judea at this time, for example, in Caesarea where he would not have had to be afraid of Herod Agrippa. It is less likely that Paul's meeting with Peter in Jerusalem was accidental, considering Paul's assertion in Galatians 2:2 that he wanted to make sure that he "was not running, or had not run, in vain."

Some scholars understand the agreement between Peter and Paul during the consultation of A.D. 44 (Gal 2:7-9) in terms of a division of the areas of missionary responsibility along geographical lines: Peter engages in missionary work in Jewish regions, Paul in Gentile regions. Other scholars interpret the agreement in the sense of a division along ethnic lines: Peter preaches among Jews, Paul among Gentiles. Both alternatives are problematic. Scholars who support the ethnic interpretation argue that the term *ta ethnē* refers in Paul's letters nearly always to Gentiles in contrast to Jews, and that we find Peter not only in Judea but in "Gentile" regions

---

[28]See I. Howard Marshall, *The Acts of the Apostles. An Introduction and Commentary*, TNTC (Leicester, U.K.: Inter-Varsity Press; Downers Grove, Ill.: InterVarsity Press, 1980), pp. 244-47; Richard N. Longenecker, *Galatians*, WBC 31 (Dallas: Word, 1990), pp. lxxii-lxxxiii; David Wenham, "Acts and the Pauline Corpus II: The Evidence of Parallels," in *The Book of Acts in Its Ancient Literary Setting*, ed. B. W. Winter and A. D. Clarke, The Book of Acts in Its First-Century Setting 1 (Exeter, U.K.: Paternoster, 1993), pp. 226-43.

as well. According to Galatians 2:11-14 he was in Antioch, and according to 1 Corinthians 9:5 Peter and his wife were engaged in missionary journeys. An interpretation in terms of a "Jewish mission" and a "Gentile mission" excludes Paul from preaching in synagogues and bars Peter from preaching the gospel before Gentiles. This scenario is entirely implausible from a historical standpoint, and it founders on the existing evidence, at least as far as Paul is concerned: according to 1 Corinthians 9:19-20 Paul preaches among Jews with the same intensity as he preaches to Gentiles, an assertion that Luke clearly and repeatedly illustrates in his account of Paul's missionary work in the book of Acts.

A division of the areas of missionary responsibility along geographical lines would have been impractical also. Jewish communities existed in all larger cities of the eastern Mediterranean that Paul would not have wanted to exclude from hearing the good news of Jesus the Messiah. And Peter would have encountered in his missionary work in synagogues outside of Judea and Galilee Gentile God-fearers, *ethnē* whom he surely would not want to exclude from hearing his preaching and teaching. The following three factors need to be considered.

First, we need to note that Galatians 2:1-10 does not describe a "division" or "separation" but a *koinōnia*, that is, a "close association involving mutual interests and sharing."[29] The subject of the consultation was not the question whether there should be two distinct or separate branches of missionary work: a mission to Jews for which Peter and the other Jerusalem apostles would be responsible, and a mission to Gentiles for which Paul would be responsible. Nor did the discussion focus on the question whether the missionary work of the early church should be organized in a unified manner with a unified authority. The issue was not whether Paul would "join" Jerusalem or whether Peter would "join" the missionary work of Paul. If Luke's account of Peter's missionary work is any indication, the Twelve did not need to "join" Paul. They were already actively preaching the gospel, also among Gentiles when possible, proclaiming the news of salvation through faith in Jesus the crucified and risen Messiah. This common

---

[29]Thus the definition of *koinōnia* in BDAG, p. 552, as the primary meaning, with the terms "association, communion, fellowship, close relationship" as suggestions for translation.

emphasis of Peter and of Paul does not exclude the possibility that questions of practical Christian behavior were answered in different ways, depending on the cultural and social contexts of Jerusalem and Judea, of Caesarea and Antioch, of Rome and Ephesus.

Second, Paul's account in Galatians 2:8 indicates that the issue was not a dispute about areas of missionary work but a consultation about the effectiveness of missionary work among Jews (Peter) and among Gentiles (Paul). The apostles recognize that in both cases the "success" of the missionary is completely dependent on God. In Galatians 2:7 the comparative particle *kathōs* ("just as") in the Greek text does not express a contrast between the two missionaries but a complementary relationship. This means that the statement in Galatians 2:8 ("for he who worked through Peter making him an apostle to the circumcised also worked through me in sending me to the Gentiles") does not describe Paul and Peter as opponents nor the relative status of the two apostles. Paul's account emphasizes that both his own missionary work and the mission of Peter depend on the power of God. This confirms that the participants in the Jerusalem consultation of A.D. 44 acknowledged the basic theological and practical unity of the early Christian mission. Both Paul (who wrote the account of the consultation in Gal 2) and the Jerusalem apostles (who recognized that God was active in the missionary work of Paul) recognized that they are involved in the same work: the work of God who is active through his servants.

Third, we should note that while Paul clearly speaks of his own concerns ("to make sure that I was not running, or had not run, in vain" [Gal 2:2]), he does not register any wishes or stipulations of the Jerusalem apostles, with the exception of financial support for the poor Christians in Jerusalem and Judea. The behavior of the "pillar apostles" is described as follows: "they contributed nothing . . . they saw . . . they recognized . . . they gave" (Gal 2:6, 7, 9). There is no evidence here that Paul was put under pressure by the Jerusalem authorities—pressure that Paul resisted, thus rescuing single-handedly the unity of the church by emphasizing the law-free gospel. Paul's concern at this consultation with Peter was focused on the recognition of his missionary work and on the recognition of the churches that he had established as having equal validity to the missionary work of Peter and of the other apostles and the churches which they had established.

The "men from James" and the Antioch incident. During the 40s, Jewish believers in Jesus came from Jerusalem to Antioch, where they managed to put Peter under pressure, eventually causing him to break off his (table-)fellowship with the Gentile believers in the city, against his theological convictions. [30] Peter caved in because he was afraid of the reaction of zealous Jews and of their potential actions against the church in Jerusalem (Gal 2:12). The "certain people from James" evidently demanded Peter's separation from the Gentile Christians who had not been circumcised and who did not follow the ritual and cultic stipulations of the Torah. Even Barnabas, who had engaged in missionary work in Antioch, Cyprus and Galatia together with Paul, was "led astray" to act in contradiction to his true convictions, withdrawing from fellowship with the Gentile Christians. When Paul returned to Antioch and realized what had happened, he confronted Peter "before them all" (Gal 2:14).

The "people from James" presumably represented James the brother of Jesus and *primus inter pares* among the elders of the church in Jerusalem. It is possible that they did not convey authoritative demands but that they presented a plea for solidarity with the Jerusalem church in view of the difficult political situation. The delegation from James appears to have acted in accordance with the agreement of the Jerusalem consultation of Galatians 2:7-9. At stake was hardly the question whether the food that was consumed during the communal meals was selected and prepared in compliance with the food laws of the Torah. Such difficulties could have been addressed by making the appropriate changes (note the decisions of the Apostles' Council). The reason why James sent envoys to the church in Antioch seems to have been informed by political considerations that were linked with the repeated persecutions of the Jerusalem church by the Jewish authorities in the 40s. James perhaps sought to reach a *modus vivendi* with the Jewish authorities in Jerusalem, a project that would have been jeopardized by news that the church

---

[30]See recently Mark Bonnington, *The Antioch Episode of Galatians 2:11-14 in Historical and Cultural Context*, Paternoster Biblical Monographs (Bletchley, U.K.: Paternoster, 2005).

tolerates Jews (Jewish believers in Jesus) to live in close fellowship with Gentiles (Gentile Christians) in Antioch, the capital of the province.

Peter's dilemma becomes understandable, considering the historical situation and the political plight of the church in Jerusalem. In Paul's view, however, these motivations were insignificant in comparison with the project of the Gentile mission in general and the Gentile Christian members of the existing churches in particular. Paul would not permit that uncircumcised followers of Jesus, Gentiles who had come to faith in Jesus as Lord and Savior, would become second-class Christians. And Paul was convinced that any differentiation between or separation of Jewish believers and Gentile Christians contradicted the logic of the gospel and denies the efficacy of Jesus' sacrificial death on the cross. This is the apostle's argument in his letter to the Galatian Christians.

The Apostles' Council (A.D. 48). Paul's next visit to Jerusalem was linked with the Apostles' Council in A.D. 48.[31] Luke reports in Acts 15:5 that Pharisees who had come to faith in Jesus Christ demanded that converted Gentiles should be circumcised and admonished to keep the Mosaic law. This was evidently a new development that appears to have taken place after the Jerusalem consultation of A.D. 44, prompting a controversy both in the church in Antioch (Acts 15:1) and in the church in Jerusalem (Acts 15:5). Luke states that the demands of these Jewish believers from Jerusalem provoked "sharp dispute and debate" (Acts 15:2 NIV) between these Judeans and Paul and Barnabas who had just returned from missionary outreach on Cyprus and in Galatia. The church of Antioch decided to send Paul, Barnabas and some other Christians to Jerusalem "to discuss this question with the apostles and the elders" (Acts 15:2). Luke's account indicates that the Twelve, the elders of the Jerusalem church and other leading missionaries such as Paul and Barnabas organized a meeting

---

[31]See Richard Bauckham, "James and the Jerusalem Church," in *The Book of Acts in its Palestinian Setting*, ed. R. Bauckham, The Book of Acts in Its First-Century Setting 4 (Exeter, U.K.: Paternoster, 1995), pp. 415-80; Richard Bauckham, "James and the Gentiles (Acts 15.13-21)," in *History, Literature, and Society in the Book of Acts*, ed. B. Witherington (Cambridge: Cambridge University Press, 1996), pp. 154-84; Holger Zeigan, *Aposteltreffen in Jerusalem. Eine forschungsgeschichtliche Studie zu Galater 2,1-10 und den möglichen lukanischen Parallelen*, Arbeiten zur Bibel und ihrer Geschichte 18 (Leipzig: Evangelische Verlagsanstalt, 2005). For details see Schnabel, *Early Christian Mission*, 2:1007-20.

where these issues should be discussed: "when they came to Jerusalem, they were welcomed by the church and the apostles and the elders, and they reported all that God had done with them" (Acts 15:4). The meeting took place in A.D. 48. Luke's account allows us to reconstruct the following sequence of events.

1. The Twelve and the elders, that is, the apostles and the leadership of the Jerusalem church, convened a meeting (Acts 15:6) in which the following groups participated: "conservative" Jewish Christians who demanded that converted Gentiles must be circumcised, Paul and Barnabas, Peter and John, and James.

2. A robust debate ensued (Acts 15:7). Some participants argued, presumably the former Pharisees who had become believers in Jesus Messiah, that the Gentile Christians should be "circumcised and ordered to keep the law of Moses" (Acts 15:5).

3. Peter reminds the participants in the discussion in a longer contribution (Acts 15:7-11), speaking as a missionary among Gentiles of the events that transpired in connection with the conversion of Cornelius in Caesarea. He emphasizes that "God made a choice" in the church already "in the early days" that the Gentiles should hear the message of the good news and come to faith (Acts 15:7), without making a distinction between Jews and Gentiles (Acts 15:8) and without imposing on the Gentiles the yoke of the law (Acts 15:9), since Gentiles are saved just like the Jews by the grace of the Lord Jesus (Acts 15:11).

4. Peter's speech reassured the participants in the meeting: "the whole assembly kept silence" (Acts 15:12). The conservative Jewish Christians had to acknowledge the fact that the Gentile mission that Paul and Barnabas and the church in Antioch had been responsible for, accepting Gentiles into the messianic people of God without circumcision, was not a Syrian aberration or a project of Paul alone (if they indeed attacked Paul as early as A.D. 48). They were forced to acknowledge that Peter himself, the *primus inter pares* of the Twelve and the first leader of the Jerusalem church, supported and taught the same theological position.

5. After the assembly had become quiet, Barnabas and Paul gave a report about the work of God "among the Gentiles" (Acts 15:12), that is, in Syria and in Cilicia, on Cyprus and in Galatia. They recounted "all the

signs and wonders" that God had done in the context of their missionary work (Acts 15:12).

6. Finally James, the brother of Jesus and the leader of the Jerusalem church, spoke (Acts 15:3). He argued in a longer contribution (Acts 15:14-21) that converted Gentiles must be accepted into the church because God has restored his people (at least in principle) and that converted Gentiles should be expected to follow only certain rules. James explains with an interpretation of Amos 9:11-12 the missionary-theological position that all apostles who were present accepted. James quotes Amos in order to establish from Scripture that the nations belong to Yahweh *as Gentiles* in the messianic era and that they worship God in the eschatological temple, which is equated with the community of the believers in Jesus the Messiah. There was perhaps no other text that demonstrated this conviction as clearly as Amos 9:11-12.

7. The Twelve and the elders, together with the delegation from Antioch and indeed the entire assembly decided to accept the theological consensus that had emerged in the contributions and arguments of Peter, Barnabas, Paul and James as the solution of the controversy (Acts 15:22). They further decided to communicate this consensus in written form to the church in Antioch through Judas/Barsabbas and Silas, "leaders among the brothers" who would accompany Paul and Barnabas on their journey back to the capital of Syria (Acts 15:23) and would be able to explain the decision orally (Acts 15:27).

8. The decree: Luke quotes the document verbatim (Acts 15:23-29). It contains the following elements: introductory formula (Acts 15:23b); review of the prehistory of the decision (Acts 15:24-27); the decision (Acts 15:28-29). Several suggestions have been offered concerning the interpretation of the stipulations of the Apostolic Decree.

a. They are practical regulations for a specific situation in which the fellowship in the Christian community between Jewish believers and Gentile Christians had become a problem. The basic demand for the Gentile Christians was that they should abandon their former religion, their pagan gods and the spiritual defilement that accompanies idolatry (cf. v. 20 with v. 29). This explanation is not fully convincing since the stipulation that forbids idolatry does not simply seek to establish "practical harmony" between Jewish believers and Gentile Christians.

b. The stipulations of the Apostles' Council correspond to the Noahic commandments that the Jews regarded as normative for humanity as a whole (cf. Jubilees 7:20). The concrete specifications of the Noahic commandments that we encounter in the rabbinic sources mention the prohibition of idolatry, blasphemy, murder, incest, stealing, perverting justice and eating meat containing blood. The stipulations of Acts 15:29 contains only the first, third, fourth and seventh command, which means that the parallel is not very striking.

c. The stipulations should be interpreted on the background of the Old Testament polemic against idolatry. The term *porneia* refers to temple prostitution, while the reference to strangled animals and blood refer to cultic practices of pagans. This interpretation has been criticized for two reasons. First, if the Apostolic Decree only wanted to direct the Gentile Christians to give up their former pagan practices and to worship the one true God, this concern could have been formulated more clearly and more easily. Second, the decree would not have said anything new and would therefore have been redundant since the renunciation of pagan practices was certainly part and parcel of the message of the missionaries who preached the gospel among Gentiles.

d. The stipulations of the decree correspond to the minimal demands that were obligatory for Jews even if their lives were in danger: idolatry, murder and incest (*y. Sanh.* 21b; *b. Sanh.* 74a). This suggestion is not fully convincing since the prohibition of eating from what has been strangled is missing from this list of minimal demands.

e. The stipulations of the Apostolic Decree should be interpreted in terms of the regulations that Leviticus 17—18 formulates for Gentiles who live among Jews as "foreigners": prohibited are *[1] porneia* (Lev 18:10, 12), specifically sexual relations between blood relatives; *[2]* what has been strangled (Lev 17:13), that is eating from animals that have not been slaughtered in a ritually proper manner as well as from animals that had a defect; *[3]* blood (Lev 17:14) as ingredient in food. If this is the conceptional background of the decree, the agreement of Acts 15:29 represents a (cultic-ritual) compromise formula that aimed at facilitating the communal fellowship of Jewish believers and Gentile Christians in "mixed churches." However, the pragmatic desire to facilitate table fellowship between Jewish believers and Gentile Christians alone does not suffice to explain the selection of the four stipulations Acts 15:20, 29. For example, stipulations for the "foreigner" such as the sabbath commandment (Ex 20:10; Deut 5:14) are missing. Richard Bauckham argues that the term *bĕtōk* ("in the midst of"), which occurs only in Leviticus 17—18, links Jeremiah 12:16/Zechariah 2:11 (via the quotation of Amos 9:11-12) with Leviticus 17—18 and thus can explain the selection of the stipulations in the Apostolic Decree. The exegetical argument of James

> which created a link between closely related prophecies and Lev 17-18 es-
> tablishes that the Law of Moses itself contains just four commandments
> which do explicitly apply to precisely those Gentiles. . . . [They] are not
> simply a pragmatic compromise, dealing with the problem of table fellow-
> ship in a context where it is not debatable that Gentile Christians do not
> have to keep the Law. In the thinking of those who formulated them, the
> same exegetical case which demonstrates conclusively that Gentile Chris-
> tians do not have to keep the Law also shows that they do have to observe
> these four prohibitions.[32]

The collection. Paul organized a collection for the church in Jerusalem throughout the churches in Macedonia and Achaia, and perhaps in the churches in the province of Asia.[33] Paul risked his life for this initiative, and it was in connection with the collection that he was arrested in Jerusalem. This collection demonstrates his connectedness with the believers in Jerusalem. The following factors are important.

1. The collection demonstrates Paul's concern for and devotion to the believers in Jerusalem. The collection was not a legal obligation for Paul or for the Jerusalem apostles, and it was not simply an initiative that was prompted by socio-cultural customs. The collection was a voluntary gift. Paul wanted to help the Christians in Jerusalem as an expression of the fellowship between Jewish and Gentile believers.

2. The collection demonstrates the central significance of Jerusalem

---

[32]Bauckham, "James and the Jerusalem Church," pp. 461-62.
[33]1 Cor 16:1-4; 2 Cor 8:1-15; 9:1-5; Rom 15:14-21; cf. Gal 2:10. Cf. Keith Fullerton Nickle, *The Collection: A Study in Paul's Strategy*, Studies in Biblical Theology 48 (London: SCM, 1966); Dieter Georgi, *Remembering the Poor: The History of Paul's Collection for Jerusalem* (Nashville: Abingdon, 1992); Stephan Joubert, *Paul as Benefactor: Reciprocity, Strategy and Theological Reflection in Paul's Collection*, WUNT 2/124 (Tübingen: Mohr Siebeck, 2000).

for Paul's missionary work. Jewish Christians from Jerusalem had been responsible for repeated interference in Paul's mission, even during the time he brought the collection to Jerusalem, interference that prompted Paul to a forceful reaction both in Antioch when he confronted Peter and in his letter to the Galatian churches. Despite this opposition, or precisely because of it, Paul traveled to Jerusalem with a good number of representatives of the churches that he had established in which Jewish believers and Gentiles Christians lived together. The gospel had originated in Jerusalem; the Gentile Christians are debtors of the believers in Jerusalem (Rom 15:27). God's revelation to Israel in the Scriptures was authoritative for Gentile Christians as well (cf. Rom 3:21). These are reasons why the collection is more than a pious work and a social deed. Paul's statement in 1 Corinthians 16:5 shows that the apostle pondered in a.d. 54 whether he should bring the collection to Jerusalem himself or not. When he wrote the comments in 2 Corinthians 1:15-16 and in Romans 15:26-27 in a.d. 55/56, he had decided to travel to Jerusalem despite the anticipated dangers. It is obvious that Paul regarded the relationship between the Jerusalem church and the Gentile Christian churches as extremely significant.

3. The collection confirms the equality of Jewish believers and Gentile Christians. The fact that Paul took uncircumcised Gentile Christians to Jerusalem was not meant as a provocation but a demonstration of what Paul regarded to be self-evident: that Jewish believers and Gentile believers should have fellowship with each other.

4. In his letter to the Christians in Rome, written in Corinth shortly before his departure to Jerusalem, Paul voices the possibility that the collection might be rejected (Rom 15:31). When Paul arrived in Jerusalem, he received a friendly welcome by James and the elders of the Jerusalem church, according to Luke's report (Acts 21:17-18). The passing reference to the collection in Paul's speech before Felix (Acts 24:17) also supports the likelihood that the financial contribution of the Gentile Christian churches was accepted.

Table 1.1 summarizes Paul's visits to Jerusalem during the twenty-five years between his conversion in A.D. 31/32 and his arrest in A.D. 57:

Table 1.1. Paul's Visits to Jerusalem

31/32	Conversion of Paul and missionary outreach in Arabia and in Damascus
33/34	First visit (Acts 9:26-29): three years after Paul's conversion, then eleven years of missionary work in Syria and Cilicia
44	Second visit (Acts 11:27-30): consultation, eleven years after the first visit, then missionary work on Cyprus and in Galatia
48	Third visit (Acts 15:1-29): Apostles' Council, three years after second visit, then missionary work in Macedonia and Achaia
51	Fourth visit (Acts 18:22): three years after the third visit, then missionary work in the Province of Asia and visit to Achaia
57	Fifth visit (Acts 21:15-17): collection visit, six years after fourth visit, arrest in Jerusalem and imprisonment in Caesarea

1.3 PAUL IN ARABIA, JERUSALEM, CILICIA AND SYRIA

Paul states in one of his earliest letters that after his conversion he preached the gospel of Jesus Christ in Arabia, and after a brief stay in Jerusalem, in Cilicia and in Syria:

> But when God, who had set me apart before I was born and called me through his grace, was pleased to reveal his Son to me, so that I might proclaim him among the Gentiles, I did not confer with any human being, nor did I go up to Jerusalem to those who were already apostles before me, but *I went away at once into Arabia*, and afterwards I returned to Damascus.
>
> Then after three years I did go up to Jerusalem to visit Cephas and stayed with him fifteen days; but I did not see any other apostle except James the Lord's brother. In what I am writing to you, before God, I do not lie! *Then I went into the regions of Syria and Cilicia*, and I was still unknown by sight to the churches of Judea that are in Christ; they only heard it said, "The one who formerly was persecuting us is now proclaiming the faith he once tried to destroy." And they glorified God because of me. (Gal 1:15-24, emphasis added)

Luke relates that right after his conversion, Paul preached the gospel in the synagogues of Damascus:

> For several days he was with the disciples in Damascus, and immediately he began to proclaim Jesus in the synagogues, saying, "He is the Son of God." All who heard him were amazed and said, "Is not this the man who made havoc in Jerusalem among those who invoked this name? And has

he not come here for the purpose of bringing them bound before the chief priests?" Saul became increasingly more powerful and *confounded the Jews who lived in Damascus by proving that Jesus was the Messiah.*" (Acts 9:19-22, emphasis added)

These texts allow us to describe the earliest phase of Paul's missionary work, albeit in a rather limited fashion due to the scarcity of information that either Paul or Luke provide.

The first period of Paul's mission: Damascus. The first period of Paul's missionary work is localized in Damascus. Paul preached in Damascus soon after his conversion (Acts 9:19-22) and again before he returned to Jerusalem (Gal 1:17; Acts 9:23-25). He proclaimed Jesus in the local synagogues as the Son of God, the promised Messiah (Acts 9:20, 22).

The fact that the Jews of Damascus succeeded in winning the support of the local representative of the Nabatean king Aretas IV for their plans to arrest Paul (2 Cor 11:32) implies that they regarded Paul's activities as a threat for their community. This indicates that Paul's preaching had considerable success and that a good number of Jews were converted to faith in Jesus Christ.

Neither Paul nor Luke provides statistics concerning the number of people converted or the number of house churches established. This is not surprising: Paul never provides statistics, and Luke gives only round numbers when he reports the growth of the church in Jerusalem and in Judea—note Acts 2:41: about 3,000 converts; Acts 4:4: about 5,000 followers of Jesus; Acts 21:20: thousands of believers.

These relatively sparse and general statistical data that Luke provides suggest two points. (1) The early Christians were not very interested in precise statistical data regarding the growth of local churches or regarding the total number of believers. Luke is the only New Testament author to provide any figures, and he limits himself to these three passages in Acts, and he gives only approximate figures for the believers in Jerusalem (Acts 2:41; 4:4; 19:7). Generally Luke describes the growth of the church with general formulations.[34] Since Luke imitates the style of the Septuagint, the Greek translation of the Hebrew Bible, the Old Testament books of

---

[34]Acts 5:14; 6:1, 7; 8:6, 12; 9:31, 35, 42; 11:21, 24; 13:43; 14:1, 21; 16:5; 18:8, 10; 21:20.

Numbers, Ezra and Nehemiah provided him with models and precedents for exact statistical information when the members of God's people are being counted. But he is clearly not interested in precise statistics. (2) On the other hand, the fact that figures are given indicates that the growth of the church is not a vague, mysterious process but a visible expansion that can be described with numbers. Luke is indeed interested to provide specific historical information to describe the quantitative and extensive growth of the Jerusalem church.[35]

The second period of Paul's mission: Arabia. Paul did not go to Arabia to work through the theological and practical consequences of his conversion.[36] He went to Arabia in order to engage in missionary work. The evidence is as follows.[37] First, Paul states in Galatians 1:17 that he obeyed God's call after his encounter with the risen Jesus Christ—he preached the gospel without first conferring with the apostles in Jerusalem when he went to Arabia.

> But when God, who had set me apart before I was born and called me through his grace, was pleased to reveal his Son to me, so that I might proclaim him among the Gentiles, I did not confer with any human being, nor did I go up to Jerusalem to those who were already apostles before me, but I went away at once into Arabia, and afterwards I returned to Damascus. (Gal 1:15-17)

Second, Paul reports in connection with a review of his sufferings and his work as an apostle that the ethnarch of King Aretas in Damascus wanted to arrest him (2 Cor 11:32-33). Luke refers to this incident as well (Acts 9:23-25).

> In Damascus, the governor [ethnarch] under King Aretas guarded the city of Damascus in order to seize me, but I was let down in a basket through a window in the wall, and escaped from his hands. (2 Cor 11:32-33)

---

[35]See Wolfgang Reinhardt, "The Population Size of Jerusalem and the Numerical Growth of the Jerusalem Church," in *The Book of Acts in its Palestinian Setting*, ed. R. Bauckham, The Book of Acts in Its First-Century Setting 4 (Exeter, U.K.: Paternoster, 1995), pp. 237-65.

[36]Such an assumption may be behind suggestions that Paul realized that the traditional Jewish attitudes concerning the Gentiles needed to be reevaluated and adjusted while he was in Arabia; cf. Gilliland, *Pauline Theology and Mission Practice*, p. 57.

[37]See Murphy-O'Connor, *Paul*, pp. 81-85; Hengel and Schwemer, *Paul Between Damascus and Antioch*, pp. 106-26; Schnabel, *Early Christian Mission*, 2:1032-45.

After some time had passed, the Jews plotted to kill him, but their plot became known to Saul. They were watching the gates day and night so that they might kill him; but his disciples took him by night and let him down through an opening in the wall, lowering him in a basket. (Acts 9:23-25)

King Aretas is the Nabatean king Aretas IV Philodemos, who ruled from 9 B.C. to A.D. 40. In Roman and in Jewish terminology, Arabia (Nabatea, see fig. 1.1) was the region to the south of the Roman province of Syria; it included Moab and Edom and extended from the Hauran Mountains in the north to the regions east and west of the Gulf of Aqaba. Most of the inhabitants of Arabia were Nabateans whose language was a precursor of modern Arabic. The Jews regarded the Nabateans as descendants of Ishmael, the son of Abraham, that is, as kindred tribes.[38] The translators of the Septuagint identified the Nabateans with Nabaioth, the firstborn of the twelve sons of Ishmael.[39] Since the Idumeans, the "descendants of Esau," were converted (by force) to Judaism by John Hyrcanus (135/34-104 B.C.), the Arab Nabateans appeared to the Jews as their closest "relatives" who were still Gentiles. Kypros, the mother of Herod I, came from a royal Nabatean family. Salome, Herod's sister, intended to marry the Nabatean prince Syllaios.[40] Herod Antipas, who ruled in Galilee as tetrarch from 4 B.C. to A.D. 39, had married his daughter in A.D. 23 but subsequently divorced her in order to be able to marry Herodias, the wife of his half-brother Philip.[41] John the Baptist was executed in A.D. 28 as a result of his criticism of this marriage. The tensions between Aretas IV and Herod Antipas intensified, eventually resulting in a war (A.D. 34-36) in which Aretas was victorious.[42]

Paul does not state in Galatians 1:15-17 why he went to Arabia. We may assume, however, that he did not travel from Damascus to Arabia in

---

[38]Hengel and Schwemer, *Paul Between Damascus and Antioch*, pp. 110-13.

[39]Cf. Gen 25:13; 28:9; 36:3; 1 Chron 1:29 (LXX).

[40]See Josephus *Bellum Judaicum* 1.181; *Antiquitates Judaicae* 14.121; 15.184; on Salome 16.220, 225, 322.

[41]Josephus *Antiquitates Judaicae* 18.109-115.

[42]See Emil Schürer, *The History of the Jewish People in the Age of Christ (175 B.C.-A.D. 135)*, rev. G. Vermes et al. (Edinburgh: T & T Clark, 1973-1987), 1:344-50; Aryeh Kasher, *Jews, Idumaeans, and Ancient Arabs: Relations of the Jews in Eretz-Israel with the Nations of the Frontier and the Desert During the Hellenistic and Roman Era (332 BCE - 70 CE)*, TSAJ 18 (Tübingen: Mohr Siebeck, 1988), pp. 176-83.

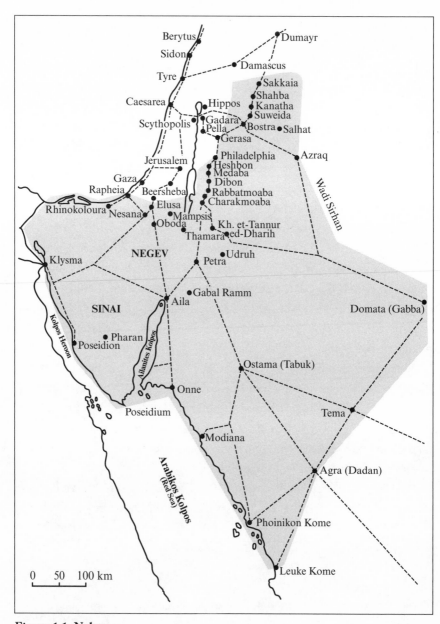

Figure 1.1. Nabatea

order to seek fellowship with God in the solitude of the desert, like Moses and Elijah, or to work through the significance of his conversion experience in order to gain theological clarity. Arabia was not only a desert but a flourishing civilization, particularly in northern Nabatea. It appears that Paul, after his conversion and after some preaching in the synagogues of Damascus, soon obeyed the divine commission to preach the gospel "among the Gentiles" (Gal 1:16). He chose to go to a region that was close to Damascus and distant enough from Jerusalem, where he might have gotten into trouble for having joined the followers of Jesus. Paul may have focused on the Gentile God-fearers and sympathizers with the Jewish faith whom he encountered in the synagogues of the Nabatean cities. Intervention of Nabatean officials suggests clearly that Paul limited his preaching not to Jewish audiences but that he reached pagan Nabateans as well.

If Paul's conversion took place in A.D. 31/32, his missionary work in Arabia should be dated to A.D. 32/33. When Paul came to Arabia in A.D. 33, the tensions between the Nabateans and the Jews had intensified.[43] King Aretas had to reckon with the intervention of the Romans. It is not out of the question that his kingdom might be annexed to the Roman province of Syria. Nabatea could not afford to appear weak, any signs of unrest had to be avoided. The activities of a Jewish missionary who wanted to win the Nabatean population for "Jewish" (Christian) convictions would certainly have met opposition. Paul managed to evade the Nabatean authorities who wanted to arrest him in Damascus. Martin Hengel suggests that "Paul's 'mission' in Nabataean Arabia was hindered and perhaps even ended by political tensions between Aretas and Antipas as the only Jewish ruler still ruling, and that therefore the apostle returned to Damascus, where he had brothers in the faith whom he knew and who trusted him."[44]

Paul evidently spent several months in Arabia, presumably in the northern part of the Nabatean kingdom, south of Damascus, that is, in the region of the modern state of Jordan. In which cities might Paul have

---

[43]For the following scenario see Jerome Murphy-O'Connor, "Paul in Arabia," *CBQ* 55 (1993): 732-37.
[44]Hengel and Schwemer, *Paul Between Damascus and Antioch*, p. 112.

preached the gospel? Hengel surmises that Paul "visited the synagogues in the larger cities during his stay of about two years, above all in the capital Petra."[45] Important Nabatean cities immediately south of Damascus that Paul could have reached include Shahba, Kanatha, Suweida (Soada), Bostra, Gerasa and Philadelphia (see fig. 1.1). Pella and Scythopolis have also been suggested as possible targets of Paul's missionary work,[46] although both cities belonged to Judea at this time. Petra, the Nabatean capital, was further south, between the southern end of the Dead Sea and the Gulf of Aqaba (approx. 370 km south of Damascus). Josephus identified Petra with Reqem and with Qadesh, and he relates the tradition that it was here that Aaron went up Mount Hor, where he was buried (according to Num 20:22 Mt. Hor was near Qadesh).[47] Such Jewish traditions may have prompted Paul to travel to Petra to preach the gospel there. Hengel suggests that Paul traveled as far as Agra (mod. Mada'in Salih), in the far south of Arabia near the southeastern border, pointing to traditions that link Hegra with Mount Sinai and with Hagar, Abraham's slave and concubine.[48] Whether such traditions might have informed Paul's missionary strategy remains hypothetical. The distance would not have been a problem: the routes that local and other international travelers used would be used by missionaries as well. On the other hand, if Paul spent only a few months in Nabatea, it becomes less likely that he penetrated to the cities further south. These cities had many of the typical elements of the infrastructure of a Greek city: *ōideion* (music hall), *bouleutērion* (council hall), *nymphaeum* (fountain), basilicas, theater, amphitheater, public baths and temples. The fact that when Paul preached again in Damascus before he traveled to Jerusalem suggests that the Christian community of Damascus was the base of Paul's missionary activity in this region.

Paul does not relate the success of his ministry in Arabia, not even in general terms. The aggressive reaction of Nabatean officials who want to eliminate Paul suggests that people had been converted in noticeable numbers, provoking unrest in various cities that caused the intervention

---

[45]Martin Hengel, "Paul in Arabia," *BBR* 12 (2002): 59.

[46]Hans Bietenhard, "Die syrische Dekapolis von Pompeius bis Trajan," in *Aufstieg und Niedergang der römischen Welt*, vol. 2.8, ed. H. Temporini and W. Haase (Berlin: De Gruyter, 1977), p. 255.

[47]Josephus *Antiquitates Judaicae* 4.82-83, 161.

[48]Hengel and Schwemer, *Paul Between Damascus and Antioch*, pp. 113-16.

of the Nabatean king.

The third period of Paul's mission: Jerusalem. Paul returned to Jerusalem, the city which he had left one or two years earlier in his quest to arrest and interrogate the followers of Jesus whose beliefs and preaching he detested, as a believer in Jesus Messiah in A.D. 33/34. The reports in Galatians 1:18-19 and in Acts 9:26-30 about this first visit in Jerusalem after his conversion complement each other.

> Then after three years I did go up to Jerusalem to visit Cephas and stayed with him fifteen days; but I did not see any other apostle except James the Lord's brother. (Gal 1:18-19)

> When he had come to Jerusalem, he attempted to join the disciples; and they were all afraid of him, for they did not believe that he was a disciple. But Barnabas took him, brought him to the apostles, and described for them how on the road he had seen the Lord, who had spoken to him, and how in Damascus he had spoken boldly in the name of Jesus. So he went in and out among them in Jerusalem, speaking boldly in the name of the Lord. He spoke and argued with the Hellenists; but they were attempting to kill him. When the believers learned of it, they brought him down to Caesarea and sent him off to Tarsus. (Acts 9:26-30)

The goal of Paul's visit to Jerusalem was to get to know Peter (Gal 1:18); the Greek verb *historein* means "to visit (for the purpose of coming to know someone)."[49] Luke reports that Paul preached in the meetings of the Christian community (Acts 9:28) and that he preached the gospel in the synagogues in which Hellenistic, Greek-speaking, Jews were meeting (cf. Acts 6:9) whom he sought to lead to faith in Jesus Messiah (Acts 9:29). The Greek formulation (imperfect tense of the verbs) suggests that Paul's preaching was not an isolated occurrence but missionary work that happened over some period of time. According to Galatians 1:18, Paul was in Jerusalem for fifteen days. Because Paul was eventually forced to leave Jerusalem, we may surmise that he would have been prepared to stay for a longer period in the Jewish capital.

The attempt of some Jews to kill Paul (Acts 9:29) may have been the

---

[49]BDAG, p. 483; cf. James D. G. Dunn, "Once More—Gal 1.18: *historēsai Kēphan*. In Reply to Otfried Hofius," *ZNW* 76 (1985): 138-39.

result of some individuals hating Paul for having converted to the new movement that he had persecuted not long ago. They may have become aggressive for the same reasons that had caused Paul to brutalize followers of Jesus. Or the plot may be an indication of the success of Paul's preaching activity in the Jerusalem synagogues whose leaders may have feared another major phase of success of the followers of Jesus. Their plan was thwarted as Paul managed to escape with the help of his fellow believers in the Jerusalem church.

The fourth period of Paul's mission: Cilicia and Syria. When Paul was forced to leave Jerusalem, he traveled via Caesarea to Tarsus in Cilicia, his home town (Acts 9:30). Paul intimates that he preached the gospel in Cilicia and in Syria. (The eastern part of Cilicia was administered by the governor of the province of Syria during this time.)

> Then I went into the regions of Syria and Cilicia, and I was still unknown by sight to the churches of Judea that are in Christ; they only heard it said, "The one who formerly was persecuting us is now proclaiming the faith he once tried to destroy." And they glorified God because of me. (Gal 1:21-24)

Luke reports in connection with the Apostles' Council (A.D. 48) that the letter that explained the apostles' decisions was addressed to the Gentile Christians in Antioch and in Syria and Cilicia: "The brothers, both the apostles and the elders, to the believers of Gentile origin in Antioch and Syria and Cilicia, greetings" (Acts 15:23). After Paul had taken the apostles' letter with Barnabas and other companions to Antioch, the Syrian capital, and after he split up with Barnabas over the suitability of John Mark as a missionary, he chose Silas as his new coworker with whom he wanted to visit the churches that he had established earlier (Acts 15:36).

Luke relates that Paul "went through Syria and Cilicia, strengthening the churches" (Acts 15:41). Since Paul and Silas had started their journey in Antioch (Acts 15:30-40), Luke's comment clearly suggests that Paul had established churches both in Cilicia and in Syria, in the latter region churches outside of Antioch.

Assuming that Paul was converted in A.D. 31/32 and that he preached in Nabatea in A.D. 32/33, he could have engaged in missionary work in

Cilicia and Syria beginning in A.D. 33/34. If we date Paul's mission to Cyprus and Galatia to A.D. 45-47 and Paul's collaboration with Barnabas in Antioch to A.D. 42-44, his mission to Cilicia and Syria (excluding the ministry in Antioch) can be dated between A.D. 33-42. This means that Paul proclaimed the gospel of Jesus Christ for about ten years in the province of Syria-Cilicia.

Neither Paul, Luke nor later Christian tradition provides any information indicating the specific cities where Paul preached between A.D. 33-44. During this time he planted the churches that he visited again after the Apostles' Council in A.D. 48 (Acts 15:41). Assuming that Paul sought out cities with Jewish communities already during this period, as Luke reports in the book of Acts for the time after A.D. 44, we would find Paul at least in those cities of Syria and Cilicia in which Jews lived.[50]

As far as Syria is concerned, a region with a large Jewish population,[51] Jewish communities are attested in Antioch, Apameia, Byblos, Berytus, Damascus, Dora, Palmyra, Phaene, Ptolemais, Sidon and Tyre.[52] Assuming that Paul traveled from Jerusalem to Syria and Cilicia along the Mediterranean coast, he could have preached the gospel in the cities in which the Greek-speaking Jewish believers from Jerusalem had already preached: perhaps in Berytus, Aphaka, Byblos, Tripolis, Arka (Caesarea ad Libanum), Arados (with Baetocaece), Antarados, Balaneae, Paltos, Gabala, Laodicea and Seleucia on the Orontes River. North of Antioch, the capital, he could have preached the gospel in Platanoi and Alexandreia; in a north-easterly direction were the cities of Imma, Gindaros, Kyrrhos and Nikopolis. It is less likely that Paul engaged in missionary work in eastern Syria, in cities such as Palmyra, Resafa, Sura, Nikephorion, Karrhai, Edessa, Charax Sidou, Zeugma (Seleucia), Hierapolis, or Barbalissos (listed from south to north). It would not have been difficult for Paul to reach these cities. However, since we later find Paul in Tarsus and in Antioch, this suggests that the apostle concentrated on western and northern Syria (see fig. 1.2, also fig. 1.1).

---

[50]For Paul's work in Syria see Schnabel, *Early Christian Mission*, 1:780-97; 2:1048-54; on Cilicia see ibid., 2:1054-69.

[51]Josephus *Bellum Judaicum* 7.43.

[52]Schürer, *History of the Jewish People*, 3:14-15.

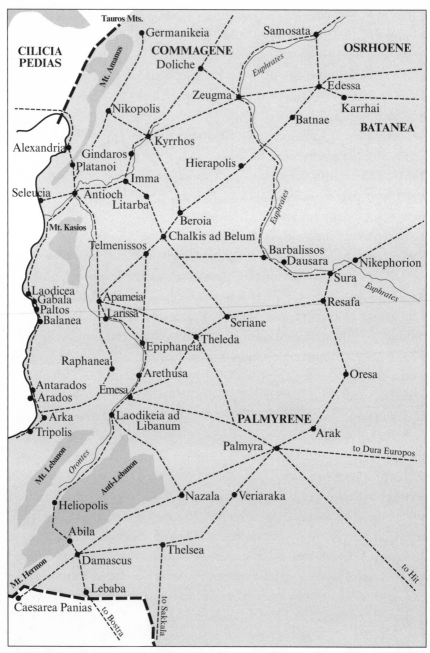

Figure 1.2. The province of Syria (North)

We may plausibly assume that Paul preached the gospel in Tarsus, his hometown, since Barnabas finds Paul there in A.D. 42, when he looked for a theologically competent missionary who could help in consolidating and expanding the Christian community in Antioch, the capital of Syria (Acts 11:25-26). Dio Chrysostom describes Tarsus as one of the three greatest cities in Asia Minor, together with Ephesus and Smyrna. Besides Luke's comment in Acts 6:9 which refers to a synagogue of Cilician Jews in Jerusalem, a funerary inscription found in Jaffa attests the presence of Jews in Tarsus: "Here lies Isaac, elder [of the assembly] of the Cappadocians, linen merchant from Tarsus."[53] Philostratus reports that some Jews had Tarsian citizenship under the emperor Titus, that is, around A.D. 80 (*Vita Apolonii* 6.34). Paul seems to have had Tarsian citizenship (Acts 21:39).[54] We have no details about Paul's work in Tarsus, apart from the report that the Jewish believers in Judea had heard that Paul was proclaiming the good news of Jesus Christ in Syria and Cilicia (Gal 1:21-24). Paul left Tarsus not because his missionary task in the city or in the region was complete (which might have been the case, but we do not know this). He left because Barnabas recruited him for ministry in Antioch (Acts 11:25-26).

In Cilicia Jews are attested in other cities besides Tarsus.[55] If Paul wanted to reach Jewish communities in Cilicia, he could have engaged in missionary work in Anazarbos, Mallos, Soloi, Sebaste, Korykos, Seleucia and Olba (listed from east to west; see fig. 1.3). If Paul preached the gospel in towns without Jewish communities as well (or in cities for which a Jewish presence has not yet been established), he could have visited (east of Tarsus) the port cities of Baiae, Issos, Katabolos, Aigaiai and Epiphaneia, as well as Hierapolis, Mopsuestia, Adana and Augusta, and (west of Tarsus) the port cities Zephyrion, Palaiai, Aphrodisias and Anemurion at the southern tip of Cilicia Tracheia. As regards travel conditions in the region, it appears that none of the roads in Cilicia was paved before A.D. 75, as the earliest milestone, discovered near Olba at the foot of the Taurus Mountains, dates to A.D. 75.[56]

---

[53]Walter Ameling, *Inscriptiones Judaicae Orientis. Band II: Kleinasien*, TSAJ 99 (Tübingen: Mohr Siebeck, 2004), no. 249.

[54]See Hemer, *Book of Acts*, p. 122; Riesner, *Paul's Early Period*, pp. 148-49.

[55]Schürer, *History of the Jewish People*, 3:33-34; Hild and Hellenkemper, *Kilikien und Isaurien*, pp. 84, 99.

[56]David French, *Roman Roads and Milestones of Asia Minor*, British Institute of Archaeology Inter-

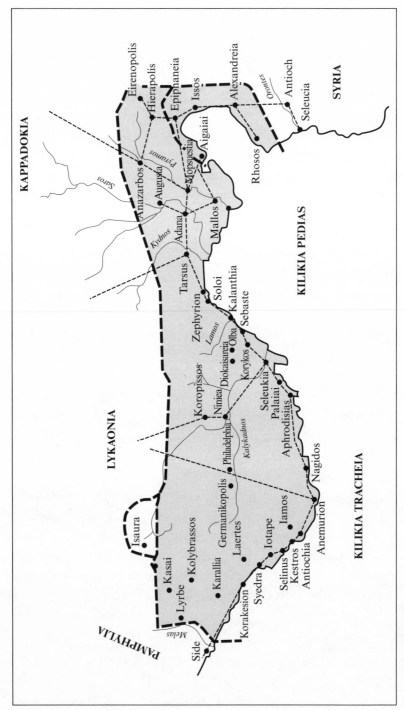

Figure 1.3. Cilicia

Because Paul provides only brief hints concerning his missionary work in Arabia, Cilicia and Syria between ca. A.D. 33-42, and Luke relates no details either, it remains an open question whether Paul worked alone or with coworkers. Since neither Paul nor Luke reports the tactical details of Paul's missionary activity between A.D. 32-44, the suggestion that he worked initially as a "solitary missionary" remains hypothetical.

The fifth period of Paul's mission: Antioch. The next period of Paul's missionary work is connected with Antioch on the Orontes, since 64 B.C. the capital of the Roman province of Syria and (after Rome and Alexandria) the third largest city of the Roman Empire, with around 250,000 inhabitants.[57] The Jewish king Herod the Great visited Antioch several times; he financed the expansion of the main street of the city to 16 meters in width; under Tiberius this main artery of the city was widened to 30-40 meters, and colonnaded halls were built along this street, using 3,200 columns of polished marble. Antioch had a large Jewish community. Seleukos I Nikator, who founded Antioch in 300 B.C., had invited Jews to live in the city. He promised them the same citizenship rights that he had granted to the 5,300 Greeks from Athens and Macedonia.[58] Recent estimates assume that the Jewish community consisted of 20,000 to 35,000 Jews, that is, about 10 percent of the population of the city. According to Josephus some Jews of Antioch had become very wealthy and supplied the temple with richly decorated and expensive gifts.[59] It also appears that a large number of Gentiles were attracted to the Jewish faith,[60] presumably many of whom regularly attended the synagogues.

The church in Antioch had been founded by Greek-speaking Jewish believers from Jerusalem who had left the Jewish capital in connection with the persecution of A.D. 31/32, following the killing of Stephen. These Jewish believers, who originally came from Cyprus and Cyrene, preached both to Jewish audiences and to Gentiles (Acts 11:20). The

---

national Series 392 (Oxford: British Institute of Archaeology at Ankara, 1981/1988), 2:430 no. 461 (Yeğenli 4).

[57]For details see Schnabel, *Early Christian Mission*, 1:781-97; 2:1069-72.

[58]Josephus *Antiquitates Judaicae* 12.119.

[59]Josephus *Antiquitates Judaicae* 17.24; *Bellum Judaicum* 7.45.

[60]Josephus *Bellum Judaicum* 7.45.

church grew rapidly in size, which prompted the apostles in Jerusalem to send Barnabas to Antioch to consolidate the missionary work in the city (Acts 11:21-24). The fact that "a great many people" were converted seems to have been the reason why Barnabas went to Tarsus to recruit Paul for the work in Antioch. It is a fair assumption that the "mass conversions"[61] in Antioch included Gentiles (Acts 11:20-21) and that Barnabas sought Paul's collaboration in Antioch for this very reason, appreciating Paul's experience in missionary work among Gentiles. Paul worked with Barnabas in Antioch "for an entire year" (Acts 11:26).

Some have suggested that the church in Antioch was "the mother-church of Christianity among non-Jews."[62] The available evidence suggests otherwise. The first Gentile about whose conversion the New Testament sources provide information was the Roman centurion Cornelius in Caesarea, who came to faith in Jesus Christ as a result of Peter's preaching (Acts 10:1-48), resulting in a lively discussion in the church in Jerusalem about the modalities of this first "Gentile mission" (Acts 11:1-18). Luke reports the origins of the church in Antioch immediately after Peter's mission to Caesarea and the subsequent discussion in Jerusalem (Acts 11:19-26), and he describes Barnabas as the personal link between Jerusalem and Antioch (Acts 11:22).

It is therefore plausible to assume that the modalities of the Gentile mission in Antioch corresponded to the missionary praxis of Peter and perhaps of other Jerusalem missionaries, a praxis that had been acknowledged by the apostles and the church in Jerusalem. When "they," that is, "the apostles and the believers who were in Judea" (Acts 11:1) heard Peter's report and explanation, "they were silenced. And they praised God, saying, 'Then God has given even to the Gentiles the repentance that leads to life' " (Acts 11:18). *Antioch seems to have been the first city in which Gentiles were converted to faith in Jesus Christ in larger numbers. But the "mother church" of the Gentile mission was Jerusalem.*

Luke concludes his brief report about Paul's missionary work in Antioch with the note that "it was in Antioch that the disciples were first called 'Christians' " (Acts 11:26). The term *Christianoi* (Lat. *Chris-*

---

[61]Jacob Jervell, *Die Apostelgeschichte*, KEK 3 (Göttingen: Vandenhoeck & Ruprecht, 1998), p. 324.
[62]Andreas Feldtkeller, "Syrien II. Zeit des Neuen Testaments," *TRE* 32 (2001): 588.

tiani) occurs in the New Testament only here and in Acts 26:28 on the lips of Herod Agrippa II during the legal proceedings involving the apostle Paul ("Are you so quickly persuading me to become a Christian?"), and in 1 Peter 4:16 in the context of Christians in Asia Minor who face the possibility of having to give an account of their beliefs before the magistrates in the cities in which they lived ("Yet if any of you suffers as a Christian, do not consider it a disgrace, but glorify God because you bear this name"). The ending *-iani* suggests that this appellation originated outside of the church in Latin-speaking circles (a Greek-speaking context would suggest formulations such as *Christeioi* or *Christikō*).[63] Jews called the followers of Jesus usually *Naṣrayya* or *Noṣrim* (Gr *Nazōraioi*), that is "Nazarenes."[64] Jews who did not acknowledge Jesus as Messiah would hardly have called the believers in Jesus "followers of the Messiah" *(Christeioi* or *Christianoi)*. It is quite possible that the term *Christianoi* was an official designation coined by the Roman authorities in Antioch for the new religious group.[65] In Rome we hear of the *Caesariani* and *Augustiani*; in Judea we encounter the "Herodians" or *Herodiani*, the relatives, clients and the supporters of the Herodian court who are also mentioned in the New Testament (Mk 3:6; 12:13).[66] The verb that is used in Acts 11:26, *chrēmatisai* ("they were called"), often occurs in official contexts. Some suggest that the new church may have had to register in the provincial capital with the magistrates of the city or with officials of the province of Syria as a Jewish "special synagogue" or as a religious association.[67] Perhaps the believers in Jesus Messiah who engaged in missionary activity in Antioch had come to the attention of the authorities in connection with the unrest of A.D. 39 provoked by Caligula's directive to

---

[63]Hengel and Schwemer, *Paul Between Damascus and Antioch*, p. 453 n. 1171.

[64]See Acts 24:5 where Tertullus uses this term in front of Felix; also Acts 26:9 (Paul before his conversion). See also Tertullian, *Adversus Marcionem* 4.8.1; Epiphanius, *Panarion* 29; Jerome, *De viris illustribus* 3; *Commentarium in Isaiam* 5.18; *Commentarium in Mattaeum* 13.53-54.

[65]Erik Peterson, *Frühkirche, Judentum und Gnosis. Studien und Untersuchungen* (Rome: Herder, 1959), pp. 269-77; cf. Glanville Downey, *A History of Antioch in Syria from Seleucus to the Arab Conquest* (Princeton, N.J.: Princeton University Press, 1961), pp. 275-76; Riesner, *Paul's Early Period*, pp. 112-13; Hengel and Schwemer, *Paul Between Damascus and Antioch*, pp. 225-30.

[66]The "Herodians" must have been a known entity in Antioch since Herod I had financed substantial building activities in the city.

[67]Hengel and Schwemer, *Paul Between Damascus and Antioch*, p. 226.

have his statue erected in the Jerusalem temple, as a very active group
of people who believed in a Jew named Jesus as Messiah *(christos)*, a
group which expanded rapidly and had to be watched.

1.4 PAUL ON CYPRUS AND IN GALATIA

When Paul and Barnabas, accompanied by John Mark, left Antioch on
the Orontes in the spring of A.D. 45 to engage in missionary work on the
island of Cyprus and in several cities in the province of Galatia, Luke
relates what precipitated this new initiative as follows:

> While they were worshiping the Lord and fasting, the Holy Spirit said,
> "Set apart for me Barnabas and Saul for the work to which I have called
> them." Then after fasting and praying they laid their hands on them and
> sent them off. (Acts 13:2-3)

This passage has often been interpreted in terms of the commissioning
of Paul by "his" local church, which sent him and Barnabas as missionaries to as yet unreached areas. This interpretation fails to take into account
the fact that, as we have seen, both Paul and Barnabas had several years
of missionary experience. Their missionary career did not begin in Antioch. Barnabas's missionary track record can be traced back to Jerusalem.
This native of Cyprus, who was a Levite and had come to live in Jerusalem where he contributed financially to the church (Acts 4:36), knew
the church in Damascus and was informed about Paul's missionaries in
this area after his conversion, and he introduced Paul to the leadership
of the Jerusalem church (Acts 9:27), evidently eager to recruit Paul for
the continued outreach in the city. It is surely no coincidence that it was
Barnabas whom the leaders of the church in Jerusalem chose to travel to
Antioch, the capital of the province of Syria, with the task of consolidating the missionary work and the growth of the new church there, a task
that he fulfilled successfully as "a great many people" were converted after
his arrival (Acts 11:22-24). And it was Barnabas who recognized Paul's
expertise and experience in outreach to Gentile audiences, prompting
him to recruit him as coworker for the ministry in Antioch in A.D. 42. If
Barnabas's mission in Antioch began in A.D. 35, he had ten years of missionary experience when he left Antioch in A.D. 45. If Paul was converted

in A.D. 31/32, the beginning of his missionary work in Damascus and in Arabia/Nabatea dates to A.D. 32/33; his missionary work in Cilicia and Syria took place between A.D. 33-42, his evangelistic and teaching ministry in Antioch in A.D. 42-44. This means that when he left Antioch in A.D. 45 for Cyprus and Galatia, Paul had nearly fifteen years of missionary experience. *Neither Barnabas nor Paul were missionary novices: they were experienced missionaries who had seen many people come to faith in Jesus Christ, both Jews and Gentiles, who had seen churches established, who had taught new believers, and who had seen churches grow.*

It is conceivable that Paul and Barnabas had planned the new missionary initiative with the goal of reaching Cyprus for some time. Luke's reference to prayer, fasting and the speaking of the Holy Spirit in Acts 13:2 does not exclude a period of prior planning. Barnabas, Paul and the other leaders of the church in Antioch may have asked God for a confirmation of their plans whose realization implied that the two leading preachers and teachers would leave the church to engage in missionary outreach in other regions. In view of these plans it would have been natural and prudent not only to seek God's guidance (Acts 13:2) but also to consult with the leaders of the church in Jerusalem (Acts 11:27-30; 12:25).

The sixth period of Paul's mission: Cyprus. Together with Barnabas and John Mark, Paul traveled from Antioch via the port city of Seleucia by ship to the city of Salamis on the eastern tip of the island of Cyprus, a Roman province since the principate of Augustus (see fig. 1.4). Luke's report about this period of Paul's missionary work in Acts 13:4-12[68] focuses on two cities. Paul and Barnabas preached in Salamis (Acts 13:5), they "went through" the whole island (Acts 13:6), perhaps indicating that they also preached in Kition, Amathus and Kourion, the major cities along the southern road, and they were active in Paphos (Acts 13:6-12). With regard to Salamis, Luke mentions a synagogue. It can be assumed that it was in the synagogue of Paphos that they met the Jewish prophet Bar-Jesus also called Elymas, who seemed to have been the court astrologer (Lat. *magus*) of the governor of the province, Sergius Paulus. In the power encounter that ensues between the Jewish astrologer and the Jewish Christian missionaries, Paul calls down

---

[68]For details see Schnabel, *Early Christian Mission*, 2:1074-89.

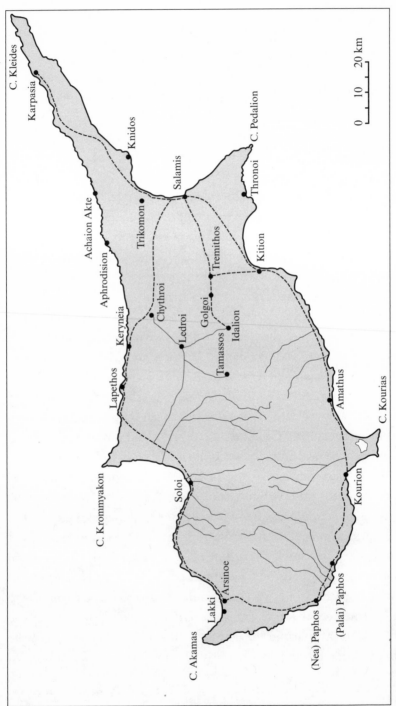

Figure. 1.4. Cyprus

divine punishment on the man who attempted to prevent the governor from considering the gospel, perhaps because he feared that he would be dismissed from his position, or he thought the message of the Jewish teachers to be seriously misguided and positively dangerous.

The governor invites Barnabas and Paul to present their message, evidently in order to establish whether it is subversive or not.[69] Elymas is struck with temporary blindness, a fact that sufficiently impressed Sergius Paulus, who had already been "astonished at the teaching about the Lord" and led him to faith in Jesus Christ (Acts 13:12). Some have suggested that the proconsul was not converted to faith in Jesus Christ because there is no reference to baptism. If this criterion is consistently applied, we would have to conclude that nobody on Cyprus and in southern Galatia was converted during the missionary work of Paul and Barnabas: Luke never mentions baptisms in Acts 13—14. The fact that Paul and Barnabas visited "churches" in Lystra, Iconium and Antioch on the journey back to Syria (Acts 14:21, 23), demonstrates, however, that there were indeed a good number of people who had been converted in these cities. Others suggest that Sergius Paulus was not baptized "on account of his political position and his senatorial status, despite his sympathy."[70] Since Luke does not regularly report baptisms, there is no reason to doubt the reliability of the Lukan account unless it is deemed impossible for a Roman proconsul to come to faith in Jesus Christ.

The seventh period of Paul's mission: Galatia. Luke's account of Paul's missionary work in Galatia (Acts 13:14—14:23) in A.D. 45-47 begins with four pieces of information. Paul and his companions set sail from Paphos. They came to Perge in Pamphylia; in Perge John Mark left them and returned to Jerusalem. Paul and Barnabas traveled from Perge to Antioch in Pisidia where they sought out the Jews who were meeting in the local synagogue on the sabbath (Acts 13:13-14).

Why didn't the missionaries engage in missionary work in Perge, since A.D. 43 the capital of the newly constituted Province Lycia-Pamphylia (see fig. 1.5), or in the other major cities in this region? This question will

---

[69]See Christoph W. Stenschke, *Luke's Portrait of Gentiles Prior to Their Coming to Faith*, WUNT 2/108 (Tübingen: Mohr Siebeck, 1999), p. 167.

[70]See Hengel and Schwemer, *Paul Between Damascus and Antioch*, p. 69.

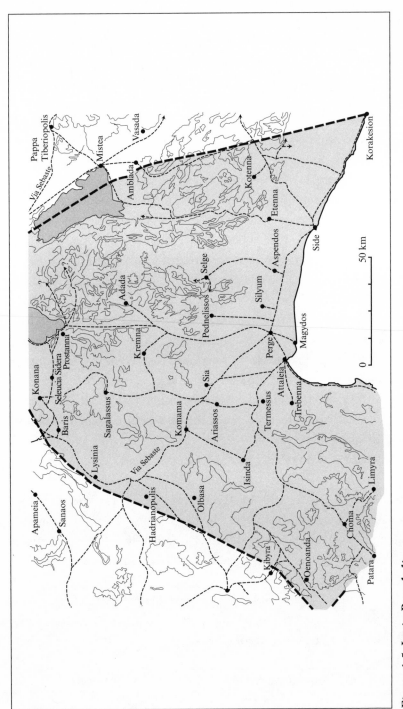

Figure 1.5. Lycia-Pamphylia

be more fully explored in chapter five. The most plausible explanation recognizes the connections between Sergius Paulus, the governor of Cyprus, and the family of the Sergii Paulli who owned estates in the region of Vetissus in the province of Galatia in central Anatolia. It is quite possible that Paul's move from Paphos to Pisidian Antioch may have been suggested by Sergius Paulus who wanted his Galatian relatives hear the gospel.[71]

Pisidian Antioch. Luke localizes Paul's first missionary outreach in southern Galatia (see fig. 1.6) in the city of Antioch (Acts 13:14-52).[72] The phrase "Antioch in Pisidia" (TNIV "Pisidian Antioch") in Acts 13:14 does not assert that Antioch was actually located in the region of Pisidia:[73] the city belonged to Phrygia.[74] The appellation "Pisidian" distinguishes this Antioch from another city named Antioch that was situated on the Maeander River and was also located in Phrygia. Luke's Greek phrase *eis Antiocheian tēn Pisidian* (Lat. *Antiocheia ad Pisidiam*) describes the closeness of this Antioch to Pisidia. In the first century, eastern Phrygia belonged to the Roman province of Galatia, as did Pisidia to the south. For convenience sake I will refer to this city as Pisidian Antioch, to distinguish it from Syrian Antioch, or Antioch-on-the-Orontes, the capital of the province of Syria.

Paul and Barnabas arrived in Antioch presumably in the summer of A.D. 46. Antioch was the most important colony in the southern region of the province of Galatia, both in military, economic and political respects. This is one of the reasons why Antioch was the center of the imperial cult in the region.[75] The city was founded by Seleukos I Nikator (358-281

---

[71]For details regarding Sergius Paulus see Schnabel, *Early Christian Mission*, 2:1084-88.

[72]For Paul's missionary work in southern Galatia see Schnabel, *Early Christian Mission*, 2:1089-1122. Luke's account of Paul's missionary work in Antioch is long (94 lines of text in the Greek New Testament of Nestle-Aland), compared with his account for Iconium (14 lines), Lystra (33 lines), Derbe (3 lines) and Perge (2 lines), and compared with his account for Philippi (72 lines), Thessalonica (24 lines), Beroea (13 lines), Athens (50 lines) and Corinth (42 lines). The account for Ephesus (103 lines) is long, mostly due to Luke's focus on the hostile reaction of the pagan citizens (46 lines).

[73]Thus erroneously the Greek geographers Ptolemaios 5.4.9 and Pliny *Naturalis historia* 5.24.94.

[74]Strabo 12.6.4 states unambiguously that this Antioch was located in Phrygia; see also Ptolemaios 5.5. In the New Testament text tradition, Codex D and the Majority Text write *Antiocheian tēs Pisidias*, with the genitive of possession indicating that the copyists assume that the city belonged to Pisidia; this reflects the political situation in the fourth century. Cf. Barbara Levick, *Roman Colonies in Southern Asia Minor* (Oxford: Clarendon, 1967), pp. 18, 33.

[75]See Thomas Witulski, *Die Adressaten des Galaterbriefes. Untersuchungen zur Gemeinde von Antio-*

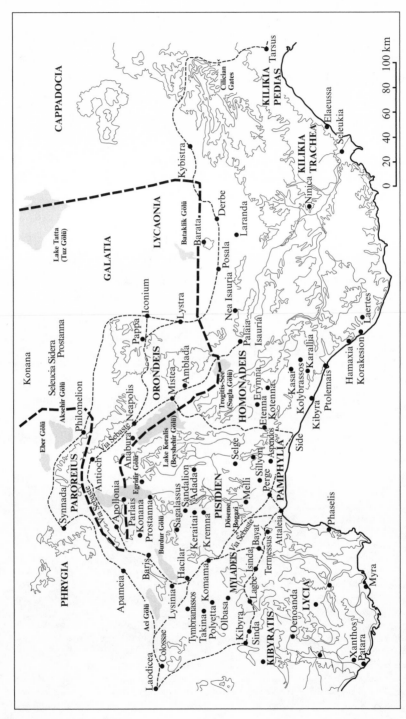

Figure 1.6. The province of Galatia (South)

B.C.) or by Antiochos II (261-246 B.C.), who settled Greek colonists from Magnesia on the Maeander (Strabo 12.8.14). The new city was intended to safeguard the Seleucid interests against the local tribes in the area. By 200 B.C. Antioch was a Greek *polis* with a constituted citizenry, a council and magistrates. Augustus refounded the city as a Roman military colony with the official name *Colonia Caesarea Antiocheia*. Augustus settled about three thousand veterans in Antioch, a city that could have had around ten thousand inhabitants.[76] Augustus stationed the *VII. legio*, a cavalry regiment *(á la Augusta Germaniciana)*, and a cohort in the city. The high number of Italian immigrants is attested by the numerous Latin inscriptions. Latin was spoken at official functions, for example, when the emperor or members of the local elite were honored. For "private" communication Greek was spoken, particularly in religious contexts in which people sought "direct communication with the deity" and on tombstones whose inscriptions express the feelings of the surviving relatives.[77] Perhaps as early as 2 B.C. an imperial temple dedicated to Augustus, emperor and founder of the colony, was built in the city center, at the eastern end of the Tiberia Platea.[78] Visitors entered the temple through a monumental gate with three arches and an inscription whose translation reads: "For the emperor Caesar Augustus, son of a god, pontifex maximus, consul for the 13th time, with tribunician power for the 22nd time, imperator for the 14th time, father of the country." Since at least the time of Antiochos III (242-187 B.C.) Jews lived in Phrygia and in Lydia.[79] The existence of a strong Jewish community (Acts 13:14) indicates that the city was attractive for merchants.[80]

Luke devotes a relatively long section to the missionary activity of Paul and Barnabas in Antioch, which he uses to give for the first time an extensive report of Paul's missionary preaching before a Jewish audience in synagogues (Acts 13:16-41; see the analysis in sec. 3.1). He emphasizes

---

chia ad Pisidiam, FRLANT 193 (Göttingen: Vandenhoeck & Ruprecht, 2000), pp. 189-90.
[76]Levick, *Roman Colonies*, pp. 93-94.
[77]Ibid., p. 136.
[78]Stephen Mitchell and Marc Waelkens, *Pisidian Antioch: The Site and Its Monuments* (London: Duckworth, 1998), pp. 113-73.
[79]Josephus *Antiquitates Judaicae* 12.147-153.
[80]Levick, *Roman Colonies*, pp. 58, 99, 189.

four elements in his description of the initial contact of Paul and Barnabas with the Jews in the synagogue: (1) reading from the Law, (2) reading from the Prophets, (3) invitation of the *archisynagōgos*, the president
of the local synagogue, to Paul to address the worshipers, (4) the homily preached by Paul. As was often the case, the synagogue served as an
"open forum for Jews of different background and persuasions."[81] At the
end of the synagogue service Paul and Barnabas are asked to come back
and to continue their teaching. Many of those who heard Paul speak in
the synagogue did not want to wait for the next sabbath to learn further
details and to receive more explanations about Paul's message of Jesus as
Messiah. It seems that people were soon converted to faith in Jesus: Luke
relates that Paul and Barnabas spoke to the people who followed them
"and urged them to continue in the grace of God" (Acts 13:43), indicating
that some of the inquirers accepted the message of the revelation of God's
grace in and through Jesus Christ.

On the following sabbath "almost the whole city" (Acts 13:44) gathered: besides the Jews, the proselytes and the God-fearers who attended
the synagogue, a larger crowd wanted to hear what these Jewish teachers
had to say. We should note that Luke does *not* assert that *all* the citizens
of Antioch gathered in the synagogue (which certainly would be too small
for the ten thousand inhabitants of the city, who may not even have found
space in the theater before the renovation of A.D. 300).

Scholars who have never witnessed a mass scene in connection with the
work of missionaries may perhaps not be able to visualize such an event.
It is not implausible to assume that Paul had the opportunity to speak to
a crowd numbering in the thousands within a week of his arrival in Antioch: he had arrived in the city possibly with a letter of introduction written by the Roman governor of Cyprus, and he may well have had contact
with the leading aristocratic families in the city during the first days of his
visit. The crowd could have gathered in front of the synagogue, or perhaps
in the plaza called Tiberia Platea in front of the temple of Augustus, or in
the plaza called Augusta Platea at the northern end of the Cardo Maximus, or perhaps in the theater located on the Decumanus Maximus.

---

[81]Lee I. Levine, *The Ancient Synagogue: The First Thousand Years* (New Haven, Conn.: Yale University Press, 2000), p. 111.

Luke relates that "the Jews" reacted to the presence of the huge crowd with "jealousy" and that they "contradicted" the proclamation of the missionaries (Acts 13:45). The term *the Jews* may refer to the leading officials of the synagogue. When Luke reports that the Jews "blasphemed" in the course of the debate, he probably means that they pronounced the curse of the law (Deut 21:22-23) against Jesus, who had been crucified; the missionaries would have interpreted this as blasphemy against God himself who had raised Jesus from the dead.

Paul reacted to the opposition of the Jewish officials by pointing to God's plan of salvation: "It was necessary that the word of God should be spoken first to you. Since you reject it and judge yourselves to be unworthy of eternal life, we are now turning to the Gentiles" (Acts 13:46). If the Jewish community decides to reject and to oppose the word of God that the missionaries are preaching, they will focus their efforts on the Gentile population of the city. Paul explains that such a turn to the Gentiles has been prophesied in the Scriptures: "For so the Lord has commanded us, saying, 'I have set you to be a light for the Gentiles, so that you may bring salvation to the ends of the earth'" (Acts 13:47). Paul's preaching of Jesus Messiah before a Gentile audience fulfills God's commission to his Servant in Isaiah 49:6, who was expected to restore Israel and to return the exiles to Israel (thus the Septuagint) and who was expected to bring salvation to the nations.[82] The phrase "light for the Gentiles" describes Paul and Barnabas as the messengers of the promised good news.

The success of the missionary work among the Gentile citizens of Antioch is described by Luke with a few terse sentences:

> When the Gentiles heard this, they were glad and praised the word of the Lord; and as many as had been destined for eternal life became believers. Thus the word of the Lord spread throughout the region. (Acts 13:48-49)

Gentiles came to faith in Jesus Christ not only in Antioch but also in some of the fifty villages within the city territory of Antioch ("throughout the region").[83]

---

[82]See David W. Pao, *Acts and the Isaianic New Exodus*, WUNT 2/130 (Tübingen: Mohr Siebeck, 2000), pp. 96-101, on the use of Is 49:6.

[83]Cilliers Breytenbach, *Paulus und Barnabas in der Provinz Galatien. Studien zu Apostelgeschichte 13f.; 16,6; 18,23 und den Adressaten des Galaterbriefes*, AGAJU 38 (Leiden: Brill, 1996), p. 50.

In the course of Paul's missionary work in Antioch, both in the synagogue and in the city more generally, he came in contact with the following people or groups of people: (1) The officials of the synagogue;[84] (2)
Jews who meet on the sabbath in the synagogue, "men of Israel," "descendants of Abraham's family";[85] (3) devout proselytes;[86] (4) God-fearers,[87]
that is, pagans who were a regular part of the synagogue community; (5)
devout Gentile women of "high standing" in the city[88] who were not part
of the regular synagogue community but who were more than sympathetic
regarding the Jewish faith; (6) Gentile inhabitants of Antioch,[89] that is,
pagan visitors of the synagogue who did not belong to the regular group of
God-fearers and sympathizers;[90] (7) the "leading men of the city,"[91] that
is, the members of the local elite in the municipal aristocracy, people who
controlled public life in Antioch on account of their social standing and
on account of their wealth which came from their estates. Luke does not
specify that Paul came into direct contact with these "leading men." If he
came to Antioch as a result of his encounter with Sergius Paulus, hoping
that he could find similar access to the aristocracy of this Roman colony
in the border region of Phrygia and Pisidia, the Jews of Antioch thwarted
the potential of this plan (Acts 13:50).

The comment on the success of Paul's missionary work in Acts 13:48-
49 is immediately followed by the observation that the Jews of the city
succeeded in using "the devout women of high standing" to prompt "the
leading men of the city" to take action against the missionaries. The "devout women of high standing" were the aristocratic women of Antioch

---

[84]*hoi archisynagōgoi* (Acts 13:15).

[85]*Ioudaioi* (Acts 13:43); *andres Israēlitai* (Acts 13:16); *huioi genous Abraam* (Acts 13:26).

[86]*sebomenoi prosēlytoi* (Acts 13:43). The adjective *sebomenoi* possibly indicates that the proselytes
who became Christians had previously had made special contributions for the Jewish community
in Antioch or that they were in some other way connected with the synagogue. They could be described as "proselytes of the first category"; cf. Bernd Wander, *Gottesfürchtige und Sympathisanten.
Studien zum heidnischen Umfeld von Diasporasynagogen*, WUNT 104 (Tübingen: Mohr Siebeck,
1998), pp. 191, 197.

[87]*hoi phoboumenoi ton theon* (Acts 13:16); *hoi en hymin phoboumenoi ton theon* (Acts 13:26).

[88]*tas sebomenas gynaikas tas euschēmonas* (Acts 13:50).

[89]*pasa hē polis* (Acts 13:44); *ta ethnē* (Acts 13:48).

[90]Wander, *Gottesfürchtige*, p. 197, distinguishes (1) model God-fearers, (2) typical God-fearers, (3)
sympathizers of the first category, (4) typical sympathizers, (5) further listeners who were present
in the synagogue.

[91]*hoi prōtoi tēs poleōs* (Acts 13:50).

who regularly attended the synagogue services, and "the leading men of the city" would have included the *duoviri*, the highest representatives of the local government who belonged to the elite families of Antioch and who played an important role in the cult of Men and presumably in the imperial cult as well. The Jews presumably argued that the activities of Paul and Barnabas jeopardized the position of the main deity of the city, a development that was unavoidable if worshipers of Men accepted the message of Paul who actively sought to recruit people to follow Jesus Christ and to abandon the traditional gods.

The aggressive, official action of the Jews of Antioch suggests that Paul's missionary work had been rather successful. The pressure that was put on the missionaries eventually resulted in their expulsion from the city. When Paul and Barnabas revisit the city a few months later on their return journey back to Syria, "they strengthened the souls of the disciples and encouraged them to continue in the faith," appointing elders *(presbyteroi)*, that is, people responsible for the new community of believers in Jesus Christ (Acts 14:22-23).

Iconium. Luke's account of Paul's missionary activity in Iconium, a city that was incorporated into the new province of Galatia in 25 B.C. (see fig. 1.6) to which Augustus added the new colony named *Iulia Augusta Iconium*, is brief (Acts 14:1-7). Paul and Barnabas "went into the Jewish synagogue and spoke in such a way that a great number of both Jews and Greeks became believers"; that is, they were able to preach the gospel to the Jews and the Gentile sympathizers who attended the meetings of the Jewish community. The unbelieving Jews who resisted Paul and Barnabas could not prevent that "they remained for a long time, speaking boldly for the Lord, who testified to the word of his grace by granting signs and wonders to be done through them."

The opposition, which eventually forced the missionaries to leave the city, was not spearheaded by representatives of the local Roman aristocracy as in Antioch, but rather by the leading Jews and Greeks of Iconium. The reference to "disciples" and to "elders" that were appointed by Paul and Barnabas during their return journey (Acts 14:21-23) implies that a community of believers had been established in Iconium.

Lystra. Paul's missionary work in Lystra is reported in Acts 14:7-20 with greater detail on account of an incident in which Paul was nearly killed. In 25 B.C. Lystra was refounded as a Roman military colony by Augustus with the name *Colonia Iulia Felix Gemina Lystra*.[92] Luke reports in a summary statement that Paul and Barnabas preached the gospel (Acts 14:7) and that a man crippled from birth was healed after he had listened to Paul's preaching and come to faith which gave him the confidence that he could be healed (Acts 14:8-10). The presence of a lame man, presumably a beggar, may suggest that Paul was preaching in the *agora*, the central square of the city, and where he interacted with the citizens who continued to speak in the local Lycaonian language besides using Greek.[93] When the crowds saw the lame man walking on his feet, they interpret the miracle in the context of their traditional religiosity (Acts 14:11-13). They regard the healing as proof of the supernatural character of the two visitors, assuming that "the gods have come down to us in human form!" They identified Barnabas with Zeus, the father of men and gods, the hurler of thunderbolts, the strongest of the gods,[94] perhaps because he had a more impressive appearance. And they identified Paul with Hermes, the messenger of the gods,[95] probably because he had been preaching. The priest of Zeus, whose temple was located outside of the city walls, brought oxen and garlands to the gates (of the temple) in preparation for a sacrifice. The priest was presumably a member of the local elite who had assumed the priesthood in the temple of Zeus for a defined period of time.[96]

The reaction of the crowd may have a specific local background. There was a legend, attested in Phrygia, according to which two local gods— perhaps Tarchunt and Runt, or Pappas and Men (in the Greek version of the legend the gods Zeus and Hermes)—wandered through the region as

---

[92]The claim by some missiologists that the culture of Lystra was relatively unaffected by Roman influence (David J. Hesselgrave and Edward Rommen, *Contextualization: Meaning, Methods and Models* [1989; reprint, Grand Rapids: Zondervan, 1992], p. 9) is uninformed.

[93]The citizens of Lystra were evidently bilingual, speaking Greek (and thus able to understand Paul's preaching) and Lycaonian, the traditional regional language. There is no indication in the text that Paul and Barnabas faced a "language problem" in Lystra, as Hesselgrave and Rommen, *Contextualization*, p. 9, assume.

[94]Walter Burkert, *Greek Religion* (Cambridge: Harvard University Press, 1985), pp. 125-31.

[95]Cf. ibid., pp. 156-59.

[96]David W. J. Gill, "Religion in a Local Setting," in *The Book of Acts in Its Graeco-Roman Setting*, ed. David W. J. Gill and Conrad Gempf, The Book of Acts in Its First-Century Setting 2 (Exeter, U.K.: Paternoster, 1994), p. 82.

human beings. Nobody provided them with hospitality, until Philemon and Baucis, an older couple, shared their supplies with the unrecognized gods. The couple was richly rewarded. They were told to climb a mountain, which they did, with the result that they escaped the flood which consumed the others (Ovid *Metamorphoses* 8.626-724). While this legend has not been attested in Lycaonia, one should note that a fragmentary inscription from Lystra possibly links Zeus, Hermes and perhaps Gē; a relief found in Lystra dedicated to Zeus Ampelites shows Zeus, Hermes and an eagle; and in the neighboring city of Sedasa an inscription dating to the third century also links Zeus and Hermes.[97] At any rate, the crowds evidently had understood so little of Paul's preaching that they saw their polytheistic and mythical traditions confirmed.

Barnabas and Paul tore their clothes, a gesture of mourning and shock, and they rushed into the crowd as an expression of self-humiliation (Acts 14:14). The missionaries clarified that they are mere mortals, not gods. And they explained that they bring the good news that they no longer have to worship their useless gods because they can turn to the only true and living God who has created everything and who wants that people experience joy in their hearts (Acts 14:15-17; for an analysis see sec. 3.2).

The missionary work in Lystra in A.D. 46/47 evidently led to the establishment of a church. Paul visited the believers in Lystra on the return journey from Derbe to Antioch (Acts 14:21-23) and again two years later in A.D. 49 on the journey from Syria to the province of Asia (Acts 16:1-3). During the latter visit in Lystra Paul recruited Timothy, the son of a Jewish woman married to a Greek husband, as coworker. Paul probably visited Lystra a fourth time when he traveled in A.D. 52 from Syria to Ephesus (Acts 18:23).

It should be noted that the oldest Christian tombstone that has been found in Isauria or Lycaonia, dating to the first century A.D., comes from the territory of Lystra. The inscription was found in Dorla, 33 kilometers southeast of the modern town of Hatunsaray (Lystra), on the hill on the western river bank. The following text is inscribed on

---

[97]See ibid., pp. 83-84; Dean Philip Bechard, *Paul Outside the Walls: A Study of Luke's Socio-Geographical Universalism in Acts 14:8-20*, Analecta biblica 143 (Rome: Editrice Pontificio Istituto Biblico, 2000), pp. 49-50.

the tombstone (which is damaged on the upper left side, where some words are missing): ". . . buried the blessed and dearest father beloved by all. The blessed father Philtatos, beloved by God. In memory." The deceased man was a certain Philtatos who was evidently wealthy and educated. His title *papas* corresponds to episkopos, which may suggest that Philtatos was a leading Christian.[98]

Derbe. The city of Derbe was the next stop of the missionaries. Luke reports that Paul and Barnabas preached the gospel in Derbe and they "made many disciples" (Acts 14:20-21). One of the Christians of Derbe was Gaius, one of Paul's coworkers in Ephesus (Acts 19:29) who accompanied Paul on his journey through Macedonia and Galatia (Acts 20:4).

Perge. After Paul and Barnabas returned from Derbe to Lystra, Iconium and Antioch, they proceeded south to the coast, traveling through Pisidia. When they arrived in Pamphylia, they preached the gospel in Perge (Acts 14:24-25). Perge was the capital of the newly constituted province Lycia-Pamphylia. Perge had the complete infrastructure of a flourishing city of the imperial period: a theater for fourteen thousand spectators, a stadium (234 meters long), monumental city gates, baths, a *nymphaeum*, an aqueduct and temples. The temple of Artemis in the city was surpassed in fame only by the temple of Artemis Ephesia in Ephesus. The buildings of Perge document the enormous wealth of the city in the first century.[99] The high level of Greek education and culture in Perge is demonstrated by inscriptions that document the presence of physicians, philosophers, philologists, athletes, actors, poets, singers, mimes, musicians and dancers, some of whom were active in other regions (in Ephesus, Pergamum, Tlos, Thyatira, Sparta and Rome).

Despite the significance of the city, Luke needs only five words of Greek text to describe Paul's missionary work in Perge. The fact that he does not record conversions or the establishment of a church does not mean that Paul's mission was unsuccessful. The other references to Paul's "speaking" *(laleō)* in Acts 13:42, 45 (Antioch); 14:1 (Iconium); 14:9 (Lystra), and in

---

[98]Gertrud Laminger-Pascher, *Die kaiserzeitlichen Inschriften Lykaoniens. Faszikel I: Der Süden,* ETAM 15 (Wien: Österreichische Akademie der Wissenschaften, 1992), pp. 215, 230. W. M. Ramsay who discovered the inscription, dated the tombstone to the third century A.D.

[99]Hartwin Brandt, *Gesellschaft und Wirtschaft Pamphyliens und Pisidiens im Altertum,* Asia-Minor Studien 7 (Bonn: Habelt, 1992), p. 102.

subsequent passages (Acts 16:6, 13, 14, 32; 17:19; 18:9) are found in the context of preaching the gospel, conversions and the establishment of new churches. This suggests that some of the people of Perge who heard Paul's preaching were indeed converted and that a church was established.

1.5 Paul in Macedonia and Achaia

Luke relates that after his return from his missionary outreach in the cities of southern Galatia, staying in Antioch in Syria for some time (Acts 14:26-28) and participating in the Apostles' Council in Jerusalem (Acts 15:1-35), Paul wanted to travel west again and visit the churches that had been established. As differences of opinion between the apostle and Barnabas over the suitability of John Mark as a missionary coworker could not be resolved, Paul recruited Silas as a companion. They "went through Syria and Cilicia, strengthening the churches" (Acts 15:41) before they reached Derbe and Lystra (Acts 16:1) and presumably Iconium and Pisidian Antioch (Acts 16:2-5).

The goal of Paul was to reach the *province of Asia* (Acts 16:6). Several options presented themselves once he had reached Pisidian Antioch (see fig. 1.7). He could have traveled in a northwesterly direction, crossing the mountain range of the Karakuş Dağı (ancient name unknown), whose peaks rise in this area to 6,500 feet (2,000 meters), just south of the sanctuary of the Xenoi Tekmoreioi.[100] Traveling southwest on a main road, Paul would have reached Apameia (Apameia Kibotos, also Celaenae, mod. Dinar). Alternatively, Paul could have traveled in a westerly and then southwesterly direction on the Via Sebastea, passing through Apollonia (Mordiaion, also Sozopolis), before reaching a junction of several roads, one of which leads to Apameia. Luke's brief notice of Asia in Acts 16:6 is usually interpreted in terms of a plan to reach Ephesus, the capital of the Roman province of Asia. This is not a certainty, however, as I will show in our discussion of the geographical scope of Paul's missionary methods (see sec. 5.1).

---

[100]See Richard J. A. Talbert, ed., *Barrington Atlas of the Greek and Roman World* (Princeton, N.J.: Princeton University Press, 2000), map 62, F5/E5. Modern maps show several small roads leading across the mountain range in this area, which are impassable for passenger cars but which present no problems for people on foot.

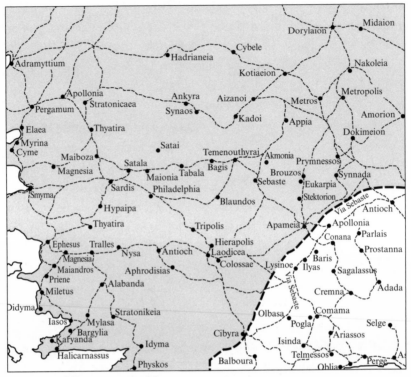

Figure 1.7. The province of Asia

When Paul was prevented by divine intervention from reaching the province of Asia, he decided to travel toward the northern regions of Asia Minor to reach cities in the *province of Bithynia-Pontus* (Acts 16:7; see fig. 1.8). When this was rendered impossible as well, Paul traveled in a westerly direction to the coastal city of Alexandria Troas (Acts 16:8).The details of the route implied in Acts 16:6-8 are unclear.[101] Paul probably reached Kotiaeion in the border region of Phrygia and Mysia, and perhaps Dorylaion, a city located at the juncture of several major north-south and west-east roads. He then evidently passed through Kadoi and, along the upper reaches of the Makestos River, through Synaos, Hadrianothera and Adramyttion before reaching Alexandria Troas. Because Paul was apparently unsure of where to focus his missionary ministry—he could not

---

[101]For the complexities of reconstructing Paul's travel route during this period see Schnabel, *Early Christian Mission*, 2:1131-50.

Figure 1.8. Bithynia-Pontus

go west to the cities in the province of Asia or north to the cities of the
province of Bithynia-Pontus, nor did he want to go back east and return to
Tarsus or Antioch—it is a distinct possibility that he preached the gospel
in these cities.

Macedonia. Prompted by a dream-vision (Acts 16:9-10), Paul and his
companions crossed over the Aegean Sea to Europe and arrived in Neapolis, a port on the Macedonian coast. From there he proceeded to preach
the gospel in *three cities in the province of Macedonia: Philippi, Thessalonica
and Beroea* (see fig. 1.9).[102] When he arrived in the summer of A.D. 49,
the region had just been reorganized five years earlier by the emperor
Claudius: from 27 B.C. to A.D. 15 Macedonia was a senatorial province;
from A.D. 15-44 Macedonia was administered together with Achaia by
the imperial legate of Moesia, with Thessalonica as the new capital; after
A.D. 44, Claudius organized Macedonia and Achaia as separate senatorial
provinces (see fig. 1.10).

Philippi. Paul's missionary work in Philippi (Acts 16:12-40) probably
took place in the months of August and October of A.D. 49. After Augustus's victory in the battle of Actium in 31 B.C., he settled Italian colonists,
including veterans of the 28th Legion and veterans of the Praetorian cohort in the city, refounding the city in 27 B.C. as a Roman colony with
the name Colonia Iulia Augusta Philippiensis.[103] As regards the religious
landscape, the influence of Thracian traditions was still evident, but in the
first century only Greco-Roman cults are attested. The religious identity
of the inhabitants was "influenced primarily by Roman religion in which
the worship of the princeps and his deified ancestors or predecessors was
central, besides the traditional Greco-Roman pantheon."[104] Philippi had
between five thousand and ten thousand inhabitants.[105]

Luke relates how Paul and his coworkers found a "place of prayer" (Gk
proseuchē), a term that commonly describes a synagogue (Acts 16:13). It

---

[102]For details on these cities see Schnabel, *Early Christian Mission*, pp. 1151-53, 1160-63, 1168.

[103]See Paul Collart, *Philippes, ville de Macédoine depuis des origines jusqu'à la fin de l'époque romaine*,
2 vols. (Paris: Boccard, 1937), pp. 224-27.

[104]Lukas Bormann, *Philippi—Stadt und Christengemeinde zur Zeit des Paulus*, NTSup 78 (Leiden:
Brill, 1995), pp. 63-64.

[105]Peter Pilhofer, *Philippi. Band I: Die erste christliche Gemeinde Europas. Band II: Katalog der Inschriften von Philippi*, WUNT 87.119 (Tübingen: Mohr Siebeck, 1995-2000), 1:76.

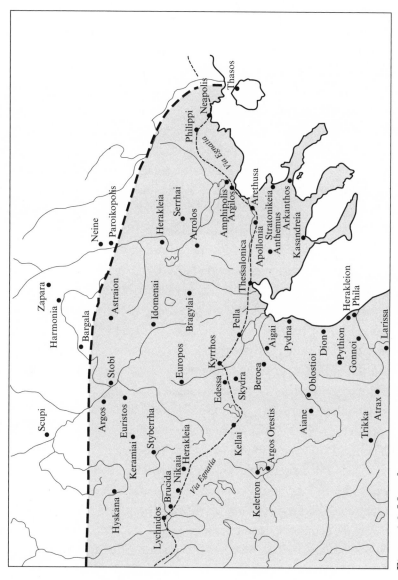

Figure 1.9. Macedonia

appears that the Jewish community in Philippi met in a house that was
located at the river Gangites, about three kilometers west of the city center.[106] The contact with Jewish women and with female sympathizers in
the synagogue leads to the conversion of Lydia, a woman from Thyatira, a
city in the region of Lydia in Asia Minor, who is introduced as a dealer in
purple cloth. She is described as a person who prayed on the sabbath, who
was hospitable, gracious and humble; she is, in other words, an ideal God-
fearer. Lydia had a house, indicating that she was well-to-do, although as
a resident alien she would hardly have been a member of the municipal
aristocracy of Philippi. When "the Lord opened her heart to listen eagerly
to what was said by Paul" (Acts 16:14), she came to faith in Jesus Christ
and was baptized together with her household, suggesting that other family members who had listened to Paul's preaching also came to faith in
Jesus Christ.

Luke reports no further missionary activity of Paul in the city. However, the continuation of the narrative indicates that Paul's preaching evidently led to numerous conversions among the inhabitants. A new situation arose when a slave girl whose owners had used her fortune-telling
powers to earn money follows the missionaries as they are active in the
city, shouting, "these men are slaves of the Most High God, who proclaim
to you a way of salvation" (Acts 16:17). Paul exorcised the demon that
possessed the girl because he was "annoyed" on account of the misleading pronouncements that she made in public: most citizens of Philippi
would have linked "the Most High God" with Zeus. Probably Paul saw
the danger that the girl's "proclamations" might confuse people who could
misunderstand Paul's own proclamation of the one true and living God
in terms of a syncretistic fusion of disparate religious ideas. The owners
of the girl dragged Paul and Silas to the forum and accused them before
the local authorities (Gk *archontai* [Acts 16:19]) as being trouble-makers
who were introducing new customs that alter the ancestral customs. Such
a charge was tantamount to revolution. Paul and Silas are described as

---

[106]Martin Hengel, "Proseuche und Synagoge: Jüdische Gemeinde, Gotteshaus und Gottesdienst
in der Diaspora und in Palästina [1971]," in *Judaica et Hellenistica I. Studien zum antiken Judentum und seiner griechisch-römischen Umwelt*, WUNT 90 (Tübingen: Mohr Siebeck, 1996), pp.
171-95.

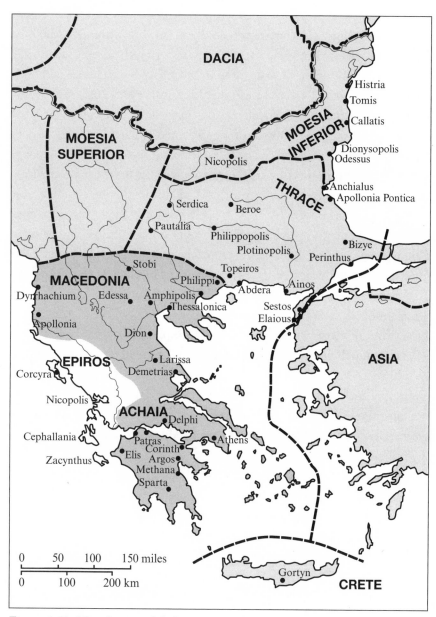

Figure 1.10. Macedonia and Achaia

newcomers, as Jews who are aliens *(peregrini)* and who therefore possess neither influence *(potentia)* nor favor *(gratia)*. The missionaries are put in prison, perhaps as a short-term penalty for misbehaving individuals or as detention before the trial. An earthquake during the night leads to the conversion of the jailer, probably a slave owned by the city who had been put in charge of the local prison,[107] and his family (Acts 16:25-34).

On the day after the earthquake the city magistrates sent the "police," that is, their attendants, the lictors, to the prison and ordered Paul and Silas to be released (Acts 16:35-36). They were evidently convinced that the flogging and the imprisonment were punishment enough for the troublemakers. It was at this point that Paul informed the authorities that he and Silas possessed Roman citizenship (Acts 16:37). His wish that the representatives of the magistrate should apologize publicly was probably fulfilled; they placated the missionaries (Acts 16:38-39), presumably since they did not want to get into trouble from the governor to whom Paul and Silas might complain.

When Paul departed, he left behind a house church: the "brothers" who are mentioned in Acts 16:40 stand for the believers who had been meeting in Lydia's house. Paul's letter to the Philippians, written twelve years after the church was established, provides us more information about the believers in Philippi.[108] The Christians in Philippi had been "sharing in the gospel from the first day until now" (Phil 1:5), a "fellowship" that was demonstrated in the financial support of the church for Paul's missionary work, which included the gift that Epaphroditus had taken to Paul (Phil 2:25-30; 4:10-20).

Thessalonica. Paul and his fellow missionaries traveled from Philippi to Thessalonica, the capital and the most populous city of Macedonia.[109] Estimates of the number of inhabitants range from twenty to sixty-five thousand.[110] Luke's account of Paul's missionary work in Thessalonica is brief (Acts 17:1-9). He first focuses on the initial phase of Paul's procla-

---

[107]See Brian Rapske, *The Book of Acts and Paul in Roman Custody*, The Book of Acts in Its First-Century Setting 3 (Exeter, U.K.: Paternoster, 1994), pp. 261-64.

[108]See O'Brien, *Philippians*, pp. 35-38.

[109]Strabo 7.7.4; Livy 45.30.4.

[110]Christoph vom Brocke, *Thessaloniki—Stadt der Kassander und Gemeinde des Paulus. Eine frühe christliche Gemeinde in ihrer heidnischen Umwelt*, WUNT 2/125 (Tübingen: Mohr Siebeck, 2001), pp. 71-72; Riesner, *Paul's Early Period*, p. 341.

mation of the gospel: Paul preached in the synagogue on three sabbaths, seeking to convince the listeners on the basis of the holy Scriptures that Jesus who suffered (and died) is the promised Messiah. The listeners included both Jews and a great number of "devout Greeks," that is, sympathizers who attended the synagogue services and who showed interest in the Jewish faith, as well as "not a few of the leading women."

Luke briefly notes the success of Paul's missionary preaching: some Jews and a larger number of Gentile God-fearers, including several women who belonged to the local aristocracy, came to faith in Jesus Christ and joined Paul and Silas (Acts 17:4), suggesting the establishment of a church. In his letter to the Thessalonian Christians, written only a few months later, Paul reminds the believers in the city how they had turned away from idols to the true and living God (1 Thess 1:9), a comment that suggests that the majority of the new Christian community consisted of former polytheists.

The second part of Luke's account (Acts 17:5-9) relates a riot scene in which the missionaries have no direct role but are nevertheless forced to leave the city (Acts 17:10). Jewish citizens and local mobs accuse Paul of having turned the entire world upside down (Acts 17:6). This accusation should be understood as a charge that seeks to make Paul appear as a criminal, using allegations from the traditional arsenal of polemics and defamation. The formulation "the (entire) *oikoumenē*" is surely meant in a hyperbolic sense: by A.D. 50 Paul had preached the gospel only in Antioch and in Damascus as far as larger cities in the Roman Empire were concerned. (He had not been in Alexandria or in Ephesus, in Corinth or in Rome.) The charge of the opponents did not need to be founded in reality to serve their agitation: formulated as Luke reports, it served its purpose of causing the city officials to take decisive action. Paul was forced to leave the city in a hurry, while Timothy and Silas stayed behind (Acts 17:14-15; 18:5) before traveling to Beroea, where they met up with Paul. Several weeks later, when Timothy traveled via Athens to Corinth where Paul had started to preach, he is soon sent back to Thessalonica with a letter from Paul (1 Thess 3:5) in which the apostle addresses theological misunderstandings that had arisen in the previous weeks.

Beroea. Luke describes Paul's ministry in Beroea in a few sentences in Acts 17:10-14. Beroea seems to have been the seat of the Macedonian provincial assembly (Koinōn) since the time of Augustus, headed by the high priest of the imperial cult of the province. Beroea flourished in the first century, the city was one of the cultural centers of the province.

Paul preached in the local synagogue, whose members were prepared to listen attentively to his message, examining whether it is in agreement with the Scriptures. Many Jews were converted and "not a few Greek women and men of high standing" (Acts 17:12). The reference to "the brothers" ("the believers" [NRSV]) in Acts 17:14 confirms the establishment of a Christian community. When Jews from Thessalonica stir up trouble, Paul is again forced to leave in a hurry. Beroean believers accompanied Paul to the coast, presumably to Pydna, the port of Beroea, and taking him by ship to Athens (Acts 17:14-15).

The ninth period of Paul's mission: Achaia. Paul arrived in the province of Achaia in the spring of A.D. 50 (see fig. 1.11). Augustus had reorganized Achaia as a senatorial province in 27 B.C. Under Tiberius and Gaius Caligula, Achaia was combined with Macedonia as an imperial province, before Claudius organized Achaia again as a separate senatorial province in A.D. 44. Achaia comprised Greece proper (the regions of Attica, Boeotia, Peloponnes) and included the regions of Thessaly and southern Epirus. The province was governed by a proconsul, appointed by lot every year, whose seat was in Corinth.

Athens. When Paul arrived in Athens early in A.D. 50., the glorious *Pentekontaetia*, the Great Fifty Years in the fifth century B.C., of this most famous of the Greek cities were long gone. In the more recent past Augustus, who had visited the city immediately after his victory in the Battle of Actium on September 2, 31 B.C., was a benefactor of the city which caused Athens to flourish again. The citizens honored Augustus by erecting a temple of Roma and Augustus on the acropolis. The economic situation remained difficult, however, seen in the fact that the Garden of Hephaistos was no longer maintained. The Romans admired Athens as the seat of the four philosophical schools: the Academy, the Peripatos, the Kepos and the Stoa.

Many think that Paul never planned to do missionary work in Athens,

Figure 1.11. Achaia

as he merely waited for Silas and Timothy, his coworkers, to arrive from Macedonia (Acts 17:15-16). Whatever Paul's original intentions were, the fact that "he argued in the synagogue with the Jews and the devout persons, and also in the marketplace every day with those who happened to be there" (Acts 17:17) demonstrates that he did indeed engage in missionary work just as he did in the other cities that he had visited. He preached in synagogues before Jews and in the central square (agora) before Gentile citizens. If Paul saw the temples that he mentioned in his speech before the Areopagus Council (Acts 17:23) in the agora, his "street preaching" took place in the old agora, the central plaza of the city, rather than in the new Market of Caesar and Augustus. Paul proclaimed the same message in Athens that he had proclaimed in other cities: "he was telling the good news about Jesus and the resurrection" (Acts 17:18).

Luke's report focuses on Paul's encounter with Epicurean and Stoic philosophers with whom he debated. Philosophical discussions in the agora were characteristic for the cultural life of Athens, as the example of Socrates demonstrates. The *Stoa Poikile* or "Painted Stoa" on the north side of the agora was a traditional location for such activities. This stoa was open to all Athenians, a popular meeting place for discussions and cultural activities, attracting jugglers, sword-swallowers, beggars, fishmongers and philosophers. Some of the people who had Paul speak concluded that he was a charlatan, an unsystematic "ragbag collector of scraps of learning" (Gk *spermologos*), while others concluded that "he seems to be a proclaimer of foreign divinities" (Acts 17:18). Perhaps they assumed that this Jewish orator from Tarsus wanted to introduce to the Athenians Jesus and Anastasis as new deities, since Paul spoke of Jesus and the resurrection (Gk *anastasis*). Paul was taken to the Council of the Areopagus, whose members promptly pointed out that they have the right to question Paul and to make a decision in this matter. The Areopagus (Gk *Areios Pagos*) was one of the ancient institutions of Athens, which increasingly functioned as the city council.

Despite the tolerant attitude concerning religious worship in the Hellenistic world, there was no "freedom of religion" in the sense that people were free to introduce new cults into the pantheon of deities that the inhabitants of a particular city would worship.[111] Even in the cosmopolitan Hellenistic period with its syncretistic tendencies, "the introduction of foreign cults and rites required the official authorization of the state."[112] An Athenian decree stipulates: "The king archon shall fix the boundaries of the sanctuaries/sacred precincts in the Pelargikon, and in the future no one shall found altars, cut the stones from the Pelargikon or take out earth or stones without (the authorization of) the council and the demos."[113]

---

[111]See Robert Garland, *Introducing New Gods: The Politics of Athenian Religion* (Ithaca, N.Y.: Cornell University Press, 1992). On the deities which were worshiped in Athens cf. John McK. Camp, *Gods and Heroes in the Athenian Agora* (Princeton, N.J.: American School of Classical Studies at Athens, 1980); see the summary in Schnabel, *Early Christian Mission*, 2:1175-77.

[112]Hendrik S. Versnel, *Ter unus: Isis, Dionysos, Hermes. Three Studies in Henotheism*, Inconsistencies in Greek and Roman Religion 1 (Leiden: Brill, 1990), p. 122; on Athenian law against foreign gods see ibid., pp. 123-46.

[113]Franciszek Sokolowski, *Lois sacrées des cités grecques* (Paris: Boccard, 1969), no. 5; Eran Lupu,

Isocrates praises the Athenians for guarding "against the elimination of any of the ancestral sacrifices and against the addition of any sacrifices outside the traditional ones."[114] Josephus relates that Ninos, a priestess of the Phrygian god Sabazios, was put to death by the Athenians "because someone accused her of initiating people into mysteries of foreign gods; this was forbidden by their law, and the penalty decreed for any who introduced a foreign god was death."[115] Maecenas's speech to Augustus suggests that this aversion to foreign and new cults persisted well into the first century A.D., as the emperor is advised:

> Do you not only yourself worship the divine Power everywhere and in every way in accordance with the traditions of our fathers, but compel all others to honour it. Those who attempt to distort our religion with strange rites you should abhor and punish, not merely for the sake of the gods (since if a man despises these he will not pay honour to any other being), but because such men, by bringing in new divinities in place of the old, persuade many to adopt foreign practices, from which spring up conspiracies, factions, and cabals, which are far from profitable to a monarchy. (Cassius Dio 52.36)

Religious laws included stipulations regulating cult calendars, the foundation of a cult, sacred land or property (statues, dedications, etc.), sacrifices, pre- and postsacrifice procedures such as purification rites, festival regulations (processions, etc.), religious offices, disciplinary penalties and funerals.

The introduction of a deity into a city would prompt the magistrates to ascertain the novelty of a cult, the desirability of allowing the cult and the requirements of the cult, such as the need for a temple or an altar, sacrifices, festivals and processions.[116] A good example is the decree permit-

---

Greek Sacred Law: A Collection of New Documents, Religions in the Graeco-Roman World 152 (Leiden: Brill, 2005), p. 36.

[114] Isocrates *Areopagiticus* 30.

[115] Josephus *Against Apion* 2.267.

[116] On religious laws in Greece and Rome see Franciszek Sokolowski, *Lois sacrées de l'Asie Mineure*, Travaux et mémoires 9 (Paris: Boccard, 1955); Franciszek Sokolowski, *Lois sacrées des cités grecques. With Supplément* (Paris: Boccard, 1962); R. C. T. Parker, "What Are Sacred Laws?" in *The Law and the Courts in Ancient Greece*, ed. E. M. Harris and L. Rubinstein (London: Duckworth, 2004), pp. 57-70; Lupu, *Greek Sacred Law* (read with the review by J.-M. Carbon, *Bryn Mawr Classical Review*, April 7, 2005); Stephen D. Lambert, "Athenian State Laws and Decrees, 352/1—322/1: II Religious Regulations," *ZPE* 154 (2005): 125-59.

ting the Citians to found a temple of Aphrodite in Athens:

> Gods. When Nikokratos was archon, in the first prytany (that of the
> tribe Aegeis): Theophilos from the deme Phegous, one of the Proedroi,
> put this matter to the vote: The Council decided (after Antidodos, son
> of Apollodoros, from the deme Sypalletos made the motion): Concern-
> ing the things that the Citians say about the foundation of the temple to
> Aphrodite, it has been voted by the Council that the Proedroi, the ones to
> be chosen by lot to serve as Proedroi at the first Assembly, should intro-
> duce the Citians and allow them to have an audience, and to share with
> the People the opinion of the Council, that the People, having heard from
> the Citians concerning the foundation of the temple, and from any other
> Athenian who wants to speak, decide to do whatever seems best. When
> Nikokrates was archon, in the second Prytany (that of the tribe Pandionis):
> Phanostratos from the deme Philaidai, one of the Proedroi, put this matter
> to the vote: The People decided (after Lycurgus, son of Lycophron, of the
> deme Boutadai made the motion): Concerning the things for which the
> Citian merchants resolved to petition, lawfully, asking the People for the
> use of a plot of land on which they might build a temple of Aphrodite, it
> has seemed best to the People to give to the merchants of the Citians the
> use of a plot of land on which they might build a temple of Aphrodite, just
> as also the Egyptians built the temple of Isis.[117]

The request of the members of the Council of the Areopagus that Paul
should present his religious teaching was polite.[118] Paul was not asked to
defend his convictions in some legal sense. He did not stand as an accused
intruder before the Council. Rather, he was questioned as an orator who
proclaimed deities that were new to the Athenians. The Council assumed
that if Paul found broad support for his religious teaching among the
Athenian citizens, he could claim for the gods he proclaimed a rightful
place in the pantheon of Athenian gods. They expected that Paul would
have to buy a piece of land in the city on which he would establish the

---

[117]IG II² 337; Lambert, "Athenian State Laws and Decrees II," p. 153, fig. 3.

[118]On the role of the Council of the Areopagus concerning religious affairs and Acts 17 see Daniel J.
Geagan, *The Athenian Constitution after Sulla*, Hesperia 12 (Princeton, N.J.: American School
of Classical Studies at Athens, 1967), p. 50; David W. J. Gill, "Achaia," in *The Book of Acts in Its
Graeco-Roman Setting*, ed. D. W. J. Gill and C. Gempf, The Book of Acts in Its First-Century
Setting 2 (Exeter, U.K.: Paternoster, 1994), p. 447.

new cult, at least building an altar for the necessary sacrificial activities. They surmised that Paul might possibly donate financial resources for the celebration of a festival to honor the new gods at least once a year and perhaps even for the support of cult personnel.

When we read Paul's speech before the Areopagus Council (Acts 17:22-31) in this context,[119] the main thrust of Paul's speech is his emphasis that he is not introducing new deities to Athens. Rather, he proclaims the deity who is honored at the altar with the inscription "To an unknown god" (Acts 17:23). He points out that the god for whom he speaks does not want to acquire a piece of land on which a sanctuary or an altar for cultic veneration should be erected, as this god neither lives in temples nor has a need for festivals or sacrifices (Acts 17:24-26). Paul thus informs the Council that he is not applying for the admission of a new deity to the pantheon of gods that are worshiped in the city of Athens. This political and social context of Paul's speech before the Council of the Areopagus suggests that Acts 17:22-31 should not be understood in terms of a summary of Paul's missionary sermons before pagan audiences, but rather as a speech in the specific context of Acts 17:16-20 (for an analysis of the speech see sec. 3.3).

Besides the question of new deities that Paul seems to want to introduce to the Athenians, the Council may have considered a second question, asking Paul to demonstrate his competence as an orator.[120] Orators who spoke in public were sometimes invited by the magistrates of the cities to demonstrate their rhetorical abilities and their philosophical orientation. The orator was usually given one day's notice to prepare his declamation on a predetermined topic. He would compose his declamation, write it down, memorize it and present it without reliance on notes. Such declamations were often copied and circulated in the city in the early imperial period; there is evidence for this practice related to Athens. It is not impossible that the speech Luke reports in

---

[119]See Bruce W. Winter, "On Introducing Gods to Athens: An Alternative Reading of Acts 17.18-20," *TynB* 47 (1996): 71-90. This historical context of Paul's summons to appear before the Council of the Areopagus is missed by most discussions of Acts 17; e.g., recently Dean E. Flemming, *Contextualization in the New Testament: Patterns for Theology and Mission* (Downers Grove, Ill.: InterVarsity Press, 2005), pp. 72-74.

[120]See Bruce W. Winter, "In Public and in Private: Early Christian Interactions with Religious Pluralism," in *One God, One Lord in a World of Religious Pluralism*, ed. A. D. Clarke and B. W. Winter (Cambridge: Tyndale House, 1991), pp. 112-34.

Acts 17:22-31 is the summary of a written source.

Contrary to the opinion of some interpreters,[121] Paul's missionary work in Athens was *not* unsuccessful.[122] Luke mentions two converts by name—Dionysius, a member of the Areopagus Council, and a woman named Damaris—and "others with them" who came to faith in Jesus Christ (Acts 17:34). The fact that Luke mentions the names of two converts is significant. He specifies only one convert by name for Paphos (Sergius Paullus [Acts 13:7, 12]), Philippi (Lydia [Acts 16:14]), Thessalonica (Jason [Acts 17:6]), and Corinth (Crispus [Acts 18:8]), and he mentions no names of converts for Pisidian Antioch, Iconium, Lystra, Derbe, Beroea or Ephesus. Also, we should note that "Athens is one of the few places on this journey where Paul is not in fact run out of town!"[123]

Corinth. Paul arrived in Corinth probably in February or March of the year A.D. 50. His missionary activity lasted for over eighteen months (Acts 18:11, 18). After having been destroyed by the Roman consul Lucius Mummius in 146 B.C., the city was refounded in 44 B.C. by Julius Caesar with the name Colonia Laus Iulia Corinthus.[124] The aristocratic families of Rome who had decided on the reestablishment of Corinth seemed to have hoped that the freedmen whom they settled in the city would be their middle men in this new commercial center on the Isthmus of Greece. By 27 B.C. Corinth was the administrative center of the senatorial province of Achaia, a center of commerce and services. One estimate of the population of Corinth in the middle of the first century assumes eighty thousand inhabitants.[125]

When Paul arrived in Corinth, he met Aquila and Priscilla, a Jewish Christian couple who had moved from Rome to Corinth "because Claudius had ordered all Jews to leave Rome" (Acts 18:2). If the Edict of Clau-

---

[121]See already William M. Ramsay, *St. Paul the Traveller and the Roman Citizen* (London: Hodder & Stoughton, 1896), p. 252.

[122]See Conrad Gempf, "Before Paul Arrived in Corinth: The Mission Strategies in 1 Corinthians 2:2 and Acts 17," in *The New Testament in its First Century Setting: Essays on Context and Background in Honor of B. W. Winter*, ed. P. J. Williams et al. (Grand Rapids: Eerdmans, 2004), p. 133.

[123]Witherington, *Acts of the Apostles*, p. 533.

[124]For details on the history of Corinth cf. Schnabel, *Early Christian Mission*, pp. 1181-86.

[125]Donald Engels, *Roman Corinth: An Alternative Model for the Classical City* (Chicago and London: University of Chicago Press, 1990), pp. 79-84, 178-81.

dius is to be dated between January 25 of A.D. 49 and January 24 of A.D. 50,[126] we may assume that Aquila and Priscilla arrived in Corinth in the fall of A.D. 49, before the closing of navigation with the onset on winter. When Paul came to Corinth in the fall of A.D. 50, Aquila and Prisca had been living in the city for about a year. The couple was presumably well-to-do: they either owned in Corinth a branch of their craftsman's business in Rome where they worked as "tentmakers" *(tabernacularii)*, that is, leather-workers,[127] or they possessed the means to open a new workshop, in which they employed other people, soon after their arrival in Corinth.

As was his custom, Paul attended the meetings of the Jewish community on the sabbath, preaching and teaching, seeking to convince Jews and Gentile sympathizers in the synagogue concerning the truth of his proclamation of Jesus as Messiah (Acts 18:1-5). Luke records that when Silas and Timothy arrived from Macedonia, Paul was able to devote himself exclusively to missionary work. Paul's preaching was successful. Crispus, the main official of the synagogue (the *archisynagōgos*) and his family were converted, as were "many of the Corinthians who heard Paul" (Acts 18:8).

After opposition in the Jewish community forced Paul to leave the synagogue as venue of his preaching and teaching, he moved to the house of Titius Justus, a God-fearer who had evidently been converted earlier and lived right next to the synagogue (Acts 18:6-7). Other converts in Corinth include Gaius who is mentioned as Paul's host in Corinth (Rom 16:23), and Stephanas and his family (1 Cor 16:15). The "many" who were converted included non-Jewish inhabitants of the city: God-fearers, polytheistic Greeks and probably descendants of the Italian colonists who held Roman citizenship. The range of problems in the young church that Paul discusses in his first letter to the Corinthians indicates that members of the local elite had become Christians as well: people who belong to the wise and powerful (1 Cor 1:26; 3:18), who expected orators to display brilliant rhetoric (1 Cor 2:1-5), who were able to initiate official legal proceedings (1 Cor 6:1-11), who visited prostitutes (1 Cor 6:12-18), who dined in

---

[126]See Riesner, *Paul's Early Period*, pp. 157-201.

[127]F. W. Danker suggests that the Greek term *skēnopoios*, which is usually translated as "tentmaker," should be interpreted in the sense of "maker of stage properties" for theatrical productions (BDAG, pp. 928-29). Note, however, the Jewish objections toward the theater; cf. Schürer, *History of the Jewish People*, 2:54-55.

the temples of the city (1 Cor 8:10), who covered their heads during the worship services of the church as signs of their superior social status, as priests did when they officiated in the temples (1 Cor 11:4), people who had time for meals in the afternoon (1 Cor 11:21-22).[128]

The fact that Paul received divine encouragement in a dream vision (Acts 18:9-10) suggests continued opposition in the city. The Lord encouraged Paul not to be silent but to preach without fear as there are "many in this city who are my people" (Acts 18:10), suggesting the further growth of the church. Paul's Jewish opponents initiated legal proceedings before the Roman governor of the province, L. Iunius Gallio, who was proconsul from July 1, A.D. 51, to June 30, A.D. 52.[129] It is possible that the Corinthian Jews believed that the new governor would be favorably disposed to their request. The legal procedure can be understood as what Roman law labeled a *cognitio extra ordinem*. In such a proceeding it was left to the discretion of the governor whether an accusation should be accepted or not.

The charge against Paul was formulated, perhaps deliberately, in an ambiguous manner: "This man is persuading people to worship God in ways that are contrary to the law" (Acts 18:13). This should probably be understood in the sense that Paul was accused of violating the laws of the Roman state: Paul's proclamation of Jesus as Messiah, Savior and Lord could easily be presented as equivalent to instigating rebellion against the emperor and his rule over the world. Alternately, Paul may have been accused of violating the edict of Claudius issued in A.D. 41 which guaranteed that the Jews were allowed to practice their customs without interference,[130] arguing that Paul disturbed the peace of their community. Gallio clearly interpreted the accusation against Paul in terms of a possible violation against the laws of the state, and he recognized that the accused

---

[128]See Bruce W. Winter, *After Paul Left Corinth: The Influence of Secular Ethics and Social Change* (Grand Rapids: Eerdmans, 2001).

[129]On the Gallio inscription see Riesner, *Paul's Early Period*, pp. 202-7. A new edition of the nine fragments has been provided by André Plassart, *Inscriptions de la terrasse du temple et de la région nord du sanctuaire, Nos. 276 à 350. Les inscriptions du Temple du IVᵉ siècle*, Fouilles de Delphes III, Épigraphie 4 (Paris: Boccard, 1970), pp. 26-32 (no. 286; plate 7). For a translation see Jerome Murphy-O'Connor, *St. Paul's Corinth: Texts and Archaeology* (Wilmington, Del.: Glazier, 1983), pp. 173-76.

[130]Josephus *Antiquitates Judaicae* 19.287-291. Cf. Miriam Pucci Ben Zeev, *Jewish Rights in the Roman World*, TSAJ 74 (Tübingen: Mohr Siebeck, 1998), pp. 328-42 (no. 29).

had not committed any such violation. The dispute was about "questions" or controversial "issues" concerning Jewish teachings, concerning Jewish persons (Jesus and the question of his identity) or Jewish law, and thus concerning matters *extra ordinem* in which a Roman official did not need get involved (Acts 18:14-16).

1.6 PAUL IN THE PROVINCE OF ASIA

When Paul traveled from Corinth via Ephesus back to Judea and Syria, visiting Jerusalem and Antioch (Acts 18:18-23), he had preached the gospel for three years in Macedonia and in Achaia. During the brief stopover in Ephesus he had promised the Jewish community there that he would return if God allows (Acts 18:21). After he spent "some time" in Antioch, he traveled overland via Cilicia to "the region of Galatia and Phrygia" to encourage the believers in the churches that he had established in these areas (Acts 18:23). The phrase "the region of Galatia and Phrygia" suggests that he visited two different areas: Lycaonian and Phrygian Galatia (the region of Phrygia that had been annexed to the province of Galatia) and Asian Phrygia (the region of Phrygia that belonged to the province of Asia).[131]

The tenth period of Paul's mission: Asia. The province of Asia (Asia Proconsularis) was organized in 133 B.C., after the death of Attalos III, the king of Pergamum, who had deeded his kingdom to the Romans. The province consisted originally of the regions Mysia, Troas, Aeolis, Lydia, Ionia, the islands along the coast, most of Caria and a corridor through Pisidia to Pamphylia. In 116 B.C. several regions of Phrygia were added. The victory of Augustus initiated a period of three hundred years of peace for the region. In the imperial period the province of Asia extended from Amorion and Philomelion in the east to the Mediterranean in the west; in the north it bordered on Bithynia, in the south on Lycia and in the east on Galatia. Ephesus was the capital of the province (see fig. 1.8).

Ephesus. Paul's first, albeit brief, visit in Ephesus in late summer of A.D. 51 during his journey from Corinth to Jerusalem (Acts 18:18-22) allowed him to speak before the Jewish community. Luke's account suggests the tentative conclusion that the origins of the church in Ephesus date to this

---

[131]See Hemer, *Book of Acts*, p. 120; for details of Paul's route see Schnabel, *Early Christian Mission*, 2:1199-1203.

brief visit. The following reasons are pertinent.

1. Paul preached in the synagogue: the Greek verb *dialegomai* (Acts 18:19) describes, as in Acts 17:2, the teaching in the synagogue in which the apostle sought to win his listeners to faith in Jesus as Messiah.

2. Luke describes Paul's departure in Acts 18:21 with the Greek verb *apotassomai*, as in Acts 18:18 where Paul's farewell from the "brothers" in Corinth is described. The verb *apotassomai* could refer to the Christians in Corinth in Acts 18:18 and to the Jews of Ephesus in Acts 18:21. However, since *apotassomai* occurs only twice in the book of Acts, and since Luke reports only farewells of Paul from Christians,132 it seems preferable to interpret Acts 18:19 in terms of a farewell from Christians.

3. The comment that Paul was asked to "stay" (Acts 18:20) also supports the possibility that Ephesian Jews were converted during Paul's brief stopover in the city. In all other passages in the book of Acts the Greek verb *menein* ("to stay"), applied in a local context with regard to people, always refers to Christian believers.133 If the Ephesians who asked Paul to stay were only sympathetic Jews who wanted to converse with him about his message, then this hardly explains the comment that Paul was asked "to stay longer" (Acts 18:20). This note also suggests that Ephesian Jews were converted during Paul's first visit.

4. The "believers" ("brothers") who provide Apollos a letter of recommendation to the "disciples" in Corinth (Acts 18:27) are Ephesian Jews who have been converted through the ministry of either Apollos (Acts 18:25-26) or Aquila and Priscilla (Acts 18:26). The possibility cannot be excluded that some of the "believers" had been converted earlier during Paul's brief visit to Ephesus.134 In other words, Paul's preaching in the synagogue in Ephesus mentioned in Acts 18:19 could have convinced Jewish listeners to come to faith in Jesus the Messiah.

When Paul returned from Jerusalem and Antioch and reached Ephesus, he was able to spend three years in the city, from the summer of A.D. 52 to the summer of A.D. 55. Ephesus had a colorful history, with Hittites, Mycenaeans, the sea people, Aeolians, Ionians, Dorians, Persians

---

132Acts 18:18; 20:1; see also Acts 13:3; 16:40; 17:10, 14; 20:36-38.
133Acts 9:43; 16:15; 18:3; 21:7, 8.
134Marshall, *Acts*, p. 304.

and Macedonians controlling the region at various times. When Julius Caesar arrived in Asia Minor in 48 B.C., during his fight with Pompey, he issued decrees in Ephesus and reorganized taxation by lowering taxes. The grateful citizens honored him with a monument; a statue base carries the following inscription: "The cities in Asia and the [Demoi] and the Ethne (honor) Gaius Iulius, son of Gaius, Caesar, Pontifex Maximus and Imperator and Consul for the second time, the god appearing (descending) from Ares and Aphrodite and the savior of human life."[135] Augustus stayed in Ephesus for several months when he reorganized the East after his victory over Mark Antony. The early first century witnessed a building boom in the city, with new temples and other large buildings being constructed. Ephesus, one of the largest cities in the empire, had about 200,000 inhabitants. The monumental temple of Artemis, one of the seven wonders of the world, attracted tourists from all areas of the Roman Empire and also functioned as the credit bank of Asia.[136]

Paul was able to teach and preach "boldly" in the synagogue for three months (Acts 19:8), that is, on at least twelve sabbaths. It appears that the officials of the synagogue were either open for Paul's message about the revelation of the kingdom of God in Jesus the Messiah (Acts 19:8), or they were at least willing to examine his message for an extended period of time. The synagogue parted ways with Paul after three months "when some stubbornly refused to believe and spoke evil of the Way before the congregation" (Acts 19:9). Some of the Jews, possibly some of the synagogue officials, opposed Paul's message and ridiculed his converts.

The next phase of Paul's mission to Ephesus lasted for two years: Paul left the synagogue with the new converts and held meetings in the lecture hall of a certain Tyrannos, teaching and "arguing" daily (Acts 19:9-10). A later textual tradition adds the comment that this happened "from the fifth to the tenth hour," that is, from ten in the morning to four in the afternoon, a comment that is at least a plausible specification for a guild hall or a lecture hall. Luke notes in Acts 19:20 that "the word of the Lord grew mightily and prevailed": Paul's preaching evidently fell on open ears, resulting in many conversions and also in miracles (Acts 19:11). When

---

[135]I. Ephesos II 251.
[136]For details on the history of Ephesus cf. Schnabel, *Early Christian Mission*, 2:1206-15.

Jewish exorcists who were active in Ephesus used the name of Jesus to manipulate their patients, perhaps as an experiment with a new magical formula, they suffered public divine punishment (Acts 19:13-16). It appears that many Ephesians concluded that Paul had superior power (Acts 19:17). These events caused many of the new converts to confess publicly their involvement with magical practices: they brought their magic texts to the church, worth 50,000 silver drachmas, and burned them publicly (Acts 19:18-19). The amount of 50,000 silver drachmas (denarii), corresponding to 200,000 sesterces, is huge: a day laborer would have to work for 50,000 days (or 137 years) to earn this sum of money.

According to Acts 19:10, "all the residents of Asia, both Jews and Greeks, heard the word of the Lord" during the time that Paul was active in Ephesus. This comment is confirmed by Paul's letter to the Corinthian Christians, written from Ephesus, in which he conveys greetings from "the churches" (plural) of Asia (1 Cor 16:19). Paul informs the Corinthian Christians in the same context that God has opened "a wide door for effective work" in Ephesus (1 Cor 16:8-9). Paul began his missionary efforts in Ephesus in A.D. 52, and he wrote his first letter to the Corinthians in the spring of A.D. 54. It appears that in the two or three years between A.D. 52-54 several churches were established in the province of Asia. Luke and Paul probably think of the churches in Laodicea, Hierapolis and Colossae in the Lykos Valley on the Upper Maeander River that were established by Epaphras (Col 1:3-8; 4:13), and perhaps of a Christian community in Miletus (cf. Acts 20:15, 17-38). It is impossible to confirm (or deny) whether the churches in Smyrna, Pergamum, Thyatira, Sardis and Philadelphia were also established during this period.

Paul had several coworkers from the province of Asia during his mission to Ephesus: Epaphras (Col 1:3-8; 4:13), Philemon (Philem 1-2), Aristarchus from Macedonia (Acts 19:29; 20:4; 27:2; Philem 23), Gaius from Corinth (Acts 19:29; 1 Cor 1:14), Tychicus and Trophimus (Acts 20:4; Col 4:7). Aquila and Priscilla were part of Paul's team of missionaries in Ephesus right from the beginning, as was Timothy (1 Cor 16:10). Later Stephanas, Fortunatus and Archaicus visited Paul in Ephesus (1 Cor 16:17). According to Acts 20:31, Paul stayed in Ephesus for three years.

The success of Paul's missionary work in Ephesus is indirectly confirmed by the hostility that Paul experienced in the city. In 1 Corinthians 15:32 Paul asserts that he was in a very dangerous situation while he was in Ephesus; his comment that he "fought with wild animals" can hardly have a literal meaning: a Roman citizen could not be sentenced *ad bestias*. In addition, hardly anybody survived a fight with animals, and Paul's extensive list of trials and suffering in 2 Corinthians 11:23-33 would probably have included a reference to such a horrific experience. The reference to a fight with wild animals is a metaphor that states that Paul had to "fight for his life" in some specific situation, perhaps in connection with the incident in which Aquila and Priscilla risked their lives for the apostles (Rom 16:3-4). Many scholars assume that Paul was thrown into prison in Ephesus, a hypothesis that cannot be confirmed.

A major incident happened evidently during the last months of Paul's missionary work in Ephesus. A silversmith with the name of Demetrios invited his colleagues from the guild of the silversmiths to a meeting. He was a large-scale entrepreneur in the manufacture and sale of devotional articles within the parameters of the rights of associations, or a dominant member of a guild whose interests coincided with those of his suppliers. The guild of the silversmiths in Ephesus is attested in inscriptions.[137] The agitated assembly in the theater that Luke mentions in Acts 19:23-40 could have taken place in connection with the Artemis festival in March or April.[138] After the riot that was caused by the guild of the silversmiths was resolved (Acts 19:21-41), Paul departed for Macedonia and Achaia (Acts 20:1-3; cf. Acts 19:21).

1.7 PAUL IN ILLYRICUM, CAESAREA, ROME, SPAIN, CRETE AND ROME

When Paul left Ephesus in the summer of A.D. 55, he intended to visit the churches in Macedonia and Achaia and make final arrangements for the collection of funds that were to be transferred to the church in Jerusalem

---

[137]I. Ephesos II 425, 547, 585, 586; III 636; VI 2212, 2441; cf. Greg H. R. Horsley and Stephen R. Llewelyn, *New Documents Illustrating Early Christianity* (North Ryde, New South Wales, Australia: Macquarie University, 1981-2002), 4:8; Peter Lampe, "Acta 19 im Spiegel der ephesischen Inschriften," *BZ* 36 (1992): 59-76.

[138]According to 1 Cor 16:8 Paul wanted to stay in Ephesus until the Feast of Pentecost, which was celebrated in the beginning of June.

(1 Cor 16:1-4). He spends some time in Alexandria Troas and preached the gospel there (2 Cor 2:12) before continuing on to Macedonia (2 Cor 2:13; Acts 20:1) and eventually to Greece (Acts 20:2).

The eleventh period of Paul's mission: Illyricum. It appears that before Paul arrived in Corinth in the fall of A.D. 56, he engaged in missionary work in Illyricum (see fig. 1.12). In his letter to the Christians in Rome, written in Corinth in the winter months of A.D. 56/57, Paul states that he preached the gospel "from Jerusalem and as far around as Illyricum" (Rom 15:19). The interpretation of this formulation is disputed, but the inclusive sense of the phrase seems to be preferable to the exclusive interpretation. In other words, Paul does not say that he preached in the regions between Jerusalem and Illyricum, with these two places excluded. Rather, as he had indeed preached in Jerusalem when he visited the Jewish capital in A.D. 33/34 for the first time after his conversion, he asserts that he preached the gospel in the Jewish capital as well as in Illyricum. When he visited the temple during this visit, Jesus confirmed his call as an apostle to the Gentiles, telling him that his testimony will be rejected in Jerusalem (Acts 22:17-18). This notice agrees with Paul's statement in Romans 15:19 that his missionary activity started in Jerusalem. If the reference to Jerusalem in Romans 15:19 is to be understood in terms of a geographical localization of Paul's missionary work, it is plausible to assume the same for the reference to Illyricum. Also, it seems significant that Paul mentions Illyricum rather than Corinth as the western limit of his missionary activities.

Paul presumably does not refer to the region in Macedonia, which was regarded as Illyrian in an ethnic sense (Strabo 7.7.4). As Romans 15:24-28 refers to Roman provinces (Spain, Macedonia, Achaia), the term *Illyricum* has a political meaning. This is confirmed by the fact that Paul uses an unusual Latinized form of the name of the province *(Illyrikon)*[139] confirms the suggestion that Paul reached the province of Illyricum on the coast of the Adriatic Sea.[140] It is possible that Paul traveled to Illyricum with the

---

[139]The traditional Greek terms were *Illyria* and *Illyris*; cf. W. Paul Bowers, "Studies in Paul's Understanding of His Mission" (Ph.D. diss. University of Cambridge, 1976), p. 21, n. 3; Marjeta Šašel Kos, "Illyricum," *BNP*, 6:732-35.

[140]See David W. J. Gill, "Macedonia," in *The Book of Acts in Its Graeco-Roman Setting*, ed. D. W. J. Gill and C. Gempf, The Book of Acts in Its First-Century Setting 2 (Exeter, U.K.: Paternoster,

goal of familiarizing himself with a region in which Latin was spoken as preparation for his planned outreach to Spain.[141]

As Paul presumably visited the churches in Philippi, Thessalonica and Beroea, we can assume that he continued along the great road called the Via Egnatia heading west, arriving on the Adriatic coast at Dyrrhachium or Apollonia. Important Illyrian cities further north included Scodra, Epetium and Tragurium.[142] As the chronology of Paul's movements during this period leaves only the summer of A.D. 56 for a mission to Illyricum, the apostle would have preached the gospel in only one or two cities, perhaps in Scadra and Risinium or in Epidaurum.

The twelfth period of Paul's mission: Caesarea. When Paul returned to Jerusalem in the spring of A.D. 57, he was arrested (Acts 21:27—22:23) and eventually transferred to Caesarea. He spent two years in Caesarea as a prisoner of the Roman governor (Acts 24:26-27), waiting for a decision to be made in the legal case that the Jewish authorities had brought against him (Acts 23:23—26:32). As Luke focuses his account in Acts 21—26 on the legal proceedings against Paul, we learn little about Paul's activities during these two years. The notice that governor Festus ordered the centurion who was responsible for Paul's imprisonment to "let him have some liberty" (Acts 24:23) may not only explain Paul's continued contact with his friends, who would have to provide him with food, but may imply a hint that Paul continued to be active in his preaching and teaching endeavors.

Paul had the opportunity to speak before the Roman governor Felix and his wife Drusilla about his faith (Acts 24:24-25). Even though the frequent contacts between Paul and the governor are attributed to the latter's hope to receive a bribe (Acts 24:26), the readers of the book of Acts who had come to know Paul as an energetic, fearless missionary would interpret the Greek verb *hōmilein* not simply in the general sense of "to converse" but in the sense of "to hold conversations with," perhaps even in the sense of "to frequent a person's lectures."[143] Later Paul had the opportunity to speak before the next Roman governor, Porcius Festus, before

---

1994), p. 399; Murphy-O'Connor, *Paul*, pp. 316-17, 322, 363.

[141]F. F. Bruce, *Paul: Apostle of the Free Spirit* (Exeter, U.K.: Paternoster, 1977), p. 317.

[142]For details see Schnabel, *Early Christian Mission*, 2:1250-1254.

[143]C. K. Barrett, *The Acts of the Apostles*, ICC (Edinburgh: T & T Clark, 1994-1998), 2:1116.

Figure 1.12. Illyricum

King Herod Agrippa I and his wife Bernice, and before the aristocratic
elite of Caesarea and high-ranking military officers (Acts 25:23), arguably
one of the most dramatic moments of Paul's missionary preaching.

The thirteenth period of Paul's mission: Rome. After Paul is transferred
from Caesarea to Rome (Acts 27:1—28:16), he spent two years (A.D.
60-62) as a prisoner of the emperor, waiting for his trial (Acts 28:17-31).[144]
He received permission from an official who reported to the *praefectus
praetorii* to stay in rented private quarters (Acts 28:16) that were evidently
large enough to receive "larger numbers" of visitors (Acts 28:23). Paul

---

[144]On Paul as a prisoner see Rapske, *Paul in Roman Custody.*

was chained to a soldier (Acts 28:20), as was customary in such situations. Otherwise he was not much restricted in what he could do. Paul initiated contacts with the leaders of the Jewish community in the city of Rome. On some occasions he spoke for several hours ("from morning until evening") about the message that he has been proclaiming, seeking to convince his visitors that the crucified and risen Jesus is the Messiah and the one who fulfills the meaning and the promises of the law and the prophets (Acts 28:23). Luke ends his account with a summary statement concerning Paul's preaching and teaching in Rome:

> He lived there two whole years at his own expense and welcomed all who came to him, proclaiming the kingdom of God and teaching about the Lord Jesus Christ with all boldness and without hindrance. (Acts 28:30-31)

The reaction to Paul's preaching is mixed, as always: some Jews believed and were converted to faith in Jesus as the Messiah, while others rejected Paul's teaching (Acts 28:24-25).

Paul asserts in his letter to the Christians in Philippi, written during his imprisonment in Rome, that the gospel was becoming known "throughout the whole praetorium" (Phil 1:13). The Latin term *praetorium* is probably a reference to the Praetorian Guard,[145] the imperial bodyguards of whom nine thousand men were stationed in the city of Rome. Presumably Paul came into contact with the Praetorians in connection with his house arrest. When Paul adds that the circumstances of his imprisonment and thus the gospel of Jesus Christ have become known "to everyone else" (Phil 1:13), he probably refers to pagans who received information about the reasons for the imprisonment of Paul, the Jewish teacher from Tarsus and from Jerusalem who was a Roman citizen. As Paul's situation became known, his teaching must have been talked about as well. According to Philippians 4:22 there were followers of Jesus in "the emperor's household," probably among the freedmen and the slaves who worked in the imperial household. We do not know whether they were converted as a result of contacts with Paul.

The fourteenth period of Paul's mission: Spain. Paul was likely released from his Roman imprisonment in A.D. 62, enabling him to engage in fur-

---

[145]See J. B. Lightfoot, *Saint Paul's Epistle to the Philippians* (London: Macmillan, 1868), pp. 99-104; O'Brien, *Philippians*, p. 93.

ther missionary work—evidently in Spain.[146] Unless Paul's case was heard by the emperor Nero himself, the apostle would have had to appear before Sextus Afranius Burrus, who had been appointed by Claudius in A.D. 51 as sole prefect of the Praetorian Guard, an office that he held until his death in A.D. 62 and that he used, together with the philosopher Seneca, to exercise a moderating influence on Nero.[147] The main argument for the assumption that Paul was released from Roman custody is the content and tone of Paul's second letter to Timothy in which he speaks of his isolation in custody (2 Tim 1:16-17; 4:11, 16), comments that do not fit the imprisonment of A.D. 60-62 but suggest a second, later imprisonment. Another, more direct piece of evidence is a comment by Clement of Rome in his letter to the Corinthians Christians, written in A.D. 95, in which Clement says concerning Paul:

> Seven times he bore chains; he was sent into exile and stoned; he served as a herald in both the East and the West; and he received the noble reputation for his faith. He taught righteousness to the whole world, and came to the limits of the West, bearing his witness before the rulers. (1 Clement 5:6-7)

In the phrase "the limits of the West," the Greek term *dysis* ("West" or "the setting [of the sun]") is sometimes used for Gaul and Britain, but usually designates Spain.[148] Spain was regarded to be at the western "end of the world." Strabo describes Gades as a city "at the end of the earth"[149] and the entire region with the "promontory of Iberia which they call the Sacred Cape" as "the most westerly point of the inhabited world." Diodorus Siculus localized Gades also "at the end of the inhabited world."[150] If Paul indeed reached "the limits of the West," he must have been released from Roman custody in A.D. 62.

Clement's comments are the earliest piece of evidence for missionary work in Spain by the apostle Paul. The assertion of Clement cannot be

---

[146]See Michael Prior, *Paul the Letter-Writer and the Second Letter to Timothy*, JSNTSup 23 (Sheffield, U.K.: JSOT Press, 1989), pp. 73-84; Murphy-O'Connor, *Paul*, pp. 359-61.

[147]See Miriam T. Griffin, *Nero: The End of a Dynasty* (1984; reprint, New York: Routledge, 2000), pp. 67-69.

[148]Josephus *Contra Apionem* 1.67; Tacitus *Historiae* 4.3; Strabo *Geographica* 1.2.31; 1.4.6; 2.1.1; 2.4.3-4; 3.1.2; 3.5.5; Philostratus *Vita Apollonii* 5.4; 4.47; Pliny *Naturalis historia* 3.1.3-7. Hermut Löhr, "Zur Paulus-Notiz in 1 Clem 5.5-7," in *Die letzte Jerusalemreise des Paulus*, ed. F. W. Horn; BZNW 106 (Berlin: De Gruyter, 2001), pp. 207-9.

[149]Strabo *Geographica* 3.1.8; cf. 1.2.31; 2.5.14; cf. 3.1.4; see also Lucanus *Pharsalia* 3.454.

[150]Diodoros Siculus 25.10.1; see also Juvenal *Satirae* 10.1-2; Silius *Punica* 17.637.

dismissed as a later fictional projection on the basis of Romans 15:24, designed to enhance the reputation of the apostle; if Paul's letter to the Romans was the only source for Clement's comment, he would probably not speak in general terms of Paul having reached the "limits of the West" but more specifically of "Spain."

Further evidence is provided by the apocryphal *Acts of Peter*, written around A.D. 190, and by the *Muratorian Canon*, dated by some to A.D. 200, by others to the fourth century.

> When Paul was at Rome confirming many in the faith . . . Quartus [a member of the guard who had come to faith] persuaded Paul to leave the city and to go wherever he pleased. Paul said to him, "If such be the will of God, he will reveal it to me." And Paul fasted three days and besought the Lord to grant what was good for him, and in a vision he saw the Lord who said to him, "Paul, arise, and be a physician to the Spaniards!" At this he related to the brethren what God had commanded him, and without hesitation he made ready to leave the city. When Paul was preparing to leave, there was a great lamentation among the brethren because they thought they would never see Paul again. (*Acts of Peter* 1)

> For the "most excellent Theophilus" Luke summarizes the several things that in his own presence have come to pass, as also by the omission of the passion of Peter he makes quite clear, and equally by (the omission) of the journey of Paul, who from the city (of Rome) proceeded to Spain. (*Muratorian Canon*, lines 35-39)

Some scholars therefore argue that the release of Paul from Roman custody is a historical fact that should be the basis for any critical reconstruction of the history of the early church.[151]

Paul had planned a mission to Spain (see fig. 1.13) at least since the winter of A.D. 56/57 when he wrote from Corinth to the Christians in the city of Rome:

> But now, with no further place for me in these regions, I desire, as I have for many years, to come to you when I go to Spain. For I do hope to see you on my journey and to be sent on by you, once I have enjoyed your company

---

[151]See Earle E. Ellis, *The Making of the New Testament Documents*, BIS 39 (Leiden: Brill, 1999), pp. 278-82.

for a little while. At present, however, I am going to Jerusalem in a ministry to the saints; for Macedonia and Achaia have been pleased to share their resources with the poor among the saints at Jerusalem. They were pleased to do this, and indeed they owe it to them; for if the Gentiles have come to share in their spiritual blessings, they ought also to be of service to them in material things. So, when I have completed this, and have delivered to them what has been collected, I will set out by way of you to Spain; and I know that when I come to you, I will come in the fullness of the blessing of Christ. (Rom 15:23-29)

Spain could be easily reached from Rome, with good sailing conditions ships needed only seven days to cover the distance between Ostia, the harbor of Rome, and Spain; an overland journey presented no obstacles either, as there was a developed network of Roman roads in this region.[152] Paul would have been able to converse in Greek with the people who came from the eastern Mediterranean and who lived in the cities of Spain, particularly with the freedmen and slaves in the urban centers of Baetica and on the Levantine coast. The Latin speaking elites in the Spanish cities spoke Greek as well. Paul may have had contacts with Spain on account of Christian believers living in Rome, or he may have had information that such contacts could be established through the Roman church.

If Paul indeed reached Spain, Tarraco, the capital of the province of Hispania Citerior on the northeast coast of Spain, would have been a natural target for missionary work. Other coastal cities include, in the northeast, Barcino, Emporiae, Celsa, Caesaraugusta and Dertosa, and in the southeast the cities of Saguntum, Valentia, Saetabis, Ilici, and Carthago Nova.[153]

The first explicit reference to Christians in Spain comes from Irenaeus, the bishop of Lyon, without any reference to Paul's missionary work, however:

> For the churches which have been planted in Germany do not believe or hand down anything different, nor do those in Spain, nor those in Gaul, nor those in the East, nor those in Egypt, nor those in Libya, nor those which have been established in the central regions of the world (i.e., in Palestine with Jerusalem). (Irenaeus *Adversus Haereses* 1.10.2)

---

[152]See John S. Richardson, *The Romans in Spain* (Oxford: Blackwell, 1996), pp. 160-62.
[153]For details see Schnabel, *Early Christian Mission*, 2:1277-81.

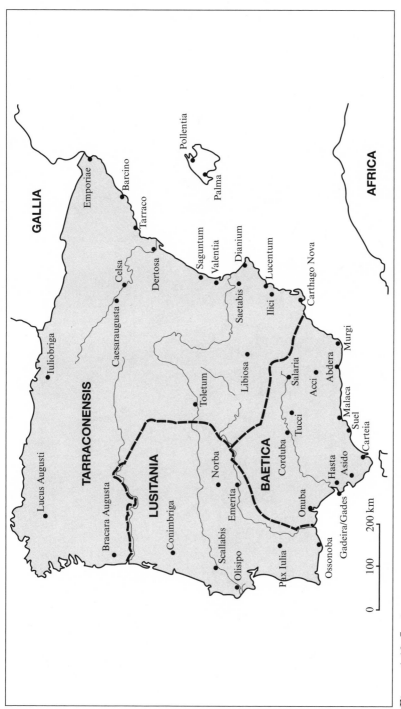

Figure 1.13. Spain

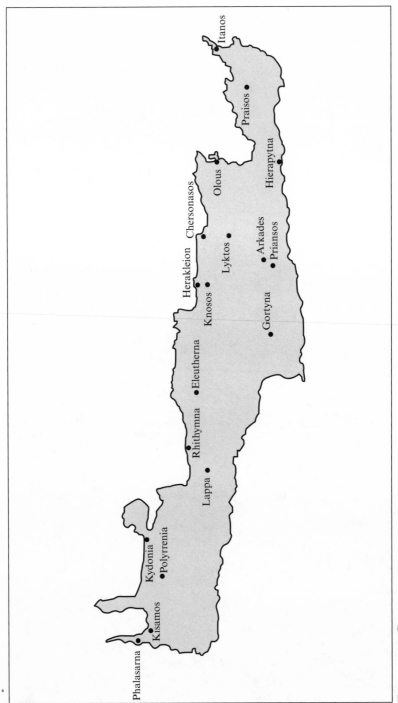

Figure 1.14. Crete

Paul cannot have been engaged in missionary work in Spain for a very long period of time. He seems to have returned to the eastern Mediterranean world within a year after his arrival. The reasons for the early interruption of his work in Spain are unknown.

The fifteenth period of Paul's mission: Crete. Evidence in Paul's letter to Titus suggests a period of missionary activity on the island of Crete (see fig. 1.14). Paul writes to Titus, one of his coworkers: "I left you behind in Crete for this reason, so that you should put in order what remained to be done, and should appoint elders in every town, as I directed you" (Tit 1:5).

There were Christian churches in several cities on Crete by the time the letter to Titus was written. It is not clear, however, who had founded these churches. In Acts 2:11 Luke mentions Jewish pilgrims from Crete who visited Jerusalem on the occasion of the Feast of Pentecost in A.D. 30. It is possible that some of these pilgrims came to faith as a result of Peter's proclamation of the gospel of Jesus the Messiah during Pentecost. If this is indeed the case, the gospel could have been brought to Crete by these new Jewish believers as early as A.D. 30. There were large Jewish communities on Crete. Philo states in his report about the letter of Herod Agrippa I to Caligula that the Greek islands are "full" of Jewish communities, specifically mentioning Crete (Philo *Legat.* 282). The Roman historian Tacitus mentions Jewish communities on Crete as well (Tacitus *Hist.* 5.11).

An alternative scenario is that Titus and perhaps other coworkers of Paul worked as missionaries in the cities of Crete, asking for the apostle's help in consolidating the new churches around A.D. 63. A mission to Crete would have been a logical project for the early Jewish Christian missionaries. If Paul arrived on Crete from the west (from Spain), he would have disembarked in the city of Kydonia on the northwest coast of the island. Traveling west he would have reached the city of Polyrrenia. Other cities on the north coast of Crete were Rhithymna, Knosos, Chersonasos and Olous.

Paul's travels: statistics. Table 1.2 shows the distances and the travel times (in days) that Paul covered as a missionary, including the visits to Jerusalem in A.D. 44 and 48, the missionary work in Arabia,[154] the mis-

---

[154]Assuming a journey from Damascus to Bostra, Philadelphia and Jerusalem, a distance of about 300 kilometers.

sionary work in Syria und Cilicia,[155] the missionary work in Galatia, the missionary work in Macedonia and in Achaia, the missionary work in the province of Asia, the journey to Spain,[156] the visit to the island of Crete,[157] and the travels before the second Roman imprisonment.[158]

Table 1.2. Paul's Travels

Arabia	300 km (12 days)		300 km (12 days)
Syria/Cilicia	1,800 km (70 days)		1,800 km (70 days)
Jerusalem (a.d. 44)	1,080 km (45 days)		1,080 km (45 days)
Galatia	1,440 km (60 days)	980 km at sea (10 days)	2,420 km (70 days)
Jerusalem (a.d. 48)	1,080 km (45 days)		1,080 km (45 days)
Macedonia/ Achaia	3,110 km (125 days)	2,060 km sea (20 days)	5,170 km (145 days)
Asia	2,900 km (115 days)	3,210 km sea (35 days)	6,110 km (150 days)
Spain	1,000 km (40 days)	1,800 km sea (15 days)	2,800 km (55 days)
Crete	120 km (5 days)	1,300 km sea	1,420 km (19 days)
Last journeys	900 km (35 days)	1,700 km sea (17 days)	2,570 km (52 days)

These figures lead to the following totals: Paul traveled ca. 25,000 kilometers (15,000 miles) as a missionary, about 14,000 kilometers (8,700 miles) by land.[159]

---

[155] Assuming a journey from Jerusalem to Damascus, a journey in Syria to Abila, Emesa, Apameia, Antioch and Kyrrhos; a journey in Cilicia from Tarsus to Adana, Mopsuestia, Anazarbus, Mallos, Korykos, Seleukia ad Kalykadnum and back to Tarsus; a journey from Tarsus to Antioch—a total of 1,800 kilometers. This is a low figure: Paul presumably traveled much more frequently during the ten years that he worked in Syria and in Cilicia.

[156] Assuming a journey from Rome to Tarraco, Barcino, Emporiae, Ilerda, Celsa, Caesaraugusta and back to Rome, a total of 1,800 kilometers by ship and 1,000 kilometers on land.

[157] Assuming a journey from Rome to Kydonia and along the coastal road to Rhithymna and by ship to Knosos, a total of 1,300 kilometers by ship and 120 kilometers on land.

[158] Assuming a journey from Knosos on Crete to Epirus and Illyricum (Nikopolis), overland to Macedonia (Thessalonica), by ship to Alexandria Troas and overland to Ephesus, a total of 900 kilometers on land and 1,700 kilometers by ship. For details cf. Schnabel, *Early Christian Mission*, 2:1287-88.

[159] For comparison: Alexander the Great traveled about 32,000 kilometers or 20,000 miles; cf. Elmer C. May et al., *Ancient and Medieval Warfare* (Wayne, N.J.: Avery, 1984), p. 29.

2

The Missionary Task
According to Paul's Letters

Paul, a servant of Jesus Christ, called to be an apostle, set apart for the
gospel of God, which he promised beforehand through his prophets in
the holy scriptures, the gospel concerning his Son, who was descended
from David according to the flesh and was declared to be Son of God
with power according to the spirit of holiness by resurrection from the
dead, Jesus Christ our Lord, through whom we have received grace and
apostleship to bring about the obedience of faith among all the Gentiles
for the sake of his name, including yourselves who are called to belong to
Jesus Christ.

ROM 1:1-6

PAUL WRITES HIS LETTERS AS A PASTOR of the churches that he or
others had established. He writes as a theologian who helps local churches
to more fully or more consistently understand the gospel. And he writes as
a missionary who is actively involved in preaching the gospel to Jews and
Gentiles as he writes (unless he is in prison, as in the case of the letters
which he wrote to the believers in Philippi, Colossae and Ephesus/Asia,
as well as to Philemon). Because Paul was called by God to be an apostle
who preaches the good news of Jesus Christ on the occasion of his conversion, Paul's identity was very much bound up with his missionary work. In
this chapter we will briefly survey Paul's letters in order to highlight some

of the major emphases and principles regarding the missionary task that he conveys to the believers in Asia Minor, Greece and Rome.

2.1 THE LETTER TO THE GALATIAN CHRISTIANS

Paul describes his conversion and his call to missionary service more extensively in Galatians 1 than he does in any other passage. This is already observable in the opening prescript in which he describes himself as the sender of the letter:

> Paul an apostle—sent neither by human commission nor from human authorities, but through Jesus Christ and God the Father, who raised him from the dead. (Gal 1:1)

Paul did not volunteer for missionary service. He was not commissioned by the apostles in Jerusalem, but he was sent by Jesus Christ and by God the Father. A few verses later Paul provides background and detail:

> But . . . God, who had set me apart before I was born and called me through his grace, was pleased to reveal his Son to me, so that I might proclaim him among the Gentiles. (Gal 1:15-16)

As Paul describes his divine calling to preach the gospel, he echoes two passages from the Old Testament in which Isaiah and Jeremiah describe their divine call:

> And now the LORD says, who formed me in the womb to be his servant, to bring Jacob back to him, and that Israel might be gathered to him, for I am honored in the sight of the LORD and my God has become my strength—he says, "It is too light a thing that you should be my servant to raise up the tribes of Jacob and to restore the survivors of Israel; I will give you as a light to the nations, that my salvation may reach to the end of the earth." (Is 49:5-6)

> Before I formed you in the womb I knew you, and before you were born I consecrated you; I appointed you a prophet to the nations. (Jer 1:5)

Like these two great prophets, Paul was chosen by God from birth, he was called by God to be his spokesperson, and he was commissioned to proclaim God's word of salvation to the nations.[1]

---

[1] Andreas J. Köstenberger and Peter T. O'Brien, *Salvation to the Ends of the Earth: A Biblical Theology of Mission*, NSBT 11 (Downers Grove, Ill.: InterVarsity Press, 2001), pp. 165-66.

Because Jewish Christian teachers had visited the Galatian Christians, seeking to disparage Paul by accusing him of lacking the full authority of an apostle, Paul is forced to defend his apostleship. He argues that there are differences in logistics when they compare his mission with the missionary work of the Jerusalem apostles, particularly the mission of Peter. And he emphasizes that he preaches the same gospel as James, Peter and John (Gal 1:1; 1:11—2:10).

While these teachers admonish the new believers in the churches in Galatia to be circumcised and to keep the law, Paul reminds the Galatian Christians of the "truth of the gospel" (Gal 2:5, 14) which he had preached to them:

> I am astonished that you are so quickly deserting the one who called you in the grace of Christ and are turning to a different gospel—not that there is another gospel, but there are some who are confusing you and want to pervert the gospel of Christ. But even if we or an angel from heaven should proclaim to you a gospel contrary to what we proclaimed to you, let that one be accursed! As we have said before, so now I repeat, if anyone proclaims to you a gospel contrary to what you received, let that one be accursed! (Gal 1:6-9)

Paul argues that it is faith in Jesus Christ alone which grants righteousness, forgiveness, salvation and adoption into God's family and the Holy Spirit. This is the message, focused on Jesus, the crucified Messiah (cf. Gal 3:1), that he preached in Galatia and he continues to preach whenever he proclaims the gospel. Because the apostles in Jerusalem had approved his calling and his preaching (Gal 2:7), there is indeed no other "good news" that can save sinners. Paul insists that the teaching of these opponents is "a different gospel" that must be rejected at all costs (Gal 1:6-9).

In the following paragraphs Paul explains that the arrival of Jesus Christ brought about a new era in which "a person is justified not by the works of the law but through faith in Jesus Christ" (Gal 2:16). As a result of this new reality, the Mosaic law no longer provides an effective, valid means for the atonement of sins (Gal 2:15—3:18). The role of the Mosaic law as a *paidagōgos*, a guardian and a guide, has come to an end with the arrival of Jesus the Messiah (Gal 3:19—4:7). If the Galatian believers submit to the teachers' demand to be circumcised and to obey the Torah, they would again submit to the enslaving powers of the world to whom they were subservient before their conversion (Gal 4:8-20). The problem of sin in the life of a believer cannot be solved with the help of the law: it is solved only in the continuing connection of the believer with the death and resurrection of Jesus Christ, in the liberation from the bondage of sin that Jesus the Messiah has brought about, and through the power of the Holy Spirit who produces "fruit" in the life of the believer (Gal 5:1—6:16).

As the missionary task is focused on preaching the gospel of Jesus Christ, Paul insists that Gentiles do not have to become Jews before they are accepted by God as followers of the Messiah. And he emphasizes that the "pillar" apostles (Gal 2:9) in Jerusalem agree with this position: faith in Jesus Christ is the only prerequisite for obtaining reconciliation from God who in gracious mercy freely forgives the sins of sinners, both for Jews and for Gentiles.

2.2 THE LETTERS TO THE CHRISTIANS IN MACEDONIA: THESSALONIANS AND PHILIPPIANS

Paul wrote three letters to the churches that he established in the province of Macedonia. He wrote two letters to the Christians in Thessalonica (in A.D. 50), and a letter to the church in Philippi (A.D. 57). In his first letter to the Thessalonian Christians, Paul's convictions concerning the task of a missionary are described.

First Thessalonians 1:4-10. In a letter to the believers in Thessalonica, written only a few months after he had established the church there, Paul reminds his converts about his preaching and about their conversion:

> For we know, brothers and sisters beloved by God, that he has chosen you, because our message of the gospel came to you not in word only, but also in power and in the Holy Spirit and with full conviction; just as you know what kind of persons we proved to be among you for your sake. And you became imitators of us and of the Lord, for in spite of persecution you received the word with joy inspired by the Holy Spirit, so that you became an example to all the believers in Macedonia and in Achaia. For the word of the Lord has sounded forth from you not only in Macedonia and Achaia, but in every place your faith in God has become known, so that we have no need to speak about it. For the people of those regions report about us what

kind of welcome we had among you, and how you turned to God from idols, to serve a living and true God, and to wait for his Son from heaven, whom he raised from the dead—Jesus, who rescues us from the wrath that is coming. (1 Thess 1:4-10)

This text shows that Paul was very much conscious of the significance of the initial contact that he had with people in a new city. The term *entrance* (Gk *eisodos* [1 Thess 1:9]) refers to the apostle's behavior during his first visit in the city (see sec 5.4). More importantly, 1 Thessalonians 1:9-10 provides a succinct summary of Paul's preaching. These two verses are often mentioned as an example of Paul's missionary proclamation before pagans in pioneer situations.[2] The following observations help us understand this text.

1. Paul's preaching focuses on God, that is, on the one true God of the Jews. As the Gentile Christians in Thessalonica had abandoned their traditional deities, Paul must have spoken of the futility of idol worship, probably along the lines of synagogue sermons that some of the Gentile listeners might have heard before. The goal of Paul's missionary preaching consisted in moving pagans to break with their idols and to worship the one true God. The break with the pagan deities is, in most cases, not the result of a theoretical acknowledgment of the truth of Jewish monotheism. Rather, it takes place in the context of a Gentile turning to the one true God whom he or she now worships, abandoning the traditional deities that had hitherto been worshiped. As Paul uses the phrase kingdom of God without explanation (1 Thess 2:12), a phrase that rarely occurs in Paul's letters,[3] we can safely infer that Paul must have spoken of God's kingly rule that has dawned with the coming of Jesus Christ in his missionary sermons. In the political context of the Roman Empire and of the imperial cult whose significance increased continuously, this was a potentially dangerous emphasis. Clearly this feature of his mis-

---

[2] Adolf von Harnack characterized this text as a "mission-preaching to pagans in a nutshell"; Adolf von Harnack, *The Mission and Expansion of Christianity in the First Three Centuries*, 4th ed. (London: Williams & Norgate, 1924), 1:89; see also Ulrich Wilckens, *Die Missionsreden der Apostelgeschichte. Form- und traditionsgeschichtliche Untersuchungen*, third rev. ed., WMANT 5 (Neukirchen-Vluyn: Neukirchener Verlag, 1974), pp. 81-86; Mauro Pesce, *Le due fasi della predicazione di Paolo. Dall'evangelizzazione alla guida delle comunità*, Studi biblici 22 (Bologna: Dehoniane, 1994), pp. 63-91.

[3] Rom 14:17; 1 Cor 4:20; 6:9-10; 15:50; Eph 5:5; Col 4:11.

sionary preaching was connected with the message about the person and the significance of Jesus Christ who proclaimed the dawn of God's kingdom; thus Paul did not dispense with this emphasis in his sermons before pagan audiences. Also, part and parcel of Paul's proclamation of the one true God was the reference to the coming day of judgment on which God's wrath will fall on all human beings who do not worship the one true God.

2. The fact that Paul used the name "Jesus" without an explanatory title such as "Christ" or "Lord" indicates that when he preached to new audiences, he recounted the life and ministry of Jesus of Nazareth before proceeding to explain the significance of his death and resurrection as central events that render his message "good news." Paul proclaimed Jesus not as a heroic figure who died for his convictions, nor did he proclaim a philosophical principle that helps people to live upright lives. Paul proclaimed Jesus as a historical person who lived and suffered, who died and who was raised from the dead.

3. Paul proclaimed Jesus as a historical person who was at the same time the Son of God. As the Roman emperors since Augustus had the title "son of god" (Lat. divi filius, abbreviated as divi f.), this emphasis was potentially dangerous because Paul could be accused of proclaiming a rival to the emperor. As regards Paul's reference to Jesus as "Son of God," we should note that the full Greek phrase (*ho huios tou theou*), in Paul's usage, always has the definite article,[4] which suggests that for Paul, Jesus' divine sonship was unique. Paul does not simply place Jesus in a class of figures who may all be regarded somehow as sons of God, such as the angels, kings, righteous individuals, miracle workers[5] or the emperors. Paul held that Jesus had a unique status and favor with God, indeed he regarded Jesus as "participating in God's attributes and roles, as sharing in the divine glory and, most importantly, as worthy to receive formal veneration with God in Christian assemblies."[6]

---

[4]Rom 1:4; 2 Cor 1:19; Gal 2:20; Eph 4:13.

[5]Angels: Gen 6:2; Ps 29:1; 89:6; in the LXX: Deut 32:8; Job 1:6; 2:1; Dan 3:25; *1 Enoch* 69:4-5; 71:1; *Jubilees* 1:24-25; the Davidic king: 2 Sam 7:14; Ps 2:7; 89:26-27; righteous individuals: *Psalms of Solomon* 13:9; 18:4; *Joseph and Aseneth* 16:14; 19:8; miracle workers: *m. Ta'anit* 3:8; *b. Ta'anit* 24b; *b. Berakhot* 17b; *b. Hullin* 86a.

[6]Larry W. Hurtado, "Son of God," *DPL*, p. 903.

4. Paul proclaimed Jesus as Savior who rescues from the coming judgment of God. Paul's consistent theological focus on Jesus' death[7] indicates that when he preached Jesus as God's Son who was raised from the dead, he focused his explanations on Jesus' death and on the fact that God forgives the sins of the people on account of the death of Jesus.

5. Paul explained to the Gentile listeners the necessity of conversion, which consists in turning away from the futile pagan gods and turning to the one true, living God. According to 1 Thessalonians 1:5-6, the reason for the effectiveness of the proclamation of the gospel was not the method of Paul's preaching but God's Spirit who convinced citizens of Thessalonica of the truth of the gospel, prompting polytheists to abandon their traditional deities and to turn to worship the one true God. According to 1 Thessalonians 2:13, the effective reality of conversion is not connected with the force of the arguments that are used but with the divine origin of the message as the word of God which is at work in people.

6. The goal of the conversion of pagans is "faith in God" (1 Thess 1:8). Faith in the one true God is faith in Jesus Christ as Savior. The effect of the conversion of pagans is "serving the true and living God" (1 Thess 1:9) in the context of their faith in Jesus Christ. In the Septuagint, the term "to serve" (*douleuein*) is "the most common term for the service of God, not in the sense of an isolated act, but in that of total commitment to the Godhead."[8] Paul uses the term *douleuein* to describe the believers' obedience to God and, more generally, the everyday life of the followers of Jesus. The goal of turning to the one true God is all-encompassing: a life lived according to the will of God.

First Thessalonians 2:3-8. In another important passage, Paul insists that the manner of his preaching corresponds with the content of the message that he proclaims.

> For our appeal does not spring from deceit or impure motives or trickery, but just as we have been approved by God to be entrusted with the message of the gospel, even so we speak, not to please mortals, but to please God who tests our hearts. As you know and as God is our witness, we never came with words of flattery or with a pretext for greed; nor did

---

[7]See Rom 3:24-26; 1 Cor 1:18-31; 15:3; 2 Cor 5:6-8, 21; Gal 1:4; 2:20; 3:1; 6:14; Phil 2:5-11.
[8]K. H. Rengstorf, *TDNT*, 2:267.

> we seek praise from mortals, whether from you or from others, though
> we might have made demands as apostles of Christ. But we were gentle
> among you, like a nurse tenderly caring for her own children. So deeply
> do we care for you that we are determined to share with you not only the
> gospel of God but also our own selves, because you have become very
> dear to us. (1 Thess 2:3-8)

Here Paul disassociates himself from deception, cunning and cajolery
as methods, and from seeking praise and from greediness as motivations
of his missionary proclamation. He emphasizes that the focus is not on
him but on God. Paul is merely the "trustee" of the message he proclaims.
He emphasizes the openness of his ministry and his clear conscience
before God, expressed in tangible love for the people before whom he
preaches the gospel. Paul asserts, by implication, that his behavior as a
preacher is very different from the demeanor of itinerant orators who are
often described by contemporaries as arrogant, self-seeking, greedy and
manipulative. Paul's conduct is controlled by the nature of the gospel, not
by considerations of expediency.

2.3 THE LETTERS TO THE CHRISTIANS IN ACHAIA: CORINTHIANS

First Corinthians 3:5-15. In 1 Corinthians 3:5-15 Paul provides the
most extensive description of his understanding of missionary work. The
problem that Paul discusses in 1 Corinthians 1—4 concerns Corinthian
Christians who believe that human "wisdom," in particular the traditional
criteria for convincing and entertaining rhetorical speech, is decisive for
evaluating the effectiveness of Christian preachers and teachers. This kind
of thinking prompted some believers to express their loyalty to a specific
teacher of the church, causing divisions in the congregation.

> What then is Apollos? What is Paul? Servants through whom you came to
> believe, as the Lord assigned to each. I planted, Apollos watered, but God
> gave the growth. So neither the one who plants nor the one who waters is
> anything, but only God who gives the growth. The one who plants and the
> one who waters have a common purpose, and each will receive wages ac-
> cording to the labor of each. For we are God's servants, working together;
> you are God's field, God's building. According to the grace of God given
> to me, like a skilled master builder I laid a foundation, and someone else is

building on it. Each builder must choose with care how to build on it. For no one can lay any foundation other than the one that has been laid; that foundation is Jesus Christ. Now if anyone builds on the foundation with gold, silver, precious stones, wood, hay, straw—the work of each builder will become visible, for the Day will disclose it, because it will be revealed with fire, and the fire will test what sort of work each has done. If what has been built on the foundation survives, the builder will receive a reward. If the work is burned up, the builder will suffer loss; the builder will be saved, but only as through fire. (1 Cor 3:5-15)

In this extended passage Paul describes his role as founder of the church as well as the role of other teachers and preachers who work in the church that he has founded. Paul's arguments express the following convictions about missionary work.

1. Paul understands himself as a "servant" (*diakonos* [1 Cor 3:5]). Since Apollos and any other teachers who have been or who are active in the church are also servants, there is no place for arrogance, vanity or self-interest. Paul's description of missionaries, preachers and teachers as "servants" turns the frame of reference of Greco-Roman society and its notion of social prestige, where personal honor and status were of paramount importance, upside down, Paul emphasizes that apostles, missionaries and teachers are servants, that is, people who get something done at the behest of a superior.[9] Paul uses metaphors from agriculture and house construction to describe the activities of missionaries, preachers and teachers: they plant, they water and they build. These are not tasks and activities that give cause for boasting.

2. God is the "Lord" (kyrios) of missionary work and of church work (1 Cor 3:5). He is the "superior" who directs the work of his "assistants" who serve him, the missionaries and the teachers. It was God who assigned tasks to each missionary and preacher, and who gave to every one different gifts. Both the task that God has assigned and the gift to carry out one's task are God's gracious gifts.[10] Both missionary ministry and pas-

---

[9]See Andrew D. Clarke, *Secular and Christian Leadership in Corinth: A Socio-Historical and Exegetical Study of 1 Corinthians 1-6*, AGAJU 18 (Leiden: Brill, 1993), pp. 119-20; for the *diakonos* as a person who gets something done, and as assistant, cf. BDAG, pp. 230-31.

[10]See Anthony C. Thiselton, *First Corinthians: A Shorter Exegetical and Pastoral Commentary* (Grand Rapids: Eerdmans, 2006), pp. 300-301.

toral ministry are tasks that God has given, work that God has assigned, commissions that God has granted.

3. The bond that ties preachers and teachers to the Lord establishes the unity of the ministry of all preachers and teachers who serve the church. The missionary who "plants" a church and the teacher who "waters" the believers in an established church are involved in one and the same task, and they are both dependent on the same Lord: they have "a common purpose" because they are "one" (1 Cor 3:8).

4. Paul understands himself as pioneer missionary, called by God to "plant" and to "lay the foundation" (1 Cor 3:6, 10), that is, to establish new churches. Apollos and other preachers and teachers "water" and "build on the foundation" (1 Cor 3:6, 10), that is, they encourage and promote the further growth of the church, teaching the believers and reaching unbelievers. Paul's statement that the Lord assigned different tasks to "each" (1 Cor 3:5) emphasizes the diversity of gifts and tasks. The context of this emphasis clarifies that Paul does not promote people focusing on their "own" ministry, which could very easily led to self-promotion. Paul criticizes the attitude of the Corinthian Christians who focus on the personality of the preacher and teacher (1 Cor 1:10-17; 3:1-4). Such a focus corresponds to the Hellenistic concerns of itinerant philosophers, but it contradicts the nature of the Christian message which preaches a crucified Savior (1 Cor 1:13, 17-18; 2:2).

5. Success always comes from God, and from God alone. This is true both for pioneer missionaries and for preachers and teachers in local congregations: only God gives growth (1 Cor 3:6-7). The effectiveness of missionary work and the effectiveness of pastoral ministry depend neither on individual persons and their gifts nor on programs or rhetorical techniques, but on God's agency. Preachers are nothing (1 Cor 3:7). The nature of the ministry of the gospel prohibits deference to and exclusivistic respect for individual preachers and teachers, as they are all instruments of God on whose work all "success" depends. Apostles and missionaries are just "coworkers," specifically "coworkers of God" (1 Cor 3:9): they are all involved in God's work.

6. The newly established churches belong neither to Paul nor to other teachers: the church is "God's field, God's building" (1 Cor 3:9). As the

growth of the church has been effected by God, the church is neither the work nor the possession of the apostle: it is the work and the possession of God. Missionaries and teachers belong together with the church to the "plantation" that is growing, to the "building" that is being constructed.

7. The responsibility of the missionary becomes apparent in the statement that "each will receive wages according to the labor of each" (1 Cor 3:8). God himself is the "employer" of the missionary and the teacher, they are all accountable to him. A second thought is implied as well: it is God alone who decides what constitutes success or failure of missionary and pastoral work, not the church. Paul does not specify the "wages" in 1 Corinthians 3:8. Later he refers to "the prize" (1 Cor 9:24), an "imperishable wreath" (1 Cor 9:25), "the crown of righteousness" (2 Tim 4:8). Paul seems to indicate in 1 Corinthians 3:8 that there are different wages as God rewards according to the work of the individual missionary, preacher or teacher. However, he does not indicate what the different wages consist of.[11] The reward

> does not depend on the degree of the giftedness nor on the scope of the success, because it is he who 'gives the growth' who decides the giftedness and the success. The reward is promised only regarding the sacrificial service of the individual. It is with this that Paul linked the expectation of a reward, without any inhibitions, 1 Corinthians 9:17, 18. Human action receives from God's action, human devotion receives God's gifts.[12]

8. Paul has been called to establish churches. The description of Paul as "skilled master builder" *(sophos architektōn)* who lays the "foundation" (1 Cor 3:10) describes the specific task that Paul received from God. Paul uses the metaphor of the master builder to describe himself as appointed and employed by God, together with a team of coworkers, to proclaim the gospel in pioneer situations, to lead people to faith in Jesus Christ and to establish new communities of believers. This is the "foundation" (a term that includes the foundation walls) without which there would be no church in the city of Corinth. The fact that Paul was active in Corinth for

---

[11]See David W. Kuck, *Judgment and Community Conflict: Paul's Use of Apocalyptic Judgement Language in 1 Corinthians 3:5-4:5*, NTSup 66 (Leiden: Brill, 1992), p. 168.

[12]Adolf Schlatter, *Paulus der Bote Jesu. Eine Deutung seiner Briefe an die Korinther* (1934; reprint, Stuttgart: Calwer, 1969), p. 131.

over one and a half years (Acts 18:2, 11, 12) clarifies that Paul regarded pioneer missionary work not as evangelistic blitz whose results should then be consolidated by other preachers and teacher in follow-up work. For Paul, to lay the foundation included instructing the new believers in the fundamental content of faith in Jesus Christ and in the basic teachings of Scripture (i.e., the Hebrew Scriptures, the Old Testament). Paul points out what every architect knows: the foundation that has been laid cannot be altered by those who continue to work on the building: if someone attempts to replace the existing foundation by another foundation he starts a different "alien" building.

9. The foundation that Paul lays is Jesus Christ himself (1 Cor 3:11), specifically Jesus the crucified Messiah (1 Cor 1:23; 2:2). The crucified and risen Jesus Christ is the content of the missionary proclamation and thus the foundation of the church as well as the critical measure of both the establishment and of the growth of the church. It is for this very reason that the decisive factor in the mission of the apostles is neither the missionary nor the teacher or the programs or the methods that are being used, but Jesus Christ who is preached. As a building has only one foundation, there can be no alternative to Jesus Christ. The existing foundation that Paul had laid in Corinth cannot be changed. When Herod the Great disregarded existing foundations during his rebuilding and renovation of the Jerusalem temple and sought to build his grandiose new edifice on newly dug foundations, they sank into the ground.[13] If a builder wants to finish the building that has been started on foundations that were laid by another architect, he has to adhere carefully to the benchmarks provided by the architect.

10. Preachers and teachers are responsible for the way they build on the "foundation Jesus Christ" (1 Cor 3:12-15) that Paul or other missionaries have laid. They have the responsibility for the priorities and for the perspectives, for the motivations and for the methods used in the (up)building of the church. Paul asserts that there is a way of erecting a building that has lasting results: when the builders follow the bench-

---

[13]Josephus *Antiquitates Judaicae* 15.391: "After removing the old foundations, he laid down others, and upon these he erected the temple, which was a hundred cubits in length and twenty more in height, but in the course of time this dropped as the foundations subsided."

marks set down by the master builder who had laid the foundations, they will successfully finish the building. And there is a way of erecting a building that is provisional: if the builders insist on new measurements and on new standards, they will erect a building that will not survive when there is a fire (a constant threat in the cities of the Mediterranean world). Materials such as gold, silver and precious stones (marble) survive a fire. In other words, missionaries and teachers who hold on to the crucified and risen Jesus Christ as the foundation, the ground and the measure of their faith and of their ministry do not have to be afraid of the fire of the Last Judgment (1 Cor 3:12-14). Wood, hay and straw burn easily and quickly. In other words, missionaries, preachers and teachers who think that they can push aside the message of the crucified and risen Savior and focus on other matters will "suffer loss" in the Last Judgment (1 Cor 3:15). They will be saved, but barely; they will experience some "deficit," perhaps the shame of the missionary who stands before God on Judgment Day without fruit after he has lost his work. Missionary work and pastoral ministry will "remain" on Judgment Day if and when Jesus, the crucified and risen Messiah and Savior, remains at the center of their preaching.

First Corinthians 9:19-23. A second significant passage is 1 Corinthians 9:19-23, where Paul describes his behavior as a missionary.

> For though I am free with respect to all, I have made myself a slave to all, so that I might win more of them. To the Jews I became as a Jew, in order to win Jews. To those under the law I became as one under the law (though I myself am not under the law) so that I might win those under the law. To those outside the law I became as one outside the law (though I am not free from God's law but am under Christ's law) so that I might win those outside the law. To the weak I became weak, so that I might win the weak. I have become all things to all people, that I might by all means save some. I do it all for the sake of the gospel, so that I may share in its blessings. (1 Cor 9:19-23)

Paul formulates the following fundamental elements of missionary work, as he understood and practiced it.

1. The basic rule of missionary existence requires the missionary to take the listener seriously (1 Cor 9:19). The behavior of the preacher is

subordinated to the preaching of the gospel. Paul is prepared to relinquish his Christian freedom if he can win people for faith in Jesus Christ.

2. Paul makes himself dependent on his listeners, he becomes their "slave" (1 Cor 9:19). Paul's "identificatory" maxim of missionary behavior means that he listens to the people so that they will listen to him, that he does what their need tells him to do, that he lives with them in order to reach them.

3. Paul does not exclude anybody from his preaching. Despite the difference in social status or ethnic background, and despite his specialized commission as missionary to Gentiles, Paul understands himself as obligated to the "people under the Torah" (1 Cor 9:20). Paul never excuses himself from preaching the message of Jesus Christ to his Jewish compatriots. His view of the church does not allow such a "separated coexistence" of Gentiles and Jews: "If Paul's call for unity is taken seriously, he did not merely want to be the apostle to the gentiles. He wants to be an apostle of all the church, for his vision was for a new community formed of all gentiles and Jews (1 Cor 9:20-22)."[14]

4. Paul's missionary accommodation formulates no limitations in advance. He becomes "all things" to all people (1 Cor 9:22). Even though he is no longer controlled by the stipulations of the Jewish law, he did not impede the potential conversion of his Jewish listeners by provocative "lawlessness." As a believer in Jesus Christ he is no longer "under the law," which means that he does not follow all stipulations of the Mosaic law, particularly the laws that distinguish between Jews and Gentiles, such as the food laws and the purity laws. But Paul emphasizes that this freedom from the law is not lawlessness: as far as the law is the law of God "in Christ," modified by the climax of God's revelation in Jesus the Messiah, it remains valid and he continues to live "in the law of Christ" (1 Cor 9:21). At the same time Paul maintains the freedom that is given with Jesus Christ as he interacts with Gentiles. He does not require them to keep the stipulations of the law: he eats what they eat, he drinks what they drink. He does not transform the new Gentile believers into Jews (which would require circumcision). We should note, however, that Paul never says that he became "a pagan to the pagans." The religious relativism of

---

[14]Alan F. Segal, *Paul the Convert: The Apostolate and Apostasy of Saul the Pharisee* (New Haven, Conn.: Yale University Press, 1990), p. 265.

Greco-Roman society makes it impossible for a missionary to live "as a Gentile" in every respect.

5. Paul seeks to win "more" people (1 Cor 9:19). The unusual Greek phrase *tous pleionas* does not mean "the majority" or "most," as Paul certainly knows from his missionary experience that usually only a few people come to faith. Perhaps he asserts that he would win fewer people if he behaved differently, for example if he always displayed the full scope of his freedom.

6. Paul emphasizes that the goal of his missionary work is to "win" people (1 Cor 9:19, 20 (2x), 21, 22). In extrabiblical Greek the verb kerdainein means "to gain, derive profit or advantage, make profit"; it is never used in a figurative sense with people as direct object (in the Septuagint the term is not used at all). To "win" a person means to "rescue" him or her, as the formulation in 1 Corinthians 9:22 demonstrates. It is the convert who "gains" as he or she receives salvation and is adopted in God's family together with other "brothers and sisters." But the apostle "profits" as well. The metaphor of building with durable materials in 1 Corinthians 3:12-15 emphasizes that Paul, as preacher of the gospel, knows he is responsible to God, who will examine his work for its durability on Judgment Day.

7. The normative center of the missionary's accommodating behavior is the gospel, not pragmatic effectiveness: "I do it all for the sake of the gospel, so that I may share in its blessings" (1 Cor 9:23). The phrase "for the sake of the gospel" excludes the abandonment of the gospel. Paul does not argue for cultural relativism but for cultural relevance. There are indeed boundaries for missionary accommodation: sin as defined by the word of God remains sin.

Second Corinthians 2:14-16. A third passage in which we can discern Paul's understanding of the missionary task is 2 Corinthians 2:14-16.

> But thanks be to God, who in Christ always leads us in triumphal procession, and through us spreads in every place the fragrance that comes from knowing him. For we are the aroma of Christ to God among those who are being saved and among those who are perishing; to the one a fragrance from death to death, to the other a fragrance from life to life. (2 Cor 2:14-16)

Paul uses the Roman triumphal procession to describe his missionary existence. The Greek term *thriambeuein* means "to celebrate a prior
victory by means of a triumph" (2 Cor 2:14), "to celebrate (by means of
a triumph) a victory over," and "to be displayed (as a prisoner of war)
in a triumph." The term regularly refers to military victories that the
Romans celebrated with a *pompa triumphalis*.[15] A triumphal procession
honored a victorious general who had been granted the imperium and
who had won a just war *(bellum iustum)* in which at least five thousand
enemies had been killed. The triumphant general sat in a carriage drawn
by four white horses clothed in a purple toga and his face painted red. A
slave held a laurel wreath above his head to remind him of his mortality.
The procession moved from the Campus Martius to the temple of Jupiter Optimus Maximus. At the head of the procession, the general's victory was portrayed on paintings and the booty was displayed, followed
by lictors with fasces wrapped in laurel, followed by prominent prisoners
and prisoners of war, then came the carriage of the triumphant general,
followed by the troops and the sacrificial animals. At the conclusion
of the procession, the prominent prisoners were generally executed, the
prisoners of war sold into slavery. The comparison of followers of Jesus
with defeated prisoners of war was hardly appealing to people living in
Roman cities in which honor and dignity were important values.

When Paul compares his missionary work with a Roman triumph, he
expresses the following conviction about his identity as a missionary.

1. Paul understands his missionary work as a public proclamation of
the victory of God who has defeated him who had once persecuted the
people of God. This victory took place, as regards Paul's biography is concerned, on the road to Damascus, a victory that is being celebrated in a
continuous triumphal procession in the missionary travels of the apostle.[16]
Paul, the great missionary to the Gentiles, never took his conversion and
his faith in Jesus Christ for granted.

2. Paul owes his calling as an apostle to God's irresistible power. This

---

[15]See Hendrik Simon Versnel, *Triumphus: An Inquiry into the Origin, Development and Meaning of
the Roman Triumph* (Leiden: Brill, 1970); Brent Roger Kinman, *Jesus' Entry into Jerusalem: In the
Context of Lukan Theology and the Politics of His Day*, AGJU 28 (Leiden: Brill, 1995), pp. 25-47.
[16]See Cilliers Breytenbach, "Paul's Proclamation and God's 'thriambos' (Notes on 2 Corinthians
2.14-16b)," *Neot* 24 (1990): 257-71.

point is a main element in Paul's metaphor of the Roman triumphal procession.[17] Paul's status as an apostle is not the result of personal achievements. Rather, his self-understanding as a missionary is determined by the conviction that God has overpowered him on the road to Damascus. The manifestation of God's power in his life and in his mission is inseparably connected with Jesus Christ (2 Cor 2:14).

3. Paul's conversion is a "fragrance" *(osmē)* and an "aroma" *(euōdia)*. It is unlikely that Paul refers here to the incense that was burned during the Roman triumphal processions (or to perfume in general) in terms of the presence of God. Some suggest that the background for the reference to "fragrance" and "aroma" is the Old Testament sacrifices, since the two Greek terms often occur together in the Septuagint,[18] and as Paul describes his missionary work as a priestly ministry in Romans 15:16. The "fragrance" of the proclamation of the gospel originates from death, that is, from the death of Jesus Christ, and it originates from life, that is, from the resurrection of Jesus. People who reject the gospel see only Jesus' death and are thus not saved from their own (eternal) death, while the people who accept it know and understand Jesus as the risen *Kyrios* and receive him as source of their (eternal) life. Whatever the background of Paul's metaphor, it remains true that many people have heard the gospel of God's revelation in Jesus Christ as a result of Paul's missionary work, even though not all the people who have heard believe.

2.4 THE LETTER TO THE CHRISTIANS IN THE CITY OF ROME

Paul's letter to the Christians in the city of Rome can be read as a missionary document.[19] As Paul prepares both himself and the Roman Christians for the missionary outreach in Spain he plans for A.D. 57, the following emphases of his letter are particularly significant.

1. Paul emphasizes the international and universal scope of his mission-

---

[17]See Margaret E. Thrall, *The Second Epistle to the Corinthians*, ICC (Edinburgh: T & T Clark, 2000), 1:195.

[18]Cf. Gen 8:21; Ex 29:18, 25, 41; Lev 1:9, 13, 17; 2:2, 9, 12; 3:5, 11, 16.

[19]See Gottlob Schrenk, "Der Römerbrief als Missionsdokument," in *Studien zu Paulus*, AThANT 26 (Zürich: Theologischer Verlag, 1954), pp. 81-106; cf. William S. Campbell, "Paul's Missionary Practice and Policy in Romans," *Irish Biblical Studies* 12 (1990): 2-25. The following summary is reproduced from Schnabel, *Early Christian Mission*, 2:1472-75.

ary ministry "from Jerusalem and as far around as Illyricum" and Spain (Rom 15:19, 24, 28). He also asserts that the responsibility of the Roman Christians has the same comprehensive scope: "For I do hope to see you on my journey and to be sent on by you, once I have enjoyed your company for a little while" (Rom 15:24). The strategy of the early Christian mission focuses on the conversion of people no matter where they live or who they are—Paul reminds the Christians in the capital of the Roman Empire of this fact.

2. Missionary work and theological reflection about the gospel depend on one another. Christian communities are, or become, centers of missionary work only if their leaders and their individual members are involved in understanding, explaining and proclaiming the gospel. This requires incisive, in-depth theological work. Paul the missionary cannot be separated from Paul the theologian. Paul the missionary, who is on his way to a new missionary initiative in Spain, expects the Christians in the city of Rome to understand his longest and most intensively theological letter.

3. In Romans 1—3 Paul explains the nature of sin and its consequences, not merely for a fictitious Gentile or Jewish dialogue partner. He describes the foundations of their faith for the Roman Christians. Only Christians who look back to their past with repentance and are thereby continuously liberated from their past are qualified coworkers among the people of the world who still live in bondage. The gospel demonstrates the "solidarity" of sinners, whether Jews or pagans. In view of God's revelation in Jesus Christ there is nobody who can escape God's judgment. A church that is active in mission and evangelism does not discharge itself from this solidarity. Missionary work presupposes that Christians remind themselves of the sin and the bondage from which they have been liberated and redeemed.

4. The salvation-historical foundation of the gospel and of the mission of God's people has specific and practical consequences for the tactical procedures of missionary work: God addresses Jews first (Rom 1:16; 2:9-10; 9—11). The Gentile mission must never emancipate itself from missionary outreach among the Jews. Did Paul expect that the Gentile Christians in the house churches in the city of Rome—probably the majority of the believers in Rome at the time of the composition of his

letter—to bring the gospel of Jesus the Messiah to the Jews living in Rome? Many answer this question in the negative, arguing that "after Auschwitz" non-Jews have no business trying to convert Jews to the Christian faith. A positive answer seems to be more likely, however. We must not forget Paul's motto for local congregations: "There is no longer Jew or Greek, there is no longer slave or free, there is no longer male and female; for all of you are one in Christ Jesus" (Gal 3:28). This is not merely a theological statement but the expression of a salvation-historical eschatological truth that has tangible consequences for the fellowship of the followers of Jesus: If Jews reach Gentiles with the gospel, there is no reason why a converted Gentile should not explain to a Jewish friend or neighbor his faith in Jesus as Israel's Messiah and Savior of the world. Of course Gentile Christians would have had no opportunities to proclaim the gospel in the synagogues. But there were other opportunities for contacts between Gentiles and Jews—opportunities in which the priority of the Jews as members of God's chosen people would have been an important conviction for the Gentile Christians as they sought to explain the gospel.

5. The missionary work of Paul and of the church is focused on the proclamation of God's salvation in the crucified and risen Jesus who is the Messiah (Rom 3:21-31). Sin can be forgiven only when the holy God himself removes his wrath. Guilt can be atoned for only when God himself procures and grants salvation. The message of God the Creator and Judge who grants salvation to sinners through Jesus the Messiah who has been sent into the world as sin-offering, dying on the cross instead of sinners (Rom 8:3), is always a missionary message. The identity of the church that confesses Jesus as Kyrios consists in the reality of having received the gift of God's righteousness and of having become a part of the Son's mission, who came into the world to save sinners. For this reason the church can be and should be a community that is involved in Jesus' mission.

6. Paul narrates the history of humankind from Adam (Rom 1:18-32; 5:12-21) and Abraham (Rom 4:1-25) to Jesus Christ, who has solved the problem of sin that dominated the world since Adam (Rom 5:1-21). God chose Abraham and his descendants, the people of Israel, in order to begin to solve the problem of sin in the world. Gentile Christians have become children of Abraham as a result of their faith in Jesus the promised Savior

(Rom 4:11), which means that they have been incorporated in the world project of salvation whose immediate climax is the death and resurrection of Jesus Christ.

7. The missionary message is not a philosophy or a hermeneutical theory. It represents a reality that is connected with the praxis of everyday life and with the continuous task of dealing with persistent sin and temptation. The justification by faith in the crucified and risen Jesus Christ that Paul preaches and describes becomes a reality in the life of the believers who live in the power of God's Spirit (Rom 6:1—8:39).

8. Missionary work always takes the specific situation of the audience into account. This is one of the reasons why Paul describes the "situation" of Israel (Rom 9:1—11:32). When missionaries offer salvation in their proclamation of the good news of Jesus the Messiah and Savior, Israel's unbelief becomes a problem. If God's old covenant people, the chosen descendants of Abraham, do not believe in Jesus the Messiah and Savior, the missionary message of Jesus' followers is either wrong or weak, some might argue. Paul thus provides theological, historical and practical insights into the condition of the Jews as seen from God's perspective. Paul speaks not only of the goals of God's plan of salvation, he also emphasizes the responsibility of the people who hear the gospel preached to them (Rom 10:14-15). And he underscores the responsibility of the (Gentile) Christian churches to provoke the Jews to jealousy, prompting them to come to faith in Jesus Messiah, as a result of the concrete realization of the messianic salvation that God has granted them in Jesus Christ and who receive visible form and shape through the work of God's Spirit (Rom 11:11-15).

9. Both Paul and the church can be effective in mission and evangelism only when God's love is realized in the midst of the church and in the life of every believer (Rom 12:1—15:29). Paul does not formulate a Christian halakhah, rules and regulations that always and for every situation tell the believers how they must behave. Paul emphasizes and explains fundamental theological, christological and pneumatological realities. His emphasis on love (Rom 12:9-10), particularly the love of one's enemies (Rom 12:19-21), is not a coincidence. Believers who are active in mission and evangelism are often attacked by "the evil one," as the Christians in

the city of Rome know only too well. As they "overcome evil with good" (Rom 12:21), they can continue to be involved in the project of the eternal God "to bring about the obedience of faith" among the Gentiles (Rom 16:26)—because they are members of God's people who have experienced the salvation effected by Jesus Christ and who live by the power of the Holy Spirit.

2.5 THE LETTERS TO THE CHRISTIANS IN ASIA: COLOSSIANS AND EPHESIANS

Paul wrote two letters to churches in the province of Asia: to the Christians in Colossae and to the believers in Ephesus, both probably written in A.D. 60 when he was a prisoner in Rome.

Colossians 1:24-29. Following a reference to the universal proclamation of the gospel in Colossians 1:23, Paul writes about his ministry as a servant of the gospel.

> I am now rejoicing in my sufferings for your sake, and in my flesh I am completing what is lacking in Christ's afflictions for the sake of his body, that is, the church. I became its servant according to God's commission that was given to me for you, to make the word of God fully known, the mystery that has been hidden throughout the ages and generations but has now been revealed to his saints. To them God chose to make known how great among the Gentiles are the riches of the glory of this mystery, which is Christ in you, the hope of glory. It is he whom we proclaim, warning everyone and teaching everyone in all wisdom, so that we may present everyone mature in Christ. For this I toil and struggle with all the energy that he powerfully inspires within me. (Col 1:24-29)

Paul describes the following central aspects of his missionary work, including the ministry of his coworkers.

1. Paul suffers as an apostle of Jesus Christ, just as Jesus suffered during his mission. Suffering is an inevitable corollary of missionary work. When Paul asserts that he "completes" in his own sufferings the sufferings of Christ (Col 1:24), he links his suffering as an itinerant missionary with the "sufferings of the Messiah," the messianic woes that are mentioned in the apocalyptic tradition. The word play with the rare Greek term *antanapleroō* (Col 1:24), a verb that occurs only here in the New

Testament, emphasizes that he has been commissioned by God to preach the word of God "fully" *(plērōsai).*[20] The context clearly refers to Paul's missionary work. This means that the messianic woes became historical reality in the suffering of Jesus the Messiah and continue in the missionary work of Paul.

2. As a "servant" *(diakonos)* of the church (Col 1:25), Paul is a "servant" of the gospel (Col 1:23). The "office" *(oikonomia)* that Paul has received from God is "to make the word of God fully known." He proclaims the word of God, which is the gospel of Jesus Christ. Paul works as a servant of the gospel and of the church of Jesus Christ. He preaches the word of God among Gentiles in the power of the Holy Spirit, with the goal that people will accept the message of Jesus Christ and come to saving faith.

3. Paul describes the process of the preaching of the word of God with different verbs (Col 1:28). He "proclaims" *(katangellomen);* that is, he announces the gospel in public. He "warns" *(nouthetountes)* people; that is, he admonishes the people concerning wrong beliefs and behavior, and he instructs in proper belief and behavior, so that the believers are fully and consistently oriented toward Jesus Christ. He "teaches" *(didaskontes)* people in all wisdom; that is, he explains the content, the roots and the consequences of the gospel for the world and for individuals. These verbs show that "clearly for Paul and his colleagues evangelistic and missionary outreach was not effected by some superficial presentation of the saving message about Christ to the world, but rather was prosecuted through warning and intensive teaching in pastoral situations."[21] Paul acknowledges that the Christians in Colossae are making progress in faith and in love (Col 1:4). However, as a missionary, pastor and teacher he is satisfied with nothing less than with the full maturity of each individual believer, which will be fully reached only when Jesus Christ returns.

4. Missionary activity is hard work *(kopos)* and regularly involves struggle *(agōnizomenos* [Col 1:29]). Paul's preaching of the gospel is hard work which demands his full attention and all his energies. At the same time Paul emphasizes that the energy and power for the hard and difficult

---

[20]See Michael Cahill, "The Neglected Parallelism in Colossians 1.24-25," *Ephemerides Theologicae Lovanienses* 68 (1992): 142-47.
[21]Peter T. O'Brien, *Colossians, Philemon,* WBC 44 (Waco, Tex.: Word, 1982), pp. 87-88.

missionary work are not his own but Christ's. Paul does not rely on his physical vitality, his rhetorical abilities, his missionary experience or his theological competence. As far as his missionary work and the success of his preaching are concerned, he relies solely on the power of God, which has become graciously available in Jesus Christ.

Ephesians 3:1-13. In Ephesians 3:1-13 Paul explains his missionary work in terms of the "mystery" that God had revealed to him:

> This is the reason that I Paul am a prisoner for Christ Jesus for the sake of you Gentiles—for surely you have already heard of the commission of God's grace that was given me for you, and how the mystery was made known to me by revelation, as I wrote above in a few words, a reading of which will enable you to perceive my understanding of the mystery of Christ. In former generations this mystery was not made known to humankind, as it has now been revealed to his holy apostles and prophets by the Spirit: that is, the Gentiles have become fellow heirs, members of the same body, and sharers in the promise in Christ Jesus through the gospel. Of this gospel I have become a servant according to the gift of God's grace that was given me by the working of his power. Although I am the very least of all the saints, this grace was given to me to bring to the Gentiles the news of the boundless riches of Christ, and to make everyone see what is the plan of the mystery hidden for ages in God who created all things; so that through the church the wisdom of God in its rich variety might now be made known to the rulers and authorities in the heavenly places. This was in accordance with the eternal purpose that he has carried out in Christ Jesus our Lord, in whom we have access to God in boldness and confidence through faith in him. I pray therefore that you may not lose heart over my sufferings for you; they are your glory. (Eph 3:1-13)

In this important passage Paul describes his missionary calling and preaching as an integral part of God's plan of salvation on account of his connection with the "mystery" that God has revealed.[22] The following four points are important.

1. Paul's calling, the content of his preaching and the conversion of the

---

[22]See Chrys C. Caragounis, *The Ephesian* Mysterion: *Meaning and Content* (Lund: Gleerup, 1977); Peter T. O'Brien, *Gospel and Mission in the Writings of Paul: An Exegetical and Theological Analysis* (Grand Rapids: Baker, 1995), pp. 12-19; Köstenberger and O'Brien, *Salvation to the Ends of the Earth*, pp. 166-67.

Gentiles are all dependent on God's grace (*charis* [Eph 3:2, 7, 8]), which is God's free gift (*dōrea* [Eph 3:7]; cf. the verb *didōmi* [Eph 3:2, 7, 8]). God's grace is the foundation and the center of Paul's personal life, of his missionary work and of the life of the new believers who have been converted and of the churches that have been established.

2. Paul received from God the "commission" or "stewardship" *(oikonomia)* of the grace of God (Eph 3:2), which is embodied in the gospel and proclaimed in Paul's ministry. Paul had not volunteered to preach among the Gentiles. Rather, God had taken the initiative in commissioning Paul to proclaim God's redeeming love among people who worship other gods. In God's "administration" of the world and of the history of salvation, Paul has been given the role of making the "mystery" known.[23] Paul emphasizes that both the commission to preach the gospel to Gentiles, which he received from God, and his missionary service through which he fulfills this calling are the result of the effective operation of the mighty power of God (Eph 3:7).[24] Paul, even as an experienced missionary who had been preaching the gospel for many years, does not take his missionary calling or the results of his missionary work for granted. Paul was always amazed at the extraordinary privilege of having been called by God to preach the gospel and of having been used by God to lead Gentiles to saving faith in Jesus Christ.[25]

3. The "mystery" *(mystērion)* that has been revealed to Paul and is part and parcel of the gospel of God's grace is the inclusion of the pagans in God's salvation, who are thus incorporated along with Jewish believers into the body of Christ, that is, into the church (Eph 3:3-6). The term *mystery* does not refer to some hidden knowledge that only Paul knows and that he now shares with is readers. Nor does it refer to some future apocalyptic event (in Eph 3:3 Paul uses the word *apokalypsis*) that is hidden in God's inscrutable plan for the world. As Paul uses the word, *mystery* generally refers to God's decisive action in the sending of Jesus Christ, the crucified

---

[23]See Peter T. O'Brien, *The Letter to the Ephesians*, PNTC (Grand Rapids: Eerdmans, 1999), pp. 227-28. Eph 3 does not address the question of the conversion of Gentiles before Paul; cf. Ernest Best, *A Critical and Exegetical Commentary on Ephesians*, ICC (Edinburgh: T & T Clark, 1998), p. 297, who emphasizes that "vv. 2-13 have no polemical edge."

[24]See Andrew T. Lincoln, *Ephesians*, WBC 42 (Dallas: Word, 1990), p. 182.

[25]See O'Brien, *Gospel and Mission in the Writings of Paul*, p. 16.

and risen Savior and Lord, as the fulfillment of God's plan of salvation.[26] In Ephesians 3:3-4, 9, the "mystery" is more specifically the "open secret" of God's plan according to which the Gentiles are being incorporated into the people of God, along with the believers among the Jewish people, on the basis of the work of Jesus Christ. The Old Testament prophets looked forward to the last days when the nations would come to Zion and worship Israel's God. It had not been revealed, however, how this would happen. Would the Gentiles become Jews (through conversion and adoption of the Mosaic law) and thus find salvation? Or would they become the recipients of God's saving purposes as Gentiles, as the Messiah would provide a new law to which the believing Gentiles would submit alongside the faithful remnant in Israel? This mystery of God's plan of salvation has been revealed: when Gentiles are converted through Paul's preaching of the gospel, God's promises to Abraham (Gen 12:1-3) are being fulfilled. And this happens in the specific manner of Gentile believers being "heirs of God" and "joint heirs with Christ" (Rom 8:17), receiving the promise of the Holy Spirit (Eph 1:13) together with Jewish believers (Eph 2:18) through Jesus' redeeming death on the cross (Eph 2:13) without first being circumcised (Eph 2:11-13) and without being required to first keep the Mosaic law (Eph 2:14-15). Thus the Gentile believers are "no longer strangers and aliens" but "citizens with the saints and also members of the household of God, built upon the foundation of the apostles and prophets, with Christ Jesus himself as the cornerstone" (Eph 2:19-20).

4. One of the results of the revelation of this mystery of God's plan of salvation is the shape of the communities of believers that have come into existence as the result of Paul's missionary work. In the churches that Paul established, Jewish and Gentile believers worship the one true God side by side, as "one new humanity" (Eph 2:15). The church was a multiracial community and as such a manifestation of the revealed "mystery" of God's plan of salvation. This is the witness of the church, apart from all missionary work (or social action) the church might be engaged in: "so that through the church the wisdom of God in its rich variety might now be made known to the rulers and authorities in the heavenly places" (Eph

---

[26]See Peter T. O'Brien, "Mystery," *DPL*, pp. 621-23.

3:10). The existence of the church, made up of Jewish and Gentile believers in Jesus Christ, is the tangible evidence of the revelation of God's mystery in Paul's missionary work.[27] This witness before the invisible world consists here specifically in the unity of the community of the followers of Jesus as the "body of Christ" in which Jews and Gentiles live together, signaling the beginning of the universal reconciliation of all things (Eph 1:9-10).[28]

Ephesians 6:10-20. In Ephesians 6:10-20, Paul describes Christian believers as being involved in a battle against the powers of evil. He specifies two reactions to the attacks of Satan who attempts to harm the believers: believers must resist the temptation, which they can do because they are protected by the armor of God, and believers must preach the gospel.

> Finally, be strong in the Lord and in the strength of his power. Put on the whole armor of God, so that you may be able to stand against the wiles of the devil. For our struggle is not against enemies of blood and flesh, but against the rulers, against the authorities, against the cosmic powers of this present darkness, against the spiritual forces of evil in the heavenly places. Therefore take up the whole armor of God, so that you may be able to withstand on that evil day, and having done everything, to stand firm. Stand therefore, and fasten the belt of truth around your waist, and put on the breastplate of righteousness. As shoes for your feet put on whatever will make you ready to proclaim the gospel of peace. With all of these [or: in all circumstances], take the shield of faith, with which you will be able to quench all the flaming arrows of the evil one. Take the helmet of salvation, and the sword of the Spirit, which is the word of God. Pray in the Spirit at all times in every prayer and supplication. To that end keep alert and always persevere in supplication for all the saints. Pray also for me, so that when I speak, a message may be given to me to make known with boldness the mystery of the gospel, for which I am an ambassador in chains. Pray that I may declare it boldly, as I must speak. (Eph 6:10-20)

The identification of the footwear with the "readiness to proclaim the

---

[27]O'Brien, *Gospel and Mission in the Writings of Paul*, p. 19, referring to Raymond E. Brown, *The Semitic Background of the Term "Mystery" in the New Testament* (Philadelphia: Fortress Press, 1968), p. 60.

[28]See Max M. B. Turner, "Mission and Meaning in Terms of 'Unity' in Ephesians," in *Mission and Meaning: Essays Presented to Peter Cotterell*, ed. A. Billington et al. (Carlisle, U.K.: Paternoster, 1995), pp. 145-48.

gospel of peace" (Eph 6:15) refers to the proclamation of the gospel. Paul asserts that authentic believers are prepared for the outward-going movement that is required for the proclamation of the gospel.[29] The reference to a weapon for battle—the "sword of the Spirit"—shows that the struggle of the Christian believer is not merely defensive but offensive as well: the "sword of the Spirit" is identified with the "word of God" (Eph 6:17). The sharp, short sword *(machaira)* was the most important weapon for close-range combat. A "defensive" interpretation is ruled out by the fact that the short sword was an offensive weapon. Paul does not want to immunize the Christians against the influences of pagan society. He describes the offensive action of Christian believers in their fight against the attacks of Satan. They engage in the active proclamation of the good news of Jesus' death on the cross by which he defeated all evil powers and of Jesus' resurrection to life. This is a message that is made effective and powerful by God's Spirit. The word of God is wielded by the Holy Spirit as a "sword"; it is the proclamation of the gospel in the midst of a world dominated by evil powers, so that people are liberated from Satan's control and find salvation.

2.6 THE LETTERS TO COWORKERS: TIMOTHY AND TITUS

Paul directs Timothy to make sure that the behavior of the believers in the churches of Asia Minor promotes the spreading of the gospel. The myths and endless genealogies in which some Christians are interested only provoke useless speculations (1 Tim 1:4). Christians should be concerned with matters that are profitable for "advancing God's work" (1 Tim 1:4 TNIV).[30] This includes the sound teaching of God's plan of salvation, as indicated by the phrase *oikonomian theou.* In 1 Timothy 1:5, Paul formulates the "aim of such instruction," which is "love that comes from a pure heart, a good conscience, and sincere faith." Timothy is directed to instruct the teachers in the churches to make sure that their ministry promotes the loving commitment of the Christians to each other. Paul emphasizes that the gospel that God has revealed is the standard for his own interpretation and proclamation of the law, the gospel that has been

---

[29]See Best, *Ephesians*, p. 599; O'Brien, *Ephesians*, pp. 476-77.
[30]See I. Howard Marshall, *The Pastoral Epistles*, ICC (Edinburgh: T & T Clark, 1999), pp. 367-68.

entrusted to him at his conversion (1 Tim 1:11-16). Paul has endeavored to preserve the content of the gospel against false teaching. His reference to his responsibilities in connection with the gospel can hardly be separated from his calling to proclaim the gospel to unbelievers.[31]

First Timothy 2:1-4. In 1 Timothy 2:1-4 Paul exhorts Christian believers to pray for all people, including "kings and all who are in high positions," who exercise authority and whose task is to safeguard a stable and peaceful society. The motivation of these prayers is the goal that the spiritual life of the believers and their witness for "God our Savior" can thrive, as God "desires everyone to be saved and to come to the knowledge of the truth."[32] The believers in the province of Asia would have known, of course, that for people to be saved there needs to be missionary preaching and teaching.

Second Timothy 4:5. In 2 Timothy 4:5, Paul exhorts Timothy to "do the work of an evangelist." When Paul writes this letter, Timothy bears the responsibility for the churches in Ephesus and in other cities in the province of Asia. In the context of 2 Timothy 4, the "work" of an evangelist is closely connected with teaching and with exercising leadership in the local congregation.[33] By implication, Paul calls on all the leaders of the churches in Asia Minor to engage in missionary work.

Titus 2:3-5. The exhortation to the "older women" in Titus 2:3-5 may be motivated by missionary concerns.

> Likewise, tell the older women to be reverent in behavior, not to be slanderers or slaves to drink; they are to teach what is good, so that they may encourage the young women to love their husbands, to love their children, to be self-controlled, chaste, good managers of the household, kind, being submissive to their husbands, so that the word of God may not be discredited. (Tit 2:3-5)

The behavior of older women should not discredit the evangelistic efforts of the church but promote them.[34] The exhortation to the Christian slaves in Titus 2:9-10 has a missionary component as well. They are called

---

[31]Royce Gordon Gruenler, "The Mission-Lifestyle Setting of 1 Tim 2:8-15," *JETS* 41 (1998): 215-38, wants to interpret 1 Tim 1:11-17 as a "missions statement."

[32]See William D. Mounce, *Pastoral Epistles*, WBC 46 (Nashville: Nelson, 2000), pp. 82-83.

[33]See Alastair Campbell, "'Do the Work of an Evangelist'," *EQ* 64 (1992): 117-29.

[34]See Philip H. Towner, *The Goal of Our Instruction: The Structure of Theology and Ethics in the Pastoral Epistles*, JSNTSup 34 (Sheffield, U.K.: JSOT Press, 1989), pp. 195-96.

"to be submissive to their masters and to give satisfaction in every respect; they are not to talk back, not to pilfer, but to show complete and perfect fidelity, so that in everything they may be an ornament to the doctrine of God our Savior." Slaves who have become believers and who are thus "free" in Jesus Christ are exhorted, as are all Christians, to put into practice the reality of the gospel in their everyday lives. They are reminded of the fact that the credibility of the gospel, which is preached in connection with the missionary activities of the local church, would be discredited if they display a rebellious attitude. Christians who happen to be slaves should be motivated by the goal of making the gospel "as attractive as possible for those around them."[35]

2.7 THE APOSTLE AS MISSIONARY, PASTOR AND THEOLOGIAN

Paul's self-understanding as apostle of Jesus Christ and thus as missionary, pastor and theological teacher can be summarized as follows.

1. God is the Kyrios, the Lord of all missionary work (1 Cor 3:5). God gives to each believer, each apostle, missionary, pastor and teacher, particular tasks and particular (spiritual) gifts. Success in missionary work is solely due to God's power and grace, as only he grants growth (1 Cor 3:6-7). Paul relies consistently and only on the power of Jesus Christ, the Son of God (Rom 15:18; 1 Cor 1:24; 2:1-5).

2. Effectiveness in missionary work and in pastoral ministry does not depend on people or programs, nor does it depend on rhetorical techniques or elaborate methods. Any "success" is the result of God's activity. Local churches do belong to neither the missionaries who established the congregations nor the teachers who are active in these communities. Rather, the church is and always remains "God's field, God's building" (1 Cor 3:9).

3. The crucified and risen Jesus Christ is the content of missionary preaching and thus the foundation, the criterion and the measure of church planting and church growth (1 Cor 1:23; 2:2; 3:11; 15:2). The decisive factor of missionary work is therefore not the missionary but Jesus Christ, who is proclaimed, not the messenger but the message.

4. Paul understands himself as a "servant" of God and of his word,

---

[35]Mounce, *Pastoral Epistles*, p. 416.

serving Jesus Christ and the church (1 Cor 3:5; Col 1:23, 25). This self-understanding excludes all self-reliance, self-interest and boasting with regard to his missionary work and his successes. Missionaries are servants whose lives are completely devoted to serving their Lord. Missionaries who preach the gospel are like clay jars: in themselves they are weak and not very impressive at all, indeed ultimately irrelevant (2 Cor 4:7). The suffering and the weaknesses of the missionary whom God uses to proclaim the gospel and to establish new churches demonstrate that success and growth are solely the result of God's power, the effect of the truth of the word of God and of the power of the Holy Spirit (2 Cor 4:7-15; Col 1:24).

5. Paul understands his missionary work as public proclamation of the victory of God, who had conquered him and leads him through the world in his triumphal procession (2 Cor 2:14-16). Paul's self-understanding is determined by his encounter with Jesus Christ on the road to Damascus. He understands himself as an ambassador of Jesus Christ who speaks as representative of the Messiah (Rom 15:18; 2 Cor 5:20; 13:3). This status is all the reputation that he requires. He does not need to boast himself or increase his importance with letters of introduction (2 Cor 3:1; 5:12).

6. Paul knows himself to be called by God to work as a pioneer missionary who "plants" churches, who lays the foundation as an "expert master builder," that is, who establishes new communities of believers (1 Cor 3:6, 10; 9:10). The metaphors of building and planting indicate that missionary work is hard work (cf. Col 1:29). Paul does not spare himself: as "servant" and "slave" he does not "take it easy" but he does the work that his Master tells him to do.

7. The central process of missionary work is the oral proclamation of the good news about Jesus the Messiah and Savior (Rom 10:14-17; 15:18; 1 Cor 15:1-2, 11; Col 1:28). Faith comes from hearing the word of God that missionaries preached and that people heard and accepted.

8. The foundational rule of missionary work is the consistent attention to the listeners: Jews have to be reached with the gospel as Jews, and Gentiles have to be reached with the gospel as Gentiles (1 Cor 9:19). All people need to hear the gospel: both the elites of the Greco-

Roman cities and the foreigners and the barbarians, both the educated and the uneducated (Rom 1:14). The behavior of the missionaries is subject to the proclamation of the gospel: the missionary is willing to become "all things to all people" (1 Cor 9:22), with the proviso that the integrity of the gospel is the normative criterion for missionary accommodation (1 Cor 9:23).

9. Paul is not satisfied with the success of his mission. He wants to reach ever more people with the gospel in the entire world (1 Cor 9:19; Rom 10:18), even though sometimes only few people come to faith, as was the case in the Jewish communities in which he preached (Rom 10:16).

10. Paul does not work alone. He surrounds himself with other missionaries and coworkers, and he reckons with the work of teachers in the churches once he leaves to engage in missionary work in other cities. Paul insists that the loyalty of every missionary and teacher of the church to the Lord establishes the unity of the ministry of all those who serve the Lord. The pioneer missionary who "plants" and the preacher and teacher who "waters" are engaged in one and the same work, and they are dependent on one and the same Lord: they are "one" (1 Cor 3:8).

11. Paul is convinced that his missionary work takes place in the last days (cf. Rom 13:11; 1 Thess 4:13-18) and that it has a significant role in God's revelation of the "mystery" of his plan of salvation (Eph 3:1-13). The conversion of Gentiles and their incorporation into God's people as believing Gentiles (and not as Gentiles who became Jews) is a visible manifestation of God's plan of salvation and thus a witness to God's redeeming and transforming grace.

12. The missionaries, preachers and teachers engaged in building up the church are responsible to God for their actions and their motivations. The reality of this responsibility will become evident and will have consequences on the Day of Judgment. There is missionary work and church ministry that will be rejected by God if and when the gospel has been compromised (1 Cor 3:12-15). Because God alone is the Lord of missionary outreach, the missionaries are responsible to God directly: each will receive his own reward "according to the labor of each" (1 Cor 3:8). As God is their master, their "employer," they are

primarily and fully accountable to him. God alone decides whether the work of the missionary, the pastor and the teacher is successful or not unsuccessful, not the church or other workers.

3

The Missionary Message
of the Apostle Paul

For I am not ashamed of the gospel; it is the power of God for salvation
to everyone who has faith, to the Jew first and also to the Greek. For in it
the righteousness of God is revealed through faith for faith; as it is written,
"The one who is righteous will live by faith."

ROM 1:16-17

For the message about the cross is foolishness to those who are perishing,
but to us who are being saved it is the power of God. For it is written, "I
will destroy the wisdom of the wise, and the discernment of the discerning
I will thwart." Where is the one who is wise? Where is the scribe? Where
is the debater of this age? Has not God made foolish the wisdom of the
world? For since, in the wisdom of God, the world did not know God
through wisdom, God decided, through the foolishness of our proclamation, to save those who believe. For Jews demand signs and Greeks desire
wisdom, but we proclaim Christ crucified, a stumbling block to Jews and
foolishness to Gentiles, but to those who are the called, both Jews and
Greeks, Christ the power of God and the wisdom of God.

1 COR 1:18-24

PAUL'S MISSIONARY SERMONS ARE NOT PRESERVED, expect for summaries that Luke records in the book of Acts. The content of Paul's mis-

sionary preaching can be reconstructed from Paul's own writings with the help of succinct summaries of the gospel[1] and of the process of conversion.[2] The description of Paul's missionary message in this chapter will begin with an analysis of three sermons of Paul as summarized by Luke (Acts 13:14-50; 14:8-18; 17:16-34). Specific aspects of his missionary preaching will then be described with the help of explanations of the gospel and its corollaries for the lives of followers of Jesus found in Paul's letters. As regards the reliability of Luke's summary of Paul's speeches in the book of Acts, we should not discount the fact that Paul may have written out some of his sermons. Contemporary orators first wrote out their public speeches before memorizing them for the public declamation;[3] it therefore is not impossible to assume that Paul kept written records of sermons he had preached in various cities.

3.1 PREACHING BEFORE JEWISH AUDIENCES

Luke illustrates Paul's missionary preaching in synagogues before Jewish audiences on the occasion of Paul's missionary work in Pisidian Antioch (Acts 13:14-50).

Acts 13:16-41. The summary in Acts 13:16-41 is the first and the longest sermon of Paul that Luke reports in the book of Acts.

> You Israelites, and others who fear God, listen. The God of this people Israel chose our ancestors and made the people great during their stay in the land of Egypt, and with uplifted arm he led them out of it. For about forty years he put up with them in the wilderness. After he had destroyed seven nations in the land of Canaan, he gave them their land as an inheritance for about four hundred fifty years. After that he gave them judges until the time of the prophet Samuel. Then they asked for a king; and God gave them Saul son of Kish, a man of the tribe of Benjamin, who reigned

---

[1]E.g., Gal 1:3-4; 2:16; 3:1, 13; 1 Cor 1:18-2:5; 15:3-4; Rom 1:3-5; 3:21-26; 5:1-2; 8:1-4, 32; 16:25-27; Eph 1:3-14.

[2]E.g., Rom 6:3-4, 17-19; 7:4-6; Eph 2:1-10; 5:8; Col 1:13-14, 21-22; 1 Thess 1:9-10.

[3]See Philostratus, *The Lives of the Sophists* (London: Heinemann, 1922), p. 580, who relates how the students of the orator Herodes Atticus humiliated Philagrus of Cilicia: when the latter seemed to be improvising an extempore speech on a topic they had suggested, "they retaliated by reading the declamation aloud" from a manuscript of Philagrus's standard speech on the suggested topic. See Glen Warren Bowersock, *Greek Sophists in the Roman Empire* (Oxford: Clarendon, 1969), p. 93. On written speeches see also Graham Anderson, *Philostratus: Biography and Belles Lettres in the Third Century A.D.* (London: Croom Helm, 1986), pp. 205-7.

for forty years. When he had removed him, he made David their king. In his testimony about him he said, "I have found David, son of Jesse, to be a man after my heart, who will carry out all my wishes." Of this man's posterity God has brought to Israel a Savior, Jesus, as he promised; before his coming John had already proclaimed a baptism of repentance to all the people of Israel. And as John was finishing his work, he said, "What do you suppose that I am? I am not he. No, but one is coming after me; I am not worthy to untie the thong of the sandals on his feet."

"My brothers, you descendants of Abraham's family, and others who fear God, to us the message of this salvation has been sent. Because the residents of Jerusalem and their leaders did not recognize him or understand the words of the prophets that are read every sabbath, they fulfilled those words by condemning him. Even though they found no cause for a sentence of death, they asked Pilate to have him killed. When they had carried out everything that was written about him, they took him down from the tree and laid him in a tomb. But God raised him from the dead; and for many days he appeared to those who came up with him from Galilee to Jerusalem, and they are now his witnesses to the people. And we bring you the good news that what God promised to our ancestors he has fulfilled for us, their children, by raising Jesus; as also it is written in the second psalm,

"You are my Son;

. . . today I have begotten you."

As to his raising him from the dead, no more to return to corruption, he has spoken in this way,

"I will give you the holy promises made to David."

Therefore he has also said in another psalm,

"You will not let your Holy One experience corruption."

For David, after he had served the purpose of God in his own generation, died, was laid beside his ancestors, and experienced corruption; but he whom God raised up experienced no corruption. Let it be known to you therefore, my brothers, that through this man forgiveness of sins is proclaimed to you; by this Jesus everyone who believes is set free from all those sins from which you could not be freed by the law of Moses. Beware, therefore, that what the prophets said does not happen to you:

"Look, you scoffers!

Be amazed and perish,
for in your days I am doing a work,

    a work that you will never believe, even if someone tells you." (Acts 13:16-41)

The threefold address of the audience (Acts 13:16, 26, 38) divides Paul's sermon into three parts which can be correlated with the traditional rhetorical parts of the *narratio* (explanation of the subject matter), *argumentatio* (proofs) and *peroratio* (conclusion).[4]

Review of salvation history (Acts 13:16b-25): Narratio.

1. address of the "Israelites" (v. 16b)
2. from the election of the patriarchs to the preview of the exile (vv. 17-20a)
3. comment on the period of the judges (v. 20b)
4. the period of the kings Saul and David (vv. 21-22)
5. the fulfillment of the promise given to David in the mission of Jesus (v. 23)
6. John the Baptist (v. 24-25)

Proclamation of the significance of Jesus (Acts 13:26-37): Argumentatio.

1. the relevance of the gospel for the audience (v. 26)
2. discussion of the culpable behavior of the citizens of Jerusalem (vv. 27-29)
3. announcement of the resurrection of Jesus (v. 30)
4. note about Jesus' postresurrection appearances (v. 31)
5. Paul and Barnabas as teachers who proclaim the fulfillment of the promise (vv. 32-33a)
6. proof from Scripture for Jesus' resurrection with Psalm 2:7; Isaiah 55:3; Psalm 16:10 (vv. 33b-37)

Call to repentance (Acts 13:38-41): Peroratio

---

[4]See Josef Pichler, *Paulusrezeption und Paulusbild in der Apostelgeschichte 13,16-52*, IThS 50 (Innsbruck: Tyrolia, 1997), pp. 124-31; cf. Joseph A. Fitzmyer, *The Acts of the Apostles*, AncB 31 (New York: Doubleday, 1998), 507-8. Some scholars suggest more elaborate divisions.

1. forgiveness of sins and the justification of the believers (vv. 38-39)
2. warning not to ignore the work of God with Habakkuk 1:5 (vv. 40-41)

In the first part of the sermon Paul reviews Israel's history of salvation, framed by the notion of Israel's election and of God's promise for Israel: God chose Israel's ancestors, that is, Abraham, Isaac and Jacob, and God promised that he would send a Savior to Israel (Acts 13:17, 23). Paul explains to the Jewish listeners that Israel's history was planned and ordered by God, that the promised coming of the Savior has taken place, and that this Savior is Jesus. Paul's review of Israel's history of salvation before Jewish listeners who hear the message of Jesus the Messiah for the first time is deliberately positive. The inclusion of personal names (Samuel, Saul, David, John) reminds the listeners not only of God's specific intervention in Israel's past, but also attests to the fact that God's promised act of salvation, which would deal with sin once and for all, would be focused on a specific redeemer figure.[5] David is particularly highlighted (Acts 13:22-23) because of his obedient service and on account of the messianic promises linked with him.

In the second part of the sermon Paul explains that God's promise of a Savior was fulfilled in the life, death and resurrection of Jesus. Paul's proclamation of the significance of Jesus of Nazareth begins with the prophet John the Baptist and his demand that "all the people of Israel" must repent (Acts 13:24-25). It ends with a description of the reaction of the citizens of Jerusalem and of the leading representatives of Israel: they rejected Jesus because they failed to recognize who Jesus was, with the result that they asked Pilate, the Roman governor, to have Jesus executed (Acts 13:27-29). The Jews in Jerusalem had not understood the significance of the words of the prophets whose prophecies they regularly heard in the temple and the synagogue. But the Jews who are sitting in the synagogue of Antioch do not yet belong to those who had heard of Jesus

---

[5] See Matthäus F.-J. Buss, *Die Missionpredigt des Apostels Paulus im Pisidischen Antiochien. Analyse von APG:13.16-41 im Hinblick auf die literarische und thematische Einheit der Paulusrede*, FzB 38 (Stuttgart: Katholisches Bibelwerk, 1980), p. 47.

but rejected him. Paul asserts that Jesus' rejection by the Jews in Jerusalem was part of God's plan. He contrasts the actions of Israel's leaders with the actions of God: God raised Jesus from the dead, and Jesus appeared to his followers for many days.

Paul substantiates this point with three quotations from Scripture. Paul uses Psalm 2:7 (a text connected with 2 Sam 7:12, 14) to demonstrate that Jesus is the messianic Son of David and the Savior of Israel whom Scripture had promised and God had begotten. Paul then uses Isaiah 55:3 (a text connected with 2 Sam 7:15-16) to assert that the rule of Jesus, whom God had raised from the dead, will last forever and thus that the salvific promises given to David are fulfilled in the rule of Jesus Christ, who is enthroned in heaven. Finally Paul uses Psalm 16:10 (a text connected with 2 Sam 7:12-13) to argue that the promise to David was fulfilled in Jesus, who was raised from the dead and who is thus the "Holy One" God promised. Paul's quotations of specific Old Testament passages and the implied allusions to other passages that are related to the explicit quotations by specific words and phrases fits the situation of a synagogue sermon. When Paul speaks before Jewish listeners who regularly attend the synagogue services where Scripture is read and explained, he uses the techniques of the rabbis who explain Scripture with Scripture. The quotations from Scripture also demonstrate Paul's intention to integrate the life of Jesus into the course of the history of Israel. And they demonstrate Paul's conviction that in the final analysis God himself is the subject of salvation history and of Jesus' history.[6]

In the third part of his sermon in the synagogue of Antioch, Paul formulates the decisive proclamation of salvation through Jesus the Messiah. He argues that Jesus, whom God has raised from the dead, is the Holy One through whom God forgives sins. Paul argues that only through faith in the risen Jesus can people have right relationship with God. The forgiveness of sins that God offers in Jesus is valid for all sins, even for the sins from which the law could not free them. And God's offer of forgiveness through Jesus justifies all people who believe (Acts 13:38-39). The

---

[6]Cf. ibid., pp. 80-81.

last statement implies that Gentiles can receive forgiveness as well if and when they believe in Jesus Christ. This applies to the Gentiles who are sitting in the synagogue of Antioch, the God-fearers and other Gentile sympathizers who hear Paul preach.

Paul explains the significance of Jesus' resurrection in four steps.[7] (1) Jesus' resurrection is the climax of Israel's history of salvation. Israel's God who had revealed himself in the history of his people through various mighty acts has sent a Savior to his people, Jesus, whom he raised from the dead as witnessed by many who saw him after his death (Acts 13:30-31). (2) Jesus' resurrection represents the fulfillment of God's promise in Psalm 2 and thus confirms Jesus as Son of God. And it represents at the same time the fulfillment of the promise in Isaiah 55:3, delivering God's gracious gifts that nobody can destroy, as the risen Son of God who, according to Psalm 16:10, cannot experience corruption (Acts 13:32-37). (3) Jesus' resurrection is the basis for God's forgiveness of sins and for the justification of everyone who believes in Jesus (Acts 13:38-39). (4) Jesus' resurrection is the amazing act of God that many do not want to believe, a fact that prompts Paul to warn the audience not to despise the work of God (Acts 13:40-41).

Paul warns his Jewish listeners not to despise God's gift of salvation. If they reject his message that salvation now comes through faith in Jesus the promised Savior, this would constitute the fulfillment of the prophecy in Habakkuk 1:5. This Scriptural passage speaks of Israel's failure to recognize the invasion of the Chaldeans, a Gentile nation, as God's judgment. Paul applies this prophecy to the danger that the Jews who hear his preaching may not grasp that Jesus is the Savior whom God has sent to his people. The "work" that God has done (Acts 13:41, quoting Hab 1:5) is the resurrection of Jesus, an event that many Jews have refused to believe.[8]

Paul did not need to convince his Jewish listeners that they were sin-

---

[7]See G. Walter Hansen, "The Preaching and Defense of Paul," in *Witness to the Gospel. The Theology of Acts*, ed. I. H. Marshall and D. Peterson (Grand Rapids: Eerdmans, 1998), pp. 300-306. Cf. Larry W. Hurtado, *Lord Jesus Christ: Devotion to Jesus in Earliest Christianity* (Grand Rapids: Eerdmans, 2003), pp. 126-33, on Jesus' redemptive death and resurrection in Paul's theology.

[8]See C. A. Joachim Pillai, *Early Missionary Preaching: A Study of Luke's Report in Acts 13* (Hicksville: Exposition Press, 1979), pp. 71-73.

ners. Pious Jews did not doubt that it was only God's grace that forgives sin; pious Jews believed that God's final answer to the problem of sin was not the Mosaic law but, rather, the arrival of the promised Messiah. What Paul needed to demonstrate in his missionary sermons before Jews was the messianic identity of Jesus. The question of whether Jesus was the Messiah or not decided the answer to the question whether the message that God forgives sins on account of Jesus' death was valid and should be accepted. Paul preached that his Jewish listeners needed to acknowledge that Jesus is the Messiah and that his death on the cross brings about God's promised salvation. This in turn implied that Israel's salvation no longer rests on being God's chosen people. It implied that circumcision no longer guarantees that Jews are the recipients of God's salvation. It implied that the sacrifices in the temple, which the Mosaic law stipulated, no longer guaranteed the forgiveness of individual Jews or the holiness of Israel as a nation. These were far-reaching implications and conclusions that depended entirely on the identity of Jesus of Nazareth as the promised Savior and on the significance of his death and resurrection. This is what Paul needed to explain to the Jews in the synagogue in Antioch.

3.2 PREACHING BEFORE GENTILE AUDIENCES

Luke provides an example of Paul's preaching of the gospel before a pagan audience in the context of his report of the apostle's missionary work in the city of Lystra (see sec. 1.3).

Acts 14:15-17. The citizens of Lystra had interpreted a miracle of healing that took place after one of Paul's sermons as a manifestation of divine power indicating that Barnabas and Paul were visiting deities in disguise—Zeus, the chief god of the Olympian gods, and Hermes, his messenger. When the citizens of Lystra make preparations to offer sacrifices, the two missionaries realize the misunderstanding that had taken place.

> "Friends, why are you doing this? We are mortals just like you, and we bring you good news, that you should turn from these worthless things to the living God, who made the heaven and the earth and the sea and all that is in them. In past generations he allowed all the nations to follow their own ways; yet he has not left himself without a witness in doing good—giving you rains from heaven and fruitful seasons, and filling you

with food and your hearts with joy." Even with these words, they scarcely restrained the crowds from offering sacrifice to them. (Acts 14:15-18)

The brief summary of Paul's sermon in Lystra, which Luke provides in the book of Acts, has the following structure:

The difference between human beings and gods (Acts 14:15a-c): Narratio.

1. address of the "men"[9] (v. 15a)
2. introductory question (v. 15b)
3. affirmation that human beings are not gods (v. 15c)

Proclamation of the one true God (Acts 14:15d-17): Argumentatio.

1. the worthlessness of the traditional gods (v. 15d)
2. the necessity of turning away from idols (v. 15d)
3. the good news of the possibility of worshiping the living God (v. 15d)
4. the one true God is the Creator of the universe (v. 15e)
5. God did not intervene in the affairs of the pagan nations in the past (v. 16)
6. God cared for the pagan nations even in the past (v. 17)

It appears that there was no conclusion of the sermon due to the reaction of the audience as they continued in their preparations to offer sacrifices to Barnabas and to Paul (Acts 14:18).

In the first part of his sermon Paul quickly clarifies that he and Barnabas are not gods that can be worshiped, they are not superhuman and thus not divine: they are mortal human beings just like the citizens of Lystra (Acts 14:15). The pagan audience would not have sharply distinguished between gods and human beings. Some gods fathered (or mothered) offspring with a mortal lover; examples of such "demigods" (Gk *hēmitheoi*) include Achilles, the son of the nymph Thetis and king Peleus; Heracles/Hercules, the son of Zeus and Alcmene; Asclepius (the famous physician), the son of Apollon and the mortal woman Coronis (or Arsinoe); Alexander the Great, according to myth the son of Queen Olympias of Macedonia and Zeus Ammon. As people attributed divine powers to images (statues)

---

[9]The NRSV translates with "friends."

of mortals,[10] deceased persons who helped (or harmed) people from the grave could be venerated as heroes.[11] Greek colonies in Asia Minor and in other regions often worshiped their founders as heroes, whose grave monument *(hērōon)* was often located in the central market square. Julius Caesar was said to trace his family line back to Aeneas, the ancestor of the Roman people, who in turn was the son of Venus, the goddess of fertility and love, and her mortal lover Anchises. The members of the imperial family in Rome, in particular the emperors themselves, were regarded as divine, a conviction that was regularly displayed in public. When visitors entered the imperial temple in Pisidian Antioch, built perhaps already in 2 B.C., they walked through a monumental gate that displayed the following inscription: "For the emperor Caesar Augustus, son of a god, pontifex maximus, consul for the 13th time, with tribunician power for the 22nd time, imperator for the 14th time, father of the country."[12] Paul emphasizes at the beginning of his speech before the citizens of Lystra that people whose activities lead to astounding miracles of healing are not gods but human beings with the same nature as theirs. Paul disputes one of the basic tenets of pagan thinking, namely, that there is no hard-and-fast dichotomy between gods and humans. This is a thoroughly Jewish point of view anchored in the Scriptures as the first of all commandments: "You shall have no other gods before me" (Ex 20:3). No human being must ever be worshiped, because humans do not deserve divine honor.

The second part of the sermon shows that Paul did not critique the religious convictions of his pagan listeners indirectly, by implication only. He was clearly rather explicit in his criticism of pagan religiosity.[13]

First, Paul emphasizes the worthlessness of the deities that the people in Lystra worship (Acts 14:15). The fact that they are willing to worship

---

[10]See Ramsay MacMullen, *Paganism in the Roman Empire* (New Haven: Yale University Press, 1981), p. 60.

[11]See Walter Burkert, *Greek Religion* (Cambridge: Harvard University Press, 1985), pp. 203-8.

[12]Stephen Mitchell and Marc Waelkens, *Pisidian Antioch: The Site and Its Monuments* (London: Duckworth, 1998), p. 147.

[13]See Marianne Fournier, *The Episode at Lystra. A Rhetorical and Semiotic Analysis of Acts 14:7-20a*, AUS 7:197 (New York: Lang, 1997); Christoph W. Stenschke, *Luke's Portrait of Gentiles Prior to Their Coming to Faith*, WUNT 2/108 (Tübingen: Mohr-Siebeck, 1999), pp. 185-90; Dean Philip Bechard, *Paul Outside the Walls: A Study of Luke's Socio-Geographical Universalism in Acts 14:8-20*, Analecta biblica 143 (Rome: Editrice Pontificio Istituto Biblico, 2000), pp. 423-27.

Barnabas and Paul, who are mere mortals who share the same experiences and feelings (Gk *homoiopatēs*) as the citizens of Lystra, demonstrates that the object of their religious devotion is not commendable. In fact, Paul argues, the deities they worship, symbolized in images of stone, wood or bronze are worthless, vain, empty, useless (Gk *mataia*). This verdict applies also to Zeus, the supreme deity! In nonbiblical Greek, the term *mataia* describes empty talk lacking truth, or vain persons who are useless. The description of pagan deities as "empty" or "worthless" is already found in the Old Testament.[14] In the Jewish literature of this period, the term *mataia* is often used to describe the gods of the pagans.[15]

Second, because the deities worshiped in Lystra are worthless, the people need to turn away from their idols (Acts 14:15). The action of "turning away" from the traditional deities involves ending the practice of bowing before the image of one's favorite deity, which perhaps stood in the central market square. Turning away meant abstaining from visiting temples and refraining from offering sacrifices. It meant no longer praying to Tyche, the god of fortune; to Asclepius, the god of healing; to Apollo, the god of youth, music and prophecy; to Artemis, the goddess of childbirth; to Aphrodite, the goddess of love and beauty; or to the Lares, the protectors of the family and the guardian spirit of the home.

Third, Paul declared that he brings the good news that it is possible to worship the living God (Acts 14:15). The one true God to whom people should turn as they abandon their traditional gods is the "living God." This expression is often used in the Greek Old Testament to emphasize the power of God over against the gods of the pagan nations whose armies the heroes of Israel defeat as they rely on the power of the living God.[16] The affirmation that there is only one God, the one true and living God of Abraham, Isaac and Jacob, is the very foundation of the Jewish faith, as many texts of Diaspora Judaism demonstrate.[17] When Cyrus, the king

---

[14]See Lev 17:7 (LXX); 1 Kings 16:2, 13 (LXX).

[15]See *Testament of Abraham* A 1:7; *Testament of Dan* 4:1; *Letter of Aristeas* 134.4; 137.1; 139.6; 205.3; 321.5; *Sibylline Oracles* 3:29; 4:4; 5:83.

[16]Cf. Deut 5:26; Josh 3:10; 1 Sam 17:26, 36; 2 Kings 19:4, 16 (= Is 37:4, 17); Dan 5:23. Cf. Cilliers Breytenbach, *Paulus und Barnabas in der Provinz Galatien*, AGAJU 38 (Leiden: Brill, 1996), pp. 60-66.

[17]Cf. Bel 5-6, 24-25; Tob 13:1-3; 2 Macc 7:33; 15:4; *Joseph and Aseneth* 8:5; 11:10; 19:8; *Testament of Job* 37:2; *Sibylline Oracles* 3:763.

of the Persians, asked Daniel why he refused to worship Bel, Daniel answered according to the apocryphal text Bel and the Dragon: "Because I do not revere idols made with hands, but the living God, who created heaven and earth and has dominion over all living creatures" (Bel 5). God is the "living God" because he is the source of life.[18] The predicate *living* also indicates that the one true God is the Creator of life who also saves from death.[19] Unlike his synagogue sermon, Paul does not quote the Old Testament explicitly for the affirmation that there is only one true and living God. His Gentile listeners would not accept the Jewish Scriptures as an authority. Paul nevertheless uses Scriptural language to insist on this axiom of divine revelation.

Fourth, Paul affirms that the one true and living God "made the heaven and the earth and the sea and all that is in them" (Acts 14:15). The living God is the Creator of the universe. The people of Lystra worship many different gods, but they do not worship the One who created the world. This emphasis is another basic axiom of Israel's faith, as demonstrated by the fact that the Hebrew Scriptures begin with an affirmation of the creation of the universe by the one God whom the Jews worship: "in the beginning when God created the heavens and the earth" (Gen 1:1).

Fifth, Paul explains that the one true and living God did not intervene in the affairs of the pagan nations in the past: "in past generations he allowed all the nations to follow their own ways" (Acts 14:16). Paul asserts that in the past God did not give the nations (Gk *ethnē*) direct revelations. He let them worship whatever objects they wanted to worship. The "ways" in which Gentiles walked when they worshiped their gods lead astray, resulting in the worship of vain and worthless entities. But in the past the one true and living God had not taken the initiative to change this. He had left the Gentile nations to themselves. Because Paul had already challenged his Gentile listeners in Lystra to turn away from their traditional gods and to worship the one true and living God, he asserts that what was true in the past is no longer true in the present. God has now taken the initiative to change the misguided ways of Gentile idol worship.

Sixth, Paul emphasizes that God cared for the pagan nations even in

---

[18]Cf. in LXX: Ps 35:10; 41:2; 83:3; Jer 2:13; 17:13.
[19]See *Testament of Abraham* A 17:11.

the past, when he let them go their own ways: "yet he has not left himself without a witness in doing good—giving you rains from heaven and fruitful seasons, and filling you with food and your hearts with joy" (Acts 14:17). God had never simply abandoned the Gentile nations. He had always revealed himself through his works in nature. He provided rain, which resulted in the fruitful seasons of the year and allowed them to reap harvests that provided them with good and resulted in rejoicing. This means that the natural order of the seasons, of harvest time and of human contentment is a witness to the goodness of God. The description of the one true and living God as the One who "does good," who "confers benefits" *(agathourgōn)* by giving rain and fruitful seasons has been explained by some scholars against the background of the veneration of Zeus as god of vegetation who controls the weather.[20] Inscriptions of the region (Phrygia and Pisidia) refer to Zeus as Zeus Kalakagathios, that is, as god "who does what is good and fruitful." The cult of Zeus Bronton, a patron of agriculture, which is also attested in the region, is connected with Hermes. If Paul was aware of these connections, his use of the rare Greek term *agathourgōn* would have implied the affirmation that the living God whom he proclaims is the only deity who truly confers benefits on human beings.

Paul thus taught the inhabitants of Lystra five truths about God.[21] (1) God is present in the works of creation, which are a silent witness of his goodness. (2) God in his goodness seeks to satisfy the needs of people, for whom he cares. (3) God wants people to experience joy in their hearts. (4) This God alone deserves to be worshiped, as he is the one true and living God. (5) God no longer permits the Gentile nations to go their own ways; he now demands that people abandon their traditional but vain objects of worship and turn to the one true and living God.

Paul's central conviction that forgiveness of sins could be obtained exclusively through faith in Jesus Christ required an explanation for Gentile audiences of who God is. It is God who punishes sinners and it is God

---

[20]See Breytenbach, *Paulus und Barnabas*, pp. 69-73; cf. the inscriptions *SEG* VI 550; *SEG* II 481; CIG 5931.

[21]See Bruce W. Winter, "In Public and in Private: Early Christian Interactions with Religious Pluralism," in *One God, One Lord in a World of Religious Pluralism*, ed. A. D. Clarke and B. W. Winter (Cambridge: Tyndale House, 1991), p. 117, for the first three points.

who forgives sins. Paul needed to convince the listeners that there is only one true God. If there is only one true God, there is probably only one true Savior from sins. One may call this "propaedeutical preaching."[22] When Paul preached before polytheists, he first needed to speak about the God of Israel as the one true and living God before he could speak about Jesus the Lord and Savior.[23]

3.3 EXPLAINING THE GOSPEL IN CIVIC SETTINGS

As we saw earlier, the main thrust of Paul's speech before the Council of the Areopagus was not the proclamation of the gospel of Jesus Christ with the goal of convincing his listeners to become followers of Jesus (sec. 1.5). Rather, Paul was asked to speak to the council as a result of his debates with Epicurean and Stoic philosophers, who came to the conclusion that Paul wanted to introduce new deities to Athens.

Acts 17:22-31. Paul's speech before the members of the council aimed at convincing the decision makers of the city that he was not introducing new deities to the pantheon of the gods worshiped in Athens.[24] Paul asserts that he proclaims the "unknown god" who is already honored at an altar in the city (Acts 17:23). He explains that the God whose spokesman he is needs neither an altar for sacrifices nor a temple for worship. He is not applying for the admission of a new deity to the register of deities that the citizens of Athens may worship. As Paul makes these points, he simultaneously addresses matters that would be of interest to the members of the council who identified with, or at least understood, the tenets of Epicurean and Stoic philosophy. At the end of Paul's speech, when he speaks of God's Day of Judgment, the members of the council must have suddenly realized that they were no longer investigating Paul and his teachings about religion but, rather, that they are under investigation themselves.

---

[22]Albrecht Oepke, *Die Missionspredigt des Apostels Paulus. Eine biblisch-theologische und religionsge-schichtliche Untersuchung*, Missionswissenschaftliche Forschungen 2 (Leipzig: Hinrichs, 1920), p. 65; cf. ibid., pp. 82-108 on "propaedeutics of preaching to pagans."

[23]For a discussion of the important text 1 Thess 1:9-10, often regarded as a succinct summary of Paul's missionary preaching before Gentiles, pp. 126-29.

[24]For a discussion of the historical context of Paul's speech before the Council of the Areopagus whose members asked Paul to explain the new deities that he wanted to introduce into the pantheon of gods worshiped in Athens see pp. 98-104 ("Athens").

Athenians, I see how extremely religious you are in every way. For as I went through the city and looked carefully at the objects of your worship, I found among them an altar with the inscription, "To an unknown god." What therefore you worship as unknown, this I proclaim to you. The God who made the world and everything in it, he who is Lord of heaven and earth, does not live in shrines made by human hands, nor is he served by human hands, as though he needed anything, since he himself gives to all mortals life and breath and all things. From one ancestor he made all nations to inhabit the whole earth, and he allotted the times of their existence and the boundaries of the places where they would live, so that they would search for God and perhaps grope for him and find him—though indeed he is not far from each one of us. For "In him we live and move and have our being"; as even some of your own poets have said, "For we too are his offspring." Since we are God's offspring, we ought not to think that the deity is like gold, or silver, or stone, an image formed by the art and imagination of mortals. While God has overlooked the times of human ignorance, now he commands all people everywhere to repent, because he has fixed a day on which he will have the world judged in righteousness by a man whom he has appointed, and of this he has given assurance to all by raising him from the dead." (Acts 17:22-31)

Paul's speech before the Council of the Areopagus can be divided into three parts:[25] the *exordium* (introduction), the *argumentatio* or *probatio* (proofs), and the *peroratio* (conclusion).

Introduction (Acts 17:22-23): Exordium.

1. Address of the "Athenians." (v. 22b)
2. Commendation of the audience *(captatio benevolentiae)*. (vv. 22c-23a)
   a. Acknowledgment of the Athenians' religiosity. (v. 22c)
   b. Reference to an Athenian altar dedicated to "an unknown god." (v. 23a)
3. Summary of the matter to be proved *(propositio)* (v. 23b):

Paul does not introduce a new deity.

---

[25]See Dean Zweck, "The Exordium of the Areopagus Speech, Acts 17.22,23," *NTS* 35 (1989): 97; cf. Ben Witherington, *The Acts of the Apostles*, p. 518.

He is the spokesman of the unknown god whom they already worship.

The Creator God, the human race, and the presence of God (Acts 17:24-29): Argumentatio.

1. Description of the Creator God whom Paul proclaims. (vv. 24-25)
   a. The Creator God made the universe and he is Lord of heaven and earth. (v. 24a)
   b. The Creator God does not live in manmade temples. (v. 24b)
   c. The Creator God does not need sacrifices. (v. 25a)
   d. The Creator God gives and sustains life. (v. 25b)
2. Description of the Creator God who created the human race.(vv. 26-27b)
   a. The human race is one due to its origins. (v. 26a)
   b. The human race was created to inhabit the whole earth in all its diversity. (v. 26b)
   c. The human race was created to be in fellowship with God. (v. 27a)
3. Description of the Creator God who is present in his creation. (vv. 27b-29)
   a. The outcome of humankind's search for God is uncertain. (v. 27b)
   b. The Creator God is not far from anyone. (v. 27c)
   c. The Creator God is the source of life who created the human race. (v. 28)
   d. God is not an image made by humans but humans have been created in God's image. (v. 29)

The Creator God commands everyone everywhere to repent (Acts 17:30-31): Peroratio.

1. Recapitulation: God overlooks the times of ignorance. (v. 30a)
2. Appeal: God commands all people to repent of their false religious notions. (v. 30b)
3. Grounds: God has fixed the day of judgment for the whole world. (v. 31)

a. God has appointed the judge who will determine the outcome at Judgment Day. (v. 31a)

b. This judge is qualified to judge the world due to his resurrection from the dead. (v. 31b)

Paul's speech before the Council of the Areopagus includes points with which the philosophically informed audience can agree, but also points that would have provoked them.

The "elements of contact" as we may call them include (1) the description of God (vv. 22-23, 24-28), (2) the critique of manmade temples (v. 24), (3) the critique of sacrifices (v. 25), (4) humanity's search for God (vv. 27-28), (5) the critique of idol images (v. 29).

The "elements of contradiction" include (1) significant elements of Paul's critique of Greco-Roman religiosity, in particular his foundational argument that there is a Creator God who made the universe and who is the Lord of heaven and earth (vv. 24-26), (2) the call to turn away from the idols to the one Creator God (v. 30), (3) the reference to God's universal judgment through a man (v. 31), (4) the reference to the one who was raised from the dead (v. 31).

Points of agreement. We note that the points of agreement are in the foreground. Paul "picks up" his listeners where they are in terms of convictions and language. Paul selects from the Old Testament and from Jewish traditions such motifs that could be immediately understood by Athenian philosophers, including terminological allusions and quotations.[26]

Five convictions that Stoic philosophers held are used by Paul to describe the Creator God whom he proclaims in Athens.

First, Stoics believed that the gods were immortal. The question of the nature of the gods was an important topic in Stoic philosophy, as writings by leading Stoic philosophers such as Cleanthes, Chrysippus and Posidonius demonstrate. Balbus asserted that the Stoics follow a fixed order in

---

[26]See Abraham J. Malherbe, *Paul and the Popular Philosophers* (Minneapolis: Fortress, 1989), pp. 147-63; David L. Balch, "The Areopagus Speech: An Appeal to the Stoic Historian Posidonius against Later Stoics and the Epicureans," in *Greeks, Romans, and Christians: Essays in Honor of Abraham J. Malherbe*, ed. D. L. Balch et al. (Minneapolis: Fortress, 1990), pp. 52-79; Winter, "Religious Pluralism"; Dean Flemming, "Contextualizing the Gospel in Athens: Paul's Areopagus Address as a Paradigm for Missionary Communication," *Missiology* 30 (2002): 199-214.

their discussion:[27] they begin by proving that the gods exist; they discuss the nature of the gods; then they show how the gods order the world; finally they explain how the gods care for the well-being of humankind. Paul argues similarly: as the Creator, God is the Lord of heaven and of the earth (Acts 17:24), he gives to human beings life and everything they need to live (v. 25), and he cares for people as he determines the "times of their existence and the boundaries of the places where they would live" (v. 26).

Second, the Stoics referred to the gods as a diverse plurality, but they were also able to speak of "god" in the singular. Cleanthes, the successor of Zenon who founded the Stoic school of philosophy, begins his hymn to Zeus with these lines:

> Noblest of immortals, many-named, always all-powerful Zeus, first cause and ruler of nature, governing everything with your law, greetings! For it is right for all mortals to address you: for we have our origin in you, bearing a likeness to God, we, alone of all that live and move as mortal creatures on earth. Therefore I shall praise you constantly; indeed I always sing of your rule.[28]

As Cleanthes depicts Zeus as the culmination of deity, the Stoic philosophers in Paul's audience would not have been bothered by Paul's use of the singular "god" and by his conviction that god rules the universe. On the other hand, Paul would have been concerned with the Stoic's easy transition from "god" to the "gods."

Third, the Stoic understanding of god was essentially pantheistic. The Stoics argued that the substance of god is "the entire world and the heavens."[29] Seneca formulates that "god is near you, with you, in you."[30] Paul stated in his speech that "in him *(en autō)* we live and move and have our being" (v. 28). If Paul's Stoic listeners understood the Greek phrase *en autō* in a spatial sense and related it to god ("in him"), they could interpret this triadic formulation in terms of the life, the movement and the existence of humankind "in god" in a pantheistic sense, in terms of the

---

[27]See the reference to Balbus in Cicero *De natura deorum* 2.3.
[28]Cleanthes, quoted in Johan Carl Thom, *Cleanthes' Hymn to Zeus: Text, Translation, and Commentary*, Studien und Texte zu Antike und Christentum 33 (Tübingen: Mohr Siebeck, 2005), p. 40.
[29]Diogenes Laertius 7.14 (Zeno).
[30]Seneca *Epistulae morales* 41.1.

immanence of all human beings in the all-pervasive deity. Paul's quotation from the Cilician poet Aratus ("for we too are his offspring" [v. 28]) could also be interpreted in *this* sense as a pantheistic statement.

Fourth, the Stoics believed in the providence of the divine. They argued that the gods rule the world by their providence. Proofs for this conviction are the divine wisdom and power, the nature of the world, the miracles of nature and the care of the gods for human beings. Paul could agree with these convictions, as his statements in verses 24-26 demonstrate.

Fifth, the subject of divine judgment was not alien to the Stoics either. At the end of his speech Paul refers to the divine judgment that would come upon all people who remain in their ignorance despite the availability of better information (v. 31).

The views of the Epicurean philosopher that Paul takes up are the following. First, Epicureans believed in the animated nature, in the immortality of the soul and in the bliss of the divine. These are concepts that Paul also can refer to.[31]

Second, Epicurus believed that the knowledge of god is apparent, a function of human reason. The Epicurean philosophers in Paul's audience would thus have understood his argument that the "unknown god" can be known (v. 23).

Third, Epicurean philosophers argued that the gods do not live in temples that humans had built. Plutarch writes that "one should not build temples of the gods."[32] They rejected what they called "the superstitions" of their contemporaries. They discussed the psychological effects of false faith in deities and they mocked the demeaning cultic practices that they observed in the temples. Paul agrees with these convictions when he writes that "the God who made the world and everything in it, he who is Lord of heaven and earth, does not live in shrines made by human hands" (v. 24).

Fourth, the Epicureans rejected the offering of sacrifices to the gods, arguing that a god does not need human things.[33] Paul agrees when he tells his listeners that God is not "served by human hands, as though he needed anything, since he himself gives to all mortals life and breath and all things" (v. 25).

---

[31]Cf. Rom 1:23; 1 Thess 1:9; 1 Tim 1:11.
[32]Plutarch *Moralia* 1034b.
[33]See Philodemus *Pros eusebeias* frag. 38; Plutarch *Moralia* 1052a; cf. Plato *Timaeus* 33d, 34b.

We thus see that Paul, in his presentation to the Areopagus, initiated by the Epicurean and Stoic philosophers of Athens, employs convictions, arguments and formulations that these intellectual Athenians were familiar with and that they would have acknowledged as valid. Exegetes and missiologists often use the term *contextualization* for this dimension of Paul's Areopagus speech.[34]

Points of contradiction. A closer look shows that Paul was not only looking for points of contact. There were also "points of contradiction."[35] Paul does not regard the Athenians' systems of faith and worship as somehow similar to the Christians' convictions concerning God, the world, humankind, history and salvation. He does not argue for an essential continuity between the revelation of the God whom he proclaims and the convictions of pagan poets and philosophers or the views of popular religion. Rather, Paul disputes the Athenians' understanding of the divine and thus their worldview[36] in at least seven respects.

First, the reference to the "unknown god" (Acts 17:23), understood in the context of Isaiah 45:15, 18-25, implies a censure of religious pagan convictions. The prophet Isaiah, after repeating Israel's monotheistic confession, "Truly, you are a God who hides himself, O God of Israel, the Savior" (Is 45:15), narrates a speech of Yahweh in which he seeks to convert the people to worshiping the one true God. If Israel's God appears to be hidden and thus an unknown God, Yahweh's words prove that he is indeed not in hiding at all:

> For thus says the LORD,
> who created the heavens

---

[34]See Joseph Osei-Bonsu, "The Contextualization of Christianity: Some New Testament Antecedents," *Irish Biblical Studies* 12 (1990): 133-37; Marcel Dumais, "La rencontre de la foi et des cultures," *Lumière et Vie* 30 (1981): 82-84; David J. Hesselgrave and Edward Rommen, *Contextualization: Meaning, Methods and Models* (1989; reprint, Grand Rapids: Zondervan, 1992), pp. 9-10; Flemming, *Contextualization*, pp. 75-84.

[35]See Bertil Gärtner, *The Areopagus Speech and Natural Revelation* (Lund: Gleerup, 1955); David W. Pao, *Acts and the Isaianic New Exodus*, WUNT 2/130 (Tübingen: Mohr-Siebeck, 2000), pp. 193-208; Richard J. Gibson, "Paul and the Evangelization of the Stoics," in *The Gospel to the Nations: Perspectives on Paul's Mission*, ed. P. Bolt and M. Thompson (Leicester, U.K.: InterVarsity Press, 2000), pp. 309-16, 318-23; see Schnabel, *Early Christian Mission*, 2:1398-1401.

[36]See D. A. Carson, "Athens Revisited," in *Telling the Truth: Evangelizing Postmoderns*, ed. D. A. Carson (Grand Rapids: Zondervan, 2000), pp. 384-98.

(he is God!),

who formed the earth and made it
(he established it;

he did not create it a chaos,
he formed it to be inhabited!):

I am the LORD, and there is no other.
I did not speak in secret,
in a land of darkness;

I did not say to the offspring of Jacob,
"Seek me in chaos."

I the LORD speak the truth,
I declare what is right. (Is 45:18-19)

Yahweh goes on to state that the nations "have no knowledge" and that "those who carry about their wooden idols" are praying to "a god that cannot save" since "there is no other god besides me, a righteous God and a Savior; there is no one besides me" (Is 45:20-21). This truth leads to an invitation:

Turn to me and be saved,
all the ends of the earth!

For I am God, and there is no other.

By myself I have sworn,
from my mouth has gone forth in righteousness

a word that shall not return:

"To me every knee shall bow,
every tongue shall swear." (Is 45:22-23)

When we read Paul's reference to the Athenians' religiosity (Acts 17:22) in the light of this dialogue between Yahweh and the nations, this is a complimentary introduction on the surface only. The reference to the altar of an "unknown god" (v. 23) is a critique of the Athenians' ignorance.

Second, Paul's reference to "the times of their existence and the boundaries of the places where they would live" (Acts 17:26), that is, to the periods of human history and to national boundaries, assumes a deeper meaning when considered against the background of Deuteronomy 32:8: "When the Most High apportioned the nations, when he divided humankind, he fixed the boundaries of the peoples according to the number of the gods."[37]

This text asserts that the diversity of nations and a diversity of deities go together, which means that Paul implies that "by the same token if God is working to unite all peoples in Christ, crossing national boundaries, then God is also working against polytheism. There would be no more concessions to human fallenness or 'times of ignorance.' "[38]

Third, Paul acknowledges that Gentiles seek God (v. 27). However, the next clause shows that he is skeptical concerning the actual outcome of this search: uncertainty is indicated (1) in the introductory phrase "in the hope that" *(ei ara ge)*, (2) by the optative mood of the Greek verbs, which indicates contingency, implying uncertainty, and (3) by the choice of the Greek verb *psēlaphaō*, which means "to touch by feeling and handling" or, as here, to look for something in uncertain fashion, *"to feel around for, grope for."*[39] The Jewish author of the following text voiced similar doubts: "For from the greatness and beauty of created things comes a corresponding perception of their Creator. Yet these people are little to be blamed, for perhaps they go astray while seeking God and desiring to find him" (Wis 13:5-6).

Fourth, when Paul states that God "is not far from each one of us" (v. 27), listeners who were aware of these Jewish convictions based on Scripture[40] would indeed wonder whether this is a reference to Stoic notions of the presence of the divine in everything that exists,[41] or, rather, a critical comment on humankind's unsuccessful attempts to find God who is "near" but not quite present. If the prepositional expression *en autō* in verse 28 is understood not in a spatial sense ("in him") but in an instrumental sense ("by him"), the triadic formulation is not an argument for humankind's kinship with God. Rather, it is a theological statement about God's past and present sovereignty in creation: human beings owe their

---

[37]The Masoretic Text and the Samaritan Pentateuch reads "the sons of Israel"; the translation of the NRSV is based on the earliest Hebrew text of the passage in 4QDeut[j] LXX. Cf. Martin Abegg, et al., *The Dead Sea Scrolls Bible* (San Francisco: HarperCollins, 1999), p. 191.

[38]Witherington, *Acts of the Apostles*, p. 527.

[39]BDAG, p. 1098, with reference to Philo *De mutatione nominum* 126.

[40]Note Ps 145:18: "The LORD is near to all who call on him, to all who call on him in truth," with the emphasis on the second part of the sentence.

[41]Seneca formulates that "God is near you, with you, in you" *(prope est a te deus, tecum est, intus est)*; *Epistulae morales* 41.1.

existence and the circumstances of their life to God—"by him we live and move and have our being."

Fifth, while the quotation from Aratos (*Phaenomena* 5)[42] in verse 28 ("for we too are his offspring") can be understood as an accommodation to the philosophical convictions of Paul's audience in the Council of the Areopagus, the context of Paul's scriptural view of creation is again significant. In *this* context the statement about people being God's offspring refers to Israel's conviction that the one true God created "the one ancestor" (i.e., Adam) from whom he made all human beings (v. 26). The knowledge of the Greek poets is partial; it becomes more fully relevant only in the context of the truth of God's revelation of his activity as Creator of "the world and everything it" (v. 24). The reference to the one ancestor in verse 26 ("from one ancestor he made all nations to inhabit the whole earth") is a reference to the biblical tradition of the beginning of all human existence in the creation of Adam, the first man whom God brought into being (Gen 1:26-27; 2:7). There is no clear parallel in Greek thought and mythology to this conviction that the human race can be traced back to one man who was created by God. Paul's use of the language of the Bible in his reference to the creation narrative of the book of Genesis conveys a biblical critique of popular polytheism and idolatry.[43]

Sixth, Paul criticizes the religious notion that God lives in man-made houses of worship. His critique of temples in verse 24 (the Creator God "does not live in shrines made by human hands") certainly reminded his listeners on the Areopagus of Epicurean arguments. At the same time this critique of pagan religious belief and practice reflects the assertion of the prophet Isaiah that the one true God insists that

> thus says the LORD:
> "Heaven is my throne
>   and the earth is my footstool;
>
> what is the house that you would build for me,
>   and what is my resting place?
>
> All these things my hand has made,

---

[42]Aratos (315-240 B.C.) of Soloi, a port city in Cilicia, was one of the most important Hellenistic poets. His *Phaenomena* was the most widely read poem after Homer's *Iliad* and *Odyssey*.

[43]C. K. Barrett, *The Acts of the Apostles*, ICC (Edinburgh: T & T Clark, 1994-1998), 2:842.

and so all these things are mine." (Is 66:1-2)

Seventh, Paul also indicts the pagan practice of sacrifices and the underlying belief that God must be "served by human hands" (v. 25). The Epicureans rejected the offering of sacrifices for the gods, arguing that a god does not need human things. Paul's critique is again biblically informed when he asserts that God "is not served by human hands, as though he needed anything, since he himself gives to all mortals life and breath and all things." The prophet Isaiah proclaims,

> Thus says God, the LORD,
>> who created the heavens and stretched them out,
>>
>> who spread out the earth and what comes from it,
>
> who gives breath to the people upon it
>> and spirit to those who walk in it. (Is 42:5)

In Israel's worship, people were regularly reminded of God's sovereign independence of human beings:

> If I were hungry, I would not tell you,
>> for the world and all that is in it is mine.
>
> Do I eat the flesh of bulls,
>> or drink the blood of goats? (Ps 50:12-13)

Eighth, after condemning temples and sacrifices, Paul also disparages the images that pagans worship: "since we are God's offspring, we ought not to think that the deity is like gold, or silver, or stone, an image formed by the art and imagination of mortals" (v. 29). This critique of idol worship is a clear indictment of popular piety with which the Stoic and the Epicurean philosophers had come to an arrangement. Both philosophical schools had accommodated their theoretical convictions to the religiosity of the population: people continued to participate in the cultic activities of the cities. Epicurus was convinced that popular piety was misguided, but he did not try to keep his followers from participation in one of the local cults. An Epicurean text, written around A.D. 50, asserts on the one hand that piety cannot be proved by the offering of sacrifices. Yet it continues with the statement that offering to the gods is permitted since it is in agreement with religious traditions (P. Oxy 215). Plutarch accuses the Stoics of contradicting themselves as they visit the mysteries in the temples and ascend the acropolis to honor the idol statues and lay down wreaths in the sanctuaries despite their convictions.[44]

The city of Athens had a temple, an altar and a cult for every taste. Zeus was worshiped on the acropolis, in the stoa on the west side of the agora, on the altar in front of the stoa and in other temples. Athena, the goddess of wisdom and the patron deity of the city, had three temples on the acropolis, a small temple in the agora, and she was worshiped in the council chamber and in the great temple of Hephaistos. Demeter, the goddess of vegetation and fertility, was worshiped in the Eleusinion located on the road from the agora to the acropolis. Apollo, the god of light and music, was worshiped in a temple located next to the stoa of Zeus; a monumental statue of the god was discovered in the area of the agora. Artemis, the sister of Apollo and the goddess of hunting and good counsel, was worshiped on the acropolis as Artemis Brauronia and in the agora as Artemis Boulaia. Aphrodite, the goddess of love, was worshiped in at least two temples located above the agora on the way up to the acropolis; over three hundred statues of Aphrodite have been discovered in excavations in the city. Other temples were dedicated to Ares, Asclepius, Dionysus, Hekate, Hephaistos, Hera, Heracles, Hermes, Hestia, Pan, Poseidon, the Twelve (Olympian?) gods, the Phrygian Mother-Goddess, the Egyptian gods Isis, Sarapis, Harpocrates and Anubis, abstractions including the Demos (the People of Athens) and Nike (Victory) as well as heroes such as Theseus, Hippothoon, Antiochos, Ajax, Leos, Erechtheus, Aigeus, Oineus, Akamas, Kekrops, Pandion, Harmodios, Aristogeiton, Eurysakes, Epitegios, Strategos, Iatros and Kallistephanos. Shortly after 27 B.C. the Athenians erected a small, round Ionic temple east of the Parthenon on the acropolis in which Roma and Caesar were venerated. A series of thirteen small altars, most of which were discovered in the vicinity of the agora, confirms the practice of the emperor cult in the lower city as well.[45]

Paul uses the quotation from Aratus as an argument against the philosophers'

---

[44]Plutarch *Moralia* 1034B-C. On the gods worshiped in Athens cf. John McK. Camp, *Gods and Heroes in the Athenian Agora* (Princeton, N.J.: American School of Classical Studies at Athens, 1980).

[45]See T. Leslie Shear, "Athens: From City-State to Provincial Town," *Hesperia* 50 (1981): 356-77, 363-65.

rapprochement with the plurality and diversity of religious cults. If human beings have been created by the Creator God, it is preposterous that human beings would create images of a god and worship statues made of gold, silver or marble. The critique of idols is not merely a philosophical argument, however. Paul takes up Old Testament affirmations and Jewish traditions that engaged in frequent polemics against idol worship and did not shrink from making sarcastic verdicts.[46] For Paul, a critique of the existing religious pluralism and diversity was an essential element of his explanation of the gospel message.[47]

On the basis of this critique of contemporary religiosity that tolerated and promoted a pluralism of gods and cults, of temples and mysteries, Paul calls the members of the Council of the Areopagus to repent and to turn to the Creator God. He asserts that "God has overlooked the times of human ignorance" (Acts 17:30). The phrase *times of ignorance* expresses the conviction that the religious beliefs and practices of the Athenians makes them guilty before God. One cannot ignore truth for too long without being responsible for one's behavior.

Because Paul's rejection of the religious beliefs and practices of the Athenians implied very practical consequences, he walked on very thin ice. Nobody would welcome abandoning the temples for which Athens was famous, or discontinuing the sacrifices that ensured the goodwill of the gods who were thought to be responsible for the prosperity of the city, or missing the opportunity to officiate in the cults of the city and thus consolidating one's superior social status. It was positively dangerous to argue, if only implicitly, that the cultic veneration of the deceased emperors—an essential and an increasingly important element of Roman culture in the larger cities—should be stopped. Shortly after 27 B.C. the Athenians erected a small temple east of the Parthenon on the acropolis in which Roma and Julius Caesar were venerated.[48] Claudius was worshiped as Apollo Patroos; Tiberius was honored

---

[46]Cf. Is 40:18-19; 44:9-20; 45:15-24; 46:5-7; see also Wis 13.

[47]Winter, "Religious Pluralism," p. 129.

[48]On the emperor cult in Athens cf. Michael C. Hoff, "The Politics and Architecture of the Athenian Imperial Cult," in *Subject and Ruler: The Cult of the Ruling Power in Classical Antiquity*, ed. A. Small, Journal of Roman Archaeology Sup 17 (Ann Arbor, Mich.: Journal of Roman Archaeology, 1996), pp. 185-200; Antony J. S. Spawforth, "The Early Reception of the Imperial Cult in Athens: Problems and Ambiguities," in *The Romanization of Athens*, ed. Michael M. C. Hoff and S. I. Rotroff, Oxbow Monograph 94 (Oxford: Oxbow Books, 1997), pp. 183-202.

with an inscription that dedicated to him the large bronze quadriga of the second century B.C. which stood in front of the stoa of Attalos. Paul's unqualified rejection of the Athenians' religious pluralism was ill-advised from the point of view of the principle of accommodation, detrimental for his missionary project in Athens, and potentially dangerous to himself and to future followers of Jesus Christ in the city.

Paul's critique of the idols is accompanied by a call to repentance: "While God has overlooked the times of human ignorance, now he commands all people everywhere to repent" (Acts 17:30). Paul's ultimate concern is not to advance a logical philosophical argument that would compel people to abandon religious pluralism. His concern was to make people see the need to change religious convictions and religious behavior. Paul grounds the need to repent and change religious beliefs and practices in the fact that there will be a day of judgment (v. 31). He emphasizes, in agreement with passages such as Psalm 9:9, 96:13 and 98:9, that God will judge the world (Gk *oikoumenē*). And he emphasizes, in agreement with early Christian teaching, that God has already appointed a judge who will carry out the divine judgment. According to Luke's account, Paul avoided mentioning the name of Jesus, perhaps because he wanted to avoid the impression that he proclaimed "foreign divinities" (v. 18).[49] When Paul points out that this judge was a man who had lived, died and was raised from the dead by God (v. 31), the reaction of the audience was divided. Some listeners wanted to hear more, while others scoffed. The notion of life after death was foreign for both the Epicureans and the Stoics, who taught the "art of dying" meant to teach people to accept their mortality. According to Aeschylus, Apollo taught the Athenians at the founding of the Areopagus that "when the dust has soaked up a person's blood, once he is dead, there is no resurrection."[50] The most widely held opinion concerning the afterlife was that "death is nothingness, eternal sleep."[51] People were not only skeptical about an afterlife, they often joked about annihilation at death: many wrote the letters *n.f.n.s.n.c* on their gravestones, an abbreviation for

---

[49]See Rudolf Pesch, *Die Apostelgeschichte*, EKK 5 (Zürich: Benziger; Neukirchen-Vluyn: Neukirchener, 1986), 2:140.

[50]Aeschylus *Eumenides* 647-48.

[51]Paul Veyne, "The Roman Empire," in *A History of Private Life*, vol.1: *From Pagan Rome to Byzantium*, ed. P. Veyne (1987; reprint, Cambridge: Harvard University Press, 2003), p. 219.

the phrase *non fui, non sum, non curo* ("I was not, I am not, I care not").

Paul's response to the religious beliefs and practices of the Athenians was, ultimately, not accommodation but confrontation.[52] While he uses terminology that could be easily understood by the intellectual Athenians, and while many of his statements and assertions are acceptable at least for some members of the council, Paul leaves no doubt that he unambiguously rejects the plurality of gods and cults and the proliferation of temples, altars and statutes in the city of Athens. Paul is convinced, and he states as much, that the religious activities of the Athenians are evidence of ignorance—none of the deities and none of the cults of the city are able to guarantee salvation on the day of universal judgment. And Paul is unafraid to point to the resurrection of the dead despite that fact that he presumably knows that the doctrine of the resurrection is a laughable concept for the Greeks, who think dualistically.

Paul could not say everything in this speech before the Council of the Areopagus, because he focused consistently on the subject that he had been invited to address. This is the reason why he describes Jesus as divine Judge rather as Savior. Paul addresses the basic assumptions of the Athenians concerning the existence and the needs of divine beings not because he wanted to create a necessary context and foundation for proclaiming the risen Christ.[53] He focuses on the one true and living God because he is being questioned concerning his apparent attempt to introduce new gods into the city of Athens.

Seen in more general context of Paul's missionary work, this speech demonstrates that

> the life and the ministry of Jesus can be understood only in the context of the presuppositions of the biblical witness concerning *God*. This is the reason why the pioneer preaching before pagans who have not been exposed to biblical influences is essentially preaching about *God*. The fact that Jesus constitutes the path to God does not mean that it is christology that opens the way

---

[52]Differently, Flemming, *Contextualization in the New Testament*, p. 83, suggests that "Paul refuses to flatly condemn the pagans or their religious and philosophical systems." The intellectual members of the Council of the Areopagus would certainly recognize Paul's "irony" (ibid., p. 75) as a provocative rejection of their religious traditions and of many of their deeply held philosophical convictions.

[53]Thus Flemming, *Contextualization in the New Testament*, p. 77.

to theology. God as Creator and Lord, humankind created in the image of God (God as Father), the prohibition of images: the unprepared pagans first need to hear the Old Testament foundations of the New Testament.[54]

In the course of providing his listeners basic instruction in the theology of Israel, Paul uses the intellectual, philosophical and linguistic traditions of his audience in a twofold manner: as bridgehead for the proclamation of Jesus the Savior of the world, since he knows their religious customs and their educational values, and as an indication that he takes them seriously as discussion partners who are willing to listen to his teaching.

3.4 IDEOLOGICAL CONFRONTATION: THE PROCLAMATION OF JESUS MESSIAH AND KYRIOS

The central emphasis of Paul's missionary preaching was the proclamation of Jesus as the Messiah of the Jewish people and the Kyrios of the world.

> Jews demand signs and Greeks desire wisdom, but we proclaim Christ [the Messiah] crucified, a stumbling block to Jews and foolishness to Gentiles, but to those who are the called, both Jews and Greeks, Christ the power of God and the wisdom of God. (1 Cor 1:22-24)

> We do not proclaim ourselves; we proclaim Jesus Christ as Lord and ourselves as your slaves for Jesus' sake. For it is the God who said, "Let light shine out of darkness," who has shone in our hearts to give the light of the knowledge of the glory of God in the face of Jesus Christ. (2 Cor 4:5-6)

Paul proclaimed Jesus of Nazareth to be the messianic Savior whom the Jews had been expecting, and he proclaimed him as the one true Savior who is Lord (Gk *kyrios*) both before Jewish audiences and polytheists. This focus of his missionary preaching does not represent an accommodation to concepts that Paul's audiences would not have found appealing. Rather many, in particular members of the local elites and officials of the cities in which he preached, would have found this emphasis to be provocatively confrontational. The link between "kingdom of God" and "Lord Jesus the Messiah" in Paul's missionary reaching implies a political dimension.

---

[54]Klaus Haacker, "Urchristliche Mission und kulturelle Identität. Beobachtungen zu Strategie und Homiletik des Apostels Paulus," *Theologische Beiträge* 19 (1988): 71.

Luke summarizes Paul's missionary preaching in the last verse of the book of Acts by pointing out that the apostle proclaimed "the kingdom of God" and that he taught "about the Lord Jesus Christ with all boldness and without hindrance" (Acts 28:31). Luke does not mention the term *kingdom* (Gk *basileia*) and the phrase "kingdom of God" (Gk *basileia tou theou*) in the book of Acts very frequently.[55] It is a term, however, that Luke repeatedly uses to summarize Paul's missionary preaching before Jewish audiences. For example, he describes Paul's arrival in the city of Ephesus and the beginnings of his missionary activity as follows: "He entered the synagogue and for three months spoke out boldly, and argued persuasively about the kingdom of God" (Acts 19:8). The direct association of "Lord" *(Kyrios)* and Messiah *(Christos)* is also rare in the book of Acts. It occurs for the first time in Peter's sermon at Pentecost.[56]

Jesus the Messiah. In Paul's letters the use of the term *Christos* as a designation for Jesus is very common.[57] The Greek term, a verbal adjective, means "capable of (liquid) being spread upon" or "besmeared, anointed"; the nominalized form *to christon* means "unguent, salve." Apart from the Greek translation of the Old Testament and the New Testament (and subsequent Christian literature), the term *Christos* is never used for persons. In the New Testament, *Christos* is used as a translation of the Hebrew term *māšîaḥ* (Gk *messias*)[58] and thus can be translated (or rather transliterated) into English as "Messiah." In the formulations "Jesus Christ" or "Christ Jesus" (thus the standard English translations) the term *Christ* or *Christos* "is not simply a proper name, but rather an epithet *(cognomen);* the predicative character does recede, but the titular meaning is preserved in its entirety, even when other statements of a titular character are added. Hence nowhere is a simple double name presupposed."[59] In other words "Jesus Christ" does not correspond to first name and the family name of "John Smith" but refers to "Jesus the Messiah." The fundamental significance of this title can be seen in the fact that the term *Christos* occurs

---

[55]Acts 1:3 (Jesus); 1:6 (the Twelve); 8:12 (Philip); 14:22 (Paul and Barnabas); 19:8; 20:25; 28:23, 31 (Paul).
[56]Acts 2:36; cf. 10:36; 11:17; 15:26; 28:31.
[57]The term *Christos* occurs 383 times in Paul's letters; cf. F. Hahn, *EDNT*, 3:479.
[58]Cf. Jn 1:41; 4:25.
[59]Hahn, *EDNT*, 3:479.

in statements about the death and the resurrection of Jesus;[60] in statements about Jesus' preexistence, his earthly existence, and his exaltation;[61] as well as in statements about the church as body and about Jesus Christ being "in you" or "in us."[62]

Paul speaks of Jesus as *Christos* in statements about his missionary activity of proclamation[63] despite the fact that pagans in the first century found it difficult to understand the designation *Christos*. This becomes evident, for example, in the misunderstanding involving the name *Chrestus*, whom Suetonius mentions in connection with measures that the emperor Claudius initiated against "men of foreign birth." He records that "since the Jews constantly made disturbances at the instigation of Chrestus, he expelled them from Rome."[64] Most scholars interpret the name *Chrestus* as a misunderstanding on the part of Suetonius and understand the text as referring to Jesus Christ. The disturbances were provoked by the missionary outreach of Jewish believers who preached Jesus as Messiah in the synagogues of Rome.[65] Neither the use of oil in pagan cults nor the anointing with ambrosia in Greek and Roman myths would have helped pagan listeners to understand the meaning of Jesus of Galilee being called *Christos*. The use of the term certainly did not facilitate Paul's missionary proclamation.[66]

The confession of Jesus as the messianic bringer of salvation was the crucial characteristic of the new movement of the followers of Jesus. This was the main reason why the followers of Jesus in Antioch were called *christianoi* ("Christians"): they were identified, probably by Ro-

---

[60]Cf. Rom 5:6, 8; 6:3-4, 9; 8:11, 34; 10:7; 14:9, 15; 15:3; 1 Cor 1:23; 2:2; 8:11; 15:3-5, 12-17, 20, 23; Gal 2:19, 21; 3:1, 13; Eph 5:2.

[61]Preexistence: 1 Cor 10:4; 11:3; earthly existence: Rom 9:5; 2 Cor 5:16; exaltation: Rom 8:34; 10:6; Col 3:1.

[62]Cf. Rom 8:10; 1 Cor 1:13; 3:23; 12:12; 2 Cor 10:7; 13:5; Gal 2:20; 3:29; 4:19; 5:24; Col 1:27; 3:3; Eph 2:5; 3:17; 4:12, 15.

[63]Cf. Rom 15:18, 20; 1 Cor 1:17, 23; 2:2; 15:12; 2 Cor 1:19; 4:5; Gal 4:14; Eph 3:4; Phil 1:15, 17, 18; Col 4:3.

[64]Suetonius *Divus Claudius* 25:4; the Latin text reads: "Judaeos impulsore Chresto assidue tumultuantes Roma expulit."

[65]See Henri Janne, "Impulsore Chresto," in *Mélanges Bidez*, Annuaire de l'Institut de philologie et d'histoire orientales 2 (Bruxelles: Secrétariat de l'Institut, 1934), pp. 531-53; cf. Irina Levinskaya, *The Book of Acts in its Diaspora Setting*, The Book of Acts in Its First-Century Setting 5 (Carlisle, U.K.: Paternoster, 1996), pp. 179-81; Schnabel, *Early Christian Mission*, 1:808-9.

[66]See Hengel and Schwemer, *Paul Between Damascus and Antioch*, pp. 456-57 n. 1189.

man authorities in the capital of the province of Syria, as the people who believe that Jesus was the Messiah (*messias*, translated into Greek as *christos*).[67] The early Christians were convinced that Jesus was the bringer of God's salvation, the Redeemer whom God had promised and for whom the Jews had been waiting. They were convinced that Jesus' life and teaching, and in particular his death and resurrection inaugurated the kingdom of God and accomplished the salvation God had promised for the last days when he would return as King. They were convinced that Jesus, after his resurrection and exaltation, sits at God's right hand and is thus Lord *(Kyrios)*. The fundamental significance of Jesus as the Messiah and Kyrios explains why these convictions were part and parcel of Paul's missionary preaching, irrespective of whether he addressed Jewish or pagan audiences.

The proclamation of Jesus as Messiah was potentially dangerous. Since the Jewish expectations concerning the promised Messiah frequently described this redeemer figure as Son of David, the term *Messiah* often had political connotations: the coming Messiah would be a king and a ruler.

Jesus the Lord. Paul did not simply preach that Jesus claimed to be the promised Messiah. This would have been harmless since a skeptical audience could conclude that Jesus' crucifixion proved that this claim was mistaken. Paul preached that Jesus has risen from the dead and that he is *now* the promised Messiah, occupying as Lord a position of authority, demanding the obedience of all human beings, whether Jews or Greeks or Romans. These convictions were risky, although a skeptical audience could still insist that dead people do not rise and therefore cannot make any demands. However, since Paul's missionary preaching included the emphasis that Jesus will return as Lord to judge the world, it often clashed with the claims concerning the imperial family in Rome, which were promoted in the provinces of the empire.

The claims that the emperor cult made on the provincials already during the Julian-Claudian reigns is often underestimated.[68] The Jews were

---

[67]For details see Schnabel, *Early Christian Mission*, 1:793-94. Hengel and Schwemer, *Paul Between Damascus and Antioch*, p. 226, suggest that "perhaps the new church had to register in the provincial capital with the magistrates of the city or of the Province of Syria as a Jewish 'special synagogue' or 'religious association,' i.e., as *collegium*."

[68]See Bruce W. Winter, "Dangers and Difficulties for the Pauline Missions," in *The Gospel to the*

excepted from participation in the emperor cult, which was basically expected of everybody (Cassius Dio 51.20.6-7), because they offered a sacrifice for the emperor in the temple in Jerusalem. What was at stake in the imperial cult not only for the emperor and for the provincial governors, but also for the members of the local elites in the cities

> was the whole web of social, political and hierarchical assumptions that bound imperial society together. Sacrifices and other religious rituals were concerned with defining and establishing relationships of power. Not to place oneself within the set of relationships between emperor, gods, élite and people was effectively to place oneself outside the mainstream of the whole world and the shared Roman understanding of humanity's place within that world.[69]

The imperial cult has been documented for nearly two hundred cities in Asia Minor, attested by altars, temples or imperial priests mentioned in inscriptions.[70] In the New Testament, twenty-three of these cities in which the imperial cult plays an important role are mentioned: Adramyttium, Pisidian Antioch, Assos, Chios, Colossae, Cos, Derbe, Ephesus, Hierapolis, Iconium, Laodicea, Miletus, Mitylene, Patara, Pergamum, Perga, Philadelphia, Rhodes, Samos, Sardis, Smyrna, Tarsus, and Thyatira.

In these urban centers, the high point of the emperor cult was an annual festival, usually celebrated on the emperor's birthday. The citizens donned white festive garments and, adorned with garlands, marched in a procession to the imperial temple, passing by houses that had been decorated in honor of the emperor. Festive banquets were given, athletic and musical contests were held, and the citizens burned incense before the statues of the emperor. It was not easy to "excuse" oneself from these civic obligations—which is exactly what Paul expects when he directs the Corinthian Christians not to attend banquets in pagan temples (1 Cor 8:4-6; 10:21).

Jesus the Crucified Savior. As Paul consistently designates Jesus as

---

Nations: Perspectives on Paul's Mission, ed. P. Bolt and M. Thompson (Leicester, U.K.: InterVarsity Press, 2000), pp. 285-95.

[69]Mary Beard et al., *Religions of Rome* (Cambridge: Cambridge University Press, 1998), 1:361.

[70]See Simon R. F. Price, *Rituals and Power: The Roman Imperial Cult in Asia Minor* (Oxford: Oxford University Press, 1984); for Ephesus see Steven Friesen, *Twice Neokoros: Ephesus, Asia and the Cult of the Flavian Imperial Family* (Leiden: Brill, 1993).

Christos and *Kyrios*, he did so in certainly conscious ideological confrontation with the claim that, for example, Augustus was a "savior" and a "son of god" and "lord." When Paul explained that Jesus was *Christos*, the promised Messiah of the Jews, he had to explain this title in terms of its Old Testament and Jewish background. In the course of such an explanation, the three main outlines of messianic conceptions in Second Temple Jewish theology could be highlighted, that is, the royal, priestly and prophetic dimensions of this term. In his missionary preaching, Paul seems to have emphasized the priestly dimension: Jesus, the messianic Savior and Lord, died on the cross as sacrifice for sins. Several texts that probably take up traditional early Christian confessions of faith, emphasize this conviction.

> For God has destined us not for wrath but for obtaining salvation through our Lord Jesus Christ, who died for us, so that whether we are awake or asleep we may live with him. (1 Thess 5:9-10)

> Who gave himself for our sins to set us free from the present evil age, according to the will of our God and Father. (Gal 1:4)

> And it is no longer I who live, but it is Christ who lives in me. And the life I now live in the flesh I live by faith in the Son of God, who loved me and gave himself for me. (Gal 2:20)

> For I handed on to you as of first importance what I in turn had received: that Christ died for our sins in accordance with the scriptures. (1 Cor 15:3)

> For Christ did not send me to baptize but to proclaim the gospel, and not with eloquent wisdom, so that the cross of Christ might not be emptied of its power. For the message about the cross is foolishness to those who are perishing, but to us who are being saved it is the power of God. (1 Cor 1:17-18)

> For I decided to know nothing among you except Jesus Christ, and him crucified. (1 Cor 2:2)

The central reference to Jesus' death was problematic, and not only for theological or religious reasons. (Why should the death of an executed criminal save from sins?) It presented a political problem as well. The affirmation that Jesus' death on the cross resulted in salvation granted by God casts doubt on the legitimacy of the Roman governor's decision to have Jesus executed, as Pilate hardly understood himself as God's instrument. If Jesus was the messianic Savior and Lord, the Roman authorities in the province of Judea should not have executed him. The focus of Paul's missionary preaching could be construed by Roman listeners as an attack on the legitimacy of the Roman provincial administration.

The proclamation of Jesus the crucified *Christos*, the messianic Savior, confronted Greek and Roman listeners with convictions that stood in stark contrast to the ideology of the city (the Greek *polis*) with its egalitarian structures that ultimately excluded the weak and the aliens. It also contradicted the new ideology of the Roman Empire, with its hierarchical structures that emphasized the divinity of the emperor and other members of the imperial family. Faith in and allegiance to a crucified Kyrios, to a Jewish Savior of the world, was scandalous. Equally nonsensical was the suggestion that a new community of people might be formed in which neither ethnic nor social differences play any role—a community in which everything and everybody is focused on faith in the God of Israel, on allegiance to the crucified Savior sent by Israel's God, on sacrificial love for all fellow believers as well as for all fellow citizens, and on the hope that Jesus Messiah would return and restore a world unmarred by any imperfection.

3.5 Cultural Confrontation: The Explication of the Gospel

Paul's missionary preaching before Jewish and pagan audiences should not be strictly separated from his pastoral teaching before followers of Jesus. There are two reasons for this. First, Paul would have had ample opportunity to explain the gospel and its consequences for those who became followers of Jesus Christ when he preached in public venues. Two scenarios quickly come to mind. Since faith in Jesus Christ was, for Paul, not a matter of theoretical or theological insight only, but a set of convictions that would influence the behavior of the converts in everyday life, it is a fair assumption that Paul's missionary preaching included pointers to the consequences of faith in Christ for those who accepted his message. Also, once there was a community of followers of Jesus whom Paul instructed, he continued his missionary preaching in the city. As his instruction of the new believers focused on explaining the corollaries of the gospel for their lives, encouraging them to apply the truth of the gospel in practical terms, their changed behavioral patterns would have come to the attention of family members and friends who would ask Paul about these matters if and when they encountered him in the city.

Paul's first letter to the Christians in Corinth helps us to see how Paul explains the gospel in terms of its significance for everyday behavior. We will look at four areas: the question of prominence, status, and Christian leadership; hedonistic lifestyle; civic ethics; and egoism versus concern for the poor.

Prominence and prestige. Paul's discussion of the behavior of Corinthian Christians in 1 Corinthians 1:18—4:21 asserts theological convictions and draws out their impact on the behavior of the congregation and its leaders. Paul's remarks in these chapters, in particular in 1:18—2:5, can most appropriately be understood against the background of the values and the behavior of contemporary orators.[71] In the eyes of the citizens of Corinth, Paul was an orator who was looking for an audience. Compared with the conventions of the contemporary orators, however, Paul was very unorthodox. The apostle asserts that his behavior was deliberate (1 Cor 2:1-5). Several terms in this brief section take up rhetorical terminology: *apodeixis* (proofs), *dynamis* (a term that is used by Isocrates and Aristotle in their definition of rhetoric: rhetoric is the "power" to detect the means of persuasion, rhetoric is the "power of speaking"), *peithō* (Lat *persuadere*, "persuade," a term often used in definitions of rhetoric),[72] *pistis* ("proof").

In other words, Paul addresses the expectations of the Corinthians regarding his rhetorical abilities. When Paul writes, "when I came to you, brothers and sisters, I did not come proclaiming the mystery of God to you in lofty words or wisdom" (1 Cor 2:1), he emphasizes the fact that when he preaches the gospel before Jewish and pagan audiences, he intentionally dispenses with the traditional conventions of contemporary rhetoric. He has no interest in being the center of attention or in being praised by

---

[71]See Duane Litfin, *St. Paul's Theology of Proclamation: 1 Corinthians 1—4 and Greco-Roman Rhetoric*, SNTSMS 79 (Cambridge: Cambridge University Press, 1994); Bruce W. Winter, *Philo and Paul Among the Sophists*, SNTSMS 96 (Cambridge: Cambridge University Press, 1997), pp. 147-65; Bruce W. Winter, *After Paul Left Corinth: The Influence of Secular Ethics and Social Change* (Grand Rapids: Eerdmans, 2001), pp. 31-43.

[72]Quintilian, *Institutio oratoria* 7.3.6, speaks of *vis persuadendi* ("quid sit rhetorice, uis persuadendi an bene dicendi scientia").

others. He does not want to gain in prestige, he does not compete with rival orators, he does not have any financial interests. And, more importantly, he knows that the character of the gospel of Jesus Christ makes it impossible to rely on the strategies of traditional rhetoric as described by Aristotle, Cicero or Quintilian. The message of a crucified Messiah is a "stumbling block" for Jewish listeners and "nonsense" for pagan listeners (1 Cor 1:23). Paul knows that the message of the cross cannot be adapted to the theological, rhetorical or aesthetic expectations of his audiences. He knows that he cannot convince his contemporaries of the truth of the gospel with the help of the traditional rhetorical arguments.[73]

It was impossible, in the first century, to speak in a rhetorically alluring manner about a man who had been executed on a cross.[74] The reality of crucifixion was too gruesome and needed too much explanation for rhetorical competence and argumentative brilliance to be of any help. When Paul taught new converts, he described Jesus as "new Adam,"[75] as the "savior of mankind"[76] and as the "Son of God."[77] These are categories that could be packaged as attractive religious content when introducing the message about Jesus to Jewish and pagan audiences. Paul asserts, however, that he never dispensed with preaching Jesus the crucified Savior in his missionary proclamation (1 Cor 2:2). Paul preaches a crucified and risen Savior because this is the message that has been given to him to pass on to those who have not heard the gospel, and because he knows that it is the almighty Lord himself, the Creator of the world, who causes Jews and pagans to come to faith. Paul relies for conversions of men and women not on the powers of rhetorical strategies and techniques, but on the power of God: "My speech and my proclamation were not with plausible words of wisdom, but with a demonstration of the Spirit and of power, so that your faith might rest not on human wisdom but on the power of God" (1 Cor 2:4-5).

---

[73]See further in section 5.5 (pp. 341-54).

[74]See Martin Hengel, *Crucifixion in the Ancient World and the Folly of the Message of the Cross* (Philadelphia: Fortress, 1978), on the shame connected with crucifixion.

[75]See Larry J. Kreitzer, "Adam and Christ," *DPL*, pp. 9-15.

[76]See David W. J. Gill, "A Saviour for the Cities of Crete: The Roman Background to the Epistle to Titus," in *The New Testament in its First Century Setting: Essays on Context and Background in Honor of B. W. Winter*, ed. P. J. Williams (Grand Rapids: Eerdmans, 2004), pp. 220-30.

[77]See Larry W. Hurtado, "Son of God," *DPL*, pp. 900-906; Hurtado, *Lord Jesus Christ*, pp. 101-8.

The consequences of this fundamental theological conviction are high-lighted in 1 Corinthians 3.[78] Paul compares missionaries and teachers to servants and agricultural workers who do the bidding of the masters (1 Cor 3:5-9), which means that social status, pledges of loyalty and "rock-star affectations" are ruled out. Paul describes his responsibility as a missionary: he lays the foundation, which is Jesus Christ crucified (vv. 10-12). The responsibility of the teachers of the church is to build carefully on this foundation, that is, to apply the significance of the cross to all aspects of the life of the church. The criterion of the foundational centrality of "Christ crucified" is of critical importance for the existence of the local church and for the way the work of missionaries and teachers will fare on the Day of Judgment (v. 11-15).

Hedonistic lifestyles. Paul comments repeatedly about the hedonistic lifestyle of some of the Corinthian believers who continue to behave in a secular manner. When he evaluates the incestuous behavior of a church member (1 Cor 5:1-13),[79] he pronounces his judgment "in the name of the Lord Jesus." He appeals to "the power of the Lord Jesus," which is present when the Corinthian believers meet and to the significance of the fact that "our paschal lamb, Christ, has been sacrificed." The gospel of Jesus Christ who has died for our sins grounds his exhortation to celebrate "not with the old yeast, the yeast of malice and evil, but with the unleavened bread of sincerity and truth" (1 Cor 5:8).

When Paul exhorts Corinthian believers to refrain from visiting prostitutes (1 Cor 6:12-20),[80] he argues that "the body is meant not for fornication but for the Lord, and the Lord for the body" (v. 13). This conviction is based on the reality of Jesus' death and resurrection: "God raised the Lord and will also raise us by his power" (v. 14). And it is based on the reality of the connection between the believer and Jesus Christ: "Do you not know that your bodies are members of Christ?" (v. 15).

---

[78]See Victor Paul Furnish, " 'Fellow Workers in God's Service,' " *JBL* 80 (1961): 364-70.

[79]See Gerald Harris, "The Beginnings of Church Discipline: 1 Corinthians 5 [1991]," in *Understanding Paul's Ethics: Twentieth-Century Approaches*, ed. B. S. Rosner (Carlisle, U.K.: Paternoster, 1995), pp. 129-51.

[80]See Renate Kirchhoff, *Die Sünde gegen den eigenen Leib. Studien zu* πορνη *und* πορνεία *in 1 Kor 6,12-20 und dem soziokulturellen Kontext der paulinischen Adressaten*, StUNT 18 (Göttingen: Vandenhoeck & Ruprecht, 1994).

When Paul addresses the life of the believer in a concise presentation of the evidence for the bodily resurrection from the dead (1 Cor 15:1-58), he presents the grounds for renouncing a hedonistic lifestyle. Note his exhortation in verse 34: "come to a sober and right mind, and sin no more; for some people have no knowledge of God." Paul begins his argument with a recapitulation of the fundamental Christian conviction "that Christ died for our sins in accordance with the scriptures, and that he was buried, and that he was raised on the third day in accordance with the scriptures, and that he appeared to Cephas, then to the twelve" (vv. 3-5). He argues that "if the dead are not raised, then Christ has not raised," and "if Christ has not been raised, your faith is futile and you are still in your sins," with the consequence that "then those also who have died in Christ have perished," because "if for this life only we have hoped in Christ, we are of all people most to be pitied" (vv. 16-19). Since, however, Jesus Christ has been bodily raised from the dead, the believers in Jesus Christ will be raised bodily as well: he is "the first fruits of those who have died" (v. 20). The "sting of death," that is, sin which triggers the death sentence for the sinner (v. 56), has been removed by God "who gives us the victory through our Lord Jesus Christ" (v. 57). God's revelation in Jesus' death and resurrection, which grants salvation in the present and hope for the future, is the reason why Christian believers can and should be "steadfast, immovable, always excelling in the work of the Lord, because you know that in the Lord your labor is not in vain" (v. 58). The reality of Jesus' resurrection from the dead and the future reality of the resurrection of the body should lead the Corinthian believers to the conclusion that what they do with their bodies is not irrelevant. It is impossible for Christians to be nonchalant concerning their lifestyles. The hedonistic position that pleasure is the greatest good and that the pursuit of pleasure is an accepted principle of ethical behavior is incompatible with the faith of the followers of Jesus. Self-indulgence and self-gratification are not Christian, but pagan.

Lawsuits and banquets in pagan temples. Paul comments on several areas of civic ethics in which Corinthian believers have failed to see the consequences of the gospel. When he admonishes Corinthian believers not to initiate lawsuits against each other (1 Cor 6:1-11),[81] he appeals to the fact that they *were* all evildoers who did not inherit the kingdom of God, but that they all "were washed, . . . sanctified, . . . justified in the name of the Lord Jesus Christ and in the Spirit of our God" (v. 11).

In the discussion about whether followers of Jesus can attend banquets in pagan temples and eat food sacrificed to idols (1 Cor 8:1—11:1),[82] Paul begins by emphasizing the fact that there is only one God, the Creator and the Lord of history, and only "one Lord, Jesus Christ, through whom are all things and through whom we exist" (1 Cor 8:6). The existence of Christians both as created human beings and as sinners who have been saved from God's wrath and who have thus been granted new (eternal) life is determined by the preexistent Jesus, whose death on the cross is the reason for the believers' new existence. Paul warns those who claim to have the right to eat in pagan temples that their behavior may destroy "those weak believers for whom Christ died" (1 Cor 8:11). Commenting further on perceived rights that some Corinthian Christians claim to have, Paul describes the rights that he has as an apostle, only to point out that "we have not made use of this right, but we endure anything rather than put an obstacle in the way of the gospel of Christ" (1 Cor 9:12). The gospel and its center—Jesus' supreme sacrifice in his death on the cross—determine Paul's behavior as a Christian and as a missionary, and it should control the behavior of the Corinthian believers as well. Paul supports his exhortation that Christians cannot attend banquets in pagan temples in 1 Corinthians 10:16 with the argument that the Lord's Supper which the church celebrates is incompatible with eating in pagan temples due to its theological reality and the christological meaning: "The cup of blessing that we bless, is it not a sharing in the blood of Christ? The bread that we break, is it not a sharing in the body of Christ?"

---

[81]See Bruce W. Winter, "Civil Litigation in Secular Corinth and the Church: The Forensic Background to 1 Corinthians 6.1-8," in *Understanding Paul's Ethics. Twentieth-Century Approaches*, ed. B. S. Rosner (Carlisle, U.K.: Paternoster, 1995), pp. 85-103.

[82]See Winter, *After Paul Left Corinth*, pp. 269-301; also Derek Newton, *Deity and Diet: The Dilemma of Sacrificial Food at Corinth*, JSNTSup 169 (Sheffield, U.K.: Sheffield Academic Press, 1998); John Fotopoulos, *Food Offered to Idols in Roman Corinth: A Social-rhetorical Reconsideration of 1 Corinthians 8:1—11:1*, WUNT 2.151 (Tübingen: Mohr Siebeck, 2003).

Egoism and concern for the poor. When Paul addresses the egoistical behavior of rich believers who do not share their food with the poor in the church (1 Cor 11:17-34), he reminds the Corinthians of the foundational reality of Jesus' self-sacrifice, recapitulating the tradition of the Lord's Supper and of Jesus' words of institution: "This is my body that is for you. Do this in remembrance of me. . . . This cup is the new covenant in my blood. Do this, as often as you drink it, in remembrance of me" (vv. 24-25). Christians who despise fellow believers "eat the bread or drink the cup of the Lord in an unworthy manner" and thus "will be answerable for the body and blood of the Lord" (v. 27).

The gospel, which is the good news of the crucified and risen Jesus Christ, the Messiah and the Lord, triggers immediate and consistent consequences for Christian behavior. Paul is not a moralist telling Christians how to behave. He is a missionary pastor and theologian who never tires of explaining the Christian message and of instructing Christians concerning areas in their lives in which the truth of this message makes a difference—such a difference, in fact, that unbelieving Jews become envious and are thus prompted to accept faith in Jesus Christ (Rom 11:11-24). Paul formulates the consequences of the gospel as follows:

> I appeal to you therefore, brothers and sisters, by the mercies of God, to present your bodies as a living sacrifice, holy and acceptable to God, which is your spiritual worship. Do not be conformed to this world, but be transformed by the renewing of your minds, so that you may discern what is the will of God—what is good and acceptable and perfect. (Rom 12:1-2)

Paul emphasizes that followers of Jesus, who continue to live in "this world," need to understand what God has done to them in Jesus Christ. This understanding results in the knowledge that they belong to God's new order and therefore cannot passively acquiesce in the worldview and the behavior of the present age that is passing away. The truth of the gospel helps them to resist the traditional social values and the cultural conventions that exert the pressure to conform to the pattern of "this age," which is hostile to God. The good news is that "they are no longer the helpless victims of tyrannizing forces, but are able to resist this pressure which comes both from without and from within, because God's merciful action in Christ has provided the basis of resistance."[83]

3.6 PASTORAL CONSOLIDATION: ENCOURAGEMENT FOR THE FOLLOWERS OF JESUS

Paul preached the gospel of Jesus Christ to Jews and Gentiles. Once people were being converted to faith in Jesus Christ, Paul established local
communities of followers of Jesus. The third phase of Paul's missionary
work was the pastoral consolidation of the faith of the new believers.[84]

Some have suggested that Paul's missionary methods were characterized by a restless rush and hectic movements. One scholar writes that

> it is perfectly astonishing to see how short a time he took in traversing the
> extensive fields where he worked, and how quickly he left scarcely founded
> churches and traveled farther, instead of taking time to care for them and
> train them. . . . The great goal of carrying the gospel to the ends of the
> earth kept him always on the move and gave him no rest.[85]

Such views ignore the fact that Paul's missionary work in Corinth and
Ephesus lasted in both cases over two years before he started new missionary initiatives in regions where the gospel had not yet been preached. The
"travel motif" that is deduced from Luke's narrative in the book of Acts
and that often controls the scholarly interpretation of Paul's missionary
work needs serious qualification.[86] Paul's missionary work was characterized by pastoral work in one location just as much as by "missionary
travels." Paul's repeated visits to the churches which he had established
demonstrates the significance of his "anxiety for all the churches" (2 Cor
11:28) in his understanding of the missionary task.

Paul's work as a missionary was not completed once a community of
followers of Jesus had been established in a city. He revisited the churches
he had established, sometimes repeatedly. Paul established the churches

---

[83]C. E. B. Cranfield, *The Epistle to the Romans*, ICC (Edinburgh: T & T Clark, 1975-1979), p. 608.

[84]See Paul Beasley-Murray, "Pastor, Paul as," *DPL*, pp. 654-58; Pesce, *Le due fasi della predicazione di Paolo. Dall'evangelizzazione alla guida delle communità;* James Thompson, *Pastoral Ministry According to Paul: A Biblical Vision* (Grand Rapids: Baker Academic, 2006).

[85]Günther Bornkamm, *Paul* (London and New York: Harper, 1971), pp. 54-55.

[86]See I. Howard Marshall, "Luke's Portrait of the Pauline Mission," in *The Gospel To the Nations: Perspectives on Paul's Mission*, ed. P. Bolt and M. Thompson (Leicester, U.K.: Inter-Varsity Press, 2000), p. 103.

in southern Galatia in A.D. 46/47 (Acts 13—14), which he revisited in A.D. 47 (Acts 14:21-23), in A.D. 49 (Acts 16:1-5), and in A.D. 52 (Acts 18:23). The fact that on the last two occasions Paul undertook the long journey from Antioch in Syria to Ephesus in the province of Asia by foot suggests that he probably visited churches in other cities in Syria and in Cilicia en route as well. After Paul was forced to leave Thessalonica, he "longed with great eagerness to see" the believers there "face to face" and thus he attempted "again and again" to return to Thessalonica, only to be blocked by Satan (1 Thess 2:17-18). When the church in Corinth was not able to deal with difficulties that had arisen, Paul interrupted his missionary work in Ephesus and traveled to Corinth (2 Cor 2:1). When he was engaged in very promising missionary work in Troas, where God had given him an "open door" (2 Cor 2:12), he was restless because the situation in the Corinthian church was still confused and because he had not received the news that he had been waiting for—so much so that he terminated his missionary work in Troas and traveled to Macedonia to meet Titus and to reestablish contact with the church in Corinth (2 Cor 2:13). It is rather interesting to note that there is no explicit evidence that Paul ever stopped his missionary work in a city on his own initiative in order to start a new project in unreached areas—apart from his mission to Corinth and Ephesus, two cities in which he stayed for over two years.[87]

Also, Paul kept in contact through coworkers who helped consolidate the newly established churches once Paul had left the city, or who were sent by Paul as emissaries with the task of solving problems that had arisen in a church. The theological, ethical and spiritual consolidation of the churches was a fundamental concern of Paul. The available evidence relates that when Paul sent his coworkers to other cities, he always sent them to existing churches he had established earlier.[88] When Paul left Macedonia and went to Achaia in order to start missionary work in Corinth, he left Timothy and Silas in Beroea, sending them later to

---

[87]W. Paul Bowers, "Fulfilling the Gospel: The Scope of the Pauline Mission," *JETS* 30 (1987): 192-93.

[88]The question whether Epaphras's missionary work in the cities of the upper Lykos Valley (Colossae, Laodicea, Hierapolis) was his own initiative or undertaken as the result of Paul's directive or suggestion cannot be answered because the sources do not address it.

the congregations in Philippi and Thessalonica (Acts 17:14; 1 Thess 3:1-8). Timothy and Titus repeatedly played an important role in the development and consolidation of the church in Corinth.[89] At a later period Timothy was sent a second time to Philippi (Phil 2:19-24), while Tychicus went to Colossae (Col 4:7-9).

We have a more extensive group of primary sources for this third phase of Paul's missionary work—the letters that Paul wrote to churches he had established in Greece (in Philippi, Thessalonica, and Corinth) and in the region of Ephesus, a letter to a church established by a coworker (the church in Colossae), a letter to a church he wanted to be involved in new missionary projects (the church in the city of Rome), as well as letters to coworkers (Timothy and Titus). The priorities of Paul's pastoral work can be briefly described as follows.

First, Paul constantly quotes or alludes to the Scriptures, that is, the Old Testament.[90] While Gentile converts may not have immediately understood these allusions, Paul probably expected the teachers of the local churches, many of them in all probability Jewish believers, to see the biblical background of his explanations of the gospel. The frequent references to Scripture also suggest that the reading and exposition of Scripture was a regular feature of the churches which Paul established. This is confirmed by Paul's advice to Timothy:

> Until I arrive, give attention to the public reading of scripture, to exorting, to teaching. Do not neglect the gift that is in you, which was given to you through prophecy with the laying on of hands by the council of elders. Put these things into practice, devote yourself to them, so that all may see your progress. Pay close attention to yourself and to your teaching; continue in these things, for in doing this you will save both yourself and your hearers. (1 Tim 4:13-16)

Second, Paul taught the new converts "the whole counsel of God" (Acts 20:27) both "publicly and from house to house" (Acts 20:20). As his letters indicate, in particular his letter to the Christians in the city of Rome, Paul's teaching focused on explaining God's revelation in Jesus Christ; the

---

[89] 1 Cor 4:17; 16:10-11; 2 Cor 2:13; 7:6-7, 13-15; 8:6, 16-17, 23; 12:18.
[90] See Gregory K. Beale and D. A. Carson, eds., *Commentary on the New Testament Use of the Old Testament* (Grand Rapids: Baker, 2007).

life and death and resurrection of Jesus; the condition of human beings without faith in the one true God and without faith in Jesus Christ; God's gift of righteousness for the repentant sinner who believes in Jesus the Messiah, Savior, and Lord; the necessity and the possibility of repentance and forgiveness for sinners, both Jews and Gentiles; the identity of the believers in Jesus Christ and the identity of their communal fellowship; the consequences of the gospel for everyday living; the transformation of the mind and of the behavior of the believers; the return of Jesus Christ and the final consummation of God's gracious revelation.[91]

Third, Paul seeks to promote the spiritual growth of the believers, in terms of not only promoting their theological understanding of the gospel but also helping them to pray,[92] to worship[93] and to be serious and consistent about living out the truth of the gospel in their everyday lives.[94]

Fourth, Paul works to strengthen the fellowship of local believers as the people, the temple and the household God, as the body of Christ, and as the community of the Spirit.[95] Paul seeks to bolster the gifts of the individual believers as they work together for the welfare of the entire

---

[91]For summaries of Paul's theology cf. James D. G. Dunn, *The Theology of Paul the Apostle* (Grand Rapids: Eerdmans, 1998); Thomas R Schreiner, *Paul, Apostle of God's Glory in Christ: A Pauline Theology* (Downers Grove, Ill.: InterVarsity Press, 2001); I. Howard Marshall, *New Testament Theology: Many Witnesses, One Gospel* (Downers Grove, Ill.: InterVarsity Press, 2004), pp. 420-69.

[92]See Gordon P. Wiles, *Paul's Intercessory Prayers: The Significance of Paul's Intercessory Prayer Passages in the Letters of St. Paul*, SNTSMS 24 (Cambridge: Cambridge University Press, 1974); David G. Peterson, "Prayer in Paul's Writings," in *Teach Us to Pray: Prayer in the Bible and the World*, ed. D. A. Carson (Grand Rapids: Baker; Exeter, U.K.: Paternoster, 1990), pp. 84-101, 325-28; Donald A. Carson, "Paul's Mission and Prayer," in *The Gospel to the Nations: Perspectives on Paul's Mission*, ed. P. Bolt and M. Thompson (Leicester, U.K.: Inter-Varsity Press, 2000), pp. 175-84.

[93]See Ralph P. Martin, *Worship in the Early Church* (London: Marshall, Morgan & Scott, 1964); Ralph P. Martin, "Worship," *DPL*, pp. 982-91; David Peterson, *Engaging with God: A Biblical Theology of Worship* (Leicester, U.K.: Inter-Varsity Press, 1992), pp. 166-227.

[94]See Eckhard J. Schnabel, "How Paul Developed His Ethics," in *Understanding Paul's Ethics: Twentieth-Century Approaches*, ed. B. S. Rosner (Carlisle, U.K.: Paternoster, 1995), pp. 267-97; Richard B. Hays, *The Moral Vision of the New Testament: Community, Cross, New Creation: A Contemporary Introduction to New Testament Ethics* (New York: HarperCollins, 1996), pp. 16-72; Winter, *After Paul Left Corinth*.

[95]See Rudolf Schnackenburg, *The Church in the New Testament* (London: Burns & Oates, 1968); Robert Banks, *Paul's Idea of Community: The Early House Churches in their Historical Setting* (Grand Rapids: Eerdmans, 1980); Richard N. Longenecker, "Paul's Vision of the Church and Community Formation in His Major Missionary Letters," in *Community Formation in the Early Church and in the Church Today*, ed. R. N. Longenecker (Peabody, Mass.: Hendrickson, 2002), pp. 73-88; Roger W. Gehring, *House Church and Mission: The Importance of Household Structures in Early Christianity* (Peabody, Mass.: Hendrickson, 2004).

congregation, which consists on the one hand in a better understanding of the nature of God and of the work of Jesus Christ, and on the other hand in an increasingly deeper realization of their status as "resident aliens" in society. He helps the churches understand their role as concrete representations of the "words of life" that they offer to the world (Phil 2:14-16).[96]

3.7 APOLOGETIC CONFRONTATION: THE DEFENSE OF THE GOSPEL

On many occasions Paul was forced to confront (Jewish) Christian teachers who had become active in the young communities of new believers. Paul's defense of the gospel that he and the other apostles had been preaching did not focus on attacks against these opponents. Rather, Paul reformulated the gospel of Jesus Christ, showing its relevance for the questions that were raised. These teachers accused Paul of failing to maintain the priority of Israel in the history of salvation. They insisted that the Mosaic law remained God's normative revelation. And they wanted to require the Gentile converts to submit to circumcision and to keep the Mosaic stipulations regarding ritual purity (e.g., the food laws) as the traditional criteria for full membership in the people of God. These teachers have often been called "Judaizers" as a result of these emphases.[97] The term *Judaizer* is taken from Galatians 2:14 ("but when I saw that they were not acting consistently with the truth of the gospel, I said to Cephas before them all, 'If you, though a Jew, live like a Gentile and not like a Jew, how can you compel the Gentiles to live like Jews?'"), where the phrase "to live like Jews" translates the Greek verb *ioudaizein*.[98] These Jewish Christian teachers in all probability came from Jerusalem. They were concerned about Paul's theological convictions and about his admitting converted Gentiles into the messianic community of salvation without circumcision and without requirement to obey the Mosaic law, particularly the purity laws and the food laws.

Paul addresses these matters in his letter to the Christians in Galatia and in Rome, as well as in his letter to the church in Colossae. For Paul,

---

[96]See Robert L. Plummer, *Paul's Understanding of the Church's Mission*, Paternoster Biblical Monographs (Bletchley, U.K.: Paternoster, 2006).
[97]See William S. Campbell, "Judaizers," *DPL*, pp. 512-16.
[98]This term also occurs in Esther 8:17; Josephus *Bellum Judaicum* 2.454.

the issue in this debate was not his own missionary work but the integrity of the gospel of Jesus Christ he proclaimed. Paul insists on the foundational significance of the Christian conviction that Jesus was the promised Messiah, that Yahweh, the God of Israel, had revealed himself in Jesus Christ, and that God had provided for the salvation of humankind in Jesus' death and resurrection. Paul specified his theology of the justification of all people alone through faith in Jesus Christ in his letters, not to legitimize his the Gentile mission, but as an authentic interpretation of the person, death and resurrection of Jesus Christ, who has brought about the salvation the prophets had promised for the last days, providing the foundation for the universality of the proclamation of the gospel. Paul was evidently convinced of the universality of the mission of Jesus' followers since the days of his conversion.[99]

This conviction was not dependent on his own calling as apostle to the Gentiles. Paul asserts that the mission to the Gentiles is a consequence of the significance of Jesus' death and resurrection, procuring the salvation of the last days as promised by the prophets, as is the equal membership of the Gentile Christians in the church of God (cf. 1 Thess 1:9-10; 2:11-12; 5:9-10).

> Paul's doctrine of justification is the radical consequence of this insight of faith. What is at issue is not merely the pragmatic argument that the Gentile mission can be much more successful without the requirement of circumcision and without an obedience to the law that includes the food laws and the purity laws. What is at stake is the conviction that the promise to Abraham in Gen 12:3 is fulfilled, which, in the context of Paul's "canonical" reading of the Torah, cannot be separated from the promise of righteousness by faith in Gen 15:6.[100]

Since the death and resurrection of Jesus the Messiah, the justification of sinners is separated from the obedience to the Mosaic law. Because God has conquered sin and death at the cross and in the resurrection of Jesus, humankind is justified only through faith in the God who has raised Jesus from the dead. As faith that justifies relies on God's grace,

---

[99]See Seyoon Kim, *The Origin of Paul's Gospel*, 2nd ed., WUNT 2/4 (Tübingen: Mohr-Siebeck, 1984), chap. 7.

[100]See Thomas Söding, "Der Skopos der paulinischen Rechtfertigungslehre," *ZThK* 97 (2000): 422 (my translation).

and as God's grace reaches all sinners, the righteousness by faith that has been promised to Abraham and that has become a reality in Jesus Christ is universal in scope. What Scripture has "foreseen" (Gal 3:8) has happened: the "fullness of time" has arrived and God's promises have become reality in the sending of his Son (Gal 4:4). The faith that God had promised "has come" (Gal 3:25). This means that in the present time all "who believe" are blessed alongside Abraham, who believed in God's promise, Jews as well as Gentiles (Gal 3:8-9). And this means that both Jews and Gentiles who believe in Jesus Christ and to whom God therefore gives the Spirit of his Son are adopted as children of God (Gal 4:5-6).

In his letter to the churches in southern Galatia Paul defends the "truth of the gospel" (Gal 2:5, 14) against Jewish Christian teachers who demand that the Gentile believers must be circumcised.[101] They seek to disparage Paul by accusing him of lacking the full authority of an apostle. Paul asserts that the teaching of these opponents represents "a different gospel" that must be rejected at all costs (Gal 1:6-9). He defends his status as an apostle with the argument that he has seen the risen Lord and that he has been called by the Lord to preach the gospel just as the other apostles have been, and that they preach the same gospel (Gal 1:1; 1:11—2:10). Paul expounds his conviction that now, in the present time that has been newly qualified by the coming of Jesus the Messiah, "a person is justified not by the works of the law but through faith in Jesus Christ" (Gal 2:16). As a result of this new reality, the Mosaic law is no longer capable of conveying salvation (Gal 2:15—3:18): the function of the law as prison warden and as a guardian and guide *(paidagōgos)* has come to an end with the arrival of Jesus Christ (Gal 3:19—4:7). Paul argues that submitting to the demand of circumcision and full Torah obedience is tantamount to submission to the enslaving powers of the world whom the Gentile believers had served before their conversion (Gal 4:8-20). Paul argues that the Gentile Christians who have been set free from sin and from the law, are already children of Sarah the freewoman and thus members of the people of God (Gal 4:21-31). In the last two chapters

---

[101]For a summary of Paul's theological argument in Gal cf. C. K. Barrett, *Freedom and Obligation: A Study of the Epistle to the Galatians* (Philadelphia: Westminster, 1985); James D. G. Dunn, *The Theology of Paul's Letter to the Galatians*, New Testament Theology (Cambridge: Cambridge University Press, 1993); Marshall, *New Testament Theology*, pp. 209-35.

of Galatians Paul emphasizes that the problems of the "flesh," that is, wrong and immoral behavior, cannot be solved with the help of the law: they are solved in the continuing union with the death and resurrection of Jesus Christ, in the liberation from bondage that Jesus the Messiah has effected, and in the power of the Holy Spirit who produces "fruit" in the life of the believer acceptable to God (Gal 5:1—6:16).

Paul's letter to the Christians in the city of Rome has been interpreted as a "statement of accountability"[102] about his theological convictions.[103] The apostle evidently anticipated a policy discussion during his upcoming visit to Jerusalem concerning his message of God's salvific revelation in Jesus Christ for all people, both Jews and Gentiles (Rom 15:30-31). Paul writes to the believers in Rome since he wants to recruit them as partners in his next project of a mission to Spain (Rom 15:23-24). He prepares his visit by writing this letter, in which he explains the message of Jesus Christ for whose proclamation he has been set apart (Rom 1:1-5) and which represents the common tradition of early Christian confession.[104] Paul explains the gospel in the first part of his letter in the form of a dialogue with a Jewish discussion partner who formulates the views of his Jewish Christian opponents who object to his gospel of the revelation of the righteousness of God in Jesus Christ without works of law. Paul focuses his exposition on

- universal sin and guilt against which God's wrath is directed (Rom 1:18—3:20)

- who Jesus is (Rom 1:3-4)

- what Jesus did as God's Messiah and Savior, securing justification by God's grace through faith, on account of his death on the cross (Rom 3:21-31)

- the nature of the new covenant people of God as children of Abraham, who was declared to be righteous on account of his faith before he was circumcised (Rom 4)

---

[102]Peter Stuhlmacher, *Paul's Letter to the Romans* (Louisville: Westminster, 1994), p. 8; the German term is *Rechenschaftsbericht*.

[103]For a summary of Paul's argument in Romans see Klaus Haacker, *The Theology of Paul's Letter to the Romans*, New Testament Theology (Cambridge: Cambridge University Press, 2003); Marshall, *New Testament Theology*, pp. 305-43.

[104]Cf. Rom 1:3-4; 3:25-26; 4:25; 6:17; 8:3; 10:9; 13:8-9; 14:17; 15:14-15.

- the believers' new relationship with God, their reconciliation with God, the experience of God's love, the reception of the Holy Spirit, justification at the final judgment (Rom 5:1-11)

- the universal availability of God's gift of righteousness and life through Jesus Christ (Rom 5:11-21)

- the new life of the believers who are no longer under compulsion to sin because they are connected by faith with Jesus' death (who died because of sin and to atone for sin), which also means that they are under obligation to obey God who has made them alive "in Christ Jesus" (Rom 6)

- the nature of sin, which manipulated God's law and forces people to violate God's commandments, thus triggering the death sentence of the law, which in and by itself is not the cause of sin (Rom 7)

- the Holy Spirit as the power of God's gracious presence who helps believers to live lives pleasing to God (Rom 8:1-17)

- the certainty of the believers' justification in the final judgment and of future glory (Rom 8:18-39)

- the unbelief of the Jewish people, the importance of the proclamation of the gospel, future conversions of Jewish people and God's faithfulness in keeping his promises (Rom 9—11)

- the new life of the believers, which is not dictated by the values and pressures of pagan, secular society but by minds transformed by God who wants his people to do his will (Rom 12—15)

In his letter to the believers in Philippi, Paul takes up matters that seem to have been introduced into the church by Jewish Christian teachers who attempt to convince the Gentile Christians in the church to submit to circumcision (Phil 3:3-4), despite the fact that their own personal behavior was anything but beyond reproach (Phil 3:17-21).[105] Paul emphasizes that "perfection," or rather maturity, is not achieved through the adoption of certain Jewish doctrines or practices. Rather, maturity is

---

[105]Peter T. O'Brien, *The Epistle to the Philippians. A Commentary on the Greek Text*, NIGTC (Grand Rapids: Eerdmans, 1991), pp. 26-35.

a goal that believers in Jesus Christ will reach only in God's future. Paul is less concerned about minor differences in the believers' understanding of the Christian faith and praxis: "Let those of us then who are mature be of the same mind; and if you think differently about anything, this too God will reveal to you" (Phil 3:15). What matters most for Christians is to "press on toward the goal for the prize of the heavenly call of God in Christ Jesus" (Phil 3:14).

In his letter to the Christians in Colossae, Paul apparently discusses the efforts of Jews who criticize the Christians' beliefs as well as their worship practices and their everyday behavior.[106] Paul encourages the believers to stay firm in their faith in Jesus Christ the Lord (Col 2:5-7) and to refuse being deceived by arguments that cast doubt on their conviction that they have "all the riches of assured understanding and have the knowledge of God's mystery, that is, Christ himself, in whom are hidden all the treasures of wisdom and knowledge" (Col 2:2-3). Paul reminds them of the fullness of divine blessing that Jesus has procured for them through his death on the cross (Col 2:8-15). He warns of the claim that there are spiritual experiences beyond their union with Jesus Christ that would move them beyond the cross of Christ. Religious experiences linked with food and drink, with festivals and sabbath celebrations, with the heavenly worship of the angels or with visions and ascetic practices, can never compete with God's revelation in Jesus Christ (Col 2:16-18). Paul assures the Colossians of the significance of their community of local believers in which the future is not merely a shadow but has already become reality (Col 2:17, 19). Paul warns of the claim that the observance of Jewish food laws and purity stipulations is something that believers in Jesus Messiah must practice (Col 2:20-23).

Paul then goes on to describe the lifestyle that results from faith in Jesus Christ. Followers of Jesus have died with Christ and have been raised with him, which means that their life is determined by this heavenly perspective and by Christ the Lord who sits at the right hand of God (Col 3:1-4). One of the significant consequences of this conviction is the fact that they are able to abandon the traditions, customs and vices that characterize the

---

[106]See James D. G. Dunn, *The Epistles to the Colossians and to Philemon: A Commentary on the Greek Text*, NIGTC (Grand Rapids: Eerdmans, 1996), pp. 23-35.

lives of their fellow citizens, in particular "fornication, impurity, passion, evil desire, and greed (which is idolatry)" (Col 3:5). Paul reminds them of the need for continual moral transformation, as God enables them to "get rid of all such things," in particular "anger, wrath, malice, slander, and abusive language from your mouth" (Col 3:8). The "new self" of a follower of Jesus overcomes the traditional social and ethnic barriers between Greeks and Jews and barbarians, and between slave and free (Col 3:10-11). The community of believers is characterized by compassion, kindness, humility, meekness and patience, by forgiveness, love and peace, and by the ministry of the word of God, accompanied by joyful and thankful singing (Col 3:12-17). Faith in Christ also has an impact on the behavior of husbands and wives, parents and children, freemen and slaves (Col 3:18—4:1).

Finally, Paul emphasizes the importance of prayer and intercession (Col 4:2-4), and he advises the believers to be wise in their dealings with their pagan fellow citizens. They should aim at conversations about their faith that are "gracious and attractive" so that they will have "the right answer for everyone" (Col 4:6 NLT).

In his letters to Timothy and Titus, Paul discusses yet again the activities of certain Jewish Christian teachers. Paul asserts that they promote foolish controversies.[107] The comment that these teachers seduce Christians (2 Tim 3:13; cf. Tit 1:10) indicates that the "nonsense" they propagate is plausible to some degree and thus convinces some believers. Their teachings focus on the Mosaic law, which they interpret in an allegorical manner, linked with Jewish myths and with circumcision,[108] with ascetic practices related to marriage and food.[109] They deny a future resurrection (2 Tim 2:18). They emphasize the participation of married women in the teaching ministry of the churches with the result that they neglect their children (1 Tim 2:11-15). And they possibly downplay the importance of missionary work among Gentiles.[110] Their teaching implied that Jesus Christ does not occupy a central position as Savior and

---

[107]Cf. 1 Tim 6:3-5; Tit 1:10; 3:9; 2 Tim 2:14-16; 2:23.
[108]1 Tim 1:4, 7; 2 Tim 4:4; Tit 1:14; on circumcision cf. Tit 1:10.
[109]Cf. 1 Tim 4:3; cf. Tit 1:15; 1 Tim 2:15; 5:23.
[110]I. Howard Marshall, *Pastoral Epistles*, p. 45; cf. 1 Tim 2:4-6, 7; 4:10; Tit 2:11; cf. 1 Tim 3:16.

as Mediator between God and humankind. Paul attacks these teachers on account of their immoral behavior (Tit 1:16; 2 Tim 3:1-5), which was demonstrated, for example, in their desire to achieve financial gain through their teaching ministry (1 Tim 6:5-10; Tit 1:11). Paul warns the Christians in the churches in Asia Minor to recognize the danger that these teachers represent and to reject them, and not to become again the kind of people they had been before their conversion.[111] Paul encourages Timothy and Titus to be concerned about the quality of character of the leaders in the local churches (1 Tim 3:1-13; Tit 1:5-9). And he emphasizes the necessity of preserving the early Christian tradition in the churches.[112]

Much more could be said, but this is not the place for an extensive interpretation of these and other passages in Paul's letters. It has become clear, however, that Paul was not content to preach the gospel to unbelievers and to establish new communities of followers of Jesus. He continued to be concerned about the churches that had come into existence and about the believers who were meeting in these local churches every week—concerned for their doctrinal authenticity and for their moral consistency, for their faith and for their life, for their leadership and for the new converts. Paul is concerned that the teachers of the churches teach correctly and that the believers in the churches believe correctly—this is why he writes his letters and why he discusses one-sided or misleading beliefs that some Christians propagate. He is not simply concerned about an authentic Christian "experience" but also about the truth of the gospel and about behaving in a manner that was consistent with the gospel (Gal 2:5, 14). Paul was concerned that some people "spin" the Christian message in the sense that they "will not put up with sound doctrine, but having itching ears, they will accumulate for themselves teachers to suit their own desires, and will turn away from listening to the truth and wander away to myths" (2 Tim 4:3-4). He was concerned that Christians might come under the harmful influence of teachers who replace the centrality of Jesus, the crucified Messiah, with an emphasis on "works" that Christians need in order to have full salvation, or with an emphasis on "lofty words

---

[111]Cf. 1 Tim 3:1-13; 5:6, 11; Tit 1:6-7; 2 Tim 2:22. Cf. Marshall, *Pastoral Epistles*, p. 43.
[112]Cf. 1 Tim 1:15-17; 2 Tim 1:13-14; 2:2, 8-13; 3:10, 14-17; Tit 2:1; 3:3-8.

of wisdom" that make the gospel message allegedly more acceptable and more attractive (Gal 3:1-2; 1 Cor 2:1-5). Paul was concerned that believers do "all for the sake of the gospel" so that they may share in its blessings (1 Cor 9:23).

4

The Missionary Goals
of the Apostle Paul

What then is Apollos? What is Paul? Servants through whom you came to believe, as the Lord assigned to each. I planted, Apollos watered, but God gave the growth. So neither the one who plants nor the one who waters is anything, but only God who gives the growth. The one who plants and the one who waters have a common purpose, and each will receive wages according to the labor of each. For we are God's servants, working together; you are God's field, God's building.

According to the grace of God given to me, like a skilled master builder I laid a foundation, and someone else is building on it. Each builder must choose with care how to build on it. For no one can lay any foundation other than the one that has been laid; that foundation is Jesus Christ. Now if anyone builds on the foundation with gold, silver, precious stones, wood, hay, straw—the work of each builder will become visible, for the Day will disclose it, because it will be revealed with fire, and the fire will test what sort of work each has done. If what has been built on the foundation survives, the builder will receive a reward. If the work is burned up, the builder will suffer loss; the builder will be saved, but only as through fire. Do you not know that you are God's temple and that God's Spirit dwells in you? If anyone destroys God's temple, God will destroy that person. For God's temple is holy, and you are that temple.

· 1 COR 3:5-17

THE FOLLOWING DESCRIPTION OF THE GOALS of Paul's missionary work can be regarded as a description of Paul's missionary strategy, which should be distinguished from his missionary methods (which will be described in chap. 5). Both chapter four and five draw conclusions from the description of Paul's missionary work, Paul's statements concerning his missionary task, and the description of Paul's missionary messages in the first three chapters. The goals of Paul's missionary work focus on preaching the gospel to Jews and Gentiles who live in cities between Jerusalem and Illyricum and Spain, entreating them to be reconciled to God through faith in Jesus the messianic Savior and Lord, teaching the new converts the whole counsel of God as he established local communities of followers of Jesus.

4.1 PREACHING THE GOSPEL

Paul's description of his missionary task (see chap. 2) focuses on the preaching of the gospel as the primary goal. This premier goal of his missionary calling is formulated in classic manner in Paul's self-description in his letter to the Christians in Rome: "Paul, a servant of Jesus Christ, called to be an apostle, *set apart for the gospel of God*" (Rom 1:1, emphasis added). Paul understood his primary task as an apostle who has been called and sent by God to preach the gospel.

The English word *gospel* goes back to the Old English word *godspel* meaning "good tidings," translating the Latin phrase *bona adnuntiatio* or *bonus nuntius* into English. The Greek word used in the New Testament is *euangelion*,[1] used fifty-six times by Paul, which means (generally good) "news" or "tidings." The verb *euangelizomai*, used nineteen times by Paul,[2] denotes, for example, the activity of the *euangelos*, the messenger in ancient Greece who was sent, for example, from the battlefield to the army's home city, which awaited the news of the victory of the army.[3] The verb often occurs in letters describing communications that bring joy: people receive the good news of the birth of a son or of an approaching wedding (but also the sad news of the death of someone). The papyrus letter that Apollonios and Sarapias, a wealthy couple who had sent four thousand

---

[1] The term *euangelion* is an adjective used as a substantive, which derives from *euangelos*.
[2] Rom 1:15; 10:15; 15:20; 1 Cor 1:17; 9:16, 18; 15:1, 2; 2 Cor 10:16; 11:7; Gal 1:8, 9, 11, 16, 23; 4:13; Eph 2:17; 3:8; 1 Thess 3:6.
[3] See G. Friedrich, *TDNT*, 2:710.

flowers to the wedding, write to a certain Dionysia, the stepmother of the bridegroom, begins with the sentence: "You filled us with joy when you announced the good news (Gk *euangelisamenē*) of most noble Sarapion's marriage."[4] These Greek terms are used for "the announcement of a message that was news to its hearers."[5]

The plural of the Greek term *euangelia* is used in connection with the emperor cult, a fact that illustrates both the non-Christian use of the term and the religious connotations that could be linked with it. A famous example of the use of "good news" language in the emperor cult is an inscription discovered in Priene, a city 46 kilometers south of Ephesus. To celebrate Augustus's gift of peace to the world after decades of civil war, the cities of the province of Asia accepted the proposal of the proconsul, Paulus Fabius Maximus, and decided in 9 B.C. to change the Macedonian calendar so that New Year's day would be observed on September 23, the birthday of the emperor Augustus.[6] A section in the second part of the document reads:

> It seemed good to the Greeks of Asia, in the opinion of the high priest Apollonius of Menophilus Azanitus: "Since Providence, which has ordered all things and is deeply interested in our life, has set in most perfect order by giving us Augustus, whom she filled with virtue that he might benefit humankind, sending him as a savior, both for us and for our descendants, that he might end war and arrange all things, and since he, Caesar, by his appearance (excelled even our anticipations), surpassing all previous benefactors, and not even leaving to posterity any hope of surpassing what he has done, and since the birthday of the god Augustus was the beginning of the good tidings *[euangelia]* for the world that came by reason of him," which Asia resolved in Smyrna.

The officials of the province proclaim that the peace achieved by Augustus and the "salvation" it brought from the civil war are "good news" for

---

[4]Greg H. R. Horsley and Stephen R. Llewelyn, *New Documents Illustrating Early Christianity* (North Ryde, New South Wales, Australia: Macquarie University, 1981-2002), 3:10-11. The papyrus letter was originally published as P. Oxy. 3313.

[5]John P. Dickson, "Gospel as News: εὐαγγελ- from Aristophanes to the Apostle Paul," *NTS* 51 (2005): 213.

[6]The inscription is published as *OGIS* II 458 (= I. Priene 105). For a convenient translation see Craig A. Evans, *Ancient Texts for New Testament Studies: A Guide to the Background Literature* (Peabody, Mass.: Hendrickson, 2005), p. 313.

the world. The Greek words for "(good) news" and "to announce (good) news" are also used to announce the birth of an heir to the emperor, his coming-of-age and his accessions.

More important than this secular use of the term *euangelion* in the Roman Empire is the use of the verb *euangelizomai* in the Greek Old Testament as the translation for the Hebrew term *biśśēr*, which in English means "to announce, tell, deliver a message." Particularly important are passages in which this term is used to describe God's kingly reign, his victory over his enemies, the arrival of salvation.[7] In the book of Isaiah, the "herald of good news" (Heb *mĕbaśśēr*, Gk *ho euangelizomenos*) announces the new era of God's kingly rule, which is inaugurated by the messenger's announcement.

> Get you up to a high mountain,
> > O Zion, *herald of good tidings*;
> lift up your voice with strength,
> > O Jerusalem, *herald of good tidings*,
> > lift it up, do not fear;
> say to the cities of Judah,
> > "Here is your God!"
> See, the Lord GOD comes with might,
> > and his arm rules for him;
> his reward is with him,
> > and his recompense before him.
> He will feed his flock like a shepherd;
> > he will gather the lambs in his arms,
> and carry them in his bosom,
> > and gently lead the mother sheep. (Is 40:9-11)
>
> How beautiful upon the mountains
> > are the feet of the messenger who announces peace,
> who brings good news,
> > who announces salvation,
> > who says to Zion, "Your God reigns." (Is 52:7)

---

[7]Cf. Ps 40:9[10]; 68:11[12]; 96:2 (LXX 95:2); Is 40:9; 41:27; 52:7; 60:6; 61:1; Nahum 1:15 (LXX Nahum 2:1). Cf. C. E. B. Cranfield, *The Epistle to the Romans*, ICC (Edinburgh: T & T Clark, 1975-1979), 1:55.

The message of this "herald of good news" is God's very own message, in his words God himself speaks. The new age is made a reality on account of and in connection with the proclamation of the "good news" of God returning to his people and taking up his reign.

Jesus understood his ministry of preaching and healing as fulfilling the role of the "herald of good tidings" of the prophet Isaiah. Mark summarizes Jesus' preaching in Galilee with the words: "The time is fulfilled, and the kingdom of God has come near; repent, and believe in the good news" (Mk 1:15). In the synagogue of Nazareth Jesus quoted Isaiah 61:1-2 (Lk 4:18-19). The full passage reads:

> The spirit of the Lord GOD is upon me,
>> because the LORD has anointed me;
> he has sent me to bring good news *[euangelisasthai]* to the oppressed,
>> to bind up the brokenhearted,
> to proclaim liberty to the captives,
>> and release to the prisoners;
> to proclaim the year of the LORD's favor,
>> and the day of vengeance of our God;
>> to comfort all who mourn;
> to provide for those who mourn in Zion—
>> to give them a garland instead of ashes,
> the oil of gladness instead of mourning,
>> the mantle of praise instead of a faint spirit.
> They will be called oaks of righteousness,
>> the planting of the LORD, to display his glory. (Is 61:1-3)

When Jesus asserts that this prophecy "has been fulfilled in your hearing" (Lk 4:21), he proclaims himself to be the *mĕbaśśēr*, the "messenger of good tidings," who announced the arrival of God's kingly rule, indeed the coming of God himself, and thus the new era of comprehensive salvation and peace. In his answer to John's question whether he is "the coming one," Jesus explains his ministry of healing and preaching as the fulfillment of Isaiah 61:1-2 (Mt 11:2-6).

It is instructive to look at the direct objects used in connection with the verb *euangelizomai*, "to announce (good) news." In Galatians 1:16 it is "him," that is, Jesus the Son of God; in Galatians 1:23 it is "the faith," that is, the faith in Jesus as the crucified Messiah; in Ephesians 3:8 it is "the boundless riches of Christ."[8] The usage of the noun *euangelion* is equally revealing. Paul refers to "the gospel of God" (Rom 1:1; 15:16; 1 Thess 2:2, 8, 9), that is, the good news that issues from God. More frequent formulations are expressions such as "the gospel of Christ" (Rom 15:19; 2 Cor 2:12; 9:13; 10:14; Gal 1:7; 1 Thess 3:2), that is, the news about the Messiah; "the gospel of the glory of Christ" (2 Cor 4:4); "the gospel of our Lord Jesus" (2 Thess 1:8); "the gospel of his son" (Rom 1:9), that is, the news concerning the Son of God; "the gospel of your salvation" (Eph 1:13); "the gospel of peace" (Eph 6:15). The *euangelion* is the good news of the arrival of Jesus the Messiah whose coming, death and resurrection bring salvation for those who accept this message. *The consistent focus of Paul's preaching was on what God had done in and through Jesus Christ, on the crucified and risen Son of God himself.*

Another term that Paul uses to describe his preaching ministry is the Greek verb *katangellō*, which is often translated as "to proclaim" and which can be defined as "to make known in public, with implication of broad dissemination."[9] The message proclaimed is "the mystery of God" (1 Cor 2:1), "the gospel" (1 Cor 9:14), "the death of the Lord" (1 Cor 11:26), "Christ" (Phil 1:17, 18), "him" (Col 1:28), that is, "Christ in you, the hope of glory" (Col 1:27). The same pattern emerges: *Paul's preaching was focused on the good news whose source is God himself—the good news of the coming of Jesus Christ and of the salvation that God offers through him, good news which is announced with authority as the word of God.*

The task of the herald in the Greco-Roman world helps us to understand Paul's proclamation of good news. Paul describes himself as a "herald" *(kēryx)* in 1 Timothy 2:7 and 2 Timothy 1:11, and he often employs the verb *kēryssein* to describe the basic process of the oral proclamation of the gospel of Jesus Christ.[10] The term *herald* (Gk *kēryx*) describes a man

---

[8]In Eph 2:13 the verb *euangelizomai* is used to describe Jesus' announcement of "peace" to Gentiles and to Jews ("to you who were far off and peace to those who were near"). In 1 Thess 3:6 the verb refers to Timothy bringing the good news of the Thessalonians faith and love to Paul, who is in Corinth. In all other occurrences, Paul uses the verb absolutely, i.e., without an object, a fact that indicates that the term had a "technical" meaning that was known to his readers.

[9]BDAG, p. 515.

[10]Rom 10:8, 14, 15; 1 Cor 1:23; 9:27; 15:11, 12; 2 Cor 1:19; 4:5; 11:4; Gal 2:2; 5:11; Phil 1:15; Col 1:23; 1 Thess 2:9; 1 Tim 3:16; cf. Acts 19:13; 20:25; 28:31.

who calls out in a clear and audible manner a message that he has been told by a ruler or the magistrates of a city-state to convey a message to the constituency. This announcement is usually "news" in the sense that its content has not been known before. The "herald" in Greco-Roman society

> is always subject to an extrinsic authority whose spokesman he is. He transmits, while being himself untouchable, the message and the viewpoint of his patron. He thus has . . . himself no room for any negotiation. His task is, at any rate, an official one . . . which is the reason why he is also the person who made court sentences public. What he makes public becomes effective as he calls it out.[11]

The missionary preaching of the gospel is the public announcement of news: the news of God's revelation in Jesus Christ that accords reconciliation with God, salvation, forgiveness of sins, peace and hope to those who accept this message as good news. The "good news," which is thus proclaimed, has been entrusted to Paul, and to other apostles and missionaries, by God and by Jesus Christ. It is news that they thus convey publicly, with divine authority and with courageous boldness.

4.2 PREACHING THE GOSPEL TO JEWS AND TO GENTILES

Paul preaches the saving news of Jesus the messianic Savior and Lord before Jewish and Gentile audiences (1 Cor 9:19-23).[12] As God addresses the Jews first (Rom 1:16; 2:9-10; 9—11), so does Paul. Because both Jews and Greeks are under the power of sin, needing forgiveness and salvation and reconciliation with God (Rom 3:9), because there is no distinction between Jews and Greeks as regards their status before God who is the "same Lord is Lord of all and is generous to all who call on him" (Rom 10:12), Greeks need to hear the saving news of Jesus Christ as well.

The Jews are called by Paul on occasion "Israelites" (Gk *Israēlitai*),[13] that is, members of God's covenant people. In Second Temple Judaism the

---

[11]Lothar Coenen, in *Theologisches Begriffslexikon zum Neuen Testament*, ed. Lothar Coenen and Klaus Haacker, Neubearbeitete Ausgabe (Wuppertal: R. Brockhaus, 1997—2000), 2:1755-56.

[12]See the discussion of 1 Cor 9:19-23 in sections 2 and 3 (pp. 131-39, 190-96).

[13]Rom 9:4; 11:1; 2 Cor 11:22. The term *Israēlitai* occurs only nine times in the New Testament; the term *Israēl* occurs sixty-eight times (in Paul seventeen times).

term *Jews* (Gk *Ioudaioi*) is used much more frequently, as it is in the texts of the New Testament.[14] The Greek expression *Ioudaioi* transliterates the Hebrew *Yehudi* and the Aramaic *Yehudai*. These terms refer in Old Testament texts to the tribe of Judah or to the ancestor of this tribe. After the division of Israel's kingdom (in the time after Solomon), it was the name of the southern kingdom, with Jerusalem as the capital city. After the destruction of Solomon's temple, the term was used for the administrative area around Jerusalem, controlled in turn by the Persians, the Ptolemies, the Seleucids and then the Romans. During this time, the term *Jews* designates the descendants of Abraham, the members of the people of Israel, without reference to membership in a particular tribe and without regard for one's place of residence. Diaspora Jews referred to themselves as "Jews," which was common in the Greek world, using terms such as *Israel* (Gk *Israēl*) or *Israelite (Israēlitai)* mostly in religious contexts.[15] In contrast, Palestinian and Babylonian Jews more commonly used the word *Israel* as a (self-)designation for the individual members of the people.

In Romans 9:4-5 Paul describes the Jews (or Israelites) as the people who are God's adopted people. They are the people who have seen God's glory on Sinai, in their history and in God's revelation. They are the people with whom God has repeatedly made covenants. They are the people to whom God gave his law. They are the people who truly worship God. They are the people to whom God has given promises regarding the restoration of God's people and of God's world. They are the people who trace their ancestry back to Abraham, Isaac and Jacob. They are the people among whom Jesus the Messiah was born. Sometimes Paul describes the Jews as the people who are circumcised.[16]

Paul is convinced that the Jews need to hear the news of Jesus the Messiah in order to be true members of God's new covenant people. In Romans 2 Paul argues that circumcision and the possession of the law are insufficient for finding favor with God and for escaping God's wrath

---

[14]For Paul cf. Rom 1:16; 2:9, 10, 17, 28, 29; 3:1, 9, 29; 9:24; 10:12; 1 Cor 1:22, 23, 24; 9:20; 10:32; 12:13; 2 Cor 11:24; Gal 2:13, 14, 15; 3:28; 1 Thess 2:14. The term *Ioudaioi* occurs 195 times in the New Testament. On *Ioudaios, Israēl /Israēlitai* and *Hebraios* see Gerhard von Rad, Karl Georg Kuhn and Walter Gutbrod, *TDNT*, 3:355-90.

[15]Cf. 3 Macc 2:6, 10; see also 3 Macc 6:32; 7:16, 23. Cf. H. Kuhli, *EDNT*, 2:194.

[16]Cf. Rom 2:25-29; 3:1; 4:9-12; 1 Cor 7:19; Gal 2:7, 8, 9, 12; Col 3:11; 4:11; Tit 1:10; cf. Phil 3:5.

of judgment (Rom 1:18). Paul asserts that the law is "holy, and the commandment is holy and just and good" (Rom 7:12). In other words, the Mosaic law is the good gift of Israel's holy God, and its individual commandments are thus holy, fair and beneficial. However, the law does not now forgive the sin of sinners: the Jews are "under sin" just as the pagans are "under sin" (Rom 3:9).[17] This can only mean that the sacrifices and other rituals that were prescribed in the Mosaic law and were God's gracious provision for the atonement for the sins of the people and for the individual Israelite no longer forgive sins. Paul preaches and writes— always—as a missionary in the time after Jesus' death and resurrection, proclaiming faith in Jesus as the Messiah who is the Son of God in whom God had revealed himself and whose death atones the sins of all people, both Jews and Gentiles.

> But now, apart from law, the righteousness of God has been disclosed, and is attested by the law and the prophets, the righteousness of God through faith in Jesus Christ for all who believe. For there is no distinction, since all have sinned and fall short of the glory of God; they are now justified by his grace as a gift, through the redemption that is in Jesus Christ, whom God put forward as a sacrifice of atonement by his blood, effective through faith. (Rom 3:21-25)

There is no distinction between Jews and Gentiles with regard to their status before God as far as their sins are concerned. They are both helplessly exposed to God's wrath, which condemns sinners (Rom 1:18—3:20). Paul argues that there is no distinction between Jews and Gentiles as regards the possibility of being justified by God, that is, of being declared "righteous" on the Day of Judgment and thus being received into the gracious and eternal presence of God. Justification of sinners is possible on account of God's free gift of salvation, to be accepted by faith in God's saving revelation in Jesus the Messiah, who died for sinners (Rom 3:21—5:21).

---

[17]On the complex question of the law in Paul's theology see Stephen Westerholm, *Israel's Law and the Church's Faith: Paul and His Recent Interpreters* (Grand Rapids: Eerdmans, 1988); Frank Thielman, *Paul and the Law: A Contextual Approach* (Downers Grove, Ill.: InterVarsity Press, 1994); Colin G. Kruse, *Paul, the Law and Justification* (Downers Grove, Ill.: InterVarsity Press, 1996); Frank Thielman, *The Law and the New Testament: The Question of Continuity* (New York: Crossroad, 1999).

Because Jews who do not believe in Jesus have no "interface" with God's new revelation in and through the Messiah and his death and resurrection, Paul has "great sorrow and unceasing anguish" in his heart (Rom 9:2). Paul knows that God has not rejected his people (Israel) as a whole (Rom 11:1), proven by the fact that he, a Jew, has come to faith in Jesus the Messiah (as have other Jews). The Jews have "zeal for God" (Rom 10:2), but they ignore the righteousness which God has now revealed (Rom 10:3). God's righteousness, that is, the gift of righteousness that God gives to his people, is bound up no longer with the Mosaic law but with Jesus the Messiah (Christ) who is the *telos* of the Mosaic law (Rom 10:4). Jesus, God's promised Messiah, is both the goal of the law (enabling God's people to live in the presence of Israel's holy God) and the end of the law (regarding its function to establish and maintain holiness and purity).[18] Divine grace and human works are no longer compatible: sinners are justified only when they put their faith in God and in Jesus Christ, acknowledging that Jesus died for their sins and that he was raised by God to new life, sitting at the right hand of God as Lord. *This is why Paul preaches to Jews—without faith in Jesus the Messiah they do not receive the gift of God's righteousness: they remain under the death sentence that the law pronounces upon sinners.*[19]

The "Gentiles" (Gk *ta ethnē*) or the "Greeks" (Gk *Hellēn*) are the people who do not belong to Israel, who are not Jewish, who are not members of God's covenant people and who are not circumcised. In the Septuagint and in the Jewish literature of the postexilic period, the Greek term *ta ethnē* does not simply designate "peoples, nations" but (1) the "nations" of

---

[18]See Robert Badenas, *Christ the End of the Law: Romans 10.4 in Pauline Perspective*, JSNTSup 10 (Sheffield, U.K.: JSOT Press, 1985).

[19]The vexing question of the meaning of Rom 11:26—whether Paul anticipates a mass conversion of Jews in the future, or whether he refers to the mode of how Jews are at present being saved, or whether he describes the sum of all Jewish and Gentile believers as "all Israel"—will not be addressed here; cf. François Refoulé, *"... et ainsi tout Israël sera sauvé." Romains 11.25-32*, LD 117 (Paris: Cerf, 1984); N. T. Wright, *The Climax of the Covenant: Christ and the Law in Pauline Theology* (Philadelphia: Fortress, 1992), pp. 231-57; Daniel J.-S. Chae, *Paul as Apostle to the Gentiles: His Apostolic Self-Awareness and its Influence on the Soteriological Argument in Romans* (Carlisle, U.K.: Paternoster, 1997), pp. 215-88; Andreas J. Köstenberger and Peter T. O'Brien, *Salvation to the Ends of the Earth: A Biblical Theology of Mission*, NSBT 11 (Downers Grove, Ill.: InterVarsity Press, 2001), pp. 185-91; Eckhard J. Schnabel, *Early Christian Mission* (Downers Grove, Ill.: InterVarsity Press, 2004), 2:1309-19.

the world, including the nation of Israel, (2) "(all) nations" in distinction to Israel, (3) the individual "pagans," that is, non-Israelites and non-Jews. Paul uses the term *ta ethnē* in this sense: as designation for the "nations" of the world, including Israel,[20] as designation for "(all) nations" in distinction to the people of Israel,[21] as designation for individual "pagans," that is, non-Jews,[22] and in the sense of "non-Jews" also for non-Jewish ("Gentile") Christians.[23]

The English term *Gentile*[24] is derived from Latin *gentilis*, which means "belonging to the same family or clan *(gens)*, stock, or race," which came to be used in later ecclesiastical language for "heathen" and "pagan," defined as "of or pertaining to any or all of the nations other than the Jewish." When Jerome translated the Bible into Latin in the fourth century, the Latin adjective *gentilis* received the negative meaning "belonging to a non-Roman, barbaric people." Jerome translated the Greek terms *Hellēn* and *Hellēnistēs* fourteen times with *gentilis*, only three times with *Graeci* ("the Greeks"); twice *gentilis* is the translation of the Greek term *ethnē* (Acts 14:5; Rom 15:27), marking the origin of the later polemical meaning of the term in the sense of "Gentile" that had come close in meaning to the Latin term *paganus*. The term *heathen* is (perhaps) etymologically linked with the Celtic-Germanic root **kaito-* meaning "forest, uncultivated tract of land," reconstructed as the Proto-Germanic cardinal form **haithanas*, from which are derived Old English (Anglo-Saxon) *hǣ´ðen*, Old Frisian *hêthin*, Old High German *heidan*, Middle High German *heiden*, English *heathen*, German *heide*.[25] The terms *Gentile* and *heathen* were used as a translation of Latin *paganus* (from *pagus*, "district, countryside"). In other words, "Gentiles" or "heathen" were "country people"—the *paganus* is the nonmilitant or the civilian, the nonspecialist or layperson, the people dwelling in the countryside, the villager. In the Vulgate, the term *paganus* is not used. Because the term *heathen* is used in all the Germanic languages in the sense "non-Christian, pagan," a meaning which could have

---

[20]Rom 4:17, 18; Gal 3:8.
[21]Rom 1:5, 13-14; 15:10-11; Gal 2:15.
[22]Rom 11:13; 1 Cor 12:2; Eph 2:11.
[23]Rom 11:13; 15:27; 16:4; Gal 2:12, 14; Eph 3:1; cf. Acts 15:19, 23.
[24]For the following see Schnabel, *Early Christian Mission*, 1:37-40.
[25]See *Oxford English Dictionary* s.v. "heathen."

arisen only after the introduction of Christianity, many scholars think that the term was probably first used in Gothic, from where it was passed on to other Germanic tribes. This is supported by Bishop Ulfilas's translation in Mark 7:26, where he translates the Latin phrase *mulier gentilis* (Gk *hē gynē ēn Hellēnis*, "the woman was a Greek") with *haipnô;* this word is probably adapted from the Gothic term *haipi* "hearth", thus "dweller on the heath" as a loose translation of Latin *paganus* ("villager"). Others suggest Armenian influence on the language of Ulfilas, with *haipnô* indicating the masculine form *haipans* which could adapt Armenian *het'anos* "heathen," a term adapted from Greek *ethnos* meaning "nation" or "non-Jewish people."

Paul agrees with the Jewish assessment that Gentiles are ungodly and wicked (Rom 1:18) because they suppress the truth which God the Creator revealed in his creation (Rom 1:18-20). They do not honor God as he must be honored, and as a result they have become futile in their thinking (Rom 1:21-22). The futility and pointlessness of all human efforts to succeed is a pervasive state of affairs, seen in the two main areas of human existence. First, as human beings seek to transcend the visible realm, acknowledging the existence of a higher being, their foolishness is proven by the fact that instead of worshiping the glory of the immortal God, they bow before images of human beings or birds or animals or reptiles that they have made themselves (Rom 1:23). Second, as human beings seek to arrange themselves in the visible world in their everyday living, their foolishness is proven by the fact that they follow their lusts and passions, they live impure lives, they dishonor their bodies, they serve the creature rather than the Creator (Rom 1:24-27). Specifically, the "base mind and improper conduct" of human beings is seen in the occurrence of "all manner of wickedness, evil, covetousness, malice. Full of envy, murder, strife, deceit, craftiness, they are gossips, slanderers, God-haters, insolent, haughty, boastful, inventors of evil, rebellious toward parents, foolish, faithless, heartless, ruthless" (Rom 1:29-31). *Since "those who practice such things deserve to die" (Rom 1:32), and since God has provided a way to life through Jesus Christ, who died for sinners and who rose to new life, Paul preaches the good news of Jesus the Savior to Gentiles.*

4.3 GEOGRAPHICAL MOVEMENT

Some have suggested that the geographical scope of Paul's missionary work can be explained with the help of Old Testament texts. One suggestion proceeds from the observation that Paul interpreted his missionary calling in terms of the mission of the Servant of the Lord in the book of Isaiah.[26] The mission of the Servant of the Lord reaches the "ends of the earth" (Is 49:6). When God comes "to gather all nations and tongues," the nations come to Zion and see God's glory (Is 66:18). From among the nations who come to Zion and see God's glory, God will send "survivors of the nations" as his messengers to the nations (Is 66:19): they first go to Tarshish (Tarsus), then they reach in a semicircular movement that proceeds in a northwesterly direction the regions of Put (Cilicia), Lud (Lydia), Meshech (Mysia), Tubal (Bithynia), Javan (Greece, Macedonia), and the distant coastlands (the regions in the far west, Spain). This geographical "program" may explain why Paul planned a mission to Spain but not a mission to Gaul (modern France).

This explanation is attractive because it acknowledges the significance of Israel's Scriptures for Paul's theology, particularly the importance of the book of Isaiah. However, it cannot ultimately explain Paul's geographical movements. First, the two geographical endpoints that Paul mentions in Romans 15:19 (Jerusalem and Illyrium) are not mentioned in the geographical "program" of Isaiah 66:19. Second, the envoys of Isaiah 66:19 are Gentiles who have survived God's judgment, a notion that can hardly be applied to Paul, who is a Jew. Third, the geographical identifications in Isaiah 66:19 do not fit Paul's movements: Tarshish is usually identified with Tartessos in Spain; and Pul (the Septuagint reads *Phoud*)[27] is perhaps a place in North Africa. It seems unlikely that Paul abandoned this tradition for the geographical identification found in the book of Judith, which links "Put and Lud" with Cilicia (Jdt 2:23). The identification of

---

[26]Rainer Riesner, *Paul's Early Period: Chronology, Mission Strategy, Theology* (Grand Rapids: Eerdmans, 1998), pp. 245-53.

[27]The most likely original reading of the Hebrew text is *Pul*. The Septuagint has *Phoud*, which is preferred by many translations and commentators because this seems to agree with the name "Put" (which occurs in Jer 46:9; Ezek 27:10; 30:5). In these texts where the Hebrew (Masoretic) text has "Put" the Septuagint translates with *Libyes* (which we would expect in Is 66:19 if "Put" was original). Cf. John N. Oswalt, *The Book of Isaiah. Chapters 40—66*, NICOT (Grand Rapids: Eerdmans, 1986), pp. 681-82 n. 62.

Meshech with Mysia and of Tubal with Bithynia—two areas in which Paul planned missionary work that he was eventually not able to carry out—is selective: in contemporary Jewish traditions, Tubal is identified not only with Bithynia but sometimes with Iberia/Spain (Josephus) and with Europe from Bulgaria to France (Jubilees); and Meshech is identified not only with Mysia but also with Cappadocia (Josephus), with Spain and France (Jubilees), and with Illyricum (Hippolytus).[28] Also, the first fifteen years of Paul's missionary work in Nabatea, in Syria and in Cilicia between A.D. 32/33-45 remain without explanation if Isaiah 66:19 provides the blueprint for Paul's mission.

Another suggestion surmises that the apostles divided the world in terms of the regions in which the descendants of Noah lived, as listed in the Table of Nations (Genesis 10). Interpreted against this background, Paul evidently saw himself as a missionary to the territory of Japheth, Noah's third son. This explains why Paul preached the gospel "from Jerusalem to Illyricum" (Rom 15:19) and why he wanted to go to Spain (Rom 15:22-24, 28-29): he engaged in missionary work in Asia Minor and in Europe, the territory in which Japheth and his descendants settled.[29]

The diverse geographical identifications in Jewish (and in early patristic) traditions and the details of Paul's actual missionary work render it doubtful whether his missionary strategy was informed by the tradition of the Table of Nations in Genesis 10. First, this explanation ignores the first fifteen years of Paul's missionary work in Nabatea, Syria and Cilicia. Paul's "independent" mission did *not* begin after the apostles' council in A.D. 48, but already in A.D. 32/33, immediately after his conversion when he went to Arabia/Nabatea and to Syria and Cilicia (cf. Gal 1:17; 2 Cor 11:32; see sec. 1.2). Arabia belongs to the territory of the descendants of Mizraim, that is, to the territory of Ham. Second, Paul's plan to preach the gospel in the "province of Asia" (Acts 16:6), that is, in the geographical region of Lydia, is a problem for this interpretation since Lud was a son of Shem (Gen 10:22). Because Paul was prevented from preaching

---

[28]See James M. Scott, *Paul and the Nations: The Old Testament and Early Jewish Background of Paul's Mission to the Nations with Special Reference to the Destination of Galatians*, WUNT 84 (1995, reprint, Tübingen: Mohr-Siebeck, 2002), pp. 8-49 (table 3).

[29]Scott, *Paul and the Nations*, pp. 135-80.

the gospel in the province of Asia according to Acts 16:6, this hypothesis survives in terms of Paul's actual movement at this point in Acts 16, but not in terms of Paul's intention. When Paul at a later stage reaches the province of Asia (Acts 19), planting a church in the city of Ephesus, the "Japheth hypothesis" is defended with the observation that Paul engaged in missionary work in the city of Ephesus, which was established by Ionian colonists—connecting this region with Javan, one of the sons of Japheth. Paul's missionary work in the province of Asia, that is, in the territory which the Greeks called Lydia (which did not belong to the territory of Japheth), has to be minimized as having been a more indirect ministry. This interpretation, as intriguing as it may appear, is not convincing. Paul's statement in Colossians 1:7 ("Epaphras . . . is a faithful minister of Christ on our behalf") suggests that he regarded Epaphras's missionary work in the Lykos Valley in the eastern part of the province of Asia as an integral part of his own missionary work. Third, the only identifications of Japheth's descendants that are not controversial in Jewish and in the patristic traditions is the identification of Javan with Ionia (or the Greeks) and the identification of Madai with the Medes. Paul did go to "Javan" (Athens, Corinth), but he did not go to Media. The suggestion that Paul understood his missionary work as being responsible for the territory of "Japheth" is not convincing.

The evidence shows that Paul preached the gospel in Damascus (Syria), Arabia, Antioch (Syria), Cilicia (Tarsus and other cities), on Cyprus (Paphos), in the province of Galatia (Pisidian Antioch, Iconium, Lystra, Derbe), Macedonia (Philippi, Thessalonica, Beroea), Achaia (Athens, Corinth), the province of Asia (Ephesus), and, if he was released from the (first) Roman imprisonment, in Spain and perhaps on Crete. When it proved impossible to reach a certain region where he had planned missionary outreach, as was the case with the project of a mission to the provinces of Asia, Bithynia and Mysia (Acts 16:7-8), Paul does not go home but goes on to visit other cities in regions whose citizens need to hear the gospel as well.

It appears that the geographical strategy which informed Paul's missionary work targeted the cities of neighboring regions and provinces. He moved from Damascus in Syria to Arabia, a region immediately to the south of Damascus. He traveled from Jerusalem to Tarsus, the main city of the region (Cilicia) north of Syria, probably because it was his home town. From Tarsus/Cilicia he moved to Antioch, the capital of the province of Syria immediately to the south of Cilicia. From Antioch in Syria he traveled to Salamis and Paphos on Cyprus, a region immediately east of Syria. Next, he moved from Cyprus to southern Galatia, a region north of Cyprus. Then he targeted cities in the province of Asia, immediately to the west of southern Galatia, the next "logical" step. When this plan could not be realized, he targeted the province of Pontus and Bithynia to the north. When this plan could not be realized, he moved to Macedonia (Philippi, Thessalonica, Beroea), the next province to the west. The move to Athens and Corinth reached cities in Achaia, the province immediately south of Macedonia.

Paul does not seem to have followed a "grand strategy" with regard to his geographical movements. The available evidence indicates that Paul moved to geographically adjacent areas that were open for missionary work. Paul preached in the regions between Damascus (the city of his conversion), Jerusalem (the city of his education) and Tarsus (the city of his birth)—Arabia, Cilicia, Syria—before reaching out to the regions further west: Cyprus and Galatia, Asia and Pontus/Bithynia (attempt aborted). With his missionary work in Macedonia and Achaia, regions again further west of Asia Minor, he reached the homeland of the Greeks. The second (successful) attempt to reach the province of Asia filled the "gap" in Paul's movement west. The next goal was Spain, the westernmost region in the northern part of the Mediterranean world. Between Italy and Spain was the province of Gaul (modern France). Did Paul intend to bypass this region, which was Hellenized and which had large cities (Massalia, Narbo) where he could have preached? We do not know the answer to this question. It is possible (but not proven) that coworkers of Paul were active in Gaul. Paul informed Timothy in his last letter from prison in Rome that Crescens went to Galatia (2 Tim 4:10). The Greek word *Galatia* can describe (1) the Roman province of Galatia in central Asia Minor, (2) the region of the Celtic Galatians in the north of the province of Galatia, and (3) the Roman province of Gaul (Lat. *Gallia*). Several New Testament manuscripts clarify the matter by reading *eis Gallian*[30] rather than *eis Galatian*). Some argue that this clarification represents the intended meaning of the original text.[31]

Paul's main burden and concern was to preach the news of God's saving revelation in Jesus Christ to as many people as possible, to Jewish and to Gentile audiences, particularly in areas where it had never been proclaimed (Gal 2:7; Rom 15:14-21). It was natural to look for audiences in geographically adjacent areas. It appears that this is exactly what Paul did.

4.4 CONVERSION OF INDIVIDUALS

The goal of Paul's missionary work is the conversion of Jews and pagans to faith in Jesus Messiah, Savior and Lord, the transformation of traditional patterns of religious, ethical and social behavior, and the integration into the community of fellow believers.[32] In Luke's description of Paul's conversion and missionary calling, he articulates the apostle's conviction that he has been called by Jesus the Messiah to help the Gentiles "turn *[epistrepsal]* from darkness to light and from the power of Satan to God" (Acts 26:18). In narratives the Greek term *epistrephō* denotes, as does the Hebrew term *šûb*, physical movements, turnings, changes of place.[33] It means "to return to a point where one has been, to turn around, to go back" or "to change direction, to turn around." Used figuratively (as here), it means "to cause a person to change belief or course of conduct, with focus on the thing to which one turns" or "to change one's mind or course of action."[34]

---

[30]The manuscripts ℵ C 81.104.326 *pc* vg[st.ww] sa bo[pt], as well as Eusebius and Epiphanius.

[31]See Ceslas Spicq, *Les Épîtres pastorales*, Quatrième édition refondue, Éditions Bibliques (Paris: Gabalda, 1969), 2:811-13; see also Joseph B. Lightfoot, *Biblical Essays*, 2nd ed. (London: MacMillan, 1904), p. 432; John N. D. Kelly, *A Commentary on the Pastoral Epistles* (1963; reprint, Grand Rapids: Thornapple Commentaries; 1986), p. 213; Victor Hasler, *Die Briefe an Timotheus und Titus (Pastoralbriefe)*, ZBK 12 (Zürich: Theologischer Verlag, 1978), pp. 79-80.

[32]On conversion cf. Richard V. Peace, *Conversion in the New Testament: Paul and the Twelve* (Grand Rapids: Eerdmans, 1999); Stephen J. Chester, *Conversion at Corinth: Perspectives on Conversion in Paul's Theology and the Corinthian Church*, Studies of the New Testament and its World (Edinburgh: T & T Clark, 2003); see also Richard N. Longenecker, *The Road from Damascus: The Impact of Paul's Conversion on His Life, Thought, and Ministry* (Grand Rapids: Eerdmans, 1997).

[33]Georg Bertram, *TDNT*, 7:723.

[34]BDAG, p. 382.

Paul asserts that when Jews "turn" (Gk *epistrephō*) to the Lord, God removes the "veil" that had covered their eyes and prevented them from understanding the Scriptures as pointing to Jesus of Nazareth as the messianic Savior (2 Cor 3:16). When polytheists are converted, they "turn *[epistrephō]* to God from idols, to serve a living and true God" (1 Thess 1:9). Paul is concerned that the believers in the churches in Galatia, after they had turned to God and come to faith in Jesus Christ, might give in to false teaching and "turn back again to the weak and beggarly elemental spirits" (Gal 4:9). In his account of Paul's missionary work, Luke refers to "conversion" (*epistrophē, epistrephō)* more frequently.[35] Whether this indicates that Paul spoke of conversion only rarely is questionable, since his letters represent only a small portion of the linguistic "register" of the apostle. Paul writes to followers of Jesus for whom consistent commitment to Jesus Christ is a more significant topic than conversion that they had already experienced. In his missionary preaching before Jews who had not yet come to faith in Jesus Christ, Paul challenged his listeners to turn away from relying on the Mosaic law, on circumcision or on good works for salvation and to come to faith in Jesus the Messiah. In his missionary preaching before Gentile audiences Paul challenged his listeners to turn away from the traditional gods they worshiped in their families and in their cities, and to turn to the one true and living God the Creator and to Jesus, who is the one and only Savior. Paul was convinced that the existence as a follower of Jesus had a definite, clear beginning, as

> he simply took it for granted that his audiences were made up of individuals who had gone through a significant transition in their experience. They had responded to Paul's (or his team's) preaching, made some kind of confessional commitment to Jesus as Lord, and been baptized in Jesus' name. They had experienced God's grace and had become members of a group whose mutual interdependence and ethos were expected to characterize their whole lives.[36]

Another term Paul uses to describe conversion is the Greek term *metanoia* (verb *metanoeō*).[37] The significant semantic connotation of the

---

[35]Acts 13:38; 17:30; 20:21; 26:18, 20.
[36]James D. G. Dunn, *The Theology of Paul the Apostle* (Grand Rapids: Eerdmans, 1998), p. 328.
[37]See Johannes Behm and Ernst Würthwein, *TDNT,* 4:975-1008; Helmut Merklein, *EDNT*

term is the concept of change (of mind), both in a good and a bad sense. The verb can mean "to perceive afterwards or too late" (to be sorry for), "to change one's mind" or "to change one's opinion." The Septuagint uses the term to translate Hebrew *niham* "to be sorry (for something)." The Hebrew term *šûb* (which the Septuagint translates as *epistrephō*) is again decisive for the use of this term in the New Testament: "repentance" is a turning away from sin (Mk 1:4-5). Repentance is prompted by the imminence of God's judgment (Mt 3:10) which nullified all recourse to the former means of salvation (Mt 3:9). In John the Baptist's preaching, repentance was indeed a return to Yahweh, but not simply a return to the law that Yahweh had given at Mount Sinai, but a return to Israel's God whose Day of Judgment is imminent and who is about to send the promised Savior. In Jesus' ministry repentance is prompted by the arrival of the kingdom of God in his words and deeds (Lk 10:9, 13; 11:32; 13:3-5) and thus entails, positively, acknowledgement of the message and the mission of Jesus and commitment to his words and deeds (Lk10:13; 11:32). In the book of Acts, repentance is connected with the forgiveness of sins (Acts 2:38; 3:19; 5:31; 8:22; 26:18, 20) and with baptism and the reception of salvation and of the Spirit (Acts 2:38; 11:18). The death and resurrection of Jesus the Messiah provide a new possibility for both Jews and Gentiles to repent and to receive the forgiveness of sins, which is to be proclaimed to all nations, beginning in Jerusalem (Acts 2:38; 3:19; 5:31; 11:18; 17:30; 20:21; 26:20). Repentance is a turning away from ignorance on the basis of God's revelation in Jesus (Acts 3:17, 19; 17:30). Positively it is a turning toward God, manifested in belief in the Lord Jesus (Acts 20:21; 26:18, 20). Paul emphasizes that it is the goodness and the patience of God that are meant to lead people to repentance (Rom 2:4).

Paul interprets the conversion of Jews and Gentiles as a "demonstration of the Spirit and power" (1 Cor 2:4; cf. 1 Thess 1:5). Turning to the true and living God and to Jesus Christ presupposes that Jews acknowledge that Jesus is the Messiah and that his death atones for sins. For Gentiles it presupposes that they acknowledge that there is one true and living

---

2:415-19. The noun *metanoia* occurs twenty-two times in the New Testament. Paul uses it in Rom 2:4; 2 Cor 7:9, 10; 2 Tim 2:25 (cf. Acts 13:24; 19:4; 20:21; 26:20). The verb *metanoeō* occurs thirty-four times in the New Testament. Paul uses it in 2 Cor 12:21 (cf. Acts 17:30; 26:20).

God, the Creator, who revealed himself in Jesus of Nazareth, who died on a cross but who rose from the dead on the third day and who is thus the one true Lord and Savior. These are matters that are not easy to believe. For Jews, faith in a crucified Messiah on account of whose death the God of Israel forgives the sins of the world is an offensive provocation. For pagans, faith in a crucified Jew whose death forgives all sins and who came back from the dead is laughable nonsense (1 Cor 1:18-25; see sec. 5.5). This is why conversions to faith in Jesus the crucified Messiah, Savior and Lord—when they happen—are the result of the powerful work of God's Spirit and power. It is only God who can cause people to come to faith in Jesus Christ.

According to Romans 10:9, conversion happens through the confession *(homologia)* by which individuals turn to God and his Messiah. The confession consists in "the acknowledgment that the believer stands before God as the transgressor who can win his salvation not by his own ability but only through God's grace and through the help of the *Kyrios*."[38]

Paul's reminder in 1 Corinthians 6:9-11 helps us to understand the apostle's understanding of the conversion of Gentiles:

> Do you not know that wrongdoers will not inherit the kingdom of God? Do not be deceived! Fornicators, idolaters, adulterers, male prostitutes, sodomites, thieves, the greedy, drunkards, revilers, robbers—none of these will inherit the kingdom of God. And this is what some of you used to be. But you were washed, you were sanctified, you were justified in the name of the Lord Jesus Christ and in the Spirit of our God.

The "vices" that Paul mentions represent, in part, accepted behavior of pagans: visiting prostitutes, worshiping various Greek, Roman and Egyptian gods, engaging in homosexual activity, being greedy and getting drunk during banquets. These activities represent behavior that did not raise eyebrows in the cities of the Greco-Roman world. Paul's missionary preaching did not present a solution to a moral crisis that his pagan listeners would have perceived as such. A proverb asserted that "bathing, wine, and Venus wear out the body but are the real stuff of life."[39] This does not

---

[38]Peter Stuhlmacher, *Biblische Theologie des Neuen Testaments* (Göttingen: Vandenhoeck & Ruprecht, 1992/1999), 1:344 (my translation), with reference to Gal 2:16; 1 Cor 1:26-30.

[39]Paul Veyne, "The Roman Empire," in *A History of Private Life*, vol.1: *From Pagan Rome to Byz-*

mean, however, that the ancients were self-indulgent, licentious sensualists who lived out every imaginable passion. The pagans were "paralyzed" by prohibitions of all sorts. Amorous passion was feared by the Romans since it could turn a free man into the slave of a woman or of a boy. But they did, of course, visit prostitutes and engage in homosexual acts. In a speech (falsely) attributed to Demosthenes, we read the famously notorious dictum that "we have courtesans for pleasure, and concubines for the daily service of our bodies, but wives for the production of legitimate offspring and to have a reliable guardian of our household property."[40] The small town of Pompeii, with a population of perhaps ten thousand inhabitants, boasted at least twenty-two brothels. A prostitute could be had for one, two or three As (a daily portion of bread cost two As).[41] If the various prohibitions of society provoked anxiety, the ancients had "tranquilizers" at hand, which they used depending on their social status: religious activity through which the offended deities would hopefully be appeased; magic through which the power of the transcendent could be made real; philosophical reflection through which the individual might obtain happiness.[42]

Paul argues in his missionary preaching that the pagans' moral contentment is the result of their failure to recognize the consequences of their behavior in view of the coming Day of Judgment, for which God has already appointed a judge, namely Jesus Christ (cf. Acts 17:30-31). Paul seeks to move his pagan listeners "from false contentment to crisis to security in Christ."[43] The transformation that conversion to faith in the Creator God and in Jesus Christ causes affects both the individual's conscience and his or her moral and social identity. Pagans recognize that what they had accepted, or at least tolerated, as reasonable or justifiable behavior made them guilty before the one true and living God, result-

---

antium, ed. P. Veyne (1987; reprint, Cambridge: Harvard University Press, 2003), p. 183; for the following discussion see ibid., pp. 202-5.

[40]Pseudo-Demosthenes *Epigramma* 59, 122; cf. Athenaeus *Deipnosophistae* 13, 573B. On prostitution in antiquity cf. Aline Rousselle, *Porneia; On Desire and the Body in Antiquity* (Oxford and New York: Blackwell, 1988); Thomas A. J. McGinn, *The Economy of Prostitution in the Roman World: A Study of Social History and the Brothel* (Ann Arbor: University of Michigan Press, 2004).

[41]See Ines Stahlmann, "Brothel," *BNP*, 2:790.

[42]Veyne, "Roman Empire," pp. 207-33.

[43]Chester, *Conversion at Corinth*, p. 147.

ing in condemnation to eternal death. They recognize that the one true
and living God expects behavior that involves a break with many of the
traditional values of society. They recognize repentance leads not only
to changed values but also to changed behavior. And they recognize (or
learn!) that the power of God's Spirit transforms their lives so that they
are no longer practicing the "works of the flesh" but manifest in their behavior the "fruit of the Spirit."

> Now the works of the flesh are obvious: fornication, impurity, licentious-
> ness, idolatry, sorcery, enmities, strife, jealousy, anger, quarrels, dissen-
> sions, factions, envy, drunkenness, carousing, and things like these. I am
> warning you, as I warned you before, those who do such things will not
> inherit the kingdom of God. By contrast, the fruit of the Spirit is love, joy,
> peace, patience, kindness, generosity, faithfulness, gentleness, self-control.
> There is no law against such things. And those who belong to Christ Jesus
> have crucified the flesh with its passions and desires. (Gal 5:19-24)

This transformation entails obedience to the Jewish Scriptures (e.g., in
the various areas of sexual behavior), to the word of Jesus Christ and to the
teaching of the apostles.

Conversion thus establishes a particular kind of relationship between
the new believer and God, his Spirit and Jesus Christ. The character of
this relationship is expressed in baptism, the action by which a person
publicly admits his or her need for purification, symbolized through immersion in water.[44] The Greek verb *baptizō* means "to immerse," the noun
baptismos means "immersion." In Greek texts this term of course does not
mean "(Christian) water baptism." The verb always means "to immerse"
and can therefore describe the "sinking" of a ship (which is "immersed" in
water) or the drowning of a person. Sometimes the verb means "to bathe,
to wash," for example, in the case of Naaman, who immersed himself
seven times in the Jordan (2 Kings 5:14). When Jews and Gentiles come
to faith in Jesus Christ they are immersed in water, that is, they are "bap-

---

[44]On baptism in the New Testament cf. James D. G. Dunn, *Baptism in the Holy Spirit: A Re-
Examination of the New Testament Teaching on the Gift of the Spirit in Relation to Pentecostalism
Today* (London: SCM, 1970); George R. Beasley-Murray, *Baptism in the New Testament*, 3rd ed.
(1962; reprint, Exeter, U.K.: Paternoster, 1979); for Paul cf. Alexander J. M. Wedderburn, *Baptism
and Resurrection: Studies in Pauline Theology Against its Graeco-Roman Background*, WUNT 44
(Tübingen: Mohr-Siebeck, 1987); George R. Beasley-Murray, "Baptism," *DPL*, pp. 60-66.

tized." This action demonstrates that they confess their sins, they admit their need for cleansing and purification, and they acknowledge their need for being reconciled with God. It also expresses their conviction that God forgives their sins on account of the death and resurrection of Jesus Christ. The reality that baptism expresses is denoted in the phrase "in the name of" (Gk *eis to onoma*). This phrase is a formula of transfer used in legal and commercial texts as a technical term meaning "to the account of (over which the name stands)." This background indicates that new believers in Jesus Christ who are immersed in water "become the possession of and come under the dedicated protection of the one whose name they bear."[45] The person who has come to faith in Jesus enters into a new relationship to God who now is Lord. The Christian belongs to God, his life is determined by Jesus Christ, and his behavior is ruled by the Holy Spirit. The fact that Paul himself did not regularly baptize the new converts (1 Cor 1:13-17) and that he did not describe his missionary task in terms of baptism (1 Cor 1:17) does not mean that he is not interested in conversions. It appears that he asked his coworkers, or recently baptized converts, to assist the new followers of Jesus when they were immersed in water.

An important corollary of conversion is joy (1 Thess 1:5-6), a gift of God's Spirit that transcends the anxieties of human existence (Rom 8:18, 22).[46] This joy was a reality that was a new experience for the Gentiles (Acts 13:48, 52; 16:34). "Smiles are rare in Greco-Roman art."[47] Followers of Jesus who had repented of their sin, turned to the one true and living God and believed in Jesus the messianic Lord and Savior experienced a joy that proved its worth even in the midst of suffering (Rom 8:31-39).

4.5 ESTABLISHING COMMUNITIES OF FOLLOWERS OF JESUS

Paul's missionary work did not end with the oral proclamation of the good news of Jesus Christ and the conversion of individuals. Paul established

---

[45]BDAG, p. 713; cf. Albrecht Oepke, *TDNT*, 1:537. Hans Bietenhard, *TDNT*, 5:274-5, derives the expression from the Hebrew term *leshem* ("with regard to the name") and suggests that it denotes (forensic) "appropriation." Similarly Lars Hartman, *EDNT* 2:522: "The expression gave the type, the basis, the purpose, and even the basic reference of a ritual. Thus, this formula would present baptism as a rite that is fundamentally determined by the person and work of Jesus."

[46]See Gerald F. Hawthorne, "Joy," *DLNTD*, pp. 600-605.

[47]Veyne, "Roman Empire," p. 229.

churches, communities of men and women who had come to faith in Jesus the Messiah and Savior, and who came together to study the Scriptures, to be instructed in the whole counsel of God, to learn and remember what Jesus Christ had done, to discover the will of God for their lives, and to celebrate God's salvation in Jesus Christ in prayers and in hymns and spiritual songs.[48]

Because Paul's preaching included the emphasis that the followers of Jesus the Messiah represent the fulfillment of God's promises regarding the restoration of Israel in the last days, it was impossible that the new converts "enjoyed" their new status as solitary Christians. The people of God exists not in the isolation of the individual member but in the corporate gathering for worship and instruction. This was true in Old Testament times when Israel regularly gathered in the temple during the great festivals that God's people were to celebrate together. And this was also true in the first century when Jews regularly gathered in the synagogues to study the Scriptures and to pray and sing.

When Jews and Gentiles were converted to faith in Jesus Christ, responding to Paul's preaching in the local synagogue or in the marketplace, Paul insisted that they continue to meet together for instruction and worship. The venue for these meetings was initially the local synagogue. As the followers of Jesus were regularly evicted by the leaders of the synagogues, they might meet in public lecture halls or, usually, in private houses.[49] When Paul writes letters to the Christians in the cities where he had engaged in missionary work, he does not write to individuals (e.g., the leaders of the church). He writes to the congregation as a whole. The establishment of local communities of believers fulfilled Jesus' missionary commission in Matthew 28:19-20 in which he emphasized that the Twelve whom he sent to the nations should "make disciples" and teach them to obey everything that he had commanded them. The missionary and the first new disciple constitute a community—a community of two

---

[48]See Robert Banks, *Paul's Idea of Community: The Early House Churches in their Historical Setting*, rev. ed. (Peabody, Mass.: Hendrickson, 1994); Everett Ferguson, *The Church of Christ: A Biblical Ecclesiology for Today* (Grand Rapids: Eerdmans, 1996); Roger W. Gehring, *House Church and Mission: The Importance of Household Structures in Early Christianity* (Peabody, Mass.: Hendrickson, 2004).

[49]For details regarding synagogues, lecture halls and private houses see section 5.2 (pp. 287-306).

people who gather in the name of Jesus, and thus a community for which Jesus had promised his presence (Mt 18:20). Since Paul was accompanied by coworkers, and since evidently a good number of people were converted already in the early stages of his missionary work, there was a community of believers in Jesus Christ right from the beginning.

In 1 Thessalonians, one of the earliest letters Paul wrote, he addresses the letter to "the church of the Thessalonians in God the Father and the Lord Jesus Christ" (1 Thess 1:1). The term *church* (Gk *ekklēsia*) has the same meaning as in Greek and Jewish circles: it describes the assembly in the city of Thessalonica as the "gathering" of the Thessalonian followers of Jesus. The continuation of Paul's greeting clarifies, however, that this gathering is different from the regular gatherings of the city council and also of the synagogue community. It is a gathering "in God the Father"; that is, it is governed by the presence and the will of God who is the Father of those who belong him as his family. And it is a gathering "in the Lord Jesus Christ"; that is, it is governed by the presence and the will of Jesus the Messiah, who is their Lord and Savior. The closing of the letter, where he requests that the letter be read to all the brothers and sisters, and that they greet each other with a holy kiss (1 Thess 5:26-27), shows that "Paul has in mind an actual gathering of the Thessalonian Christians."[50]

Paul describes the church as belonging to God, through whose power Jews and pagans found faith in Jesus, the crucified and risen Messiah and Savior.

> To the church of God that is in Corinth, to those who are sanctified in Christ Jesus, called to be saints, together with all those who in every place call on the name of our Lord Jesus Christ, both their Lord and ours. (1 Cor 1:2)
>
> To the church of God that is in Corinth, including all the saints throughout Achaia. (2 Cor 1:1)

The expression "church of God" means "the church that God brought into existence" and which therefore belongs to God.[51] In Romans 16:16 the parallel expression "the churches of Christ" denotes the local com-

---

[50]Peter T. O'Brien, "Church," *DPL*, p. 124.
[51]In technical grammatical terms, the genitive "of God" (Gk *tou theou*) is a subjective or a possessive genitive.

munities of people who belong to the Messiah. "Such an *ekklēsia* was not simply a human association or a religious club, but a divinely created entity. As in the case of ancient Israel, the gatherings referred to by our term were in order to hear the word of God and to worship."[52]

In several passages Paul describes the community of the followers of Jesus as a heavenly gathering.

> Giving thanks to the Father, who has enabled you to share in the inheritance of the saints in the light. He has rescued us from the power of darkness and transferred us into the kingdom of his beloved Son, in whom we have redemption, the forgiveness of sins. . . .
>
> He is the head of the body, the church; he is the beginning, the firstborn from the dead, so that he might come to have first place in everything. (Col 1:12-14, 18)

> And he has put all things under his feet and has made him the head over all things for the church, which is his body, the fullness of him who fills all in all. (Eph 1:22-23)

> But God, who is rich in mercy, out of the great love with which he loved us even when we were dead through our trespasses, made us alive together with Christ—by grace you have been saved—and raised us up with him and seated us with him in the heavenly places in Christ Jesus. (Eph 2:4-6)

The designation of the church as "the body of Christ" asserts that Jesus Christ is the "head" of the church. This means that the local community of the followers of Jesus owes its existence to Jesus Christ. It also means that the life of the Christian community is directed by Jesus Christ. These passages are often interpreted in terms of the church universal, the totality of followers of Jesus scattered throughout the world. The point that Paul makes has a somewhat different focus, however. Paul emphasizes that the followers of Jesus Christ presently exist in a heavenly realm. The local gatherings of Christians, meeting in private houses, were earthly manifestations of that heavenly gathering around the crucified and risen Jesus Christ. The fellowship of believers in Jesus Christ represents a gathering that takes place in heaven where Jesus Christ is exalted at the right hand of God. This means that Christians participate in this heavenly reality

---

[52]O'Brien, "Church," p. 125.

as they go about their ordinary daily tasks. They are already gathered around Christ, and this is another way of saying that they now enjoy fellowship with him . . . to speak of their membership of this heavenly gathering assembled around Christ is another way of referring to this new relationship with him. They and other Christians were to assemble in local congregations here on earth, for this was an important way in which their fellowship with Christ was expressed. Further, as they came together with others who were in fellowship with him, so they not only met with each other—they also met with Christ himself who indwelt them corporately and individually.[53]

The metaphors that Paul uses for the church emphasize the fundamental significance of the local gatherings of the believers. The church is the "temple" of God (1 Cor 3:16-17; 2 Cor 6:16-18; Eph 2:20-22), that is, the place of his holy presence. This means that the church and indeed all the individual believers should live holy lives and recognize their essential unity. The church is the "body of Christ" (1 Cor 12:12-17; Rom 12:4-5; Eph 5:22-33). This means, again, that Jesus Christ is the life of the church and gives direction to the church, and that the believers in the local congregations form a unity in the midst of diversity. The church is a household (1 Tim 3:15), a family in which God is the Father (Rom 8:15; Gal 4:6) and the believers are God's children (Rom 8:14-17; Gal 4:1-7). This means that the believers should strive to glorify God and to care for one another.

The purpose of the gatherings of the followers of Jesus is formulated by Paul in terms of "edification" or "upbuilding" (Gk *oikodomē*), a metaphor that fits the image of the church as a temple (1 Cor 14:3–5, 12, 17, 26; Eph 4:11-16; 1 Thess 5:11). Paul emphasizes that the Messiah builds his church[54] through the people he has given to the congregations as apostles, prophets, evangelists and pastor-teachers (Eph 4:7, 11). The process of edification is integrally linked with the ministry of the word of the apostles and prophets (Eph 2:20-22) and other preachers and teachers (Eph 4:11).

---

[53]O'Brien, "Church," p. 126; cf. Peter T. O'Brien, "The Church as a Heavenly and Eschatological Entity," in *The Church in the Bible and the World*, ed. D. A. Carson (1987; reprint, Grand Rapids: Baker, 1993), pp. 88-119, 307-11.

[54]Note the Old Testament text where God promises to prepare a people for himself; cf. Jer 24:6; 31:4; 33:7.

They have the task of equipping the believers "for the work of ministry, for building up the body of Christ" (Eph 4:12). The goal of the ministry of the word, and thus the purpose of the gathering of the believers, is to "come to the unity of the faith and of the knowledge of the Son of God, to maturity, to the measure of the stature of the fullness of Christ" (Eph 4:13), that is, to become mature Christians who are ready and eager to meet their Lord when he returns.

The edification of the believers happens when they come together, hearing and learning the Word of God, the words of Jesus Christ and the teaching of the apostles. "This would take place when the Scriptures were formally expounded and taught, or when believers informally exhorted one another in the congregation to live out their obedience to the gospel."[55] In hearing and heeding the Word of God they meet with Jesus Christ.

> Let the word of Christ dwell in you richly; teach and admonish one another in all wisdom; and with gratitude in your hearts sing psalms, and hymns, and spiritual songs to God. (Col 3:16)

> Be filled with the Spirit, as you sing psalms and hymns and spiritual songs among yourselves, singing and making melody to the Lord in your hearts, giving thanks to God the Father at all times in the name of our Lord Jesus Christ. (Eph 5:18-20)

As the followers of Jesus read and learned the Word of God, and as they sang psalms, hymns and spiritual songs with gratitude in their hearts, the "word of Christ" dwelt among them and thus Christ himself was present in their midst.

4.6 TEACHING NEW CONVERTS

The challenges of establishing and consolidating new churches were enormous. The integration of Jewish believers and Gentile Christians was not easy. Jewish believers needed to learn new ways of behavior, abandoning legal traditions that had regulated their dealings with pagans and made fellowship (e.g., during meals) with pagans difficult or impossible. Even more challenging was the integration of converted pagans into the new

---

[55]O'Brien, "Church," p. 129.

messianic people of God. They needed to learn new values and new patterns of behavior in many different areas, not the least in terms of their sexual activities. This explains why one of the main goals of gathering the believers in local communities was instruction. Paul describes himself as a teacher "in every church" (1 Cor 4:17). His rulings on theological and ethical questions are relevant for "all the churches" (1 Cor 7:17; cf. 11:16; 14:33; 16:1). Paul's letters reveal the following focal points.

Theological instruction. A first major focus was the theological instruction of the believers. When Paul taught Jews who had been converted to faith in Jesus Messiah, he could rely on their knowledge of the Scriptures. He entered new territory when he explained the significance of Jesus' death on the cross and when he insisted that they have integrated (table) fellowship with their formerly pagan brothers and sisters.

Paul would have had to promote change in practical-theological matters as well: when Jewish believers continued to circumcise their children (which is a plausible assumption), they needed to understand that circumcision was no longer a sign of membership in God's covenant people. Jewish believers had to be instructed to recognize the central significance of Jesus' death on the cross as the normative criterion for the authority of God's revelation in the Torah of the "old" covenant. They had to understand, for example, that the purity laws and the food laws of the Torah are no longer valid, as holiness has been established and granted by Jesus Christ once and for all. This made true integration of Jewish believers and Gentile believers possible.

Paul's theological instruction of Gentile Christians could refer to some elements of pagan conceptions of the divine, but only in very general terms. Basically everything that Paul needed to say about God and his revelation in the history of Israel, about Jesus the Son of God and the Messiah, about sin and the forgiveness of sins, and about the identity of the followers of Jesus as the people of God of the last days, was novel and unprecedented.

Ethical instruction. The second major focus was the ethical instruction of the new believers. Instruction concerning moral behavior was imperative for Gentile Christians, who had to learn the general thrust and the details of the revealed will of God, both in theory and in practice. In the course of his ethical instruction Paul could refer to some of the religious and philosophical traditions of the Greco-Roman world. But in many areas of morality he had to train the new Gentile converts in new ways of behavior. A primary example is the area of sexual activities, questions such as the appropriateness of visiting prostitutes or of homosexual activities (1 Cor 6:12-19; Rom 1:24-27).

The ethical instruction of the new believers had immediate and inevitable social consequences. The Gentile Christians were no longer able to visit the theater, the amphitheater or the circus because the performances were integrated into a traditional pagan religious framework and promoted values that the new converts were leaving behind. Depending on the specific local situation, Christians could no longer visit the public baths, at least those who were scrupulous in terms of public nudity. Believers who came from the higher classes would have found it difficult to fulfill all the traditional obligations linked with public offices in the city, which often required participation in religious (cultic) activities. To become a Christian implied in some respects a loss of or a removal from the traditional culture.[56] Paul exhorts the Christians in the city of Rome: "Do not be conformed to this world, but be transformed by the renewing of your minds, so that you may discern what is the will of God—what is good and acceptable and perfect" (Rom 12:2).

However, Paul does not argue that Christians should avoid non-Christians. He clarifies that Christians do not have to be afraid of having contacts with pagans. A Christian woman does not need to divorce her pagan husband (1 Cor 7:16). A Christian can eat the meat that is sold in the market without having scruples (1 Cor 10:25-26). Christians should ensure that unbelievers can attend their gatherings (1 Cor 14:23-24). And Erastus could stay the city treasurer of Corinth (Rom 16:23). The challenges of Paul's ethical instruction of Christians find expression in his prayer for the Gentile Christians in Colossae:

> For this reason, since the day we heard it, we have not ceased praying for you and asking that you may be filled with the knowledge of God's will in

---

[56]Christoph Burchard, "Erfahrungen multikulturellen Zusammenlebens im Neuen Testament," in *Multikulturelles Zusammenleben: Theologische Erfahrungen*, ed. J. Micksch (Frankfurt: Limbeck, 1984), p. 30. See further below section 5.3 (pp. 306-34).

all spiritual wisdom and understanding, so that you may lead lives worthy of the Lord, fully pleasing to him, as you bear fruit in every good work and as you grow in the knowledge of God. May you be made strong with all the strength that comes from his glorious power, and may you be prepared to endure everything with patience, while joyfully giving thanks to the Father, who has enabled you to share in the inheritance of the saints in the light. He has rescued us from the power of darkness and transferred us into the kingdom of his beloved Son, in whom we have redemption, the forgiveness of sins. (Col 1:9-14)

Instruction concerning the life of the church. A third focus was instruction relating to the life of the church. Paul had to instruct the new believers in new religious forms and in new modes of behavior during the gatherings of the congregation. Jewish believers who were no longer able to visit the local synagogue had to get used to meeting in a private house for worship, perhaps a house owned by a converted Gentile. For the converted Gentiles, the gatherings of the followers of Jesus were strange. The Gentile Christians had essentially no possibility

> to express their new faith in forms that they were familiar with from dealing with their gods: there were no temples and no altars where priests offered sacrifices and invited the people to dine with the deity. In the houses in which they gathered there was no image—neither of God nor of Jesus Christ his son—in front of which the individual believer could pray and express with incense and dedicatory offerings his personal thankfulness and reverence. Christians also did not organize processions or games in honor of their god in which the former Gentiles could have participated in festive celebration. The forms through which they could, together with other Christians, express their faith in God were baptism, the Lord's Supper (which did not require particular purification rites nor particular implements, types of behavior or clothes) and prayer. For the "nations" Christ was the end of their ancestral religion.[57]

When Jewish Christian teachers demanded that converted Gentiles undergo circumcision (Gal 5:2-3; 6:12-13), observe the festivals of the Jewish calendar (Gal 4:10; Col 2:16), and obey stipulations concerning

---

[57]Meinrad Limbeck, "Die Religionen im Neuen Testament," *Theologische Quartalschrift* 169 (1989): 53.

food and the worship of angels (Col 2:16-23), Paul consistently and ve-
hemently rejected all such attempts to "enrich" the spiritual life of the
Christians. As they have come to faith in Jesus Christ, they have already
received the Holy Spirit and the blessing promised to Abraham (Gal 3:2,
14), they have access to "the riches of the glory" of God's revelation in
Jesus Christ (Col 1:27), they already possess "all the treasures of wisdom
and knowledge" (Col 2:3).

When persons of high social standing were converted, their behavior
concerning the freedmen and the slaves, the so-called *humiliores*, needed
to be transformed. The challenge that this entailed can be illustrated with
the exhortation concerning head-coverings. While the male members of
the Corinthian elite were used to cover their heads when they officiated
during religious activities in the local temples, pulling their toga over their
head and signaling their elevated social status, they are now instructed to
refrain from such ostentatious actions when they pray in the Christian assembly (1 Cor 11:4).[58] To flaunt one's social status in the gathering of the
followers of Jesus dishonors Jesus, the "head" of all believers.

Another example is the understanding of leadership in the local church.
In 1 Corinthians 1—6, Paul reproaches the Corinthian believers for adopting the secular ("fleshly") values of Roman society in their understanding
of leadership in the Christian community.[59] He criticizes their loyalty to
particular persons, their emphasis on status, their boasting with regard to
people, their preference for the wisdom of leading personalities in society or for successful orators, their tolerance of the sexual immorality of a
church member of high social standing and their willingness to take other
believers to court. The Corinthian believers must learn and understand
that leading Christians, including the apostles whom they put on a pedestal, do not distinguish themselves through wealth or personal authority,
nor through status symbols or the kind of prestige that the citizens in Roman Corinth emphasize. Rather, they are "servants," like the workers in
agriculture and in building construction. They are not esteemed patrons

---

[58]See David W. J. Gill, "The Importance of Roman Portraiture for Head Coverings in 1 Corinthians 11.2-16," *TynB* 41 (1990): 245-60; Winter, *After Paul Left Corinth*, pp. 121-41.

[59]Andrew D. Clarke, *Secular and Christian Leadership in Corinth: A Socio-Historical and Exegetical
Study of 1 Corinthians 1-6*, AGAJU 18 (Leiden: Brill, 1993), pp. 109-18; Winter, *After Paul Left
Corinth*, pp. 31-120.

(1 Cor 3:5-9), they are people who have been placed "last of all, as though sentenced to death" like the prisoners who come last in a Roman triumphal procession (1 Cor 4:8-13).

Example: Paul's instruction in 1 Corinthians. Paul did not neatly distinguish between theological, ethical and ecclesiological instruction. The integration of these perspectives can be seen in the way he discusses various issues in his first letter to the Corinthians that resulted from the religious pluralism in the city of Corinth and presented a challenge for the local Christians.[60]

Paul insists that when Corinthian Christians compare the rhetorical capabilities of Paul and of Apollos, that they make the mistake of being "of the flesh" and of "behaving according to human inclinations," that is, of being controlled by the standards of the current philosophical schools such as the Sophists (1 Cor 3:3). Paul argues five points. First, all Christian teachers belong, without exception, to the church and not vice versa (1 Cor 3:21-22). Second, Christian teachers should be evaluated with regard not to their status but to their function (1 Cor 3:5-8). Third, all Christian teachers are servants of Christ and stewards of God's revelation for the benefit of the church (1 Cor 4:1). Fourth, he, Paul, consciously renounced impressive rhetorical fireworks to ensure that their faith rests squarely on the power of God (1 Cor 2:1-5). Fifth, he does not attempt to win followers for himself when he preached and taught in Corinth but acted like a father (1 Cor 4:15), and they are brothers and sisters since they all believe in Jesus Christ the Son of God and thus belong together to God's family. Paul therefore challenges the Christians in Corinth to critically rethink the influences of the Greek and Roman traditions of education and erudition of their city and society, abandoning their criteria and norms in important respects.

The Corinthian Christians presently refuse to abandon the fellowship with a young man who lives in an incestuous relationship with his (step) mother; rather, they "boast" (1 Cor 5:2, 6), presumably with regard to

---

[60]For the following discussion see Bruce W. Winter, "Theological and Ethical Responses to Religious Pluralism—1 Corinthians 8—10," *TynB* 41 (1990): 209-26; Winter, *After Paul Left Corinth*.

the high social status of the man living in sin.[61] If they continue to tolerate this man's scandalous behavior, they function within the customs of Roman society, in which profitable social relationships with people of high social standing are more important than moral integrity or obeying existing laws (1 Cor 5:1). Paul demands that the believers in Corinth stop having any contact with this man, even if this means breaking with the social etiquette of the day (1 Cor 5:1-13). We should note that under Roman law both this man and his stepmother would be sentenced to exile on an island, his possessions would be confiscated, and his social status would be repealed.

Christians in Corinth who belonged to the local elite continued to use the Roman legal system for their power struggles and quarrels about the smallest cases (1 Cor 6:2). Such litigation was rather common among rich Roman citizens who regarded personal insults or disagreements as sufficient reason to initiate *inimicitiae* (hostile litigation, private warfare) before a civil court.[62] Paul argues that the failure to put the Christian faith into practice is so evident that they should be ashamed (1 Cor 6:5). Christians must not allow the quarrels about power, influence and prestige that characterized Roman society to influence their behavior (1 Cor 6:1-8).

Corinthian Christians, particularly members of the social elite who had the financial resources to finance a lifestyle corresponding to their high social status, evidently lived according to the motto, "All things are lawful for me" (1 Cor 6:12; 10:23). This slogan served to rationalize their permissive lifestyle that they indulged in at banquets where the "dessert" of the meal included sexual pleasures (1 Cor 6:13). Perhaps Paul thinks specifically of young men who received the *toga virilis* at the age of eighteen years, that is, who achieved the full legal age, which included the right to attend banquets on their own. (Note that Paul accuses them in 1 Corinthians 6:13 of *porneia*, "immorality" or "fornication," rather than *moicheia*, "adultery.")[63] Paul rejects this attitude of ethical *laissez-faire* with

---

[61]Clarke, *Secular and Christian Leadership*, pp. 73-88.

[62]See John M. Kelly, *Roman Litigation* (Oxford: Clarendon Press, 1966), pp. 62-72, 98-99; Peter Garnsey, *Social Status and Legal Privilege in the Roman Empire* (Oxford: Clarendon, 1970), pp. 181-87, 199-209; David F. Epstein, *Personal Enmity in Roman Politics 218-43 B.C.* (London: Routledge, 1989), pp. 90-103.

[63]See Alan Booth, "The Age for Reclining and Its Attendant Perils," in *Dining in a Classical Con-*

strong words. People who behave in this way cannot inherit the kingdom of God (1 Cor 6:8-10). People who think and act in this manner have not understood that God's revelation in Jesus Christ and the presence of the Holy Spirit have created an entirely new situation for the believer that is characterized by purity, holiness and righteousness (1 Cor 6:11). Paul insists that they cannot attend public banquets held in the local temples (1 Cor 8:1—11:1) where they eat, drink, dance and fornicate (1 Cor 10:7-8).

It appears that some Corinthian Christians insisted on their civic "right" to recline at banquets in the temple (1 Cor 8:10). The historical background for this insistence can be illustrated with the banquet which Lucius Castricus Regulus, the president of the Isthmian Games, organized on the occasion of the return of the games from the city of Sikyon to Corinth. He invited all Roman citizens of the city *(epulumo omnibus colonis)*,[64] possibly in A.D. 51, the year in which Paul lived in Corinth. Paul alleges that such an insistence implies that for these Christians status, entertainment and fun are more important than the fellowship of the believers in Jesus Christ. In the family of the believers in Jesus Christ, the principle not to give offense to the brother or sister applies (1 Cor 8:13). The encouragement and support of the brother and the sister are more important than one's perceived rights. Believers are willing to renounce their rights for the sake of the well-being of their fellow Christians (1 Cor 10:23-33). The behavior of Christians is controlled by the example of Jesus Christ (1 Cor 11:1). Paul rejects the principle that everything is permitted (for members of the elite), that nobody has the right to criticize the lifestyle of another person. This principle does not apply to Christians, who are members of the people of God and members of God's family. Prominent Christians of high social standing must not rely on their traditional privileges or think of themselves as exceptions, especially not with the slogan "all is permitted," irrespective of the Roman laws in the city of Corinth or the traditional customs of society. The fellowship of the

---

text, ed. W. J. Slater (Ann Arbor: University of Michigan Press, 1991), pp. 105-20; Anthony Corbeill, "Dining Deviants in Roman Political Invective," in *Roman Sexualities*, ed. J. P. Hallett and M. B. Skinner (Princeton, N.J.: Princeton University Press, 1997), pp. 99-128. Cf. Juvenal *Satirae* 11, 162-170; Cicero *Pro Murena* 13; *In Verrem* 2, 5, 92-94; *Orationes philippicae* 2, 104-5.

[64]John Harvey Kent, *Corinth VIII, iii: The Inscriptions 1926-1950* (Princeton, N.J.: American School of Classical Studies at Athens, 1966), p. 153; cf. Winter, *After Paul Left Corinth*, pp. 94, 276-78.

followers of Jesus does not allow an ethical behavior of the powerful, rich and prominent Christians that would be any different from the life of the other believers.

Evangelistic outreach. There is sufficient evidence to conclude that Paul's teaching included the encouragement of the believers to share their faith in Jesus Christ with other people. Luke describes the church in Antioch as actively involved in sending missionaries: Barnabas and Paul (Acts 13:1-2). This means that we have to reckon with local congregations who sent missionaries to regions that had not yet been reached with the news of Jesus. The fact that Paul repeatedly revisited the church in Antioch suggests that both Paul and Luke, who reports about Paul's lasting connection with the church in Antioch, regard the involvement of this church in the missionary task of the church as exemplary and as a model for other churches. We should also note that Paul knows other Christians who are involved in missionary work: the apostles (1 Cor 9:5; 12:28-29) and the Christians in the city of Rome who are not legitimized by some specific "title" (Phil 1:14-18).

Paul praises the missionary commitment of the church in Thessalonica on account of the fact that "the word of the Lord has sounded forth from you not only in Macedonia and Achaia, but in every place your faith in God has become known, so that we have no need to speak about it" (1 Thess 1:8). This description has been interpreted in the sense that "Paul sketches a picture of active preaching by the Thessalonians in Macedonia and Achaia and beyond."[65] In 1 Thessalonians 3:12, Paul prays that the love of the believers in Thessalonica "for one another and for all" might increase. He reminds them that they should not allow the new community and fellowship that they enjoy as new converts to be solidified as a "closed group" that insulates itself against society, a behavior which would prevent others from hearing the news of Jesus.

When Paul discusses the behavior of the Corinthian Christians, he notes in passing that outsiders attend the meetings of the congregation (1 Cor 14:23-24). It was evidently common that unbelievers attended the gatherings of the Christian communities. The meetings of the local churches were

---

[65] Abraham J. Malherbe, *The Letters to the Thessalonians*, AncB 32B (New York: Doubleday, 2000), p. 117.

no exclusive assemblies of a closed society. He insists that what is being said in their gatherings should be intelligible for visitors. This is the reason why he limits the practice of the gift of speaking in unlearned languages (glossolalia) in their meetings. When a Christian is married to an unbelieving spouse, he faces a missionary situation which is, however, open, as Paul states: "Wife, for all you know, you might save your husband. Husband, for all you know, you might save your wife" (1 Cor 7:16).

Paul thanks the Christians in Philippi for their "sharing in the gospel" (Phil 1:5). The phrase "in the gospel" *(eis to euangelion)* describes an active participation of the church in Philippi in his own missionary work. They cooperated in the preaching of the gospel not only through their financial support for Paul (Phil 4:15-16) and through their prayers (Phil 1:19), but also in terms of passing on the news of Jesus.[66] Since Paul in the same context refers to the "progress of the gospel" (Phil 1:12), the "fellowship of the gospel" is centrally connected with this progress. The believers in Philippi contribute to the "progress of the gospel" through their financial support of the apostle and through their own missionary activity in Philippi. The fact that Paul mentions the evangelistic activity of believers in Rome (assuming a Roman imprisonment of Paul) in Philippians 1:14 in passing indicates that it was a matter of course for Paul that individual Christians preach the gospel in their city. The "messengers" that the churches send out (2 Cor 8:23; Phil 2:25, 30) represent the missionary responsibility of the Pauline churches.

In Ephesians 4:11, Paul mentions "evangelists" (Gk *euangelistas*), between the apostles and prophets and the shepherds/pastors and teachers, as leaders in the church. The *charismata* that the Holy Spirit gives to the church for "building up the body of Christ" (Eph 4:12) include the task of proclaiming the news of Jesus. The orientation of this task toward the nurture of the church does not diminish the primary meaning of the word: evangelists, particularly if they are not at the same time "shepherds" and teachers, proclaim the gospel of Jesus Christ *also* and perhaps primarily before people who have not yet heard the gospel or who have not yet come to faith in Jesus Christ.[67]

---

[66]See Peter T. O'Brien, *The Epistle to the Philippians. A Commentary on the Greek Text*, NIGTC (Grand Rapids: Eerdmans, 1991), pp. 62-63.
[67]I. Howard Marshall, "Who Were the Evangelists?" in *The Mission of the Early Church to Jews and*

In Ephesians 6:10-20, Paul describes the existence of the believer as a battle against the powers of evil. He specifies two reactions to the attacks of Satan, who attempts, together with the cosmic powers and spiritual forces that he controls, to harm the believers. First, believers must resist the temptation, which they can do because they are protected by the armor of God. Second, believers shall preach the gospel. The identification of the footwear in the believers' spiritual "armor" with the "readiness to proclaim the gospel of peace" (Eph 6:15) refers to the proclamation of the gospel. The term *hetoimasia* ("ready"), used only here in the New Testament, does not describe the "firmness" of the footwear that guarantees the stability of the soldier in battle; rather, it refers to "readiness." Paul asserts that believers who are equipped with God's armor can be certain that they are prepared for all eventualities. The connection with the feet refers to active readiness. The Greek genitive construction *hetoimasia tou euangeliou* ("ready to proclaim the gospel") is best interpreted in terms of an objective genitive: Paul speaks of the readiness of the outward-going movement (footwear) required for the proclamation of the news of Jesus.[68] The one reference to a weapon for battle shows that the struggle of the believers is not merely defensive but offensive as well: the "sword of the Spirit," which is identified with the "word of God" (Eph 6:17). The sharp, short sword *(machaira)* was the most important weapon for close-range combat. A "defensive" interpretation does not make sense since the short sword was an offensive weapon. The apostle does not want to "immunize" the Christians against the influences of pagan society. Paul describes here the primary offensive action of Christians in the fight against the attacks of Satan, which consists in the active proclamation of the good news of Jesus' death on the cross by which he defeated all evil powers and of Jesus' resurrection to life.[69] This message is made effective and powerful by God's Spirit. The word of God is wielded by the Holy Spirit as "sword," it is the proclamation of the gospel in the midst of a world dominated by

---

Gentiles, ed. J. Adna and H. Kvalbein, WUNT 127 (Tübingen: Mohr-Siebeck, 2000), pp. 251-63, 261.

[68]Peter T. O'Brien, *The Letter to the Ephesians*, PNTC (Grand Rapids: Eerdmans, 1999), pp. 476-77.

[69]See Robert L. Plummer, *Paul's Understanding of the Church's Mission*, Paternoster Biblical Monographs (Bletchley, U.K.: Paternoster, 2006), pp. 77-80.

evil powers so that people are liberated from Satan's control and find salvation. Paul challenges the Christians in the province of Asia to remain steadfast against temptations and at the same time to offensively proclaim the gospel.

The final qualification of the elders mentioned by Paul in 1 Timothy 3:7 can be seen in a missionary context as well: "He must also have a good reputation *(martyria)* with outsiders, so that he will not fall into disgrace and into the devil's trap" (TNIV). This criterion is formulated from a "defensive" perspective: slander and actual moral improprieties and failures damage their reputation and destroy their credibility. At the same time, however, this criterion is also connected with the role of the church in God's plan of salvation "for all people" (1 Tim 2:1-6; 4:9-10). Thus it is linked with the effectiveness of the mission of the congregations.[70] The "good reputation" *(martyria)* of the elders determines the witness *(martyria)* of the church. Both the elders and the congregation are committed to the obligation to represent, display and communicate the will of God who wants to save sinners.

In 2 Timothy 4:5, the apostle exhorts Timothy, who carries the responsibility for the churches in Ephesus and other cities in the province of Asia, to "do the work of an evangelist." In the context of 2 Timothy 4, the "work" *(ergon)* of an evangelist is closely connected with teaching and with exercising leadership in the local congregation.[71] The leaders of the congregations are called upon to proclaim the gospel, evidently before people who have not yet heard the message of Jesus Christ. The congregations are not to wait for traveling missionaries who pass through. Rather, they are to make sure that people hear the gospel.

The exhortation to the "older women" in Titus 2:3-5 may be motivated by missionary concerns. They are called

> to be reverent in behavior, not to be slanderers or slaves to drink; they are
> to teach what is good, so that they may encourage the young women to love
> their husbands, to love their children, to be self-controlled, chaste, good
> managers of the household, kind, being submissive to their husbands, so
> that the word of God may not be discredited.

---

[70]Marshall, *Pastoral Epistles*, p. 484.
[71]Ibid., p. 804.

Their behavior should not discredit the evangelistic efforts of the church but promote them.[72]

The exhortation to the Christian slaves has a missionary component as well. They are called "to be submissive to their masters and to give satisfaction in every respect; they are not to talk back, not to pilfer, but to show complete and perfect fidelity, so that in everything they may be an ornament to the doctrine of God our Savior" (Tit 2:9-10). Slaves who have become believers and are thus "free" in Jesus Christ are exhorted, as are all Christians, to put into practice the reality of the gospel in everyday life (cf. Rom 12:1-2), and to be aware of the fact that the credibility of the gospel, which is preached in connection with the missionary activities of the local church, would be discredited if they display a rebellious attitude.[73] The Christian slaves are encouraged "to make the gospel as attractive as possible for those around them."[74]

4.7 TRAINING NEW MISSIONARIES

A further goal of Paul's missionary work was the training of new missionaries. The coworkers who accompanied Paul on his travels[75] participated in his missionary activities and can thus be seen as trainees, much like Jesus' disciples who had been chosen by Jesus to be with him (Mk 3:13-15) and to be trained as "fishers of people" (Mk 1:17).[76] The New Testament sources do not state explicitly that Paul surrounded himself with a circle of coworkers for the express purpose of preparing them for missionary service. This is a plausible assumption, however, as they did not simply carry out menial tasks: they were involved in the same type of activities that Paul focused on. Of the approximately one hundred names that are

---

[72]Philip H. Towner, *The Goal of Our Instruction: The Structure of Theology and Ethics in the Pastoral Epistles*, JSNTSup 34 (Sheffield, U.K.: JSOT Press, 1989), pp. 195-96.

[73]Plummer, *Paul's Understanding of the Church's Mission*, pp. 100-103.

[74]William D. Mounce, *Pastoral Epistles*, WBC 46 (Nashville: Nelson, 2000), p. 416.

[75]See Earle E. Ellis, "Paul and His Co-Workers," *NTS* 17 (1971): 437-52; Wolf-Henning Ollrog, *Paulus und seine Mitarbeiter*, WMANT 50 (Neukirchen-Vluyn: Neukirchener Verlag, 1979); Wayne A. Meeks, *The First Urban Christians: The Social World of the Apostle Paul* (New Haven, Conn.: Yale University Press, 1983), pp. 51-73; John P. Dickson, *Mission-Commitment in Ancient Judaism and in the Pauline Communities: The Shape, Extent and Background of Early Christian Mission*, WUNT 159 (Tübingen: Mohr-Siebeck, 2003), pp. 86-132; Schnabel, *Early Christian Mission*, 2:1425-45. For a list see Schnabel, *Early Christian Mission*, 2:1426-27.

[76]On the Twelve see Schnabel, *Early Christian Mission*, 1:263-315.

connected with Paul in the book of Acts and in the Pauline letters, thirty-eight are coworkers of the apostle.

Paul uses nine different designations for the coworkers who are listed: brother, apostle or envoy, servant, slave (fellow-slave), companion or partner, worker, soldier (fellow-soldier), fellow-prisoner, and fellow-worker.[77] Further expressions that are used for some of Paul's coworkers include prophet, teacher, traveling companion, shepherd, proclaimer of the gospel ("evangelist," Gk *euangelistēs*), servant or minister, manager or administrator, helper or assistant.[78] This list illustrates the fact that these coworkers fully shared in Paul's missionary work. When they are called "servants," "slaves" or "helpers," they are not Paul's servants, slaves or helpers but—just like Paul himself—the servants, slaves and helpers of God and of the Lord Jesus Christ. Some of these terms indicate that many of the tasks that Paul's coworkers were involved in entailed missionary work.

The most frequent terms are "worker" *(ergatēs)* or "coworker" *(synergos)*, terms which are generally used by Paul to describe companions who traveled with him. The term *ergatēs* describes "one who is engaged in work" and specifically the person who works for money, the "worker" or "laborer," including slaves.[79] The term *synergos* describes the "fellow worker," the person who works alongside another laborer. Some scholars maintain that *ergatēs* is a technical term for early Christian missionaries.[80] There is no clear evidence for this suggestion, however. Christians who have leadership responsibilities in the local congregation also "work" without being missionaries.

---

[77]On brother *(adelphos):* Acts 25:22; Rom 16:23; 1 Cor 1:1; 16:12; 2 Cor 1:1; 2:13; Eph 6:21; Phil 2:25; Col 1:1; 4:7, 9; 1 Thess 3:2; Philem 1; apostle *(apostolos):* Acts 14:4, 14; Rom 1:1; 16:7; Phil 2:25; 1 Thess 2:7; servant *(diakonos):* 1 Cor 3:5; 2 Cor 3:6; 6:4; Eph 6:21; Col 1:7; 4:7; slave/fellow-slave *(doulos/syndoulos):* Phil 1:1; Col 1:7; 4:7, 12; 2 Tim 2:24; partner *(koinōnos):* 2 Cor 8:23; Philem 17; the one who works *(ho kopiōn):* Rom 16:6, 12; 2 Tim 2:6; fellow-soldier *(stratiōtēs, systratiōtēs):* Phil 2:25; 2 Tim 2:3; Philem 2; fellow-prisoner *(synaichmalōtos):* Rom 16:7; Col 4:10; Philem 23; fellow-worker *(synergos):* Rom 15:21; 16:3, 9, 21; 1 Cor 3:9; 2 Cor 8:23; Phil 2:25; 4:2-3; Col 4:10-11; 1 Thess 3:2; Philem 1, 24.

[78]Prophet: Acts 13:1; 15:32; teacher: Acts 13:1: traveling companion: Acts 19:29; shepherd: 1 Cor 9:7; Eph 4:11; evangelist *(euangelistēs):* 2 Tim 4:5; Eph 4:11; minister *(leitourgos):* Phil 2:25; Rom 15:16; manager *(oikonomos):* 1 Cor 4:1-2; cf. Tit 1:7; helper *(hypēretēs):* 1 Cor 4:1.

[79]Roman Heiligenthal, *EDNT*, 2:49.

[80]Dieter Georgi, *The Opponents of Paul in Second Corinthians* (Philadelphia: Fortress, 1986), p. 40; Takaaki Haraguchi, "Das Unterhaltsrecht des frühchristlichen Verkündigers. Eine Untersuchung zur Bezeichnung ἐργάτης im Neuen Testament," *ZNW* 84 (1993): 178.

Paul describes himself and his fellow missionaries as "God's co-workers" (1 Cor 3:9 TNIV). This expression acknowledges that the effectiveness
of missionary preaching leading people to come to faith in Jesus Christ
is caused by God alone (1 Cor 2:5). At the same time the expression recognizes that Paul and other Christians are called to engage in the work
of preaching the good news. The activities of the missionary team day in
and day out indeed represent "work" that is often hard and difficult. The
study of the Scriptures, the proclamation of the gospel in public and in
private, answering questions from the audience, caring for the new converts, interacting with local opponents, the often dangerous travel to other
cities, the search for living quarters, the concern for food and drink—all
this is indeed hard work. The Greek term *kopos* describes an "activity that
is burdensome," hence "work, labor, toil."[81] It describes not only Paul's
physical labor, by which he earns his living expenses (1 Thess 2:9; 2 Thess
3:8) but all labor that he undertakes as a missionary (2 Cor 6:5; 11:23,
27). The term *kopos* is thus a term for missionary work (1 Cor 3:8; 2 Cor
10:15; 1 Thess 3:5) and for the work in the local church (1 Cor 15:58;
1 Thess 1:3; 1 Tim 5:17).[82] The "workers" whom Paul mentions in his
letters describe a specific group of coworkers who presumably have been
recruited by Paul himself.

Among the more frequently mentioned coworkers of Paul are the following: Barnabas from Jerusalem (Judea), who was active in Antioch, Cyprus and Galatia;[83] Timothy from Lystra (Lycaonia), who accompanied
Paul in Macedonia, Achaia, Thessalonica, Ephesus and Corinth;[84] Luke
from Antioch (Syria), who was active in Antioch(?) and Philippi; Aquila
and Priscilla from Rome, who were active in Corinth, Ephesus and in
Rome;[85] Silas/Silvanus from Jerusalem, who was active in Macedonia and
in Achaia;[86] Titus, who worked with Paul in Antioch and in Corinth and
who later worked on the island of Crete and in Dalmatia;[87] Tychicus from

---

[81]BDAG, p. 558.
[82]Friedrich Hauck, *TDNT*, 3:827-30; Herbert Fendrich, *EDNT*, 2:307-8; Manfred Seitz, *NIDNTT*,
  1:262-63.
[83]Acts 11:19-26; 13—14.
[84]Acts 17—18; 1 Thess 3:1-6; Acts 19:22; 1 Cor 16:10-11; 1 Tim 1:3.
[85]Acts 18:26; 1 Cor 16:19; Rom 16:4.
[86]Acts 15:40; 16:19; 17:4, 10, 15; 18:1; 2 Cor 1:19; 1 Thess 1:1; 2 Thess 1:1; 1 Pet 5:12.
[87]2 Cor 7:6-7, 13-15; 8:6; Tit 1:5; 2 Tim 4:10.

an unknown city in the province of Asia, who was active in Colossae and Ephesus and on Crete;[88] Apollos from Alexandria (Egypt), who was active in Corinth and Ephesus and later on Crete.[89] The circle of Paul's coworkers included a considerable number of women. It has been estimated that 18 percent of Paul's missionary coworkers were women.[90] In the list of greetings in his letter to the Romans, Paul mentions the following female coworkers who are now residing in Rome: Phoebe (Rom 16:1-2), Priscilla (Rom 16:3), Mary (Rom 16:6), Junia (Rom 16:7), Tryphaena and Tryphosa (Rom 16:12), and Persis (Rom 16:12). Other women whom Paul's description reveals to be coworkers are Apphia (Philem 2), Euodia and Syntyche (Phil 4:2-3). Their participation in Paul's missionary work is indicated by the Greek affix *syn* ("with"): they have struggled "with" Paul for the gospel (Phil 4:3). They evidently preached the gospel beside Paul.[91]

Timothy serves as an illustration of the work that Paul's coworkers were involved in. Timothy was evidently converted in the course of Paul's missionary activities in Galatia in A.D. 46, presumably during his mission to Lystra (Acts 14:6-20). Three years later Paul recruited him as a coworker when he was en route to the province of Asia, being eventually diverted to Macedonia and Achaia (Acts 16:1-3). After Paul had to leave Thessalonica in a hurry when the local Jews threatened his life, Timothy evidently stayed in the city. He seemed to have traveled to Beroea a few weeks later to join Paul again (Acts 17:14). When Paul was forced to leave Beroea, Timothy stayed behind, together with Silas (Acts 17:14). A few weeks later he joined Paul in Athens (Acts 17:15), who promptly sent him back to Thessalonica with the task of consolidating the believers there (1 Thess 3:1-5). Several months later Timothy traveled to Corinth with good news about the church in Thessalonica (1 Thess 3:6) and with the request to deal with questions that had arisen in the church (1 Thess 4:9, 13; 5:1). If the traditional localization of Paul's letters to Timothy is reliable,

---

[88]Col 4:7-9; Eph 6:21; 2 Tim 4:12; Tit 3:12.

[89]Acts 18:27; 1 Cor 3:5-6:9; 16:12; Tit 3:13.

[90]See Andreas J. Köstenberger, "Women in the Pauline Mission," in *The Gospel to the Nations: Perspectives on Paul's Mission*, ed. P. Bolt and M. Thompson (Leicester, U.K.: Inter-Varsity Press, 2000), pp. 221-47.

[91]See Walter L. Liefeld, "Women and Evangelism in the Early Church," *Missiology* 15 (1987): 291-98.

then Timothy carried the responsibility for the churches in the province of Asia, perhaps after A.D. 62 when Paul had been arrested.

Titus is another example of a very active coworker. Paul took Titus with him to Jerusalem when he traveled from Antioch to Jerusalem in A.D. 47 (Gal 2:3). The purpose of this visit was the famine relief that had been collected by the Antiochene believers, and apparently Paul wanted to have a private consultation with the apostles, perhaps regarding planned missionary initiative that took him and Barnabas to Cyprus and to southern Galatia. Paul recounts that the Jerusalem apostles did not require Titus to be circumcised, which indicates that he was a Gentile Christian, perhaps a God-fearer who had been converted to faith in Jesus Christ. Titus evidently worked with Paul and Barnabas in Antioch between A.D. 45-47. It is not clear whether Antioch was his home town. He could have been converted in the course of Paul's missionary work in Syria and Cilicia between A.D. 34-42. At the end of Paul's missionary work in Ephesus in A.D. 52-55, Titus appears as a coworker who was responsible for the practical aspects of organizing the collection for the poor Christians in Jerusalem, which Paul had initiated in the churches of Macedonia and Achaia.[92] The suggestion that Paul recruited Titus as a coworker only for the specific task of the collection[93] is not plausible, as the following survey of his activities demonstrates. When Paul was engaged in missionary work in Ephesus and corresponded with the church in Corinth, Titus evidently was one of the most important of his companions. Paul entrusted him with the delicate task of taking the "letter of tears" (2 Cor 2:4) to the Corinthian church and to help achieve reconciliation between the Corinthian Christians and Paul.[94] Paul describes Titus as "my partner and co-worker in your service" (2 Cor 8:23). Second, Titus was accompanied by a brother "who is famous among all the churches for his proclaiming the good news" (2 Cor 8:18), as well as a second brother "whom we have often tested and found eager in many matters, but who is now more eager than ever because of his great confidence in you" (2 Cor 8:22). These bio-

---

[92]Cf. 2 Cor 8:6, 10, 16-17; 12:17-18.

[93]Ollrog, *Paulus und seine Mitarbeiter*, p. 95.

[94]Cf. 2 Cor 2:13; 7:6-7, 13-14; 8:6, 16, 23; 12:18. Cf. Margaret E. Thrall, *The Second Epistle to the Corinthians*, ICC (Edinburgh: T & T Clark, 2000), 1:186.

graphical descriptions and testimonials suggest a similar (if not superior) reputation and giftedness of Titus. Third, according to 2 Timothy 4:10, Titus was later active in Dalmatia; that is, he was engaged in missionary work in Illyricum. And according to Titus 1:4-5, Titus was responsible for the new churches on Crete, at least since Paul's imprisonment in A.D. 57.

The missionary work of Paul's coworkers should not be interpreted as an inferior substitute for Paul's own presence and ministry. It has been suggested that the apostolic authority and effectivity was tied, first, to the apostle's personal presence *(parousia)*, second, to the presence of the apostle mediated by envoys and, third, to the letters that he writes to churches as substitute for his presence.[95] This typology of the forms of true apostolic "presence" may be helpful for analytical purposes. It is unwarranted, however, to maintain that the greatest effectivity was connected with the personal presence of the apostle and that the presence of envoys (or the sending of letters) was but an inferior substitute. In the Greco-Roman world, envoys fully represented the person (or the city) that had sent the messenger. The envoy is engaged in the work of his patron with the latter's full authority. Thus the envoy must be accepted and treated according to the status of his patron with dignity and respect. John formulates in John 13:20 the general principle that characterized the formal and the informal relationships in Greco-Roman society succinctly when he reports Jesus as saying, "whoever receives one whom I send receives me; and whoever receives me receives him who sent me." What is true for the sending of Jesus by God and for the sending of the disciples by Jesus is true not only for the sending of the apostle Paul by Jesus but also for Paul's "sending" of Timothy, Titus and Epaphroditus. Paul directs the churches to receive these messengers as they would receive him.

> If Timothy comes, see that he has nothing to fear among you, for he is doing the work of the Lord just as I am; therefore let no one despise him. Send him on his way in peace, so that he may come to me; for I am expecting him with the brothers. (1 Cor 16:10-11)

---

[95]Robert W. Funk, "The Apostolic *Parousia:* Form and Significance," in *Christian History and Interpretation: Studies Presented to John Knox*, ed. W. R. Farmer (Cambridge: Cambridge University Press, 1967), pp. 249-69; this essay was very influential. For the following critique see Margaret M. Mitchell, "New Testament Envoys in the Context of Greco-Roman Diplomatic and Epistolary Conventions: The Example of Timothy and Titus," *JBL* 111 (1992): 641-62.

But God, who consoles the downcast, consoled us by the arrival of Titus, and not only by his coming, but also by the consolation with which he was consoled about you, as he told us of your longing, your mourning, your zeal for me, so that I rejoiced still more. . . . And his heart goes out all the more to you, as he remembers the obedience of all of you, and how you welcomed him with fear and trembling. (2 Cor 7:6-7, 15)

Welcome him [i.e., Epaphroditus] then in the Lord with all joy, and honor such people. (Phil 2:29)

Timothy, as Paul's envoy, can speak directly for Paul because he knows him and his message, and because he teaches nothing that Paul would not teach himself. This is why Paul writes, "For this reason I sent you Timothy, who is my beloved and faithful child in the Lord, to remind you of my ways in Christ Jesus, as I teach them everywhere in every church" (1 Cor 4:17). The role of Timothy in Thessalonica and the role of Titus in Corinth is hardly a "weak substitute" for Paul's presence. They perform important tasks that Paul will not or cannot perform himself at that particular time.

Stephanas, the "first convert in Achaia" who had devoted himself together with his family "to the service of the saints" (1 Cor 16:15), apparently engaged in a *diakonia* in Corinth and the surrounding areas, which went beyond practical assistance to include a preaching and teaching activity. Paul writes, "I urge you to put yourselves at the service of such people, and of everyone who works and toils with them" (1 Cor 16:16). Stephanas and his family represented the nucleus of the growing church in Corinth and in Achaia. The loyal work and the committed witness of this family is the beginning, the foundation and the promise of the growth of the church.

Paul repeatedly mentions coworkers who teach and preach in the local congregations and who establish churches in the surrounding areas. A significant example is Epaphras's missionary work in the cities of the Lykos Valley, in Colossae, Hierapolis and Laodicea.[96] It can be safely assumed that Paul trained these local coworkers during his initial stay in the city—Stephanas in Corinth, Epaphras in Ephesus.

---

[96]Gal 6:6; Phil 1:1; 4:2-3; 1 Thess 5:12-13; 2 Thess 3:6-11. For Epaphras see Col 1:7-8; 2:1; 3:16; 4:12, 16.

The majority of Paul's coworkers came from the new churches that he had established. Some came to Paul as "delegates" of their home churches (Col 1:7; 4:12-13; Philem 13). They represent the "messengers of the churches" (*apostoloi ekklēsiōn*; 2 Cor 8:23; cf. Phil 2:25). The "home churches" of these coworkers acknowledge that they share in the responsibility for the expansion of the kingdom of God by providing missionary workers who help Paul. Their participation in Paul's mission "makes up" what their churches owe to Paul (1 Cor 16:17; Phil 2:30). The churches participate through their envoys in Paul's mission. The role of Paul's coworkers

> cannot be determined only along psychological lines on the basis of the need for fellowship, nor along organizational lines in terms of maximizing the missionary effectiveness, nor along pedagogical lines in terms of training workers for the time after Paul. Rather, Paul emphasizes the coresponsibility and the participation of the churches because he regards missionary work and ministry as a function of the entire church (thus the great fluctuation in his team of coworkers).[97]

---

[97]Wolfgang Schrage, *Der erste Brief an die Korinther*, EKK 7 (Zürich: Benziger; Neukirchen-Vluyn: Neukirchener Verlag, 1991-2001), 1:101.

5

The Missionary Methods
of the Apostle Paul

You yourselves know, brothers and sisters, that our coming to you was not in vain, but though we had already suffered and been shamefully mistreated at Philippi, as you know, we had courage in our God to declare to you the gospel of God in spite of great opposition. For our appeal does not spring from deceit or impure motives or trickery, but just as we have been approved by God to be entrusted with the message of the gospel, even so we speak, not to please mortals, but to please God who tests our hearts. As you know and as God is our witness, we never came with words of flattery or with a pretext for greed; nor did we seek praise from mortals, whether from you or from others, though we might have made demands as apostles of Christ. But we were gentle among you, like a nurse tenderly caring for her own children. So deeply do we care for you that we are determined to share with you not only the gospel of God but also our own selves, because you have become very dear to us. You remember our labor and toil, brothers and sisters; we worked night and day, so that we might not burden any of you while we proclaimed to you the gospel of God. You are witnesses, and God also, how pure, upright, and blameless our conduct was toward you believers. As you know, we dealt with each one of you like a father with his children, urging and encouraging you and pleading that you lead a life worthy of God, who calls you into his own kingdom and glory.

1 THESS 2:1-12

When I came to you, brothers and sisters, I did not come proclaiming the mystery of God to you in lofty words or wisdom. For I decided to know nothing among you except Jesus Christ, and him crucified. And I came to you in weakness and in fear and in much trembling. My speech and my proclamation were not with plausible words of wisdom, but with a demonstration of the Spirit and of power, so that your faith might rest not on human wisdom but on the power of God.

1 COR 2:1-5

IRRESPECTIVE OF THE DETAILS OF DEFINITIONS of strategy and method, it is obvious that Paul planned his missionary initiatives in the context of a general strategy that shaped specific decisions. The survey of Paul's activities in the previous chapters demonstrates that he was neither stubborn nor mystical. Had Paul been inflexible, he would have been killed early in his ministry—in Damascus or in Jerusalem as early as A.D. 32/33.[1] Had Paul followed merely inner promptings, he would not have preached in Athens and would not have stayed in Corinth for nearly two years from February/March A.D. 50 to September 51.[2]

The directive to proclaim the news of God's redemptive intervention in the person and work of Jesus the crucified and risen Messiah and Savior results quite naturally in a basic method of missionary work. Paul's missionary methods can be presented along the following lines.

First, people need to hear the message about Jesus Christ. This means that both Jews and pagans need to be reached in such a fashion that the news of Jesus Christ could be shared, whether this be in public speeches or sermons and/or in private conversations.

Second, people live in cities, towns and villages. In order for people to hear the gospel, Paul had to travel to the cities, towns and villages where people live. Paul did not expect people to come to him: he went to the places where people lived.

Third, as the cities and the towns of the Mediterranean world were part of the political structure of the Roman Empire, apostles who preach the gospel will have to travel in Roman provinces.

---

[1]For Damascus see Gal 1:15-17; 2 Cor 11:32-33; Acts 9:19-25; for Jerusalem see Acts 9:26-30.
[2]For Athens see Acts 17:15-16; 18:1, 5; for Corinth see Acts 18:9-11.

Fourth, for people to hear the gospel, they will have to be sought out in places where they are willing to listen to discourses and are willing to engage in conversations. For Jews, the natural place for religious discourse and discussion is the synagogue. For pagans, the central square of the city—in Greek cities the marketplace *(agora)*, in Roman cities the forum—is the space where people are accustomed to hearing and listening to speeches. Workshops and private houses provide further opportunities to reach people with sermons and private conversations.

Fifth, matters of ethnic identity and class, culture and gender were relevant matters to be considered, as the apostles sought to reach not only Jews but also pagans, not only the rich but also the poor, not only the educated but also the large crowds of the uneducated, not only men but also women.

Sixth, as people in antiquity were used to encounter and listen to traveling orators, the rhetorical principles that are employed in such encounters and the expectations that are raised in the audience—both negative and positive, both helpful and obstructive—had to be considered.

Seventh, as the missionaries successfully established communities of people who had accepted their preaching and responded with faith to the gospel of Jesus Christ, the question of what makes missionary work successful was posed.

These matters will be addressed in the following discussion. Paul himself explicitly addresses mostly the sixth factor, the behavior and the rhetoric of the itinerant orators of his time. The other elements of Paul's missionary method need to be deduced from hints in his letters and from Luke's report in the book of Acts. This chapter thus draws conclusions from the description of Paul's missionary work (chap. 1), from Paul's statements about his missionary task (chap. 2), and from Paul's missionary message (chap. 3).

5.1 CITIES, REGIONS AND PROVINCES

How did Paul select the cities, regions or provinces where he preached the news of Jesus Christ? Neither Luke nor Paul explicitly comment on this matter. We will examine the available evidence in the book of Acts and in Paul's letters in order to establish whether Paul's choices were the result of a particular missionary method.

The cities of Paul's missionary work. The first period of Paul's mission-ary work is connected with Damascus (Acts 9:19-21, 23-25; Gal 1:17; see sec. 1.2). Why did Paul begin his missionary work in Damascus? Paul's reference to the events in Damascus in Galatians 1:15-17 singles out five elements: (1) God called him to proclaim Jesus Christ among the Gentiles, (2) he did not confer with any other human being, (3) he did not return to Jerusalem immediately after his conversion to consult with the apostles, (4) he went to Arabia, and (5) he eventually returned to Damascus. Be-cause Damascus was a Gentile city, Paul presumably chose Damascus as the location for missionary work because the city was instantly "available" as the place where he was to be obedient to God's call. He left the city not because he had successfully carried out a plan but because local Jews plot-ted to kill him, forcing him to leave in a hurry in the middle of the night, escaping over the city walls (Acts 9:23-25).

The second period of Paul's missionary work was Arabia (Gal 1:17; 2 Cor 11:32; see sec. 1.2). Why did Paul evangelize in Arabia/Nabatea? The answer may be as simple as the fact that this was the Gentile region immediately to the south of Damascus and thus easily reachable. Paul left the area on account of an arrest warrant issued by Nabatean officials (on the advice of or at least with the cooperation of the local Jews; cf. Acts 9:23-25; 2 Cor 11:32).

The third location of Paul's mission was Jerusalem (Acts 9:26-29). Luke does not explain why Paul traveled to Jerusalem after he had to leave Damascus in a hurry. In Galatians 1:18 Paul states that three years after his conversion he left Damascus and went to Jerusalem "to visit Cephas." The formulation of the Greek text indicates that Paul wanted to make the acquaintance of the apostle Peter.[3] The purpose of Paul's visit was not to evangelize in Jerusalem. However, as he understood his divine calling to relate to "the Jew first and also the Greek" (Rom 1:16; cf. Rom 9:1-3), he joined the followers of Jesus in Jerusalem in their outreach to their fellow

---

[3]Paul uses the verb *historēsai*, which means "to visit (for the purpose of coming to know someone)"; cf. BDAG, p. 483; see the discussion of James D. G. Dunn, "The Relationship Between Paul and Jerusalem According to Galatians 1 and 2," *NTS* 28 (1982): 461-78; Otfried Hofius, "Gal 1,18: ἱστορῆσαι Κηφᾶν [1989]," in *Paulusstudien* (Tübingen: Mohr Siebeck, 1994), pp. 255-67; James D. G. Dunn, "Once More—Gal 1.18: *historesai Kephan*. In Reply to Otfried Hofius," *ZNW* 76 (1985).

Jews. He was particularly active among the Greek-speaking Jews in the city (Acts 9:29). He explained the news of Jesus to Jews who did not yet believe in Jesus as the Messiah, proclaiming a message he always conveyed to people wherever he went. In 1 Corinthians 9:16 Paul asserts that when he proclaims the gospel this gives him no ground for boasting, "for an obligation is laid on me, and woe to me if I do not proclaim the gospel." Paul's departure from Jerusalem was not planned but was again the consequence of a plot to kill him (Acts 9:29-30).

The fourth period of Paul's missionary work sees him in Syria and Cilicia (Gal 1:21; see sec. 1.2). Paul preached at least in Tarsus (Acts 9:30; 11:25-26). The other cities in which he evangelized are not specified in our sources. Tarsus was a plausible target for Paul's missionary efforts for at least five reasons: (1) Tarsus was his home town. He presumably had relatives, friends and acquaintances in the city who would not only be a natural first audience but also a helpful base of operations for reaching other cities in the region. (2) The Tarsian citizenship that Paul evidently possessed gave him protection, a factor that was not merely theoretical after his experience in Nabatea and in Jerusalem. (3) Tarsus was the most significant city in the region after Antioch. (4) Tarsus had a Jewish community. (5) Due to its location on the Mediterranean coast and on the main road across the Taurus Mountains, Tarsus was not only ideal as a base of missionary activity in Syria and in Cilicia but also in the regions to the north and to the west. Whether the last consideration played any part in Paul's thinking, we do not know, however.

The fifth period of Paul's missionary work is linked with Antioch, the capital of the province of Syria (Acts 11:26-30; 13:1; see sec. 1.2). We do not know why Paul accepted Barnabas's invitation to join in the outreach in Antioch, where Gentiles were being converted in larger numbers (Acts 11:20-24). It has been suggested that

> perhaps the apostle's activity in Cilicia, as later in Corinth and Ephesus or then in the eastern Mediterranean generally, had come to a certain conclusion. Presumably the communities which he had founded had to some degree become independent. On the other hand, Barnabas, who must have regarded Paul as a missionary authority "with equal rights," must have convinced him,

with the theological agreements which were fundamental to him, that he was *urgently needed* in Antioch, at least at that very moment.[4]

Perhaps because the situation in the capital of the province of Syria "became more critical, so that a theologian with Paul's competence in the scriptures, capacity to argue strongly, resolution and capacity for organization was urgently needed."[5] It is unclear whether the ecstatic experience that Paul refers to in 2 Corinthians 12:2, dating around A.D. 42, played a role in Paul's move from Tarsus to Antioch.[6] Paul leaves Antioch as the result of divine intervention. If the reference to fasting in Acts 13:2 implies a deliberate searching for God's guidance,[7] which is a plausible assumption—fasting is mentioned very rarely in Acts 13:2, 3; 14:23—the leadership of the church in Antioch may already have considered a new missionary initiative in areas that had not yet been reached with the gospel.

The sixth period of Paul's ministry is connected with Cyprus (see sec 1.3). Why did Paul and Barnabas travel to Cyprus? Luke does not explain the apostles' strategy. It is plausible to assume that two factors were decisive. First, Barnabas was a native of Cyprus (Acts 4:36). As Barnabas had recruited coworkers for the evangelistic and pastoral ministry in Antioch, he was probably instrumental in suggesting Cyprus as the next geographical area where they might preach the gospel. Second, Luke reports that some of the Jewish believers who had to leave Jerusalem in A.D. 31/32 in the persecution that followed Stephen's murder engaged in missionary work in cities on the Phoenician coast and on Cyprus (Acts 11:19). Barnabas surely knew these Greek-speaking Jewish believers from Jerusalem. Just as Barnabas had been asked by the leaders of the Jerusalem church to go to Antioch and to consolidate the missionary work and the emerging church in that city (Acts 11:22), it is plausible to assume that the leadership of the church in Antioch tasked these two experienced missionaries

---

[4]Martin Hengel and Anna Maria Schwemer, *Paul Between Damascus and Antioch: The Unknown Years* (London: SCM; Lousiville, Ky.: Westminster John Knox, 1997), pp. 179-80.
[5]Ibid., p. 218.
[6]See Rainer Riesner, *Paul's Early Period: Chronology, Mission Strategy, Theology* (Grand Rapids: Eerdmans, 1998), pp. 272, 320.
[7]See I. Howard Marshall, *The Acts of the Apostles. An Introduction and Commentary*, TNTC (Leicester, U.K.: Inter-Varsity Press; Downers Grove, Ill.: InterVarsity Press, 1980), p. 216; also James D. G. Dunn, *The Acts of the Apostles*, EpComm (London: Epworth, 1996), p. 173, with reference to Neh 1:3-4; Lk 2:37.

to consolidate and to expand the missionary work in the cities of Cyprus. It is probably not a coincidence that Barnabas felt responsible for the missionary work on Cyprus at a later date as well (Acts 15:39).

Why did Paul and Barnabas first preach in Salamis? This location was presumably determined by the fact that Salamis was the first port of call of the ship that brought the missionaries from Syria to Cyprus. Salamis was an important enough city. It remained one of the most eminent cities of Cyprus in the Roman period even after it was replaced as capital by Paphos after having been severely damaged in an earthquake in 15 B.C. The Jewish community in the city was certainly another draw.

The Greek verb *dierchesthai* in Acts 13:6, which is translated as "to go through," perhaps indicates that the missionaries engaged in missionary outreach in cities situated between Salamis and Paphos (e.g., in Kition, Amathus and Kourion). In Acts 8:4 the same verb describes missionary activity: "Now those who were scattered went from place to place [*dielthon*], proclaiming the word." Luke is not concerned with describing a particular strategy or method that Paul and Barnabas executed, however. They eventually came to Paphos, the capital of the province, where they reach the Jewish community as well as Gentiles. Luke's narrative focuses on the contact with Sergius Paullus, the Roman governor. We do not know what prompted Paul to end his missionary work in Paphos.

The seventh period of Paul's missionary work is connected to four cities in the southern part of the province of Galatia: Pisidian Antioch in Phrygia, Iconium, Lystra and Derbe in Lycaonia (Acts 13:14—14:23; see sec. 1.3). Why did Paul travel from Paphos on Cyprus straight to Pisidian Antioch?[8] Why did he travel through the newly constituted Roman province of Pamphylia-Lycia (A.D. 43), which included southern Pisidia,[9] without evangelizing among the inhabitants of the numerous and often important cities in this area? It might have been strategically expeditious

---

[8]Luke mentions Perga in Acts 13:13 as a stop on the journey from Paphos to Antioch, evidently as the location of making landfall in Asia Minor (according to Strabo *Geography* 14.42, it was possible then to sail up the river Kestros and reach Perga, seven miles from the coast, by ship) and as the location of John Mark's departure. It is only in Acts 14:25 that a preaching ministry in Perga is mentioned. Cf. David Magie, *Roman Rule in Asia Minor to the End of the Third Century after Christ* (1950; reprint, New York: Arno, 1975), 2:1134 n. 7.

[9]See Stephen Mitchell, *Anatolia: Land, Men, and Gods in Asia Minor* (Oxford: Oxford University Press, 1995), 2:153-4.

to work in the new province, constituted only three years before Paul and Barnabas arrived in A.D. 46. Side and Attaleia were important port cities. Perga, Aspendos and Etenna were significant cities in the Pamphylian plain. Further sizable cities included Sillyon, Lyrba and Cotenna. The leading family of the city of Attaleia, the Calpurnii, whose members held senatorial office during the first century, had landholding interests in the province of Asia as well as in Galatia. Augustus had settled military colonists in Attaleia, whose infrastructure has been described in terms of "civic opulence."[10] Side was a Roman naval base. Perga was a flourishing city, with lively building activity in the early first century. The temple of Artemis was surpassed in fame only by the temple of Artemis Ephesia in Ephesus. The significance of Perga is illustrated by the numerous inscriptions that record the presence of physicians, philosophers, philologists, athletes, actors, poets, singers, mimes, musicians and dancers in the city, some of whom had traveled to Ephesus, Pergamum, Tlos, Thyatira, Sparta and Rome. Inscriptions attest citizens from Side, Aspendos, Selge and Tarsus who visited Perga to see the temple of Artemis.[11] Side competed with Perga for preeminence in the province. Both of these cities are arguably more significant for a missionary strategy that focuses on urban centers than Pisidian Antioch or Lycaonian Iconium. In southern Pisidia, Selge, Termessus and Sagalassus had a more developed urban infrastructure than Pisidian Antioch, and were certainly more important than Iconium, Lystra or Derbe. The Pisidian cities of Ariassos, Kremna, Komama, Pogla, Andeda, Sibidunda, Olbasa, Lysinia, Ilyas, Eudoxiopolis, Apollonia and Tymandos were regional centers—Kremna, Komama and Olbasa were Roman colonies—whose significance was certainly comparable to that of Lystra and Derbe.

One explanation for Paul's journey from Paphos on Cyprus to Pisidian Antioch in southern Galatia is the possibility that Paul had contracted malaria in Pamphylia and that this was the reason why he traveled to southern Galatia, with its higher elevations: he came to Galatia and preached the

---

[10]Ibid., 1:152; for the Calpurnii see ibid., 1:153.
[11]Hartwin Brandt, *Gesellschaft und Wirtschaft Pamphyliens und Pisidiens im Altertum*, Asia-Minor Studien 7 (Bonn: Habelt, 1992), p. 145.

gospel there "because of a physical infirmity" (Gal 4:13).[12] This scenario is certainly possible. It does not exclude the plausibility of another suggestion that links Sergius Paullus, the governor of Cyprus, who according to Acts 13:12 was converted as a result of Paul's preaching, with the family of the Sergii Paulli who owned estates in the region of Vetissus (modern Emirler) in the province of Galatia in central Anatolia.[13] It has been surmised that Paul's move from Paphos to Pisidian Antioch may have been suggested by Sergius Paulus who proposed "that he make it his next port of call, no doubt proving him with letters of introduction to aid his passage and his stay."[14] The implications of this potential effort to reach the leading citizens for Paul's missionary strategy will be explored later (see sec. 5.3).

Pisidian Antioch was certainly an important city—the principal Roman colony in the Greek East, divided into seven districts in analogy to the city of Rome and thus evidently established as a "new Rome" in the border area of Phrygia and Pisidia.[15] The importance of Antioch can be seen in the erection of a large imperial temple, dedicated to the worship of the emperor Augustus. The semi-circular temple was hardly finished when Paul arrived in the city. Luke records the conversion of Jews, proselytes and Gentiles (Acts 13:43, 48). The brief note that "the word of the Lord spread throughout the region" (Acts 13:49) suggests that Paul's preaching in Antioch also affected the fifty villages in the territory controlled by the city, which has been estimated at 540 square miles, with a population of perhaps fifty thousand in addition to the ten thousand people living in

---

[12]William M. Ramsay, *St. Paul the Traveller and the Roman Citizen* (London: Hodder & Stoughton, 1896), pp. 92-97; cf. F. F. Bruce, *Commentary on Galatians*, NIGTC (Grand Rapids: Eerdmans, 1982), pp. 208-9.

[13]See Schnabel, *Early Christian Mission*, 2:1085-86; cf. Riesner, *Paul's Early Period*, 124-25; Cilliers Breytenbach, *Paulus und Barnabas in der Provinz Galatien. Studien zu Apostelgeschichte 13f.; 16,6; 18,23 und den Adressaten des Galaterbriefes*, AGAJU 38 (Leiden: Brill, 1996), pp. 38-45. For a different interpretation of the evidence cf. Douglas A. Campbell, "Possible Inscriptional Attestation to Sergius Paul[l]us (Acts 13:6-12), and the Implications for Pauline Chronology," *JTS* 56 (2005): 1-29. The latest discussion of the Sergii Paulii and their relationship to Pisidian Antioch is the French study of Michel Christol and Thomas Drew-Bear, "Les Sergii Paulli et Antioche," in *Actes du Ier congres international sur Antioche de Pisidie*, ed. T. Drew-Bear et al., Collection archéologie et histoire de l'antiquité 5 (Lyon: Université Lumière-Lyon; Paris : Boccard, 2002), pp. 177-91.

[14]Mitchell, *Anatolia*, 2:7.

[15]See Levick, *Roman Colonies*, p. 78; Stephen Mitchell and Marc Waelkens, *Pisidian Antioch: The Site and Its Monuments* (London: Duckworth, 1998), p. 9.

Antioch itself.[16] Luke's formulation does not indicate whether Paul moved to Antioch in order to reach the people living in this densely populated region. If Paul indeed came to Antioch to reach the local elites—the leading families of the city were the Caristanii, the Sergii, the Munatii, the Flavonii and the Iulii[17]—he was in the end not successful. The "leading men of the city" and the "devout women of high standing" eventually reacted negatively to Paul's activities and expelled the missionaries from the region (Acts 13:50).

The missionary activity of the following months concentrated on three cities in southern Galatia east of Antioch that were located on the Via Sebaste, the strategically important east-west route: Iconium, Lystra and Derbe. As Paul traveled from Antioch to Iconium, he passed through Neapolis and Pappa; on the journey from Lystra to Derbe he passed through Dalisandos, Kodylessos, Laranda and Posala—cities that were not particularly insignificant.[18] As the missionary work in Derbe is narrated rather briefly (Acts 14:20-21, three lines in the Greek text), it can be assumed that Paul and Barnabas did not preach in these cities between Iconium, Lystra and Derbe.

Would the missionaries have moved on quickly if people did not respond positively to the gospel? This is possible, but not very likely. Luke could mention missionary work in these cities without reporting conversions, as he does in the case of Perga at the end of this journey (Acts 14:25). As no explanation is given, we have no information about Paul's geographical strategy after he left Pisidian Antioch. Perhaps Paul intended to travel east on the Via Sebaste, all the way back to Tarsus, a plan that he might have seen fit to alter in view of the fact that he and Barnabas had been driven out of Antioch, Iconium and Lystra. Luke reports for Derbe that the missionaries "made many disciples" (Acts 14:21), evidently without encountering the active resistance of the residents. Rather than moving further east, Paul may have come to the conviction that they should return

---

[16]Mitchell and Waelkens, *Pisidian Antioch*, pp. 3, 15; cf. Barbara Levick, "Antiocheia 15," in *Real-Encyclopädie der classischen Altertumswissenschaft*, vol. Supplement XI, ed. A. F. von Pauly and G. Wissowa (Stuttgart: Metzler, 1968), p. 56.

[17]Levick, *Roman Colonies*, pp. 113-17; Brandt, *Gesellschaft*, p. 126.

[18]Laranda was located at the juncture of several roads that led from the west and the north to five passes across the Taurus Mountains. For details on these cities cf. Schnabel, *Early Christian Mission*, 2:1110, 1120-21.

the way they had come and visit the new believers in Lystra, Iconium and Antioch, and consolidate the churches in these cities. Luke only reports:

> They returned to Lystra, then on to Iconium and Antioch. There they strengthened the souls of the disciples and encouraged them to continue in the faith, saying, "It is through many persecutions that we must enter the kingdom of God." And after they had appointed elders for them in each church, with prayer and fasting they entrusted them to the Lord in whom they had come to believe. (Acts 14:21-23)

Luke's next statement shows again that his reporting is selective:

> Then they passed through Pisidia and came to Pamphylia. When they had spoken the word in Perge, they went down to Attalia. From there they sailed back to Antioch. (Acts 14:24-26)

Did Paul preach while he "passed through" (Gk *dielthontes*) the region of Pisidia in the cities that previously mentioned (Ariassos, Kremna, Komama, Pogla, Andeda, Sibidunda, Olbasa, Lysinia, Ilyas, Eudoxiopolis, Apollonia, Tymandos)? This is possible, perhaps even likely, but the larger chronological framework does not allow much time for missionary activities in the Pisidian cities south of Antioch. Luke reports that Paul preached in Perge, the capital of Pamphylia: he needs only five words of Greek text to state this, and he does not record either conversions or the establishment of a church. Both are likely, however, as we have seen earlier.

Given the political and economic significance of Perge, this very brief remark in Acts 14:25 indicates three facts. First, Luke knows much more than he tells us, his reporting is very selective. Second, we are not given any reasons why Luke sometimes provides more information, while at other times he omits entire episodes or includes only hints. Literary reasons that perhaps may explain the details of Luke's report are equally elusive as historical or contextual explanations. Third, we need to exercise caution in our evaluation of Paul's missionary methods, as the extant evidence is not a complete picture of what transpired. Thus the suggestion that the alleged "fiasco of miscommunication at Lystra"[19] may have prompted Paul

---

[19]Conrad Gempf, "Before Paul Arrived in Corinth: The Mission Strategies in 1 Corinthians 2:2 and Acts 17," in *The New Testament in its First Century Setting: Essays on Context and Background in*

to avoid smaller towns and to concentrate on major metropolitan centers[20] remains entirely hypothetical.

The eighth period of Paul's missionary work begins with a long overland journey from Syrian Antioch via Tarsus and the Cilician Gates in a westerly direction on the Via Sebaste. The goal of Paul was to preach the gospel in the province of Asia (Acts 16:6). This brief notice is usually interpreted in terms of a plan to reach Ephesus, the capital of the Roman province of Asia.[21] While certainly plausible, this is not a foregone conclusion, since Paul had not set his sights on large metropolitan centers before. His missionary work in Damascus (Acts 9:19-20) was not a strategic decision but a natural choice: he preached in the city where he happened to be right after his conversion. His move to Jerusalem (Acts 9:26) was caused by a plot in Damascus to kill him and prompted by a desire to meet with Peter (Gal 1:18) and to return to the city where he had lived as a student for many years and had friends and relatives. His move to Tarsus (Acts 9:30) can most plausibly be explained by the fact that this was his home town where his family lived. The move to Antioch was the result of an invitation by Barnabas (Acts 11:25-26); whatever "strategic" reasons Paul may have had to relocate to the capital of the province of Syria, he did not initiate this move.

Because Paul wanted to preach the gospel in the province of Asia, he would have first traveled to Apameia (note the survey of Paul's itinerary in sec. 1.4). Strabo describes Apameia as a large commercial city that was surpassed in Asia Minor only by Ephesus (Strabo *Geography* 12.8.15). In the Roman period Apameia was an assize center (Lat *conventus,* Gk *dioikēsis*) and the hub of a large region—not only for the regions of Phrygia, Lydia and Caria, but also for Cappadocia, Pamphylia and Pisidia. Apameia had the largest Jewish community of central Anatolia. In a famous case dating to 62 B.C., the Jews of Asia Minor took L. Valerius Flaccus, the proconsul

---

Honor of B. W. Winter, ed. P. J. Williams et al. (Grand Rapids: Eerdmans, 2004), p. 127.

[20]Conrad Gempf, "Mission and Misunderstanding: Paul and Barnabas in Lystra (Acts 14:8-20)," in *Mission and Meaning: Essays Presented to Peter Cotterell,* ed. A. Billington et al. (Carlisle, U.K.: Paternoster, 1995), pp. 58-59.

[21]F. F. Bruce, *The Book of the Acts,* rev. ed., NICNT (Grand Rapids: Eerdmans, 1988), p. 306; Marshall, *Acts of the Apostles,* p. 261; Dunn, *Acts of the Apostles,* p. 217; Witherington, *The Acts of the Apostles,* p. 477; Schnabel, *Early Christian Mission,* 2:1131.

of the province of Asia, to court for prohibiting the transfer of monies to the temple in Jerusalem. He was accused of having confiscated twenty pounds of gold from Laodicea and one hundred pounds from Apameia (in today's currency about \$1 million and \$5 million respectively).[22] Cicero, the famous senator of Republican Rome, defended Flaccus. His narration in *Pro Flacco* 67-68 provides evidence that the contributions in gold that the Jews sent annually to Jerusalem were collected in the centers of the assize districts into which Roman Asia Minor had been divided and which continued to be a key element of the provincial administration.[23] It is obvious that Apameia would have been a strategic location for missionary work in this region.

From Apameia Paul could have traveled southwest and west to the Lykos Valley in the region of the upper Maeander River, with the important cities of Laodicea and Hierapolis, and the smaller cities of Colossae and Tripolis ad Maeandrum.[24] Laodicea, also an assize center, was one of the three cities of Asia Minor that were permitted to name its games after the emperor Claudius. It had two theaters, a stadium and an odeion (a small theater for musical presentations) as well as large public baths. The Jewish community in Laodicea was the subject of a letter that the magistrates of the city wrote to the Roman proconsul Gaius Rabirius, raising the issue of how to treat the local Jews.[25] Hierapolis, birthplace of the philosopher Epictetus (born in A.D. 50), was an economic center due to its wool, dye works and the tourism connected with its thermal springs. Traveling west in the Maeander Valley, Paul would have found several cities that were at least as large as the cities in southern Galatia, which he had just visited: Antiochia ad Maeandrum, Nysa, Tralles, Magnesia ad Maeandrum, Priene and the port city of Miletus.[26] The theater of Miletus was one of the largest in Asia Minor.

---

[22]See Lee I. Levine, *Jerusalem: Portrait of the City in the Second Temple Period (538 B.C.E. - 70 C.E.)* (Philadelphia: Jewish Publication Society, 2002), p. 247.

[23]See Stephen Mitchell, "The Administration of Roman Asia from 133 BC to AD 250," in *Lokale Autonomie und römische Ordnungsmacht in den kaiserzeitlichen Provinzen vom 1. bis 3. Jahrhundert*, ed. W. Eck and E. Müller-Luckner, Schriften des Historischen Kollegs 42 (München: Oldenbourg, 1999), p. 27.

[24]For details on these cities see Schnabel, *Early Christian Mission*, 2:1235-46.

[25]Josephus *Antiquitates Judaicae* 14.241.

[26]For details see Schnabel, *Early Christian Mission*, 2:1231-36.

The significance of the Jewish community in Miletus can be seen in the fact that the translator of the book of Ezekiel from Hebrew into Greek smuggled the city into the text of Ezekiel 27:18 (translating the phrase "wool from Zahar" with "wool from Miletus").[27] From Miletus, Paul could have easily reached Ephesus via the cities of Priene and Maiandros in a two or three day journey traveling north.

If Paul had followed a more northerly route after leaving Apameia, he would have reached Eumeneia, Sebaste, Akmonia, Temenouthyrai and Blaundos[28] before reaching the valley of the Hermos River, in which Philadelphia and Sardis were located. Sardis, an old royal city, had perhaps as many as 100,000 inhabitants. It owed its wealth to the city's location at the crossroads of major roads leading to Ephesus, Smyrna, Pergamum and into the interior regions of Anatolia. The influence of the Jewish community in Sardis is illustrated by the fact that both a Roman official and the city council of Sardis confirmed the Jews' considerable autonomy rights. Lucius Antonius, the proquaestor and propraetor in the province of Asia, wrote to the city of Sardis in 49 B.C. to confirm the rights of the Jewish citizens.[29] The city of Sardis issued a decree, sometime after October 47 B.C., formally recognizing three specific rights for which the Jews had asked: the right to assemble, the right to adjudicate legal matters among themselves, and the right to maintain a meeting place for worship.[30] From Sardis, Paul could have easily reached Thyatira and Pergamum to the north or Smyrna to the west.[31] From Smyrna, Paul could have reached Ephesus, located to the south, in two days.

Thus, instead of linking Acts 16:6 with the project of a mission to Ephesus, Paul might have been planning to preach the gospel in any (or all) of these cities: Apameia, Laodicea, Hierapolis, Colossae, Tripolis ad Maeandrum, Antiochia ad Maeandrum, Nysa, Tralles, Magnesia ad Maeandrum, Priene and Miletus in the south-central regions of the

---

[27]Wool from Miletus was both famous and expensive; for details see Peter Herrmann, "Milesischer Purpur," *Istanbuler Mitteilungen* 25 (1975): 141-47.

[28]For details see Schnabel, *Early Christian Mission*, 2:1200-1203.

[29]Josephus *Antiquitates Judaicae* 14.235.

[30]Ibid., 14.259-261. Cf. Miriam Pucci Ben Zeev, *Jewish Rights in the Roman World: The Greek and Roman Documents Quoted by Josephus Flavius*, TSAJ 74 (Tübingen: Mohr Siebeck, 1998), pp. 216-25.

[31]For details on these cities see Schnabel, *Early Christian Mission*, 1:819-38.

province of Asia, and Eumeneia, Sebaste, Akmonia, Temenouthyrai, Blaundos, Philadelphia, Sardis, Thyatira, Pergamum, and Smyrna in the north-central regions of the province. We should not read the concept of a "metropolis" mission into Luke's account of Paul's missionary activity during these years.

After Paul had to abandon the project of preaching the gospel in the province of Asia due to an intervention by God (Acts 16:6), he drew up a new plan, aiming at cities in the province of Bithynia-Pontus. Presumably Paul wanted to preach the gospel in the cities of Nicaea, Nikomedia and Chalcedon.[32] As this plan had to be abandoned (Acts 16:7), Paul passed by Mysia and eventually came to Troas.

The move across the Macedonicum Mare, the northern part of the Aegean Sea, was not motivated by a strategic decision to reach cities in Europe. Rather, according to Luke's report, it was prompted by a dream-vision: "During the night Paul had a vision: there stood a man of Macedonia pleading with him and saying, 'Come over to Macedonia and help us.' When he had seen the vision, we immediately tried to cross over to Macedonia, being convinced that God had called us to proclaim the good news to them" (Acts 16:9-10).

After the sea passage from Troas to Neapolis, Paul evangelized in three cities in the province of Macedonia: Philippi, Thessalonica and Beroea (see sec. 1.4). Philippi, the first stop of Paul's move to Europe, is often mentioned by Greek and Roman historians; it was here that Brutus and Cassius, who had eliminated Julius Caesar, fought the famous battle against Mark Antony and Octavian (Augustus). Augustus refounded the city as a Roman colony in 27 B.C. as Colonia Iulia Augusta Philippiensis and settled Italian colonists and veterans of the Praetorian cohort in the city. In the early imperial period Philippi was the most important city of Eastern Macedonia, although it was not a very large city: it had between five thousand and ten thousand inhabitants in the first century.[33] According to Acts 16:13 there was a Jewish synagogue at the river Gangites, about three kilometers west of the city center.

---

[32]For details see Schnabel, *Early Christian Mission*, 1:842-48.

[33]Peter Pilhofer, *Philippi. Band I: Die erste christliche Gemeinde Europas. Band II: Katalog der Inschriften von Philippi*, WUNT 87.119 (Tübingen: Mohr-Siebeck, 1995-2000), 1:76.

Why did Paul go to Philippi first? The answer to this question is to be found, perhaps, not so much in a particular strategy of Paul but in the schedule of the ship on which the missionaries sailed across the Aegean. Before docking in Amphipolis, an important city further west, the first port of call of ships arriving from Asia Minor was Neapolis, the harbor controlled by Philippi. If Paul was familiar with the local history of Philippi and Amphipolis, the latter might have been a better choice for gaining a foothold for the gospel in Macedonia. When the region came under Roman control in 168 B.C., Amphipolis became the capital of the first Macedonian region but then suffered a decline that only recently had been reversed; the city was flourishing again under the emperor Augustus. An up-and-coming city would have been a less exposed location for missionary work, a welcome relief after the experiences in the province of Galatia and after the abortive attempt to engage in missionary work in the province of Asia. Preaching the news of Jesus Christ the Son of God and the Lord and Savior of the world in Philippi risked hostile reactions from the start, as the citizens were staunch supporters of the worship of the emperor and of his deified ancestors. Inscriptions attest officials and priests of the cult of the "divine Augustus," women officiating in the cult honoring Livia, the wife of Augustus, as well as *seviri Augustales,* that is, freedmen who were responsible for the festivals honoring Augustus. A series of coins minted in Philippi shows on the obverse the head of the emperor Augustus with the legend "Colonia Augusta Iulia Philippensis iussu Augusti" (the Augustan colony of Julian Philippi on the command of Augustus). The reverse of the coins depicts a statue of Augustus on a pedestal being crowned by Julius Caesar, with the legend "Augustus Divi Filius Divo Iulio" (Augustus, son of the Divine, for the Divine Julius).[34]

Paul and his coworkers left Philippi after this incident and traveled on the Via Egnatia westwards via Amphipolis to Thessalonica, situated at the junction of the roads from Asia Minor to the Adriatic Sea and from the Balkans through the Axios Valley to the Danube region. This and the fact that the city's harbor controlled the maritime connections with the Bosporus soon lead to Thessalonica, surpassing the old Macedonian capi-

---

[34]Lukas Bormann, *Philippi—Stadt und Christengemeinde zur Zeit des Paulus,* NTSup 78 (Leiden: Brill, 1995), pp. 63-64; for the inscriptions cf. ibid., pp. 42-46, for the coins ibid., pp. 34-35.

tal Pella in importance, about 40 kilometers (25 miles) to the northwest. Thessalonica was the most populous city of Macedonia (Strabo *Geography* 7.7.4), which can be regarded as another reason why the city was an ideal location for missionary work. When Claudius reorganized Macedonia as a senatorial province in A.D. 44, Thessalonica became the capital.

It is unclear why Paul traveled to Beroea next. It would have been plausible to continue on the Via Egnatia, the main Roman road that ran from Byzantium (Constantinople) via Philippi, Thessalonica, Pella and Edessa to Dyrrhachium and Apollonia, port cities on the Adriatic Sea. Pella, the old capital of Macedonia, a city with impressive palaces, had been destroyed by an earthquake in the first century B.C. The recently founded Roman colony of Pella (Colonia Pellensis), established in A.D. 30 west of old Pella, would have been an acceptable candidate for missionary work, as was Edessa, a city that had been granted autonomy and the right to mint coins by Augustus. We have no evidence for Jews living in Pella or Edessa during the early Roman Empire, a factor (if not a literary or archaeological coincidence) that may explain why Paul did not continue his journey on the Via Egnatia. Paul could have decided to travel south on the major north-south route to the province of Achaia. Instead, he moved to Beroea, a city situated at the southwestern end of the Macedonian Plain on the southernmost of the three passes across the Bermion Mountains. Beroea seems to have been the seat of the Macedonian provincial assembly (Koinon), headed up by the high priest of the imperial cult of the province. This means that Beroea was not necessarily a more attractive destination than Pella or Edessa for missionaries who had just been forced to leave the capital of the province in a hurry. Perhaps the Jewish community was the reason why Paul and Silas went to Beroea. The new Jewish converts in Thessalonica who "sent Paul and Silas off to Beroea" (Acts 17:10) may have used connections to relatives or friends there in their effort to bring the missionaries to safety.[35]

The ninth period of Paul's missionary work is linked with the cities of Athens and Corinth in the province of Achaia (see sec. 1.4). When Paul

---

[35]The earliest evidence for Jews in Beroea outside of Acts 17:10-11 are Jewish tombstones dating to the fourth and fifth century; cf. David Noy et al., *Inscriptiones Judaicae Orientis*, vol. I: *Eastern Europe*, TSAJ 101 (Tübingen: Mohr-Siebeck, 2004), pp. 76-87.

was forced to leave Beroea on account of hostile Jews from Thessalonica who had stirred up trouble for the missionaries, "the believers immediately sent Paul away to the coast, but Silas and Timothy remained behind. Those who conducted Paul brought him as far as Athens" (Acts 17:14-15). It is again unclear what Paul's strategy was. He could have continued on the Via Egnatia to evangelize cities further west. Instead, he decided to leave Macedonia, perhaps to avoid further troubles. Luke's geographical references make it difficult to discern a strategy on Paul's part. Several of the new converts from Beroea "conducted Paul" to the coast and "brought him as far as Athens," where Paul gave them instructions "to have Silas and Timothy join him as soon as possible" (Acts 17:15). Luke's next comment states that "while Paul was waiting for them in Athens, he was deeply distressed to see that the city was full of idols" (Acts 17:16), which prompts the remark: "so he argued in the synagogue with the Jews and the devout persons, and also in the marketplace every day with those who happened to be there" (Acts 17:17).

Did Paul plan missionary work in Athens when he left Beroea? Or was his visit in Athens a stopover during his journey further south to Corinth that Paul, ever the eager missionary, could not help but use as an opportunity to preach the gospel? The coordinating conjunction *men oun* in the Greek text of Acts 17:17, generally translated "so," denotes continuation; as a characteristic expression in the book of Acts the phrase introduces a development in the narrative.[36] The formulation cannot be taken as evidence that Paul's missionary work in Athens resulted from his exasperation about the idols that were on display in the city. The fact that Luke provides an extensive account of Paul's visit (Acts 17:16-34) suggests, perhaps, that Paul's preaching in Athens was not incidental. The summary statement in Acts 17:17 indicates that Paul pursued missionary work in Athens as he did in other cities. He preached in the local synagogue to Jewish audiences and in the marketplace to Gentile audiences: "He argued in the synagogue with the Jews and the devout persons, and also in the marketplace every day with those who happened to be there" (Acts 17:17).

---

[36]BDAG, p. 630; cf. Barrett, *The Acts of the Apostles*, 1:75; 2:828.

Even though the heyday of Athens was long in the past, the city remained an important cultural and intellectual center in the Mediterranean world, despite economic difficulties during the first century.[37] Another draw for Paul was the Jewish community. Jews had lived in Athens since the fourth century B.C.[38] As Paul walked through the city, he would have been able to see statues of King Herod I, whose support for the city had been honored by the Athenians.[39] One statue base, found behind the Parthenon on the acropolis, had the following inscription: "The people to King Herod / friend of Romans / because of his good works and good will toward the city." The chronology of Paul's travels leaves a period of several months (January through March, A.D. 50) for his missionary work in Athens.

Luke does not inform his readers why Paul left Athens. The apostle waited for the arrival of his coworkers (Acts 17:15) who had stayed behind in Beroea (Acts 17:14), with Timothy being active in Thessalonica as well (1 Thess 3:1-5). They met Paul in Athens, who sent them back to Macedonia with new assignments: Timothy evidently went to Thessalonica (1 Thess 3:1-5) and Silas to Philippi (2 Cor 11:9; Phil 4:14).[40] They later rejoined Paul in Corinth (Acts 18:5). Luke reports neither official sanctions nor an increasingly hostile opposition that forced Paul to leave the city. He remarks laconically that "after this Paul left Athens and went to Corinth" (Acts 18:1). The phrase "after this" (Gk *meta tauta*) simply means "after the Athenian episode was over."[41]

No reason is given why Paul moved to Corinth. Luke reports that Paul quickly established connections with the Jewish community, that he preached in the local synagogue and that he proclaimed the gospel to Jewish and Gentile audiences (Acts 18:2-4). Corinth, one of the major cities

---

[37]For details on Athens see Schnabel, *Early Christian Mission*, 2:1170-77.

[38]See Irina Levinskaya, *The Book of Acts in its Diaspora Setting*, The Book of Acts in Its First-Century Setting 5 (Carlisle, U.K.: Paternoster, 1996), pp. 158-62; Noy et al., *Inscriptiones Judaicae Orientis I*, pp. 144-64.

[39]Josephus *Bellum Judaicum* 1.422-425. Cf. Peter Richardson, *Herod: King of the Jews and Friend of the Romans* (1996; reprint, Minneapolis: Fortress, 1999), p. 177; see ibid., pp. 207-8 (nos. 6-8) for the text of the three inscriptions (published as *OGIS* 414; *OGIS* 427; *SEG* XII 150) discovered in Athens attesting a benefaction that named Herod.

[40]See Marshall, *Acts*, p. 281; Abraham J. Malherbe, *The Letters to the Thessalonians*, AncB 32B (New York: Doubleday, 2000), p. 70.

[41]Barrett, *Acts of the Apostles*, 2:860.

of ancient Greece, minted its own coins since 600 B.C.[42] The city had been destroyed in 146 B.C. by the Roman consul Lucius Mummius as punishment for its role in the resistance of the Greek cities against Rome. Julius Caesar refounded the city in 44 B.C. as a Roman colony with the official name Colonia Laus Iulia Corinthus, settling several thousand freed slaves and veterans in the city.[43] The new colony was intended to safeguard Roman control of the trade from Rome to the eastern Mediterranean.[44] The aristocratic families of the Senate in Rome evidently hoped that the freedmen which they settled in the colony would be their middlemen in the new commercial center on the Isthmus of Greece. Scholars estimate that Roman Corinth (including the harbor of Lechaeum) had a population of approximately 80,000 people. If the inhabitants of the five larger cities in the area—Krommyon, Cenchreae, Tenea, Ayios Charalambos, and Asprokambos—and of the forty-five smaller towns and villages that belonged to the territory of Corinth are included, the population of "greater Corinth" was about 100,000 people.[45] The proconsul (governor) of the province of Achaia resided in Corinth. Because the city had a Jewish community (Acts 18:4-8),[46] this thriving economic and political center was a strategic location for missionary work. Paul arrived in Corinth in February or March A.D. 50 and engaged in missionary activity for over eighteen months (Acts 18:11, 18), leaving the city in September(?) A.D. 51.

The divine encouragement that Paul received in a dream during his mis-

---

[42]For details on the city of Corinth see Schnabel, *Early Christian Mission*, 2:1181-86.

[43]See Strabo *Geographica* 8.6.23; Plutarch *De Caesar* 57; Cassius Dio *Historiae Romanae* 43.50.3-4; Appian *Libyca*. 136. Cf. David W. J. Gill, "Corinth: A Roman Colony in Achaea," *BZ* 37 (1993): 259-64; Mary E. H. Walbank, "The Foundation and Planning of Early Roman Corinth," *JRA* 10 (1997): 95-130. Some sources call the city Laus Iulia Corinthiensis.

[44]See Charles K. Williams, "Roman Corinth as a Commercial Center," in *The Corinthia in the Roman Period*, ed. T. E. Gregory, JRASup 8 (Ann Arbor, Mich.: Journal of Roman Archaeology, 1993), pp. 31-46.

[45]See Donald Engels, *Roman Corinth: An Alternative Model for the Classical City* (Chicago and London: University of Chicago Press, 1990), pp. 79-84, 178-81. David G. Romano, "A Tale of Two Cities: Roman Colonies at Corinth," in *Romanization and the City: Creation, Transformations, and Failures*, ed. E. Fentress, JRASup 38 (Portsmouth, R.I.: Journal of Roman Archaeology, 2000), p. 103 n. 71, thinks that these figures are too high for the time before the foundation of a second colony in Corinth (Colonia Iulia Flavia Augusta Corinthiensis) under Vespasian after A.D. 70.

[46]The lintel with the inscription "synagogue of the Hebrews" that was discovered in Corinth was initially dated to the first century A.D. Today most scholars prefer a date in the second/third or in the fourth century; cf. Noy et al., *Inscriptiones Judaicae Orientis I*, pp. 182-84; Levinskaya, *Diaspora*, pp. 162-65.

sionary work in Corinth presupposes the continued opposition of members of the local Jewish community, who are reported to have abused Paul (Acts 18:6). Paul heard the Lord say to him, "Do not be afraid, but speak and do not be silent; for I am with you, and no one will lay a hand on you to harm you, for there are many in this city who are my people" (Acts 18:9-10).

The following verse asserts that "he stayed there a year and six months, teaching the word of God among them" (Acts 18:11). This sequence of comments has been interpreted as marking a change of missionary strategy: while Paul had reacted to strong opposition to his preaching with hurried departures, he now stays in Corinth despite continued opposition of the Jews, prompted by God to continue his missionary work over a longer period of time.[47] While it is possible that the divine intervention preempted a hasty departure by Paul, Luke does not actually state this. He does not link Paul's dream (Acts 18:9) with the opposition of the Jews (Acts 18:6) but with his report of the conversion of Crispus, the synagogue official, and of many Corinthians who heard Paul preach (Acts 18:8). The Gallio inscription that has been found in Delphi[48] allows us to date the proconsulship of L. Iunius Gallio to the year from July 1, A.D. 51, to June 30, A.D. 52, which means that the legal proceedings before Gallio that Paul's Jewish opponents wanted to initiate should probably be dated to the summer of A.D. 51. It is also not plausible to assume that the Gallio incident might have been the reason for a planned departure of Paul, which was averted on account of divine intervention. In other words, because the text is silent about Paul's potential plans, and because the reference to God's words of encouragement is neither linked with the Jewish opposition to Paul in the spring of A.D. 50 nor with the Gallio incident in the summer of A.D. 51, it is impossible to know the reasons that prompted the dream. Moreover, God's words of encouragement only imply an anxiety on Paul's part, which is left unexplained, without reference to a planned

---

[47]See Philip H. Towner, "Mission Practice and Theology under Construction (Acts 18—20)," in *Witness to the Gospel. The Theology of Acts*, ed. I. H. Marshall and D. Peterson (Grand Rapids: Eerdmans, 1998), pp. 417-36.

[48]See André Plassart, *Inscriptions de la terrasse du temple et de la region nord du sanctuaire, Nos. 276 à 350. Les inscriptions du Temple du IVᵉ siècle*, Fouilles de Delphes III, Épigraphie 4 (Paris: Boccard, 1970), pp. 26-32 (no. 286; plate 7); Jerome Murphy-O'Connor, *St. Paul's Corinth: Texts and Archaeology* (Wilmington, Del.: Glazier, 1983), pp. 173-76; Riesner, *Paul's Early Period*, pp. 203-4.

departure. Speculations about a change in Paul's missionary methods have no foundation in the text.

Luke gives no reasons for Paul's eventual departure from Corinth. It is evident, however, that Paul was not driven out by local opposition. He left because he decided that it was time to move on. "After staying there for a considerable time, Paul said farewell to the believers and sailed for Syria, accompanied by Priscilla and Aquila. At Cenchreae he had his hair cut, for he was under a vow" (Acts 18:18).

The vow is difficult to interpret. First, it is not entirely clear whether the statement "he had his hair cut, for he was under a vow" refers to Aquila or to Paul. The grammar of the Greek sentence allows for both possibilities. However, because Luke's focus is on Paul, it is more plausible to take Paul as the subject of the sentence. The traditional understanding that Paul had his hair cut is most likely to be correct. Second, it is not clear whether the vow should be understood against a Jewish or a Greek background. Some suggest that Paul's action should be understood in terms of a standard reaction, attested among Greeks, to a dream in which a god gave guidance. Many understand the vow to refer to a Nazirite vow (cf. Num 6:1-21), which required the hair to be cut off at the end of the period during which the vow was operative.[49] The text does not indicate whether the vow was related to Paul's missionary work in Corinth or to his departure from the city.

The tenth period of Paul's missionary work comprises the three years from A.D. 52 to 55, during which he preached the gospel in Ephesus, the capital of the province of Asia (see sec. 1.5). I have already discussed the possibility that the initial goal of the eighth phase of Paul's missionary work, the preaching of the gospel in the province of Asia (Acts 16:6), targeted Ephesus, an inference that is plausible but not necessarily accurate. Paul's return journey from Corinth to Syria (Acts 18:18, 22-23) took him to Ephesus. Paul was accompanied by Aquila and Priscilla, a Jewish Christian couple who had to leave Rome on account of the edict of Emperor Claudius ordering the expulsion of the Jews from the city as a result of continued disturbances caused by Jewish Christians and their

---

[49]See Witherington, *Acts of the Apostles*, p. 557.

preaching of the gospel (Acts 18:2).[50] It appears that Aquila and Priscilla had branches of their tentmaking (or leather) business in Corinth and in Ephesus. Perhaps Paul accompanied Aquila and Priscilla, who may have traveled to Ephesus in order to look after their business venture there. It is also possible that the ship with which they wanted to reach Syria put into Ephesus as a regular port of call. On the other hand, it is not impossible to assume that the journey to Ephesus in the late summer or fall of A.D. 51 was a strategic decision: Paul may have organized a visit that was meant to explore the possibility of a later extended period of missionary work in the city. At any rate, Paul takes the opportunity of this visit to contact the Jewish community in Ephesus.

When the Jewish community of Ephesus asks Paul to stay, he declines but promises a visit, "if God wills," in the not too distant future (Acts 18:21). Unless we understand this expression as a pious formula Jews and Greeks tended to use in these sorts of contexts, Luke conveys Paul's conviction that his movements as a preacher and teacher depend on God.[51] Luke does not explain why Paul does not stay in Ephesus.

The expansion of the Western text, which is also found in the Byzantine textual tradition, provides a motivation for Paul's departure from Ephesus. It reads in Acts 18:21: "I must at all costs keep the approaching festival in Jerusalem" (Codex D). In the year A.D. 51 the Day of Atonement (Yom Kippur) fell on October 2, the festival of Tabernacles (Sukkot) on October 7-15. If Paul left Corinth in September, he did not have much time to reach Jerusalem. This clarification in later manuscripts does not explain, however, why Paul wanted to be in Jerusalem for one of the Jewish festivals.

It is preferable to either look for a more plausible explanation or to acknowledge that we do not know the reason for Paul's refusal to stay in Ephesus at this particular time. A reasonable suggestion surmises that

> Paul, profoundly disturbed by opposition that had already made itself felt in Galatia and may have begun to affect Corinth and other centres also, made his way to Jerusalem to find out how far the Jerusalem authorities were behind the trouble-makers, and if possible to stop the trouble at its

---

[50]For details cf. Schnabel, *Early Christian Mission*, 1:806-11.
[51]Cf. 1 Cor 4:19; 16:7; see also Heb 6:3; Jas 4:15.

source. This might account for the speed of his journey—he was not at this point concerned to visit churches en route but to get to his destination as quickly as possible—and also for Luke's silence; he did not wish to dig up old troubles."[52]

After Paul visited Caesarea, Jerusalem[53] and Antioch, he traveled to Galatia and Phrygia and taught the believers in the churches he had established in these areas (Acts 18:22-23). This itinerary indicates that, for Paul, the consolidation of Christians was as important as pioneer missionary work in new cities.

After finally reaching Ephesus in late spring or summer of the year A.D. 52 (Acts 19:1), Paul taught disciples of John the Baptist, in the synagogue and in the lecture hall of Tyrannus (Acts 19:2-9). Ephesus was one of the most important urban centers of the Mediterranean world—one of the largest cities of the Roman Empire with about 200,000 inhabitants, and the residence city of the governor of the province of Asia.[54] Luke reports the success of Paul's missionary work in Ephesus in a manner that is unique in the book of Acts: "This continued for two years, so that all the residents of the province of Asia, both Jews and Greeks, heard the word of the Lord" (Acts 19:10).

What is remarkable is not only the length of Paul's stay in the city, but also the effects of his missionary work on the entire province. The information that Luke provides is confirmed by a comment in 1 Corinthians 16:19 where Paul, writing from Ephesus, conveys greetings from "the churches of Asia" to the Christians in Corinth, informing the Corinthian Christians that God has opened "a wide door for effective work" in Ephesus (1 Cor 16:8-9). Luke does not clarify his comment in geographical terms or in terms of Paul's missionary methods.

The eleventh phase of Paul's mission is his short stay in the province of Illyricum, which is hinted at in Romans 15:19. No details are known about this time (see sec. 1.6).

---

[52]Barrett, *Acts of the Apostles*, 2:881.

[53]The Greek text does not actually mention Jerusalem. The verbs that Luke uses in Acts 18:22 ("When he had landed at Caesarea, *he went up* and greeted the church and then *went down* to Antioch") are appropriate for a journey from Caesarea "up" (into the Judean hills) to Jerusalem and from there "down" to Antioch in Syria; a journey from Caesarea to Antioch would not be described with the verbs "he went up" and "he went down." Also, the expression "the church" (*hē ekklēsia*; with the definite article) is more plausibly linked with the church in Jerusalem.

[54]For details cf. Schnabel, *Early Christian Mission*, 2:1204-15.

The twelfth phase of Paul's missionary work is linked with his un-planned stay in Caesarea Maritima (see sec. 1.6). Paul's plans for fu-ture missionary ministry focused on a visit to Rome (Acts 19:21; Rom 1:11-15; 15:23) and to Spain (Rom 15:24, 28). Paul had decided that he needed to travel to Jerusalem and to hand over the collection that he asked the churches in Macedonia and Achaia to put together for the needy believers in Jerusalem.[55] During the visit to Jerusalem, Jews from the province of Asia who saw Paul in the temple seized him and tried to kill him. Paul was rescued by the Roman officer of the army detach-ment stationed in Jerusalem and eventually transferred to Caesarea on the coast. Paul was a prisoner in Caesarea for two years (A.D. 57-59), waiting for his trial and eventually for his transfer to Rome, after he had used his right as a Roman citizen to appeal to the emperor to decide his case. During this time Paul used any opportunity that presented itself to speak about Jesus Christ. This included appearances before the highest Roman officials of the province of Judea: before governor Felix (Acts 24:1-27) and before governor Festus (Acts 25:1—26:32). And Paul spoke before the highest representatives of the Jewish commonwealth: the high priest Ananias (Acts 24:1), the chief priests (Acts 25:2-7) and king Agrippa (Acts 25:13; 26:1). Luke includes no comment about the results of Paul's witness in Caesarea.

The thirteenth phase of Paul's mission is linked with the two or three years of imprisonment in Rome from A.D. 60-62. Paul was able to meet the leaders of the Jewish community in the city of Rome (Acts 28:17-28). The initiative for these contacts is attributed to Paul (Acts 28:17), in the course of which Paul had the opportunity to speak for several hours before a larger number of Jews about his message, "trying to convince them about Jesus both from the law of Moses and from the prophets" (Acts 28:23). His proclamation of the news of Jesus the Messiah led to conversions in the Jewish community (Acts 28:24).

The fourteenth phase of Paul's missionary work is linked with Spain, if we accept the evidence of the second century sources (for details see sec. 1.6). Paul had intended to reach Spain since A.D. 56/57 at the latest: he

---

[55]Cf. Rom 15:25-28, 30-31; 1 Cor 16:1-4; 2 Cor 8—9.

mentions this new missionary initiative in his letter written to the Christians in the city of Rome written at this time (cf. Rom 15:23-28). Why did Paul plan to begin missionary work in Spain? The Greek and the Hebrew notion that in the West the "end of the earth" was located in Gades or in Tarshish probably played an important role.[56] In other words, Paul might have considered a mission to Spain with the goal of contributing to the literal fulfillment of Jesus' command to reach the "ends of the earth" (Acts 1:8). If Paul was indeed released from his incarceration in Rome and then traveled to Spain, he might have attempted to preach in Tarraco, the provincial capital of Hispania Citerior. There is no information about Paul's missionary work there.

A fifteenth phase of Paul's missionary work places the apostle on the island of Crete. Paul's comment in Titus 1:5 suggests that after Paul returned from Spain he spent some time in the cities of Crete. However, there is no hard evidence for the kind of missionary work or teaching ministry that Paul was engaged in.

Paul and cities: Preliminary conclusions. When we survey the evidence presented in this section it becomes obvious that it is a significant overstatement to say that Paul's passion was the planting of churches in metropolitan centers or in the "strategic cities" of the Roman Empire.[57] Paul's missionary work in Cilicia may have focused on Tarsus, but this is not certain. His ministry in Antioch was certainly a "metropolis mission." When he moved to Cyprus, he did not go straight to Paphos, the capital of the province, but to cities on the eastern and southern coast of the island. When he reached Asia Minor, he bypassed the large cities in the

---

[56]See W. Paul Bowers, "Studies in Paul's Understanding of His Mission" (Ph.D. diss. University of Cambridge, 1976), pp. 53-62; Bernd Wander, "Die letzte Jerusalemreise des Paulus," in *Warum wollte Paulus nach Spanien? Ein forschungs- und motivgeschichtlicher Überblick*, ed. F. W. Horn, BZNW 106 (Berlin: De Gruyter, 2001), pp. 175-95.

[57]See Odo Haas, *Paulus der Missionar. Ziel, Grundsätze und Methoden der Missionstätigkeit des Apostels Paulus nach seinen eigenen Aussagen* (Münsterschwarzach: Vier-Türme-Verlag, 1971), pp. 83-86; David J. Bosch, *Transforming Mission: Paradigm Shifts in the Theology of Mission*, American Society of Missiology Series 16 (1991; reprint, Maryknoll: Orbis, 1999), pp. 129-30; Howard Peskett and Vinoth Ramachandra, *The Message of Mission: The Glory of Christ in All Time and Space* (Downers Grove, Ill.: InterVarsity Press, 2003), p. 225; Roger S. Greenway, "Success in the City: Paul's Urban Mission Strategy: Acts 14:1-28," in *Mission in Acts: Ancient Narratives in Contemporary Context*, ed. R. L. Gallagher and Paul P. Hertig, American Society of Missiology Series 34 (Maryknoll, N.Y.: Orbis Books, 2004), pp. 183-95.

province of Pamphylia to evangelize in relatively small towns in southern Galatia, without attempting to reach Ancyra, the capital of the province of Galatia in the north. When he reached the province of Macedonia, he did not go straight to Thessalonica, the provincial capital, which could be reached by ship, but to Philippi. When he had to leave Thessalonica, he did not go east on the Via Egnatia to reach larger cities further west, nor did he travel straight to Corinth, the capital of the province of Achaia, but to Athens, a city with a great history and reputation but with a more humble present role.

Paul certainly focused on cities rather than on villages. Reading the gospels, this may come indeed as a surprise: Jesus visited the small towns and the villages of Galilee, a focus that would naturally have served as a model for the apostles. On the other hand, Jesus is portrayed as preaching in front of audiences that numbered in the thousands. The conclusion seems obvious: Jesus sought to reach people wherever they lived, he preached before as many people as possible. This was Paul's burden as well: to reach as many Jews and Gentiles as possible with the message of salvation in Jesus Christ, wherever they lived. As Paul always sought to seek out Jews, he was bound to focus on cities: in the provinces outside of Judea, Jewish communities could only be found in cities.

Did Paul focus on cities in the expectation that establishment of a church in a metropolis (lit. "mother city") would naturally, perhaps automatically, radiate to other cities? This is what Roland Allen assumed: "St Paul's theory of evangelizing a province was not to preach in every place in it himself, but to establish centres of Christian life in two or three important places from which the knowledge might spread into the country round [sic]."[58] This proposition is questionable for the following reasons.

First, many if not most of the cities in which Paul preached the gospel were Greek (Hellenistic) cities that were organized as a polis in which the citizens governed their own affairs.[59] A "radiation effect" of developments in a particular city would generally end at the borders of the territory

---

[58] Allen, *Missionary Methods*, p. 12.

[59] See Oswyn Murray, "Polis," *OCD*, pp. 1205-6; A. H. M. Jones, *The Greek City from Alexander to Justinian* (1940; reprint, Oxford: Clarendon, 1998); Oswyn Murray and Simon Price, *The Greek City: From Homer to Alexander* (Oxford: Clarendon, 1991); Peter J. Rhodes, "Polis II," *ANP* 11 (2007): 470-73.

(*chōra*) that the city controlled, delimited by mountains, the sea or the territory of another city.

Second, as Greek cities competed with each other for preeminence in the province, the "radiation effect" of establishing churches in "strategic urban centers" would have worked only in rural areas with smaller towns. People living in Attaleia would not be much affected by events that transpired in the city of Perge, especially not by religious developments emanating from local Jewish communities.

Third, as social identity was closely bound up with the city in which one was born and lived, any sense of "community" was generally limited to the city. The significance of the city for identity can be seen in the coinage of the cities in the Roman provinces.[60] The imagery on the coinage depicts local gods (such as Artemis Ephesia in Ephesus or Zeus Laodiceus in Laodicea), temples of the city (such as the temple of Augustus on coins of Herod Philip), local mythologies (such as founding heroes of the city depicted on coins), dating on coins by local magistrates or priests or by marked turning points in the history of the city (such as the foundation of the city or the achievement of independence), and local geography (such as a reference to local games). Because the existing evidence for an emphasis on provincial identity (Asians, Galatians), regional identity (Phrygians, Lycaonians) and ethnic identity (Cilicians, Ionians)[61] is rather limited (see sec. 5.3), the news of Jesus Christ would not have naturally been disseminated from a particular city to other areas.

Fourth, standard characteristics of urbanism in the Roman world were more obstructive than helpful for the missionary penetration of a region or province. The aspirations of the urban communities "for a higher place in the formal hierarchy of city status" and "their claims to favor, based on the past and present attainment of their citizens" were central features of city

---

[60]During the 350 years between Julius Caesar and Diocletian, over five hundred provincial cities issued up to 100,000 coin types; Christopher Howgego, "Coinage and Identity in the Roman Provinces," in *Coinage and Identity in the Roman Provinces*, ed. C. Howgego et al. (Oxford: Oxford University Press, 2004), p. 2; for the following examples see ibid., pp. 2-14. Cf. also Simon Price, "Local Mythologies in the Greek East," in *Coinage and Identity in the Roman Provinces*, ed. C. Howgego et al. (Oxford: Oxford University Press, 2004), pp. 115-24.

[61]See Eckhard Stephan, *Honoratioren, Griechen, Polisbürger. Kollektive Identitäten innerhalb der Oberschicht des kaiserzeitlichen Kleinasien*, Hypomnemata 143 (Göttingen: Vandenhoeck & Ruprecht, 2002), pp. 178-99.

life in the Roman Empire.[62] These priorities contradicted the truth of the gospel, which was focused on the death of a Jewish provincial on a Roman cross. And they contradicted fundamental values of the gospel in which it is the "poor in spirit" who inherit the kingdom of God. In the churches that Paul established, the majority of believers were "foolish," that is, uneducated; "weak," that is, without influence in the affairs of the city; "low and despised" and regarded as being "nothing," that is, at the receiving end of discrimination and marginalization by the wise, the powerful and the noble of birth (1 Cor 1:26-28).

The cities were certainly centers of communication. But as the focus of the local, regional and provincial administration, they were also "the base for supervision."[63] It was much easier to control the activities of people in the city than in the smaller towns and villages that were not governed by a council. Planting churches in cities certainly had strategic value. But it was no guarantee that the gospel would spread from the cities into the countryside. Roland Allen is indeed correct when he asserts that concentrated missionary activity in a strategic center radiates to other areas only if "the center," that is, the church in the metropolis, is evangelistic and is actively involved in planting "daughter" churches.[64]

A good example of this reality is the establishment of churches in Laodicea, Hierapolis and Colossae in the Lykos Valley on the upper Maeander River (Col 1:7; 4:13). The missionary activity of Epaphras in these cities was not a "radiation effect" from Paul's ministry in Ephesus. These cities were neither controlled by nor beholden to Ephesus. Visits to Ephesus by people living in the Lykos Valley might have been prompted by the lure of the famous temple of Artemis. But if traders needed a sea port, they would have used Miletus (which was at the mouth of the Maeander River) and not Ephesus, which could be reached from the Maeander Valley only by crossing a mountain range. Epaphras, who may have been converted during Paul's ministry in Ephesus (although this is not certain), evidently evangelized in the Lykos Valley because he hailed from this region ("Epa-

---

[62]John E. Stambaugh, *The Ancient Roman City* (Baltimore: Johns Hopkins University Press, 1988).
[63]N. Purcell, "Urbanism II. Roman," *OCD*, p. 1573.
[64]Allen, *Missionary Method*, p. 17. Note his graphic statement that "in great cities are great prisons as well as great railway stations." Today we would refer to great airports as well.

phras, who is one of you:" [Col 4:12]). There is no indication that he was sent by Paul as part of a particular method of missionary work (although, again, this is possible). We only learn that Paul commended Epaphras for hard work (Col 4:12-13).

Paul and villages. Paul's missionary ministry is not described in terms of preaching tours through villages. This may have two different explanations. First, the focus on cities may have been indeed a strategic decision of Paul, based on the expectation that the new believers would carry the gospel to the villages in the territory controlled by the city and to other more remote cities.

Second, the focus on cities may be a literary decision of Luke, who wanted to demonstrate to his reading audience that while Paul was often attacked by Jews, he received exemplary treatment at the hand of Roman officials.[65] This means that Paul may well have preached in villages, an activity that Luke simply omits from his narrative.

The fact that Luke mentions "the church" in Galilee (Acts 9:31) and "the church throughout Judea" (Acts 9:31; cf. Acts 11:1, 29) without mentioning missionary activity in Galilean or Judean villages suggests that the second explanation is certainly possible.

Two texts render this possibility a near certainty. In Acts 14:6-7 Luke relates the aftermath of Paul's and Barnabas' expulsion from Iconium: "The apostles learned of it and fled to Lystra and Derbe, cities of Lycaonia, and to the surrounding country; and there they continued proclaiming the good news."

The Greek term *perichōros* ("surrounding country") means "the region around" or "the people living around them." When Paul and Barnabas left Iconium, they preached not only in the cities of Lystra and Derbe but evidently also in the towns and villages controlled by these two cities. According to Acts 26:19-20, Paul relates his actions after his conversion in his address to King Agrippa:

> After that, King Agrippa, I was not disobedient to the heavenly vision, but declared first to those in Damascus, then in Jerusalem and throughout the countryside of Judea, and also to the Gentiles, that they should repent and

---

[65]Thus already Ramsay, *St. Paul the Traveller and the Roman Citizen*, p. 304.

turn to God and do deeds consistent with repentance.

The Greek term *chōra* ("countryside") refers here to the region that makes up the province of Judea. This certainly implies towns and perhaps villages outside of Jerusalem. Paul asserts, in other words, that when he visited Jerusalem in A.D. 33/34 after his conversion, he engaged in missionary work not only in Jerusalem but also in some of the smaller towns (and perhaps villages) of Judea.

Paul did focus his missionary ministry on cities. But he evidently did not refrain from preaching in smaller towns and perhaps in villages as well.

Paul and Roman provinces. The opinion that "in St Paul's view the unit was the province rather than the city"[66] needs to be abandoned. It is certainly correct that Paul was (initially) prevented from preaching the gospel in the province of Asia and that he was called to come over to Macedonia (Acts 16:6, 9-10), and that he refers to "Achaia" as being ready to contribute to the collection for the believers in Jerusalem (2 Cor 9:2). This, however, does not prove that Paul focused on provinces rather than on cities.

References such as Acts 16:6, 9-10, and 2 Corinthians 9:2 can easily be explained by the fact that when Luke (or Paul) wanted to refer to several cities in a particular region, they could use (1) regional names or (2) provincial names. As far as regional names are concerned, Luke mentions Phrygia three times, Pisidia twice and Lycaonia once.[67] As far as provincial names are concerned, Luke mentions Syria five times, Cilicia seven times, Pamphylia five times, Galatia twice, the province of Asia fourteen times, Macedonia ten times, and Achaia three times.[68] Paul mentions Syria and Cilicia once, Galatia three times, the province of Asia times four, Macedonia fourteen times, Achaia six times, and Spain twice.[69]

---

[66]Allen, *Missionary Method*, p. 12.

[67]Phrygia: Acts 2:10; 16:6; 18:23. Pisidia: Acts 13:14; 14:24. Lycaonia: Acts 14:6; cf. in Acts 14:11 the reference to the Lycaonian language.

[68]Syria: Acts 15:23, 41; 18:18; 20:3; 21:3. Cilicia: Acts 6:9; 15:23, 41; 21:39; 22:3; 23:34; 27:5. Pamphylia: Acts 2:10; 13:13; 14:24; 15:38; 27:5. Province of Asia: Acts 2:9; 6:9; 16:6; 19:10, 22, 26, 27, 31; 20:4, 16, 18; 21:27; 24:19; 27:2. Galatia: Acts 16:6; 18:23. Macedonia: Acts 16:9, 10, 12; 18:5; 19:21, 22, 29; 20:1, 3; 27:2. Achaia: Acts 18:12, 27; 19:21.

[69]Syria and Cilicia: Gal 1:21. Galatia: Gal 1:2; 1 Cor 16:1; 2 Tim 4:10. Province of Asia: 1 Cor 16:19; 2 Cor 1:8; Rom 16:5; 2 Tim 1:15. Macedonia: 1 Thess 1:7, 8; 4:10; 1 Cor 16:5; 2 Cor 1:16; 2:13; 7:5; 8:1; 9:2, 4; 11:9; Phil 4:15; 1 Tim 1:3. Achaia: 1 Thess 1:7, 8; 1 Cor 16:15; 2 Cor 1:1; 9:2;

It is implausible to assume that Paul intentionally focused on the provincial administration of the Roman Empire. He was quite certainly not guided by the "desire to obtain for himself and for his people the security afforded by a strong government."[70] While Paul may indeed expect the protection of Roman officials against local opposition on account of his Roman citizenship, this applied only to himself and a few coworkers, such as Silas (Acts 16:37). Paul's Roman citizenship could not protect fellow missionaries, such as Barnabas or Timothy, who were Jewish (or half Jewish). Moreover we know that Paul was not in the habit of insisting on his rights (1 Cor 9:12). Paul's experience in the cities of southern Galatia demonstrates that the magistrates of the Roman colonies where Paul preached did nothing to prevent his expulsion. As we have seen earlier (see sec. 4.3), Paul worked his way from Syria—from Damascus, the city of his conversion—toward the west, initiating missionary work in Arabia, Cilicia, Cyprus, Galatia, Asia (after an initially abortive attempt), Macedonia, Achaia and probably Spain.

Paul and cities, regions and provinces: Summary. My earlier conclusion concerning the question whether Paul had a geographical strategy has been confirmed. The geographical scope of Paul's missionary work was not controlled by a "grand strategy" that helped him decide in which cities to begin a new missionary initiative. The evidence indicates that Paul moved to geographically adjacent areas that were open for missionary work. This is true for provinces, regions and cities.

Paul's burning desire was to "win as many as possible" (1 Cor 9:19) for faith in Jesus Christ, whether Jews or Gentiles (1 Cor 9:20-21). Jews lived in the cities of the Roman provinces: this is an important reason why Paul focused on cities. As an apostle whose ministry focuses on Gentiles, he targets cities because they are major population centers and centers of communication and of education where people certainly speak Greek.

5.2 Synagogues, Marketplaces, Lecture Halls, Workshops and Private Houses

When I affirm that Paul focused his missionary work on cities, I need to clarify which urban venues were available to Paul's preaching. The

---

11:10; Rom 15:26. Spain: Rom 15:24, 28.
[70]Allen, *Missionary Method,* p. 13.

evidence in Paul's letters and in the book of Acts indicates five locations of missionary work in the city: synagogues, marketplaces, lecture
halls, workshops and private houses. Giving religious speeches in the
city's council chamber *(bouleutērion)*, the music hall *(ōideion)* or the
theater *(theatron)* would have required the sponsorship of a local patron
and thus was not a strategic option for pioneer missionaries such as
Paul. The following exposition will first review the evidence and then
survey the architectural and social characteristics and possibilities of
these locations.

Synagogues. Because Paul wanted to reach his fellow Jews with the
message of Jesus Messiah, the obvious location for initial contacts were
the synagogues in the cities where he engaged in missionary work.

In Damascus Paul shared the news of Jesus in the local synagogues
(Acts 9:20). He would have preached during the regular meetings of the
Jewish community, confounding, as Luke relates, the Jews as he provided
evidence for his message that Jesus was the promised Messiah (Acts 9:22).
This means that they debated the validity of his message, presumably entering into a dialogue with his listeners, fielding questions, countering
objections and solidifying his arguments.

The attempt of the ethnarch in Damascus who wanted to arrest
Paul, evidently on the orders of the Nabatean king Aretas IV (Acts
9:23-25; 2 Cor 11:32), indicates that Paul's preaching had provoked
unrest in Nabatean cities. Luke's report of Paul's later missionary work
in Jerusalem, southern Galatia and Achaia suggests that he preached
in synagogues that Jesus is the Messiah and that he led Gentiles to
faith in Jesus Christ, admitting them into the people of God without
circumcision.

Luke's account of Paul's missionary work in Antioch highlights two activities. Paul and Barnabas "came together" (Gk *synagō*) with the congregation of Jewish and Gentile Christians, and they "taught" (Gk *didaskō*)
a large number of people (Acts 11:26). The verb teach may refer to the
instruction of new converts and of the believers in the church, that is, to
the "great many people" of Acts 11:24 who had been converted through
the missionary work of the Jewish believers from Jerusalem. Or it may refer to missionary teaching in the synagogues of Antioch. The Greek term

ochlos (defined as "a large number of people gathered together, crowd")[71] refers in Acts 6:7, 11:24, 19:26 to people who have been converted. In Acts 13:45 it designates the curious listeners in the synagogue of Pisidian Antioch. The term is not missionary terminology referring to mass conversions per se,[72] but it certainly suggests the continued growth of the church.

In Salamis on the island of Cyprus, Paul "proclaimed the word of God" in the synagogues (Acts 13:5). With regard to Paphos, the seat of the Roman governor, the focus is on the power encounter with a Jewish magician and on the conversion of the governor. We can safely assume that they met the Jewish prophet Bar-Jesus (Acts 13:6-7) in the synagogue, but this is not explicitly stated. The preaching of the word of God is mentioned only in connection with the governor Sergius Paullus, who took the initiative to summon Barnabas and Paul because "he wanted to hear the word of God" (Acts 13:7).

When we continue to work our way through Luke's account in the book of Acts, Paul's missionary preaching in synagogues is further attested for Pisidian Antioch (Acts 13:14), Iconium (Acts 14:1), Philippi (Acts 16:12-13), Thessalonica (Acts 17:1), Beroea (Acts 17:10), Athens (Acts 17:17), Corinth (Acts 18:1, 4) and Ephesus (Acts 18:19; 19:8). The Jewish communities in Corinth and Ephesus were curious enough about Paul's teaching that they asked (or at least allowed) him to preach for several weeks. In Ephesus Paul was able to teach in the synagogue for three months (Acts 19:8). Luke connects his most extensive summary of Paul's preaching with the synagogue in Pisidian Antioch (Acts 13:16-41).

Since none of the synagogue buildings Paul preached in has been discovered by archaeologists, we are dependent on other sites to provide us with some insight into architectural details. A good example is the synagogue in Ostia, the port city of Rome, which was located near the harbor (see fig. 5.1).[73] The synagogue remains that have been excavated date to

---

[71]BDAG, p. 746. Cf. Rudolf Meyer, *TDNT*, 5:581-90; Horst Balz, *EDNT*, 2:553-4; Hans Bietenhard, *NIDNTT*, 2:800.

[72]Thus Jacob Jervell, *Die Apostelgeschichte*, KEK 3 (Göttingen: Vandenhoeck & Ruprecht, 1998), p. 324.

[73]See L. Michael White, *The Social Origins of Christian Architecture*, HTS 42 (Valley Forge, Penn.: Trinity Press International, 1996/1997), 2:379-94; L. Michael White, "Synagogue and Society in Imperial Ostia: Archaeological and Epigraphic Evidence," in *Judaism and Christianity in First-Century Rome*, ed. K. P. Donfried and P. Richardson (Grand Rapids: Eerdmans, 1998), pp. 30-68;

the fourth century A.D., but the earlier stages of the building go back to the late first or early second century.[74] The original building (the opis reticulatum structure), consisting of the three rooms, D, B/C and G, was probably part of a private house complex (insula) which contained domestic quarters as well as shops (or work space). It is possible that a collegial hall was part of an insula. A visitor entering the synagogue from the Via Severiana (after the original building was renovated in the middle to later second century) accessed the building at Area C1. The entry court area (B + C)[75] had a floor of cocciopesto, a packed floor of crushed earthenware mixed with plaster. At the southern end a passage (the later Room B3) led to a kitchen (Room G), with a marble table near the door and an oven in the southwest corner. The main hall (Room D) was lined with benches along the sidewalls. At the western end of the slightly curved wall was a bema, a platform used for the reading of Scripture. (The large apsidal aedicula platform for the Torah shrine belongs to a later phase of the building.) At the southwestern end of the entry hall area B + C (later Room C3) there seems to have been a stairway leading to rooms on the upper floor.

An inscription from the synagogue in Stobi, a city in central Macedonia, provides us with important details about Diaspora synagogues:[76]

> [Claudius] Tiberius Polycharmos, also (called) Achyrius, father of the synagogue at Stobi, having lived my whole life according to the (prescriptions of) Judaism, in fulfilment of a vow (have donated) the rooms(?) to the holy place, and the triclinium with the tetrastoa out of my personal accounts without touching the sacred (funds) at all. All the right of all the upper (rooms of the building) and the ownership is to be held by me, Claudius Tiberius Polycharmos, and my heirs for all (our?) life. If someone wishes to make changes beyond my decisions, he shall give the Patriarch 250,000 denarii. For thus have I agreed. As for the upkeep of the roof tiles of the

---

Lee I. Levine, *The Ancient Synagogue: The First Thousand Years* (New Haven, Conn.: Yale University Press, 2000), pp. 255-58. The plan in fig. 5.1 is adapted from White's 1997 publication.

[74]The main excavator, M. F. Squarciapino, dates the earliest phase to the first century and believes that the building was erected *de novo* as a synagogue building; cf. Maria Floriani Squarciapino, "The Synagogue at Ostia," *Archaeology* 16 (1963): 194-203.

[75]Entry court area B+C: 10.9 x 9.67 m (35.6 x 31.7 ft); main hall Room D: 14.31 x 12.5 m (46.9 x 41.0 ft); kitchen Room G: 6.20 x 10.32 m (20.3 x 33.8 ft).

[76]For a discussion of the inscription see Noy et al., *Inscriptiones Judaicae Orientis I*, pp. 56-71; see also Levine, *Synagogue*, pp. 252-55. The date at the beginning of the inscription has been lost.

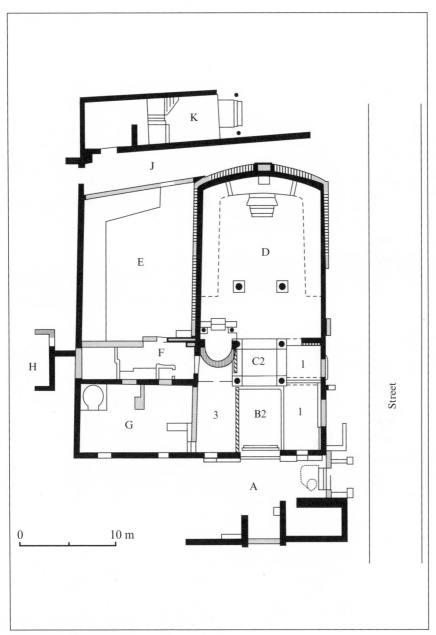

Figure 5.1. The synagogue in Ostia

upper (rooms of the building), it will be done by me and my heirs.

This inscription shows that synagogue buildings were sometimes do-
nated by a benefactor. The donor in this case was Claudius Tiberius Polycharmos, who was evidently a prominent member of the Jewish community and perhaps also a prominent citizen of Stobi, as the combination of
Latin and Greek names suggests. The title "father of the synagogue" was
probably honorific, describing Polycharmos as a distinguished benefactor
of the Jewish community. The explicit reference to his obedience to the
Torah may indicate that he was a proselyte. Polycharmos's donation included several rooms, probably from his private residence. The synagogue
was a two-story structure, the upper rooms of which were reserved for
use by his family. The synagogue (or the main hall) is called "holy place."
The synagogue included a triclinium, that is, a dining room, as well as
a tetrastoon, that is, a hall (or atrium) with four rows of columns or four
porticoes which served perhaps as a study room. The "patriarch" who is to
be paid an enormous sum of money as a fine by the person who breaches
Polyarchmos's will is most probably the Patriarch, the leader of the Jewish
commonwealth in Palestine, the first of whom was Judah ha-Nasi (A.D.
135-220).

The available evidence concerning Diaspora synagogues makes it abun-
dantly clear that no synagogue was exactly the same as other synagogues,
both in terms of architectural styles and artistic features, as well as in
terms of the titles and the offices of leaders and governing bodies.[77] Common features include the orientation of the synagogue's interior toward
Jerusalem, the prominence of the Torah shrine (especially in later buildings), symbols such as the menorah (the candelabrum with seven candles)
and the shofar (a ram's horn, which was blown like a trumpet during Rosh
Hashanah and Yom Kippur), the status as religious institutions, and the
concern for purification. The latter explains the location of many synagogues near rivers or near the sea, and the presence of basins, fountains or
wells in courtyards or entrance ways. Titles that designate leaders of Jewish communities in the Diaspora include *didaskalos* (teacher), *mathētēs
sophōn* (a disciple of the wise), *nomomathēs* (one learned in the Law),

---

[77]Levine, *Synagogue*, pp. 278-79; for the following comment cf. ibid., pp. 279-86.

and *sophos* (a wise person). It appears that synagogue communities in the Diaspora used the local vernacular, usually Greek, in their liturgy.

Paul always understood himself as a Jew, even and especially as a missionary among the Gentiles. This is seen in the fact that he accepted the Jewish jurisdiction of the synagogues for himself: according to 2 Corinthians 11:24 he was punished five times with the "forty minus one" lashes. Apart from being the meeting place of local Jews, the synagogues provided the opportunity to meet Gentiles who already believed in Israel's God—Gentiles who had converted to the Jewish faith (the proselytes), Gentiles who regularly attended the synagogue services and probably observed some Jewish laws (God-fearers) and other Gentile sympathizers who were attracted by the ethical monotheism of the Jewish faith.

It does not require a "method" to figure out that a Jewish Christian missionary who wants to preach the gospel to Gentiles should begin missionary work in the local synagogue, the only location in the city where he could meet both Jews and Gentiles. It may well be true that perhaps the majority of the non-Jewish believers in the first century came from the group of the God-fearers and other Gentile sympathizers who attended synagogue services before encountering Christian missionaries. It is telling that Paul could presuppose that the believers in the churches that he had established who were reading his letters, at least the leading pastors and teachers among them, were familiar with the Septuagint as holy Scripture and with Jewish customs.[78]

Marketplaces. A wider range of people could be reached in the central square of a Greek or Roman city.[79] In Greek cities, the central square, the agora, was the political and commercial center of the city. In Roman cities and colonies, the central plaza (the forum) was the political and religious

---

[78]See Martin Hengel, "Einleitung," in *Die Heiden. Juden, Christen und das Problem des Fremden,* ed. R. Feldmeier and U. Heckel, WUNT 70 (Tübingen: Mohr-Siebeck, 1994), p. x; cf. Stephen Mitchell, "The Cult of Theos Hypsistos Between Pagans, Jews, and Christians," in *Pagan Monotheism in Late Antiquity,* ed. P. Athanassiadi and M. Frede (Oxford: Clarendon, 1999), pp. 121-22.

[79]See Richard A. Tomlinson, "Agora," *OCD,* pp. 42-43; Janet DeLaine, "Forum," *OCD,* pp. 606-7; Malcolm Todd, "Forum and Capitolium in the Early Empire," in *Roman Urban Topography in Britain and the Western Empire,* proceedings of the Third Conference on Urban Archaeology, ed. F. Grew and B. Hobley (London: Council for British Archaeology, 1985), pp. 56-66. On public spaces in Greek cities cf. Tonio Hölscher, *Öffentliche Räume in frühen griechischen Städten* (Heidelberg: Universitätsverlag C. Winter, 1998).

center of the city, with market activities taking place in specifically built markets in various city quarters.

We have only one explicit piece of evidence for Paul seeking to establish contact with the citizens in the large square in the center of the city. According to Acts 17:17, Paul went "every day" to the marketplace (Gk *agora*) and spoke "with those who happened to be there." The grammar of the Greek sentence (present participle) indicates that going to the agora and speaking with passersby was a routine that the apostle adopted regularly. Some suggest that the discussion with the Epicurean and Stoic philosophers in the agora of Athens took place in the Royal Stoa (the *Stoa basileios*) at the northwest corner of the agora.[80]

The city center of Roman Corinth, the forum in the early Roman period, may serve as an example (see fig. 5.2). The forum was an enormous open space (c. 200 x 100 m or 656 x 330 ft).[81] The forum was divided by a row of shops into the upper forum (with the south stoa) and the lower forum. In the center of this row of shops was a monumental speaker's platform (Gk *bēma*, Lat *rostra*) on which the governor would hold court. A small temple and fourteen rooms extended east of the bema. West of the bema were three rooms (2.2 x 3 m) decorated with frescoes, used either by merchants in precious metals or by bankers. On the south side of the forum stood the two-story south stoa (164 x 25 m), with 71 Doric and 34 Ionic columns, the largest public building in Greece, built in the fourth century B.C. and restored by the Romans. The thirty-three shops in the southern part of the building were torn down in the first century and replaced by buildings of the Roman administration: the office of the official who organized the Isthmian Games *(agōnothetēs)*, the office of the governor of the province, the South Basilica, the city council *(bouleutērion)*, a public bath, and the office of the city magistrates (the duoviri). The most important Roman building phase dates to A.D. 50 (the year in which Paul arrived in Corinth) and later. The skyline on the northern side of

---

[80]Justin Taylor, *Les Actes des deux Apôtres*, Études Biblique (Paris: Lecoffre, 1990-2000), 5:304-6; cf. Barrett, *Acts of the Apostles*, 2:831.

[81]For the following description cf. Schnabel, *Early Christian Mission*, 1184-85; Guy D. R. Sanders, "Urban Corinth: An Introduction," in *Urban Religion in Roman Corinth: Interdisciplinary Approaches*, ed. D. N. Schowalter and S. J. Friesen, Harvard Theological Studies 53 (Cambridge, Mass.: Harvard University Press, 2005), pp. 22-23; see also Williams, "Roman Corinth."

the forum was dominated by the ancient temple of Apollo on Temple Hill (100 x 80 m), flanked by colonnades to the north and the south. The colonnaded hall adjacent to the forum was large (101 x 9.2 m), with forty-seven Doric columns. Between Temple Hill and the monumental arch of the Lechaion Road stood a long basilica. East of the Lechaion Road was the Fountain of Peirene, with a rectangular pool enclosed by a two-story court. On the eastern end of the forum stood the Julian Basilica which had a cryptoporticus basement; fourteen steps led to the first story, which was a large rectangular space (38 x 24 m). This floor of the building housed statues of the imperial family, including a statue of Augustus dressed in a toga, with a fold draped over his head (capite velato), engaged in a sacrificial act. The Julian Basilica thus had important civic functions. The building on the southeast corner of the forum served administrative purposes as well, mostly as Tabularium, that is, as the archive for public and private documents. (The suggestion that is was a library is less likely.) On the west side of the forum stood the temple of Venus Victrix (temple F), the temple of Roma, the Senate and the Emperors (temple G), the Fountain of Poseidon, the Babbius Monument with a temple (temple K, perhaps the Pantheion, or a temple of Apollo), and a temple of Tyche (temple D, identified by some scholars as the temple of Hermes).

As far as Corinth is concerned, it seems more likely that Paul preached in the forum rather than in the market buildings that stood at some distance from the city center. The following markets have been identified in Corinth: the market near the Fountain of Peirene (over the east side of which the Peribolos of Apollo was later built), the market north of the basilica on the Lechaion Road, the market north of the temple of Apollo, or the market west of Temple Hill (northwest of temple E). People who lived in any of the suburbs of the city would regularly walk to and across the forum on their way to the government offices, the moneylenders, the dealers of precious metals, the market buildings, the workshops and to the port cities of Lechaion and Cenchreae.

When Paul proclaimed the news of Jesus Christ in the central plaza of a city, he would have been able to meet large numbers of people and reach a diverse audience, which might include on some occasions the decision makers of the city. In Athens, Paul's missionary activities in the city center

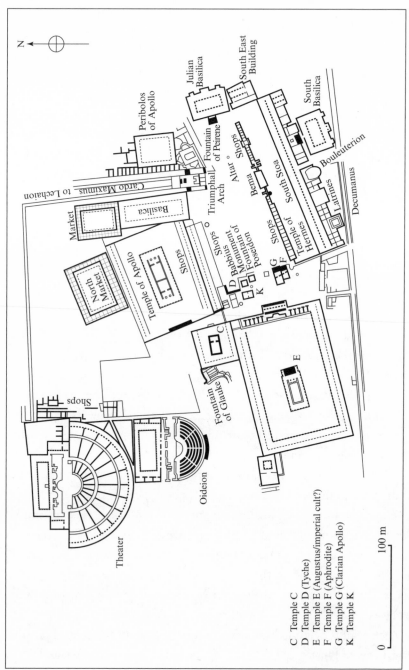

Figure 5.2. The forum in Corinth

C   Temple C
D   Temple D (Tyche)
E   Temple E (Augustus/imperial cult?)
F   Temple F (Aphrodite)
G   Temple G (Clarian Apollo)
K   Temple K

included discussions with Epicurean and Stoic philosophers who eventually took him to the venerable Council of the Areopagus (Acts 17:18-19; see secs. 1.4 [pp. 74-89] and 3.3 [pp. 169-84]). It would be inappropriate, however, to interpret Paul's preaching in the central city square as "mass evangelism," particularly if one thinks of the organized mass rallies of later evangelists such as George Whitefield or Billy Graham.

Lecture halls. According to Acts 19:9, Paul taught daily in the lecture hall *(scholē)* of Tyrannus when he preached the gospel in Corinth. The (later) Western Text adds the comment that this happened "from the fifth to the tenth hour," that is, from ten in the morning to four in the afternoon. This comment might represent information that was reliably handed down. It is at least a plausible clarification for a lecture hall. The name Tyrannos is frequently attested both in western Asia Minor and in Ephesus.[82] He may have been a philosopher who lectured in a class room, or otherwise the owner of the building.[83]

Since privacy was not a priority for teachers in antiquity, it is theoretically possible that the *scholē* of Tyrannus was located under the arcades of the forum. In Pompeii, graffiti mark the site of an elementary school under the arcades of the forum.[84] Since advanced education needed less distracting settings, grammarians and rhetors seemed to have gathered their students in a rented room or even in their own residence. It is also possible that the "school" of Tyrannus was located in a gymnasium, in the baths, in a room in one of the basilicas or in a room on the upper story of one of the colonnaded halls in the forum.

In Alexandria, the remains of a building near the theater and the baths have been identified as the possible site of a lecture hall or a school: "A central auditorium with the dais for the teacher (or speaker) and seats all around is flanked by two sets of smaller rooms provided with seats."[85]

Workshops. It is often suggested that Paul's occupation as a "tentmaker"

---

[82]See Colin J. Hemer, *The Book of Acts in the Setting of Hellenistic History*, ed. C. H. Gempf, WUNT 49 (Tübingen: Mohr-Siebeck, 1989), pp. 120-21, 243.

[83]Barrett, *Acts of the Apostles*, 2:905.

[84]Stanley F. Bonner, *Education in Ancient Rome: From the Elder Cato to the Younger Pliny* (London: Methuen, 1977), p. 118.

[85]Raffaella Cribiore, *Gymnastics of the Mind: Greek Education in Hellenistic and Roman Egypt* (Princeton, N.J.: Princeton University Press, 2001), p. 34. A *dais* is "the raised platform at one end of a hall for the high table, or for seats of honour" *(OED).*

or leatherworker (Acts 18:3)[86] allowed him to teach in the natural environment of a workshop where he would have been able to meet people from all walks of life.[87] This scenario is certainly plausible. It needs to be recognized, however, that working as a leatherworker was not a "method" that Paul employed in order to meet people. Rather, this was a financial necessity when his funds had run low.

In Pompeii, over half of the houses either are or incorporate shops *(tabernae)*, workshops *(officina)* or horticultural plots *(horti)*. The *officina*, in which "industrial" production took place, represents the workshops of bakers, fullers, dyers, metalworkers, leatherworkers and lampmakers. The average size of the workshops in Pompeii is 76 square meters. A good example of the location and the size of a medium workshop is the *officina* of a cabinetmaker or a metalworker in the Casa del Fabbro in Pompeii (see fig. 5.3). This relatively modest house had an atrium (room 3) flanked by three *cubicula* (rooms 2, 4, 5) which served as bedrooms or as places for the reception of friends and the conducting of confidential business; two large rooms (triclinia), finely decorated, served as dining rooms or reception rooms (rooms 8 and 9), both oriented toward the garden (which a single colonnade and a wooden outdoor triclinium). Stairs in rooms 1 and 10 lead to the second floor, which had six rooms. Tools which were found in room 10 suggest that this large space was a workshop, either of a cabinetmaker or of a metalworker.[88]

Working in the officina of Aquila and Priscilla would have brought Paul in contact with people who already trusted this couple—presumably not only Jews but also Gentile customers. Sharing the news of Jesus in a workshop in a private house would not have been much different than preaching to unbelievers who visited the Christian meetings that took

---

[86]F. W. Danker suggests that *skēnopoios* should be interpreted in terms of a "maker of stage properties" for theatrical productions; cf. BDAG, pp. 928-29.

[87]See Ronald F. Hock, *The Social Context of Paul's Ministry: Tentmaking and Apostleship* (Philadelphia: Fortress, 1980); Wayne A. Meeks, *The First Urban Christians: The Social World of the Apostle Paul* (New Haven, Conn.: Yale University Press, 1983), p. 29.

[88]Andrew Wallace-Hadrill, *Houses and Society in Pompeii and Herculaneum* (Princeton, N.J.: Princeton University Press, 1994), pp. 56-57, 136-37, 193. On room 10 in the Casa del Fabbro as the workshop of a cabinetmaker cf. Olga Elia, "Pompei—Relazione sullo scavo dell'Insula X della Regio I," *Notizie degli Scavi di Antichità* 10 (1934): 292; as the workshop of a metalworker cf. Bettine Gralfs, *Metallverarbeitende Produktionsstätten in Pompeji*, BAR International Series 433 (Oxford: British Institute of Archaeology, 1988), pp. 50-52.

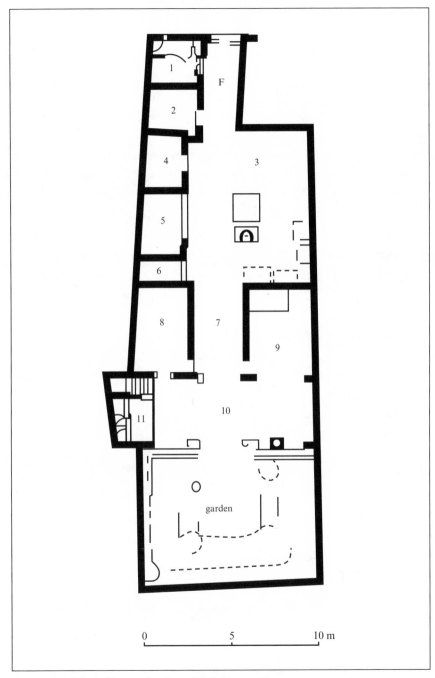

Figure 5.3. Workshop in the Casa del Fabbra in Pompeii

place in the houses of a believer, apart from the fact that the former would have taken place in the morning and early afternoon while the latter took place in late afternoon or in the evening.

Private houses. The successful establishment of new communities of followers of Jesus as well as the life of the new churches were closely connected with private houses. In the ancient world, the Greek term *oikos* (Lat *familia*) describes the house both as living space and as the domestic household of the family. In Paul's missionary work, the *oikos*, that is, the private house and the family of the houseowner was "the base of missionary work, the foundational center of a local church, the location of the assembly for worship, the lodging for the missionaries and envoys and at the same time, of course, the primary and decisive place of Christian life and formation."[89] The "house" or "family" was the most fundamental social reality in the ancient world. The "house" included not only husband and wife, parents and children, but other dependents, relatives and friends, as well as slaves.

Perhaps 90 percent of the free citizens and an even higher percentage of the rest of the population, slaves included, lived in apartment buildings.[90] The multistory tenement houses in the cities are called in Latin *insulae;* because they occupied an entire city block, one could go around them. Families who could afford them had sufficiently large apartments *(cenacula).* Freedmen and their families had to make do with very small units: many families lived in a single room measuring 10 sq. meters (12 sq. yards).[91] These tenement apartments are not the "houses" in which the early Christians were meeting. It was not possible to accommodate more than a handful of people in these apartments for worship or sermons, let alone for a common meal. When the number of followers of Jesus continued to grow, and when Paul looked for accommodations for regular weekly meetings, he needed to find larger rooms, which generally meant

---

[89]Jürgen Becker, "Paulus und seine Gemeinden," in *Die Anfänge des Christentums: Alte Welt und neue Hoffnung,* ed. J. Becker (Stuttgart: Kohlhammer, 1987), pp. 125-26.

[90]See Bruce W. Frier, *Landlords and Tenants in Imperial Rome* (Princeton, N.J.: Princeton University Press, 1980).

[91]These living arrangements explain the high population density of the large Roman cities: in Rome about 750 people lived per one hectare (2.4 acres), nearly 2.5 times as many as in Calcutta and 3 times as many as in Manhattan. Cf. Robert Jewett, "Tenement Churches and Pauline Love Feasts," *Quarterly Review* 14 (1994): 49.

that he had to locate a private house the new church could meet in.

In the Greco-Roman world we find two main types of private houses. The Greek-Hellenistic peristyle house consisted of an atrium section and one or several atrium-like peristyle courtyards, that is, rectangular or square courtyards that were surrounded on all four sides with colonnaded corridors behind which the living quarters and rooms for sleeping were located. In some cities a grand peristyle house could occupy an entire city block. In the Roman atrium house the living and sleeping quarters, the kitchen, and any other domestic rooms, usually closed by curtains, were built around the atrium, a rectangular space open to the sky at the center so that sunlight and fresh air could enter. In the more elaborate houses the atrium was surrounded with columns at all four sides. Visitors entered the house through a vestibule on one side of the atrium.

A good example of a large private house is Terrace House 2 in Ephesus (see fig. 5.4).[92] This house occupied about 4,000 sq. meters on three terraces with identical dimensions in the first phase of construction. In the first century A.D. two separate housing units were built in the form of peristyle houses. The entrance into housing unit 6 was at the western end of the Stoa of Alytarch on Curetes Street. A stairway led directly to the peristyle courtyard (room 31a) which was lined on all four sides by colonnaded corridors. The courtyard, surrounded by twelve marble columns, was paved and in the center open to the sky. On the northern and western side of the courtyard were the living quarters (rooms 31b-c, 42, 36c-e), which were accessed from the courtyard through wide doors. One of the rooms (room 31b) was devoted to the house cult; the bench-like socles probably supported cupboards made of wood. A room in the southeastern part of the unit housed a latrine (room 36b) whose walls were paneled with marble. The latrine could be used by four or five persons simultaneously. On the south side of the courtyard was the entrance to the so-called marble room (room 31), a large room (180 sq. meters) that served representative purposes. This room was decorated with expensive marble panels and other colorful stones; at the center of the southern wall stood

---

[92]Selahattin Erdemgil, *The Terrace Houses in Ephesus* (Ephesus Museum; Istanbul: Hitit, 2000). One can consult the plans drawn up by the Austrian archaeologists working in Ephesus at <www .oeaw.ac.at/antike/ephesos/hh/einstieg.html>.

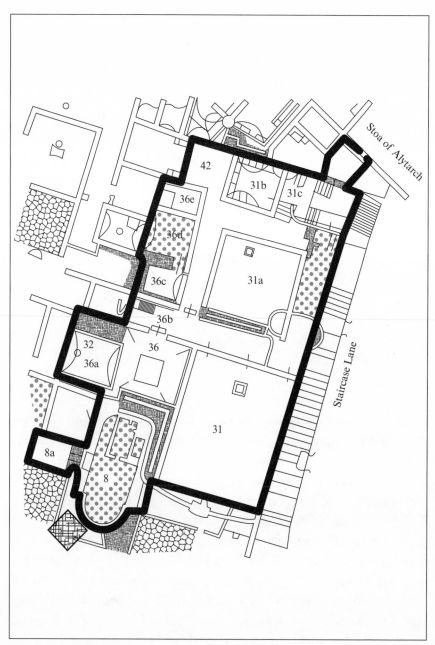

Figure 5.4. Private house (Terrace House 2) in Ephesus

a water basin with a fountain. The atrium (room 36) was equipped with a water basin in the center of the hall. The atrium gave access to a second large banquet hall (12 x 7 meters) called the basilica, a barrel-vaulted room about 11.5 meters high and decorated with frescoes (room 8). This room was equipped with underfloor heating and a water basin on the northwest corner. The so-called stucco room (room 8a) on the west side of the atrium was decorated with murals depicting scenes from the Dionysos myth. A stairway behind the basilica room led to the upper level of the house, which had a living room, a kitchen and other work-related rooms.

The largest rooms in an atrium house could accommodate between thirty and forty people. This fact has led to the suggestion that the size of the houses in which the early Christians met limited the size of the houses churches to about thirty to forty people.[93] This is not necessarily the case, however, since people could sit outside of the larger room of a house in the atrium hall, or following the preaching, from adjacent rooms.

The following reasons explain why the early missionaries chose private homes as meeting places of the new Christian communities.[94] First, the houses of converted Jews and Gentiles did not need any remodeling in order to be used as meeting places since the meetings of the followers of Jesus did not require any special architectural features. Second, Jews were accustomed to meeting in private houses. Many synagogues were initially rooms in a private residence. Jews, proselytes and God-fearers who converted to faith in Jesus Christ would thus not have been surprised about the choice of private homes as meeting places for religious activities. Third, a private home provided excellent conditions for important elements of the meetings of Christian believers, including the common meals during which the Lord's Supper was celebrated. Four private houses allowed the Christians to meet in a relatively inconspicuous manner, which became a pressing necessity as soon as the local synagogues no longer tolerated the believers in Jesus Messiah.

Paul's missionary work led to the conversion not only of individuals but

---

[93]See Murphy-O'Connor, *St. Paul's Corinth*, p. 156.
[94]See Bradley B. Blue, "Acts and the House Church," in *The Book of Acts in Its Graeco-Roman Literary Setting*, ed. D. W. J. Gill and C. Gempf, The Book of Acts in Its First-Century Setting (Exeter, U.K.: Paternoster, 1994), 2:119-222; Roger W. Gehring, *House Church and Mission: The Importance of Household Structures in Early Christianity* (Peabody, Mass.: Hendrickson, 2004).

sometimes of entire "houses," that is, of households or families. In Philippi, the household of Lydia the purple merchant and the household of the prison official became Christians (Acts 16:14-15, 32-34). In Corinth, the household of Crispus the synagogue ruler and the household of Stephanas became believers in Jesus Christ (Acts 18:8; 1 Cor 1:16; 16:15).

The importance of private houses and of the family is illustrated by Paul's exhortation that believers should not divorce their Gentile spouses but to continue to live with them, an exhortation that is motivated in part by a missionary concern: "Wife, for all you know, you might save your husband. Husband, for all you know, you might save your wife" (1 Cor 7:16). Paul assumes as a matter of course that unbelievers are visiting the meetings of the church. He asserts in connection with his discussion about the spiritual gift of speaking in unlearnt languages:

> If, therefore, the whole church comes together and all speak in tongues, and outsiders or unbelievers enter, will they not say that you are out of your mind? But if all prophesy, an unbeliever or outsider who enters is reproved by all and called to account by all. After the secrets of the unbeliever's heart are disclosed, that person will bow down before God and worship him, declaring, "God is really among you." (1 Cor 14:23-25)

Private houses were less accessible than synagogues or lecture halls, not to mention the central plaza of the city. Visitors would enter a private house only when they had been invited. In other words, existing relationships were as essential as the willingness of the new converts to invite their friends. The households of newly converted believers were important centers of Paul's missionary work. And they were centers of the life of the newly established communities who met as churches in the houses of believers.

Missionary methods. Does Paul's missionary preaching in synagogues, marketplaces, lecture halls, workshops and private houses represent a missionary "method" or strategy? The only "strategy" was the utilization of all venues that allowed the spreading of the news of Jesus Christ. The fact that Paul first contacted the Jewish community and preached in synagogues was not a method but the rather obvious first option of a traveling Jewish teacher who visited cities in which Jews met for prayer and instruction in the Torah. Because the synagogue services were attended not only by Jews but also by proselytes and God-fearers who had Gentile relatives and friends, it did not require much insight to realize that the synagogues were ideal places to talk about matters that arose out of the Scriptures and the Jewish faith.

When Paul was no longer allowed to use rooms in the synagogue building for his teaching and preaching, he was willing to move to other venues that allowed him to continue his teaching, such as local lecture halls. When Paul was forced to work in a workshop, he used the contacts with customers who might be curious about the new leatherworker who was educated and who had given speeches in the local synagogue or in a public lecture hall. Preaching in private houses did not require a "plan" either, as Paul would be invited into private homes only by people who knew him and who would expect him to speak about the news concerning Jesus Christ.

The only location that would require methodical strategizing was the central plaza of the city, the agora or the forum. Drawing a crowd in the central square was acceptable for lawyers and magistrates, that is, for the members of the local elites who spoke about local, provincial or imperial matters. Traveling philosophers were known to deliver discourses about historical and ethical matters, sometimes speaking in the forum. Religious activity in the open air was unconventional. The *theologoi*, that is, the people who discoursed about the gods, were often involved in mystery religions, presumably not in the central plaza but in the temple of the god. For the mysteries of Demeter Thesmophoros at Smyrna two female *theologoi* are attested who spoke in honor of the goddess.[95] At Pergamum and at Smyrna, *theologoi* who were also *hymnologoi* are attested for the ruler cult.[96]

Paul was accused of throwing the city into an uproar by advocating foreign customs (Acts 16:20-21) and of causing trouble by preaching Jesus as king and thus defying the emperor (Acts 17:6-7). Proclaiming the news of Jesus as Savior and Lord in the central plaza of a Greek or Roman city was thus potentially risky. Neither Luke nor Paul himself provide any details on

---

[95]Martin P. Nilsson, *Geschichte der griechischen Religion*, 4th ed. HdA V.2 (1950; reprint, München: Beck, 1992), 2:357.

[96]Duncan Fishwick, *The Imperial Cult in the Latin West* (Leiden: Brill, 1987-2002), 2:571. The inscriptions are published as *IGR* IV 353 and *IGR* IV 1431.

how Paul handled the challenge of preaching in the agora. We may confidently assume, however, that the long and varied experience of many years of missionary preaching made Paul skillful in considering the potential dangers, the local situation and new developments that affected his missionary preaching in the agora. Paul knew what it meant to be in danger from Jews and Gentiles, in danger in the city and in the countryside (2 Cor 11:26). As Christ's ambassador (2 Cor 5:20), Paul was willing to be beaten with rods and to be pelted with stones (2 Cor 11:25), to endure insults, hardships, persecutions and difficulties (2 Cor 12:10), if only he could explain, and help other people accept and believe in, the grace of the Lord Jesus Christ, the love of God, and the fellowship of the Holy Spirit (2 Cor 13:14).

5.3 ETHNIC IDENTITY, CLASS AND CULTURE

The next question that needs to be addressed concerns Paul's missionary praxis with respect to ethnic and social groups and with regard to cultural factors and gender issues.

Ethnic identity: Jews and Gentiles. Paul is generally described as the apostle to the Gentiles.[97] This description is certainly correct, as Paul speaks of the grace given to him by God "to be a minister of Christ Jesus to the Gentiles in the priestly service of the gospel of God" (Rom 15:16). In a more extended passage in which Paul gives us some insight into his understanding of the missionary task, he writes,

> To the Jews I became as a Jew, in order to win Jews. To those under the law I became as one under the law (though I myself am not under the law) so that I might win those under the law. To those outside the law I became as one outside the law (though I am not free from God's law but am under Christ's law) so that I might win those outside the law. To the weak I became weak, so that I might win the weak. I have become all things to all people, that I might by all means save some. I do it all for the sake of the gospel, so that I may share in its blessings. (1 Cor 9:20-23)

Paul preached to Jews who practice the Mosaic law, and he preached to Gentiles who do not follow the stipulations of the Jewish law. Paul

---

[97]See Jürgen Becker, *Paul: Apostle to the Gentiles* (Louisville: Westminster, 1993); Daniel J.-S. Chae, *Paul as Apostle to the Gentiles: His Apostolic Self-Awareness and its Influence on the Soteriological Argument in Romans* (Carlisle, U.K.: Paternoster, 1997).

excluded nobody from his missionary preaching. He was not a "Gentile specialist" who had mastered the art of winning pagans for the gospel. Nor was he so anxious about winning his fellow Jews for faith in Jesus the Messiah that he neglected or minimized missionary work among Gentiles. Paul was not naive. He was aware of the traditional ethnic and social distinctions and divisions in Greco-Roman society. Paul knew that there are Jews and Gentiles, Greeks and Romans, Lycaonians and Phrygians, and barbarians such as the Scythians (cf. Col 3:11).

This evidence shows that Paul did not pursue a missionary strategy that focused on a particular ethnic group. He was concerned to preach the gospel to all people in any given city, irrespective of ethnic origin. This may be the reason why Luke does not describe the ethnic and cultural diversity of cities such as Pisidian Antioch, in which he would have encountered native Phrygians and Pisidians, descendants of the Seleucid colonists, descendants of Augustus's Italian veterans, Greeks and Jews.[98] If Paul and the other early Christian missionaries, who were all Jewish, did not pay much attention to ethnic differences among the Gentiles, it is entirely appropriate that Luke and Paul use the term *ethnē* ("Gentiles") as a technical term for non-Jews.[99]

Social class: The elites and the disenfranchised. Paul also knew that there were the powerful and the powerless, the small number of the influential and rich decision makers and the large and usually "silent" majority of the poor. He knew that there are men and women, freeborn and freedmen, slaves, the educated and the uneducated. The following passages illustrate this awareness.

> There is no longer Jew or Greek, there is no longer slave or free, there is no longer male and female; for all of you are one in Christ Jesus. (Gal 3:28)

> Consider your own call, brothers and sisters: not many of you were wise by human standards, not many were powerful, not many were of noble birth. But God chose what is foolish in the world to shame the wise; God chose

---

[98]See Robert L. Mowery, "Paul and Caristanius at Pisidian Antioch," *Biblica* 87 (2006): 221-42, 230-32, 241.

[99]See Dean Philip Bechard, *Paul Outside the Walls: A Study of Luke's Socio-Geographical Universalism in Acts 14:8-20*, Analecta biblica 143 (Rome: Editrice Pontificio Istituto Biblico, 2000), pp. 152-53.

what is weak in the world to shame the strong; God chose what is low and despised in the world, things that are not, to reduce to nothing things that are, so that no one might boast in the presence of God. (1 Cor 1:26-29)

For in the one Spirit we were all baptized into one body—Jews or Greeks, slaves or free—and we were all made to drink of one Spirit. (1 Cor 12:13)

I am a debtor both to Greeks and to barbarians, both to the wise and to the foolish—hence my eagerness to proclaim the gospel to you also who are in Rome. For I am not ashamed of the gospel; it is the power of God for salvation to everyone who has faith, to the Jew first and also to the Greek. (Rom 1:14-16)

In that renewal there is no longer Greek and Jew, circumcised and uncircumcised, barbarian, Scythian, slave and free; but Christ is all and in all! (Col 3:11)

In 1 Corinthians 1:26-29 Paul refers to the two main classes of Greco-Roman society. On the one hand are "the wise" *(sophoi)*, that is, the educated citizens, the intellectuals. They are more or less identical with "the powerful" *(dynatoi)*, that is, with those who are influential, who belong to the decision makers of the city, former or present members of the city council and their families, people whose wealth of very often the basis for their high social status. They are the people "of noble birth" *(eugeneis)*, the members of the local elite who control the decisions that affect the lives of the people living in the city. On the other end of the social spectrum, comprising perhaps 95 percent of the population of a city in the first century, are "the foolish" *(mōra)*, that is, those who did not have the privilege of learning to read and write. They are more or less identical with "the weak" (*asthenē*), that is, with the people who have no political or economic power and thus no influence. They are "the despised" *(exouthenēmena)* by the members of the local aristocracy, regarded as "things that are not" *(to mē onta)*, as people who are ultimately irrelevant.[100] The wise, the powerful and those of noble birth were the people who occupied the positions of the cursus honorum, the municipal and provincial career path in the cities of the Roman Empire. The majority of the people living

---

[100]See Johannes Munck, *Paul and the Salvation of Mankind* (1959; reprint, Atlanta: Knox, 1977), p. 161; Bruce W. Winter, *Philo and Paul Among the Sophists*, SNTSMS 96 (Cambridge: Cambridge University Press, 1997), pp. 186-94; Anthony C. Thiselton, *The First Epistle to the Corinthians*, NIGTC (Grand Rapids: Eerdmans, 2000), pp. 182-85.

in the cities, even more so in the countryside, were uneducated, powerless, without influence, of humble origins—people whom the elites would regard as foolish, weak, low, despised, indeed as "nothing."

Plutarch, a philosopher (born A.D. 45) who studied in Athens and later taught philosophy in Rome, epitomized the social status of the powerful and rich in his treatise "How to Tell a Flatterer from a Friend," in which he writes that "flatterers proclaim that kings and wealthy persons and rulers are not only prosperous and blessed, but that they also rank first in understanding, technical skill, and every form of virtue" (Plutarch *Moralia* 58e).

Greco-Roman society was deeply divided. Philo, the Jewish theologian of the first century who lived in Alexandria in Egypt, describes how sophist orators defended their lifestyle.[101] They expounded on their wealth, glory, honor and authority, proclaiming themselves to be

> men of mark and wealth, holding leading positions, praised on all hands, recipients of honours, portly, healthy and robust, revelling in luxurious and riotous living, knowing nothing of labour, conversant with pleasures which carry the sweets of life to the all-welcoming soul by every channel of sense.

They argued that their opponents were

> almost without exception obscure people, looked down upon, of mean estate, destitute of the necessities of life, not enjoying the privileges of subject peoples or even of slaves, filthy, sallow, reduced to skeletons, with a hungry look from want of food, the prey of disease, in training for dying. (Philo *That the Worse Attacks the Better* 34)

Paul is fully aware of these distinctions and differences, about the near abyss that existed between the local elites and the mass of the poor and disenfranchised. However, despite his differentiation of audiences and despite his specialized commission as missionary to Gentiles, Paul understands himself to be obligated to "become all things to all people" so that some people might come to saving faith in Jesus Christ (1 Cor 9:22). The reason for this comprehensive approach to missionary outreach is given in the next sentence, where Paul asserts, "I do it all for the sake of the gospel" (1 Cor 9:23). The saving news of Jesus Christ does not allow the missionary to omit a particular ethnic group or a particular social group from the preaching of

---

[101]See Winter, *Philo and Paul*, pp. 107-9.

the gospel. Everybody needs to hear the gospel, because there is no salvation apart from faith in the crucified and risen Jesus Christ.

Paul never excuses himself from preaching the message of Jesus Christ to his Jewish compatriots with the excuse that he has been called to preach to the Gentiles. And when he preaches before Greek and Roman audiences, he does not exclude the powerful, the influential or the intellectuals from the proclamation of the gospel with the excuse that they have caused Jesus' death and continue to cause trouble for the missionaries of the church. As Paul calls for the unity of the church, he cannot be an apostle to the Gentiles only. "He wants to be an apostle of all the church, for his vision was for a new community formed of all gentiles and Jews (1 Cor 9:20-22)."[102]

Luke's account of Paul's missionary work confirms that the apostle did not limit his preaching to specific groups but targeted anyone who was willing to listen. In Salamis he preaches to Jews in the synagogues (Acts 13:5). In Paphos he engages the Jewish community (in particular a Jewish sorcerer) and the governor of the province (Acts 13:6-7). In Pisidian Antioch he preaches to Jews; he engages proselytes and God-fearers who attended the synagogue; he reaches Gentile citizens (Acts 13:14, 16, 26, 42-43, 48). In Iconium he preaches to Jews and Gentiles (Acts 14:1). In Lystra he preaches to Jews (Acts 14:7) and to pagan citizens, including a priest of Zeus (Acts 14:13-17). Luke's report of Paul's missionary work in Lystra illustrates that he evangelizes not only the educated but also the rural population, not only Greeks but also "barbarians" who speak a "foreign" language (in this case Lycaonian), not only in the centers of Greek culture but also in the politically unimportant hinterland of Lycaonia. In Philippi Paul preaches before Jews and God-fearers in the synagogue and before a Gentile official of the city who was in charge of the local prison (Acts 16:13-15, 29-31). In Thessalonica he preaches to Jews, God-fearers and other Gentile sympathizers with the Jewish faith, including several women from prominent families (Acts 17:2, 4). In Beroea he preaches to Jews and to Gentiles, the latter again including aristocratic women (Acts 17:10, 12). In Athens he preaches to Jews, to God-fearers and to Gen-

---

[102]Alan F. Segal, *Paul the Convert: The Apostolate and Apostasy of Saul the Pharisee* (New Haven, Conn.: Yale University Press, 1990), p. 265.

tiles, including philosophers and city officials (Acts 17:16-19, 32-34). In Corinth he preaches to Jews and Greeks (Acts 18:4), as he does in Ephesus (Acts 19:8-10, 17). Paul preaches to the poor and to the powerful, to people belonging to the lower classes and to members of the local or provincial elites.

The names that are mentioned in Paul's letters and in the book of Acts in connection with Paul's missionary work provide information about the social status of some of the converts, some of whom became his coworkers.[103]

The person with the highest social status who converted to faith in Jesus Christ as a result of Paul's preaching was Sergius Paullus, the governor of the senatorial province of Cyprus, with the rank of proconsul (Gk *anthypatos* [Acts 13:12]).[104] The proconsul Sergius Paullus is possibly identical with Lucius Sergius Paullus who is mentioned in an inscription from Rome where he is described as one of five curators of the Tiber River *(curatores riparum et alvei Tiberis)*, who were responsible for regulating the flow of the Tiber during the principate of Claudius between A.D. 41-47.[105] The position of his name in the Tiber inscription suggests that he was praetor at the time, which would fit a subsequent career as the proconsul of a senatorial province.

As we have seen earlier, Paul's move from Paphos on Cyprus to Pisidian Antioch (Acts 13:13-14) may have been prompted by the proconsul Sergius Paullus, whose family owned estates in the area of Pisidian Antioch. The proconsul may have suggested to Paul to contact the members of the Pisidian branch of his family in southern Galatia. If this reconstruction of events is historically accurate, this would have been an occasion where Paul deliberately visited representatives of the aristocracy in connection with his missionary work, aiming at "the Romanised provincial elite"[106] in the military, political and commercial capital of south Galatia.[107]

---

[103]See Meeks, *First Urban Christians*, pp. 55-63; cf. Edwin A. Judge, *The Social Pattern of Christian Groups in the First Century* (London: Tyndale, 1960); Abraham J. Malherbe, *Social Aspects of Early Christianity*, 2nd ed. (Philadelphia: Fortress, 1983); Gerd Theissen, *The Social Setting of Pauline Christianity* (Philadelphia: Fortress, 1982).

[104]See Schnabel, *Early Christian Mission*, 2:1082-88.

[105]See Mitchell, *Anatolia*, 2:6-7; Alanna Nobbs, "Cyprus," in *The Book of Acts in Its Graeco-Roman Setting*, ed. D. W. J. Gill and C. Gempf, The Book of Acts in Its First-Century Setting (Exeter, U.K.: Paternoster, 1994), 2:284-87; Riesner, *Paul's Early Period*, pp. 139-41.

[106]Mitchell and Waelkens, *Pisidian Antioch*, p. 12.

[107]Levick, *Roman Colonies*, p. 126.

Luke relates that on the second sabbath of Paul's visit to Pisidian Antioch "almost the whole city gathered to hear the word of the Lord" (Acts 13:44), a crowd that probably included "the devout women of high standing and the leading men of the city" that Luke mentions later (Acts 13:50). These men and women would have been the descendants of Augustus's Italian veterans. A Latin inscription that was recently discovered near Pisidian Antioch[108] helps us to understand the political, social and cultural context in which Paul preached the gospel.[109] A certain C. Caristanius Fronto Caisianus Iullus had fulfilled a vow he had made to one of the deities of the city on behalf of Emperor Claudius's safety and victory during the invasion of Britain (A.D. 43/44). Caristanius held the office of *duumvir* for the third time, he was a priest (pontifex) and an officer in the Roman army. Lines 11-13 of the inscription assert that Caristanius fulfilled his vow by paying for four benefactions: a statue, games, sacrifices and a *venatio*. The statue, probably a life-like image of Emperor Claudius, stood on the base on which the inscription is inscribed. The games were specified as *ludi iuvenales,* games involving the youth. The sacrifices *(hostias)* would probably have been offered in the large temple in the center of Pisidian Antioch, dedicated to the worship of Augustus and Roma; Caristanius would have followed tradition and chosen the animals himself. The fourth benefaction, the *venatio,* was an event involving wild animals, either a beast hunt or a fight with wild beasts. These benefactions were probably offered in the year A.D. 45/46—Paul arrived in Pisidian Antioch probably in A.D. 46. Caristanius's fulfillment of his vow must have duly impressed the citizens of Pisidian Antioch, especially the other prominent families of the city. The huge statue reminded them "of the power of Rome, the power of the emperor, the power of the Roman legions, and, by implication, the pagan divine power that aided and protected Claudius and his legions."[110]

If Paul indeed traveled to Pisidian Antioch in order to contact the Sergii Paulii and other leading families of the city, Luke's account leads

---

[108]See Michel Christol et al., "L'empereur Claude, le chevalier C. Caristanius Fronto Caesianus Iullus et le culte impérial à Antioche de Pisidie," *Tyche* 16 (2001): 1-20.
[109]See Mowery, "Paul and Caristanius," 221-42.
[110]Ibid., p. 242.

us to conclude that this strategy was not successful. On the contrary, he recounts that the Jews who rejected Paul's message were able to incite "the leading men of the city" against Paul and Barnabas and expel them from the city (Acts 13:50-51).

Luke reports that Paul used the opportunity of his trial in Caesarea Maritima to explain the gospel of Jesus Christ to two Roman governors of Judea: Antonius Felix and Porcius Festus, as well as to the Jewish king Herod Agrippa II.[111] Another contact with a proconsul is reported for Corinth: the Jews of the city accuse Paul before L. Iunius Gallio, the proconsul of the province of Achaia (Acts 18:12-16). According to Luke, Paul did not get an opportunity to defend himself because Gallio refused to hear the case. We therefore do not know whether Paul was able to explain the news of Jesus he proclaimed in Corinth to the proconsul.

In Caesarea and in Rome Paul is able to explain the gospel before high-ranking military officials in the capital of the province of Judea and in the capital of the Roman Empire.[112] As Paul was imprisoned in Rome for at least two years, the comment in Philippians 1:13 that "it has become known throughout the whole imperial guard and to everyone else that my imprisonment is for Christ" suggests that Paul used his imprisonment to explain the gospel to the Praetorian Guard (assuming that the letter to the Philippians was written in Rome). The Praetorian Guard *(praetorium)* was stationed since A.D. 23 in a permanent camp in the eastern suburbs of Rome. Lucius Vitellius, consul in A.D. 47 for the third time, had increased the guard to sixteen cohorts of 1,000 men each. The role of the Praetorian Guard was to protect the emperor and the members of the imperial family, to discourage plots in the city of Rome, and to suppress disturbances.[113] The statement in Philippians 1:13 does not mean that all sixteen thousand soldiers heard the gospel. However, as Paul's guard changed regularly, over the course of two years a good number of the legionaries of the Praetorian Guard would have heard an explanation of the gospel, presumably also the prefect of the Praetorian Guard, the *praefectus castrorum,*

---

[111]Acts 24:2, 22-25; 25:13-24; 26:24-25, 28, 32.
[112]Acts 25:23; Phil 1:13. On Paul's imprisonment in the city of Rome, cf. Acts 28:16, 30-31.
[113]See J. Brian Campbell, "Praetorians," *OCD*, p. 1241; J. Brian Campbell, "Praetorians,"*BNP* 11 (2007): 773-75.

a position that was occupied during the time of Paul's imprisonment by Afranius Burrus.[114]

In Philippians 4:22 Paul mentions "saints," that is, Christian believers in "the emperor's household." As Paul is probably in Roman imprisonment when he writes to the Christians in the city of Philippi, this means that imperial slaves and freedmen (from whose ranks the civil service of the Roman Empire was staffed) had heard the gospel and had come to faith in Jesus Christ.[115]

According to 2 Timothy 4:17 Paul used his trial in Rome as an opportunity for explaining the gospel: "The Lord stood by me and gave me strength, so that through me the message might be fully proclaimed and all the Gentiles might hear it. So I was rescued from the lion's mouth." The context of this statement suggests that Paul refers to his second trial (in A.D. 64?) in Rome, specifically to his defense in the *prima actio,* the preliminary proceedings in which the legally relevant material was presented.[116] Again, Paul uses the opportunity of a trial to explain the gospel to high government officials.

Luke relates that Paul had friends among the Asiarchs (Acts 19:31), high officials of the city who introduced motions in the assemblies of the city council, who dedicated buildings, who built statues and who organized festivals and games.[117] These officials were prepared to protect Paul during disturbances in the city. It is a plausible assumption to surmise that this acquaintance was related in some way to Paul's missionary activity in Ephesus. These provincial officials would not have been unaware of the message that Paul proclaimed in the city. On Malta, Paul had friendly contacts with Publius, the "chief man of the island" who had given shelter to shipwrecked prisoners and crew (Acts 28:7). We can assume that Paul explained the gospel to him.

---

[114]See Barrett, *Acts of the Apostles,* 2:1232-33, on the Western text, which specifies that Paul was committed to the *stratopedarchos,* i.e., to the *praefectus castrorum,* the chief administrative officer of the Praetorian Guard.

[115]See Meeks, *First Urban Christians,* p. 63; Peter T. O'Brien, *The Epistle to the Philippians. A Commentary on the Greek Text,* NIGTC (Grand Rapids: Eerdmans, 1991), p. 554.

[116]See William D. Mounce, *Pastoral Epistles,* WBC 46 (Nashville: Nelson, 2000), p. 595.

[117]See Rosalinde A. Kearsley, "The Asiarchs," in *The Book of Acts in Its Graeco-Roman Literary Setting,* ed. D. W. J. Gill and C. Gempf, The Book of Acts in Its First-Century Setting 2 (Exeter, U.K.: Paternoster, 1994), pp. 363-76.

Erastus of Corinth has not only a Latin name but he is described as a city treasurer (*oikonomos tēs poleōs* [Rom 16:23; cf. Acts 19:22; 2 Tim 4:20]). An inscription discovered in Corinth honors an Erastus as the benefactor who financed the pavement of the plaza east of the theater. The inscription reads: "Erastus, in gratitude for his aedileship, laid this pavement at his own expense."[118] This Erastus, evidently a freedman who had acquired considerable wealth, which allowed him to be one of the benefactors in the city of Corinth, is very probably identical with the Erastus of the New Testament.[119]

Phoebe of Cenchreae near Corinth (Rom 16:1-2) is described as a "benefactor" *(prostatis)*.[120] She is an independent woman who travels from Corinth to Rome and who evidently has some wealth. She was probably converted when Paul was preaching in Corinth. Luke mentions that several "Greek women of high standing" were converted to faith in Jesus Christ through Paul's preaching in Thessalonica and in Beroea (Acts 17:4, 12).

Gaius of Corinth (1 Cor 1:14; Rom 16:22, 23) has a common Roman praenomen. He has a house in Corinth in which he can accommodate Paul, who wrote the epistle to the Romans as his guest. The secretary who took down Paul's dictation with the name of Tertius is a further indication that Gaius is a man of some wealth: Tertius may have been in the employ of Gaius.

Achaicus, Fortunatus, Lucius and Quartus in Corinth and Clement in Philippi have Latin names (1 Cor 16:17; Rom 16:21, 23; Phil 4:3), which suggests, perhaps, that they came from families who belonged to the original colonists when these two cities were (re-)founded as Roman colonies. The name "Achaicus" (lit. "from Achaia") suggests that this Corinthian Christian, or his father, lived for a time in Italy, where he was given this

---

[118]John Harvey Kent, *Corinth VIII, iii: The Inscriptions 1926-1950* (Princeton, N.J.: American School of Classical Studies at Athens, 1966), p. 99. Cf. David W. J. Gill, "Erastus the Aedile," *Tyndale Bulletin* 40 (1989): 293-301; Andrew D. Clarke, *Secular and Christian Leadership in Corinth: A Socio-Historical and Exegetical Study of 1 Corinthians 1-6*, AGAJU 18 (Leiden: Brill, 1993), pp. 46-56; Schnabel, *Early Christian Mission*, 2:1141-43.

[119]See Theissen, *Social Setting of Pauline Christianity*, pp. 243-45; Jerome Murphy-O'Connor, *Paul: A Critical Life* (Oxford: Oxford University Press, 1996), pp. 268-70; Bruce W. Winter, *Seek the Welfare of the City: Christians as Benefactors and Citizens* (Carlisle, U.K.: Paternoster; Grand Rapids: Eerdmans, 1994), pp. 179-97.

[120]The term *prostatis* used in Rom 16:2 is evidently the equivalent of Greek *euergetēs* and the Latin *patrona*. Cf. Meeks, *First Urban Christians*, p. 60.

geographical appellation, before returning to Corinth, perhaps as one of the freedmen who settled in the newly established colony. Freedmen, especially those who settled in new Roman colonies, belonged to the very few groups who had greater opportunities for social advancement than the majority of the people. The fact that Corinthian Christians initiate lawsuits against fellow believers (1 Cor 6:1-11) suggests people of high social status, as the disenfranchised did not have access to the law courts. The problem of believers making a point of praying with their head covered (1 Cor 11:4) also points to people of high social status, as members of the elite regularly officiated in the cults of the city with their heads covered *(capite velato)*.[121] The same conclusion can be drawn from the insistence of some Corinthian believers that they have the right to attend banquets in the temples of the city (1 Cor 8:9).[122]

Crispus of Corinth (1 Cor 1:14; Acts 18:8) also has a Latin *praenomen*. Because he had achieved the office of president of the synagogue *(archisynagōgos),* he enjoyed prestige at least in the local Jewish community, if not in the city. He was probably a man of some wealth as well. Luke, a coworker of Paul, also has a Latin name. The fact that he was a physician (Col 4:14) indicates that he might have been a *medicus* in a Roman family who received the name of his master (Lucius) when he was manumitted—doctors were often slaves.

Prisca and Aquila (Acts 18:2-3; 1 Cor 16:19; Rom 16:3-5) were leatherworkers, artisans who worked independently in several major cities; their occupation indicates low status; their Jewish identity, coupled with the fact that they operated in several cities rather than in one city only, surely gave them an outsider status in the Roman society of Rome, Corinth and Ephesus.

Gaius of Macedonia, Secundus of Thessalonica and Gaius of Derbe have also Latin names and are free to travel (Acts 19:29; 20:4), but we have no information about their social background. Sometimes slaves traveled as agents of their masters. The Greek names of Lydia (Acts 16:14-15), Euodia and Syntyche (Phil 4:2-3), members of the church in Philippi,

---

[121]See David W. J. Gill, "The Importance of Roman Portraiture for Head Coverings in 1 Corinthians 11.2-16," *TynB* 41 (1990); Winter, *After Paul Left Corinth*, pp. 121-41.

[122]In 1 Cor 8:9, the word *exousia* should not be translated as "liberty" but as "right" that some Corinthians claim to have; cf. Winter, *Seek the Welfare of the City*, pp. 166-68.

suggest that they belonged to the merchant groups who consisted of free persons who lived temporarily, or permanently, in the city. A "foreigner" living in a city was called *metoikos* (translated as "metic"). That Lydia was a dealer in purple fabrics and the owner of a house in which she could accommodate Paul and some of his coworkers indicates that she was a woman of some wealth. Chloe of Corinth (1 Cor 1:11) was also a woman of means, as she had slaves (or slaves who had become freedmen), but we do not know whether she was a Christian.

Several names suggest that Christians who were converted through Paul's ministry or were coworkers of Paul were slaves, perhaps freedmen. The names Ampliatus and Epaenetus (Rom 16:5, 8), whom Paul knew in the East before they moved to Rome, were common Latin slave names: they were Christians who had been slaves or continued to be slaves. The "people of Chloe" (1 Cor 1:11) who traveled from Corinth to Ephesus to visit Paul are either slaves or freedmen. Onesimus (Philem 10; Col 4:9) was a slave of Philemon who lived in Colossae. He had become a Christian after he had run away and met Paul in Ephesus. Slaves are mentioned as members of the church in Corinth (1 Cor 7:20-24; 12:13), and presumably in the churches in Galatia (Gal 3:28) and in the province of Asia (Eph 6:5-8), also in the church in Colossae (Col 3:11, 22), which had been established by Paul's coworker Epaphras.

This evidence shows that Paul did not pursue a missionary strategy that focused on particular social groups. He was concerned to preach the gospel to all people in a city, irrespective of social class.

Culture: Was Paul a crosscultural missionary? This is the point at which we must ask the question whether Paul was a crosscultural missionary who took into account and adapted to the cultural differences between the various ethnic groups. It is generally assumed, at least by missiologists and missionaries who write in the twentieth or twenty-first century, that Paul was a crosscultural missionary, indeed the model par excellence for crosscultural missions.[123] Before we can answer this question, we need to explore the definition of culture. A definition that is often used by evangelicals understands culture as "the more or less integrated systems of ideas,

---

[123]See Christopher R. Little, *Mission in the Way of Paul: Biblical Mission for the Church in the Twenty-First Century*, Studies in Biblical Literature 80 (New York: Peter Lang, 2005), p. 60.

feelings, and values and their associated patterns of behavior and products shared by a group of people."[124] A more general definition understands culture as a shared set of assumptions about the way things are, a worldview. However, the problem with such definitions is that "worldviews may vary considerably depending on peoples' age group, socioeconomic status, ethnic identity, religion, education, or family background."[125]

A general anthropological definition of culture makes it difficult, if not impossible, to distinguish between culture and subcultures, between subcultures and ethnic groups or between social groups and religious affiliation. A general definition does not clarify the distinction between or overlap of culture, society, civilization, ethnicity and identity. And a general definition of culture is insufficient to appropriately address the problems of interculturality. When Cicero asserts, "cultura autem animi philosophia est" ("philosophy is the care/culture of the soul"),[126] the point of reference is the philosophical contemplation of human nature.[127] It has been pointed out that

> the metaphoric relation between the words "cultura" and "agri-cultura" hints at the conviction that philosophical-cultural points of reference for human self care are as reliable as the natural conditions of farming, provided one strives towards knowledge about physical and metaphysical norms and laws. Cultures, which are metaphysically stabilized in such a way, do not yet even require their own notion of culture, because any such notion would always already contain the suspicion of a lack of substance. However, the etymological continuity from "cultura" to "culture" covered up deep conceptual and epistemological ruptures, which became more and more apparent only in the course of the 18th century.

Some philosophers of culture have therefore argued that culture, as a

---

[124]Paul G. Hiebert, *Anthropological Insights for Missionaries* (Grand Rapids: Baker, 1985), p. 30; Paul G. Hiebert and Eloise Meneses Hiebert, *Incarnational Ministry: Planting Churches in Band, Tribal, Peasant, and Urban Societies* (Grand Rapids: Baker, 1995), p. 37. Cf. Flemming, *Contextualization in the New Testament*, p. 118, who adds that "culture embraces both our beliefs and our social practices, that is, the ways people live out their everyday lives in society."

[125]Flemming, *Contextualization in the New Testament*, pp. 118-19.

[126]Cicero *Tusculanae Disputationes* 2.13.9.

[127]See Paul Geyer, "A Critical Theory of Culture," paper presented at "XXVII. Deutscher Romanistentag," Munich, October 10, 2001 <www.romanistik.uni-bonn.de/www/Romanistik/Seminar/Lehreude/geyer/Schriften/bilder/Schriftenverzeichnis.pdf>. For the following comments see ibid.

concept, "becomes possible only in modern society, which, being able for the first time to reflect upon itself as structurally contingent, ceases to be able to reflect upon itself in any other way."[128]

It is not surprising that in contemporary cultural studies the term culture has the wider meaning, often absorbing the notion of civilization. A famous definition understands culture as "the way of life of a particular people living together in one place."[129] Others define culture as

> the whole of institutions, actions, processes and symbolic forms, which, aided by planned techniques, transform 'existent nature' into a space of social living, maintain and improve this space, preserve and develop the required skills (cultural techniques, knowledge), consolidate leading values through special rites ('cultus') and, thus, create social orders and communicative symbolic worlds, which sustain community formations.[130]

In North American cultural anthropology, culture is "essentially a matter of ideas and values, a collective cast of mind. The ideas and values, the cosmology, morality, and aesthetics, are expressed in symbols."[131] The understanding of the term culture has

> shifted in use from an implication of a privileged body of artistic materials (and a set of attitudes surrounding them), which transcends localism and links the generations of civilized humans . . . to an idea of a conglomeration of protocols, behavioural patterns, micro-social expectations and ideological formations—"the culture of the University"; "the culture of cigarettes."[132]

Culture can thus be defined as "a description of a particular way of life which expresses certain meanings and values not only in art and learning but also in institutions and ordinary behavior. The analysis of culture, from such a definition, is the clarification of the meanings and values im-

---

[128]Niklas Luhmann, "Kultur als historischer Begriff," in *Gesellschaftsstruktur und Semantik. Studien zur Wissenssoziologie der modernen Gesellschaft. Band 4* (Frankfurt: Suhrkamp, 1995), p. 51.

[129]T. S. Eliot, *Notes Towards the Definition of Culture* (New York: Harcourt, Brace, 1949), p. 120.

[130]Hartmut Böhme et al., *Orientierung Kulturwissenschaft* (Reinbek: Rowohlt, 2000), p. 104.

[131]Adam Kuper, *Culture: The Anthropologists' Account* (Cambridge: Harvard University Press, 1999), p. 227.

[132]Simon Goldhill, "Introduction. Setting an Agenda: 'Everything is Greece to the Wise,' " in *Being Greek Under Rome: Cultural Identity, the Second Sophistic and the Development of Empire*, ed. S. Goldhill (Cambridge: Cambridge University Press, 2001), p. 15.

plicit and explicit in a particular way of life, a particular culture."[133]

A recent example of such a general approach to the understanding of culture is an article in the *Journal of General Internal Medicine* in which the author acknowledges that culture is a broad and complex concept but then goes on to comment on the trend to focus on "cultural differences" between patients and physicians as the "principal culprit" of inequalities in the quantity and quality of medical care.[134] The author comments on the tendency to conflate the concept of culture with race and ethnicity, and raises the concern that

> physicians may use race and ethnicity as proxies for culture, bluntly ap-
> plying cross-cultural skills according to the presence or absence of racial
> or ethnic discordance. The ability to gauge cultural distance might help
> physicians more deftly apply cross-cultural skills according to the degree
> and nature of cultural differences (just as they may approach counseling on
> diet and exercise differently for patients with mild vs severe obesity or dys-
> lipidemia). In trying to meet patients where they are culturally, physicians
> would need to recognize that people do not occupy fixed positions on the
> cultural landscape. Culture is multifaceted and dynamic; individuals may
> employ different perspectives for different issues, or even for the same issue
> at different points in time.

Such general definitions of culture render any conversation between a wealthy member of the local elite in a Greek city with a poor freedman a "crosscultural" event, as would be the conversation of a Jew who believes in the existence of only one true God and a pagan who accepts the existence of many gods a "cross-cultural" event, or the conversation between a believer in the crucified and risen Jesus as Messiah and Savior with a Jewish or pagan person who has either not heard the news of Jesus or rejects it as unbelievable or irrelevant.

General anthropological definitions of culture are not easily applied

---

[133]Raymond Williams, *The Long Revolution* (London: Chatto & Windus, 1961), p. 41. Williams is regarded as the founding father of British cultural studies.

[134]Sarah Somnath, "The Relevance of Cultural Distance Between Patients and Physicians to Racial Disparities in Health Care," *Journal of General Internal Medicine* 21, no. 2 (2006): 203-5. The following quotations are from ibid. She refers to the "Executive Summary" published in 2001 by the Office of Minority Health in the U. S. Department of Health and Human Services in Washington D.C. with the title "National Standards for Culturally and Linguistically Appropriate Services in Health Care."

to the realities of the Greco-Roman world.[135] Neither the Oxford Classical Dictionary nor Brill's New Pauly, the most comprehensive encyclopedia of the ancient world, have entries with the heading "Culture."[136] A prominent specialist of the Roman world argues in a book that has been hailed as providing "an authoritative synoptic view of the entire Roman Near East" that "if we think of a 'culture' in the full sense, as a tradition, an educational system, a set of customs and above all a collective understanding of the past, then we can find in the Roman Near East only two established cultures: Greek and Jewish."[137] Some historians have voiced disagreement, suggesting that Western prejudice in favor of Greek culture prevents scholars from viewing the Roman Empire from the perspective of the East, with the result that the existence of a Near Eastern culture (or Syrian, Arabic, Mesopotamian culture) is minimized:

> Scratch a Temple of Zeus and we find a Baal or a Hadad, scratch a "Roman" city and we find something that is Near Eastern. The Corinthian colonnades vanish like a mirage to reveal forms and ideas rooted in the East, not West. The influences of Greek and Roman rule are there, of course. But the real picture now emerging is of cities, religious practices, lifestyles, architecture and a civilization that remained overwhelmingly Near Eastern throughout the nine centuries of domination by Macedonians and Romans.[138]

If we were to simply combine these approaches, we could speak of three or four "cultures" in the Hellenistic world: Greek, Roman, Near Eastern or Syrian, and Jewish culture (unless the latter is included in the Near Eastern culture).

But even these broad distinctions are not easy to define in specific contexts. Plutarch, born in the first century in the 40s in Chaeronia in Boeotia, a region in Greece, served as a priest at the nearby oracle of Apollo in Delphi. He had Roman citizenship and traveled extensively both in the eastern

---

[135]See Goldhill, "Introduction," pp. 15-17.

[136]The *OCD* has only an entry on "Culture-bringers," i.e., "mythical figures who are credited with the inventions of important cultural achievements" (p. 412).

[137]Fergus Millar, *The Roman Near East, 31 BC - AD 337* (Cambridge: Harvard University Press, 1993), p. 517. The praise comes from noted classical scholar G. W. Bowersock on the dust jacket of the book.

[138]Warwick Ball, *Rome in the East: The Transformation of an Empire* (London: Routledge, 2000), p. 449.

part of the Roman Empire as well as in Italy. His works *Roman Questions* and *Greek Questions* demonstrate that his relationship with Roman identity "is complex, even contradictory," as he was both inside and outside Roman culture, although "he was more of an insider to Greek culture than to Roman."[139] The *Roman Questions* do not allow us to conclude with certainty "how far Roman culture is to be seen as an autonomous entity, or as a mere copy of Greek culture," because "the Romans seem to be Hellenized barbarians, and to be some other, separate, but civilized kind of people." Moreover, the perception "that by the imperial period Italy was united, at peace and had become fully Romanised" needs to be revisited in the light of the evidence for example of Pompeii, which demonstrates that "identifying an assemblage of material is not sufficient in itself for the recognition of a cultural identity." Roman or "Romanized" styles of material may not demonstrate the presence of a Roman identity but may be asserting social status.[140]

Scholars who have investigated the process of Romanization in the early first century point out that regarding personal demeanor the Roman intruders in the East (e.g., in Asia Minor) deferred to local custom.[141] They sought local public offices and priesthoods and the presidency of the gymnasium or of festival games. They performed pious acts to local deities. Unless they lived in their own colonies, they evidently were determined to fit in, willing even to deny their ancestral culture. Descendants of Italian immigrants to the East lost their Latin within a generation or two. And when they died, their effect on their neighbors came to an end. The imperial cult was a novelty, but "it cannot have amounted to much more than the acquainting of the audience with the physical appearance of the imperial family."[142] Roman culture was most evident in the military,

---

[139]Rebecca Preston, "Roman Questions, Greek Answers: Plutarch and the Construction of Identity," in *Being Greek Under Rome: Cultural Identity, the Second Sophistic and the Development of Empire*, ed. S. Goldhill (Cambridge: Cambridge University Press, 2001), pp. 86-119, 118-19; the following quotations from ibid., p. 118.

[140]Mark Grahame, "Material Culture and Roman Identity: The Spatial Layout of Pomopeian Houses and the Problem of Ethnicity," in *Cultural Identity in the Roman Empire*, ed. R. Laurence and J. Berry (London: Routledge, 1998), pp. 156-78, 175-76.

[141]See Ramsay MacMullen, *Romanization in the Time of Augustus* (New Haven, Conn.: Yale University Press, 2000), pp. 1-29. On Romanization in Cilicia, the province in which Paul was born, cf. Susanne Pilhofer, *Romanisierung in Kilikien? Das Zeugnis der Inschriften*, Quellen und Forschungen zur Antiken Welt 46 (München: Herbert Utz, 2006).

[142]MacMullen, *Romanization in the Time of Augustus*, p. 15.

in the administration of cities and provinces, and in practical technology: Roman novelties included gladiatorial exhibitions, land surveying *(centuriatio)*, road building, city wall construction, aqueducts, the size and arrangement of baths, food market buildings *(macellum)*, the use of brick and cement, and the technique of setting small stones on concrete in a net pattern *(opus reticulatum)*. And it is important to remember that many people were bilingual and intermarried, which resulted in the fact that gradually the East transformed the Roman colonies.[143]

How did people in the provinces think of themselves? The members of the local and provincial elites in Asia Minor can be described in terms of several collective identities that complemented one another harmoniously. They were members of the social elite, citizens of their hometown (and perhaps of other towns), members of an *ethnos* (e.g., of the province of Asia), members of the commonwealth of the Greeks, and Roman citizens.[144] The collective identities of the people living in the villages focused on the village. The identity of the villagers was characterized by a dependence on the weather, by illnesses and by other forces of nature that could not be controlled, resulting in a more pronounced role of religion.

Ethnic factors in cultural self-identification are difficult to assess with regard to the early Roman Empire, particularly in the provinces, mostly because of a lack of evidence. The view that the *polis* ("city state") represents the endpoint of the development of the state in Greece while *ethnos* ("tribe") constituted an earlier form has been replaced by more sophisticated views that reckon with parallel developments and different living conditions; geographically scattered large *ethnē*, such as the Achaeans, the Ionians and the Dorians, never were primordial tribes but communities of descent whose genesis is dated to the eighth and seventh centuries B.C., although "there is still considerable controversy regarding the development of a sense of affiliation and shared traits in cult, calendar system, institu-

---

[143]For a somewhat different assessment see Benjamin H. Isaac, *The Invention of Racism in Classical Antiquity* (Princeton, N.J.: Princeton University Press, 2004), pp. 381-405, who highlights the hostility and the patronizing attitudes of Romans concerning Greeks. On bilingualism as expression of double identity in the Greco-Roman world cf. James Adams, N. Swain and Simon Swain, "Introduction," in *Bilingualism in Ancient Society: Language Contact and the Written Text*, ed. J. N. Adams et al. (Oxford: Oxford University Press, 2002), pp. 1-20, 2, 7-8.

[144]Stephan, *Honoratioren*, pp. 329-36 (conclusions); on the collective identities in rural Asia Minor see ibid., pp. 261-94.

tions, etc."[145] Scholars who research ethnicity in the Greek world point
out that ethnicity is a social rather than a biological phenomenon. What
some describe as an ethnic group cannot be defined by genetic, linguistic,
religious or common cultural features. Such groups exist only in conscious
opposition to other "ethnic" identities by virtue of their association with a
specific territory and a shared narrative of descent. Moreover, the sources
demonstrate that the boundaries of ethnic groups are permeable.[146] If this
is indeed correct, we understand why neither regions nor ethnicity seemed
to have played a major role in Asia Minor, and why the cities were the
central points of crystallization of collective identities.

Instructive is Strabo (64 B.C.-A.D. 21), the geographer from Amaseia
in Pontus.[147] He describes numerous regions, including Cappadocia,
Pontus, Bithynia, Mysia, Phrygia, Ionia, Pamphylia and Cilicia, with a
focus on geographical and topographical details.[148] Occasionally he mentions the ethnic affiliation of populations. He describes, for example, the
Bithynians as an *ethnos* derived from the Thracians, and the Pamphylians
as descendants of Amphilochos and Kalchas, who had come from Troy
(Strabo 12.3.3; 14.4.3). An ethnic group is described in terms of having a
common ancestor, although in the end the "ethnic" Pamphylians cannot
be isolated from the region of Pamphylia. Strabo readily admits that he
has difficulties distinguishing the Bithynians, Phrygians and Mysians:
these peoples are different, but it is not clear how they are different. Even
a geographical description fails, because there are no natural boundaries
between these peoples or regions (Strabo 12.4.4-5).

Funerary and honorary inscriptions sometimes mention ethnic terms. In
Rome, a certain Aurelius Marcus honors Zeus Olybrios, a local deity from

---

[145]Klaus Freitag, "Ethnos," in *Brill's New Pauly*, ed. H. Cancik and H. Schneider (Leiden: Brill,
2004), 5:88-89, 88.

[146]See Jonathan M. Hall, *Ethnic Identity in Greek Antiquity* (1997; reprint, Cambridge: Cambridge
University Press, 2000), pp. 17-33. For the notion of ethnicity in ancient Greece before the Hellenistic period cf. Noel Robertson, "The Religious Criterion in Greek Ethnicity," *American Journal
of Ancient History* 1 (2002): 5-74.

[147]See Ronald Syme, *Anatolica: Studies in Strabo*, ed. A. Birley (Oxford: Clarendon, 1995); Daniela
Dueck, *Strabo of Amasia: A Greek Man of Letters in Augustan Rome* (London and New York: Rout-
ledge, 2000); Daniela Dueck et al., *Strabo's Cultural Geography: The Making of a* Kolossourgia
(Cambridge: Cambridge University Press, 2005).

[148]Strabo *Geographica*, 12.1.1-3 (Cappadocia), 12.3.1 (Pontus), 12.4.1-3 (Bithynia), 12.4.4-5 (Mysia), 12.8.1 (Phrygia), 14.1.3-4 (Ionia), 14.4.1-3 (Pamphylia), 14.5.1 (Cilicia).

Asia Minor, which is described as the patron of the Cilicians and as the patron of the citizens of Anazarbus. The inscription reads: "To Zeus Olybrios of the ethnos of the Cilicians (and) of the most glorious metropolis Anazarbus, from Aurelius Marcus, the stator (usher), on the occasion of a vow."[149]

Aurelius Marcus, a Cilician living in Rome, evidently thought it important to express his loyalty not only to the city of Anazarbus (where he was born?) but also to the *ethnos* of the Cilicians. Villagers in rural areas sometimes used the name of their village as an "ethnic" term. A dedicatory inscription from Phrygia, set up by a certain Tychasios for the Anatolian deity Men reads: "Tychasios, son of Apollonios, resident of Koliakome, (erected) for Men the stele."[150]

The leading officials of the regional assembly *(Koinon)*, are called Asiarchs in Asia, Lyciarchs in Lycia, and Galatarchs in Galatia. But these regional assemblies do not seem to have represented a major factor in the collective identities of the population.[151] The main focus of personal identification and pride was the *polis*, the city in which one was born, raised and educated, and in which one lived (and died).

Regarding the cultural identity of Jews and Greeks in the early Roman Empire, the cultural distinction "is more notional than real, and so unlikely to have been particularly visible," even in Palestine.[152] For the Jewish historian Josephus, the term Greeks describes non-Jews, including the mercenaries of the Jewish king Alexander Jannaeus, even though they were actually Pisidians and Cilicians. Sometimes the Greeks are "us," that is, the Jews, contrasted with barbarians.[153] In one passage he describes the Jews who translated Jewish-writings into Greek as "Greeks."[154] Often the "Greeks" are the people living in the large cities, the people living in rural areas are sometimes called "Syrians."[155] If indeed "Greeks" are simply the

---

[149]Stephan, *Honoratioren*, p. 194; the inscription is published as *IGR* I 72.

[150]MAMA V 209.

[151]See Stephan, *Honoratioren*, pp. 184-94.

[152]Tessa Rajak, "The Location of Cultures in Second Temple Palestine: The Evidence of Josephus," in *The Book of Acts in its Palestinian Setting*, ed. R. Bauckham (Exeter, U.K.: Paternoster, 1995), p. 5.

[153]Josephus *Bellum Judaicum* 1.94.

[154]Ibid., 1.17.

[155]Ibid., 2.458; the villagers around Caesarea are described as Syrians, while the neighboring cities are not included in the Syrian area.

citizens of the cities, "then we do not learn much from the term about the ethnicity or culture of those thus described."[156] For Jews in the first century, identity was a combination of both ancestry (ethnicity) and religion (including dietary and moral customs).[157] In many definitions of Jewishness, "religion" could be replaced by "culture."

On one end of the continuum were some Jews who had assimilated to Hellenistic culture to such a degree that they had abandoned most Jewish customs and whose Jewishness was not much more than a matter of Jewish lineage. On the other end of the continuum were proselytes, Gentiles who had converted to Judaism, who were Jews not by biological descent but by a thorough resocialization through which they acquired a new "ethnicity" in kinship and custom. The terms that Diaspora Jews used to describe themselves include *ethnos* ("people, nation"), *phylon* ("tribe, nation"), *genos* ("race, people by descent"), and *laos* ("people"), distinguishing between *homoethneis* or *homophyloi* ("fellow nationals" or "people of the same race") and *alloethneis, allogeneis* or *allophyloi* ("foreigners" or "people of other races"). When political authorities challenged the rights of Jews to assemble, celebrate the sabbath or send money to Jerusalem, the Jews living in Diaspora cities appealed to their right to practice their "ancestral customs" *(ta patria ethnē)* and to live in accordance with their "ancestral laws" *(hoi patrioi nomoi).*[158]

An illustration of the complex situation is the very diverse customs that can be observed in the case of Jews who received Roman citizenship. The primary source material shows that with regard to the adoption of Roman names, Diaspora Jews used several options.[159] Some used purely Roman names, for example, a Jew in Akmonia in Phrygia who adopted the

---

[156]Rajak, "Location of Cultures," p. 13.

[157]See John M. G. Barclay, *Jews in the Mediterranean Diaspora: From Alexander to Trajan (323 BCE - 117 CE)* (Edinburgh: T & T Clark, 1996), pp. 402-13. See also Shaye J. D. Cohen, *The Beginnings of Jewishness: Boundaries, Varieties, Uncertainties,* Hellenistic Culture and Society 31 (Berkeley: University of California Press, 1999), pp. 13-197; Jonathan L. Reed, *Archaeology and the Galilean Jesus: A Re-Examination of the Evidence* (Harrisburg, Penn.: Trinity Press International, 2000), pp. 28-43.

[158]Barclay, *Jews in the Mediterranean Diaspora,* pp. 405-7. On the Jewish rights to practice their ancestral customs cf. Pucci Ben Zeev, *Jewish Rights.*

[159]See Schnabel, *Early Christian Mission,* 1:577; see Pantelis M. Nigdelis, "Synagoge(n) und Gemeinde der Juden in Thessaloniki: Fragen aufgrund einer neuen jüdischen Grabinschrift der Kaiserzeit," *ZPE* 102 (1994): 297-306, 302-3.

name Publius Turronius Claudius. Some Jews added a Roman or Greek patronymic to their Roman name (e.g., Aurelius Phrygianos Menokritou in Akmonia). Some Jews used a Greek name followed by a Roman name (e.g., Loukios Loukiou in Akmonia). Some Jews used a Roman or Greek name with or without a patronymic (e.g., Roupheina in Smyrna and Straton Tyrannou in Magnesia). Some Jews used a Jewish name, a Greek patronymic and a toponymic (e.g., a certain Aurelius Eusanbatios Menandrou Korykiotes from the city of Korykos). Some Jews used a Jewish name combined with a Roman or Greek *supernomen* (e.g., Beniames ho kai Dometios in Thessalonica and Iakob he ke Apellion in Aphrodisias). Some Jews used a Greek *cognomen* followed by a Jewish *supernomen* (e.g., Claudius Tiberius Polycharmos ho kai Achyrios in Stoboi). Jewish identity or descent is often, but not always, indicated on funerary epitaphs by religious symbols (e.g., the menorah), by titles (e.g., *archisynagōgos*), or by the addition of an ethnicon *(Ioudaios* or *Hebraios)*.

These names do not tell us much, if anything, about the cultural assimilation or the cultural values of the Jewish families that set up these inscriptions. A very conservative Jewish family that avoided all nonessential contacts with their pagan neighbors in a Greek city would not have wanted to receive Roman citizenship. A totally assimilated family that did not care about the details of the Jewish law would probably not have wanted to be identified as Jewish on a gravestone. Most Diaspora Jews lived somewhere between these two extremes. They were people who did not worship in the pagan temples of the city they lived in. Nor did they participate in local religious rites or in processions dedicated to one of the local deities. They regularly attended the local synagogue where they worshiped and studied Torah. They did not eat certain foods that their pagan fellow citizens would regularly consume, such as meat from pigs. Many if not most Diaspora Jews would not have been comfortable with the sexual mores of their fellow citizens, especially with regard to homosexuality, prostitution or sexual intercourse with slaves. However, their language, dress, houses, material possessions, professions and in some cases even their education would have not been different from that of their pagan neighbors.

Of course there were Jews living in Judea and in Galilee whose cul-

tural identity differed considerably from their brothers and sisters in the
Diaspora. It is a safe assumption that a member of the Essene community
who lived in the desert near the Dead Sea and who embarked on a journey
via Jerusalem and Alexandria to the city of Rome would certainly experience a passage through several cultures: from a traditional conservative
Jewish rural culture in the desert to an urban Jewish Greek culture in
Jerusalem, from there to the Greek-Hellenistic culture of Alexandria and
finally to the Roman culture in the capital of the Empire.

By contrast, members of the Jewish Diaspora community in Tarsus
who had studied in Jerusalem and who traveled from Jerusalem via Antioch to Ephesus, Athens and Corinth would have had an entirely different
experience, especially if they have both Tarsian and Roman citizenship.
They are at least bilingual or trilingual: they can speak Hebrew, Greek
and Aramaic, possibly even some Latin. In Jerusalem they converse in
Hebrew with the Torah experts, and speak Greek when they visit the
synagogue of the Cilician Jews (according to Acts 6:9 Paul had such an
affiliation). In Antioch, the metropolitan capital of the province of Syria,
they converse with fellow Jews in Aramaic; in conversations with local
Syrians they speak either Aramaic or Greek, depending on the individual's education and preference; in encounters with the descendants of the
Greek settlers and with Roman officials they speak in Greek, with the
latter perhaps in Latin. In Ephesus, Athens and Corinth they can use
Greek with everybody; even the descendants of the Roman colonists in
Corinth can converse in Greek, at least in the middle of the first century.
If they speak some Latin, they would use that in encounters with Roman officials. In Antioch, Ephesus, Athens and Corinth, Jewish beliefs
and practices—belief in one God, circumcision, the regular reading of the
Scriptures, the Jewish festivals, the weekly gatherings on the sabbath in
the synagogue—differentiate Jewish travelers from the non-Jewish citizens.
Differences in terms of lifestyle are largely limited to the abstention from
work on the sabbath and to the consumption or nonconsumption of particular food items. The material culture of a Jewish home in Ephesus, Athens or
Corinth in which the traveling Diaspora Jews may have found accommodations was virtually indistinguishable from that of the Greek neighbors. The
only exception was the *lalarium*, the house altar where pagans worshiped

the *lares,* the house gods. As Jewish travelers from Tarsus may have participated in the gymnasium education in Tarsus[160] while at the same time being introduced to and perhaps even trained in the traditions of the Hebrew
Bible and the Jewish traditions, they were certainly at home in two cultures
and thus did not have to "cross" cultures. People who are bicultural do not
cross cultures, or alternately, they are hardly aware of constantly crossing
between two cultures in which they are equally at home.

Diaspora Jews, according to Erich Gruen, "did not promote private
enclaves or segregated seclusion. Jews strove to engender circumstances
that would enable them to maintain their ancient heritage while engaging
comfortably and productively in the lands of the classical world wherein
they dwelled."[161] For Philo, Roman citizenship and "Jewish citizenship"
are not mutually exclusive.[162] Diaspora Jews did not deplore their fate or
yearn to return to the land of their ancestors, as Gruen points out:

> The respect and awe paid to the Holy Land by Jews living elsewhere stood
> in full harmony with commitment to local community and allegiance to
> Gentile governance. . . . Palestine mattered, and it mattered in a territorial
> sense—but not as a required residence. Gifts to the Temple and pilgrimages
> to Jerusalem announced simultaneously a devotion to the symbolic heart
> of Judaism and a singular pride in the accomplishments of the Diaspora.
> Jewish Hellenistic writers took the concurrence for granted. They were not
> driven to apologia. Nor did they feel obliged to reconcile the contradiction.
> As they saw it, there was none.[163]

Paul was bicultural both in the cognitive and in the functional sense.[164]
As a Jew whose family maintained conservative "Hebrew" traditions while
living in the Greek Diaspora city of Tarsus, Paul understood both Jewish
and Greco-Roman cultures. He was at least bilingual, probably trilingual:
he was fluent in Aramaic and in Greek, and in all probability also in Hebrew. He was evidently able to function comfortably, without consciously

---

[160]See Erich S. Gruen, *Diaspora: Jews amidst Greeks and Romans* (Cambridge: Harvard University
    Press, 2002), pp. 123-24.
[161]Ibid., p. 103.
[162]See Philo *De legatione ad Gaium* 157, with regard to the Jews living in the city of Rome.
[163]Gruen, *Diaspora*, p. 252.
[164]For these terms cf. A. Scott Moreau, "Biculturalism," *EDWM*, p. 131. For the following defini-
    tion of "root biculturalism," cf. ibid. On Paul's view concerning ethnicity, cf. Charles H. Cos-
    grove, "Did Paul Value Ethnicity?" *Catholic Biblical Quarterly* 68 (2006): 268-90.

"crossing over" into one or the other culture, both in Jewish culture and in Greco-Roman culture. He could give an expository sermon explaining the significance of Jesus the promised Messiah on Saturday morning in the local synagogue, and speak before the intellectual elite of Athens in the Council of the Areopagus perhaps on Sunday morning. If "root biculturalism" is defined as "the ability of the person to truly and naturally identify at the root level of both cultures emotionally and cognitively," then no pious Jews would ever be "root biculturalists." They might cognitively grasp the "meaning" of pagan religiosity, but they would never "identify emotionally" with the worship of idols.

The only example of a truly crosscultural situation in Paul's missionary ministry may be his encounter with Lycaonians in Lystra (Acts 14:8-18)—if indeed the crowds who are explicitly said to have used the Lycaonian language (Acts 14:11) did not understand Paul's preaching due to the language barrier.[165] The text assumes, however, that the crowds were able to understand Paul's speech (Acts 14:15-17, 18), which suggests that they were bilingual, speaking both Greek and Lycaonian.

In conclusion, the cultural realities of the Greek-speaking regions in the East of the Roman Empire suggest that the notion that Paul was a "crosscultural" missionary is a modern construct that is not helpful as an analytical tool for understanding Paul's missionary work. Most of the comments on Paul as a crosscultural missionary come from missiologists or missionaries who base their analyses on the missionary realities of the nineteenth and twentieth centuries without really knowing the cultural realities of the first century. The cultural distance between a missionary from Great Britain or North America and the local population in the villages of China, India or Kenya is as enormous as the cultural distance between a missionary from Korea, Singapore or Thailand and the urban centers in Africa, Eastern Europe or South America. They may all share the experience of eating in Western-style fast food restaurants, but the differences in language, political tradition, educational systems, social customs and the collective understanding of the past are so considerable that these missionaries need several years of cultural

---

[165]Thus argued by Glen L. Thompson, "In Darkest Lycaonia: Paul as Foreign Missionary at Lystra," a paper read at the Evangelical Theological Society Annual Meeting; San Diego 2007.

studies, including the study of the local language(s), before they can function appropriately and practically in their host culture. The cultural distance between the Greek-speaking Torah expert and Christian missionary Paul from Tarsus, and the Greek-speaking philosophers of the Epicurean or Stoic schools of thought in Athens was much shorter: Paul spoke their language, he had some experience of the same educational system, he shared the political tradition of the last one hundred years (since the reorganization of the East by Pompey between 66-62 B.C.), he understood the political administration of Greek cities, he was familiar with the urban infrastructure of the city, he knew their philosophy and their poets. Paul's understanding of the past, being a traditionalist Jew (a "Hebrew of Hebrews"), was determined by God's revelation to Israel from Abraham to Moses, from David to the prophets. Thus there were major differences between himself and the Athenian philosophers, and indeed the entire non-Jewish population of the city, particularly in the area of worship, religious practice and moral behavior. But such differences existed within the city between the skeptical Epicureans and worshipers of Artemis who celebrated the birth of the deity in May during the festival of Thargelion,[166] or the devotees of the Egyptians gods who strode through the dark passageways between the inside and outside walls of the sanctuary where they observed the statues of Sarapis, Isis, Anubis, Harpokrates and Apis.[167] The "culture" of the Jews in Tarsus, and the "culture" of the Greek-speaking Jews living in Jerusalem was in many ways largely indistinguishable from the "culture" of the citizens of Antioch, Ephesus or Corinth. When Tarsian Jews conversed with their Greek neighbors about their faith in one true and living God, this was as little "crosscultural" as was Paul's conversation with fellow Jews about faith in Jesus as the promised Messiah.

---

[166]On festival processions in Ephesus cf. Dieter Knibbe, "Via Sacra Ephesiaca: New Aspects of the Cult of Artemis Ephesia," in *Ephesos, Metropolos of Asia: An Interdisciplinary Approach to its Archaeology, Religion, and Culture,* ed. H. Koester, HTS 41 (Valley Forge, Penn.: Trinity Press International, 1995), pp. 141-55.

[167]See Regina Salditt-Trappmann, *Tempel der ägyptischen Götter in Griechenland und an der Westküste Kleinasiens,* EPRO 15 (Leiden: Brill, 1970), p. 31; James C. Walters, "Egyptian Religions in Ephesos," in *Ephesos, Metropolos of Asia: An Interdisciplinary Approach to its Archaeology, Religion, and Culture,* ed. H. Koester, HTS 41 (Valley Forge, Penn.: Trinity Press International, 1995), pp. 297-98, 302-3.

Paul was crosscultural in the sense that he gave "instruction in Judaism" to pagan listeners who had had no prior contacts with the local synagogues. Paul expected pagan converts to renounce the pagan gods and to turn to the one true and living God, the God of the Jews, the God of Israel's holy Scriptures, the one true God who was almighty, who was different from the divine supreme power of the Epicureans and from the divine immanence of the Stoics, the God who had chosen the strange people of the Jews and who had made their history the peculiar place of his interventions and of his revelation, the God who intervened in history, the God who had given specific promises to the Jews that he would fulfill in the future, the God who had promised a Messiah.[168]

When Jewish Christians visited the churches that Paul had established in Galatia and demanded that the Gentile Christians should be circumcised in order to qualify as full members of Abraham's family and thus of God's people, Paul is evidently not at all surprised that the Galatian Christians want to belong to "Abraham's family." He was only surprised that they let themselves be convinced that circumcision was a necessary prerequisite for being included among Abraham's descendants. This is the reason why Paul writes,

> Just as Abraham "believed God, and it was reckoned to him as righteousness," so, you see, those who believe are the descendants of Abraham. And the scripture, foreseeing that God would justify the Gentiles by faith, declared the gospel beforehand to Abraham, saying, "All the Gentiles shall be blessed in you." For this reason, those who believe are blessed with Abraham who believed. . . . Christ redeemed us from the curse of the law by becoming a curse for us—for it is written, "Cursed is everyone who hangs on a tree"—in order that in Christ Jesus the blessing of Abraham might come to the Gentiles, so that we might receive the promise of the Spirit through faith. (Gal 3:6-9, 13-14, with quotations from Gen 15:6 and Deut 21:23)

When Paul explained that Jesus is Savior on account of his death on the cross, which was difficult enough, if not impossible, to understand, he needed to explain why Jesus was crucified if he was not executed as a

---

[168]See C. K. Barrett, *Jesus and the Word and Other Essays*, PTMS 41 (Allison Park, Penn.: Pickwick, 1995), pp. 149-62.

criminal slave, a political usurper or a rebel who had taken up arms. Paul had to give a report of the life of Jesus, who had a Jewish biography.

As polytheists converted to faith in Jesus Christ, they had to abandon not only beliefs about their traditional gods and beliefs about the past, present and future of the world. They also had to abandon their traditional superstitions and their magical practices. They no longer visited pagan temples and participated in pagan cults. They now visited the gatherings of the followers of Jesus, which were established by Jewish believers (in most if not all cases in the first century) and were often led by Jewish believers in Jesus.

And, which was probably even more difficult, they had to abandon the traditional, universally accepted (the Jews excepted!) moral laxness, including sexual immorality, adultery, prostitution, homosexual behavior, greed, revelries, drunkenness (cf. 1 Cor 5:11; 6:9-10). These vices were not regarded as depraved or degrading behavior by most contemporaries, at least when excesses and undue publicity were avoided.

Paul certainly did not seek to transform pagan converts into Jews. He always insisted that Gentiles do not need to be circumcised or keep the food and purity laws and the festival calendar of the Mosaic law (Rom 4; 14—15; Gal 3—4; Col 2). However, the pagans who watched their pagan neighbors and friends accept faith in Jesus would have found their new behavior to be rather "Jewish"—these followers of Jesus rejected the traditional gods; they believed in a Jewish Savior; they followed the moral standards of the Jews' holy book; they gathered weekly for religious instruction and for worship. It is in this sense that Paul formulates a "crosscultural" agenda when he writes to the church in the city of Rome, which was largely composed of Gentile Christians at the time of writing:

> I appeal to you therefore, brothers and sisters, by the mercies of God, to present your bodies as a living sacrifice, holy and acceptable to God, which is your spiritual worship. Do not be conformed to this world, but be transformed by the renewing of your minds, so that you may discern what is the will of God—what is good and acceptable and perfect. (Rom 12:1-2)

The behavior of the followers of Jesus is not controlled by the traditions, customs, values and practices of the city they live in, or by the social class they belong to. Rather, they are informed and transformed by the revelation of the one true and living Creator God in the "Jewish" Scriptures and in Jesus the Messiah, Lord and Savior. Followers of Jesus "cross over" to a fellowship of people for whom it is true that

> now that faith has come, we are no longer subject to a disciplinarian, for in Christ Jesus you are all children of God through faith. As many of you as were baptized into Christ have clothed yourselves with Christ. There is no longer Jew or Greek, there is no longer slave or free, there is no longer male and female; for all of you are one in Christ Jesus. And if you belong to Christ, then you are Abraham's offspring, heirs according to the promise. (Gal 3:25-29)

In the new fellowship of the followers of Jesus, Gentiles need to believe the "Jewish" truths of the one true and living God, and of the coming of the Messiah as Savior and Lord. And they need to learn to live according to God's will as revealed in the Jewish Scriptures in the area of their personal morality. And Jews need to believe in Jesus as the promised Messiah and in the arrival of the kingdom of God that was promised for the last days. And they need to accept the influx of Gentile believers in Jesus as members of the new covenant. Both Jews and Gentiles experience estrangement and opposition: from fellow Jews in the local synagogues, and from pagan relatives and friends in their families and at their workplace. They lose a part—in the case of the Gentiles a large part—of their cultural affiliation. But they gain a new family in which all are "one" in Jesus Christ. Using language that Peter uses (1 Pet 1:1; 2:11), followers of Jesus—both Jews and Gentiles—are "resident aliens" in their society.

5.4 ESTABLISHING CONTACT AS A PUBLIC SPEAKER

When Paul arrived in a city in which there was no community of believers in Jesus Christ, he came uninvited. There was no one waiting for him. Nobody prepared for his visit. Nobody made an effort to make his stay comfortable or enjoyable. No one waited for the news that he was proclaiming. No one thought that they needed his preaching. Paul is clearly aware of this. Several passages demonstrate that he contemplated the factors and the conditions that come into play during the process of establishing initial contacts with Jewish and Gentile listeners.

> For the people of those regions report about us what kind of welcome we had among you, and how you turned to God from idols, to serve a living and true God. (1 Thess 1:9)

> Though my condition put you to the test, you did not scorn or despise me, but welcomed me as an angel of God, as Christ Jesus. (Gal 4:14)

> When I came to you, brothers and sisters, I did not come proclaiming the mystery of God to you in lofty words or wisdom. For I decided to know nothing among you except Jesus Christ, and him crucified. (1 Cor 2:1-2)

> When I came to Troas to proclaim the good news of Christ, a door was opened for me in the Lord. (2 Cor 2:12)

We have already encountered the basic approach that Paul followed when he entered a city in which he had not yet proclaimed the news of Jesus. Paul first visited the local synagogue. As a former student of the renowned Rabbi Gamaliel, he could reckon with the opportunity to explain the Law and the Prophets for the synagogue congregation. In his synagogue sermons, he used the readings from the Torah and the Prophets to proclaim Jesus of Nazareth as the promised Messiah.

Contacts with Gentiles were established in the synagogue where proselytes, God-fearers and other sympathizers are present. Further, Paul engaged in conversations with people in the central plaza of the city, the agora or the forum. In this open, public space he was able to encounter, at least potentially, both the powerful and the poor, the freeborn, the freedmen and slaves, men and women. Paul sometimes taught in lecture halls, and he spoke with people in workshops and in private homes. The expectation of the people whom he encountered varied. The educated members of the local elites were confounded by this public discourse, which they regarded as lacking in rhetorical refinement (see sec. 5.5). The vast majority of the people were uneducated, powerless, noninfluential, hardworking, trying to make a decent living, generally religious. They would have been somewhat surprised to be treated as bona fide conversation partners by an educated orator who had international experience, who was a Jew, who wanted to start what looked like a new religion, who treated them not as objects but as persons, who did not want something from them but who offered them something.

We have seen that Paul's conduct as a preacher of the news of Jesus was predicated on the principle that his behavior must be subordinated to the task of reaching Jews and Gentiles with the message of Jesus, with the goal of leading them to faith in Jesus Christ (1 Cor 9; see sec. 2.3). The freedom of the gospel is freedom from the death sentence of the law, and it is the freedom of repentant people who have come to faith in Jesus, who died for their sins and rose from the dead, thus effecting their adoption into God's family as his children. As a result it is a freedom that obligates the believer and especially the missionary to take action for the benefit of others. Paul is prepared to relinquish his freedom if he can win people for faith in Jesus Christ. Paul's willingness to became "all things to all people" (1 Cor 9:22) is the result of the message he proclaims. Since Jesus, the messianic Son who was sent by God to sacrifice himself so that sinners can be forgiven, so missionaries who are sent to proclaim the gospel of Jesus Christ are prepared to do anything in their power in order to reach people who need to hear this message. This is the reason why Paul goes to people wherever they are "at home" in terms of space, class, gender, education or language.

Paul makes himself dependent on his listeners, he becomes their "slave" (1 Cor 9:19). This means that the needs of Jews and Gentiles inform his behavior, because it is their salvation that he desires. "He listens to them so that they will listen to him, and because he expects them to do what he demands of them, he does what they ask of him."[169]

Paul applies this "principle of identification" to the sociocultural realities of his missionary work. He affirms that God has commissioned him to proclaim the gospel to all people without any distinction, "to Greeks and to barbarians, both to the wise and to the foolish" (Rom 1:14). Paul preached to the elites of the Greco-Roman world. And he preached to the foreigners, the people who did not speak Greek, who had no Greek culture and whom the elites excluded from all decision-making processes. He preached to the people who had had the privilege of formal education.

---

[169]See Adolf Schlatter, *Paulus der Bote Jesu. Eine Deutung seiner Briefe an die Korinther* (1934; reprint, Stuttgart: Calwer, 1969), p. 279.

And he preached to uneducated people, the large majority of people who had no or only rudimentary schooling and who belonged to the powerless working class.

Paul's commitment to preach to anyone in any given city demonstrates that his "principle of identification" has specific consequences for his missionary work. He deliberately disregards the social and cultural classifications that were defined and maintained by the elites. He sees himself obligated to exclude neither the privileged members of the local elites at the top nor the alien barbarians and the slaves "at the bottom" of a city's social spectrum. The gospel concerns everybody, it needs to reach everybody, without concern for social, racial or educational boundaries.[170]

We have no examples of Paul preaching to barbarians, that is, to people who speak a non-Greek language (besides Aramaic or Hebrew) and who are thus recognized as foreigners. The Scythian mentioned in Colossians 3:11 is a barbarian, and the Spaniards Paul wants to reach (cf. Rom 15:24, 28) were regarded as barbarians if they did not speak Latin or Greek.

The people of Lystra who speak "in the Lycaonian language" (Acts 14:11) would be regarded as barbarians if they were speaking only Lycaonian, unable to communicate in Greek. Lystra was a Roman colony, established at the site of an old Greek town. Coins and inscriptions document the veneration of Augustus, Ceres, Mercurius/Hermes, Minerva and Tyche, that is, of Greek and Roman deities and of members of the imperial family.[171] The major temple was dedicated to the worship of the Greek deity Zeus (Acts 14:13). The inscriptions that have been discovered in the city are in Greek and Latin (more inscriptions have survived of Lystra than of any other colony that Augustus founded in Asia Minor).[172] This evidence allows the conclusion that the population

---

[170]Some interpret Paul's principle of "identification" as indicative of "incarnational mission." The description of missionary identification with the term *incarnation* is not helpful—not because it might detract from Jesus' "becoming flesh" (Lat. *incarnatio*) when he, the messianic Son of Man and Son of God, became a human being, but because despite all efforts of identification, an American missionary will rarely learn to speak Japanese without an accent, a black Nigerian missionary will never look like a Chinese, an English missionary from a privileged background will probably never fully understand the angst of an Argentinean campesino.

[171]Levick, *Roman Colonies*, pp. 99, 154-56 n. 3.

[172]Gertrud Laminger-Pascher, *Die kaiserzeitlichen Inschriften Lykaoniens. Faszikel I: Der Süden*, ETAM 15 (Wien: Österreichische Akademie der Wissenschaften, 1992), pp. 125-49.

of Lystra was "Greek" both in the linguistic and in the cultural sense of the word. When Paul preached in Lystra (Acts 14:15-18), his audience was Greek, not barbarian.

The only text in the book of Acts in which the term *barbarian* occurs is Luke's report of the shipwreck of the ship on which Paul the prisoner was transported to Rome. When the survivors of the ordeal ended up on an island that they eventually learned was the island of Malta, they were shown kindness by "the barbarians" *(oi barbaroi)*;[173] when Paul was bitten by a viper, "the barbarians" expect that the justice of the gods would cause him to swell up or to drop dead (Acts 28:2-4). We should not conclude from the reference to "barbarians" that these people spoke a local language, Paul was not able to communicate with them and thus did not proclaim the gospel.[174] Certainly Luke does not mention any missionary activity of Paul. However, he relates that healings took place (Acts 28:8-9), that the healed citizens bestowed "many honors" on the Christians, and that they gave them provisions when they were about to set sail (Acts 28:10). These activities all require communication. It can be assumed that somehow communication was possible, that Paul prayed for the sick in the name of Jesus Christ, and that he explained who Jesus was and why faith in Jesus was necessary.[175] However, since Luke provides no details, we do not know how Paul explained the gospel.

Luke's account in the book of Acts illustrates Paul's preaching to Greeks, particularly to the "wise," that is, to people who were educated. The most important example of Paul preaching to the sophisticated is the report of his missionary work in Athens (Acts 17:16-34; see sec. 1.4). During his outreach in Athens in the central plaza, his audience included Epicurean and Stoic philosophers (Acts 17:18). When they determined that this Jewish orator evidently wanted to introduce new deities to be worshiped in Athens, he is summoned to appear before the Council of the Areopagus to explain his religious views. Paul gives a speech in which he relates to

---

[173]The NASB and NRSV translates "the natives"; NIV and TNIV, "the islanders"; NLT, "the people of the island"; TEV, "the natives"; NET, "the local inhabitants" and "the local people."

[174]Thus Amy L. Wordelman, "Cultural Divides and Dual Realities: A Greco-Roman Context for Acts 14," in *Contextualizing Acts: Lukan Narrative and Greco-Roman Discourse*, SBL Symposium 20, ed. T. C. Penner and C. Vander Stichele (Leiden: Brill, 2004), p. 217.

[175]See Stenschke, *Luke's Portrait of Gentiles*, p. 236.

his philosophical audience both in linguistic and in conceptual terms (for a fuller analysis of Paul's speech before the Council of the Areopagus see sec. 3.3). Paul's missionary "principle of identification" explains why he selects from the Hebrew Scriptures and from Jewish traditions motifs and formulations that could be easily understood by the Stoic and Epicurean philosophers. And he chooses formulations and voices convictions with which the philosophically educated audience was familiar and with which they would have had to agree.

As we have seen, however, Paul clarifies that the religious, cosmological and historical convictions of the Athenians are not somehow similar to the message he proclaims. He does not argue that there is in the end no difference between the God he proclaims and the religious beliefs and practices of the Athenians. Rather, Paul indeed disputes his audience's understanding of the divine. The reference to the "unknown god" (Acts 17:23) is meant as a censure of the local religious practices: rather than acknowledging their religious sophistication, Paul criticizes their ignorance. He acknowledges that they seek God, but he clearly implies that this search is unsuccessful: God is near but not present. And this is of course the main focus in his missionary preaching: the presence of God not only in his creation but in Jesus the Savior and Lord, who will be the judge when all people will have to appear before the one true and living God. Paul's reference to the "times of ignorance" that God has so far overlooked and his announcement that the Creator God now commands all people everywhere to repent (Acts 17:30) constitute an indictment of the popular religious piety which the Stoic and the Epicurean philosophers never sought to change. Paul rejects any accommodation to popular religiosity.[176] Paul leaves no doubt that he rejects the plurality of gods and cults, and the proliferation of temples, altars and statues in the city of Athens. He ends his speech with the declaration that the one true God who created the world has fixed a Day of Judgment and appointed a judge (Acts 17:31). Paul thus gave expression to his conviction that the religious beliefs and practices of the people living in Athenians will not be able to save them on the day of universal judgment.

---

[176]See Winter, "Religious Pluralism," pp. 126-30.

In a wider historical context that includes later missionary activity, especially in the early medieval period, it is important to point out that Paul did not visit the local temples with the express purpose of proclaiming the gospel before pagan worshipers present in the temple precincts. He did not knock down statues or destroy sacred trees. There is no evidence for such tactics in the early Christian texts, nor is such a strategy likely. Given his upbringing as a Diaspora Jews in Tarsus, and given his varied experiences as a missionary, Paul certainly had a realistic view of the political, social and religious power structures of the empire. Both the missionaries and the small communities of followers of Jesus had to abstain from provocative actions if they wanted to be tolerated in the Greek and Roman cities. Even though Hellenistic culture and the Roman state were fundamentally tolerant, the experiences of the Jewish communities demonstrated that minorities who insisted on their peculiar form of worship that forbade them to visit the great temples of the city, linked with regular and frequent meetings, could come under pressure from local and provincial authorities.[177] Since the Christians, unlike the Jews, had no legal protection, their political and social status in the cities of the Greco-Roman world was always precarious. Paul was certainly no fool: preaching the message of the one true God, who allows no other gods besides him in the precinct of a pagan temple, would only provoke the local magistrates responsible for maintaining the ancestral traditions and public order. Contrast this with the early medieval missionaries who took calculated action against pagan sanctuaries: they profaned images of deities, altars, sacred groves and sacred springs, and they destroyed temples and cult places.[178] Paul accuses Jews of "robbing temples" (Rom 2:22), an accusation has can be understood either in terms of Jews illegally removing objects from temples of pagan shrines,[179] or in terms of Jews who are trading objects that have been stolen from pagan temples.[180] This accusation implies that Paul could never have used force in order to advance the gospel among pagans.

Nor did Paul carry objects with him or engage in public religious ac-

---

[177]See Ben Zeev, *Jewish Rights*.

[178]See Lutz E. von Padberg, *Mission und Christianisierung. Formen und Folgen bei Angelsachsen und Franken im 7. und 8. Jahrhundert* (Stuttgart: Steiner, 1995), pp. 146-51.

[179]See James D. G. Dunn, *Romans*, WBC 38 (Dallas: Word, 1988), 1:114-15.

[180]See Ernst Käsemann, *Commentary on Romans* (Grand Rapids: Eerdmans, 1980), p. 71.

tivities that could have enhanced the acceptance of his message. We hear nothing of prayers or of liturgical hymns recited or sung in public. We hear nothing of organized processions through the streets of the city. Contrast again the early medieval missionaries. They carried with them mobile altars, containers for consecrated oil and for sacrificial substances, crosses, pictorial representations of Jesus Christ on wooden boards, as well as sacred relics and priestly garments. They entered pagan territories with supplicatory processions during which hymns of confession, hymns of praise and petitions were sung. They wanted their outward appearance to reflect the dignity and the authority of Jesus Christ.[181]

Paul made an effort to adopt traditional and accepted practices of pagan religiosity in order to make it easier for Gentiles to accept faith in the crucified and risen Jesus Christ. The only steps that Paul took to mitigate the unbridgeable contrast between pagan religiosity and Christian faith were linguistic in nature. He sought to take into account the categories of thought and the possibilities of linguistic expression of his listeners as he formulated his missionary sermons. The speech before the Council of the Areopagus in Athens is the classic example for this. We do not know whether Paul spent more time and rhetorical energy on a discussion of the pagan deities worshiped locally and on the problem of the veneration of a plurality of deities, or on arguments supporting the reality of the one true God, the God of Israel. It is a fair assumption that Paul's emphasis would depend on the requirements of the particular situation. Paul's argumentation in Romans 1:18-32 certainly demonstrates that he could write (and speak) with commitment and skill about pagan religiosity and its consequences for society and the individual. And the Areopagus speech in Acts 17:22-31 shows that Paul was able to lecture with penetrating logic in a philosophically informed manner about false and valid concepts of God.

5.5 THE PERSUASIVENESS OF THE MESSAGE: THE PROBLEM OF RHETORIC

When Paul arrived in a city and started to proclaim the gospel in settings with a non-Jewish audience, he was regarded as one of the orators that pe-

---

[181]Padberg, *Mission und Christianisierung*, pp. 113-25.

riodically came to visit and deliver public speeches. He was a visitor to the
city, he gave speeches in public venues, and he hoped to gain a following.
Quite apart from his subject matter, there were several aspects of his behavior in general and of his performance as a public speaker in particular
which would have been regarded as strange by Gentile audiences. First,
he was not sponsored by a member of the local elites. Second, he did not
seek fame for himself or influence over the families in the city. Third, his
speeches did not exhibit the features that contemporary rhetorical schools
and handbooks expected in public discourses.

Paul and rhetoric. Paul is very much aware of his style of preaching the
news of Jesus when he had arrived in a city. He reminds the Corinthian
Christians of the manner of his proclamation when he first visited the city:

> When I came to you, brothers and sisters, I did not come proclaiming the
> mystery of God to you in lofty words or wisdom. For I decided to know
> nothing among you except Jesus Christ, and him crucified. And I came
> to you in weakness and in fear and in much trembling. My speech and my
> proclamation were not with plausible words of wisdom, but with a dem-
> onstration of the Spirit and of power, so that your faith might rest not on
> human wisdom but on the power of God. (1 Cor 2:1-5)

The point that Paul makes in this passage needs to be understood against
the background of the popular philosophers and the orators of the Second
Sophistic. The latter movement is dated to the period from the middle of
the first century A.D. to the third century, "when declamation became the
most prestigious literary activity in the Greek world," prominently so in
Athens and in the great cities of western Asia Minor.[182] Famous orators
include Dio Chrysostom (born A.D. 40/50), Polemon of Laodicea (born
A.D. 88), Favorinus of Arles (born c. A.D. 90), Herodes Atticus of Athens
(born A.D. 101), and Aristides of Hadrianotherae (born A.D. 117).

The phrase "when I came to you" (1 Cor 2:1) recalls the arrival of such
orators in a city. A popular philosopher could attain to great fame if he

---

[182]Ewan L. Bowie, "Second Sophistic," *OCD*, p. 1377. Cf. Glen Warren Bowersock, *Greek Sophists
in the Roman Empire* (Oxford: Clarendon, 1969); George A. Kennedy, *The Art of Rhetoric in the
Roman World, 300 B.C. - A.D. 300* (Princeton, N.J.: Princeton University Press, 1972); Donald A.
Russell, *Greek Declamation* (Cambridge: Cambridge University Press, 1983); Graham Anderson,
The Second Sophistic: A Cultural Phenomenon in the Roman Empire (London: Routledge, 1993);
Winter, *Philo and Paul*, pp. 17-144.

managed to establish himself as a dramatic and effective speaker, creating a following among the educated and thus gaining influence in the affairs of the city and even of the province. The very first visit of an itinerant orator gave him the opportunity to provide the citizens with a taste of his oratorical skills. Favorinus, an orator in Corinth at the time of Emperor Hadrian, reminded the Corinthians of his first visit in the city when he proved his rhetorical skills and when he established friendly relations both with the citizens and the municipal authorities.[183]

A good example for the entry of a popular philosopher in a city is the arrival of Aristides in Smyrna.[184] When Aristides visited for the first time, the citizens came out to greet him. The most gifted young people of the city presented themselves as students, a date for a lecture by Aristides was set and an invitation was formulated and sent out. Before the day of the lecture arrived, Aristides had a dream in which he was told to declaim in the council chamber at ten o'clock that very day. He was able to arrange this "impromptu" appearance at very short notice. Even though hardly anybody had heard of this turn of events, the council chamber was so packed "that it was impossible to see anything except men's heads, and there was not even room to shove your hand between the people." Aristides delivered the preliminary speech *(dialēxis)* sitting down, the following formal declamation *(meletē)* was presented standing up. The excited audience was entranced throughout his delivery, so much so that "every man counted it his gain if he should bestow some very great compliment on me." The "dream" of Aristides was probably prompted by a rival sophist, "an Egyptian" who was scheduled to present a declamation in the Oideion on that particular day after having had two days' notice for the preparation of his speech. Aristides was thus able to carry off a complete victory over the Egyptian, whose event attracted only seventeen people. This story confirms what other sources tell us: the sophistic ora-

---

[183]The Corinthian speech of Favorinus is found in Dio Chrysostom *Orationes* 37 ("Corinthiaca"). Cf. Bruce W. Winter, "Acts and the Pauline Corpus: I. Ancient Literary Parallels. III. Favorinus, Gellius and Philostratus," in *The Book of Acts in Its Ancient Literary Setting*, ed. B. W. Winter and A. D. Clarke (Exeter, U.K.: Paternoster, 1993), pp. 196-205; Maud W. Gleason, *Making Men: Sophists and Self-Presentation in Ancient Rome* (Princeton, N.J.: Princeton University Press, 1995), pp. 3-20; Winter, *Philo and Paul*, pp. 132-37.

[184]Aristides *Orationes* 51.29-34. Cf. Russell, *Greek Declamation*, pp. 76-77; Winter, *Philo and Paul*, pp. 149-50.

tors wanted to impress their audiences with their declamations, both the young men of the leading families as well as the invited guests and other people who would pay for the experience of listening to visiting orator. If the orator was successful, he could profit financially and gain not only in prestige but in influence.

In the eyes of the citizens of Corinth, Paul was at first sight a traveling orator looking for an audience. Compared with the conventions that controlled the declamations of the popular philosophers, Paul's conduct was unconventional, however. Paul asserts in 1 Corinthians 2:1-5 that his behavior was deliberate: "For I decided to know nothing among you except Jesus Christ, and him crucified" (1 Cor 2:2).

Paul uses in this passage several terms that have a firm place in Greco-Roman rhetoric. The term "lofty" or "superiority, excellence" (*hyperochē* [v. 1]) is used to describe the superiority of eloquence over against incompetent speakers.[185] The term "demonstration" (*apodeixis* [v. 4]) is one of the three proofs in rhetorical logic. The word "power" (*dynamis* [v. 4]) is used by Isocrates and Aristotle in their definition of rhetoric, which is described as the "power" to detect the means of persuasion; rhetoric is the "power of speaking"; Quintilian speaks of rhetoric as *vis persuadendi,* the power to convince; Dio Chrysostom describes the gift of oratory as dynamis.[186] The term plausible, derived from the verb "to convince" (*peithō* [v. 4]) is often used in definitions of rhetoric. The term faith (*pistis* [v. 5]) in Greek logic and rhetoric means "confidence" or "conviction"; Aristotle linked *pistis* with the combined application of three proofs.[187]

Greco-Roman rhetoric. To understand Paul's disclaimer concerning his missionary preaching, it will be helpful to examine the basic elements of Greco-Roman rhetoric.[188] An orator has five tasks. First, he has to find the relevant material, which includes arguments and proofs *(inventio).* He collects the facts of the case *(materia)* and determines

---

[185] Aristotle *Rhetorica* 2.2.7.

[186] Ibid., 1.2.2.1; Quintilian *Institutio Oratoria,* 2.15.2-4; 5.10.7; Cicero *Academica* 2.8; Dio Chrysostom *Orationes* 33.1.4-6.

[187] Aristotle *Rhetorica* 1.1.1356a.

[188] See Kennedy, *Art of Rhetoric*; George A. Kennedy, *A New History of Classical Rhetoric* (Princeton, N.J.: Princeton University Press, 1994); Stanley E. Porter, ed., *Handbook of Classical Rhetoric in the Hellenistic Period, 330 B.C. - A.D. 400* (Leiden: Brill, 2001); Heinrich Lausberg, *Handbook of Literary Rhetoric: A Foundation for Literary Study* (Leiden: Brill, 1998).

the nature of the case *(status)*. Second, the orator composes the speech according to established rules *(dispositio)*. The speech begins with an introduction into the subject matter *(exordium)*, which includes the effort to gain the interest of the audience *(attentum parare)* or even the goodwill of the audience *(captatio benevolentiae)*. The next sections present the facts of the case as the basis of the following presentation *(narratio)* and provide a review of the case and of the goals of the speech *(partitio)*. The central section of the speech contains the exposition of the case *(argumentatio)*, in which the orator presents the arguments for the case that he seeks to make *(probatio)* as well as the arguments that refute the case of the opposition *(refutatio)*. The speech finishes with a summation of the case and a direct or indirect charge or admonition *(conclusio* or *peroratio)*. Third, the orator formulates and writes down the speech *(elocutio)* using figures of speech such as rhetorical questions or irony, as well as appropriate tropes (metaphor, metonymy, hyperbole, allegory). Important qualities of rhetorical excellence are *puritas* (purity of expression), *perspicuitas* (clarity), *aptum* and *decorum* (appropriateness as regards the content and the goals of the speech), *ornatus* (ornamentation, embellishment), and *brevitas* (conciseness). Fourth, the orator memorizes the speech *(memoria);* reading a speech is regarded as inferior, a testimony to the ineptitude of the orator. Fifth, the orator presents the speech with appropriate modulation *(pronuntiatio)* and gestures *(actio)*.

The rhetorical experts distinguished two types of proofs that could be advanced in the *argumentatio* (or *probatio*, Gk *pistis*), the central section of the speech, which presented the evidence for the position that was argued for by the orator.[189]

First, the "inartificial proofs" *(genus inartificiale probationum)*. These are arguments presented without the help of rhetoric devices. They include the written or oral eyewitness statements and past decisions of the courts.

Second, the "artificial proofs" or factual arguments *(genus artificiale probationum)* are proofs deduced from the subject matter by rhetorical

---

[189]Lausberg, *Handbook*, §348; for the following cf. ibid. §§348-430; Walter F. Veit, "Argumentatio," in *Historisches Wörterbuch der Rhetorik*, ed. G. Ueding (Tübingen: Niemeyer, 1992-2007), 1:904-10.

means with the help of intellectual reflection. Ancient rhetoricians distinguish three artificial proofs: *ēthos* (the trustworthy character of the orator), *pathos* (the arousal of passions in the listeners), and *apodeixis* (the logical consistency of the presentation of the subject matter).

The first "artificial proof" is called *ēthos*. The orator persuades by *ēthos* when he delivers his speech in a manner that demonstrates he, the orator and philosopher, is worthy to be trusted. For Aristotle, this was the most effective proof. The term *ēthos* describes the good character and thus the credibility that the orator seeks to establish in order to gain a hearing and a following. In order to be believed, in order to be successful, he needs to convey a sympathetic picture of himself as a credible and likable person. In order to achieve this he needs to identify and study the particular qualities of his listeners so that he can anticipate their reactions to his declamation.

The second proof is *pathos*. This term describes the feelings of the listeners that can be utilized strategically in order to guarantee the effectiveness of the speech. Aristotle describes ten types of feelings, the circumstances in which they might be evoked, the type of person in whom they can be evoked and against whom they can be directed.

The third proof is called *apodeixis*. This term describes the method by which an orator can prove what is not certain, namely, by referring to what is certain, that is, to specific, logical arguments. Quintilian describes *apodeixis* as "clear proofs."

The "artificial proofs" include the following three elements: (1) *signa* (Gk *sēmeia*), that is, a fact or event that can be ascertained by the senses that accompany another fact or event and thus allows a conclusion concerning the subject matter; (2) *argumenta* (Gk *enthymēmata*), that is, proofs that can be developed rationally, in terms of logical deductions, from the facts of the case, such as psychological or physical causes; (3) *exempla* (Gk *paradeigmata*), that is, examples that resemble the subject matter and can confirm what is to be proven (e.g., a similar event in history).

In order to link an example *(exemplum)* with the case (which is achieved by induction), the orator needs a fact or a state of affairs that exists outside of the case to be argued for *(causa)* and which is unquestioned. The *exemplum* is related to the concept of authority *(auctoritas):* a general proverbial wisdom saying from folklore or from poetry that also belongs to the proofs which lie outside of the *causa* and is also based on a historical incident. In rhetoric, "every persuasive strategy has to start with fundamental notions which are already generally shared by people and which are thus plausible and compelling if one wants to successfully convince people of something which would remain debatable or implausible without explanation, proof, or example."[190]

Paul's preaching in Corinth. In his autobiographical account of his arrival in the city of Corinth, Paul describes the methods of his proclamation.[191] He explains his missionary preaching on the occasion of his first contact with the citizens of Corinth. He proclaimed the message of the cross not with "the wisdom of words" (1 Cor 1:17) because he does not want to show off his eloquence: "When I came to you, brothers and sisters, I did not come proclaiming the mystery of God to you in lofty words or wisdom" (1 Cor 2:1). His focus is not on himself but on the crucified Jesus Christ. Paul emphasizes that he dispenses intentionally with the fireworks of rhetoric when he preaches the gospel. He had no interest in being the center of attention or praised by others. The term *proclaim* (1 Cor 2:1) explains Paul's conduct as a public speaker. His task was the proclamation of the news of Jesus as the crucified Messiah. The proclamation of news is not the same as a declamation on a certain subject with the assumption that rhetorical brilliance can convince any audience.

Paul's public proclamation of the news of Jesus could not be compared with the artificially constructed orations on historical events involving tyrants, pirates or rape with which orators entertained the crowds, seeking to make a political point (deliberative rhetoric). They were not speeches about controversial matters, such as the question whether a man who started a civil war and then halted it should be rewarded (forensic rheto-

---

[190]Peter Ptassek, "Endoxa," in *Historisches Wörterbuch der Rhetorik*, ed. Gert Ueding (Tübingen: Niemeyer, 1992-2011), 2:1134.

[191]See Duane Litfin, *St. Paul's Theology of Proclamation: 1 Corinthians 1—4 and Greco-Roman Rhetoric*, SNTSMS 79 (Cambridge: Cambridge University Press, 1994); Winter, *Philo and Paul*, pp. 145-202; Eckhard J. Schnabel, *Der erste Brief des Paulus an die Korinther*, Historisch-Theologische Auslegung (Wuppertal: R. Brockhaus, 2006), pp. 111-59. See also Corin Mihaila, "The Paul-Apollos Relationship and Paul's Stance toward Greco-Roman Rhetoric: An Exegetical and Socio-Historical Study," (Ph.D. diss., Louisville: Southeastern Baptist Theological Seminary, 2006).

ric). They were not speeches commemorating a memorable event, such as the dedication of a temple or the charitable giving of a prominent citizen (epideictic rhetoric).

Nor did Paul need suggestions for a subject that he could take up in a public declamation in order to receive the applause and the approval of the citizens. The subject matter on which Paul spoke had been determined long before he arrived in the city. Paul reminds the Corinthians of the fact that when he first came to Corinth, he proclaimed Jesus, the crucified Messiah and Savior: "I decided to know nothing among you except Jesus Christ, and him crucified" (1 Cor 2:2). He did not allow himself to be distracted by any other subject when he initiated contact with the citizens of Corinth.

Before we further explore the problem that traditional Greek rhetoric causes for the proclamation of the cross, it needs to be pointed out that Paul's renunciation of rhetorical techniques should not be confused with a weak public appearance. The view that public speaking was not Paul's forte and that this was the reason why Paul resorted to other means of communication is misguided. Equally erroneous is the argument that the (alleged) lack of success of Paul's speech before the Council of the Areopagus in Athens proves that Paul lacked the rhetorical education and the rhetorical expertise that both the cultural elite and the citizens more generally expected. According to 2 Corinthians 10:1, 10-11, Corinthian Christians reproached Paul that his writing was strong and audacious while he was personally weak, that his speeches were contemptible, having no merit. Another accusation was the suggestion, put forward by some Christians in Corinth, that he was "untrained in speech" (2 Cor 11:6), that is, that he was an amateur (Gk *idiotēs*), managing only a botched job when he speaks. Paul answers these criticisms not in terms of defending his speaking style, that is, his rhetoric, but with reference to the fact that in his opinion such accusations are aimed, in the final analysis, against Jesus Christ himself: the "meekness and gentleness of Christ" (2 Cor 10:1) consist, according to Philippians 2:1-11, in self-abasement. Paul's behavior as a missionary preacher, as a teacher who speaks in public, is characterized not by brilliant rhetoric but by humility because Jesus Christ's conduct and demeanor was characterized by humility as well.

Paul argues in 1 Corinthians 1:18—2:5 that the message of the gospel, which focuses on God's revelation in Jesus' death and resurrection, cannot be adapted to the requirements and categories of traditional formal rhetoric. This is the reason Paul asserts that he deliberately dispenses with the traditional criteria of rhetoric when he preaches the gospel of Jesus, the crucified Messiah. The character of the gospel of Jesus Christ makes it impossible to rely on the strategies of traditional rhetoric as described by Aristotle or Cicero. Paul declares, "For Jews demand signs and Greeks desire wisdom, but we proclaim Christ [the Messiah] crucified, a stumbling block to Jews and foolishness to Greeks" (1 Cor 1:22-23).

As a Jewish theologian, Paul can very well distinguish between the religious convictions of Jews and Greeks. However, as he has been speaking to hundreds, probably thousands of people about the gospel, he knows how both Gentiles and Jews react to his preaching.

Paul summarizes the expectations of Jewish audiences with the sentence "Jews demand signs." The phrase "Christ the power of God" in 1 Corinthians 1:24, which Paul contrasts with the demands of Jewish listeners, suggests that they wanted a proof that would allow them to conclude that God's saving power was effectively revealed in Jesus' death on the cross. In view of Paul's proclamation that Jesus was the promised Messiah, these "signs" that Jewish listeners demanded were perhaps some specific cosmic manifestations or a proof from social and political transformation that were expected to accompany the arrival of the Messiah.[192] Jews believed that since God have given them the law, they already possess divine wisdom. But they needed signs that would allow them to localize their position in salvation history, if indeed the last days, the days of the Messiah, had arrived.[193] Because Paul could point to such signs, many Jewish listeners regarded his message as a "stumbling block" (Gk *skandalon*). The term *skandalon* here describes "that which causes offense or revulsion and results in opposition, disapproval, or hostility."[194] The preaching of a crucified Messiah arouses opposition.

---

[192]See David E. Garland, *1 Corinthians*, BECNT (Grand Rapids: Baker, 2003), p. 69. For similar demands that scribes and Pharisees raised in disputes with Jesus see Mt 12:38-39; 16:1-4; Mk 8:11-13; Lk 11:16.29-32; Jn 2:18-22; 6:30.

[193]See Thiselton, *First Epistle to the Corinthians*, p. 170.

[194]BDAG, p. 926, *skandalon* 3.

The dialogue between Justin, a leading Christian teacher in the second century, and Tryphon the Jew illustrates the revulsion that some Jews felt concerning the Christians' preaching of a crucified Messiah. Trypho says that "Bring us on, then, by the Scriptures, that we may also be persuaded by you; for we know that he should suffer and be led as a sheep. But prove to us whether he must be crucified and die so disgracefully and so dishonorably by the death cursed in the law. For we cannot bring ourselves even to think of this" (Justin *Dialogus* 90.1).

Jews generally expected a victorious Messiah who would save his people.[195] The Essene community evidently wanted to use the punishment of crucifixion for treason and interpreted this type of execution as a divine curse, with reference to Deuteronomy 21:23 ("for anyone hung on a tree is under God's curse").[196] The proclamation of a crucified Messiah did not correspond to the Jewish interpretation of the Scriptures, to their view of God or to their expectation of God's intervention in the last days.

For pagan audiences the message of a crucified Jewish savior is "non-sense" (Gk *mōria*), sheer absurdity, positively silly, ridiculously crazy. Greeks are renowned for their quest for wisdom. Aelius Aristides describes the Athenians as people who are preeminent in all matters of wisdom (*Orationes* 1.330). The Greeks linked wisdom *(sophia)* with rhetoric[197] and, because wisdom was connected with advanced education, with social status and influence. The educated elites would have regarded already the proclamation of a Jewish savior of the world as an impertinence. It certainly was an imposition on their intelligence and experience that they would need to be instructed in the fundamental beliefs of the Jewish faith and in the Jewish expectations concerning the future. For a Greek audience Paul's insistence that salvation is bound up with the acceptance of the news of a crucified Jew was not only a contradiction of the principles of logic. This "news" was incongruous with the beauty of human wisdom. And it was a violation of good taste. Cicero called crucifixion "a most cruel and disgusting punishment." He asserts:

---

[195]See, for example, *Psalms of Solomon* 17:21-45.

[196]The text is found in the so-called Temple Scroll: 11QTemple LXIV 6-13.

[197]Isocrates *Antidosis* 293-296; *Panegyricus* 45-50; Philostratus *Vitae sophistarum* 571, 588, 613, 617. Cf. Litfin, *St. Paul's Theology of Proclamation*, p. 200.

Wretched is the loss of one's good name in the public courts, wretched, too, a monetary fine exacted from one's property, and wretched is exile, but, still, in each calamity there is retained some trace of liberty. Even if death is set before us, we may die in freedom. But the executioner, the veiling of heads, and the very word "cross," let them all be far removed from not only the bodies of Roman citizens but even from their thoughts, their eyes, and their ears. The results and suffering from these doings as well as the situation, even anticipation, of their enablement, and, in the end, the mere mention of them are unworthy of a Roman citizen and a free man. Or is that, while the kindness of their masters frees our slaves from the fear of all these punishments with one stroke of the staff of manumission, neither our exploits nor the lives we have lived nor honors you have bestowed will liberate us from scourging, from the hook, and, finally, from the terror of the cross? (Cicero *Pro Rabirio Postumo* 16)

This text illustrates the horror crucifixions generated in the ancient world. In the Palatine Museum in Rome visitors can see a graffito that depicts a crucified man with a donkey's head and a line of text which reads "Alexamenos prays to his god," mocking a Christian with the name of Alexamenos. The deities of Greece and Rome were immortal. The proclamation of a Savior who was the Son of the one true God and who died the most ignominious of deaths would quite naturally be regarded as nonsense. Paul's proclamation of a crucified Savior contradicted pagan religiosity in general and the view of the divine in particular. The message of a crucified Savior cannot be verified with the help of wisdom nor understood with the categories of reason.

Paul knows that the message of the cross cannot be adapted to the religious convictions, the rhetorical traditions or the aesthetic expectations of his audiences. Paul preached Jesus as "new Adam" and "savior of mankind," as "Son of God" and "firstborn of the dead." These were terms and concepts that could indeed be packaged as attractive religious content. However, Paul never dispensed with linking the significance of Jesus with his death on the cross: "For I decided to know nothing among you except Jesus Christ, and him crucified" (1 Cor 2:2). It was impossible, in the first century, to speak in an aesthetically pleasing manner about a man who had been executed on a cross by the Roman authorities. The reality of crucifixion was too gruesome and needed too much explanation for rhetorical competence and brilliance to be of much help. Paul knows that he cannot convince his contemporaries of the truth of the gospel with the traditional rhetorical arguments. Which rhetorical devices might Paul have contemplated?[198]

Paul had good "inartificial proofs" *(genus inartificiale probationum):* the eyewitness testimony of people who had seen Jesus alive after his resurrection (1 Cor 15:5-8). But the event that these witnesses testified to would remind Greek and Roman listeners of mythological tales. This would certainly prompt them quickly to doubt the authenticity of this particular argument. Moreover, the conviction that Jesus' death on the cross represents the ultimate and universal rescue operation of the one true Creator God could not be proven with an appeal to people who claimed to have seen the crucified Jesus as risen from the dead.

The repertoire of material proofs *(genus artificiale probationum)* was of limited help. Paul would not have been able to find *signa* or *argumenta* to corroborate the conviction that Jesus' death on the cross conveys salvation from personal sins and reconciliation with the one true God. As regards *exempla,* Paul could have referred to people who had the courage to die for their convictions, the classical example being Socrates. But such examples do not demonstrate that the death of a man who was the Jewish Messiah brings salvation, forgiveness of sin and adoption into God's family. Nor do they prove that all one has to do to receive these benefits is to rely on the death of this Jewish man for the forgiveness of one's sins, accepting his death as one's own death.

Neither would Paul have been able to appeal to the authority *(auctoritas)* of a generally acknowledged proposition *(endoxa)* that is therefore plausible and compelling, nor could he appeal to a generally recognized wisdom saying. Paul did have personal credibility *(ethos)* as a Roman citizen and a Jewish Torah scholar who had traveled internationally, but the shamefulness of the crucifixion of Jesus could not be overcome by even the most impressive credentials or a charismatic personality. And the passions *(pathos)* that Paul could have aroused in the audience as an orator who

---

[198]See Schnabel, *Der erste Brief des Paulus an die Korinther,* pp. 105-7.

spoke about a crucified savior would have consisted in sympathy at best, revulsion at worst.

Aristotle defines the comedy as "an imitation of base men . . . characterized not by every kind of vice but specifically by 'the ridiculous,' some error or ugliness that is painless and has no harmful effects." Paul's pagan listeners may have interpreted his discourse about a crucified savior of the world as a comedy that produces laughs. Similarly, if they recalled Cicero's understanding of the ridiculous *(ridiculum)* as "a certain ugliness or defectiveness,"[199] then the message of a crucified Jew who is presented as the Savior of mankind must have made a comical *(comicus)* impression on the listeners.

Paul preached a crucified and risen Savior because this was the central content of the news that God had made known to him and to the other apostles, and because this was the truth he had personally encountered when he was converted near Damascus. This was the message that God had entrusted to him to pass on to those who had not heard of Jesus the Savior.

Paul knows that it is the almighty God himself, the Creator of the world, who causes Jews and pagans to come to faith. He relies for conversions of men and women not on the powers of rhetorical strategies and techniques but on the power of God. The "proof" *(apodeixis)* for the validity of the news that Jesus, the crucified Messiah, is the Savior of the world whose death atones sin and who reconciles sinners with the Creator God cannot be discovered by the application of logical inference or rhetorical deduction. The "proof" for the truth of the gospel is to be found in the power of the Holy Spirit, that is, in the presence of God himself. When Paul proclaims the gospel, he speaks "not with plausible words of wisdom." Rather, he relies "on the demonstration *(apodeixei)* of the Spirit and of power" (1 Cor 2:4). The preaching of the gospel goes hand in hand with the demonstration or "proof" effected by the Spirit and by "power," that is, by God himself. In other words, the powerful Spirit of God "proves" the truth of the proclamation of God's redemptive revelation in Jesus Christ's death and resurrection.[200] This "proof" is the

---

[199]Aristotle *Poetica* 1449a; Cicero *De oratore* 2.58.236.
[200]See Garland, *1 Corinthians*, p. 87; Florian Voss, *Das Wort vom Kreuz und die menschliche Vernunft. Eine Untersuchung zur Soteriologie des 1. Korintherbriefes*, FRLANT 199 (Göttingen: Vanden-

fact that Jews and pagans living in Corinth have been persuaded to accept the message of Jesus the crucified and risen Messiah. The supernatural proof for the validity of Paul's missionary proclamation is the conversion of Jews and pagans to faith in Jesus, the crucified Messiah and Lord. In 1 Corinthians 2:5, Paul reaffirms why he renounces traditional rhetorical methods: "so that your faith might rest not on human wisdom but on the power of God."

5.6 THE CREDIBILITY OF THE MESSENGER

Personal credibility is an important factor when an orator visits a city for the first time and seeks to establish contact with the citizens. Credibility is in fact always important for an orator, as knowledge concerning the good character of a speaker might move an audience much more effectively to believe him than arguments might. This aspect of public speaking was called, as we have seen earlier, *ēthos*. The experts in rhetoric taught that in order to be believed, an orator needs to convey a sympathetic picture of himself as a credible and likable person. In order to achieve this he needs to identify and study the particular qualities of his listeners so that he can anticipate their reactions to his declamation.

When Paul arrived in a city as a pioneer missionary, the issue of personal credibility played a different role in the two social locations in which he proclaimed the news of Jesus. In the local synagogue he had credibility on account of his training as a rabbi in Jerusalem under Gamaliel, a famous rabbi with whom the synagogue audience might be familiar. And he had credibility on account of his competence in interpreting the Scriptures.

Pagan audiences would have been impressed by his Roman and Tarsian citizenship if they were aware of it, by his international travels, by the miracles that on occasion accompanied his missionary work, by his character as a man whose personal behavior is above reproach, by his astounding personal commitment to his teaching activity, and by his astonishing courage against immense odds. However, in view of the competition of various philosophical schools and religious cults in the first century, this initial credibility would have been quickly compensated for

---

hoeck & Ruprecht, 2002), p. 131; Hans-Christian Kammler, *Kreuz und Weisheit. Eine exegetische Untersuchung zu 1 Kor 1,10—3,4*, WUNT 159 (Tübingen: Mohr Siebeck, 2003), p. 171.

by the content of Paul's message, which focused on a crucified Jew as the Savior of the world.

When Paul was forced to assert his personal credibility, he refers to his missionary work and to his personal behavior. He points to his often dangerous travels, to the fact that he had no home and thus no social "power" base, to his economic independence, to his personal relationship with the people who have come to faith in Jesus Christ through his preaching, and to the historical origins of the local Christian community.[201] He rejects recommendations by others, including letters of recommendation (2 Cor 3:1-3). Paul is concerned that at least the Christians know that his missionary work is no money-making business (2 Cor 2:17; 1 Thess 2:5). Paul emphasizes that he pursues his missionary work independently of whether he has "success" and whether he receives recognition and praise (Gal 1:10; 1 Thess 2:6). His motivation is neither prestige nor success, but his conviction that God called him to proclaim Jesus as Messiah and Savior.

> For our appeal does not spring from deceit or impure motives or trickery, but just as we have been approved by God to be entrusted with the message of the gospel, even so we speak, not to please mortals, but to please God who tests our hearts. As you know and as God is our witness, we never came with words of flattery or with a pretext for greed; nor did we seek praise from mortals, whether from you or from others, though we might have made demands as apostles of Christ. But we were gentle among you, like a nurse tenderly caring for her own children. So deeply do we care for you that we are determined to share with you not only the gospel of God but also our own selves, because you have become very dear to us. (1 Thess 2:3-8)

Paul disassociates himself in this passage from deception, cunning, cajolery and strong-arm stuff as methods of missionary work. And he distances himself from praise and from pleasing people (Gal 1:10) as well as from greediness (cf. 2 Cor 2:17) as motivations of missionary work. Paul emphasizes his role as trustee (1 Thess 2:4), the openness of his ministry and his responsibility before God, expressed in love for the people before whom he proclaims the gospel.

---

[201] See 1 Thess 1:4—3:10; 1 Cor 4:11-12; 9:6-18; 2 Cor 6:5; 10:7—11:33.

Paul did not adapt his personal conduct as public speaker to the customs of contemporary itinerant orators. His conduct was controlled by the nature of the gospel of Jesus, the crucified Messiah and Savior. This explains why Paul was willing to risk isolation, loneliness and social discrimination. The credibility of the preacher of the gospel is certainly important for the proclamation of the truth of the gospel. However, Paul did not establish his credibility by drawing attention to his capabilities and successes but by living out the truth of the gospel in his own personal life. A public speaker can distract an audience from favorably accepting his speech or even from listening to what he has to say. In the case of Paul, this would happen if he drew attention to himself thus pushing the message into the background. Paul as the messenger of the news of Jesus Christ "becomes, for the world, a part of his true message. Paul gave to the world not only a word, he also gave himself."[202]

Paul's fundamental commitment to the truth of the good news of Jesus Christ explains why he disassociates himself from certain methods of contemporary public speaking. Paul was very much aware of the problematic nature and the appropriateness of rhetorical methods for the proclamation of the gospel. He writes to the Corinthians, "For if someone comes and proclaims another Jesus than the one we proclaimed, or if you receive a different spirit from the one you received, or a different gospel from the one you accepted, you submit to it readily enough" (2 Cor 11:4).

Paul describes in this text the active process of communication as "proclaiming Jesus" and the reception of the message as "accepting the gospel." The third factor of communication that is inserted between communication and reception is the element "receiving the Spirit." This third factor is, evidently, decisive. Paul insists that the method of communication that he practices corresponds with the content of the message that he proclaims.

5.7 EXPLANATIONS FOR MISSIONARY SUCCESS

Why was Paul's missionary work successful? Why did people, both Jews and Gentiles, both men and women, both free and slaves, come to faith

---

[202]Traugott Holtz, *Der erste Brief an die Thessalonicher*, EKK 13 (Neukirchen-Vluyn: Neukirchener; Zürich: Benziger, 1986), p. 95.

in Jesus, the crucified and risen Messiah, Savior and Lord? Why was Paul able to establish congregations of followers of Jesus in the cities in which he preached the news of Jesus Christ?

One obvious answer would be to point to the attractiveness of the gospel message. Paul focuses his summaries of the gospel on the offer of salvation from sin and reconciliation with God (e.g., 1 Thess 1:9-10; 2 Cor 5:18-21). The offer of salvation as complete liberation from guilt and sin, the offer of hope for a perfect existence after death, the offer of fellowship with people from all walks of life and all classes of society were certainly attractive.

One should note, however, the last item in this list would be true only for members of the lower classes, including slaves, but not for the members of the elite. A poor cabinetmaker would certainly feel appreciated and honored to call a prominent lawyer who had been one of the two chief magistrates in the city two years earlier his "brother" and to be able to report that they were having a chat over dinner. If this lawyer would be asked by his friends where he had been the evening before, his story of having sat next to a cabinetmaker on one side and a slave on the other side would have earned him only laughs.

The attractiveness of these important elements of the Christian message could not hide the fact that the central emphasis of Paul's proclamation was a scandal for Jews and nonsense for Greeks (1 Cor 1:18-23; 2:14; 3:19). Paul asserts repeatedly that the gospel is ultimately accepted and believed by the listeners only because God himself is effectively present in the proclamation of the gospel.[203] Paul knows that God is the primary "communicator" while the apostles are God's envoys, messengers who have been sent. They are the channel of the message; they are not the source of the gospel message themselves. Paul expresses this conviction in 1 Thessalonians 2:13 and 2 Corinthians 5:18-21:

> We also constantly give thanks to God for this, that when you received the word of God that you heard from us, you accepted it not as a human word

---

[203]See Don N. Howell, "Mission in Paul's Epistles: Genesis, Pattern, and Dynamics," in *Mission in the New Testament. An Evangelical Approach*, ed. W. J. Larkin and J. F. Williams, ASMS 27 (New York: Orbis, 1998), pp. 63-91, 77-84, with reference to 1 Thess 1:5-6; 4:8; 5:16-24; 2 Thess 1:11; 2:13.

but as what it really is, God's word, which is also at work in you believers. (1 Thess 2:13)

All this is from God, who reconciled us to himself through Christ, and has given us the ministry of reconciliation; that is, in Christ God was reconciling the world to himself, not counting their trespasses against them, and entrusting the message of reconciliation to us. So we are ambassadors for Christ, since God is making his appeal through us; we entreat you on behalf of Christ, be reconciled to God. For our sake he made him to be sin who knew no sin, so that in him we might become the righteousness of God. (2 Cor 5:18-21)

This focus on God's power in convincing people of the truth of the gospel can be illustrated from Paul's missionary work in Thessalonica. Paul had to leave the city in a hurry two or three months after his arrival since the local opposition had become too dangerous. He left Timothy behind, a young believer and new coworker whom he had given the task to look after the church (Acts 17:10, 14, 15; 1 Thess 3:1-5). Despite these difficult beginnings of the church in Thessalonica, Paul asserts in his first letter to the Thessalonian believers, written only a few months after the foundation of the church,

Our message of the gospel came to you not in word only, but also in power and in the Holy Spirit and with full conviction; just as you know what kind of persons we proved to be among you for your sake. And you became imitators of us and of the Lord, for in spite of persecution you received the word with joy inspired by the Holy Spirit. (1 Thess 1:5-6)

The preaching and teaching of the gospel had been fruitful not because of effective missionary methods, but because the Spirit of God had convinced citizens of Thessalonica of the truth of the gospel, causing them to become followers of Jesus and to join the community of believers in the city—all this despite the fact that the new believers came under immense pressure. It was precisely this reliance on and confidence in the work of the Holy Spirit that allowed Paul to involve young and inexperienced coworkers such as Timothy in pioneer situations and to entrust them with demanding responsibilities.

The search for factors that might explain the success of Paul's missionary work is understandable. Once such factors are identified, they can be copied and applied by other missionaries. Some have argued that Paul's success in winning pagans for the gospel is linked with the fact that he abandoned the traditional characteristics of his Jewish heritage that had controlled the boundaries of acceptance in and exclusion from the people of God: ethnic Jews were "in" while Gentiles were "out" unless they became Jews. Instead, Paul preached Jesus Christ "as God's universal, dynamic center of life and thought that meshed spontaneously with the cultural particularity of his Gentile converts." It is suggested that Paul did not require the new converts from paganism "to deny their culture, to abandon their heritage, to learn a new language, to be circumcised, to eat certain foods and not others, to observe certain days and not others, to attend feasts, to present offerings."[204] This analysis is only partially correct. Paul certainly did not ask new Gentile believers to learn a new language, to be circumcised, to eat kosher food or to celebrate the Jewish holidays and festivals. But Paul certainly asked converts from a pagan background to abandon important parts of their heritage and to give up central convictions and patterns of behavior of their culture. When polytheists in Ephesus were converted to faith in Jesus Christ, they no longer visited the temple of Artemis Ephesia, no longer participated in the sacrificial rites of her cult, no longer marched in processions held in her honor. When the street where they lived was decorated for the festival of the Artemisia, which was celebrated in March (or April), they did not participate in these activities. When they walked across the State Agora, they no longer worshiped Augustus in the Basilike Stoa as they used to do before becoming followers of Jesus. They no longer dined in the temple, no longer observed the traditional rituals on the doorstep of his house, removed the statues of deities that stood in the cult niche in their living rooms. Gentile converts without doubt abandoned important practices of their culture and heritage—rather publicly, not to be missed by their Gentile relatives and friends.

Eusebius, the bishop of the church in Caesarea from A.D. 313 to 339, the first historian of the church, believed that even though God's providence and sovereignty ultimately and specifically explain the growth of

---

[204]George Shillington, "Paul's Success in the Conversion of Gentiles: Dynamic Center in Cultural Diversity," *Direction* 20 (1991): 126, 128.

the Christian church, there were social factors that need to be considered as well.[205] Since then historians have attempted to explain the success of the early Christian mission, pointing to various external and internal conditions.[206]

The first factor that is often mentioned in connection with the appearance and the growth of the Christian church are the generally favorable conditions of the Pax Romana: (1) The political stability that the Roman Empire guaranteed, allowing travelers to use the excellent network of Roman roads in relative safety and with shorter travel times. (2) The cultural unity of the Greco-Roman world, with widely shared religious and philosophical ideas, facilitating communication across ethnic divides. (3) The Greek language as a single lingua franca from Syria in the East and to the cities of Spain in the West. (4) The Hellenistic idea of the unity of the human race. (5) The general religious tolerance of the Roman emperors and their provincial governors. These factors clearly facilitated the missionary outreach of the early Christians and the growth of the church.

However, we need to contrast these favorable conditions with unfavorable factors that hindered the missionary expansion of the churches.[207] These unfavorable factors include (1) the persecutions directed at Christians which did not only hinder and in some cases prevent missionary work (one example is Paul's plan for a mission to the province of Asia and the province of Bithynia-Pontus) but which must have caused fear among potential converts. (2) The Christian missionaries proclaimed convictions that Gentiles found very difficult to accept: the existence of only one God, the redemptive significance of a crucified Jew, the bodily resurrection

---

[205]Eusebius *Historia ecclesiastica* 8.1.5-9; *Demonstratio Evangelica* 3.7.30-35. Cf. Aryeh Kofsky, *Eusebius of Caesarea Against Paganism* (Leiden: Brill, 2002), pp. 74-99.

[206]See Adolf von Harnack, *The Mission and Expansion of Christianity in the First Three Centuries*, 4th ed. (London: Williams & Norgate, 1924), 1:1-23; Ramsay MacMullen, *Paganism in the Roman Empire* (New Haven, Conn.: Yale University Press, 1981), pp. 49-112; Ramsay MacMullen, *Christianizing the Roman Empire (A.D. 100-400)* (New Haven, Conn.: Yale University Press, 1984), pp. 17-42; Robin Lane Fox, *Pagans and Christians in the Mediterranean World from the Second Century A.D. to the Conversion of Constantine* (1986; reprint, London: Penguin, 1988); L. Michael White, "Adolf Harnack and the 'Expansion' of Early Christianity: A Reappraisal of Social History," *Second Century* 5 (1985-86): 97-127; Danny Praet, "Explaining the Christianization of the Roman Empire: Older Theories and Recent Developments," *Sacris Erudiri* 33 (1992-93): 5-119.

[207]See Norbert Brox, *A History of the Early Church* (London: SCM, 1994).

from the dead, and the claim that salvation is tied exclusively to faith in Jesus Christ. Christian convictions that were difficult to accept for Jews included the redemptive significance of a crucified Messiah, the resurrection of Jesus from the dead before the day of the resurrection at the end of time, the epiphany of God in Jesus Christ, the redefinition of temple and Torah, and the acceptance of uncircumcised Gentiles in the people of God. (3) The external forms of the Christian community clashed with the traditional religious praxis of both Jews and Gentiles. The followers of Jesus had no temple(s), no altars, no images of their deity, no processions. These unfavorable factors make it difficult to recognize the auspicious conditions of the Hellenistic world and of the Pax Romana as satisfactory explanations for the successful expansion of the Christian faith in the first century.

A second factor that has often been mentioned is the rational critique of polytheism by Platonist and Stoic philosophers. The philosophical critique of the depiction of the gods in terms of possessing qualities of human thought, will, emotion and experience prompted Greek intellectuals to deny the reality of the Olympian gods.[208] It has often been claimed that this critique paved the way for a monotheistic alternative. However, this factor cannot explain the success of the early Christian missionaries. The philosophical critique of polytheism never had any practical consequences for the participation of the majority of the people in pagan cults. Since pagan religiosity knew no explicit "confession of faith," no theological doctrine, the myths about the gods were essentially irrelevant for the cultic practices. The critique of the myths had no influence on the religious rites that were practiced in the temples. Moreover, we do not know who listened to the Epicureans and Stoics.[209] And a critique of popular religion does not prepare people for belief in the message of a coming final judgment and of a bodily resurrection. When Paul spoke before the Council of the Areopagus (Acts 17:22-31), he was able to draw on some of the convictions of the Epicurean and Stoic philosophers who were present. Many of his statements would have elicited a positive response. But when he

---

[208]See Eric R. Dodds, *The Greeks and the Irrational*, Sather Classical Lectures (Berkeley: University of California Press, 1951), p. 258.

[209]See MacMullen, *Paganism in the Roman Empire*, pp. 71-82.

came to speak of the resurrection of the dead, "some of them sneered, but others said, 'We want to hear you again on this subject' " (Acts 17:32).

The religious syncretism of the Hellenistic world with its religious tolerance and its tendency to fuse several gods into a single deity did not lead to monotheism. At best it promoted a hierarchical polytheism.[210] The notion that god is one but his force is many, "expressed in the various familiar divine personalities," was a quite abstract doctrine, taught in the philosophical schools, a doctrine that left the gods "in fact quite undisturbed and independent entities, so far as ordinary worship was concerned."[211] The philosophers who had connections with or belonged to the Council of the Areopagus might indeed believe that we as human beings all live and move and have our being in one supreme deity. But the majority of the people living in Athens worshiped the traditional gods. The daily religious activity did not remotely correspond to tendencies toward monotheism.

The exclusiveness of the Christian faith, which rejected all compromises with syncretistic forms and practices, may be attractive for some people, perhaps as a noble, radical stance opposing the status quo. But people in general did not complain about the numerous religious options that were available. Polytheism has its advantages![212] In the context of the emperor cult, which was becoming more prominent during the first century, and in the context of the precarious nature of the Christian congregations' legal status, which were not officially registered, the uncompromising exclusiveness of the Christian message was more a problem than a blessing. Even the Jews whose legal status and rights had been confirmed by Julius Caesar and by Augustus[213] continued to come under local political pressure. Responding to unrest in the city of Alexandria, Emperor Claudius issued an edict in A.D. 41[214] (a year before Paul started his ministry in Antioch in Syria) in which he reminded the Jews of their loyalty and friendship to the Romans and stipulated that the Jews should

---

[210]Fox, *Pagans and Christians*, pp. 34-35.

[211]MacMullen, *Paganism in the Roman Empire*, pp. 87, 89.

[212]Fox, *Pagans and Christians*, p. 575.

[213]See Josephus *Antiquitates Judaicae* 14.190-195; 14.213-216; 16.162-166. For the relevant documents and their interpretation see Pucci Ben Zeev, *Jewish Rights*, pp. 31-106, 121-36, 342, 443-44.

[214]Josephus *Antiquitates Judaicae* 19.287-291. Pucci Ben Zeev, *Jewish Rights*, pp. 328-42.

be allowed to "observe the customs of their fathers without let or hindrance." The edict continues:

> I enjoin upon them also by these presents to avail themselves of this kindness in a more reasonable spirit, and not to set at nought the beliefs about the gods held by other peoples, but to keep their own laws. It is my will that the ruling bodies of the cities and colonies and municipia in Italy and outside Italy, and the kings and other authorities through their own ambassadors, shall cause this edict of mine to be inscribed, and keep it posted for not less than thirty days in a place where it can plainly be read from the ground." (Josephus *Antiquitates Judaicae* 19.290-291)

Since Jews generally did not seek to win Gentiles for faith in Yahweh as the only true God (pagans became Jewish proselytes of their own accord), the stipulation "not to set at nought the beliefs about the gods held by other peoples" was not a hardship. The exclusive monotheism of the Diaspora Jews did not threaten the customs and laws of their pagan neighbors. This was different for the followers of Jesus in general and for Paul in particular, who not only believed that there is only one true God but actively propagated this conviction, seeking to win as many Gentile converts as possible. A further and more serious complication was the fact that Paul could not speak of God without speaking of Jesus as the messianic King of the Jews and the Savior of the world. In Thessalonica and in Corinth, and probably in other cities as well, Paul's preaching about God created personal and legal difficulties for him. In the Macedonian capital, Paul's sermons irritated some opponents to such a degree that they dragged him before the politarchs, the city authorities, and accused him with the words, "they are all acting contrary to the decrees of the emperor, saying that there is another king named Jesus" (Acts 17:7). In Corinth, the capital of Achaia, the Jewish opponents hoped that Gallio, the governor of the province, could be pushed to indict Paul. They accused him with the charge that "This man is persuading people to worship God in ways that are contrary to the law" (Acts 18:13). What Paul had to say about God and his revelation in Jesus, Messiah and Savior, was irritating not only for Jewish dissenters but, at least in the latter's opinion, it was an offense that city officials and governors should deal with. Paul's convictions about the one true God and his revelation in the crucified and risen Christ was not an attraction, but a liability.

A third factor that is sometimes mentioned focuses on the disintegration of the system of the Greek city-state (polis). Some have argued that the gods lost credit and credibility as a result of the defeat of the polis and the general decline of the city-states. This hypothesis focuses too much on Greece, and it is irrelevant for the Greek cities of the first century. Cities such as Pisidian Antioch and Corinth were newly established Roman colonies that were thriving centers of culture and commerce, with numerous temples in daily use and with new temples dedicated to the worship of the emperor inaugurated in the recent past.

Fourth, some suggest that the Hellenistic ruler cult was a factor in the success of the early Christian mission, since it introduced the concept of a god-man. This suggested parallel that is attested for some traditions of pagan religiosity explains neither the incarnation of Jesus nor a crucified Messiah. The worship of the Roman emperors did not make missionary preaching any easier, on the contrary. Paul's conviction that "there is one God, the Father, from whom are all things and for whom we exist, and one Lord, Jesus Christ, through whom are all things and through whom we exist" (1 Cor 8:6), created a potentially serious conflict with the imperial ideology, since there was no room beside God the Father and the Lord Jesus Christ for any other gods who claimed to be saviors.

Fifth, it has often been suggested that the decline of pagan religiosity, especially in the third century A.D., explains the success of Christianity.[215] However, the hypothesis of a general religious crisis in the Greco-Roman world has either been abandoned or heavily modified. This theory ignores clear and ample evidence for the vitality and the unbroken spirit of paganism in the third century. It was not the priests who became more and more silent but the stonecutters who produce inscriptions that we can study today: "Religion, like many other aspects of life, rises and falls on the quantity of surviving evidence like a boat on the tide."[216] As regards the first century, Paul's experience in Lystra il-

---

[215]Eric R. Dodds, *Pagan and Christian in an Age of Anxiety: Some Aspects of Religious Experience from Marcus Aurelius to Constantine* (Cambridge: Cambridge University Press, 1965), pp. 132-33.
[216]MacMullen, *Paganism in the Roman Empire*, pp. 127; cf. Fox, *Pagans and Christians*, pp. 52-55, 75-82, 574-75.

lustrates the emotional vitality of pagan religiosity: the people of Lystra quickly integrated the miracle they witnessed into their traditional religiosity (see sec. 1.3). The old polytheistic and mythical traditions were very much alive.

A sixth factor that has been mentioned is the notion of status inconsistency, that is, the diverging evaluation of the social position (status) of a person by that person him- or herself or by others, especially in an urban context. Some scholars suggest that "independent women with moderate wealth, Jews with wealth in a pagan society, freedmen with skill and money but stigmatized by origin," thus criss-crossing categories of social status, would more easily convert to the Christian faith. For these kind of people "the intimacy of the Christian groups become a welcome refuge, the emotion-charged language of family and affection and the image of a caring, personal God powerful antidotes."[217]

This explanation does not fit the available data, nor does it reckon with the complex manner people think about themselves or their social status.[218] It should be noted that people's views of their social status are rather complex. Regarding "Jews with wealth," they did not need persecuted churches to find a satisfying role, they had their synagogues. The social stigma that attached to released slaves (the freedmen) should not be exaggerated, their "status inconsistency" was probably short-lived, and they could gain prestige in the emperor cult. Regarding the "independent women," there is no clear evidence that they did not accept their "reduced" social status in antiquity; if they wanted to find satisfaction in a greater role, they could seek the priesthood of various cults. There is no evidence whatsoever that Christian converts were conscious "victims" of status inconsistency that drove them to accept the Christian faith. And it should be noted that the Christian communities were opposed to the personal, open pursuit of power: "it did not resolve 'inconsistency' by offering a new outlet; rather, it claimed to sidestep status and power altogether."[219] Thus Paul requests Christian men not to pray or prophesy with their heads covered *(capite velato)*, a practice that signaled in religious contexts, at least

---

[217]Meeks, *First Urban Christians*, p. 191.
[218]See Fox, *Pagans and Christians*, pp. 319-22.
[219]Ibid., p. 321.

in a Roman city such as Corinth in the first century, high social status.[220] And he tells Christian women to pray or prophesy with their heads covered and thus to continue to wear the traditional costume for married women, who had a veil *(palla)* over their head as a symbol of the chaste married women, and not to dishonor their husbands.[221] Paul comments on social mobility as follows:

> However that may be, let each of you lead the life that the Lord has assigned, to which God called you. This is my rule in all the churches. Was anyone at the time of his call already circumcised? Let him not seek to remove the marks of circumcision. Was anyone at the time of his call uncircumcised? Let him not seek circumcision. Circumcision is nothing, and uncircumcision is nothing; but obeying the commandments of God is everything. Let each of you remain in the condition in which you were called. Were you a slave when called? Do not be concerned about it. Even if you can gain your freedom, make use of your present condition now more than ever. For whoever was called in the Lord as a slave is a freed person belonging to the Lord, just as whoever was free when called is a slave of Christ. You were bought with a price; do not become slaves of human masters. In whatever condition you were called, brothers and sisters, there remain with God. (1 Cor 7:17-24)

Paul mentions three groups of people who might wish to be upwardly mobile in society: Christian Jews who might contemplate the removal of their circumcision *(epispasm)*,[222] Christian slaves who might aspire freedom, and Christian free men who might be willing to sell themselves into slavery (with an aristocratic family) for social and financial benefits, as a route perhaps to Roman citizenship. Paul states that Christians should remain in the "condition," that is, in the class in which they have become Christians. Paul teaches that the "calling" of each Christian, which includes social status and ethnic identity, has been providentially ordered for each Christian by the Lord. Those who are "in Christ" are never deficient, whether they are slaves, underprivileged or stigmatized by others in pagan society. "Those Christians who yearned to join the 'class' of the

---

[220]See Gill, "Importance of Roman Portraiture for Head Coverings."
[221]See Winter, *After Paul Left Corinth*, pp. 123-41.
[222]See the description in the medical handbook by Aulus Cornelius Celsus *De medicina* 7.25.

'wise, mighty and well-born' whose significance was most visible in the public place were forbidden to do so. Their aspirations represent a failure thankfully to acknowledge what they were by virtue of their calling in Christ (1:26-31)."[223]

A seventh factor that has been suggested as explanation for the success of the missionary work of Paul and of other early Christians are the feelings of anxiety, insecurity and helplessness, and the Hellenistic "yearning for salvation" caused by material and moral insecurity, by the political alienation of people in absolutist monarchies, or by the threat of slavery.[224] This explanation does not convince, either. There is abundant evidence for the general optimism of people in the first, second and third century, as well as for the fact that the religious commitments of people in the various gods of the Greek and Roman pantheon, continued during this time. Popular religiosity more than neutralizes the "anxieties" of some Greek or Roman intellectuals.[225] Moreover, Paul's experience as a missionary, who was expelled from cities, beaten in synagogues and thrown into prisons, was not a particularly attractive example of an anxiety-free life.

Eighth, the Christian belief in life after death has been suggested as a powerful motivation to convert to faith in Jesus in a pagan society in which death was regarded as the conclusion of human existence.[226] However, the very idea of a bodily resurrection remained unacceptable for many pagans. We have seen earlier that people were not only skeptical about an afterlife, but they joked about annihilation at death. It comes as no surprise that Paul needs to write a long text arguing for the plausibility and the logic of the expectation of a bodily resurrection (1 Cor 15:1-58). And the message of a second coming of Jesus and of eternal damnation was not easy to believe, either. Paul's speech before the Council of the Areopagus and his summary of the message that he preached in Thessalonica show that these were not topics for advanced believers, but matters that he addressed in his missionary preaching (Acts 17:30-31; 1 Thess 1:9-10).

---

[223]Winter, *Seek the Welfare of the City*, p. 164.
[224]Dodds, *Pagan and Christian*, pp. 3-4, 137.
[225]Fox, *Pagans and Christians*, pp. 65-66.
[226]See MacMullen, *Paganism in the Roman Empire*, pp. 53-57.

Ninth, another explanation for the success of the early Christian missionary expansion has been defended by several scholars. According to historians of Roman religion, miracles and exorcisms are the most important if not only reason for the conversions to Christianity.[227] There is no question that miracles and exorcisms played an important role in the missionary work of the early Christians.[228] But they explain neither individual conversions nor the continuous expansion of the Christian faith.[229] Pagans turned to their gods in times of illness and other kinds of distress as well, and experienced miracles in response to their prayers, pledges, donations or sacrifices, as thousands of votive inscriptions illustrate. Also, miracles impress only eyewitnesses. And even eyewitnesses do not always draw the correct conclusions. The awe and excitement that people displayed when miracles happened did not necessarily lead to acceptance of faith in Jesus Christ with its exclusive claims, as the experience of Paul and Barnabas in Lycaonian Lystra demonstrates (Acts 14:8-19).

Moreover, miracles are always ambiguous: pagan philosophers would certainly have been able to offer some other explanation. And we should not forget that Paul himself was not healthy: when he arrived in southern Galatia, he suffered from a physical infirmity (Gal 4:13); the "thorn in the flesh" that Paul had to endure despite repeated prayers (2 Cor 12:7) is generally interpreted as an illness, perhaps malaria, possibly contracted in Pamphylia, the physical infirmity that may have prompted him to travel to the Anatolian highlands.[230] Moreover, he was surrounded by coworkers who fell ill: Epaphroditus of Philippi had become seriously ill and nearly died (Phil 2:26-27); Timothy is admonished to no longer drink only water but to "take a little wine for the sake of your stomach and your frequent ailments" (1 Tim 5:23); and Trophimus had to be left behind in Miletus because he had become ill (2 Tim 4:20).

Tenth, another explanation is the courage of the Christian martyrs, which impressed the crowds who watched them die in the arena for their

---

[227]Ibid., pp. 49-112; MacMullen, *Christianizing the Roman Empire*, pp. 17-42.
[228]See Peter H. Davids, "Miracles in Acts," *DLNTD*, pp. 746-52; "Signs and Wonders," *DLNTD*, pp. 1093-95; Graham H. Twelftree, "Signs, Wonders, Miracles," *DPL*, pp. 875-77.
[229]Fox, *Pagans and Christians*, pp. 329-30.
[230]Ramsay, *St. Paul the Traveller and the Roman Citizen*, pp. 92-97.

faith in Jesus Christ.[231] There is no doubt that the death of martyrs impressed many pagans, as Tertullian confirms, who asserted that the blood of the martyrs is the seed of the church.[232] On the other hand we find the philosopher Epictetus and the philosopher-emperor Marcus Aurelius had less flattering explanations for the willingness of the Christians to die for their faith. They saw theatrical affectations, foolish stubbornness and an irrational death wish.[233] Also, even if spectators were impressed by the courageous steadfastness of the Christian martyrs, they would not automatically have accepted the Christian message, since they would have certainly pondered the possibly deadly consequences of such a decision. Paul came under attack in nearly every city where he preached: Damascus, Jerusalem, Pisidian Antioch, Iconium, Lystra, Philippi, Thessalonica, Beroea, Corinth and Ephesus. When Paul explains his missionary work with the metaphor of the Roman triumphal procession, the *pompa triumphalis*, the blunt seriousness of his experiences are evident (2 Cor 2:14-16).

Eleven, the ideal of brotherly love and the praxis of Christian charity are often singled out as key factors in the success of the early Christian mission. The love of the Christian believers for each other and also for unbelievers indeed impressed many pagans.[234] However, we should not assume that all pagans were heartless.[235] And there were more than a handful of Christians who displayed intolerance, even hatred for fellow believers who held different theological views, sentiments that did not go unnoticed in the ancient world.[236] The social inclusiveness of the Christian faith and the Christian congregations indeed transcended national and ethnical ties as well as social and fi-

---

[231]Dodds, *Pagan and Christian*, p. 132; MacMullen, *Christianizing the Roman Empire*, p. 30; Rodney Stark, *The Rise of Christianity* (HarperCollins: San Francisco, 1997), pp. 163-89.

[232]Tertullian *Apologeticus* 50.13: "semen est sanguis Christianorum."

[233]Arrian *Dissertationes* 4.7.6; Marcus Aurelius *Meditationes* 11.3. Cf. Praet, "Explaining the Christianization of the Roman Empire," pp. 29-30.

[234]See Stark, *Rise of Christianity*, pp. 73-94, with regard to the (smallpox?) epidemic of A.D. 165-180 in which a quarter to a third of the population of the Roman Empire may have perished.

[235]MacMullen, *Paganism in the Roman Empire*, pp. 37, 42; Fox, *Pagans and Christians*, pp. 61-62, 591.

[236]Ammianus Marcellinus *Resgestae* 22.5.4. For a critique of Rodney Stark see J. T. Sanders, "Christians and Jews in the Roman Empire: A Conversation with Rodney Stark," *Sociological Analysis* 53 (1992): 433-45. For the fourth and later centuries cf. Ramsay MacMullen, *Voting about God in Early Church Councils* (New Haven, Conn.: Yale University Press, 2006).

nancial barriers, bringing Jews and Gentiles together, slaves and free, men and women. However, this inclusiveness is an attraction only for people who were at the lower end of the social ladder, whereas wealthy citizens would have complained about the impertinence of having to submit to "elders" who were slaves but more mature as Christians. The social networks of the Christian churches allowed for vertical connections in the hierarchal social structures of Roman society.[237] Personal connections within a "house" (or *familia*) that included slaves and servants were certainly a factor in the spread of the gospel. However, the example of Sergius Paullus, the Roman governor of Cyprus and of his relatives in Pisidian Antiocheia shows that social networks, though potentially useful for conversions, did not automatically lead to successful encounters, nor can they explain conversions.

Twelve, the historical foundation of the Christian faith, including the unique personality of Jesus is sometimes regarded as another factor in the success of the Christian missionaries. The mythologies of pagan gods was indeed complex. However, pagan intellectuals such as Celsus countered this argument, at least in the second century, by asking why the Christian Savior came so late, leaving generations of people without salvation, and what he really accomplished for his faithful devotees other than persecution.[238] Since we do not have an extended summary of Paul's missionary preaching before Gentiles, we cannot know how much historical background pagan listeners would be given when they heard Paul preach. The problem with the historical background of Paul's pagan audiences was the fact that it was tied to Jewish history and had no connections at all with the highs or lows of Greek history. And when Paul told the story of Jesus, he could not point to a superior education nor to a celebrated career: Jesus was not even accepted by the leaders of his own people in Jerusalem, so why should the citizens of Corinth or Ephesus listen to what he said after his death?

None of these factors and no combination of some individual factors explain the expansion of the Christian mission—not in the first century

---

[237]L. Michael White, "Finding the Ties That Bind: Issues from Social Description," *Semeia* 56 (1991): 3-22; Stark, *Rise of Christianity*, pp. 55-57.
[238]Origen *Contra Celsum* 4.7; 8.69.

or in later centuries. To believe the Christian message that the missionaries or Christian relatives, friends and neighbors proclaimed was not easy. To accept faith in a crucified Savior as necessary condition for salvation was rationally impossible, as was faith in a bodily resurrection. And to join a local congregation of followers of Jesus was potentially dangerous.

Why was Paul's preaching successful? Why did people become convinced that allegiance to Jesus Christ is the only path to salvation? Paul preached a crucified and risen Savior because he knew that it is God himself, the Creator of the world, who causes Jews and pagans to come to faith in the crucified Jesus, Messiah and Savior (1 Cor 1:18—2:5). Paul relies for the "success" of his missionary work not on the powers of rhetorical strategies and techniques, and certainly not on social or psychological factors. He relies on the power of God, which is present in the preaching of the gospel of the crucified and risen Jesus Christ. The "proof" for the validity of the gospel of Jesus Christ is not to be found through the application of logical inference or deduction, or in mere rhetorical brilliance. The "proof" for the truth of the gospel is to be found in the power of the Holy Spirit. When Paul proclaims the gospel, he speaks "not with plausible words of wisdom," but he relies on the "demonstration of the Spirit and of power" (1 Cor 2:4). The preaching of the gospel is a demonstration effected by the Spirit and by the power of the presence of God. The powerful Spirit of God "proves" the truth of the proclamation of God's redemptive revelation in Jesus Christ's death and resurrection in the hearts and minds of Jews and Gentiles, free and slaves, men and women. The proof "of the Spirit and of power" is the fact that Jews and pagans living in Corinth, and elsewhere, are being persuaded to accept the message of Jesus the crucified and risen Messiah.

Since Paul does not rely on a "method" understood in terms of "a defined, and regular plan" for the success of his missionary preaching but, rather, on the power of God, he regularly asks for prayer:

Beloved, pray for us. (1 Thess 5:25)

As you also join in helping us by your prayers, so that many will give thanks on our behalf for the blessing granted us through the prayers of many. (2 Cor 1:11)

Pray also for me, so that when I speak, a message may be given to me to make known with boldness the mystery of the gospel, for which I am an ambassador in chains. Pray that I may declare it boldly, as I must speak. (Eph 6:19-20)

At the same time pray for us as well that God will open to us a door for the word, that we may declare the mystery of Christ, for which I am in prison, so that I may reveal it clearly, as I should. (Col 4:3-4)

Finally, brothers and sisters, pray for us, so that the word of the Lord may spread rapidly and be glorified everywhere, just as it is among you. (2 Thess 3:1)

Paul requests the cooperation of the Corinthian believers in petitioning God for the blessing of deliverance from suffering. Such deliverance is an undeserved blessing (Gk *charisma*), but it is intimately, albeit mysteriously, linked with the intercessory prayers of fellow believers.[239]

Paul prays, and asks others to pray, for courage, openness, and clarity (Gk *parrēsia*, translated as "boldness") when he proclaims the gospel and its corollaries for Jewish and Gentile believers. Past boldness[240] does not guarantee boldness in the future, since the life of the Christian and particularly the life of a missionary is a struggle in the presence of "the wiles of the devil" against "the rulers, against the authorities, against the cosmic powers of this present darkness, against the spiritual forces of evil in the heavenly places," a struggle in which "the whole armor of God" is needed. This armor includes "shoes" symbolizing the readiness "to proclaim the gospel of peace" and "sword of the Spirit, which is the word of God" (Eph 6:10-17).

Paul asks the Christians in Colossae, whom he does not know personally, to pray for an open "door for the word" (Gk *thyra tou logou*)—that God will give him the opportunity to preach in captivity, that God will remove hindrances from his listeners so that they understand and accept the gospel, and that God may use his proclamation to make known the

---

[239]Murray J. Harris, *The Second Epistle to the Corinthians*, NIGTC (Grand Rapids: Eerdmans, 2005), p. 160.

[240]Examples of Paul's boldness in his missionary work are Acts 9:27; 13:46; 14:3; 19:8, and can be deduced from 2 Cor 3:12; Phil 1:20; 1 Thess 2:2. Cf. Ernest Best, *A Critical and Exegetical Commentary on Ephesians*, ICC (Edinburgh: T & T Clark, 1998), p. 609.

"mystery" of the good news of Jesus Christ. Understood in the latter sense, Paul's request for intercessory prayer emphasizes that the proclamation of the gospel "is not in the power of the proclaimer but that it is constantly dependent on God" to reveal the truth and the consequences of the gospel through his words.[241]

As Paul engages in missionary work in Corinth, he asks the believers in Thessalonica to support him with their prayers, petitioning God that the message of the gospel—treated "almost as a separate entity with a life of its own"[242]—may be swiftly accepted by many people who give praise and honor to the gospel as they receive it with faith and thanksgiving.

When Paul prays for fellow believers, he first and foremost gives thanks to God (cf. Eph 1:15-16; Phil 1:3-8; Col 1:3-6)—thanks for the reality of the transforming power of the gospel in their lives, as they have come to faith in Jesus Christ, as they love their fellow believers, as they continue to grow in maturity, and as the gospel continues to bears fruit among them from the day that they have heard the gospel and "truly comprehended the grace of God" (Col 1:6).[243] When Paul petitions God to continue his work in the lives of the believers, he prays for their growth in spiritual maturity, consisting in "the knowledge of God's will in all spiritual wisdom and understanding" so that they may "lead lives worthy of the Lord, fully pleasing to him" as they bear fruit in every good work and as they grow in the knowledge of God (Col 1:9-10). He prays that God will give them strength, endurance, patience, love and joy. He prays that God will help them to be obedient to the gospel and to persevere to the end.

---

[241]Markus Barth and Helmut Blanke, *Colossians*, AncB 34B (New York: Doubleday, 1994), p. 453. Paul does not ask for prayer to be released from prison: he sees "the fulfillment of his missionary charge in his suffering" (ibid., with reference to Col 1:24—2:5).

[242]I. Howard Marshall, *1 and 2 Thessalonians*, New Century Bible Commentary (Grand Rapids: Eerdmans, 1983), p. 213.

[243]On Paul's prayers of thanksgiving cf. Peter O'Brien, *Introductory Thanksgivings in the Letters of Paul*, NTSup 49 (Leiden: Brill, 1977); David W. Pao, *Thanksgiving: An Investigation of a Pauline Theme*, NSBT (Downers Grove, Ill.: InterVarsity Press, 2002). On Paul's intercessory prayers cf. Donald A. Carson, "Paul's Mission and Prayer," in *The Gospel to the Nations: Perspectives on Paul's Mission*, ed. P. Bolt and M. Thompson (Leicester, U.K.: Inter-Varsity Press, 2000), p. 180, with reference to Rom 15:30-33; Eph 1:15-23; 3:14-21; Phil 1:9-11; Col 1:9-14; 1 Thess 3:11-13.

6

The Task of Missionary
Work in the Twenty-First Century

You yourselves know how I lived among you the entire time from the first day that I set foot in Asia, serving the Lord with all humility and with tears, enduring the trials that came to me through the plots of the Jews. I did not shrink from doing anything helpful, proclaiming the message to you and teaching you publicly and from house to house, as I testified to both Jews and Greeks about repentance toward God and faith toward our Lord Jesus. And now, as a captive to the Spirit, I am on my way to Jerusalem, not knowing what will happen to me there, except that the Holy Spirit testifies to me in every city that imprisonment and persecutions are waiting for me. But I do not count my life of any value to myself, if only I may finish my course and the ministry that I received from the Lord Jesus, to testify to the good news of God's grace.

ACTS 20:18-24

WHEN WE CALL OURSELVES "CHRISTIANS," we can define this designation in very general terms as referring to a person "who believes or professes the religion of Christ; an adherent of Christianity," the first definition listed in the *Oxford English Dictionary*. Or we can define it, using the *OED*'s second definition, as referring to a person "who exhibits the spirit, and follows the precepts and example, of Christ; a believer in Christ who is characterized by genuine piety." The first definition suggests only a very loose connection between one's beliefs and the person, teaching and work of Jesus Christ, while the second definition reflects the conviction that Jesus' ministry in word and deed is authoritative for a person who confesses allegiance to Jesus Christ. Historically, this allegiance pertains not only to the example and teaching of Jesus of Nazareth, but also to the example and teaching of the apostles. In other words, people who call themselves Christians regard not only the four Gospels as the norm for their faith and life, but the entire canon of the Old Testament and New Testament texts. Christians are people who accept God's revelation in Israel's history and in the history of Jesus and the apostles as authority for their commitment to respond to the grace and to the mandate of the one true and living God in an authentic manner.

In the first three chapters I described the missionary work, the missionary task and the missionary message of the apostle Paul. In chapters four and five I integrated this description into an analysis of the goals and the methods of Paul's mission. In this final chapter I take up the challenge of bridging the historical distance between Paul, who engaged in missionary work in the first century, and the realities of and the challenges for missionary work in the twenty-first century. I will focus on the pragmatic task of applying the biblical text to the Christian churches of the present as well as to the mission societies and to the missionaries who are actively engaged in proclaiming the gospel and establishing new communities of followers of Jesus in the twenty-first century. It goes without saying that this chapter does not aim at commenting on or evaluating the whole range of the numerous and immensely diverse strategies, methods and techniques of missionary work and church planting. The churches and Christian denominations on all continents and in thousands of people groups are too numerous, the missionary initiatives are too diverse, and the methods of evangelism and church growth are too manifold to be discussed here (the world is indeed not a village!). A few examples must suffice to demonstrate the need for critical theological thought, thorough exegetical work and flexible adaptation of methods and techniques that are used by missionaries, church planters, pastors and teachers who serve God in proclaiming and explaining the good news of Jesus Christ.

Before I outline some of the consequences that follow from my description and analysis of Paul's missionary work for the missionary work of the church today, a few brief comments on the hermeneutical process are necessary.[1]

First, it should be apparent that theologians, missiologists, church leaders, missionaries and pastors who have engaged in a close reading of the relevant New Testament texts will produce more compelling results than those who read the texts only casually or who refer to biblical texts only as proof-texts. The need for serious exegesis is permanent and continuing.

The "application" of Acts 13, which contrasts the church in Antioch with the church in Jerusalem, arguing that the latter was monocultural and thus unable to provide the impetus for the spreading of the gospel to other cultures, while the former was composed of "the hybrid people" who were bicultural and thus able to send out the first missionaries[2] reveals an astonishing lack of understanding the relevant texts and of first-century realities. Luke credits precisely the church in Jerusalem with the impetus for spreading the gospel to other "cultures": Philip goes from Jerusalem to Samaria, and Peter moves from Jerusalem to Caesarea; Peter is instrumental in leading the first Gentile to faith in Jesus Christ; Peter puts forward important arguments during the Apostles' Council in which some of the criteria for the Gentile mission are discussed. Jerusalem was neither "monocultural" nor unable to engage in international missionary work. And both Paul and Barnabas, who set out from Antioch to do missionary work on Cyprus and in Galatia, are both firmly located by Luke in Jerusalem.

Second, we find several characteristic modes of presentation in the New Testament texts concerning Paul's missionary work, which need to be taken seriously and which all need to be incorporated in proposals for the missionary task in the modern-postmodern world.

---

[1] I rely for the following discussion on Richard B. Hays, *The Moral Vision of the New Testament: Community, Cross, New Creation: A Contemporary Introduction to New Testament Ethics* (New York: HarperCollins, 1996), pp. 207-14, 291-98, who provides "normative reflections" for the application of New Testament ethics to the ethical behavior of Christians today.

[2] John S. Leonard, "The Church in Between Cultures," *EMQ* 40 (2004): 69. Leonard's overall argument—multicultural churches have more missionary relevance than monocultural churches—is valid, despite the questionable exegesis of New Testament texts.

Luke tells the story of the missionary work of Paul (and of Peter, Stephen, Philip and Barnabas). The authority of Scripture is connected not only with its content but also with its form. The proverbs of the Old Testament are not divine promises for the individual; legal stipulations are not prophecies. The narratives in the book of Acts should not be turned into rules or principles. For example, someone may argue that since Paul always visited the local synagogue first, the missionary work of Christians today must begin by outreach to the Jewish community. Nobody argues this, but some of the "applications" of New Testament texts sound rather similar. The narrative of Paul's missionary work provides a paradigm, a model for the mission of the church. Note, for example, the fact that Paul's sermons before Jewish audiences are very different in terms of the argumentative flow and in terms of his appeal to authoritative sources (i.e., the Old Testament, in his synagogue sermon), compared to his speeches given before Gentile audiences. This "contextualizing" flexibility provides a model for missionary preaching. The ethnic, religious and social identity of the audience helps to shape the structure, content and linguistic formulations of sermons and speeches. Paul's description of his missionary behavior in his letters belongs to the same mode of discourse: the apostle challenges the churches he writes to follow his behavior. For example, in 1 Corinthians 9 he argues that just as he is willing to give up the right to be financially supported as a missionary, the Corinthian Christians who claim to have a right to participate in banquets in pagan temples should be willing to give up this right. Paul does not formulate a general principle (Christians should give up their rights) or a rule (no pioneer missionary should accept financial support).

In Paul's letters in particular we find a second mode of discourse. As a theologian who is also a missionary, he formulates principles for the mission of the church, general frameworks that need to govern decisions concerning missionary work. For example, in 1 Corinthians 14 Paul argues for the principle of intelligibility of the various contributions during the weekly gathering of the Christians, which ensure that everybody present understands what is being said and is consequently built up, visitors who are unbelievers included. The rule that Paul formulates in this context relates to the practice of speaking in unlearned languages (glossolalia). This translates into the principle that missionaries behave in such a manner that their message can be clearly heard, and to avoid everything that provokes mere puzzlement. This means, in a most basic manner, that authentic missionaries are willing to learn the language of the people to whom they want to preach the gospel, even if this takes years of hard work, rather than speaking through a translator. Another example is Hudson Taylor (1832-1905) who abandoned Western dress and wore Chinese garments when he realized that many listeners were more interested in his black coat rather than in what he preached.

A third mode of discourse in the New Testament is the formulation of rules, of direct commandments or prohibitions of specific conduct. Rules are more common in ethical texts (e.g., the prohibition of divorce in Mk 10:2-12) than in mission texts, since Paul does not explicitly exhort the churches to engage in missionary work. An example is Paul's prohibition in Galatians 1:9-10 to preach "another gospel," that is, to add other elements to the message of the crucified Jesus, who is God's Messiah and Savior by virtue of his identity as the promised seed of Abraham and by virtue of his death and resurrection. This rule translates directly into the contemporary mandate to evaluate emphases, activities and initiatives in the church and in missionary work today that relegate Jesus Christ and his death and resurrection to the sidelines.

A fourth mode of discourse is the symbolic world that provides fundamental categories through which we are to understand and interpret reality, in our case the missionary task. Examples are the representation of missionaries as "slaves" and "workers" who fulfill the tasks that have been given to them because of the status and authority of their Master, the Lord Jesus Christ and God himself.

We need to take care that we do not read the "missionary texts" of the New Testament only in one mode: only as rules or only as principles or only as paradigms. We do not find only rules, nor do we find only timeless principles, nor do we simply have entertaining stories, "paradigms" that are so open-ended that the modern interpreter moves beyond the New Testament texts so completely that they lose their normative authority. Also, we need to be careful not to use one mode of appeal to

New Testament texts in order to override the emphasis of another mode. A principle such as the centrality of Jesus the crucified Savior for the missionary message (1 Cor 1:18—2:5) cannot be dodged by appealing to the paradigm of Paul's behavior who seeks to "become all things to all people" (1 Cor 9:22).

Most of the mission texts in the New Testament, in particular in the book of Acts, are presented in the form of story. Most of Paul's statements about the missionary task describe paradigmatically his own missionary work. Consequently, the Christian church that seeks to take the form of these texts seriously will be drawn to the paradigmatic mode in the endeavor to be faithful to Jesus Christ's great missionary commission to go to all nations to the ends of the earth and to make disciples who obey what Jesus has commanded. Luke's narrative of Paul's (and Peter's) missionary work are fundamental resources for the normative task of missions today. The picture that will emerge is then complemented by the principles and the rules concerning the task of reaching people with the news of salvation through Jesus Christ, modes of discourse that we also find in the New Testament texts.

As we seek to engage the New Testament texts on the task of missionary work in our generation today, we do not operate in a vacuum. There are other sources of wisdom that inform our conclusions and the missionary practices that result from these conclusions. The role of tradition is one of these sources. Tradition—the tradition of the church, including missionary traditions—needs to be considered both when we seek to determine the meaning of New Testament texts and when we seek to formulate principles and rules that undergird and govern missionary work. It would be foolish to disregard the traditions that have arisen since the nineteenth century concerning the theory and practice of missionary work and church planting. Protestants since Martin Luther have always insisted that tradition must be submitted to critical evaluation in the light of the Word of God as revealed in the Old and New Testaments. Paul's warning against following human tradition (Col 2:8), formulated in the context of teachings that undermined the centrality of Jesus Christ, is fundamentally significant. When traditions, including missionary traditions, conflict with biblical paradigms, principles and rules for the life and the mission of the followers of Jesus Christ, "the time is at hand for judgment, repentance, and reformation."[3]

Another source of wisdom is reason, which helps interpreters to clarify their understanding of the meaning of Scripture and to determine the correlation of Scripture, tradition and experience. Like tradition, the function of reason is not unambiguous, since the intellectual faculty of human beings has been tainted by their rebellion against God as well. This is particularly significant to note with regard to the missionary message of Jesus the crucified Messiah and Savior, "news" that is certainly not "good news" for unbelieving Jews and Greeks and that cannot be contextualized in the sense that it would make the missionary's message more palatable or more persuasive (1 Cor 1:18-31). When reason comes into conflict with New Testament emphases, we need to reevaluate our thinking.

A final source of wisdom is experience. The work of thousands of missionaries throughout the ages is instructive both in positive and in negative ways when we move from the interpretation of Scripture as a historical text to the application of Scripture in the present. It is important in this context to point out, particularly for churches and Christians in the highly individualistic West, that I refer here, when I speak of sources of guidance for the application of Scripture, not to the experience of individuals or of individual churches, but to the experience of the community of the followers of Jesus Christ collectively. What "works" in one location, in one ethnic group, in one affluent suburb, in the ministry of one charismatic missionary or pastor, may not work in other places. When we interpret New Testament texts and apply them to the churches in which we worship and to the ministries in which we are active, we are shaped by our personal experience of God and the world and by our personal experience of communicating the gospel across cultural boundaries. Just as tradition and reason can come into conflict with Scripture, so can experience. And just as tradition and reason need to be submitted to the witness of God's revelation in Scripture and to the truth of the gospel, experience never trumps the normative voice of Scripture.

---

[3]Hays, *Moral Vision of the New Testament*, p. 297.

It is not easy to keep Scripture, tradition, reason and experience in the right kind of balance. The Reformers of the sixteenth century fought for the authority of Scripture over against the preeminence of tradition. The orthodox theologians of the seventeenth and eighteenth centuries fought for the authority of Scripture over against the preeminence of reason. The evangelical theologians of the twentieth century fought for the authority of Scripture over against the preeminence of experience, which appears to continue to be a major battle in the beginning of the twenty-first century. In our endeavor to apply New Testament texts that speak of the missionary task of the church to the mission of the church in the twenty-first century, we need what Paul asks God for when he intercedes for Christian communities:

> For this reason, since the day we heard it, we have not ceased praying for you and asking that you may be filled with the knowledge of God's will in all spiritual wisdom and understanding, so that you may lead lives worthy of the Lord, fully pleasing to him, as you bear fruit in every good work and as you grow in the knowledge of God. May you be made strong with all the strength that comes from his glorious power, and may you be prepared to endure everything with patience, while joyfully giving thanks to the Father, who has enabled you to share in the inheritance of the saints in the light. (Col 1:9-12)

Neither the reading of Scripture nor the application of Scripture is a mathematical or mechanistic process where a clever formula guarantees success. Schemes such as "ten steps for church growth"[4] immediately raise red flags, as do books with subtitles such as "Your One-Stop Resource for Effective Ministry."[5] The notion that we human beings can figure out how to guarantee that we achieve our goals is as old as the project of the Tower of Babel in Genesis 11. We utilize elaborate exegetical and hermeneutical skills, we are proud of our traditions, we use our reason and its analytical capabilities, we factor in our experience and our expertise, and we are thankful for advances in numerous academic fields of study which

---

[4]Thus the unfortunate title of an otherwise informative book by Donald A. McGavran and Winfield C. Arn, *Ten Steps for Church Growth* (San Francisco: Harper & Row, 1977).

[5]Gary L. McIntosh, *Church That Works: Your One-Stop Resource for Effective Ministry* (Grand Rapids: Baker, 2004). The introduction promises that "each chapter takes only minutes to read" (ibid., p. 8), which is evidently regarded as a positive feature.

help us understand the world and how human beings "work." At the same time, as followers of Jesus we know that it is ultimately and primarily the almighty and merciful God himself who provides us with the kind of knowledge that does not become outdated tomorrow but that helps us grasp and apply truth which is true spiritual wisdom. And it is only the latter that allows us to understand something of the reality of God and of the world, and thus helps us to see more clearly the missionary task of the church.

6.1 THE CALLING AND SENDING OF MISSIONARIES

In the New Testament neither the Twelve nor other apostles, such as Paul, volunteered for missionary ministry. They became involved in the task of reaching other people with the news of the arrival of the kingdom of God and, after Easter, with the news of the arrival of the promised Messiah, through whose death Israel's God forgives the sins of sinners, because Jesus had taken the initiative.

The calling of missionaries. Paul was called to proclaim the news of Jesus the Savior in conjunction with his conversion to faith in Jesus two or three years after Jesus' crucifixion and resurrection (see sec. 1.1). As Paul was converted to faith in Jesus Christ, he was called to proclaim the good news of Jesus and was sent to audiences who either had not heard or who did not believe in Jesus. In Paul's experience, conversion and call to missionary service were simultaneous events. The situation of the Twelve was in some respects similar, in other respects different. When they were called to follow Jesus and be his disciples, they were told that they would be transformed into followers who "fish" for other people, that is, into people whose task would be to attract others to follow Jesus also (Mk 1:17). If we call this moment the disciples' "conversion," then their calling to reach other people with the good news also happened simultaneously with their conversion. On the other hand, several of the Twelve had been disciples of John the Baptist and had encountered Jesus in connection with John's ministry before they became Jesus' disciples (Jn 1:35-42). It is difficult to determine what "conversion" meant in the case of the Twelve. According to John 1:41, Andrew realized right from the beginning that Jesus was the Messiah, whereas Mark 8:27-30 relates that Peter expressed his conviction that Jesus was the Messiah at a later time, while failing to grasp that the messiahship of Jesus was characterized by suffering, death and resurrection (Mk 8:31-33). It was only after Easter that the disciples grasped who Jesus was.

Both the experience of the Twelve as well as the experience of Paul are told in narratives that provide a paradigm for the summons to follow Jesus and to believe him as the crucified, risen and exalted messianic Son of Man and Son of God (Mt 4:19; Gal 1:15-16). They provide a paradigm for the reality that following Jesus entails a life of discipleship, that is, a life of learning from and about Jesus (Mt 28:20). They provide a paradigm for the reality that coming to faith in Jesus involves a transformation of sinners into people who are holy as a result of God's merciful grace through Jesus' death on the cross and who are called to be holy as a result of the presence of God's Spirit (Rom 1:7; 1 Cor 1:2; 1 Thess 4:4). The question is whether they also provide a paradigm for the call to missionary work.

The repeated references in the Gospels to the calling of the Twelve to missionary work in connection with their calling to follow Jesus, and the temporal connection between Paul's conversion and call may suggest that all believers who have been called to be followers of Jesus are also called to proclaim the news of Jesus to others.

First, we need to note that both the Twelve and Paul were called into what we call today "full-time" or vocational ministry. The Twelve were called to "leave their nets," that is, to give up their professions and to devote their entire time and energy to be trained by Jesus to become "fishers of people" and then to be sent into the world to proclaim the news of the kingdom of God and of Jesus the Messiah and Savior. Paul as a Jewish rabbi (or Torah expert) had already devoted his life to the interpretation and explanation of the Scriptures. When he came to faith in Christ and was called to be sent out to be a witness to "all the world" (Acts 22:15), he received a commission that could only be carried out by full-time ministry. This does not mean that Paul would not sometimes have to work in his profession as a tentmaker when funds were low (Acts 18:1-3). But it means that whenever possible he would devote his time and energy to proclaiming the news of Jesus the Messiah (Acts 18:5).

The paradigm of the call of the Twelve and of Paul can be correlated with the call that God extended to the tribe of Levi (Ex 32:25-29). The descendants of Levi did not volunteer for full-time priestly ministry. Rather, God in his sovereignty chose Levi "to stand and minister in the name of the LORD" (Deut 18:5). The Levites received no tribal territory in Israel: they were to devote their time and energy not to farming but to serve God (Deut 10:8-9). One Levitical family, Aaron and his descendants, was appointed (or "called") to serve as priests in the tabernacle and eventually in the temple (Num 18).

Second, Paul's emphasis that there is a variety of gifts of the Spirit, a variety of services connected with these gifts, and a variety of manifestations of God's power in the ministry connected with these gifts (1 Cor 12:4-5), suggests that not every Christian is called in order to be sent into missionary service. Paul argues in 1 Corinthians 12 that all believers have been gifted by God's Spirit to engage in a ministry that contributes to the building of the church, but that not everybody has the same gift or the same ministry. Paul asserts that "God has appointed in the church first apostles, second prophets, third teachers; then deeds of power, then gifts of healing, forms of assistance, forms of leadership, various kinds of tongues" (1 Cor 12:28). Then he asks a series of questions: "Are all apostles? Are all prophets? Are all teachers? Do all work miracles? Do all possess gifts of healing? Do all speak in tongues? Do all interpret?" (1 Cor 12:29-30). These are rhetorical questions: in light of Paul's previous discussion in 1 Corinthians 12, and in light of the reality of the church in Corinth and in other cities, the answer to these questions is well known—no, not all believers are apostles; no, not all believers are have the gift of prophecy; no, not all are teachers in the church; not all work miracles, not all have the gift of healing, not all speak in unlearned languages.

Only some followers of Jesus are called to vocational ministry. If all believers without exception would be called to missionary work thus understood, there would be no local communities of followers of Jesus, that is, no churches, because new converts would immediately (or perhaps after some period devoted to training) embark on missionary travels. And this is clearly not the case in the New Testament period. If not all Christians are called to missionary service, the question still remains whether those who are called to missionary service—to travel to other cities, regions and provinces in order proclaim the news of Jesus— should expect to be called to this task as Paul and the Twelve were called by Jesus to be fishers of people.

The narratives of the call given to the Twelve and to Paul—the latter narrated repeatedly in the book of Acts (Acts 9:15-16; 22:14-15; cf. Acts 26:16-18)—indeed suggest that later followers of Jesus may expect a similar supernatural call by the risen Lord to engage in full-time ministry. They provide a model of how people are called to full-time ministry for Jesus. On the other hand, Paul's reference to the various gifts that God has given to the church through the Holy Spirit suggests that since these gifts and ministries are grouped together, and since apostleship is one among many ministries that do not seem to require a supernatural "direct address" by the risen Lord, that these narratives concerning the "missionary call" of the Twelve and of Paul should not be reduced to a principle (a missionary call is necessary) nor to a rule (all missionaries must have been directly called by Jesus to full-time missionary ministry). The example of Barnabas confirms this: he was sent by the Jerusalem church to Antioch for the specific task of consolidating the work of missionaries who were already active in the city (Acts 11:22). His later missionary activities are not linked with a specific divine call.

Paul does not formulate principles, let alone rules, concerning a divine call as prerequisite for proclaiming the news of Jesus to people who are not followers of Jesus. On the other hand, the repeated narratives concerning Paul and the Twelve model for other believers entry into full-time ministry in the service of the kingdom of God.

It is this ambiguity of the New Testament evidence that seems to be responsible for the uncertainty concerning the "missionary call." A recent introduction to missionary work first details eight misunderstandings before elaborating on the biblical concept of God "calling" people: (1) the missionary call is a definite event; (2) Paul's "Macedonian call" in Acts 16:9-10 is a model of the missionary call; (3) the missionary call always comes through a mystical experience; (4) Christians cannot become successful missionaries without a call; (5) a missionary call is the best test of fitness for missionary service; (6) a call to full-time Christian ministry is given only to people who are especially gifted; (7) a missionary call is completely irrelevant to becoming a missionary; (8) a missionary call involves only God and the person who is called.[6]

A helpful way forward is to make two distinctions. First, we should distinguish between Jesus' call to all of his followers to be the salt of the earth and the light of the world (Mt 5:13-16) and Jesus' call to some of his followers to leave their professions and devote their lives to proclaiming the news of the arrival of the kingdom of God (Mt 4:19; Acts 26:16-18). When Paul writes in 2 Corinthians 5:18—6:2 that "we are ambassadors for Christ" he distinguishes between himself and the other apostles ("we") and the churches and the church members ("you").[7] At the same time he exhorts the believers in the city of Corinth to make sure that everything that is being said in their gatherings is intelligible so that unbelievers can understand (1 Cor 14:23-24). These followers of Jesus thus have a responsibility to unbelievers who should be able to follow what is being said. The church in Philippi participated in the "progress of the gospel" through Paul's missionary work on account of its financial support and prayers (Phil 1:5, 12, 19; 4:15-16). And Paul seeks to recruit the Christians in the city of Rome as active participants in his future missionary work in Spain (Rom 15:14-29).

Second, we should distinguish between God's call to full-time service and personal guidance that involves the assignment of specific tasks.[8] Jesus called the Twelve to be trained as "fishers of people" (Mt 4:19), and later he sent them out to a particular preaching tour through the towns and villages of Galilee (Mt 10:1-15). In the case of Paul, he was called by the risen Jesus Christ, who appeared to him on the road to Damascus to devote his life from now on to the proclamation of the news that Jesus is indeed the promised Messiah (Acts 9:15-16; 22:14-15). When the leaders of the church in Antioch sent him, together with Barnabas, to engage in missionary work on the island of Cyprus (Acts 13:1-4), this was not a "missionary call" but the commission for a new missionary initiative, the

---

[6]A. Scott Moreau et al., *Introducing World Missions: A Biblical, Historical, and Practical Survey* (Grand Rapids: Baker Academic, 2003), pp. 160-64.

[7]See W. Paul Bowers, "Church and Mission in Paul," *JSNT* 44 (1991): 89-111.

[8]The same distinction made by Kane, *Understanding Christian Missions*, pp. 45-46.

assignment of a new sphere of ministry, specific guidance to travel to cities further West in which the news of Jesus needed to be preached.

The paradigm of Paul's and the Twelve's call to full-time ministry suggests that Jesus Christ takes the initiative in calling specific believers to the specific life of ministry that is fully devoted in terms of time, energy and work to the task of proclaiming the news of Jesus and of teaching the new disciples. Since we also find missionaries in the early church (e.g., Barnabas) for whom such a specific divine call is not reported but who are sent by churches and are engaged in preaching and teaching, this paradigm cannot be reduced to a rule on whose application the church must insist.

We can thus conclude that the church should expect that leaders who commit themselves to a life of full-time ministry in proclaiming the news of Jesus and in teaching the followers of Jesus to be specifically called by Jesus Christ to this task. But we also conclude that this call can come in different ways: through direct spiritual encounters with Jesus Christ (through vision-dreams, through the still, small voice speaking in the heart, through a growing conviction) or through the initiative of the leaders of a local church who commission an experienced colleague for a ministry of preaching and teaching.

The questions that Harold Cook formulated for believers who consider applying to missionary societies half a century ago are still pertinent today for Christians who ask themselves whether God has called them to full-time missionary service:

> Are you sure that your motives in seeking appointment are the right ones? . . . What is your real reason for wanting to go out as a missionary? Is it the work that intrigues you, the life of the missionary, or the opportunity to do good? Do you feel that it is simply the highest form of Christian service? Are you more interested in the country or the people? Are you more concerned about their physical plight or their spiritual destitution? Do you merely want to go, or do you feel that you must go? In other words, are you going on your own initiative or is the Spirit of Christ really sending you? Are you more concerned about finding our own "place in life" or about doing what He wants you to do?[9]

---

[9]Harold R. Cook, *Missionary Life and Work: A Discussion of Principles and Practices of Missions* (Chicago: Moody, 1959), p. 16.

The evidence of the New Testament suggests that both the range and the geographical location of full-time missionary ministry is secondary: Paul does not insist in reaching the province of Asia; he is willing to change his plans and travel to other Roman provinces. He wants to focus on reaching non-Jews as an apostle called to proclaim the news of Jesus to Gentiles, but at the same time he seeks out the Jewish communities in the local synagogues of the cities where he does missionary work. The calling to serve God is permanent, the specific ministries and locations may be temporary.

Preparatory training. Followers of Jesus who have been called to full-time or vocational ministry as missionaries prepare themselves. Paul's biography does not provide a helpful paradigm for the preparatory training of missionaries. When Jesus Christ called Paul to proclaim the news of the arrival of the Savior, he had just persecuted the church. The time in Arabia was not a time for preparation, as we have seen (see sec. 1.2), but the first phase of his missionary work. However, we should not forget that Paul was a Jewish Torah scholar who had been trained "at the feet of Gamaliel" (Acts 22:3). These long years of exegetical and theological studies were Paul's preparation for missionary service: when he was forced to acknowledge on the road to Damascus that Jesus is indeed the promised Messiah and Savior, he would not have necessarily needed a long time to rearrange and reinterpret his Jewish convictions concerning God's promises for Israel, concerning the scope of the validity of the Mosaic law, concerning the righteousness of God and the forgiveness of sins, concerning the new covenant of the last days and the new people of God.[10] It is a plausible assumption that when Paul chose Timothy (Acts 16:1-4) and other believers as his coworkers, he trained them while they traveled for hundreds of kilometers on the roads of Asia Minor and Greece, and by involving them in his ongoing missionary work. Since Paul expects the leaders of the local churches to be skillful in teaching (1 Tim 3:2), and since missionary work involved proclaiming and explaining the news of Jesus, which also involved teaching, he would as a matter of course have been concerned that his coworkers know the Scriptures, the sound inter-

---

[10]See Seyoon Kim, *The Origin of Paul's Gospel*, 2nd ed., WUNT 2/4 (Tübingen: Mohr-Siebeck, 1984).

pretation of the Scriptures in the light of the coming of Jesus the Messiah, the words of Jesus, the tradition of the apostles, the content of the gospel. However, neither Luke's report in the book of Acts nor Paul in his letters provides details concerning the training of new missionaries.

A more explicit paradigm is Jesus' training of the Twelve, which lasted about three years from the initial call to follow Jesus in order to be transformed into fishers of people to their being sent into the world after Jesus' resurrection. Their "missionary" tour through the towns and villages of Galilee (Mt 10) apparently was a short-term training exercise in proclaiming the news of the arrival of the kingdom of God.[11]

The paradigms of training for missionary ministry in the New Testament are thus both informal (unintentional learning through the daily events of life), nonformal (intentional learning outside a formal school setting) and formal (intentional learning in a formal school setting).

Regarding the training of future missionaries, some missiologists distinguish four areas: character, commitment, competence and culture.[12] The significance of character and commitment are paramount in the New Testament texts. The requirements that Paul formulates for church leaders (1 Tim 3; Tit 1) and that are surely the fundamental requirements for the missionaries who establish churches also focus exclusively on the character of the leader. A person who has leadership responsibilities in the church

> must be above reproach, married only once, temperate, sensible, respectable, hospitable, an apt teacher, not a drunkard, not violent but gentle, not quarrelsome, and not a lover of money. He must manage his own household well, keeping his children submissive and respectful in every way—for if someone does not know how to manage his own household, how can he take care of God's church? He must not be a recent convert, or he may be puffed up with conceit and fall into the condemnation of the devil. Moreover, he must be well thought of by outsiders, so that he may not fall into disgrace and the snare of the devil. (1 Tim 3:2-7)

Paul often emphasizes his own commitment to the task of preaching the gospel to Jews and Gentiles, to the educated and to the uneducated

---

[11]See Schnabel, *Early Christian Mission*, 1:263-315, on Mt 10 (Mk 6; Lk 9); cf. ibid., pp. 290-315.
[12]See Tom A. Steffen, "Training of Missionaries," *EDWM*, pp. 964-65; cf. William David Taylor, ed., *Internationalizing Missionary Training: A Global Perspective* (Grand Rapids: Baker, 1991).

(see chap. 2). He would expect no less from other missionaries. In his last letter he writes to Timothy:

> For this reason I remind you to rekindle the gift of God that is within you through the laying on of my hands; for God did not give us a spirit of cowardice, but rather a spirit of power and of love and of self-discipline. Do not be ashamed, then, of the testimony about our Lord or of me his prisoner, but join with me in suffering for the gospel, relying on the power of God. . . . Hold to the standard of sound teaching that you have heard from me, in the faith and love that are in Christ Jesus. Guard the good treasure entrusted to you, with the help of the Holy Spirit living in us. (2 Tim 1:6-8, 13-14)

The question of competency is seldom raised explicitly in Paul's letters. Paul asserts that his competency as a "minister of the new covenant" comes from God: "Not that we are competent of ourselves to claim anything as coming from us; our competence is from God, who has made us competent to be ministers of a new covenant" (2 Cor 3:5-6).

Paul regards self-commendation a serious mistake (2 Cor 3:1) and insists that he does not claim competence for himself. He disowns "any qualification to claim credit for himself for any aspect of his ministry."[13] He insists, however, quite forcefully that people who teach others must be qualified to teach, as his instructions to Timothy and Titus demonstrate: "And what you have heard from me through many witnesses entrust to faithful people who will be able to teach others as well" (2 Tim 2:2). The overseer "must have a firm grasp of the word that is trustworthy in accordance with the teaching, so that he may be able both to preach with sound doctrine and to refute those who contradict it" (Tit 1:9).

Training missionary candidates in understanding culture is a modern phenomenon. We have seen (see sec. 5.3) that Paul's missionary work is not really "crosscultural" in the modern sense of the term. Paul did not need to learn a new language. He did not need to learn the meaning of cultural institutions or symbols. He did not need to learn the way of thinking, the values and the allegiances of the people who lived in the cities in which he proclaimed the news of Jesus. As a Diaspora Jew who was born and lived for

---

[13]Murray J. Harris, *The Second Epistle to the Corinthians*, NIGTC (Grand Rapids: Eerdmans, 2005), p. 268.

some time in Tarsus and who spoke Greek as well as Aramaic and Hebrew, he felt at home in Tarsus as much as in Jerusalem, in Antioch in Syria as much as in Corinth. Paul was bicultural and thus able to understand and to function comfortably in Jewish synagogues as well as in a lecture hall of a Greek city. Paul's bicultural identity enabled him to move with relative ease from a Jewish context to a Gentile context. If Paul indeed reached Spain after the release from his (first) imprisonment,[14] missionary work among the Latin-speaking population in the cities would have been a challenge, perhaps the reason why he sought the support of the churches in the city of Rome (Rom 15:22-29). Had Paul traveled to India with the goal of preaching the gospel and establishing churches there, as the apostle Thomas perhaps did,[15] the cultural divide would have been vast, requiring him to learn new languages, new customs and new worldviews.

Most missionaries today have grown up in a single culture and thus need to learn the worldview, values, symbols and appropriate modes of behavior of the "target culture" in which they seek to proclaim the gospel. The much more fragmented and distinct cultures of our own day (compared with the Hellenistic culture of the cities in the Roman Empire) require serious and sustained training of new missionaries in cultural competence. The paradigms of the New Testament texts do not provide much help in this regard. Paul's description of his behavior as a missionary who relinquishes the rights that he has and who becomes a "slave" to all so that people might be saved (1 Cor 9:19-23) provides a general paradigm for crosscultural ministry and for the necessary training for such ministry. New missionaries must learn to be humble, unpretentious, genuine. They need to learn not to seek their own advantage. They must learn not to be concerned about their own prestige. They need to learn flexibility, for example, in eating foods they have not eaten before, in wearing clothes they have not worn before, and—more seriously—in appreciating values and opinions that they have never heard about or which they thought strange, in withholding criticism of cultural patterns which they may not under-

---

[14]On Paul's mission to Spain cf. Schnabel, *Early Christian Mission*, 2:1271-83; on the likelihood of his release from prison see ibid., 2:1270; Jerome Murphy-O'Connor, *Paul: A Critical Life* (Oxford: Oxford University Press, 1996), pp. 359-60.

[15]On the plausibility of Thomas's mission to India, mentioned in the *Acts of Thomas* as well as in Indian oral sources, cf. Schnabel, *Early Christian Mission*, 1:880-911; on India, see ibid., 1:479-98.

stand, in avoiding facile black-and-white judgments, to mention only a few areas of culture learning. They need to be willing to spend years, if necessary, to master a new and perhaps difficult language, or even multiple languages in some regions.

The sending of missionaries. The Twelve are sent by Jesus, as is Paul (Mt 4:19; 28:18-20; Gal 1:15-16; Acts 9:15-16; 22:14-15; 26:16-18). When Paul and Barnabas leave the church in Antioch to engage in missionary work on the island of Cyprus (Acts 13:1-4), they are not sent by the church but by the Holy Spirit (Acts 13:2, 4). When Luke reports that "after fasting and praying they laid their hands on them and sent them off" (Acts 13:3), the Greek of the last verb (*apolyō*, translated as "sent") means "to permit or cause someone to leave a particular location, let go, send away, dismiss."[16] This is not a term that describes an official action of the church. As we have seen, Paul and Barnabas may have pondered the possibility of initiating a new phase of missionary work for some time, during which they consulted with Peter in Jerusalem (see secs. 1.3 and 1.7). The reference to the prayer and the fasting of the leaders of the church in Antioch suggests, however, that Paul's decision to move to Cyprus was made in consultation with the local church in which he was active at the time. The church of Antioch was involved in the new missionary initiative: they asked God to guide the missionaries and to give them strength for the missionary work they embarked on.

Paul's missionary work in Damascus and Arabia immediately after his conversion and without first consulting the apostles in Jerusalem (Gal 1:17) constitutes a different paradigm. Paul initiates missionary work evidently without the explicit direction of a local church. (Although the possibility cannot be ruled out that the church in Damascus provided guidance.) Sometimes Paul seems to act in accordance with plans that he had drawn up (e.g., Paul's plan to do missionary work in the province of Asia [Acts 16:6]). Sometimes he acts in response to an explicit directive from God (e.g., Paul's move to Macedonia [Acts 16:9-10]). The New Testament texts provide no consistent paradigms, principles or rules for the sending of missionaries.

---

[16]BDAG, p. 117.

The sending of missionaries has been long connected with mission agencies. This is another area where Paul's missionary work provides neither a paradigm nor principles or rules. A well-known example of using the New Testament for contemporary missiological purposes, here for explaining mission societies, is Ralph Winter's argument that the modern mission society resembles the missionary team of Paul and his coworkers.[17] He suggests that from a sociological perspective the church can be understood as a "modality," that is, as a structured community in which there are no differences of gender or age. The missionary team is a "sodality," that is, a structured community in which membership is determined by a second "decision" and limited as the result of age, gender or marital status. Theologically the function of the church is important, not its form or structures. This analysis has been critiqued for the following reasons.[18] (1) The missionary teams in the first century were not a "church." The New Testament provides very little data about these teams, which means that all evaluations of their self-understanding remain hypothetical. It should be noted, however, that they are never described as *ekklēsia*. They did not exist as "organizations" independent of the church. As soon as the missionary team arrived in a city and as soon the first people were converted, the missionaries and thus the "team" belonged to the local congregation, for example to the *ekklēsia* of Antioch, Corinth or Rome. (2) The claim that Paul's missionary team had the full authority of a local church and thus can be described as a "traveling church" is erroneous. The authority of Paul was not focused on his team of missionary coworkers but on the church(es) of Jesus Christ. There is no evidence for the "authority" of a missionary team in the New Testament. (3) If a "sodality" limits its members (according to the definition given), it cannot be a "church" since an *ekklēsia* is always defined as a community in which every follower of Jesus is a member, whether a woman or man, slave or freeborn, Jew or Gentile. Since missionary teams and mission agencies as "sodalities" require a "second decision" of

---

[17]Ralph D. Winter, "The Two Structures of God's Redemptive Mission," *Missiology* 2 (1974): 121-39; "Momentum Building in Global Missions," *International Journal of Frontier Missions* 7 (1990): 49-59; "Sodality and Modality," *EDWM*, pp. 894-95.

[18]See Bruce K. Camp, "A Theological Examination of the Two-Structure Theory," *Missiology* 23 (1995): 197-209.

their potential members (a certain age, certain experiences, a particular expertise) they cannot constitute a "church."

A mission agency has been the most effective means of initiating and supporting missionary work in distant regions due to its knowledge in terms of country, culture, language and politics of the particular region. The specialized knowledge the mission agency possesses and the wealth of experiences and trial-and-error efforts leading to improved methods are generally not available to the leaders of a local church or to an independent missionary. There is no biblical rule that would require Christians to find a specific biblical warrant for everything they do, for example establish and maintain missionary agencies. However, it stands to reason to pool knowledge, expertise and resources in sending missionaries. Experience has demonstrated that mission agencies are effective tools for sending missionaries into crosscultural situations. And there has been a long tradition of maintaining mission agencies, shared by most denominations. The question of the relationship between a mission agency and the local church, and the question of the responsibilities of a mission agency with regard to the local congregation, is complex.[19] However, such questions must not be solved by removing the church and the local congregations from their primary responsibility for the task of mission and evangelism.[20]

6.2 The Content of Missionary Proclamation

Biblical narratives are paradigms that provide us with models for our own faithful and authentic response to God's revelation. The narratives concerning Paul's missionary work (in the book of Acts, and also in Paul's letters) provide us with examples that highlight the priorities of missionaries and some of the methods they use. As we turn to

---

[19]For a discussion of these matters cf. Charles van Engen, *God's Missionary People: Rethinking the Purpose of the Local Church* (Grand Rapids: Baker, 1991); Samuel F. Metcalf, "When Local Churches Act Like Agencies," *EMQ* 29 (1993): 142-49; Andrew F. Walls, *The Missionary Movement in Christian History: Studies in the Transmission of Faith* (Maryknoll, N.Y.: Orbis, 1996), pp. 241-54; Tom Telford and Lois Shaw, *Missions in the Twenty-First Century: Getting the Church into the Game* (Wheaton, Ill.: Shaw, 1998); Paul Borthwick, "What Local Churches Are Saying to Mission Agencies," *EMQ* 35 (1999): 324-33; Stan Guthrie, *Missions in the Third Millennium: 21 Key Trends for the 21st Century*, rev. ed. (Bletchley, U.K.: Paternoster, 2004), pp. 3-10.

[20]See Hesselgrave, *Planting Churches Cross-Culturally*, pp. 413-21; Bosch, *Transforming Mission: Paradigm Shifts in the Theology of Mission*, pp. 368-89.

discuss the content of the missionary message, we are no longer dealing mostly with texts in the book of Acts, but more consistently with texts in Paul's letters, which are not narrative but argumentative and prescriptive. In other words, the form in which the missionary proclamation of Paul is presented in the New Testament reflects the conviction that the content of Paul's preaching is not simply a paradigm, an "example" how one might preach the news of Jesus. Rather, the form of the description of Paul's preaching (in Paul's letters, and also in the book of Acts) signifies that here we encounter principles and indeed rules that govern the missionary proclamation of people who accept the authority of Scripture.

In chapter three we analyzed key texts and themes of Paul's missionary message. Paul's first letter to the followers of Jesus in the city of Thessalonica helps us to summarize the content of the apostle's missionary proclamation.[21]

1. There is only one living and true God (1 Thess 1:9).

2. Gentiles who worship other entities as gods need to acknowledge the futility of their religious commitment (1 Thess 1:9).

3. Gentiles who are committed to lustful passions and unholy behavior will be judged by God (1 Thess 4:3-8).

4. Jews who reject Jesus the Messiah and Lord are exposed to God's wrath (1 Thess 2:15-16).

5. God's judgment will come suddenly and unexpectedly (1 Thess 1:10; 4:15—5:10).

6. Gentiles who worship other deities must commit themselves to the one living and true God in order to be saved (1 Thess 1:9; 5:9).

7. Jews need to give up their opposition to the proclamation of Jesus as the Messiah and accept this message if they want to please God and be saved (1 Thess 2:14-16; 5:9).

8. Jesus is the Son of God, the promised Messiah and Lord (1 Thess 1:1, 10; 3:2; 5:9).

---

[21]For a similar, briefer summary cf. Dean S. Gilliland, *Pauline Theology and Mission Practice* (Grand Rapids: Baker, 1983), p. 271.

9. Jesus has died, but he was raised from the dead by God (1 Thess 1:10; 4:14; 5:9-10).

10. Jesus is the one through whom God grants salvation to Jews and Gentiles, saving them from the coming judgment (1 Thess 1:10; 5:9-10).

11. Followers of Jesus expect the return of Jesus from heaven (1 Thess 1:10; 4:13-17).

12. Followers of Jesus will share in God's new world of glory (1 Thess 1:10; 4:14-17).

13. Followers of Jesus are Jews and Gentiles who become members of the kingdom of God (1 Thess 2:9-12).

14. Followers of Jesus are governed by the will of the one living and true God, a holy God whose people live holy lives, distinct from the values and behavioral patterns of pagan society, empowered by the Holy Spirit (1 Thess 2:9-12; 4:1-8).

Paul taught these truths in his earliest missionary sermons. In his first letter to the Christians in the city of Corinth he insists that these emphases, focused on the proclamation of Jesus, the crucified and risen Messiah and Savior,[22] are not personal idiosyncrasies but the indispensable and irreplaceable foundation of the church everywhere (1 Cor 1:18—2:5; 3:10-15; 15:1-11). The content of Paul's missionary proclamation provides us not with a general paradigm for missionary preaching but with normative principles and rules concerning its content.

Paul and Jewish audiences. Paul informs Jewish audiences in no uncertain terms about the failure of the Jewish authorities in Jerusalem to properly understand the Scriptures as far as the announcement of the coming of the messianic Savior was concerned. He asserts that Jesus' rejection in Jerusalem, which caused his death was part of God's plan, and warns his audience not to make the same mistake. Since God raised Jesus from the dead, they should acknowledge that he is indeed the Messiah and Savior, and recognize that God now forgives sins no longer through the Mosaic law but through faith in Jesus.

---

[22]This consistent focus of Paul's missionary preaching has been missed by Bosch, *Transforming Mission*, pp. 170-78.

Paul argued, as his letters to the Christians in Galatia and in Rome demonstrate, that God's saving revelation in the death of Jesus the Messiah, who was vindicated in his resurrection from the dead, has far-reaching consequences—the salvation of the Jewish people no longer rests on their being God's chosen people; circumcision no longer guarantees that Jews are the recipients of God's salvation; the sacrifices in the temple, which the Mosaic law stipulated, no longer guarantee the forgiveness of individual Jews nor the holiness of Israel as a nation.

Paul is not eager to ingratiate himself to Jewish audiences. He does not smooth over the failure of the leadership in Jerusalem. He does not politely gloss over facts, arguments or controversies that might constitute an obstacle to belief or might be repugnant to their prejudices. The goal of leading Jewish people to find faith in Jesus the Messiah does not dictate the content of his message. The end does not justify the means.

The news of Israel's God saving sinners through faith in Jesus the Messiah, whose death on the cross atones for the sins of humanity, of Jews and of Gentiles, is the center of Paul's missionary preaching. Paul uses Scripture, God's sovereignty in Israel's history and the demonstrable fact of Jesus' resurrection. But he knows that Jews will not be persuaded with logical arguments. Nor can he meet the demands of Jewish audiences for (cosmic) signs that would clearly demonstrate that the days of the Messiah had arrived. The news of Jesus the Messiah, whose death on the cross atones for the sins of the world, will be accepted only by people in whom God's Holy Spirit works understanding and faith (1 Cor 1:18—2:5).

Paul before Gentile audiences. Paul proclaims essentially the same news before Gentile audiences as he did before Jewish audiences. Certainly he adapts his missionary sermons to the possibilities of comprehension of pagans, taking into account their religious and educational traditions. He evidently does not use quotations from Israel's Scriptures or reviews of Israel's history. He elaborates more vigorously on the nature of the God whom he proclaims. However, even though a discussion about the nature of God might seem like a more neutral topic that many pagans find interesting and even congenial, he insists on sharply distinguishing between gods and human beings (Acts 14:15). This distinction undermined not only traditional emphases of generally accepted religiosity. More seriously, it undermined the recently established and increasingly popular emperor cult. Paul unequivocally calls pagans who listen to his preaching to abandon their traditional gods and to turn to the one true and living God who created the world (Acts 17:30-31; 1 Thess 1:9). And he insisted that sins can be forgiven only through faith in Jesus, a Jew from Nazareth, who died on a cross for the sins of the world, whom God raised from the dead and who will return to judge the world. Paul knows that pagans must regard this news as intellectual and religious nonsense. He knows that it is only God himself who can cause Greeks to believe in Jesus the messianic Savior and Lord (1 Cor 1:17—2:5).

Paul is not eager to ingratiate himself to pagan audiences, whether he discourses on the subject of the supreme deity he proclaims or when he explains the news of Jesus, the Savior of sinners. He does not smooth over the failure of the traditional religiosity of his pagan listeners. He does not politely gloss over facts, arguments or controversies that might constitute an obstacle to his pagan listeners' sympathy or might be repugnant to their prejudices. The goal of leading pagans to find faith in Jesus the Savior does not dictate the content of his message. The end does not justify the means.

The center of the gospel. Paul's missionary preaching is not expedient. He does not streamline the content of his message in order to guarantee its acceptance. He does not redesign the content of his preaching depending on the likes and dislikes of his audiences in order to make coming to faith easier or more convenient. He adapts the form of his preaching to different audiences, but he never downplays or omits the central truths of the gospel that audiences might find unreasonable or impertinent. He adapts the linguistic expression of the news he proclaims to his audiences, but he always focuses on the significance of Jesus' death on the cross and of his resurrection from the dead.[23] And he never hides the fact that pagans need to worship Israel's God and that Jesus is a Jewish savior, the Messiah (Gk *Christos*) who is Lord.

Paul insists that this is the message that must be preached. When people change this basic content of Christian preaching and teaching, suggesting

---

[23]Cf. Rom 3:21-26; 4:25; 5:6-11; 8:3, 32-35; 14:9; 1 Cor 1:18—3:20; 8:11; 11:23-25; 15:3-5; 2 Cor 5:14—6:2; Gal 1:1-5; 2:19-21; 3:1, 10-14; Phil 2:6-11, 16; Col 1:20; 2:13-14; 1 Thess 5:10; 1 Tim 6:13.

alternate contours of understanding the news of God's grace because they seek human approval, they preach a perverted the gospel, an action which provokes God's curse (Gal 1:6-10). Paul insists that the news of Jesus the crucified Messiah and Savior is the foundation of the faith of followers of Jesus. When people suggest that the Christian message should be adapted to the intellectual and rhetorical needs and expectations of a Greek audience, Paul argues, they ignore the foundation that has been laid and start constructing a building that will surely collapse because the normative parameters of the foundation have been defied. These people will be judged by God (1 Cor 3:10-15).

It has been suggested that

> the old wineskins of traditional theological categories are often inadequate to build adequate cultural bridges for communication to most postmodern people today. . . . The explanation that the death of Christ on the cross is an example of God's capital punishment against wrongdoers in order to meet legal requirements that are objectively necessary to maintain some inflexible universal law of justice is simply incomprehensible.[24]

The same author argues that "if we are serious about following the biblical precedent of contextualizing the faith into forms understandable to the receiver culture, we need to look at our expressions of atonement afresh. As the central tenet of salvation, the atonement must make sense to a very relationally oriented culture."[25]

That is exactly Paul's point: the atonement for sins that God provides for sinners through Jesus' death on a cross does not make sense—not for Jews and not for Greeks. If we avoid speaking of God's wrath, of God's

---

[24]R. Larry Shelton, *Cross and Covenant: Interpreting the Atonement for 21st Century Mission* (Carlisle, U.K.: Paternoster, 2006), pp. 3-4.

[25]Ibid., p. 4. See also Joel B. Green and Mark D. Baker, *Recovering the Scandal of the Cross: Atonement in New Testament & Contemporary Contexts* (Downers Grove, Ill.: InterVarsity Press, 2000), who question whether the "theory" of penal substitution—"the view that Jesus' death was a self-offering to God, whereby he bore the punishment God would otherwise have inflicted on us, thus turning God's hostility away from us" (p. 23)—faithfully represents the relevant New Testament texts. The reasons for this critique are, among others, the fear that "a central tenet of our faith might have little or nothing to say about racial reconciliation, for example, or issues of wealth and poverty, or our relationship to the cosmos" (p. 31), and the belief that the "commitment to penal substitutionary atonement has had ill effects in the life of the church in the United States and has little to offer the global church and mission by way of understanding or embodying the message of Jesus Christ" (pp. 220-21).

justice, of the coming day of divine judgment, of Jesus' death as an atoning sacrifice for us, we are not changing the form of the missionary presentation of the gospel but its content. The foundational centrality of "Christ crucified" is of critical importance for the existence of the local church. In mission and evangelism the search for a presentation of the gospel that will convince listeners is misguided if the fact of Jesus' death on the cross and the significance of this death are not central to that message.

The cross has been and always will be regarded as a religious scandal and as intellectual nonsense. The search for a message that is more easily comprehensible must never attempt to eliminate the provocative nature of the news of Jesus the messianic Son of God who came to die so that sinners can be forgiven by God who hates sin and judges sinners on the Day of Judgment. Paul knows that it is only the power of God, the "proof" of God's Spirit working in people, that convinces unbelievers of the truth of the news of Jesus and that leads them to faith in Jesus the Messiah and Savior.[26]

6.3 The Proclamation of the Gospel and Church Planting

Paul insists that the content of missionary preaching governs the form of presenting the news of Jesus. As we have seen earlier, Paul rejects the expectations of some Corinthian Christians who demand that effective preaching should adhere to the stipulations of the "science" of rhetoric, stipulations which guarantee that people are impressed and accept what is being said (see sec. 5.5). In missionary proclamation, rhetorical strategies have an ambiguous value. Every verbal address that presents a case to an audience has by definition rhetorical elements. Paul's letters demonstrate that he was not only capable but also willing to employ (at least basic) rhetorical schemes. However, Paul asserts in 1 Corinthians 1—4 that the proclamation of the news of Jesus the crucified Messiah and Savior suffers abuse when it is submerged into the categories of the Greco-Roman rhetoric of his day. There are times and subjects where the preacher needs

---

[26]See Gilliland, *Pauline Theology and Mission Practice*, pp. 44-45, 108-9, 124-26; Don N. Howell, "Confidence in the Spirit as the Governing Ethos of the Pauline Mission," in *The Holy Spirit and Mission Dynamics*, ed. C. D. McConnell, Evangelical Missiological Society Series 5 (Pasadena, Calif.: William Carey Library, 1997), pp. 36-65.

to tone down or entirely abandon rhetorical strategies in favor of a retelling of the narrative of Jesus' life, death and resurrection, and in favor of a presentation of God's call to repentance and faith. The fundamental significance of the cross affects the rhetorical methods that are used in the proclamation of the news of Jesus Christ.

In mission and evangelism the search for a method that will guarantee success in our attempt to convince listeners of the truth of the gospel of Jesus Christ is misguided. It is never a particular method which convinces people that Jesus of Nazareth is the messianic Son of God, the Savior and Kyrios whose death on the cross atoned the sins of the world. There is no fool-proof method for successful missionary work, no method that is "simple and straightforward so as to respond even to the most inexperienced or careless handling" and is thus "safeguarded against every sort of accident."[27]

Mission and God's power. The cause of missionary "success" is not rhetorical brilliance, refined communication strategies or any other method or technique of evangelism or church administration. The effective cause of people coming to faith in Jesus Christ and becoming active members of local communities of followers of Jesus is the power of God and of the Holy Spirit (see sec. 6.7). Content is more important than rhetoric, substance is more consequential than form, the presence of God is more effective than the communication techniques of the missionary or preacher. The immense growth of the church in China demonstrates this point: millions of people found faith in Jesus Christ in a very hostile environment in which most pastors had been silenced, often through imprisonment, in which theological seminaries and other training facilities had been closed, in which public preaching was illegal and severely punished, in which there were no Chinese Christian seminaries, organizations or experts who advised the churches, and in which foreign missionaries had been forced to leave the country.

Precisely because content is more important than method, and because it is God and his Spirit who speak in the proclamation of the news of Jesus Christ and who cause people to come to faith, neither the gospel nor God

---

[27]Thus the definition of "fool-proof" in the *Oxford English Dictionary*.

and his Spirit should be taken for granted.[28] If we use a standard model of communication,[29] the source or communicator formulates a message that is transmitted via a gatekeeper or opinion leader to a receiver or audience. The gatekeeper (e.g., a journalist) sends the message in connection with his or her knowledge of reality to the audience. The audience or receiver sends feedback to the source of the communication. At the same time there is feedback from the gatekeeper to the source and from the receiver to the gatekeeper. In communication, particularly in mass communication, "noise" is a further element: the transmission of a message is generally accompanied by disturbances, unwanted stimuli that can influence the accuracy of the message, for example, static interference during a phone conversation or hecklers who interrupt a speaker.

Most Christian communication models define the "sender" or communicator of the message as the missionary, evangelist, pastor or the Christian who seeks to speak with others about the gospel of Jesus Christ. All too often God is "taken for granted" in the construction of an "effective" communication strategy in which the preacher or missionary seeks to "create" understanding in the listeners. In view of the position that Paul takes on principle, this view needs to be thoroughly rethought. Paul asserts that God is the primary communicator, while he and other missionaries are *apostoloi*, "sent ones" or "envoys" of God; they are his "coworkers." They are messengers who have been "sent," which means that they are the medium or channel of the message. They are not the source of the message themselves. God and Jesus Christ are the source of the message, and they speak as the gospel is being proclaimed.

> We also constantly give thanks to God for this, that when you received
> the word of God that you heard from us, you accepted it not as a human

---

[28]Viggo Søgaard, *Media in Church and Mission: Communicating the Gospel* (Pasadena, Calif.: Carey Library, 1993), p. 26, writes: "permeating all our ministry are certain constant factors which set Christian communication apart. It is on this basis that we propose our strategy, and as such it is not necessary for us to make constant references to the work of the Holy spirit [sic]. It is taken for granted." While "constant references" to the powerful presence of God in the preaching of is Word may indeed not be necessary, it certainly needs explication and explanation at key points.

[29]See Michael Burgoon et al., *Human Communication*, 3rd ed. (London: Sage, 1994), pp. 26-31; Denis McQuail, *McQuail's Mass Communication Theory*, 5th ed. (Thousand Oaks, Calif.: Sage, 2005), pp. 49-76. See also Søgaard, *Media in Church and Mission*, pp. 39-51; Schnabel, *Early Christian Mission*, 2:1321.

word but as what it really is, God's word, which is also at work in you believers. (1 Thess 2:13)

What, after all, is Apollos? And what is Paul? Only servants, through whom you came to believe—as the Lord has assigned to each his task. I planted the seed, Apollos watered it, but God has been making it grow. So neither the one who plants nor the one who waters is anything, but only God, who makes things grow. The one who plants and the one who waters have one purpose, and they each will be rewarded according to their own labor. For we are God's co-workers; you are God's field, God's building. (1 Cor 3:5-9 TNIV)

All this is from God, who reconciled us to himself through Christ, and has given us the ministry of reconciliation; that is, in Christ God was reconciling the world to himself, not counting their trespasses against them, and entrusting the message of reconciliation to us. So we are ambassadors for Christ, since God is making his appeal through us; we entreat you on behalf of Christ, be reconciled to God. For our sake he made him to be sin who knew no sin, so that in him we might become the righteousness of God. (2 Cor 5:18-21)

The offer of salvation as liberation from guilt and sin, the offer of hope for a perfect existence after death, the offer of a transformed life of victory over impure passions, and the offer of fellowship with people from all walks of life were attractive and powerful convictions and realities that Paul could place in the center of his missionary proclamation. However, since salvation, hope, transformation and fellowship are all predicated on Jesus' death on the cross, Paul insisted that the latter is the foundation for everything else that the teachers of the church explain, and thus the center of missionary preaching. And this is precisely the problem that no communication theory can solve: despite the attractiveness of important elements of the beliefs of the early Christians, the central emphasis on Jesus the crucified Jewish Messiah, Savior and Lord was and remained a "scandal" for Jewish audiences and "nonsense" for Greek audiences (1 Cor 1:18-23; 2:14; 3:19). Paul can be optimistic about Jews and Greeks actually accepting faith in Jesus the crucified Savior only because he knows that the almighty God himself speaks when the news of Jesus is being proclaimed.[30] Conversions to faith in Jesus the crucified Savior are always a miracle, an event or a process caused by the effective power of the Spirit of the gracious and merciful God of Israel.

Certainly the presentation of the gospel should be as effective as possible, if we understand "effective" in the sense of "powerful in effect." In other words missionaries, evangelists and teachers of the church want to proclaim and explain the news of Jesus in ways God's Spirit can use to powerful effect. However, missionary proclamation is never "effective" in the sense that it produces the conditions in which conversions occur, let alone the event of conversion itself. Missionaries, evangelists and teachers who have understood both the scandal of the cross and the irreplaceable and foundational significance of the news of Jesus the crucified and risen Messiah and Savior will not rely on strategies, models, methods or techniques. They rely on the presence of God when they proclaim Jesus Christ, and on the effective power of the Holy Spirit. This dependence on God rather than on methods liberates them from following every new fad, from using only one particular method, from using always the same techniques, and from copying methods and techniques from others whose ministry is deemed successful. Preachers of the gospel who understand that the primary cause of people coming to faith in Jesus the crucified Savior and Lord is the power of God become truly flexible, able to become a Jew for Jews and a Greek for Greeks. They are authentically flexible because they are motivated not by the pressure of demonstrating the "effectiveness" of their methods or the "success" of their ministry but by their commitment to God and by their commitment to the people they seek to reach with the news of Jesus, a twofold commitment that is characterized by sacrificial love, faith and hope.

Targeting homogeneous people groups. One of the methods that has been suggested as an effective means of missionary work and church planting is the consistent focus on "people groups" or "homogeneous units," defined as "a section of society in which all the members have some characteristic in common."[31] Another, more precise description of the "ho-

---

[30]See Schnabel, *Early Christian Mission*, 2:1356-58. See Reinhold Reck, *Kommunikation und Gemeindeaufbau* (Stuttgart: Katholisches Bibelwerk, 1991), pp. 180-83.

[31]Donald A. McGavran, *Understanding Church Growth*, 3rd ed., rev. and ed. C. P. Wagner (Grand

mogeneous unit" defines it "a significantly large sociological grouping of individuals who perceive themselves to have a common affinity for one another" where this "common affinity" can be based "on any combination of culture, language, religion, economics, ethnicity, residence, occupation, class, caste, life situation, or other significant characteristics which provide ties which bind the individuals in the group together."[32] Missiologists connected with Donald McGavran, who introduced the "people group principle" into missiological thinking,[33] proceed from the assumption that "people like to become Christians without crossing racial, linguistic, or class barriers."[34] It is claimed that "church planters who enable unbelievers to become Christians without crossing such barriers are much more effective than those who place them in their way."[35] This claim formulates the primary rationale for the "people group principle": it makes missionary work effective. This conviction reflects the assumption that the main barrier to conversion is not religious or theological but sociological.

The popularity of the "people group principle" is waning among missiologists. However, it still serves as an example for how contemporary missionary methods can, or should, be related to the New Testament. Evaluating the "people group principle," the pragmatic argument of effectiveness clearly is not sufficient to justify its use in missionary work

Rapids: Eerdmans, 1990), p. 69.

[32]C. Peter Wagner, "Homogeneous Unit Principle," *EDWM*, p. 455.

[33]See Donald Anderson McGavran, *The Bridges of God: A Study in the Strategy of Missions* (New York: Friendship Press, 1955); *Understanding Church Growth* (Grand Rapids: Eerdmans, 1970), and the influential plenary address at the Lausanne Congress on World Evangelism (1974) by Ralph D. Winter, "The Highest Priority: Cross-Cultural Evangelism," in *Let the Earth Hear His Voice*, Official Reference Volume: Papers and Responses, ed. J. D. Douglas (Minneapolis: World Wide Publications, 1975), pp. 213-41.

[34]Thus the famous dictum of McGavran; cf. McGavran, *Understanding Church Growth*, p. 163, repeated ibid., p. 166. Thus Ed Stetzer, *Planting New Churches in a Postmodern Age* (Nashville: Broadman & Holman, 2003), pp. 177-85, advises church planters that they have to choose a "focus group," i.e., select the group that the church will reach, which happens through a process of profiling factors, in a North American context: "values, income, education, and lifestyle preferences" (p. 178).

[35]McGavran, *Understanding Church Growth*, p. 168. Cf. also H. Cornell Goerner, *All Nations in God's Purpose: What the Bible Teaches About Missions* (Nashville: Broadman, 1979); Edward R. Dayton and David A. Fraser, *Planning Strategies for World Evangelization* (Grand Rapids: Eerdmans, 1980), pp. 107-92; C. Peter Wagner and Edward R. Dayton, "The People-Group Approach to World Evangelization," in *Unreached Peoples '81* (Elgin, Ill.: Cook, 1981), pp. 19-35; Thom S. Rainer, *The Book of Church Growth: History, Theology, and Principles* (Nashville: Broadman, 1993); C. Peter Wagner, "Church Growth Movement," *EDWM*, pp. 199-200.

that aims at establishing new communities of followers of Jesus. Paul's letters provide us both with a paradigm and with a biblical principle for evaluating methods of proclaiming the news of Jesus and of establishing communities of followers of Jesus. As we have seen,[36] most clearly in my analysis of passages from Paul's first letter to the Christians in Corinth, Paul insists on the fundamental significance of the proclamation of Jesus the crucified and risen Messiah and Savior not only for one's personal salvation[37] but for all areas of the life of the new converts and of the church as a whole, including the use of rhetoric in missionary sermons. Paul's emphasis on the unity of a local congregation in which Jews, proselytes, God-fearers and Greek and Romans who have come to faith in Jesus Christ live and learn and worship together proceeds from the foundational significance of the missionary message he preaches. Since there is "one God, the Father, from whom are all things and for whom we exist, and one Lord, Jesus Christ, through whom are all things and through whom we exist" (1 Cor 8:6), the unity of the believers in a local congregation follows.[38]

The unity of the believers in a local church, whether they are new converts from a Jewish or Greek background, is the subject of Paul's narrative concerning developments in the church in Antioch:

> But when Cephas came to Antioch, I opposed him to his face, because he stood self-condemned; for until certain people came from James, he used to eat with the Gentiles. But after they came, he drew back and kept himself separate for fear of the circumcision faction. And the other Jews joined him in this hypocrisy, so that even Barnabas was led astray by their hypocrisy. But when I saw that they were not acting consistently with the truth of the gospel, I said to Cephas before them all, "If you, though a Jew, live like a Gentile and not like a Jew, how can you compel the Gentiles to live like Jews?" (Gal 2:11-14)

---

[36]See particularly sections 2.3, 3.5, 5.5 (pp. 130-39, 189-96, 341-54).

[37]McGavran, *Understanding Church Growth*, p. 168, insists on not removing the "offense of the cross" as one of the basic barriers of becoming Christian.

[38]For a critique of the "church growth movement," see René Padilla, "The Unity of the Church and the Homogeneous Unit Principle," *International Bulletin of Missionary Research* 6, no. 1 (1982): 23-30; and Gary L. McIntosh, ed., *Evaluating the Church Growth Movement: Five Views* (Grand Rapids: Zondervan, 2004).

Paul risked a public clash with Peter in his effort to maintain the unity of Jewish and Greek Christians in the church in Antioch. In the next section (Gal 2:15-21) Paul argues that since both Jews and Gentiles are saved by faith in Jesus Christ apart from the law, the Gentile believers must not be asked to follow the stipulations of the law before they can be bona fide members of God's people, which is the gathering of believers in Jesus Christ. Paul argues that if he were made to accept that Gentile believers should keep the law, his whole life as a Christian and his entire ministry as a missionary who reaches out to Gentiles would become "one long act of transgression."[39] To argue that this means precisely that people from different "people groups" should not be made to cross barriers misses the point entirely: Paul insists that Peter and Barnabas and the other Jewish believers in the church in Antioch must continue to fellowship and worship in the same church as Gentile Christians do, which includes eating meals together. In other words, Paul expects the Jewish believers—whether veteran leaders such as Peter or new Jewish converts—to belong to the same local congregation as the Gentile Christians do.

Paul accuses Peter of hypocrisy because he knows that Peter shares his own theological convictions concerning the abandonment of the barriers that Jews (and indeed the Mosaic law) had erected against Greeks. During the proceedings of the Apostles' Council, Peter had reminded the leaders who were present that

> you know that in the early days God made a choice among you, that I should be the one through whom the Gentiles would hear the message of the good news and become believers. And God, who knows the human heart, testified to them by giving them the Holy Spirit, just as he did to us; and in cleansing their hearts by faith he has made no distinction between them and us. Now therefore why are you putting God to the test by placing on the neck of the disciples a yoke that neither our ancestors nor we have been able to bear? On the contrary, we believe that we will be saved through the grace of the Lord Jesus, just as they will. (Acts 15:7-11)

---

[39]James D. G. Dunn, *A Commentary on the Epistle to the Galatians*, BNTC (London: Black, 1993), p. 143, commenting on Gal 2:18: "But if I build up again the very things that I once tore down, then I demonstrate that I am a transgressor."

Paul did not establish separate local congregations for Jewish and Gentile believers. This would have been certainly convenient and would have saved him a lot of trouble—even his life: Paul risked his life for the collection he organized in the churches in Macedonia and Achaia (and perhaps in the churches in the province of Asia) for the church in Jerusalem (see sec. 1.7 [pp. 112-23]).[40] The collection aimed at demonstrating the unity of the Jewish believers and the churches of Paul's mission in which both Jewish believers and Gentile converts worshiped together, a project which got him arrested in Jerusalem.

The paradigm of Paul's argumentation in Antioch, repeated for the churches in Galatia, would be enough to question the "people group principle," which insists that the most effective manner of missionary work and church planting is not to ask potential converts to cross any barriers. The paradigm of Paul's missionary work and church planting strategy is reinforced by principles he formulates, particularly in 1 Corinthians 12:12-13 and Ephesians 2:11-22.

> For just as the body is one and has many members, and all the members of the body, though many, are one body, so it is with Christ. For in the one Spirit we were all baptized into one body—Jews or Greeks, slaves or free—and we were all made to drink of one Spirit. (1 Cor 12:12-13)

> So then, remember that at one time you Gentiles by birth, called "the uncircumcision" by those who are called "the circumcision"—a physical circumcision made in the flesh by human hands—remember that you were at that time without Christ, being aliens from the commonwealth of Israel, and strangers to the covenants of promise, having no hope and without God in the world. But now in Christ Jesus you who once were far off have been brought near by the blood of Christ. For he is our peace; in his flesh he has made both groups into one and has broken down the dividing wall, that is, the hostility between us. He has abolished the law with its commandments and ordinances, that he might create in himself one new humanity in place of the two, thus making peace, and might reconcile both groups to God in one body through the cross, thus putting to death that hostility through it. So he came and proclaimed peace to you who were far off and peace to those who were near; for through

---

[40]Cf. 1 Cor 16:1-4; 2 Cor 8:1-15; 9:1-5; Rom 15:14-21; cf. Gal 2:10.

him both of us have access in one Spirit to the Father. So then you are no longer strangers and aliens, but you are citizens with the saints and also members of the household of God, built upon the foundation of the apostles and prophets, with Christ Jesus himself as the cornerstone. In him the whole structure is joined together and grows into a holy temple in the Lord; in whom you also are built together spiritually into a dwelling place for God. (Eph 2:11-22)

Clearly, the unity of the church is a basic theological and missiological principle for Paul—not only in general terms for the church worldwide but for the local gatherings of the followers of Jesus.

Proponents of the homogeneous-unit principle claim that this approach to missionary work and church planting describes "the way in which unbelievers become followers of Jesus Christ and responsible members of His church," not the ideal way in which Christians should relate to each other.[41] This explanation separates missionary work and church planting from an "ideal" church in a manner which leaves the question unanswered when this ideal should be reached or whether it can be realized at all. Also, this explanation is a typically Protestant explanation—Protestants seem to have accepted the fragmentation of the church in countless denominations, independent churches and "parachurch" ministries,[42] with little or no desire to move beyond general references to the unity of the church, regarding the formation of local congregations that truly embody the unity in diversity as an unrealistic vision.

Paul did not establish separate local congregations for Gentile slaves and for Gentile freedmen, or separate congregations for the members of the social elite and for the vast majority of the poor. There is no evidence for the claim that "Paul could see that it was natural for people to come to Christ together with their own kind."[43] Paul established local assemblies

---

[41]C. Peter Wagner, *Church Growth and the Whole Gospel: A Biblical Mandate* (San Francisco: Harper & Row, 1987), p. 168; cf. Gilliland, *Pauline Theology and Mission Practice*, p. 206.

[42]For helpful discussions of parachurch agencies cf. John W. Nyquist, "Parachurch Agencies and Mission," *EDWM*, pp. 722-23; Jerry White, *The Church and the Parachurch: An Uneasy Marriage* (Portland, Ore.: Multnomah, 1983); Wesley K. Willmer et al., *The Prospering Parachurch: Enlarging the Boundaries of God's Kingdom* (San Francisco: Jossey-Bass, 1998).

[43]Gilliland, *Pauline Theology and Mission Practice*, p. 205.

of followers of Jesus irrespective of their ethnic, cultural or social identity, insisting on the unity of the local expression of the people of God.

Donald McGavran comes close to accusing Paul of not understanding this "universal principle" of church growth and of being responsible for the resistance of Jews to the gospel throughout history. He writes,

> As soon as numerous Gentiles had become Christians, however, to be a Christian often involved for a Jew leaving the Jewish people and joining a conglomerate society. Admitting Gentiles created a racial barrier for Jews. Indeed, it is a reasonable conjecture that as soon as becoming a Christian meant joining a house church full of Gentiles and sitting down to agape feasts where on occasion pork was served, would-be Jewish converts found the racial and cultural barriers too high and turned sorrowfully away. Jews have been largely resistant to the gospel ever since.[44]

A similar confidence in modern methods underlies the assertions of a Christian advertising specialist who suggests that

> back in Jerusalem where the church started, God performed a miracle there on the day of Pentecost. They didn't have the benefits of buttons and media, so God had to do a little supernatural work there. But today, with our technology, we have available to us the opportunity to create the same kind of interest in a secular society.[45]

If we understand Paul's missionary work and his "missionary theology" correctly, however, the positive concern for attractiveness and numerical growth must not be allowed to dodge the question of the logic of the gospel of one true God and one crucified and risen Savior, and its consequences for the identity and the life of local congregations.

It is revealing that Ralph Winter, in his plenary address at the Lausanne Congress on World Evangelism in 1974, writes that after having struggled with the question of the unity of the church, he now realizes "that Christian unity cannot be healthy if it infringes upon Christian liberty."[46] He argues that "unity does not have to require uniformity" and refers to the analogy of a symphony orchestra in which not everybody plays the violin. He misses the

---

[44]McGavran, *Understanding Church Growth*, p. 170.
[45]Quoted by Os Guinness, *Dining with the Devil: The Megachurch Movement Flirts with Modernity* (Grand Rapids: Baker, 1993), p. 38.
[46]Winter, "Highest Priority," p. 237; for his analogy of the orchestra, see ibid.

point that for an orchestra to be an orchestra, the violin players and the cello players, the clarinets and the oboes, the flutes and the trumpets and the timpani all sit and play in the same symphony hall. If the violins were playing on the ground floor, the cellos on the second floor, the clarinets on the roof, the oboes and the flutes in a building across the street, and the trumpets and the timpani in a building on the other side of town, you certainly have liberty and you have eliminated uniformity, but you do not have an orchestra. The arguments based on liberty and freedom, coupled with the criteria of effectiveness and success, are corollaries of the individualistic and the pragmatic premises of Western culture (and in particular of Western business models and management tools) rather than corollaries of the gospel of the one true God and the one Savior Jesus Christ. Christian liberty properly understood is not the freedom to do what I personally prefer but freedom from the curse of the law, freedom from the power of sin, freedom from the values of a secular culture that are not in tune with the revealed will of God, freedom from the focus on myself, freedom to serve others.

Regarding the unity of the church, consisting of believers who may be Jews or Gentiles, slaves or free, men or women, black or white, rich or poor, Paul gives us not only a paradigm and fundamental principles. He formulates this deep conviction as a rule as well.

> Now I appeal to you, brothers and sisters, by the name of our Lord Jesus Christ, that all of you be in agreement and that there be no divisions among you, but that you be united in the same mind and the same purpose. (1 Cor 1:10)

> If then there is any encouragement in Christ, any consolation from love, any sharing in the Spirit, any compassion and sympathy, make my joy complete: be of the same mind, having the same love, being in full accord and of one mind. Do nothing from selfish ambition or conceit, but in humility regard others as better than yourselves. Let each of you look not to your own interests, but to the interests of others. Let the same mind be in you that was in Christ Jesus. (Phil 2:1-5)

> I therefore, the prisoner in the Lord, beg you to lead a life worthy of the calling to which you have been called, with all humility and gentleness, with patience, bearing with one another in love, making every effort to maintain the unity of the Spirit in the bond of peace. There is one body and one Spirit, just as you were called to the one hope of your calling, one

Lord, one faith, one baptism, one God and Father of all, who is above all and through all and in all. (Eph 4:1-6)

It is simply incorrect to state that "nothing in the Bible, for instance, requires that in becoming a Christian a believer must cross linguistic, racial, and class barriers. To require that they do so is to take the spotlight off the three essential biblical acts and focus it on human requirements."[47] When people become Christians, they not only experience repentance, salvation and transformation on a personal level. They experience repentance, salvation and transformation in all areas of their worldview, their cultural values, their social affiliations and so on. Neither Paul's theology nor his missionary practice provides even the slightest grounds for justifying the apartheid of people in a local congregation.[48] As Paul is a debtor "both to Greeks and to barbarians, both to the wise and to the foolish" (Rom 1:14), he reaches people wherever they are willing to listen—in the synagogue or in a lecture hall, in the central plaza of the city or in a private house—and he gathers those who believe into one local community of followers of Jesus.

Finally, the symbolic world of Paul's missionary work confirms the paradigm, the principles and the rules of the accounts in his letters and in the book of Acts. Paul uses numerous metaphors to describe the identity of the local gathering of the followers of Jesus,[49] many of which unequivocally imply the unity of the believers who come together to worship God and to learn from Jesus Christ. This is immediately evident in the following images: the church is a local assembly of the citi-

---

[47]McGavran, *Understanding Church Growth*, pp. 168-69. The "three essential biblical acts" are accepting the truth that we are sinners whose salvation depends entirely on accepting what Jesus Christ has done on the cross, repenting of sins and turning from them, and openly confessing Christ before others in baptism (ibid., p. 168).

[48]Aubrey Malphurs, *Planting Growing Churches for the 21st Century: A Comprehensive Guide for New Churches and Those Desiring Renewal* (Grand Rapids: Baker, 2004), p. 169, defends McGavran against the charge of advocating a racist church growth model.

[49]See Paul S. Minear, *Images of the Church in the New Testament* (Philadelphia: Westminster, 1960); Jürgen Roloff, *Die Kirche im Neuen Testament*, Grundrisse zum Neuen Testament 10 (Göttingen: Vandenhoeck & Ruprecht, 1993), pp. 86-143; Robert Banks, *Paul's Idea of Community: The Early House Churches in Their Historical Setting* (Grand Rapids: Eerdmans, 1980), pp. 26-66; Everett Ferguson, *The Church of Christ: A Biblical Ecclesiology for Today* (Grand Rapids: Eerdmans, 1996), pp. 71-133; James D. G. Dunn, *The Theology of Paul the Apostle* (Grand Rapids: Eerdmans, 1998), pp. 533-64.

zens of God's new society,[50] a family,[51] brothers (and sisters),[52] a letter from Christ,[53] an olive tree,[54] God's plantation and God's building/temple,[55] the body of Christ,[56] the bride of Christ,[57] the people of God,[58] Israel (Gal 6:16), the true circumcision,[59] the descendants of Abraham,[60] the new creation,[61] a fellowship.[62] The local community of the followers of Jesus is not a religious club, a "single-purpose gathering that people join on the basis of self-interest."[63] It is a family in whose gathering the one true and living God is present.

The sociological focus of the church-growth movement is certainly helpful in one respect. It challenges churches to analyze and study the various social groups and subgroups that live in the city, region, province and country. A local church should know which social groups their members belong to, which social groups are underrepresented and which social groups are totally ignored. As the pastors and teachers of the church seek to preach the whole counsel of God, they want to reach all people who are willing to listen to the news of Jesus. They do not want to reach only Jews or only Greeks but both Jews and Greeks, not only slaves or only the free but both slaves and free, not only men or only women but both men and women.

Example: Television as a missionary tool. The use of television as a tool for missionary work and evangelism is a good example that illustrates the

---

[50]Paul uses the Greek term *ekklēsia* ("assembly") sixty-two times.

[51]Gal 4:19: Paul "birthing" the church; 1 Cor 4:15, 17; Phil 2:22; 1 Thess 2:11: Paul as father and the local church as child; cf. the so-called household codes in Col 3:18—4:1; Eph 5:22—6:9; 1 Tim 2:8-15; 6:1-2; Tit 2:1-10.

[52]Cf. Rom 8:29; 14:10, 13, 21; 1 Cor 6:5-8; 8:11-13; 15:58; 1 Thess 1:4; 4:6; Phil 4:1.

[53]2 Cor 3:2-3.

[54]Rom 11:13-24.

[55]1 Cor 3:9, 16; 14:3; 2 Cor 6:16; Rom 14:19; 15:2.

[56]1 Cor 12:12-13, 27; Rom 12:4-5; cf. Gal 3:27-29; 1 Cor 1:13; 6:15; 10:16-17; Rom 10:12.

[57]2 Cor 11:1-2.

[58]Rom 9:25-26; 2 Cor 6:16.

[59]Phil 3:3.

[60]Gal 3:7, 29; 4:7, 28; Rom 4:1, 12, 16; 9:7; 11:1; 2 Cor 11:22.

[61]2 Cor 5:17; Gal 6:15.

[62]1 Cor 1:9; 10:16; 2 Cor 8:4; 13:13; Phil 1:5; 2:1. The Greek term is *koinōnia* which means "close association involving mutual interests and sharing, *association, communion, fellowship, close relationship*" (BDAG 552). The believers are *koinōnia* (2 Cor 1:7; 8:23; Philem 17).

[63]Thus the warning of Paul G. Hiebert and Eloise Meneses Hiebert, *Incarnational Ministry: Planting Churches in Band, Tribal, Peasant, and Urban Societies* (Grand Rapids: Baker, 1995), p. 347.

information and expertise that are needed and the critical questions that need to be asked before decisions concerning the methods of missionary proclamation are made. Viggo Søgaard details the strength and weaknesses of the use of television as follows.[64] The use of public or Christian television, including the closed-circuit television broadcasts from a megachurch to satellite churches, can have the following advantages. (1) Television reaches many people simultaneously. (2) It is effective because it combines audio and visual communication. (3) It tends to draw the audience into the action as people become emotionally involved. (4) Television brings a sense of closeness and intimacy with the persons and the events that appear on the screen. (5) Television suggests an immediacy of the events portrayed. (6) Television is regarded by many if not most people as a credible medium.

The weaknesses of television are: (1) Television is a very expensive medium; since only well-financed groups can afford to produce and to broadcast television programs, it is not a very "democratic" medium because it is controlled by gatekeepers and by commercial conglomerates. (2) Television programs tend to cater to the lowest common denominator in order to successfully reach a wide audience. (3) Television tends to stay away from complex and deep issues. It is mostly used for entertainment. Research indicates that television generally reinforces opinions and beliefs that the viewers already hold, which explains why TV preachers who refrain from challenging viewers' beliefs seem to be so successful. (4) Television lacks continuity as not every viewer watches every program. (5) Television is impersonal, since the "face-to-face" relationship between the performer and the audience is an illusion. (6) Television does not allow the audience to ask questions or voice criticism; opportunities for feedback are delayed in time and used by a small minority of viewers.

In some countries and for some churches the costs involved in using television for missionary and evangelistic work are prohibitive. In other countries and in other churches ministry leaders may come to the conclusion that since the weaknesses of this medium far outweigh the advan-

---

[64]See Søgaard, *Media in Church and Mission*, pp. 114-29, for the following summary and discussion.

tages, television stations or television programs should not be part of the missionary strategy of the church. Others may conclude that television can be effectively used for some purposes but not for others. If it is indeed true that television writes its own rules, requiring "scenery, people, motion, and visual effects" while dealing largely with "simple solutions to human problems,"[65] Christian television will have to produce shows, news and dramas with a high entertainment value and with the goal of making the audience feel good because otherwise people will switch to another channel. Profitability forces Christian television stations to engage in high-pressure fundraising campaigns on the air or through computer generated letters, with prayer requests of members of the audience "handled" by the computer. Here serious questions about authenticity, illusions and truth emerge.[66]

Since television is not a neutral medium that simply duplicates, for example, a worship service for an audience in another building and for people sitting in their La-Z-Boys at home, the interference with reality that television creates needs to be taken seriously. Søgaard comments that

> there is the interference of the television director with his crew and equipment. The television director now resumes the role of a "mediator" between the minister and the viewers. This "unseen" television director decides—by manipulating the use of cameras and microphones—what the viewers are going to see and hear on their living-room television sets. The television director becomes both receiver and transmitter. He or she receives the message from the original sender (the minister), records it, and sends it through the television chain out to another set of receivers, who are separated by hundreds of miles, and are in totally different environments. The communication process involved is totally different from the one in the church itself.[67]

---

[65]Ibid., pp. 118-20.

[66]For a critique of the negative effects of television cf. Malcolm Muggeridge, *Christ and the Media* (Grand Rapids: Eerdmans, 1977); Virginia Stem Owens, *The Total Image, or, Selling Jesus in the Modern Age* (Grand Rapids: Eerdmans, 1980); William F. Fore, *Television and Religion: The Shaping of Faith, Values, and Culture* (Minneapolis: Augsburg, 1987); John Stott, *Between Two Worlds: The Art of Preaching in the Twentieth Century* (Grand Rapids: Eerdmans, 1987), pp. 70-76.

[67]Søgaard, *Media in Church and Mission*, p. 124, referring to Johan G. Hahn, "Liturgy on Television or 'Television-Liturgy,' " in *Media Development 3* (London: World Association for Christian Communication, 1984), pp. 9-11.

Television can be helpful in providing information and background concerning the beliefs of Christians and the content of the Bible. But it can never replace the consistent proclamation of the news of Jesus with arguments and emphases that are adapted to the particular audience, expecting the listeners to give immediate feedback in terms of questions that need to be addressed or of a positive response of listeners who want to know how they can become Christians. Paul became a Jew when he proclaimed the gospel to Jewish audiences, and he became a Gentile when he preached before pagans. Television preachers cannot do that, they are "somebody for everybody" in the impersonal medialand. Wise missionaries and church leaders will therefore insist on a media mix that minimizes the weaknesses and harnesses the strength of the medium of television. If the medium of television determines that there should be no extended times of prayer in a worship service and no extended readings from Scripture, because both liturgical practices are unsuitable for a viewing audience, it seems obvious that such media requirements do not trump the identity of the community of followers of Jesus who call on God in prayer and who read the Word of God. And if the only demands that "Christian television" make on the viewing audience are financial contributions, the authenticity of the fellowship of the followers of God's people has completely fallen victim to marketing forces and to the financial burdens that this medium places on people.

Methods and following Jesus Christ. Missionaries and evangelists, pastors and teachers should not be motivated by what they see everyone else doing or what "works" in the ministry of a "successful" colleague. They should not be motivated by mere novelty or by what seems attractive to the greatest number of people. And they should certainly not become dependent on some particular method, on a specific communication strategy in the sense that they become convinced that a particular method or "strategy" guarantees "success." Missionaries and church planters from the technological societies in the West face the temptation of placing their faith and confidence in methods and techniques. The first and the main question is not which method promises the best results, but which method corresponds most closely with the news of Jesus the risen and crucified Messiah and Savior. When missionaries and church planters think that there are strategies and methods which guarantee results, they have fallen prey to the utopia that human beings always get what they want. And they underestimate the adverse effects of technology on the missionary, on converts and on the churches that are being established.

If missionaries adopted a consistently "capitalist" approach to missionary work, they might simply decide to buy converts: if the power of money guarantees "results" in the marketplace, why should we not use the immense financial resources of Western churches to give money (or a house, car or computer) to "seekers" if they promise to stay in the new church for at least a year? Fortunately, such a suggestion would quickly and generally be regarded as unethical and as a contradiction to the gospel. This example demonstrates, however, that what works is not automatically what missionaries and church planters should be doing. The fundamental criterion for missionary and evangelistic ministry is not the perceived (or even real) effectiveness but the connection with the message of the gospel, which speaks of repentance of sin, of faith in the one true and living God and in Jesus the crucified and living Savior, of love for and commitment to God, to the Lord Jesus Christ, and to the Holy Spirit. All missionary methods, whatever their pedigree or their promise, must be subjected to the compatibility test in which the news of Jesus Messiah and Lord is the benchmark for evaluating its appropriateness for gospel ministry.

All this also means that the value of missionaries in particular and of preachers in general cannot be established on the basis of their rhetorical competence, argumentative brilliance, methodological expertise or technological savvy, or on the basis of the quantitative "success" of their work. The caliber of Christian workers is solely determined on the basis of their faithfulness to the gospel of Jesus, the crucified Messiah and Savior (1 Cor 3:1-23).

The symbolical world of Paul's description of the work of the missionaries and teachers of the church is instructive. Missionaries and teachers are "servants" (Gk *diakonoi*), God's "coworkers" (Gk *synergoi*), farm hands who plant and water (1 Cor 3:5-9). Missionaries and the teachers of the church are valued not on the basis of the number of their converts or the size of their church but on the basis of their faithfulness to the gospel of Jesus, the crucified and risen Messiah and Savior. In the light of Paul's description of the functional identity of the teachers and the leaders of the church, the praise and attention that is heaped on individual preachers owes more to the star-struck pop culture of our day than to the logic of the gospel. Observers have repeatedly pointed out that evangelicals seem to be enamored with their high-profile stars. The humility of Billy Graham was never in doubt. Younger evangelical leaders may not promote their star appeal themselves, but some do not seem to mind when they are cheered. Sometimes the craving for attention and the sense of self-importance is rather transparent. Why would a pastor of a megachurch otherwise point out in a nationally televised interview that he is being regularly called by the White House? Why would webmasters of some megachurches suggest that it is a privilege to have one's picture taken with "the pastor"? Should high-profile missionaries, evangelists and pastors establish independent ministries whose title includes their personal names? It is quite conceivable that the Jewish Christian "conservatives" in Jerusalem who opposed Paul on theological grounds called his missionary team "Paul of Tarsus Ministries." Whether Paul would have used such a name seems rather unlikely, given his critique of self-commendation (cf. 2 Cor 3:1; 10:12, 18), his insistence that servants of God commend themselves by their great endurance in afflictions, hardships and calamities (2 Cor 6:4) and by his self-introduction as "slave" of Jesus Christ (Rom 1:1).

The missionaries, teachers and preachers of the church are and remain sinners saved by God's grace and servants of Jesus Christ who labor for the glory of God and whose "success"—evaluated from the eternal perspective of God's Day of Judgment—is the result of the power of the Spirit of God, who honors their faithfulness to the truth of the gospel of the crucified Jesus Christ. It is only on the Day of Judgment that we will know what is valuable and what is worthless, the criterion for "value" being faithfulness to the message of the crucified and risen Jesus Christ. Visible success may not mean much at all—note the "wealth" of the church in Laodicea (Rev 3:14-20)—faithfulness to Christ crucified means everything, "in the long run" under the horizon of the coming day of God's judgment where his "coworkers" will be held accountable.

There is much more that can be discussed: the migration of people from many ethnic and cultural backgrounds often to our own neighborhoods; the segregation of listeners according to age group or education, often in neglect of the family unit; the disappearance of traditional family structures in the West; the role of women in ministry; the opportunities for retired seniors in the third phrase of their lives; the role of money; the impact of digital forms of communication. But this book is already too long. Biblical scholars and missiologists, pastors and missionaries will continually face the challenge of assessing contemporary developments in the light of the paradigms, principles and rules of Scripture as they fulfill Jesus Christ's commission to take the good news to all people.

6.4 THE TEACHING OF THE FOLLOWERS OF JESUS

Paul spent much of his time as a missionary teaching the new converts (see secs. 3.5-7 [pp. 190-201] and 4.6 [pp. 236-48]). Is Paul's twofold focus of theological and ethical instruction, with theological instruction being foundational and thus primary, a paradigm, a principle or a rule? It is certainly a paradigm: Paul's letters consistently have this twofold focus. In his letters to the Christians in Galatia and Rome he first focuses on what we may call theology (Gal 1—4; Rom 1—11) before he draws out general and specific consequences of the gospel for the life of the believers and of the church (Gal 5—6; Rom 12—15). In his first letter to the Christians in Corinth, he addresses ethical problems of the new believers by deriving general guidelines and specific solutions from theology, that is, from the truth of the gospel that he had preached in Corinth and the Corinthian Christians know. When I speak of a Pauline paradigm of focusing teaching on theology and on ethics, I do not imply that each is a compartmentalized discipline. Paul's theological discussion in Romans 1—11 includes sections that are intensely ethical (Rom 6—8). And his ethical discussion in 1 Corinthians is saturated with theological arguments. Still, the distinction between what followers of Jesus believe and how they live is a valid one, and Paul's example suggests that missionaries and pastors teach in both areas.

The fact that Paul repeatedly mentions teachers as an integral part of each local congregation[68] establishes a principle: when followers of Jesus

---

[68]Cf. Rom 12:7; 1 Cor 12:28-29; 14:6; Gal 6:6; Eph 4:11; 1 Tim 3:2.

gather in their weekly meetings, they are taught from the Scriptures (the Old Testament),[69] from the Jesus tradition[70] and from the foundational traditions of the apostles[71] (among them Paul himself) who explicate the meaning of the life, death and resurrection of Jesus the Messiah and Savior. Christians come together not for entertainment but for instruction and worship. The phrase "do you not know," which Paul uses fourteen times,[72] refers to both the theological information and ethical knowledge which Christians were familiar with, whether they fully understood all the ramifications or not. The same is true when Paul refers to the traditions that the believers have been taught,[73] to various confessional formulas,[74] perhaps to hymnic texts[75] and to doxologies[76] that he includes in his letters.

Unavoidably there was the expectation that the teachers of the new believers would have mastered and were responsible for the traditions of the church. This explains why "it is not surprising that teachers are the first of the regular ministries to take on a more professional aura" since their time-consuming responsibilities "might well require financial support."[77]

---

[69]Cf. 2 Tim 3:16 and the numerous quotations from the Old Testament in Paul's letters. Cf. Moisés Silva, "Old Testament in Paul," *DPL*, pp. 630-42; Gregory K. Beale and D. A. Carson, eds., *Commentary on the New Testament Use of the Old Testament* (Grand Rapids: Baker, 2007).

[70]Seyoon Kim, "Jesus, Sayings of," *DPL*, pp. 474-91; John M. G. Barclay, "Jesus and Paul," *DPL*, pp. 492-503; David Wenham, *Paul: Follower of Jesus or Founder of Christianity?* (Grand Rapids: Eerdmans, 1995).

[71]Michael B. Thompson, "Tradition," *DPL*, pp. 943-45; F. F. Bruce, *Tradition Old and New* (Exeter, U.K.: Paternoster, 1970); James I. H. McDonald, *Kerygma and Didache: The Articulation and Structure of the Earliest Christian Message*, SNTSMS 37 (1980; reprint, Cambridge: Cambridge University Press, 2004), pp. 101-25.

[72]Rom 6:3, 16; 7:1; 11:2; 1 Cor 3:16; 5:2; 6:2, 3, 9, 15, 16, 19; 9:13, 24.

[73]1 Cor 11:2, 23-26; 2 Thess 2:15; 3:6. Cf. I. H. Marshall, "Lord's Supper," *DPL*, pp. 569-75; Thomas R Schreiner, *Paul, Apostle of God's Glory in Christ: A Pauline Theology* (Downers Grove, Ill.: InterVarsity Press, 2001), pp. 390-91.

[74]Cf. 1 Cor 12:3; 15:3-5; Rom 10:9-10; 1 Tim 3:16. Cf. Julie L. Wu, "Liturgical Elements," *DPL*, pp. 655-65.

[75]Cf. Col 1:15-20; Phil 2:6-11; Eph 2:14-16; 5:14; 1 Tim 3:16. Cf. Ralph P. Martin, "Hymns, Hymn Fragments, Songs, Spiritual Songs," *DPL*, pp. 419-23.

[76]Cf. Rom 1:25; 9:5; 11:33-36; 16:25-27; 2 Cor 1:3-11; 11:31; Gal 1:5; Eph 1:3-14; 3:21; Phil 4:20; 1 Tim 1:17; 6:16; 2 Tim 4:18.

[77]Dunn, *Theology of Paul the Apostle*, p. 582. Note Gal 6:6: "Those who are taught the word must share in all good things with their teacher," and 1 Tim 5:17-18: "Let the elders who rule well be considered worthy of double compensation [honor], especially those who labor in preaching and teaching; for the scripture says, 'You shall not muzzle an ox while it is treading out the grain,' and, 'The laborer deserves to be paid.' " The term *timē*, usually translated as "honor," means also "compensation," which in 1 Tim 5:17 is the contextual meaning (BDAG, p. 1005 no. 3; NRSV has "compensation" in the margin).

Paul formulates the task of teaching also in the form of imperatives, that is, a rule for the leaders of the churches.[78]

The work of missionaries in the nineteenth and twentieth centuries has generally placed a consistent emphasis on teaching the new believers in the newly established churches.[79] The reason for this is linked with the nature of missionary work, which proclaims the "news" of Jesus and is thus inherently educational. And it is connected with the Great Commission in Matthew 28:19-20, which emphasizes the teaching of new disciples.[80] Missionaries and church planters teach in personal encounters with other individuals. They teach the Bible in the homes of people who have expressed interest in the gospel (or in their own homes). Once a fellowship of followers of Jesus has been established, they teach in the room or in the building in which the new church meets. They may use Bible correspondence courses as an evangelistic tool or as a instructional tool for new Christians.[81] Radio programs and in particular literature ministries also aim at teaching new converts, as do translation projects that seek to provide the Bible or at least parts of the Bible to Christians in their own language.

Established churches traditionally focus on teaching as well: in the preaching services on Sunday morning and in educational programs such as Sunday school or adult Bible fellowship classes, catechism classes, baptismal classes, mid-week Bible studies, small group Bible studies, youth group meetings, Bible camps, conferences (for men, women, pastors, theologians, etc.) and other educational opportunities.[82]

---

[78]Cf. 1 Tim 4:11; 6:2; Tit 2:1, 3.

[79]Roland Allen and Charles Gore, *Educational Principles and Missionary Methods: The Application of Educational Principles to Missionary Evangelism* (London: Robert Scott, 1919); Roland Allen, *Education in the Native Church* (London: World Dominion Press, 1926); and Peter F. Penner, ed., *Theological Education as Mission* (Schwarzenfeld, Germany: Neufeld Verlag, 2005).

[80]See Robert W. Ferris, "Educational Mission Work," *EDWM*, p. 303. Cf. Perry G. Downs, *Teaching for Spiritual Growth* (Grand Rapids: Zondervan, 1994).

[81]See Justice C. Anderson, "Theological Education by Extension," *EDWM*, p. 944; Ralph D. Winter, ed., *Theological Education by Extension* (Pasadena, Calif.: William Carey Library, 1969); Wayne C. Weld, *The World Directory of Theological Education by Extension* (Pasadena, Calif.: William Carey Library, 1973); Vergil Gerber, ed., *Discipling Through Theological Education by Extension: A Fresh Approach to Theological Education in the 1980s* (Chicago: Moody, 1980).

[82]See Kendig Brubaker Cully, ed., *The Westminster Dictionary of Christian Education* (Philadelphia: Westminster, 1963); Bruce P. Powers, ed., *Christian Education Handbook* (Nashville: Broadman & Holman, 1996); Michael J. Anthony, ed., *Evangelical Dictionary of Christian Education* (Grand Rapids: Baker Academic, 2001); Michael J. Anthony, ed., *Introducing Christian Education: Foundations for the Twenty-First Century* (Grand Rapids: Baker Academic, 2001).

Finally, teaching takes place in institutional settings: in discipleship training centers, Bible colleges, seminaries and divinity schools at universities.[83] In most countries the national church(es) or missionary agencies maintain training institutions for Christian workers—pastors, ministry leaders, educators, counselors, missionaries.

6.5 THE PURPOSE AND THE WORK OF THE LOCAL CHURCH

For Paul the main purpose of the local gatherings of the followers of Jesus is twofold: edification through instruction,[84] and meeting with Jesus Christ through the singing of psalms, hymns and spiritual songs, and through the celebration of the Lord's Supper.[85] The leaders of the churches—the pastors who are also teachers (Eph 4:11)—have the task of equipping the believers "for the work of ministry, for building up the body of Christ" so that the believers "come to the unity of the faith and of the knowledge of the Son of God, to maturity, to the measure of the stature of the fullness of Christ" (Eph 4:12-13). Paul's emphasis in this and in other passages establishes the instruction of the followers of Jesus as the primary task of the local church.

Which task is primary: edification through teaching, or meeting with Christ? The answer is that neither is possible without the other. If churches place the emphasis on meeting with Jesus Christ, downplaying instruction, they face the danger that the believers (and the "seekers") who are present are more concerned with having a rich experience rather than being instructed in the Word of God—the problem of the church in Laodicea (Rev 3:14-22). If churches focus on the ministry of the Word and hence on teaching and instruction, downplaying meeting with Jesus Christ, they face the danger of having knowledge but not much love—the problem of the church in Ephesus (Rev 2:1-7). The church in Laodicea certainly had the bigger problem: it is told that Jesus Christ is not even

---

[83]The International Council on Evangelical Theological Education, sponsored by seven continental networks of theological schools under the World Evangelical Fellowship, seeks to "encourage international contact and collaboration among all those concerned for excellence and renewal in evangelical theological education worldwide," cf. <www.icete-edu.org>.

[84]Cf. 1 Cor 14:3-5, 12, 17, 26; 1 Thess 5:11; Eph 4:11-16.

[85]Cf. Eph 5:19-20; Col 3:16. Cf. Peter T. O'Brien, "Church," *DPL*, pp. 129-30; Ferguson, *Church of Christ*, pp. 244-79.

present when they meet. But the orthodox and faithful church in Ephesus is censured for having "fallen" and being in need of repentance. Both are essential for the life of the church: instruction in the Word of God and meeting with Jesus Christ in prayer and song.

If indeed the proclamation of the Word of God is central both for missionary and church work, then Jesus the crucified and risen Messiah and Savior—the embodiment of God's new Word for the people of the new covenant—must be central in the instruction of the followers of Jesus. The reasons for the centrality of Jesus the Messiah and Savior are obvious: he is the climactic center of salvation history and of the Scriptures, he is God's answer to the needs of sinful human beings, he achieved the salvation of sinners, and he is the cause and source of the transformation of sinners.[86]

Evangelism and missionary work. Apart from the tasks of edification and meeting with Christ, the church has the task of making sure that the people in the neighborhood, the city, the region and more remote areas hear the news of Jesus. Since the followers of Jesus in the local congregations love the one true and living God who created the universe, and since they love the Lord Jesus Christ who gave his life to save sinners, and since they are filled with the Holy Spirit who gives them power to be witnesses, they seek to reach the immediate vicinity and the remoter regions with the news of Jesus. This task involves both evangelism and missionary work. Churches have a responsibility to reach the people who live in the neighborhood and the same city with the news of Jesus. And they have a responsibility to help those believers whom God has called to proclaim the news of Jesus in regions and cities that require more extended travel.

This distinction between the local evangelist and the traveling missionary is based on Ephesians 4:11, where Paul mentions "evangelists" between apostles (and prophets) and the pastors (and teachers): "The gifts he gave were that some would be apostles, some prophets, some evangelists, some pastors and teachers."

In the multiethnic and multicultural societies of megacities such as New York City, Chicago, Los Angeles or London, the "local" evangelist may

---

[86]See Colin Smith, "Keeping Christ Central in Preaching," in *Telling the Truth: Evangelizing Postmoderns*, ed. D. A. Carson (Grand Rapids: Zondervan, 2000), pp. 111-22.

have to learn a new culture just as a "foreign" missionary does who travels from Chicago to Banda Aceh in Indonesia or from Seoul to N'Djamena in the Republic of Chad. Whatever term one uses for people who devote their lives to the proclamation of the gospel to people who have not yet heard or who have not yet come to faith in Jesus Christ—all followers of Jesus in the local congregation seek to be the salt of the earth and the light of the world through who they are, through what they say and through how they live, reaching out to the people living around them—just as the messengers of the gospel that the congregation sends to other places.

Church planting and church growth. The paradigm of Paul's missionary work, the principles and the rules concerning the life of the local congregation, and the symbolic world of his description of the church all lead to the conclusion that a local church has the responsibility to reach people with the news of Jesus Christ. If followers of Jesus are indeed light of the world and salt of the earth, their everyday life, transformed by the presence of the power of God and his Spirit, will prompt non-Christians to ask questions. Also, if followers of Jesus indeed believe that faith in Jesus Christ reconciles with God, forgives sin, transforms their lives and gives a firm hope for the future, they would naturally share this news with family and neighbors, with friends and coworkers. They would invite people to their gatherings. They are eager to answer questions. And thus existing churches grow, and new fellowships of followers of Jesus come into existence.

In recent decades the principles of the church-growth movement have been applied to the evangelistic task of the local congregation. The so-called seeker-driven (mega)churches are motivated by the desire to see churches grow. The centrality of the church; the emphasis on making the gospel understood; the desire to reach people with the gospel; the expectation of the (numerical) growth of local congregations; the mobilization of believers who are encouraged to speak to their neighbors, friends and colleagues about God, the gospel and the church; the acknowledgment of the significance of culture are all important and helpful elements.[87]

---

[87]Guinness, *Dining with the Devil*, p. 22; cf. Os Guinness, "Sounding Out the Idols of Church Growth," in *No God But God*, ed. O. Guinness and J. Seel (Chicago: Moody, 1992), pp. 151-74, 152-53.

The following evaluation is intended to provide an example of how the paradigm, principles, rules and symbolic world of Paul's missionary work must inform contemporary efforts of local congregations to reach people in their own culture with the gospel of Jesus Christ.

Some have suggested that

> if the goal is to reach, attract, welcome, serve, include, assimilate, and challenge the generations born after 1965, then that often means a congregation has to (1) excel in presenting the gospel in what is perceived as relevant terms (and that often includes growing weekday ministries); (2) be able to earn a reputation for high quality in worship, teaching, training, and other aspects of congregational life; and (3) provide people with a broad range of attractive choices in worship, leaning, involvement in doing ministry, facilitating their individual personal spiritual pilgrimage, helping them rear children, and finding a sense of community.[88]

Regarding the demand that the presentation of the gospel needs to "excel" in being relevant for particular audiences (such as the contemporary generation of unchurched people), it should be noted that indeed Paul adapts the proclamation of the gospel to the audience before whom he explains the news of Jesus the crucified Savior. Ultimately, however, he did not allow his audiences to determine the terms in which he proclaims the gospel. Paul never downplayed the shameful reality of the cross, although this "news" would clearly not have been perceived as "relevant" by either pagan or Jewish listeners. Paul did not proceed from the felt needs as potential seekers might define them: the pagans of his day where quite happy in their temples, and the Jews certainly did not find the idea of a crucified Messiah entertaining. The paradigm and the principles of Paul's missionary preaching suggest that the question is not what people want but what God has revealed in Jesus Christ.

Regarding the second point, the criterion of the ability to "earn a reputation for high quality in worship, teaching, training" is problematic, not only because the insistence that "relevance, quality, and choices cost money" but because here "quality" is not linked with faithfulness to

---

[88]Lyle E. Schaller, *The Very Large Church: New Rules for Leaders* (Nashville: Abingdon, 2000), p. 31. In fairness to Schaller, we should also note his book *Small Congregation, Big Potential: Ministry in the Small Membership Church* (Nashville: Abingdon, 2003).

the Word of God or with theological or exegetical expertise, but with technology and stage performance. Paul's exposition on the quality of his rhetoric, on the weakness and foolishness of the cross, and on the real locus of God's power reveals this criterion to be highly questionable and defective.

Regarding the third point, providing people with a broad range of attractive choices, observers point out that some megachurches have become almost like self-contained villages that provide "a safe environment which is drug-free and where the ailments of a morally eroded society are kept outside. These complexes are secure, safe, 'gated communities' for the spiritual which are secure from the harsh world outside."[89] Churches are not supermarkets where the customers know what they want and how to get what they want, with money the only criterion for the question whether they can afford what they want. The suggested vision for "very large churches" that offer "choices" allows for a church with consumer-driven services: "The weekend schedule may include five different worship experiences: one for seekers, one for new believers, one for learners, one for those ready to be transformed into disciples, and one for disciples ready to be challenged to become apostles."[90] We miss a choice for seekers who drive Japanese cars (and German cars), a "worship experience" for people with postgraduate degrees (and with low IQs), for blacks (and whites), for legal residents (and immigrants), for people wearing ties (and Hawaii shirts). For Paul the reality of authentic communities of followers of Jesus is not governed by the perceived needs of seekers that need to be met by activities they choose for themselves at the time of their convenience. The concept of the unity of the local church, so emphatically emphasized by Paul is a nonnegotiable principle (1 Cor 12:12-26; Eph 2:11-22), is also formulated as a rule (1 Cor 1:10; Phil 2:2, 5; 3:15) that exposes such suggestions as destructive.

Rather disturbing is the view that "achievement is a product of the combination of high expectations, very high-quality ministries, a sur-

---

[89]David F. Wells, *Above All Earthly Pow'rs: Christ in a Postmodern World* (Grand Rapids: Eerdmans, 2005), p. 292, referring to Patricia Leigh Brown, "Megachurches as Minitowns," *New York Times*, May 9, 2002, p. F1.
[90]Schaller, *Very Large Church*, p. 99.

plus of off-street parking, a creative staff, and an extensive seven-day-a-week program."[91] In this scenario of "effectiveness," neither God nor the Holy Spirit seem to be needed. There are examples of missionaries and church leaders who had high expectations, implemented professional approaches and even had good parking, but failed miserably. High expectations can be arrogant. Low expectations (at least compared with the "expectations" of megachurch pastors) may result from a lack of faith, but sometimes they are based on a realistic assessment of the situation, shared by other Christian leaders. Missionary work and church planting in regions where the majority of the population is atheist or Muslim is but one example. The optimism of "high expectations" is sometimes not much more than market-driven triumphalism that knows nothing about suffering. It seems beyond arrogant to argue that the "vision-driven entrepreneurial pastor" will be successful because "the transformational power of Christianity is a predictable consequence of its being a religion that projects high expectations of anyone who commits to being a disciple of Jesus Christ."[92] In such optimistic visions there is no place for Christian leaders whose high expectations reckon with the real possibility that they will be martyred for their faith and their leadership.

The language of such descriptions is the language of the marketplace. This is a problem in itself, if the business columnist Robert Samuelson is right, who warned that "our corporate elites are awash in empty jargon that masquerades as serious thought."[93] When the buildings of the so-called megachurches include food courts, coffee shops, fast-food restaurants, water slides, climbing walls, gyms and saunas, one realizes that this is an updated version of the missionary theory of the church-growth movement, which stipulates that people do not like to cross barriers. The founders of churches that are driven by the preferences of the seekers identify the latter (at least in the white megachurches) generally as typically suburban, middle-class, relatively wealthy, well-educated baby boomers who enjoy technologically advanced presentations, like pop songs and rock bands—

---

[91]Ibid., p. 112; the following quotations are from ibid., pp. 124-25.
[92]Ibid., p. 125.
[93]Robert Samuelson, quoted in Guinness, *Dining with the Devil*, p. 75.

and, because they are often stressed and in debt, look for help, which the seeker churches assure they can provide.

The local congregation, whatever the size, is not a religious corporation in which all "relevant" people have paid positions, in which the "management" is controlled by quantifiable and projected growth objectives, in which the audience is treated as consumers, in which attractiveness is therefore paramount, and in which the primary service offered is entertainment.[94] In this vision of ministry the centrality of theology, which has been pushed to the periphery, is replaced by claims to specialized and professionalized competence. The criteria and methods for a "successful" ministry are no longer grounded in theology but drawn from sociological and cultural trends.[95]

Church growth and methods. When one reads the literature of the influential "purpose-driven church" movement,[96] the conscious effort to be faithful to the paradigms and principles of the Scriptures, and in particular of the New Testament, stand out. The purpose-driven church is described as "a church health model that provides your pastoral team with a unique, biblically-based approach to establishing, transforming, and maintaining a balanced, growing congregation that seeks to fulfill the God-given purposes of worship, fellowship, discipleship, ministry, and missions."[97] The foundation for this model is explicitly "the Bible— with an intentional emphasis on the Great Commandment (Matthew 22:37-40) and the Great Commission (Matthew 28:19-20)." The em-

---

[94]Paul Hiebert and Eloise Hiebert Menenses *Incarnational Ministry*, pp. 348-49. Note Robert H. Welch, *Church Administration: Creating Efficiency for Effective Ministry* (Nashville: Broadman & Holman, 2005), pp. 123-36, 199, 224-25, 246, 268, 294, 299, who provides an in-depth discussion of "the salary plan" and includes a space utilization plan, a chart for the "inspection and maintenance record," a "daily toilet cleaning checklist," a chart for deciding which files to keep and which to discard, a chart for motion sensors (under the heading "security"), and a parking space planning chart.

[95]See Guinness, *Dining with the Devil*, p. 26: "Discussion of the traditional marks of the church is virtually nonexistent. Instead, methodology is at the center and in control."

[96]See Rick Warren, *The Purpose-Driven Church: Growth Without Compromising Your Message & Mission* (Grand Rapids: Zondervan, 1995); cf. the follow-up title by Doug Fields, *Purpose-Driven Youth Ministry: Nine Essential Foundations for Healthy Growth* (Grand Rapids: Zondervan, 1998). The title of the management study by Perry Pascarella and Mark A. Frohman, *The Purpose-Driven Organization: Unleashing the Power of Direction and Commitment* (San Francisco: Jossey-Bass Publishers, 1989) and the title of the "hands on" book by Daryl Covington, *Purpose Driven Martial Arts* (Blountsville: Fifth Estate, 2006), seem to be a coincidence.

[97]This and the following quotations are from Rick Warren's "PurposeDriven" website <www .purposedriven.com/en-US/Home.htm>.

phasis on worship and fellowship is derived from Matthew 22:37-40, and the emphasis on discipleship, ministry and missions is based on Matthew 28:19-20. It is argued that the balanced combination of these five essential elements are basic for "a healthy, growing, biblically-based church." None of this is new, of course—apart from the packaging and the catchy (trademark protected) slogan "purpose driven." Perhaps some Christians in some countries need strategic packaging in order to become serious about being a Christian. Perhaps some pastors in some countries need catchy slogans in order to emphasize what they should have discovered and taught all along had they studied the New Testament and what theologians had written about the nature and the ministry of the church throughout the ages.

The question that the purpose-driven-church movement asks is certainly appropriate: "How balanced is your church related to these purposes?" The question that proponents of the purpose-driven-church model should ponder is whether this is just one more method that method-driven evangelicals in the West have formulated. Under the tab "common myths," the website PurposeDriven.com disputes that the purpose-driven-church model just chases after a quickly fading fad ("PD is about being biblical and eternal"), that it is limited to boomer seekers ("Purpose Driven is not about a particular style; rather it's about balancing the purposes and establishing a target group to evangelize"), or that it represents a seeker-sensitive approach ("PD does not require any specific method for evangelism or even a seeker-oriented worship service"). However, the fact that the label "PD" is used, that the word *model* is often omitted (the phrase "Purpose Driven" is evidently regarded as self-explanatory), and that the term "Purpose Driven" is capitalized and used as an adjective (e.g., "Purpose Driven congregations" or "PD congregations") suggests that apart from the focus being on the Bible and on what the Bible says about followers of Jesus and their gatherings in local congregations, there is indeed a consistent focus on a particular method with particular slogans.

This is confirmed by descriptions such as this: "Purpose Driven provides a simple, effective strategy and the necessary tools to bring these biblical purposes into balance." There is never anything simple about being a Christian, being a leader of a church, or being a missionary, church planter, or evangelist. And while there certainly are tools which are necessary for being an authentic follower of Jesus or a church truly devoted to the one true and living God, and to Jesus the Messiah and Savior, there is never anything automatically effective about any strategy that church leaders formulate. Perhaps the promise of "a simple, effective strategy" is simply hype, a term that Merriam-Webster defines as (1) deception, put-on, the act of deceiving, (2) publicity, especially: promotional publicity of an extravagant or contrived kind. Under the heading "Purpose Driven congregations have 12 essential characteristics," we read that "we've seen church after church dynamically transformed by simply adapting Purpose Driven methods into their overall strategy." Again, what is being claimed? Do "Purpose Driven methods" transform churches, or does God transform churches? Is the transformation of seemingly weak churches into strong churches really simple when "Purpose Driven methods" are used? Are churches that use other methods doomed to a difficult road ahead simply because they do not follow PD?

If there is a simple method for the transformation of a church, is there also a simple method for teaching junior high school students? Or a simple method for transforming convicts into productive members of society? Or a simple method for avoiding marriage breakdowns? The sequence of the twelve "essential characteristics" suggests that the focus on method is much stronger than the focus on content. After describing the formulation of a purpose statement, the drafting of a "Purpose Driven strategy," the organization of the church around a "Purpose Driven structure," the development of "ministry strategies by purpose" and the staffing "by purpose," it is only the sixth characteristic that touches on content: "PD congregations are led by pastors who preach by purpose. Sermons, including series, are planned so that the congregation receives a balanced emphasis on each of the purposes." The last six characteristics focus again on method: they describe the formation of "small groups on purpose," the scheduling of events "by purpose," the budgeting "by purpose," the construction of buildings "by purpose," the self-evaluation "by purpose" and the strategy of building congregations "from the outside-in." Apart from the redundant use of the word *purpose*, the focus is on method and process, and organization and management.

Every method that missionaries or churches utilize in the proclamation and explanation of the gospel has strengths and weaknesses. This does not mean that all methods (or media) are equally suitable in every context for the proclamation of the gospel or for teaching followers of Jesus. It means, however, that there are no simple methods, there are no simple methods that guarantee success, and there are no complex methods that guarantee success. The success of missionary work and of pastoral ministry—the conversion of unbelievers and the growth of the local church—is always the result of the gracious presence of God and his Holy Spirit. Evangelicals need to stop paying lip service to this conviction, which they generally do hold. They need to retool their strategies and reformulate their methods so that their proposals are not only somehow, somewhere, "biblically based." The Word of God forms not only the basis of the church but also the center of the church and the content of what is being preached and taught. Pastors for whom the Word of God is both basic and central do not preach purpose-driven emphases or any other program, but the Word of God as revealed in the texts of the Old and New Testaments.

Missionaries and church planters for whom the Word of God is basic and central make sure that the truth of the gospel of Jesus the crucified and risen Messiah and Savior is the content of what they preach and teach, and also governs the strategies and methods they formulate. The content, contours and consequences of the gospel of Jesus Christ provide the theological and missiological criteria for deciding on the specific methods and on the appropriate use of the methods that missionaries, church planters and preachers use.

Seeker-driven churches. In David Well's analysis,[98] the ambition "to do church effectively" and to grow local congregations numerically represents a deliberate response to cultural changes in North-American society in five ways that are seriously flawed in several respects.

First, the seeker-driven churches cater to people who seek spirituality without theology. They offer spiritual help of a therapeutic nature: how to maintain lasting relationships, how to handle the breakdown of relationships (or of marriages), how to handle stress, how to handle financial debt, how to handle

---

[98]Wells, *Above All Earthly Pow'rs*, pp. 263-309; cf. Guinness, *Dining with the Devil.*

conflict, how to raise children. The pastors of evangelical megachurches are generally orthodox in doctrine, but doctrine is regarded as more or less irrelevant with regard to the method of reaching people who are looking for answers. It is suggested that preachers should answer the questions people have, not questions nobody is asking. It is suggested that baby boomers do not look for truth but for solutions to life issues that work.

In this new method of planting and growing churches, theology is pushed to the periphery while what is regarded as "practical" becomes the new center. In the tradition of missionary work and pastoral ministry that goes back to Paul the apostle, what is "practical" is not detached from theology, derived from social and cultural sources of knowledge. The practical methods and the tools of missionary and evangelistic work are implied in and governed by theology. *Theology* is not a word to be avoided or an activity for intellectuals, but a term that describes the knowledge of God and the transformation of the missionaries', evangelists' and pastors' life, which this knowledge produced. Theology relates to the wisdom of those who grow in their knowledge and love for God to know what to do in ministry as they strive to know and love the people they seek to reach with the news of Jesus. Theology governs the aspiration and the calling to serve God and to proclaim his Word. In the "modern ministry" of the professionalized "services" of the "very large church" the focus of ministry is arguably not God but the church, or the seekers that the church wants to attract. This results in a situation in which methods and techniques regarded as essential for a "successful" and "relevant" ministry determine what aspects of theology should be studied and how much theology should be included in sermons. Truth itself appears to be no longer important.[99]

Second, the seeker-driven churches present a solution to the problem of stagnant churches. Some have suggested that the vast majority of Protestant churches in America are either stagnating or dying.[100] While some

---

[99]See David F. Wells, *No Place for Truth, or, Whatever Happened to Evangelical Theology?* (Grand Rapids: Eerdmans, 1993), pp. 250-57.

[100]Leith Anderson, *Dying for Change: An Arresting Look at the New Realities Confronting Churches and Para-Church Ministries* (Minneapolis: Bethany, 1990), p. 10, mentions the figure of 85 percent, a figure which seems to come from surveys conducted by George Barna, published in *User Friendly Churches: What Christians Need to Know About the Churches People Love to Go To* (Ventura, Calif.: Regal Books, 1991), p. 10; cf. Wells, *Above All Earthly Pow'rs*, 270 n. 6.

dispute this analysis,[101] it is certainly true that the megachurch movement has helpfully raised the question of the growth of local congregations and of ways to reach the unchurched. It should be noted, however, that predictions that the regional megachurch is the new paradigm seems to be contradicted by the facts. Studies found that "large size" was the third strongest negative(!) factor in the minds of people, on par with "liberalism" and "traditionalism." Smaller churches were growing faster than large churches: churches that had under one hundred worshipers grew at sixteen times the rate of megachurches with an average attendance of 2,856 people.[102]

Third, the seeker-driven churches accept that local congregations operate in a marketplace environment. People find it easy to leave one church and transfer to other churches. They look for churches they find attractive. And attractiveness is judged on the basis of whether newcomers can feel at home in a church and what programs the church offers. The Disney approach to business is regarded as a helpful model for "doing church." The people at Disney know how to create an atmosphere that is safe, optimistic and fun. They know how to provide an "experience" the customer desires. They know what attracts people, how to attract people and how to get them back for multiple visits. Thus both entrepreneurial marketing techniques are justified, as is entertainment as a major criterion for how "to do" church.[103] One church-growth consultant claims that five or ten million baby boomers would come back to church within a month if churches adopted three simple changes: first, advertise; second, let people know about "product" benefits; third, be nice to people.[104]

---

[101]See Carl S. Dudley and David A. Roozen, *Faith Communities Today: A Report on Religion in the United States Today* (Hartford, Conn.: Hartford Institute for Religious Research, 2001), p. 26; cf. Wells, *Above All Earthly Pow'rs*, p. 270 n. 6.

[102]Wells, *Above All Earthly Pow'rs*, p. 275 n. 12, who refers to Christian A. Schwarz, *Natural Church Development: A Guide to Eight Essential Qualities of Healthy Churches* (Carol Stream, Ill.: ChurchSmart Resources, 1996), pp. 46-48.

[103]See George Barna, *Marketing the Church: What They Never Taught You About Church Growth* (Colorado Springs: NavPress, 1988); Norman Shawchuck et al., *Marketing for Congregations: Choosing to Serve People More Effectively* (Nashville: Abingdon, 1992); Kirbyjon Caldwell and Walt Kallestad, *Entrepreneurial Faith: Launching Bold Initiatives to Expand God's Kingdom* (Colorado Springs: WaterBrook, 2004); Walt Kallestad, *Entertainment Evangelism: Taking the Church Public* (Nashville: Abingdon, 1996).

[104]Quoted in Guinness, *Dining with the Devil*, p. 38.

David Wells asks some incisive questions:

How serious can Christian faith be in such a context? And how serious can it afford to be if it is to succeed? A faith serious enough to engage with the modern world as it really is with its loss of truth, meaning, and hope might very well become an impediment to spiritual seekers in the marketplace today. Theirs is a world of technique not of truth, a world where reality contracts into the self, and the self into feelings and intuitions, and evil is often just a bad day.[105]

Fourth, the seeker-driven churches have adapted to the complex realities of contemporary society and to new ways people shop. In the urban centers of North America, people no longer drive into the city centers to shop: they shop in large malls in the suburbs. People no longer find identity in the neighborhoods (suburbs have no center and thus no character), but in nongeographical networks (e.g., in clubs). Products such as pharmaceutical drugs are no longer advertised in journals that doctors read but marketed on television directly to the consumer; there is a shift from the producer (the doctor) to the consumer (the patient). Traditional churches were "producer" churches that prescribed what people need, while seeker-driven churches are "consumer" churches in which the customers define their own needs.[106] One of the many corollaries of the consumer approach can be seen in sermons for sale or for download from the Internet, for pastors who are too busy to prepare sermons, for pastors who are not as "gifted" as the pastor of a large church. Motorists in the greater Chicago area can see a sign that reads, "Worship with the largest church in America. You'll love it." The "small print" underneath the very large letters of this advertisement reveal that "the largest church in America" is not on the other side of the road but in another state (in Texas), and that the services of this church are used via "live simulcast." If "large" is identified with good and attractive, and if the criterion for church services is no longer the truth but the number of the people who show up on Sunday mornings, then such advertisements make sense—and only then.

---

[105]Wells, *Above All Earthly Pow'rs*, p. 274.
[106]See Lyle E. Schaller, *Church Marketing: Breaking Ground for the Harvest* (Ventura, Calif.: Regal Books, 1992).

Fifth, the seeker-driven churches claim to offer a model of how to "do church" that is contemporary and thus relevant, and thus avoids becoming an irrelevant relic of the past. It is suggested that what the church has been traditionally offering to people is no longer what people want. Since the church is out of step with the world as it is, it is not growing—so goes the claim. Proponents who advance this kind of argument evidently do not know church history. Exactly the same argument was used by liberal theologians and church leaders in Europe in the nineteenth and twentieth centuries who argued that the church must adapt to the new social, cultural and ideological trends that shape how people think and behave. They were ready and willing to abandon what they regarded as traditional in their quest to attract people to the church. Liberal church people adapted their theology; megachurch strategists claim that they only adapt the form of delivery.

David Wells wonders, however, whether the similarity of strategy will not indeed risk the demise of the orthodox faith in these churches. Seeker-driven churches

> represent a coalition bound together not by a theological vision of the world but by a common strategy for reaching particular segments of society and by a common methodology for accomplishing this. . . . [T]here is no theological truth upon which the methodology is predicated and upon which it insists, because theological truth, it is thought, is not what builds churches.[107]

The consumer approach, almost by necessity, produces a spirituality that is located in the privatized realm of the individual, as these churches offer choices for individuals who look for meaning and for help in areas in which they cannot help themselves.[108]

> It is this acutely privatized dimension that explains why so few of these churches have any kind of social involvement. But it also explains why these churches are appealing to so many people who are looking for a spiritual dimension to life but who may want to distance themselves from religion. Here is a spirituality without theology, spirituality which is privatized and

---

[107]Wells, *Above All Earthly Pow'rs*, p. 281.
[108]Some megachurches pastors have "discovered" social involvement in Africa or missionary work in Asia after decades of focusing on building the very large church they serve.

therefore, to some extent, freed from the external rhythms and authority of a practiced faith. . . .

The question of truth degenerates into a question as to whether it works and that degenerates further into the question as to whether it even matters.[109]

It is not surprising that the sermons preached in seeker-driven churches politely affirm the "guests" who have come. In one sermon God was introduced as someone "who loves you, is proud of you, believes in you, and will give you strength to stand up to the forces of evil in the world," and sin is described in terms of how it "harms the individual, rather than how it offends a holy God. Sin, in short, prevents us from realizing our full potential."[110]

It is not surprising that the buildings of seeker-driven churches often look like corporate headquarters or country clubs. This is quite deliberate: the barrier of "looking like a church" is removed. Inside the auditorium, the front is occupied not by an altar or a pulpit, but by a stage for performances.[111] The problem in a technological society in which refined consumer analysis and market techniques manage to sell just about anything is that the methods for marketing a pleasant church experience are indeed so effective that these seeker-driven churches seem to need very little truth in order to have success.[112]

The only truth in marketing is the success that it produces, success which is defined numerically in the context of market forces. The exterior and interior of church buildings, the professional light and sound effects, the uplifting music, the entertaining drama, the playful humor, the inspirational speech and the many other elements of church can indeed be arranged in such a manner that people who are used to responding daily to multimedia experiences also respond positively and fill the "auditorium" in the building in which "seekers" are sought in increasing numbers. This is not meant as a comparison, but we

---

[109]Wells, *Above All Earthly Pow'rs*, pp. 282, 304.

[110]Kimon Howland Sargeant, *Seeker Churches: Promoting Traditional Religion in a Nontraditional Way* (New Brunswick, N.J.: Rutgers University Press, 2000), p. 86; he points out that the gospel is presented "in the friendly guise of an egalitarian, fulfillment-enhancing, fun, religious encounter with God" (ibid.); cf. Wells, *Above All Earthly Pow'rs*, p. 306.

[111]See Jeanne Halgren Kilde, *When Church Became Theatre: The Transformation of Evangelical Architecture and Worship in Nineteenth-Century America* (New York: Oxford University Press, 2002).

[112]Wells, *Above All Earthly Pow'rs*, p. 307.

should not forget that the media-savvy leaders of the National Socialist movement in Germany in the 1930s had a pretty good idea how they could fulfill the longing for meaning, achievement, solidarity and entertainment, and how they could thus gain the people's confidence and move in the direction they wanted the masses to march.[113]

In his analysis of the megachurch movement, Os Guinness points out that Christians dare not forget to know what the decisive authority was in the early church. When Christians substitute the authority of God's revealed truth for something else, the church is no longer church, and Christians "risk living unauthorized lives of faith, exercising unauthorized ministries, and proclaiming an unauthorized gospel."[114]

Sending missionaries. As we have seen (sec. 4.6), Paul expected the churches, their leaders as well as their members, to participate in the ministry of communicating the news of Jesus. The paradigm of Paul's own missionary work, as well as the principles and rules he formulates, suggests that the church is always committed to the missionary mandate of sharing the gospel with other people.[115]

The logic of the gospel implies not only a commitment to Jesus Christ but also a commitment to the progress of the gospel in the world.[116] In the opening paragraph of his letter to the Christians in the city of Rome (Rom 1:1-17), Paul describes his personal involvement in the gospel. He was called by God to be an apostle "called by God to preach the Good News" (Rom 1:1 TEV). The goal of his ministry is "to bring about the obedience of faith among all the Gentiles" (Rom 1:5). His ministry is tireless (Rom 1:9). He wants to come to Rome and preach the gospel there as well (Rom 1:15). He is not ashamed of the gospel because "it is the power of

---

[113]See Hilmar Hoffmann, *The Triumph of Propaganda: Film and National Socialism, 1933-1945* (Providence: Berghahn, 1996); Ulrike Bartels, *Die Wochenschau im Dritten Reich: Entwicklung und Funktion eines Massenmediums unter besonderer Berücksichtigung völkisch-nationaler Inhalte* (Frankfurt: Lang, 2004).

[114]Guinness, *Dining with the Devil*, p. 61. He predicts that since "many superchurches are simply artificially inflated local churches with charismatically inflated super-pastors" they will not be able "to survive their supergrowth" (ibid., p. 29).

[115]Differently Bob Finley, *Reformation in Foreign Missions* (Longwood, Fla.: Xulon, 2005), pp. 15-21, 198-99, argues that (Western) churches should only send money to the Christians in poorer countries who can be much more effective missionaries than crosscultural workers can be.

[116]See Peter T. O'Brien, *Gospel and Mission in the Writings of Paul: An Exegetical and Theological Analysis* (Grand Rapids: Baker, 1995), pp. 53-77.

God for salvation to everyone who has faith, to the Jew first and also to the Greek" (Rom 1:16).

At the same time Paul describes the role and the function of the gospel in salvation history. The gospel had been announced beforehand in the holy Scriptures (Rom 1:1-2). The content of the gospel is Jesus Christ the Son of David and the Son of God, who was raised from the dead (Rom 1:3-4). The goal of the gospel is the lordship of the risen Messiah over the new people of God, which includes converted Gentiles (Rom 1:5). The gospel is the saving power of God, who fulfills his promise to Abraham (Rom 1:16-17; 4:16-17). One of the reasons Paul writes to the Christians in the city of Rome is to provide them with a fuller understanding of the saving power of the gospel in a world that has rebelled against God and that helplessly faces God's wrath. And he writes to help them understand better the faithfulness of God with regard to his covenant promises that he had given to Abraham and that implied the integration of the nations in the people of God. "The dynamic of the gospel's logic meant for these believers in Rome and for other Christians, including ourselves, a deeper commitment to its ongoing, powerful advance, as well as to the person at its centre, Jesus Christ, God's Son."[117]

The biblical understanding of a messenger who is sent by God (and who is thus a "missionary") to proclaim the news of Jesus to people who have not heard or not yet accepted the gospel is not tied as such to crossing cultures. Paul, the Jew from Tarsus who was trained in Jerusalem and who was at home in both Greek and Jewish culture, did not have to cross a massive cultural gap when he proclaimed the gospel to either Jews or Greeks. The Jewish believers from Jerusalem, at home in Galilee and in Judea, on the other hand, had to be willing to adapt culturally in many areas as they traveled to cities such as Caesarea, Antioch or Rome.

The argument that the sending of missionaries to people in other cultures has no basis in the New Testament because the only crosscultural event is Pentecost, where "foreign visitors" came to Jerusalem where they met the apostles from whom they heard the gospel[118] seriously misunderstands Acts 2. The people "from every nation" that are mentioned in

---

[117]Ibid., pp. 76-77.
[118]Finley, *Reformation in Foreign Missions*, pp. 20-21, 23-24.

Acts 2:5 were "devout Jews" who were "living in Jerusalem" (Acts 2:5). They were not "foreign nationals" but Diaspora Jews who either visited Jerusalem as pilgrims during the Jewish festival of Pentecost or who had come to live in Jerusalem, perhaps older Jews who wanted to be buried in Jerusalem.[119] The Twelve did not "concentrate on winning immigrants and visitors from 'mission field' countries" at Pentecost.[120] They witnessed to Jews. It is equally erroneous to think that "none of those original disciples could speak a foreign language."[121] Many Jews who lived in Galilee and in Judea could speak Greek, beside Aramaic and Hebrew.[122] About a third of the 250 inscriptions that have been found in or near Jerusalem dating to the period of the Second Temple are written in Greek (7 percent are bilingual). This suggests that Jesus' disciples were indeed linguistically equipped to proclaim the gospel to Greeks living in other regions beyond Judea and Galilee. Moreover, the determining characteristic of the apostles and of other missionaries in the New Testament period is not the need to learn another language or to cross cultural divides. Rather, they are characterized by Jesus' call and commission to proclaim the good news of God's saving action to all people, Jews and Greeks, no matter where they lived—whether in the same city, in the neighboring region or in another Roman province.

An important trend is the dramatic increase in so-called short-term mission trips that attract hundreds of thousands of young and older Christians every year who travel to the "mission field" for often only a week or two to "do missions." While this is not the place to fully evaluate this phenomenon, the following comments summarize the concerns of many observers. First, these "short-term mission trips" force us to consider again, and carefully, what "missionary work" is. When (sometimes very young) people who do not have much theological understanding or any training in communicating with people of other faiths return from such trips reporting how much

---

[119]See Ben Witherington, *The Acts of the Apostles: A Socio-Rhetorical Commentary* (Grand Rapids: Eerdmans, 1998), p. 135.

[120]Finley, *Reformation in Foreign Missions*, p. 199.

[121]Ibid., p. 20.

[122]See Eric M. Meyers and James F. Strange, *Archaeology, the Rabbis and Early Christianity* (Nashville: Parthenon, 1981), pp. 62-91; Stanley Porter, "Jesus and the Use of Greek in Galilee," in *Studying the Historical Jesus. Evaluations of the State of Current Research*, ed. B. Chilton and C. A. Evans, NTTS 19 (Leiden: Brill, 1994), pp. 123-54; Schnabel, *Early Christian Mission*, 1:201-2.

they have learned and how they have been challenged, it becomes obvious that the designation "missionary work" should be withheld from many such ventures, replaced by designations such as "sanctification experience in exotic places," which could be handily abbreviated as SEEP. The benefit for the short-termers and their congregations "at home" far outweighs the strategic impact on the city or the area visited. Second, despite often laudable intentions, the insensitivity concerning the culture the short-termers visit has sometimes done immense damage to the local churches.[123] Third, the amount of money that North American churches spend on such short-term trips is astronomical, while at the same time career missionaries are struggling to maintain their support. Fourth, the notion that missionary work can be done as a "drive through" venture is as erroneous as is the notion that authentic missionary work is a matter of preference, choice and convenience rather than a matter of calling and obedience. Notwithstanding these and similar criticisms, many established missions organizations have excellent programs that place "visiting Christians" (as we may want to call short-termers) in ministry situations in which they can make a valuable contribution as they follow the lead of experienced national and foreign missionaries and pastors, while preparing them as thoroughly as possible for their future full-time involvement overseas.

In the twenty-first century it is no longer Western churches who send missionaries to other countries. Churches in Korea and Singapore, in Japan and Thailand, in India and the Philippines, in Kenya and Nigeria, in Brazil and Argentina commission Christians to do missionary work in unreached regions within their own country as well as in other countries.[124] In the mid-1990s there were about 88,000 crosscultural missionary workers sent out by approximately 1,600 non-Western organizations

---

[123]For this and the following points see Moreau et al., *Introducing World Missions*, pp. 191-94, 254-55, 279-82.

[124]See Marlin L. Nelson, ed., *Readings in Third World Missions: A Collection of Essential Documents* (South Pasadena, Calif.: William Carey Library, 1976); Lawrence E. Keyes, *The Last Age of Missions: A Study of Third World Missionary Societies* (Pasadena, Calif.: William Carey Library, 1983); Larry D. Pate, *From Every People: A Handbook of Two-Thirds World Missions with Directory* (Monrovia, Calif.: MARC, 1989); Samuel Escobar, *The New Global Mission: The Gospel from Everywhere to Everyone* (Downers Grove, Ill.: InterVarsity Press, 2003); Martin Klauber and Scott M. Manetsch, *The Great Commission: Evangelicals and the History of World Missions* (Nashville: Broadman & Holman, 2007), particularly the contributions by J. E. Pluedemann, J. D. Salinas, R. R. Cook and T. Tiénou.

in Africa, Asia, Latin America and Oceania.[125] Jim Chew from Singapore asserts that what he calls the crosscultural messenger "is not a temporary but an abiding necessity for the life of the church, provided always that the movement of mission is multidirectional, all churches both sending and receiving."[126]

The global context. Since sending and receiving missionaries happens in a globalized context, the relationship between Western churches and the churches of the former "mission fields," and between Western mission organizations and the mission agencies of the Two-Thirds World (or what many now call the "Majority World") have become complex and challenging. Some missions experts have argued that Western churches should stop sending missionaries to foreign countries and instead send money. They argue that it is cheaper and more effective to support indigenous missionary workers, church planters and evangelists. Missions experts and evangelical church leaders both in the West and in the Two-Thirds World argue, on the other hand, that while the commitment to missionary work of the younger missionary movement is to be applauded, there is so much work to be done that a call for a moratorium for sending missionaries is uncalled for. Non-Western missionaries are seen to make some of the same mistakes as Western missionaries made in the past. The sending, training and support of non-Western missionaries by their home base is seen by many as in need of consolidation.[127]

A key term in these discussions is *partnership*, defined by Luis Bush as "an association of two or more Christian autonomous bodies who have formed a trusting relationship and fulfill agreed-upon expectations by sharing complementary strengths and resources to reach their mutual goal."[128] Mission experts who support this approach point out that part-

---

[125]Larry E. Keyes, "Non-Western Mission Boards and Societies," *EDWM*, p. 696.

[126]Jim Chew, *When You Cross Cultures: Vital Issues Facing Christian Missions* (Singapore: Navigators, 1990); William D. Taylor, "Missionary," *EDWM*, p. 644.

[127]See Stanley M. Guthrie, "Globalization," *EDWM*, p. 395.

[128]Luis Bush, "In Pursuit of True Christian Partnership: A Biblical Basis from Philippians," in *Partners in the Gospel: The Strategic Role of Partnership in World Evangelization*, ed. J. H. Kraakevik and D. Welliver (Wheaton: Billy Graham Center, 1992), p. 3. Cf. Steven Downey, "Partnership Re-Visited," *EMQ* 42 (2006): 200-202, who reprints the "Covenant of Partnership: An Emerging Vision for a Radical New Commitment to Global Christian Community" of Partners International.

nerships thus understood protect the identity of the receiving national church as well as the sending church or institution. Others argue that "the complexity of ethnic relationships, economic levels, and so forth, make this theory extremely difficult to accomplish."[129]

Craig Ott points out that the support of national missionary workers by Western organizations is a model that national churches outside the West cannot reproduce (thus they are not really partners), that financial partnerships seem to be based on the assumption that the proclamation of the gospel and the establishment of new churches depends on money, that financial partnerships often create dependencies which reinforce feelings of inferiority, that the financial support by Western agencies can create a mercenary spirit, and that this model "can rob the national church of the joy of being a truly missionary church."[130] Christopher Little has provided the most recent study of the historical, anthropological, structural and missiological issues related to what he calls the "international partner-ship movement."[131] He agrees with other studies that have concluded that these international missionary partnerships are "problematic at best, and at worst, counterproductive to the goals of the missio Dei."

Concerns that are raised by many missions experts include the dilemma that it is often the power of money that sets the agenda. Some have com-pared such partnerships with a dance between an elephant and a mouse, in which the mouse is thrown in whatever direction the elephant moves, and the mouse is eventually trampled.[132] There is the problem of national churches not being able to become truly self-governing and self-supporting due to the influx of Western money. Control over the financial resources raises the issue who controls the resources. There is the problem that West-ern churches and organizations are in kingdom-building mode, meaning that they build their own kingdoms using the "growth by acquisition" ap-proach. There is the problem that some Western missions organizations who are involved in partnerships are often just as paternalistic as they

---

[129]Thus the report in Tom A. Steffen, "Partnership," *EDWM*, p. 727.
[130]Craig Ott, "Let the Buyer Beware," *EMQ* 29 (1993): 290.
[131]Christopher R. Little, *Mission in the Way of Paul: Biblical Mission for the Church in the Twenty-First Century*, Studies in Biblical Literature 80 (New York: Peter Lang, 2005); conclusion in ibid., p. 231.
[132]David Neff, "Stepping on Toes," *EMQ* 36 (2000): 238-42.

have been in the past. There is the problem of the affluence of Western churches who depend on expensive strategies and technology, which most churches outside the West cannot emulate.[133] There is the problem of the heavy commitment of such partnerships to relief and development programs, to the neglect of the proclamation of the gospel and church planting. There is the dilemma of cultural differences (accountability is understood differently in Western organizations, which operate with a marketing business model compared with the understanding in under-developed countries). There is the problem of a very one-sided partnership, as hardly anything flows back from the churches in the Majority World to the Western churches. Some missions experts are more optimistic about the possibilities and the usefulness of carefully nurtured partnerships be-tween Western missions organizations and churches and their counter-parts in other areas of the world.[134]

Paul's missionary work does not provide a model for such partnerships. The famine relief of the church in Antioch for the church in Jerusalem, a project in which Paul played a role (Acts 11:27-30),[135] is certainly a model for Christians in one region providing humanitarian assistance to needy Christians in another region. However, it needs to be pointed out that this was an emergency situation due to a severe famine, that the church in An-tioch did not provide financial assistance for the missionary outreach of the Jerusalem believers, and that this was evidently a one-time event that did not create a long-term dependency. The collection which Paul orga-nized in the churches he had established[136] can hardly constitute the bib-lical precedent for modern partnerships between missions organizations and national churches. Paul's main concern was the promotion of unity between the churches he had established as an apostle to the Gentiles and

---

[133]Jonathan J. Bonk, *Missions and Money: Affluence as a Western Missionary Problem* (Maryknoll, N.Y.: Orbis, 1991), pp. 70-72; George Verwer, *Out of the Comfort Zone* (Minneapolis: Bethany House, 2000), pp. 103-4.

[134]See Daniel Rickett, *Making Your Partnership Work* (Enumclaw, Wash.: WinePress, 2002); Moreau et al., *Introducing World Missions*, pp. 286-87.

[135]See Schnabel, *Early Christian Mission*, 2:987-1000; cf. Gilliland, *Pauline Theology and Mission Practice*, pp. 252-56.

[136]1 Cor 16:1-4; 2 Cor 8:1-15; 9:1-5; Rom 15:14-21; cf. Gal 2:10. Cf. Stephan Joubert, *Paul as Bene-factor: Reciprocity, Strategy and Theological Reflection in Paul's Collection*, WUNT 2/124 (Tübin-gen: Mohr-Siebeck, 2000); Alexander J. M. Wedderburn, "Paul's Collection: Chronology and History," *NTS* 48 (2002): 95-110; Schnabel, *Early Christian Mission*, 2:1000-1003.

the Jewish believers in Jerusalem, perhaps linked with the hope that this project may prompt skeptical Jews to come to faith in Jesus the Messiah when they see "the nations" come to Zion. If Paul's collection were to be used as a precedent, then the "receiving churches" in the majority world would need to offer gifts to the "sending churches" as a sign of appreciation for having sent out missionaries.[137]

Since the missionary situation today is very different from Paul's time, it would not seem to be necessary to find a biblical warrant for organizational models that are set up to facilitate missionary work. Paul's understanding of the missionary task and of the nature of the church provides the basic principles that must be observed by any missionary in any situation, whatever personal or organizational relationships are the context for his or her work. In the first place, the submission and the obedience to God the Father that governed the mission of Jesus the Son provide the controlling norms for the behavior of all believers.

> Let the same mind be in you that was in Christ Jesus, who, though he was in the form of God, did not regard equality with God as something to be exploited, but emptied himself, taking the form of a slave, being born in human likeness. And being found in human form, he humbled himself and became obedient to the point of death—even death on a cross. (Phil 2:5-8)

In the second place, the fruit of the Holy Spirit as described in Galatians 5:22-26 must govern the behavior of the followers of Jesus, the missionaries (especially) included:

> The fruit of the Spirit is love, joy, peace, patience, kindness, generosity, faithfulness, gentleness, and self-control. There is no law against such things. And those who belong to Christ Jesus have crucified the flesh with its passions and desires. If we live by the Spirit, let us also be guided by the Spirit. Let us not become conceited, competing against one another, envying one another.

Missionaries—whether from the West or from the East, whether from the North or from the South—who live "close to the cross" will not have all the answers to the often complex problems outlined. They will often

---

[137]Little, *Mission in the Way of Paul*, pp. 147-70.

be "perplexed, but not driven to despair" (2 Cor 4:8), sharing Paul's focus on Jesus:

> Always carrying in the body the death of Jesus, so that the life of Jesus may also be made visible in our bodies. For while we live, we are always being given up to death for Jesus' sake, so that the life of Jesus may be made visible in our mortal flesh. So death is at work in us, but life in you. (2 Cor 4:10-12)

6.6 THE CHALLENGE OF CULTURE

The challenge of missionary work has always been a challenge for churches. When Peter and the other apostles proclaimed their conviction that Jesus, albeit crucified, was the Messiah, the political and spiritual leaders of the Jewish people in Jerusalem had them imprisoned (Acts 4—5). When Stephen reached out to Greek-speaking Jews in the Jerusalem synagogues, emphasizing that a new situation had arisen as a result of the death and resurrection of Jesus, and that the temple and its sacrificial cult had become redundant, he was killed by members of his audience (Acts 6—7). When Peter had been forced by a divine revelation that he should no longer regard Gentiles as unclean people with whom contact should be minimized, but as people whom God now invites to join his new people of followers of Jesus Christ, he had to convince the church in Jerusalem that this was an "innovation" sanctioned by God himself (Acts 10—11). When an increasing number of Greeks came to faith in Jesus Christ, the insistence of Peter and Paul that Gentiles are saved as Gentiles, without the need to undergo circumcision and to adhere to the purity stipulations of the Mosaic law, caused a clash with an influential group of Jewish Christians (Acts 15). When Paul proclaimed the news of Jesus in the larger and smaller cities of Asia Minor and of Europe, he was repeatedly attacked and accused by enraged individuals, both Jews and Gentiles, who accused him of introducing religious and social innovations that should be rejected as illegal, and who on more than one occasion wanted to harm him physically (Acts 13—19). When he returned to Jerusalem in the spring of A.D. 57, Jews from the province of Asia accused him of "teaching everyone everywhere against our people, our law, and this place" and of bringing Greeks into the Temple and having thus "defiled this holy place" (Acts

21:28), resulting in his imprisonment first in Caesarea and eventually in Rome (Acts 22—28). Some Gentile Christians evidently believed that the Christian faith does not require a separation from traditional aspects of Greco-Roman culture such as attending the temples and enjoying the carnal pleasures of the city (1 Cor 6; 8—10; Rev 2—3).

The expansion of the early church was prompted by bold new initiatives of "famous" missionaries, such as Peter and Paul as well as by numerous nameless missionaries such as the Greek speaking Jewish believers from Jerusalem who took the news of Jesus to cities in Phoenicia, Cyprus and Syria (Acts 11:19). Time and again, Paul and his fellow missionaries clashed with Jews, Greeks and sometimes with Christians who resisted change. Jews of Jerusalem were incensed at the suggestion that the Jesus of Nazareth whose life had ended in a crucifixion was the Messiah after all, vindicated by God in his resurrection, his death God's ultimate solution of the sin problem of humankind. Greeks in Philippi and in Ephesus were enraged at the prospect of an increasing number of their fellow citizens becoming followers of Jesus whose change of religious affiliation would change the traditional customs that the entire population had practiced. Some Jewish Christians disagreed with the argument that the Mosaic law is no longer central. Some Gentile Christians disagreed with the insistence that followers of Jesus discontinue the custom of attending banquets in pagan temples and visiting prostitutes.

While all of these difficulties are connected with theological convictions, they also involve the challenge of culture. The proclamation of the news of Jesus in the first century caused cultural dissonance both with regard to the traditional culture of the Jews and with regard to the traditional culture of the Greeks and Romans. The challenge of culture is at least twofold.

First, Christians can resist cultural change that is necessary on account of the "logic" of the gospel. Peter and Paul were able to convince many of the Jewish believers in Jerusalem that a new situation had arisen with the coming of Jesus the Messiah, indeed a new era of salvation in which the Mosaic law underwent a change due to Jesus' saving death on the cross and to the triumph of God's grace, which became apparent on the day of Jesus' resurrection from the dead. In this new era of salvation

Gentiles come to faith in Jesus the Messiah and Savior as well, in fulfillment of God's promises through Israel's prophets, without having to become Jews through circumcision and Torah obedience before joining God's people.

Second, Christians can insist on cultural adaptation in areas that contradict the truth and logic of the gospel. The motivation for such an insistence may be understandable. Who wants to die as a witness for the gospel if this can be avoided by paying token homage to the emperor on some altar in some temple? Why should Christians insist on forfeiting sexual entertainment if everyone else is "doing it" and if Christians have their sins forgiven once and for all already?

Followers of Jesus live their lives as "resident aliens" or "exiles" (1 Pet 1:1; 2:11) whose real home is not in this world but in God's world (Jn 17:14-16) and whose mission is to be sanctified in the truth of the Word of God so that they can be sent into the world (Jn 17:17-18). The life of a "resident alien" is a life between two cultures: the host culture and the home culture. Followers of Jesus are part of the culture they happen to live in this world, and they are part of the "culture" of God's world, which has been revealed in his Word. They are similar to their contemporaries in many ways, kindred spirits of their family members, friends and acquaintances. And they are similar to Jesus Christ, whom they follow and imitate, kindred spirits of the Holy Spirit who transforms their lives as people who are called to be holy in an unholy world. Andrew Walls speaks of the "pilgrim principle," which is in some respects a universalizing factor, standing next to the "indigenizing principle," which associates Christians with the particulars of their culture and group.[138]

As Christians thus live "between two worlds," they can err in both directions. They can be so "this-worldly" that their Christian identity is at best obscured, at worst compromised. Or they can be so "other-worldly" that their contact with their contemporaries becomes problematic or impossible. The consequences of the first kind of lopsidedness, leaning to the left, can be observed in the "liberals," from the Gnostics of the

---

[138]See Walls, *Missionary Movement in Christian History*, pp. 8-9.

second and third century[139] to the more recent theologians of the nineteenth and twentieth century, who are unrestrained by Scripture which they deny to be the normative Word of God[140] and who are thus willing, sometimes eager, to support homosexual relationships and unions as these have become accepted in Western society. The consequences of the second kind of lopsidedness, leaning to the right, can be observed in the "conservatives," from some parts of the monastic movement, where monks built walls in order to keep the world out in their effort to enhance their personal holiness,[141] to some parts of the fundamentalist movement for whom using a radio or riding a train was a sin that needed to be shunned.[142]

In some areas the necessity for cultural transformation is evident: not many people who call themselves Christians have argued for "free love" or for polygamy. In some areas there is a dispute about the level of contextualization that is acceptable: some Christians argue for a counter-cultural lifestyle that helps them to decide not to buy (for example) luxury cars, while others argue that Christians are free to make their own choices as consumers. What is crucial from our study of the missionary work of the apostle Paul is the recognition that there should be no dispute about the centrality of faith in the one true and living God, faith in Jesus the Messiah and Savior, faith in the Holy Spirit whose power transforms the lives of the believers. In other words, there should be no dispute about the centrality of truth—biblical truth, theological truth, spiritual truth. There should be no dispute about the primacy of the truth of the reality of God, of his Word, of his saving revelation in Jesus Christ, and of the transforming power of his Spirit. Any other entity that seeks to compete

[139]See for example Edmondo Lupieri, *The Mandaeans: The Last Gnostics*, Italian Texts and Studies on Religion and Society (Grand Rapids: Eerdmans, 2002).

[140]See Karl Barth, *Protestant Theology in the Nineteenth Century: Its Background and History* (Grand Rapids: Eerdmans, 2002); Harold O. J. Brown, *Heresies: The Image of Christ in the Mirror of Heresy and Orthodoxy from the Apostles to the Present* (Grand Rapids: Baker, 1988).

[141]See Douglas Burton-Christie, *The Word in the Desert: Scripture and the Quest for Holiness in Early Christian Monasticism* (Oxford: Oxford University Press, 1993).

[142]See Carl F. H. Henry, *The Uneasy Conscience of Modern Fundamentalism* (1947; reprint, Grand Rapids: Eerdmans, 2003); George M. Marsden, *Understanding Fundamentalism and Evangelicalism* (Grand Rapids: Eerdmans, 1991).

with the centrality and the primacy of God's truth for the identity and the mission of God's people is an idol—whether this is another belief or conviction, a method or a technique.

As the evaluation of important features of the church-growth and the megachurch movements has demonstrated, the lure of modernity, with its comforts and effectiveness, its material wealth and emphasis on personal experience and satisfaction, pulls Christians who are committed to missionary work and to church planting more in the direction of cultural compromise. Missiologists often emphasize the need for contextualization, that is, the need to adapt theological content and Christian forms to the traditions and customs of the people group hearing the gospel of Jesus Christ. Not many have emphasized the need for decontextualization, that is, the need to help Christians move away from those traditions and customs of their culture that contradict the truth of the gospel (apart from the standard warnings not to compromise the gospel, caveats which are typical for evangelicals).[143] Andrew Walls uses the term *pilgrim principle* to describe this process:

> Not only does God in Christ take people as they are: He takes them in order to transform them into what He wants them to be. Along with the indigenizing principle which makes his faith a place to feel at home, the Christian inherits the pilgrim principle, which whispers to him that he has no abiding city and warns him that to be faithful to Christ will put him out of step with his society; for that society never existed, in East or West, ancient time or modern, which could absorb the word of Christ painlessly into its system.[144]

Authentic biblical contextualization does not exploit a culture "for the Church's own gain even as Christian faith is not about exploiting God for what we want."[145] Paul's willingness to "become all things to all people" (1 Cor 9:22) is governed by the truth and logic of the gospel: "I do it all

---

[143]Much needed recent studies that emphasize not only the need for cultural awareness or the need of missionaries and church planters to adapt to the culture of the people they seek to reach with the gospel, but also the need to recognize the cultural areas of disobedience to the will of God which require biblical transformation are Sherwood G. Lingenfelter, *Transforming Culture: A Challenge for Christian Mission*, 2nd ed. (Grand Rapids: Baker, 1998); *Agents of Transformation: A Guide for Effective Cross-Cultural Ministry* (Grand Rapids: Baker, 1996).

[144]Walls, *Missionary Movement in Christian History*, p. 8.

[145]Wells, *Above All Earthly Pow'rs*, p. 307.

for the sake of the gospel" (1 Cor 9:23). The gospel contradicts all human culture since humankind's rebellion against God (Genesis 3). This is why followers of Jesus who belong to God's people never simply belong to a culture, where the term *belong* means "to be the rightful property or possession of"—authentic Christians are not owned by the culture in which they were born and live. Rather, they belong to the one true and living God, they belong to and serve the Lord Jesus Christ, and they belong to God's people, a diverse yet unified body that transcends ethnic, social and cultural divisions. When potential Christians—seekers who are unbelievers, the unchurched who are agnostics, future converts who may stay atheists—who are indeed "owned" by their culture, determine the form and ultimately also the content of what is being preached, it is difficult to see how seeker-driven churches can maintain their Christian authenticity in the long run, during which the "noise" of culture disturbs the communication of the Word of God but also threatens to drown out the truth of God's Word.

The utter uniqueness and holiness of the one true and living God render all attempts to overhaul and retool the news of Jesus the Messiah and Savior to the preferences of secular or pagan audiences idolatrous. In a consumer culture the consumer is king: the consumer owns what he or she buys, and because successful selling and buying trumps everything else, consumer preferences and wishes control not only the form of the product but more basically what is being produced in the first place. The one true and living God cannot be bought, he cannot be owned. Likewise, his Word cannot be bought. Sinners who are dead on account of their rebellion against God (Eph 2:1) do not have any "life" which would allow them to make demands on God. Since the holy God who holds sinners to account is also a merciful God who loves to forgive the sinner who repents, God's saving word comes in ways that can and should be understood by the people who are remote from God. And thus missionaries, church planters and evangelists who have been sent to proclaim the news of Jesus who saves from the wrath of God (Rom 3:21—5:21, following Rom 1:18—3:20) certainly preach and teach in such a manner that people can clearly hear and, on account of the prompting of the Holy Spirit, understand the gospel. The language they speak is the language of the culture in which they speak. The locations in which they proclaim the gospel are locations in which the people of that particular culture are willing to listen to people speak about the deep questions of life. The content which they proclaim, however, is governed not by the content which that particular culture deems "relevant" and apropos, but by the truth of God's revelation in the Scriptures, supremely by the saving news of Jesus, the crucified and risen Messiah and Savior.

The church is not the retailing outlet, offering selections of God's truth to bargain hunters. Authentic Christian faith can only be had on God's terms, as a whole, inevitably confronting culture.[146] Authentic missionary work does not aim at niches of class, ethnic identity, gender, generation or economic status. Authentic missionaries and church planters do not look for special interest groups that may guarantee the success of their efforts. Like the apostle Paul, they will be constrained to proclaim the news of Jesus to all who are willing to listen—Jews and Greeks, blacks and whites, rich and poor, men and women, citizens and aliens. Authentic missionaries do not have a narrow vision that focuses on one particular group, and they are certainly not driven by a vision that is motivated by the promise and projection of success. In today's world, good marketing can guarantee success, at least success as defined by the consumer. Authentic missionaries have a large vision—the calling to sacrificially proclaim the news of Jesus to all levels and all segments of society and to establish communities of followers of Jesus who have experienced the miracle of coming to faith in Jesus Christ, who are experiencing the miracle of the transforming presence of the holy God in their lives, and who rejoice in the miracle of a fellowship in which "there is no longer Jew or Greek, there is no longer slave or free, there is no longer male and female" because all are "one in Christ Jesus" (Gal 3:28).

6.7 THE POWER OF GOD

Before Paul became a Christian and a missionary, he persecuted Christians. As an envoy from the Jewish authorities in Jerusalem, he knew something about power—political power that was capable of eliminating

---

[146]Ibid., pp. 308-9; for the following comment cf. ibid., p. 313.

dissenters, social and cultural power that pressured people to conform to traditions and customs and long-held beliefs, legal power that was in a position to punish troublemakers. Then Paul met the risen Lord Jesus Christ on the road to Damascus—an encounter that he had not sought, but whose reality and meaning he could not deny, an encounter whose significance changed his life. Paul became an apostle because the risen Lord called and sent him. He proclaimed the news of Jesus the Messiah and Savior and saw people come to faith in Jesus and churches established because the power of God was present in his preaching.

> For I will not venture to speak of anything except what Christ has accomplished through me to win obedience from the Gentiles, by word and deed, by the power of signs and wonders, by the power of the Spirit of God, so that from Jerusalem and as far around as Illyricum I have fully proclaimed the good news of Christ. (Rom 15:18-19)

In a lengthy passage, that deserves to be quoted in full, Paul develops the same conviction.

> For the message about the cross is foolishness to those who are perishing, but to us who are being saved it is the power of God. For it is written,
>
> > "I will destroy the wisdom of the wise,
> > . . . and the discernment of the discerning I will thwart."
>
> Where is the one who is wise? Where is the scribe? Where is the debater of this age? Has not God made foolish the wisdom of the world? For since, in the wisdom of God, the world did not know God through wisdom, God decided, through the foolishness of our proclamation, to save those who believe. For Jews demand signs and Greeks desire wisdom, but we proclaim Christ crucified, a stumbling block to Jews and foolishness to Gentiles, but to those who are the called, both Jews and Greeks, Christ the power of God and the wisdom of God. For God's foolishness is wiser than human wisdom, and God's weakness is stronger than human strength.
>
> Consider your own call, brothers and sisters: not many of you were wise by human standards, not many were powerful, not many were of noble birth. But God chose what is foolish in the world to shame the wise; God chose what is weak in the world to shame the strong; God chose what is low and despised in the world, things that are not, to

reduce to nothing things that are, so that no one might boast in the presence of God. He is the source of your life in Christ Jesus, who became for us wisdom from God, and righteousness and sanctification and redemption, in order that, as it is written, "Let the one who boasts, boast in the Lord."

When I came to you, brothers and sisters, I did not come proclaiming the mystery of God to you in lofty words or wisdom. For I decided to know nothing among you except Jesus Christ, and him crucified. And I came to you in weakness and in fear and in much trembling. My speech and my proclamation were not with plausible words of wisdom, but with a demonstration of the Spirit and of power, so that your faith might rest not on human wisdom but on the power of God. (1 Cor 1:18—2:5)

Paul insists that is the power of God alone that convicts people of sin, brings them to repentance and unites them in their weekly gatherings. Neither methods nor miracles guarantee the success of missionary preaching. Only God himself can cause Jews and Greeks to accept and believe a message that seems scandalous and nonsensical. Only God's Spirit can create righteousness, holiness and redemption.[147]

We have examined Paul's deliberate choice to renounce rhetorical methods to enhance the effectiveness of his proclamation of the gospel, and we have seen how this choice provides an important criterion for missionaries, church planters and pastors today when they assess the suitability of methods and techniques. Methods are not simply neutral tools but routines that influence the way human beings live and behave. In the case of the proclamation of the news of Jesus, methods influence the content of what is being communicated.

Os Guinness warns that "the insights and tools of modernity can be so brilliant and effective that there no longer appears to be any need for

---

[147]On the role of the Holy Spirit in the missionary task, see David F. Wells, *God the Evangelist: How the Holy Spirit Works to Bring Men and Women to Faith* (Grand Rapids: Eerdmans, 1987); John M. Penney, *The Missionary Emphasis of Lukan Pneumatology*, JPTSup 12 (Sheffield, U.K.: Academic Press, 1996); Robertson McQuilkin, "The Role of the Holy Spirit in Missions," in *The Holy Spirit and Mission Dynamics*, ed. C. D. McConnell, Evangelical Missiological Society Series 5 (Pasadena, Calif.: William Carey Library, 1997); and Peter T. O'Brien, "Mission, Witness, and the Coming of the Spirit," *BBR* 9 (1999): 203-14.

God."[148] David Wells also emphasizes this point when he asserts,

> technology is concerned with effects and with producing those effects in
> the most efficient way. It is not concerned with those who devise or use
> it, nor is it concerned with those who are affected by it, since the tacit
> operative assumption is that what is efficient is right. If technology can
> produce its results efficiently, then questions of moral or a reflective na-
> ture become redundant. It is not difficult to see how easily this mind-set
> can influence and eventually control the preaching of the gospel. Evan-
> gelism can be viewed as a human endeavor whose object is to achieve
> results in the shortest possible time. And if results efficiently achieved,
> can be reported, questions about the character of the evangelist and the
> means employed to carry out the evangelism seem redundant or irrel-
> evant. This approach, however, not only departs from the biblical pattern
> but is positively injurious to it. The character of the evangelist and the
> means he or she uses must be consistent with the message proclaimed.
> And the message proclaimed has the power to do its work not because
> of the evangelist's personality or skills of persuasion but because of the
> mighty power of the Holy Spirit, who alone is able to turn rebellious sin-
> ners into obedient followers of Christ.[149]

Missionary work and pastoral ministry that acknowledge the authority of Scripture and want to pay more than lip service to the centrality of
the gospel of Jesus the crucified and risen Savior will always recognize
the power of God as the primary cause of repentance and conversion, of
change and transformation.

The power of God should not be confused with experiencing miracles. The assertion that the miracle promotes faith and should thus be
an integral part of the mission and evangelism of the church[150] is neither
confirmed by Paul, by Luke's narrative of the apostles' missionary work
in the book of Acts or by the history of the church. It is simply incorrect
when some assert that "there is a pattern of growth and expansion of
the church that followed these recorded miracles in Scripture."[151] Some

---

[148]Guinness, *Dining with the Devil*, p. 29.

[149]Wells, *God the Evangelist*, p. 46.

[150]See John Wimber, *Power Evangelism: Signs and Wonders Today* (London: Hodder & Stoughton,
1985); Wagner, *Church Growth and the Whole Gospel*.

[151]Mark Wagner, "Signs and Wonders," *EDWM*, p. 875.

passages indeed link the numerical growth of the church with miracles: Acts 5:15-16 (Jerusalem); 9:34-35 (Lydda and Sharon); 9:40-42 (Joppa). They are all linked with the missionary work of Peter. This does not constitute a pattern. The picture is complex. When miraculous signs took place in Samaria when Philip proclaimed the news of Jesus there, the people were indeed amazed (Acts 8:5-8); but conversions and baptisms are linked not with miracles but with Philip "who was proclaiming the good news about the kingdom of God and the name of Jesus Christ" (Acts 8:12). In Paphos, the governor Sergius Paullus reacts to the miraculous punishment of his court astrologer who is struck with blindness, but the cause of his faith is connected by Luke with Paul's teaching about the Lord Jesus Christ (Acts 13:12). In Iconium, Paul's mission was accompanied by signs and wonders (Acts 14:3); however, Luke does not link these events with conversions but with the comment that "the residents of the city were divided; some sided with the Jews, and some with the apostles" (Acts 14:4). The citizens of Lystra who witnessed Paul's healing of a crippled man interpreted the miracle not as the decisive authentication of the missionaries and their message. Rather, they integrated the miracle into their traditional religiosity (Acts 14:11). They evidently had understood so little of Paul's preaching that they believed their polytheistic and mythical traditions to be confirmed by the miracle. Luke's report only implicitly mentions the conversions of people in the city (Acts 14:20); there is no explicit reference to establishment of a church, let alone explosive growth.

In the first century (and today) miraculous events take place not only in the context of the work of Christian missionaries but in pagan contexts as well. The significance of miracles is therefore always ambiguous, needing interpretation. It is not a question whether God has the power to work miracles, which on occasion may indeed prompt people to listen to the proclamation of the gospel with more openness. Of course God has not abdicated his creative and healing powers to modern physicians and psychologists. And it is certainly true that Western Christians and missionaries can be so secular and materialistic in their expectations that they do not expect God to intervene and heal people. And it is certainly correct that in many cultures "power encounters" are an important part of the religious experience of people and should therefore be expected to be a significant element of missionary work.

It is a matter of concern, however, when language is used which suggests that missionaries, evangelists and pastors should use signs and wonders as tools in their ministry. The notion that Christian missionaries can "use" miracles implies that they can cause miracles to happen, which in turn would imply that they can manipulate God in causing miracles to take place. The problem with the signs and wonders movement is not only that miracles often take center stage (literally), at the expense of the proclamation of the gospel, that some practices approach the techniques of traditional magic or that sometimes claims of miracles are made where nothing happened.[152] The main problem is that the apparent reliance on God for working a miracle becomes trust in the tool of signs and wonders that is used whenever the missionary and evangelist sees a need and an opportunity.[153] Sometimes God works through miracles. The ambiguity of miracles suggests that God never works only through miracles to bring people to faith in Jesus Christ. God always works through the proclamation of his Word in which the power of his Holy Spirit is present.

A similar danger of unwittingly adopting magical practices has been suggested for the so-called spiritual warfare movement,[154] which has been influencing many Christians and missionaries. A key element in this missionary "tool" is to identify spirits or demons, understood to be fallen angels, who hold sway over cities, regions and countries controlling the spiritual receptiveness of people to the gospel, and then "neutralizing" them through prayer, resulting in an increased openness of people to the gospel. The notion that spiritual powers can be manipu-

---

[152]Thus the critique of ibid., p. 876. We should not forget that the death rate and the life expectancy of Christians who belong to churches that do not emphasize the miraculous do not seem to be different from those in churches that emphasize signs and wonders.

[153]See Ebbie C. Smith, "Miracles in Mission," *EDWM*, p. 631, who asserts that "missionaries must affirm that miracles, signs, and wonders are not necessary for evangelism or other missionary work" and that "power resides in the gospel itself, not in miracles."

[154]See C. Peter Wagner, *Confronting the Powers: How the New Testament Church Experienced the Power of Strategic-Level Spiritual Warfare* (Ventura: Regal Books, 1996); Charles H. Kraft, "'Christian Animism' or God-Given Authority?" in *Spiritual Power and Missions: Raising the Issues*, ed. E. Rommen (Pasadena, Calif.: William Carey Library, 1995), pp. 88-135.

lated by human activity is described by critics as animistic and magical rather than biblical.[155] Again, when we consider Paul's paradigm and principles concerning missionary work and the truth of the gospel, there is no doubt that Christians are in a "state of war" on account of the activities and the influence of Satan, God's enemy (Eph 6:10-18). And there is no doubt that missionaries and pastors encounter the reality of the spirit world as they proclaim the news of Jesus Christ and seek to help new converts to grasp and apply the consequences of the gospel for their lives. Whatever territorial "responsibilities" some demons might have—Scripture is far from giving a clear and unified teaching on these matters—it appears to be the Western technocratic spirit that transforms prayer against the attacks of Satan into a strategic tool that is expected to make missionary work more effective.

This review and evaluation of missionary strategies, church planting methods and church-growth techniques are not exhaustive. To borrow an analogy from nuclear physics, the half-life of a particular contemporary method in missions and evangelism seems to be diminishing constantly. What is a trend today may be obsolete next year. The discussion in this chapter is meant to illustrate how new projects and paradigms, new models and methods should be evaluated in the light of the biblical witness, which prominently includes the missionary theology and work of the apostle Paul.

Followers of Jesus follow Jesus. They have come to faith in the one true and living God, the God of Abraham, Isaac and Israel. They have come to faith in Jesus, the Son of Man and Son of God, the Messiah and Savior whom God had promised to solve the problem of human sin once and for all. They have come to enjoy the presence of God and of the Lord Jesus Christ in their lives as God's Holy Spirit prompts them to worship God, transforms their lives and equips them to be light of the world and salt of the earth.

---

[155]See Robert J. Priest et al., "Missiological Syncretism: The New Animistic Paradigm," in *Spiritual Power and Missions: Raising the Issues*, ed. E. Rommen (Pasadena, Calif.: William Carey Library, 1995), pp. 143-68. See the discussion in Clinton E. Arnold, *Three Crucial Questions about Spiritual Warfare* (Grand Rapids: Baker, 1997); Chuck Lowe, *Territorial Spirits and World Evangelisation?* (Sevenoaks, U.K.: Mentor/Overseas Missionary Fellowship, 1998); Moreau et al., *Introducing World Missions*, pp. 287-90.

Followers of Jesus follow Jesus as they are committed to the one true God and his Word. They are committed to love God and Jesus Christ. Since authentic love presupposes and coalesces around knowing and understanding the person one loves, their love for God and for Jesus Christ seeks to "overflow more and more with knowledge and full insight" in order to be able "to determine what is best" and in order to be "pure and blameless" on the day of Jesus' return and of God's judgment (Phil 1:9-10).

Followers of Jesus have thus a spiritual identity, focused on understanding God the Father, Jesus the messianic Son of God and God's Holy Spirit. This means that theology, the discipline which teaches followers of Jesus about God, the Son and the Spirit, is central and must remain foundational for churches and for their missionary work, no matter where they are geographically, ethnically or socially located.[156]

Certainly, the local gathering of the followers of Jesus is more than a spiritual gathering of people learning and living theology. The church is also a family whose members enjoy each other's company, encouraging and helping each other. But the church is never less. First things must be truly first in the people of God. If first things are pushed to the periphery because "second things" are more attractive, the church worships idols.

Christians truly worship the one true and living God only when they let God be God. And when they do, they will be a light to the world and the salt of the earth. When they do, some of them will be willing to be called and sent by God to devote their lives to proclaiming the news of Jesus in places where his name is not acknowledged. When they go and serve, they will trust in the power of God to use their proclamation of Jesus Christ, and whatever else they do to help people in need, so that Jews and Greeks, slaves and free, men and women understand the news of Jesus, accept the Messiah and Savior, and live to the glory of God until Jesus Christ returns.

---

[156]See Guthrie, *Missions in the Third Millennium*, pp. 28-29, who is convinced that the cure for the missionary malaise in the Western churches "will not come in a new marketing strategy, but in a new look at Scripture, for it is there that we see God clearly."

Bibliography

Abegg, Martin, Peter Flint and Eugene Ulrich. *The Dead Sea Scrolls Bible*. San Francisco: HarperCollins, 1999.

Adams, N. James, and Simon Swain. "Introduction." In *Bilingualism in Ancient Society: Language Contact and the Written Text*, edited by J. N. Adams, M. Janse, and S. Swaine, 1-20. Oxford: Oxford University Press, 2002.

Allen, Hubert J. B. *Roland Allen: Pioneer, Priest, and Prophet*. Cincinnati: Forward Movement Publications; Grand Rapids: Eerdmans, 1995.

Allen, Roland. *Education in the Native Church*. London: World Dominion Press, 1926.

———. *Missionary Methods: St. Paul's or Ours? A Study of the Church in the Four Provinces*. Library of Historic Theology. London: Robert Scott Roxburghe, 1912.

———. *Missionary Methods: St. Paul's or Ours?* Reprint. Grand Rapids: Eerdmans, 2001.

Allen, Roland, and Charles Gore. *Educational Principles and Missionary Methods: The Application of Educational Principles to Missionary Evangelism*. London: Robert Scott, 1919.

Ameling, Walter. *Inscriptiones Judaicae Orientis. Band II: Kleinasien*. TSAJ 99. Tübingen: Mohr-Siebeck, 2004.

Anderson, Graham. *Philostratus: Biography and Belles Lettres in the Third Century A.D.* London: Croom Helm, 1986.

———. *The Second Sophistic: A Cultural Phenomenon in the Roman Empire*. London: Routledge, 1993.

Anderson, Leith. *Dying for Change: An Arresting Look at the New Realities Confronting Churches and Para-Church Ministries*. Minneapolis: Bethany, 1990.

Anthony, Michael J., ed. *Evangelical Dictionary of Christian Education*. Grand Rapids: Baker Academic, 2001.

————. *Introducing Christian Education: Foundations for the Twenty-First Century.* Grand Rapids: Baker Academic, 2001.

Arnold, Clinton E. *Three Crucial Questions About Spiritual Warfare.* Grand Rapids: Baker, 1997.

Bachmann, Philipp. *Der erste Brief des Paulus an die Korinther.* 4th ed. Leipzig: Deichert, 1936.

Badenas, Robert. *Christ the End of the Law: Romans 10.4 in Pauline Perspective.* JSNTSup 10. Sheffield, U.K.: JSOT Press, 1985.

Balch, David L. "The Areopagus Speech: An Appeal to the Stoic Historian Posidonius against Later Stoics and the Epicureans." In *Greeks, Romans, and Christians: Essays in Honor of Abraham J. Malherbe,* edited by D. L. Balch, E. Ferguson and W. A. Meeks, 52-79. Minneapolis: Fortress, 1990.

Ball, Warwick. *Rome in the East: The Transformation of an Empire.* London: Routledge, 2000.

Balz, Horst, and Gerhard Schneider, eds. *Exegetical Dictionary of the New Testament.* 3 vols. Grand Rapids: Eerdmans, 1990-1993.

Banks, Robert. *Paul's Idea of Community: The Early House Churches in their Historical Setting.* Rev. ed. Peabody, Mass.: Hendrickson, 1994.

Barclay, John M. G. *Jews in the Mediterranean Diaspora: From Alexander to Trajan (323 BCE—117 CE).* Edinburgh: T & T Clark, 1996.

Barna, George. *Marketing the Church: What They Never Taught You About Church Growth.* Colorado Springs: NavPress, 1988.

————. *User Friendly Churches: What Christians Need to Know About the Churches People Love to Go To.* Ventura: Regal Books, 1991.

Barrett, C. K. *The Acts of the Apostles.* ICC. Edinburgh: T & T Clark, 1994-98.

————. *Freedom and Obligation: A Study of the Epistle to the Galatians.* Philadelphia: Westminster, 1985.

————. *Jesus and the Word and Other Essays.* PTMS 41. Allison Park, Penn.: Pickwick, 1995.

Bartels, Ulrike. *Die Wochenschau im Dritten Reich: Entwicklung und Funktion eines Massenmediums unter besonderer Berücksichtigung völkisch-nationaler Inhalte.* Frankfurt: Lang, 2004.

Barth, Karl. *Protestant Theology in the Nineteenth Century: Its Background and History.* Grand Rapids: Eerdmans, 2002.

Barth, Markus, and Helmut Blanke. *Colossians.* AncB 34B. New York: Doubleday, 1994.

Bauckham, Richard. "James and the Gentiles (Acts 15.13-21)." In *History, Literature, and Society in the Book of Acts*, edited by B. Witherington, 154-84. Cambridge: Cambridge University Press, 1996.

―――. "James and the Jerusalem Church." In *The Book of Acts in its Palestinian Setting*, edited by R. Bauckham, 415-80. The Book of Acts in Its First-Century Setting 4. Exeter, U.K.: Paternoster, 1995.

Bauer, Walter, Frederick W. Danker, William F. Arndt and F. Wilbur Gingrich. *A Greek-English Lexicon of the New Testament and Other Early Christian Literature*. 3rd ed. Chicago: Chicago University Press, 2000.

Baugh, Steven M. "Paul and Ephesus: The Apostle Among His Contemporaries." Ph.D. Dissertation. University of California, Irvine, 1990.

Beale, G. K., and D. A. Carson, eds. *Commentary on the New Testament Use of the Old Testament*. Grand Rapids: Baker, 2007.

Beard, Mary, John North and Simon Price. *Religions of Rome*. Cambridge: Cambridge University Press, 1998.

Beasley-Murray, George R. *Baptism in the New Testament*. 3rd Edition. Exeter, U.K.: Paternoster, 1979.

―――. *Jesus and the Kingdom of God*. Grand Rapids: Eerdmans, 1986.

Bechard, Dean Philip. *Paul Outside the Walls: A Study of Luke's Socio-Geographical Universalism in Acts 14:8-20*. Analecta biblica 143. Rome: Editrice Pontificio Istituto Biblico, 2000.

Becker, Jürgen. *Paul: Apostle to the Gentiles*, translated by O. C. Dean Jr. Louisville: Westminster/John Knox Press, 1993.

―――. "Paulus und seine Gemeinden." In *Die Anfänge des Christentums: Alte Welt und neue Hoffnung*, edited by J. Becker, 102-59. Stuttgart: Kohlhammer, 1987.

Best, Ernest. *A Critical and Exegetical Commentary on Ephesians*. ICC. Edinburgh: T & T Clark, 1998.

Bietenhard, Hans. "Die syrische Dekapolis von Pompeius bis Trajan." In *Aufstieg und Niedergang der römischen Welt*. Vol. II.8. Edited by H. Temporini and W. Haase, 220-61. Berlin: De Gruyter, 1977.

Blue, Bradley B. "Acts and the House Church." In *The Book of Acts in Its Graeco-Roman Literary Setting*, edited by D. W. J. Gill and C. Gempf, 119-222. The Book of Acts in Its First-Century Setting 2. Exeter, U.K.: Paternoster, 1994.

Bonk, Jonathan J. *Missions and Money: Affluence as a Western Missionary Problem*. Maryknoll: Orbis Books, 1991.

Bonner, Stanley F. *Education in Ancient Rome: From the Elder Cato to the Younger*

Pliny. London: Methuen, 1977.

Bonnington, Mark. *The Antioch Episode of Galatians 2:11-14 in Historical and Cultural Context*. Paternoster Biblical Monographs. Bletchley: Paternoster, 2005.

Booth, Alan. "The Age for Reclining and Its Attendant Perils." In *Dining in a Classical Context*, edited by W. J. Slater, 105-20. Ann Arbor: University of Michigan Press, 1991.

Bormann, Lukas. *Philippi—Stadt und Christengemeinde zur Zeit des Paulus*. NT-Sup 78. Leiden: Brill, 1995.

Bornkamm, Günther. *Paul*. London and New York: Harper, 1971.

Borthwick, Paul. "What Local Churches are Saying to Mission Agencies." *EMQ* 35 (1999): 324-33.

Bosch, David J. *Transforming Mission: Paradigm Shifts in the Theology of Mission*. American Society of Missiology Series 16. Maryknoll: Orbis, 1991.

Bowers, W. Paul. "Church and Mission in Paul." *JSNT* 44 (1991): 89-111.

———. "Fulfilling the Gospel: The Scope of the Pauline Mission." *JETS* 30 (1987): 185-98.

———. "Studies in Paul's Understanding of His Mission." Ph.D. Dissertation. University of Cambridge, 1976.

Bowersock, Glen Warren. *Greek Sophists in the Roman Empire*. Oxford: Clarendon, 1969.

Böhme, Hartmut, Peter Matussek and Lothar Müller. *Orientierung Kulturwissenschaft*. Reinbek: Rowohlt, 2000.

Brandt, Hartwin. *Gesellschaft und Wirtschaft Pamphyliens und Pisidiens im Altertum*. Asia-Minor Studien 7. Bonn: Habelt, 1992.

Breytenbach, Cilliers. "Paul's Proclamation and God's 'thriambos' (Notes on 2 Corinthians 2.14-16b)." *Neot.* 24 (1990): 257-71.

———. *Paulus und Barnabas in der Provinz Galatien. Studien zu Apostelgeschichte 13f.; 16,6; 18,23 und den Adressaten des Galaterbriefes*. AGAJU 38. Leiden: Brill, 1996.

———. *Paulus und Barnabas in der Provinz Galatien*. AGAJU 38. Leiden: Brill, 1996.

Brocke, Christoph vom. *Thessaloniki—Stadt der Kassander und Gemeinde des Paulus. Eine frühe christliche Gemeinde in ihrer heidnischen Umwelt*. WUNT 2.125. Tübingen: Mohr-Siebeck, 2001.

Brown, Colin, ed. *The New International Dictionary of New Testament Theology*. 4 vols. Grand Rapids: Eerdmans, 1975-1978.

Brown, Harold O. J. *Heresies: The Image of Christ in the Mirror of Heresy and Or-*

thodoxy from the Apostles to the Present. Grand Rapids: Baker, 1988.

Brown, Raymond E. *The Semitic Background of the Term "Mystery" in the New Testament*. Philadelphia: Fortress Press, 1968.

Brox, Norbert. *A History of the Early Church*. London: SCM, 1994.

Bruce, F. F. *The Book of the Acts*. Rev. ed. NICNT. Grand Rapids: Eerdmans, 1988.

————. *Commentary on Galatians*. NIGTC. Grand Rapids: Eerdmans, 1982.

————. *Paul: Apostle of the Free Spirit*. Exeter, U.K.: Paternoster, 1977.

————. *Tradition Old and New*. Exeter, U.K.: Paternoster, 1970.

Burchard, Christoph. "Erfahrungen multikulturellen Zusammenlebens im Neuen Testament." In *Multikulturelles Zusammenleben: Theologische Erfahrungen*, edited by J. Micksch, 24-41. Frankfurt: Limbeck, 1984.

Burgoon, Michael, Frank G. Hunsaker and Edwin J. Dawson. *Human Communication*. 3rd ed. London: Sage, 1994.

Burkert, Walter. *Greek Religion*. Cambridge, Mass.: Harvard University Press, 1985.

Burton-Christie, Douglas. *The Word in the Desert: Scripture and the Quest for Holiness in Early Christian Monasticism*. Oxford: Oxford University Press, 1993.

Bush, Luis. "In Pursuit of True Christian Partnership: A Biblical Basis from Philippians." In *Partners in the Gospel: The Strategic Role of Partnership in World Evangelization*, edited by J. H. Kraakevik and D. Welliver, 3-15. Wheaton, Ill.: Billy Graham Center, 1992.

Buss, Matthäus F.-J. *Die Missionpredigt des Apostels Paulus im Pisidischen Antiochien. Analyse von APG:13.16-41 im Hinblick auf die literarische und thematische Einheit der Paulusrede*. FzB 38. Stuttgart: Katholisches Bibelwerk, 1980.

Cahill, Michael. "The Neglected Parallelism in Colossians 1.24-25." *Ephemerides Theologicae Lovanienses* 68 (1992): 142-47.

Caldwell, Kirbyjon, and Walt Kallestad. *Entrepreneurial Faith: Launching Bold Initiatives to Expand God's Kingdom*. Colorado Springs: WaterBrook, 2004.

Camp, Bruce K. "A Theological Examination of the Two-Structure Theory." *Missiology* 23 (1995): 197-209.

Camp, John McK. *Gods and Heroes in the Athenian Agora*. Princeton, N.J.: American School of Classical Studies at Athens, 1980.

Campbell, Alastair. "'Do the Work of an Evangelist'." *EVQ* 64 (1992): 117-29.

Campbell, Douglas A. "Possible Inscriptional Attestation to Sergius Paul[l]us (Acts 13:6-12), and the Implications for Pauline Chronology." *JTS* 56 (April 2005): 1-29.

Campbell, William S. "Paul's Missionary Practice and Policy in Romans." *Irish Biblical Studies* 12 (1990): 2-25.

Cancik, Hubert, and Helmuth Schneider, eds. *Der Neue Pauly. Enzyklopädie der Antike.* 26 vols. Stuttgart and Weimar: Metzler, 1996-2009. English: *Brill's New Pauly: Encyclopedia of the Ancient World.* 20 vols. Leiden: Brill, 2002-

Caragounis, Chrys C. *The Ephesian Mysterion: Meaning and Content.* Lund: Gleerup, 1977.

Carson, Donald A. "Athens Revisited." In *Telling the Truth: Evangelizing Postmoderns,* edited by D. A. Carson, 384-98. Grand Rapids: Zondervan, 2000.

————."Paul's Mission and Prayer." In *The Gospel to the Nations: Perspectives on Paul's Mission,* edited by P. Bolt and M. Thompson, 175-84. Leicester, U.K.: Inter-Varsity Press, 2000.

Casson, Lionel. *Travel in the Ancient World.* 1974. Reprint, Baltimore: Johns Hopkins University Press, 1994.

Chae, Daniel J.-S. *Paul as Apostle to the Gentiles: His Apostolic Self-Awareness and its Influence on the Soteriological Argument in Romans.* Carlisle, U.K.: Paternoster, 1997.

Chester, Stephen J. *Conversion at Corinth: Perspectives on Conversion in Paul's Theology and the Corinthian Church.* Studies of the New Testament and its World. Edinburgh: T & T Clark, 2003.

Chew, Jim. *When You Cross Cultures: Vital Issues Facing Christian Missions.* Singapore: Navigators, 1990.

Christol, Michel, Thomas Drew-Bear and Mehmet Tahlialan. "L'empereur Claude, le chevalier C. Caristanius Fronto Caesianus Iullus et le culte impérial à Antioche de Pisidie." *Tyche* 16 (2001): 1-20.

Christol, Michel, and Thomas Drew-Bear. "Les Sergii Paulli et Antioche." In *Actes du Ier congres international sur Antioche de Pisidie,* edited by T. Drew-Bear, M. Tashalan and C. J. Thomas, 177-91. Collection archéologie et histoire de l'antiquité 5. Lyon: Université Lumière-Lyon ; Paris: Boccard, 2002.

Clarke, Andrew D. *Secular and Christian Leadership in Corinth: A Socio-Historical and Exegetical Study of 1 Corinthians 1-6.* AGAJU 18. Leiden: Brill, 1993.

Coenen, Lothar, and Klaus Haacker, eds. *Theologisches Begriffslexikon zum Neuen Testament.* Neubearbeitete Ausgabe. Wuppertal: R. Brockhaus, 1997/2000.

Cohen. Shaye J. D. *The Beginnings of Jewishness: Boundaries, Varieties, Uncertainties. Hellenistic Culture and Society* 31. Berkeley: University of California Press, 1999.

Collart, Paul. *Philippes, ville de Macédonie depuis des origines jusqu'à la fin de l'époque romaine.* 2 vols. Paris: Boccard, 1937.

Cook, Harold R. *Missionary Life and Work: A Discussion of Principles and Practices of Missions*. Chicago: Moody Press, 1959.

Corbeill, Anthony. "Dining Deviants in Roman Political Invective." In *Roman Sexualities*, edited by J. P. Hallett and M. B. Skinner, 99-128. Princeton, N.J.: Princeton University Press, 1997.

Cosgrove, Charles H. "Did Paul Value Ethnicity?" *CBQ* 68 (2006): 268-90.

Covington, Daryl. *Purpose Driven Martial Arts*. Blountsville: Fifth Estate, 2006.

Cranfield, C. E. B. *The Epistle to the Romans*. ICC. Edinburgh: T & T Clark, 1975-79.

Cribiore, Raffaella. *Gymnastics of the Mind: Greek Education in Hellenistic and Roman Egypt*. Princeton, N.J.: Princeton University Press, 2001.

Cully, Kendig Brubaker, ed. *The Westminster Dictionary of Christian Education*. Philadelphia: Westminster, 1963.

Davids, Peter H., and Ralph P. Martin, eds. *Dictionary of the Later New Testament and Its Developments*. Downers Grove, Ill.: InterVarsity Press, 1997.

Dayton, Edward R., and David A. Fraser. *Planning Strategies for World Evangelization*. Grand Rapids: Eerdmans, 1980.

Dickson, John P. "Gospel as News: εὐαγγελ- from Aristophanes to the Apostle Paul." *NTS* 51 (2005): 212-30.

———. *Mission-Commitment in Ancient Judaism and in the Pauline Communities: The Shape, Extent and Background of Early Christian Mission*. WUNT 159. Tübingen: Mohr Siebeck, 2003.

Dodds, Eric R. *The Greeks and the Irrational*. Sather Classical Lectures. Berkeley: University of California Press, 1951.

———. *Pagan and Christian in an Age of Anxiety: Some Aspects of Religious Experience from Marcus Aurelius to Constantine*. Cambridge: Cambridge University Press, 1965.

Downey, Glanville. *A History of Antioch in Syria from Seleucus to the Arab Conquest*. Princeton, N.J.: Princeton University Press, 1961.

Downey, Steven. "Partnership Re-Visited." *EMQ* 42 (2006): 200-202.

Downs, Perry G. *Teaching for Spiritual Growth*. Grand Rapids: Zondervan, 1994.

DuBose, Francis M. *God Who Sends: A Fresh Quest for Biblical Mission*. Nashville: Broadman, 1983.

Dudley, Carl S., and David A. Roozen. *Faith Communities Today: A Report on Religion in the United States Today*. Hartford: Hartford Institute for Religious Research, 2001.

Dueck, Daniela. *Strabo of Amasia: A Greek Man of Letters in Augustan Rome*. London and New York: Routledge, 2000.

Dueck, Daniela, Hugh Lindsay and Sarah Pothecary, eds. *Strabo's Cultural Geography: The Making of a Kolossourgia*. Cambridge: Cambridge University Press, 2005.

Dumais, Marcel. "La rencontre de la foi et des cultures." *Lumière et Vie* 30 (1981): 72-86.

Dunn, James D. G. *A Commentary on the Epistle to the Galatians*. BNTC. London: Black, 1993.

———. *The Epistles to the Colossians and to Philemon: A Commentary on the Greek Text*. NIGTC. Grand Rapids: Eerdmans, 1996.

———. *The Acts of the Apostles*. EpComm. London: Epworth, 1996.

———. *Baptism in the Holy Spirit: A Re-examination of the New Testament Teaching on the Gift of the Spirit in Relation to Pentecostalism Today*. London: SCM, 1970.

———. "Once More—Gal 1.18: historēsai Kēphan. In Reply to Otfried Hofius." *ZNW* 76 (1985): 138-39.

———. "The Relationship Between Paul and Jerusalem According to Galatians 1 and 2." *NTS* 28 (1982): 461-78.

———. *Romans*. WBC 38. Dallas: Word, 1988.

———. *The Theology of Paul the Apostle*. Grand Rapids: Eerdmans, 1998.

———. *The Theology of Paul's Letter to the Galatians*. New Testament Theology. Cambridge: Cambridge University Press, 1993.

Elia, Olga. "Pompei—Relazione sullo scavo dell'Insula X della Regio I." *Notizie degli Scavi di Antichità* 10 (1934): 264-344.

Eliot, Thomas S. *Notes Towards the Definition of Culture*. New York: Harcourt, Brace, 1949.

Ellis, E. Earle. The Making of the New Testament Documents. *BIS* 39. Leiden: Brill, 1999.

———. "Paul and His Co-Workers." *NTS* 17 (1971): 437-52.

Engels, Donald. *Roman Corinth: An Alternative Model for the Classical City*. Chicago and London: University of Chicago Press, 1990.

Epstein, David F. *Personal Enmity in Roman Politics 218-43 B.C.* London: Routledge, 1989.

Erdemgil, Selahattin. *The Terrace Houses in Ephesus. Ephesus Museum*. Istanbul: Hitit, 2000.

Escobar, Samuel. *The New Global Mission: The Gospel from Everywhere to Everyone*. Downers Grove, Ill.: InterVarsity Press, 2003.

Evans, Craig A. *Ancient Texts for New Testament Studies: A Guide to the Background Literature*. Peabody, Mass.: Hendrickson, 2005.

Feldtkeller, Andreas. "Syrien II. Zeit des Neuen Testaments." *TRE* 32 (2001): 587-89.

Ferguson, Everett. *The Church of Christ: A Biblical Ecclesiology for Today*. Grand Rapids: Eerdmans, 1996.

Fields, Doug. *Purpose-Driven Youth Ministry: Nine Essential Foundations for Healthy Growth*. Grand Rapids: Zondervan, 1998.

Finley, Bob. *Reformation in Foreign Missions*. Longwood, Fla.: Xulon, 2005.

Fishwick, Duncan. *The Imperial Cult in the Latin West*. Leiden: Brill, 1987-2002.

Fitzmyer, Joseph A. *The Acts of the Apostles*. AncB 31. New York: Doubleday, 1998.

Flemming, Dean E. *Contextualization in the New Testament: Patterns for Theology and Mission*. Downers Grove, Ill.: InterVarsity Press, 2005.

Flemming, Dean E. "Contextualizing the Gospel in Athens: Paul's Areopagus Address as a Paradigm for Missionary Communication." *Missiology* 30 (2002): 199-214.

Fore, William F. *Television and Religion: The Shaping of Faith, Values, and Culture*. Minneapolis: Augsburg, 1987.

Fotopoulos, John. *Food Offered to Idols in Roman Corinth: A Social-Rhetorical Reconsideration of 1 Corinthians 8:1—11:1*. WUNT 2.151. Tübingen: Mohr Siebeck, 2003.

Fournier, Marianne. *The Episode at Lystra. A Rhetorical and Semiotic Analysis of Acts 14:7-20a*. AUS 7:197. New York: Lang, 1997.

French, David. *Roman Roads and Milestones of Asia Minor*. British Institute of Archaeology International Series 392. Oxford: British Institute of Archaeology at Ankara, 1988.

Frier, Bruce W. *Landlords and Tenants in Imperial Rome*. Princeton, N.J.: Princeton University Press, 1980.

Friesen, Steven. *Twice Neokoros: Ephesus, Asia and the Cult of the Flavian Imperial Family*. Leiden: Brill, 1993.

Funk, Robert W. "The Apostolic *Parousia*: Form and Significance." In *Christian History and Interpretation: Studies Presented to John Knox*, ed. W. R. Farmer, 249-69. Cambridge: Cambridge University Press, 1967.

Furnish, Victor Paul. "Fellow Workers in God's Service." *JBL* 80 (1961): 364-70.

Gadamer, Hans-Georg. *Truth and Method*. London: Sheed and Ward, 1975.

Garland, David E. *1 Corinthians*. BECNT. Grand Rapids: Baker, 2003.

Garland, Robert. *Introducing New Gods: The Politics of Athenian Religion*. Ithaca, N.Y.: Cornell University Press, 1992.

Garnsey, Peter. *Social Status and Legal Privilege in the Roman Empire*. Oxford: Clarendon, 1970.

Gärtner, Bertil. *The Areopagus Speech and Natural Revelation*. Lund: Gleerup, 1955.

Geagan, Daniel J. *The Athenian Constitution after Sulla*. Hesperia 12. Princeton, N.J.: American School of Classical Studies at Athens, 1967.

Gehring, Roger W. *House Church and Mission: The Importance of Household Structures in Early Christianity*. Peabody, Mass.: Hendrickson, 2004.

Gempf, Conrad. "Before Paul Arrived in Corinth: The Mission Strategies in 1 Corinthians 2:2 and Acts 17." In *The New Testament in its First Century Setting: Essays on Context and Background in Honor of B. W. Winter*, edited by P. J. Williams et al., 126-42. Grand Rapids: Eerdmans, 2004.

———. "Mission and Misunderstanding: Paul and Barnabas in Lystra (Acts 14:8-20)." In *Mission and Meaning: Essays Presented to Peter Cotterell*, edited by A. Billington et al., 56-69. Carlisle, U.K.: Paternoster, 1995.

Georgi, Dieter. *The Opponents of Paul in Second Corinthians*. Philadelphia: Fortress, 1986.

———. *Remembering the Poor: The History of Paul's Collection for Jerusalem*. Nashville: Abingdon, 1992.

Gerber, Vergil, ed. *Discipling Through Theological Education by Extension: A Fresh Approach to Theological Education in the 1980s*. Chicago: Moody Press, 1980.

Geyer, Paul. "A Critical Theory of Culture." *XXVII*. Deutscher Romanistentag: Munich, 2001.

Gibson, Richard J. "Paul and the Evangelization of the Stoics." In *The Gospel to the Nations: Perspectives on Paul's Mission*, edited by P. Bolt and M. Thompson, 309-26. Leicester, U.K.: Inter-Varsity Press, 2000.

Gill, David W. J. "Achaia." In *The Book of Acts in Its Graeco-Roman Setting*, edited by David W. J. Gill and Conrad Gempf, 433-53. The Book of Acts in Its First-Century Setting 2. Exeter, U.K.: Paternoster, 1994.

———. "Corinth: A Roman Colony in Achaea." *BZ* 37 (1993): 259-64.

———. "Erastus the Aedile." *TynB* 40 (1989): 293-301.

———. "The Importance of Roman Portraiture for Head Coverings in 1 Corinthians 11.2-16." *TynB* 41 (1990): 245-60.

———. "Macedonia." In *The Book of Acts in Its Graeco-Roman Setting*, edited by David W. J. Gill and Conrad Gempf, 397-417. The Book of Acts in Its First-Century Setting 2. Exeter, U.K.: Paternoster, 1994.

———. "Religion in a Local Setting." In *The Book of Acts in Its Graeco-Roman Setting*, edited by David W. J. Gill and Conrad Gempf, 79-92. The Book of Acts in Its First-Century Setting 2. Exeter, U.K.: Paternoster, 1994.

———. "A Saviour for the Cities of Crete: The Roman Background to the Epistle to Titus." In *The New Testament in its First Century Setting: Essays on Context and Background in Honor of B. W. Winter*, edited by P. J. Williams, 220-30. Grand Rapids: Eerdmans, 2004.

Gilliland, Dean S. *Pauline Theology and Mission Practice*. Grand Rapids: Baker, 1983.

Gleason, Maud W. *Making Men: Sophists and Self-Presentation in Ancient Rome*. Princeton, N.J.: Princeton University Press, 1995.

Goerner, H. Cornell. *All Nations in God's Purpose: What the Bible Teaches about Missions*. Nashville: Broadman, 1979.

Goldhill, Simon. "Introduction. Setting an Agenda: 'Everything is Greece to the Wise.' " In *Being Greek under Rome: Cultural Identity, the Second Sophistic and the Development of Empire*, edited by S. Goldhill, 1-25. Cambridge: Cambridge University Press, 2001.

Goodman, Martin. *Mission and Conversion: Proselytizing in the Religious History of the Roman Empire*. Oxford: Clarendon, 1994.

Grahame, Mark. "Material Culture and Roman Identity: The Spatial Layout of Pomopeian Houses and the Problem of Ethnicity." In *Cultural Identity in the Roman Empire*, edited by R. Laurence and J. Berry, 156-78. London: Routledge, 1998.

Gralfs, Bettine. *Metallverarbeitende Produktionsstätten in Pompeji*. BAR International Series 433. Oxford: British Institute of Archaeology, 1988.

Green, Joel B., and Mark D. Baker. *Recovering the Scandal of the Cross: Atonement in New Testament & Contemporary Contexts*. Downers Grove, Ill.: InterVarsity Press, 2000.

Greenway, Roger S. "Success in the City: Paul's Urban Mission Strategy: Acts 14:1-28." In *Mission in Acts: Ancient Narratives in Contemporary Context*, edited by R. L. Gallagher and Paul P. Hertig, 183-95. American Society of Missiology Series 34. Maryknoll: Orbis Books, 2004.

Griffin, Miriam T. *Nero: The End of a Dynasty*. 1984. Reprint, New York: Routledge, 2000.

Gritz, S. H. *Paul, Women Teachers, and the Mother Goddess at Ephesus. A Study of 1 Timothy 2.9-15 in Light of the Religious and Cultural Milieu of the First Century.* Lanham, Md.: University Press of America, 1991.

Gruen, Erich S. *Diaspora: Jews amidst Greeks and Romans.* Cambridge: Harvard University Press, 2002.

Gruenler, Royce Gordon. "The Mission-Lifestyle Setting of 1 Tim 2:8-15." *JETS* 41 (1998): 215-38.

Guinness, Os. *Dining with the Devil: The Megachurch Movement Flirts with Modernity.* Grand Rapids: Baker, 1993.

———— "Sounding Out the Idols of Church Growth." In *No God But God*, edited by O. Guinness and J. Seel, 151-74. Chicago: Moody, 1992.

Guthrie, Stan. *Missions in the Third Millennium: 21 Key Trends for the 21st Century.* Rev. ed. Bletchley, U.K.: Paternoster, 2004.

Haacker, Klaus. *The Theology of Paul's Letter to the Romans.* New Testament Theology. Cambridge: Cambridge University Press, 2003.

————. "Urchristliche Mission und kulturelle Identität. Beobachtungen zu Strategie und Homiletik des Apostels Paulus." *Theologische Beiträge* 19 (1988): 61-72.

Haas, Odo. *Paulus der Missionar. Ziel, Grundsätze und Methoden der Missionstätigkeit des Apostels Paulus nach seinen eigenen Aussagen.* Münsterschwarzach: Vier-Türme-Verlag, 1971.

Hahn, Johan G. "Liturgy on Television or 'Television-Liturgy.' " in *Media Development 3*, 9-11. London: World Association for Christian Communication, 1984.

Hall, Jonathan M. *Ethnic Identity in Greek Antiquity.* Cambridge: Cambridge University Press, 2000.

Hansen, G. Walter. "The Preaching and Defense of Paul." In *Witness to the Gospel. The Theology of Acts*, edited by I. H. Marshall and D. Peterson, 295-324. Grand Rapids: Eerdmans, 1998.

Haraguchi, Takaaki. "Das Unterhaltsrecht des frühchristlichen Verkündigers. Eine Untersuchung zur Bezeichnung ἐργάτης im Neuen Testament." *ZNW* 84 (1993): 178-95.

Harnack, Adolf von. *The Mission and Expansion of Christianity in the First Three Centuries.* 4th ed. London: Williams & Norgate, 1924.

Harris, Gerald. "The Beginnings of Church Discipline: 1 Corinthians 5." In *Understanding Paul's Ethics: Twentieth-Century Approaches*, edited by B. S. Rosner, 129-51. 1991. Carlisle, U.K.: Paternoster, 1995.

Harris, Murray J. *The Second Epistle to the Corinthians*. NIGTC. Grand Rapids: Eerdmans, 2005.

Hasler, Victor. *Die Briefe an Timotheus und Titus (Pastoralbriefe)*. ZBK 12. Zürich: Theologischer Verlag, 1978.

Hawthorne, Gerald F., Ralph P. Martin and Daniel G. Reid, eds. *Dictionary of Paul and His Letters*. Downers Grove, Ill.: InterVarsity Press, 1993.

Hays, Richard B. *The Moral Vision of the New Testament: Community, Cross, New Creation: A Contemporary Introduction to New Testament Ethics*. New York: HarperCollins, 1996.

———. "Scripture-Shaped Community: The Problem of Method in New Testament Ethics." *Interpretation* 44 (1990): 42-55.

Hemer, Colin J. *The Book of Acts in the Setting of Hellenistic History*. Edited by C. H. Gempf. WUNT 49. Tübingen: Mohr-Siebeck, 1989.

Hengel, Martin. *Crucifixion in the Ancient World and the Folly of the Message of the Cross*. Philadelphia: Fortress, 1978.

———. "Einleitung." In *Die Heiden. Juden, Christen und das Problem des Fremden*, edited by R. Feldmeier and U. Heckel, ix-xviii. WUNT 70. Tübingen: Mohr-Siebeck, 1994.

———. "Paul in Arabia." *BBR* 12 (2002): 47-66.

———. "Proseuche und Synagoge: Jüdische Gemeinde, Gotteshaus und Gottesdienst in der Diaspora und in Palästina." In *Judaica et Hellenistica I*. Studien zum antiken Judentum und seiner griechisch-römischen Umwelt, 171-95. 1971. WUNT 90. Tübingen: Mohr-Siebeck, 1996.

——— "Der vorchristliche Paulus." In *Paulus und das antike Judentum*. Tübingen-Durham-Symposium im Gedenken an den 50. Todestag Adolf Schlatters. Edited by M. Hengel and U. Heckel, 177-293. WUNT 58. Tübingen: Mohr-Siebeck, 1991.

Hengel, Martin, and Anna Maria Schwemer. *Paul Between Damascus and Antioch: The Unknown Years*. London: SCM Press; Louisville: Westminster John Knox, 1997.

Henry, Carl F. *The Uneasy Conscience of Modern Fundamentalism*. 1947. Reprint, Grand Rapids: Eerdmans, 2003.

Herrmann, Peter. "Milesischer Purpur." *Istanbuler Mitteilungen* 25 (1975): 141-47.

Hesselgrave, David J. *Planting Churches Cross-Culturally*. 2nd ed. Grand Rapids: Baker, 2000.

Hesselgrave, David J., and Edward Rommen. *Contextualization: Meaning, Methods and Models*. 1992. Grand Rapids: Zondervan, 1989.

Hiebert, Paul G. *Anthropological Insights for Missionaries*. Grand Rapids: Baker, 1985.

Hiebert, Paul G., and Eloise Meneses Hiebert. *Incarnational Ministry: Planting Churches in Band, Tribal, Peasant, and Urban Societies*. Grand Rapids: Baker, 1995.

Hild, Friedrich, and Hansgerd Hellenkemper. *Kilikien und Isaurien*. Tabula Imperii Byzantini 5. Wien: Österreichische Akademie der Wissenschaften, 1990.

Hock, Ronald F. *The Social Context of Paul's Ministry: Tentmaking and Apostleship*. Philadelphia: Fortress, 1980.

Hoff, Michael C. "The Politics and Architecture of the Athenian Imperial Cult." In *Subject and Ruler: The Cult of the Ruling Power in Classical Antiquity*, edited by A. Small, 185-200. Journal of Roman Archaeology Sup 17. Ann Arbor, Mich.: Journal of Roman Archaeology, 1996.

Hoffmann, Hilmar. *The Triumph of Propaganda: Film and National Socialism, 1933-1945*. Providence: Berghahn, 1996.

Hofius, Otfried. "Gal 1,18: ἱστορῆσαι Κηφᾶν." In *Paulusstudien*, 255-67. 1989. Tübingen: Mohr Siebeck, 1994.

Hollander, Harm W., and Gijsbert E. van der Hout. "The Apostle Paul Calling Himself an Abortion: 1 Cor. 15:8 Within the Context of 1 Cor. 15:8-10." *NT* 38 (1996): 224-36.

Holtz, Traugott. *Der erste Brief an die Thessalonicher*. EKK 13. Neukirchen-Vluyn: Neukirchener Verlag; Zürich: Benziger, 1986.

Horsley, Greg H. R., and Stephen R. Llewelyn. *New Documents Illustrating Early Christianity*. North Ryde, New South Wales, Australia: Macquarie University, 1981-2002.

Howell, Don N. "Confidence in the Spirit as the Governing Ethos of the Pauline Mission." In *The Holy Spirit and Mission Dynamics*, edited by C. D. McConnell, 36-65. Evangelical Missiological Society Series 5. Pasadena, Calif.: William Carey Library, 1997.

———. "Mission in Paul's Epistles: Genesis, Pattern, and Dynamics." In *Mission in the New Testament. An Evangelical Approach*, edited by W. J. Larkin and J. F. Williams, 63-91. ASMS 27. New York: Orbis, 1998.

Hölscher, Tonio. *Öffentliche Räume in frühen griechischen Städten*. Heidelberg: Winter, 1998.

Hornblower, Simon, and Antony Spawforth, eds. *Oxford Classical Dictionary*. 3rd ed. Oxford: Oxford University Press, 1996.

Howgego, Christopher. "Coinage and Identity in the Roman Provinces." In *Coinage and Identity in the Roman Provinces*, edited by C. Howgego, V. Heuchert and A. Burnett, 1-17. Oxford: Oxford University Press, 2004.

Hurtado, Larry W. *Lord Jesus Christ: Devotion to Jesus in Earliest Christianity*. Grand Rapids: Eerdmans, 2003.

Hvalvik, Reidar. *The Struggle for Scripture and Covenant: The Purpose of the Epistle of Barnabas and Jewish-Christian Competition in the Second Century*. WUNT 2.82. Tübingen: Mohr-Siebeck, 1996.

Isaac, Benjamin H. *The Invention of Racism in Classical Antiquity*. Princeton, N.J.: Princeton University Press, 2004.

Janne, Henri. "Impulsore Chresto." In *Mélanges Bidez. Annuaire de l'Institut de philologie et d'histoire orientales 2*, 531-53. Bruxelles: Secrétariat de l'Institut, 1934.

Jervell, Jacob. *Die Apostelgeschichte*. KEK 3. Göttingen: Vandenhoeck & Ruprecht, 1998.

Jewett, Robert. "Tenement Churches and Pauline Love Feasts." *Quarterly Review* 14 (1994): 43-58.

Jones, A. H. M. *The Greek City from Alexander to Justinian*. 1940. Reprint, Oxford: Clarendon, 1998.

Joubert, Stephan. *Paul as Benefactor: Reciprocity, Strategy and Theological Reflection in Paul's Collection*. WUNT 2.124. Tübingen: Mohr-Siebeck, 2000.

Judge, Edwin A. *The Social Pattern of Christian Groups in the First Century*. London: Tyndale, 1960.

Kallestad, Walt. *Entertainment Evangelism: Taking the Church Public*. Nashville: Abingdon, 1996.

Kammler, Hans-Christian. *Kreuz und Weisheit. Eine exegetische Untersuchung zu 1 Kor 1,10—3,4*. WUNT 159. Tübingen: Mohr Siebeck, 2003.

Kane, J. Herbert. *Christian Missions in Biblical Perspective*. Grand Rapids: Baker, 1976.

―――. *Understanding Christian Missions*. Rev. ed. Grand Rapids: Baker, 1981.

Kasher, Aryeh. *Jews, Idumaeans, and Ancient Arabs: Relations of the Jews in Eretz-Israel with the Nations of the Frontier and the Desert During the Hellenistic and Roman Era (332 BCE - 70 CE)*. TSAJ 18. Tübingen: Mohr-Siebeck, 1988.

Käsemann, Ernst. *Commentary on Romans*. Grand Rapids: Eerdmans, 1980.

Kearsley, Rosalinde A. "The Asiarchs." In *The Book of Acts in Its Graeco-Roman Literary Setting*, edited by D. W. J. Gill and C. Gempf, 363-76. The Book of Acts in Its First-Century Setting 2. Exeter, U.K.: Paternoster, 1994.

Kelly, John M. *Roman Litigation*. Oxford: Clarendon Press, 1966.

Kelly, John N. D. *A Commentary on the Pastoral Epistles*. 1963. Reprint, Grand Rapids: Thornapple Commentaries, 1986.

Kennedy, George A. *The Art of Rhetoric in the Roman World, 300 B.C. - A.D. 300*. Princeton, N.J.: Princeton University Press, 1972.

————. *A New History of Classical Rhetoric*. Princeton, N.J.: Princeton University Press, 1994.

Kent, John Harvey. *Corinth VIII, iii: The Inscriptions 1926-1950*. Princeton, N.J.: American School of Classical Studies at Athens, 1966.

Keyes, Lawrence E. *The Last Age of Missions: A Study of Third World Missionary Societies*. Pasadena, Calif.: William Carey Library, 1983.

Kilde, Jeanne Halgren. *When Church became Theatre: The Transformation of Evangelical Architecture and Worship in Nineteenth-Century America*. New York: Oxford University Press, 2002.

Kim, Seyoon. *The Origin of Paul's Gospel*. 2nd ed. WUNT 2.4. Tübingen: Mohr-Siebeck, 1984.

Kinman, Brent Roger. *Jesus' Entry into Jerusalem: In the Context of Lukan Theology and the Politics of His Day*. AGJU 28. Leiden: Brill, 1995.

Kirchhoff, Renate. *Die Sünde gegen den eigenen Leib. Studien zu* πόρνη *und* πορνεία *in 1 Kor 6,12-20 und dem soziokulturellen Kontext der paulinischen Adressaten*. StUNT 18. Göttingen: Vandenhoeck & Ruprecht, 1994.

Kittel, Gerhard, and Gerhard Friedrich, eds. *Theological Dictionary of the New Testament*. 10 vols. Grand Rapids: Eerdmans, 1964-1976.

Klauber, Martin, and Scott M. Manetsch. *The Great Commission: Evangelicals and the History of World Missions*. Nashville: Broadman & Holman, 2007.

Knibbe, Dieter. "Via Sacra Ephesiaca: New Aspects of the Cult of Artemis Ephesia." In *Ephesos, Metropolos of Asia: An Interdisciplinary Approach to its Archaeology, Religion, and Culture*, edited by H. Koester, 141-55. HTS 41. Valley Forge, Penn.: Trinity Press International, 1995.

Kofsky, Aryeh. *Eusebius of Caesarea Against Paganism*. Leiden: Brill, 2002.

Köstenberger, Andreas J. *The Missions of Jesus and the Disciples according to the Fourth Gospel. With Implications for the Fourth Gospel's Purpose and the Mission of the Contemporary Church*. Grand Rapids: Eerdmans, 1998.

————. "Women in the Pauline Mission." In *The Gospel to the Nations: Perspectives on Paul's Mission*, edited by P. Bolt and M. Thompson, pp. 221-47. Leicester, U.K.: Inter-Varsity Press, 2000.

Köstenberger, Andreas J., and Peter T. O'Brien. *Salvation to the Ends of the Earth: A Biblical Theology of Mission.* NSBT 11. Downers Grove, Ill.: InterVarsity Press, 2001.

Kraft, Charles H. "'Christian Animism' or God-given Authority?" In *Spiritual Power and Missions: Raising the Issues,* edited by E. Rommen, 88-135. Pasadena, Calif.: William Carey Library, 1995.

Krause, Gerhard, and Gerhard Müller, eds. *Theologische Realenzyklopädie.* 36 vols. Berlin: De Gruyter, 1977-2007.

Kruse, Colin G. *Paul, the Law and Justification.* Downers Grove, Ill.: InterVarsity Press, 1996.

Kuck, David W. *Judgment and Community Conflict: Paul's Use of Apocalyptic Judgement Language in 1 Corinthians 3:5—4:5.* NTSup Leiden: Brill, 1992.

Kuper, Adam. *Culture: The Anthropologists' Account.* Cambridge, Mass.: Harvard University Press, 1999.

Lambert, Stephen D. "Athenian State Laws and Decrees, 352/1—322/1: II Religious Regulations." *ZPE* 154 (2005): 125-59.

Laminger-Pascher, Gertrud. *Die kaiserzeitlichen Inschriften Lykaoniens. Faszikel I: Der Süden.* ETAM 15. Wien: Österreichische Akademie der Wissenschaften, 1992.

Lampe, Peter. "Acta 19 im Spiegel der ephesischen Inschriften." *BZ* 36 (1992): 59-76.

Lane Fox, Robin. *Pagans and Christians in the Mediterranean World from the Second Century A.D. to the Conversion of Constantine.* Harmondsworth, U.K.: Viking, 1986.

Lausberg, Heinrich. *Handbook of Literary Rhetoric: A Foundation for Literary Study.* Leiden: Brill, 1998.

Leonard, John S. "The Church in Between Cultures." *EMQ* 40 (2004): 62-70.

Levick, Barbara. "Antiocheia 15." In *Real-Encyclopädie der classischen Altertumswissenschaft, Supplement XI,* edited by A. F. von Pauly and G. Wissowa, 49-61. Stuttgart: Metzler, 1968.

———. *Roman Colonies in Southern Asia Minor.* Oxford: Clarendon, 1967.

Levine, Lee I. *The Ancient Synagogue: The First Thousand Years.* New Haven, Conn.: Yale University Press, 2000.

———. *Jerusalem: Portrait of the City in the Second Temple Period (538 B.C.E.—70 C.E.).* Philadelphia: Jewish Publication Society, 2002.

Levinskaya, Irina. *The Book of Acts in its Diaspora Setting.* The Book of Acts in Its First-Century Setting 5. Carlisle, U.K.: Paternoster, 1996.

Liefeld, Walter L. "Women and Evangelism in the Early Church." *Missiology* 15 (1987): 291-98.

Lightfoot, J. B. *Biblical Essays*. 2nd ed. London: MacMillan, 1904.

———. *Saint Paul's Epistle to the Philippians*. London: Macmillan, 1868.

Limbeck, Meinrad. "Die Religionen im Neuen Testament." *Theologische Quartalschrift* 169 (1989): 44-56.

Lincoln, Andrew T. *Ephesians*. WBC 42. Dallas: Word, 1990.

Lingenfelter, Sherwood G. *Agents of Transformation: A Guide for Effective Cross-Cultural Ministry*. Grand Rapids: Baker, 1996.

———. *Transforming Culture: A Challenge for Christian Mission*. 2nd ed. Grand Rapids: Baker, 1998.

Litfin, Duane. *St. Paul's Theology of Proclamation: 1 Corinthians 1—4 and Greco-Roman Rhetoric*. SNTSMS 79. Cambridge: Cambridge University Press, 1994.

Little, Christopher R. *Mission in the Way of Paul: Biblical Mission for the Church in the Twenty-First Century*. Studies in Biblical Literature 80. New York: Peter Lang, 2005.

Löhr, Hermut. "Zur Paulus-Notiz in 1 Clem 5.5-7." In *Die letzte Jerusalemreise des Paulus*, edited by F. W. Horn, 197-213. BZNW 106. Berlin: De Gruyter, 2001.

Longenecker, Richard N. *Galatians*. WBC 31. Dallas: Word, 1990.

———. "Paul's Vision of the Church and Community Formation in His Major Missionary Letters." In *Community Formation in the Early Church and in the Church Today*, edited by R. N. Longenecker, 73-88. Peabody, Mass.: Hendrickson, 2002.

Longenecker, Richard N., ed. *The Road from Damascus: The Impact of Paul's Conversion on His Life, Thought, and Ministry*. Grand Rapids: Eerdmans, 1997.

Lowe, Chuck. *Territorial Spirits and World Evangelisation?* Sevenoaks, U.K.: Mentor/Overseas Missionary Fellowship, 1998.

Luhmann, Niklas. "Kultur als historischer Begriff." In *Gesellschaftsstruktur und Semantik. Studien zur Wissenssoziologie der modernen Gesellschaft. Band 4*, 31-54. Frankfurt: Suhrkamp, 1995.

Lupieri, Edmondo. *The Mandaeans: The Last Gnostics*. Italian Texts and Studies on Religion and Society. Grand Rapids: Eerdmans, 2002.

Lupu, Eran. *Greek Sacred Law: A Collection of New Documents*. Religions in the Graeco-Roman World 152. Leiden: Brill, 2005.

MacMullen, Ramsay. *Christianizing the Roman Empire (A.D. 100-400)*. New Haven, Conn.: Yale University Press, 1984.

—————. *Paganism in the Roman Empire.* New Haven, Conn.: Yale University Press, 1981.

—————. *Romanization in the Time of Augustus.* New Haven, Conn.: Yale University Press, 2000.

—————. *Voting about God in Early Church Councils.* New Haven, Conn.: Yale University Press, 2006.

Magie, David. *Roman Rule in Asia Minor to the End of the Third Century After Christ.* 1950. Reprint, New York: Arno, 1975.

Malherbe, Abraham J. *The Letters to the Thessalonians.* AncB 32B. New York: Doubleday, 2000.

—————. *Paul and the Popular Philosophers.* Minneapolis: Fortress, 1989.

—————. *Social Aspects of Early Christianity.* 2nd ed. Philadelphia: Fortress, 1983.

Malphurs, Aubrey. *Planting Growing Churches for the 21st Century: A Comprehensive Guide for New Churches and those Desiring Renewal.* Grand Rapids: Baker, 2004.

Marsden, George M. *Understanding Fundamentalism and Evangelicalism.* Grand Rapids: Eerdmans, 1991.

Marshall, I. Howard. *The Acts of the Apostles. An Introduction and Commentary.* TNTC. Leicester, U.K.: Inter-Varsity Press, 1980.

—————. *1 and 2 Thessalonians.* New Century Bible Commentary. Grand Rapids: Eerdmans, 1983.

—————. "Luke's Portrait of the Pauline Mission." In *The Gospel to the Nations: Perspectives on Paul's Mission,* edited by P. Bolt and M. Thompson, 99-113. Leicester, U.K.: Inter-Varsity Press, 2000.

—————. *New Testament Theology: Many Witnesses, One Gospel.* Downers Grove, Ill.: InterVarsity Press, 2004.

—————. *The Pastoral Epistles.* ICC. Edinburgh: T & T Clark, 1999.

—————. "Who Were the Evangelists?" In *The Mission of the Early Church to Jews and Gentiles,* edited by J. Adna and H. Kvalbein, 251-63. WUNT 127. Tübingen: Mohr-Siebeck, 2000.

Martin, Ralph P. *Worship in the Early Church.* London: Marshall, Morgan & Scott, 1964.

May, Elmer C., Gerald P. Stadler and John F. Votaw. *Ancient and Medieval Warfare.* Wayne: Avery, 1984.

McDonald, James I. H. *Kerygma and Didache: The Articulation and Structure of the Earliest Christian Message.* SNTSMS 37. 1980. Reprint, Cambridge: Cambridge University Press, 2004.

McGavran, Donald Anderson. *The Bridges of God: A Study in the Strategy of Missions*. New York: Friendship Press, 1955.

———. *Understanding Church Growth*. Grand Rapids: Eerdmans, 1970.

———. *Understanding Church Growth*. 3rd ed. Revised and edited by C. P. Wagner. Grand Rapids: Eerdmans, 1990.

McGavran, Donald A., and Winfield C. Arn. *Ten Steps for Church Growth*. San Francisco: Harper & Row, 1977.

McGinn, Thomas A. J. *The Economy of Prostitution in the Roman World: A Study of Social History and the Brothel*. Ann Arbor: University of Michigan Press, 2004.

McIntosh, Gary L. *Church That Works: Your One-Stop Resource for Effective Ministry*. Grand Rapids: Baker, 2004.

McIntosh, Gary L., ed. *Evaluating the Church Growth Movement: Five Views*. Grand Rapids: Zondervan, 2004.

McQuail, Denis. *McQuail's Mass Communication Theory*. 5th ed. Thousand Oaks, Calif.: Sage, 2005.

McQuilkin, Robertson. "The Role of the Holy Spirit in Missions." In *The Holy Spirit and Mission Dynamics*, edited by C. D. McConnell. Evangelical Missiological Society Series 5. Pasadena, Calif.: William Carey Library, 1997.

Meeks, Wayne A. *The First Urban Christians: The Social World of the Apostle Paul*. New Haven, Conn.: Yale University Press, 1983.

Metcalf, Samuel F. "When Local Churches Act Like Agencies." *EMQ* 29 (1993): 142-49.

Meyers, Eric M., and James F. Strange. *Archaeology, the Rabbis and Early Christianity*. Nashville: Parthenon, 1981.

Mihaila, Corin. "The Paul-Apollos Relationship and Paul's Stance Toward Greco-Roman Rhetoric: An Exegetical and Socio-Historical Study." Ph.D. Dissertation. Louisville: Southeastern Baptist Theological Seminary, 2006.

Millar, Fergus. *The Roman Empire and its Neighbours*. 2nd ed. 1996. London: Duckworth, 1981.

———. *The Roman Near East, 31 BC—AD 337*. Cambridge: Harvard University Press, 1993.

Minear, Paul S. *Images of the Church in the New Testament*. Philadelphia: Westminster, 1960.

Mitchell, Margaret M. "New Testament Envoys in the Context of Greco-Roman Diplomatic and Epistolary Conventions: The Example of Timothy and Titus." *JBL* 111 (1992): 641-62.

Mitchell, Stephen. "The Administration of Roman Asia from 133 B.C. to A.D. 250." In *Lokale Autonomie und römische Ordnungsmacht in den kaiserzeitlichen Provinzen vom 1. bis 3. Jahrhundert*, edited by W. Eck and E. Müller-Luckner, 17-46. Schriften des Historischen Kollegs 42. München: Oldenbourg, 1999.

———. *Anatolia: Land, Men, and Gods in Asia Minor.* Oxford: Oxford University Press, 1995.

———. "The Cult of Theos Hypsistos between Pagans, Jews, and Christians." In *Pagan Monotheism in Late Antiquity*, edited by P. Athanassiadi and M. Frede, 81-148. Oxford: Clarendon, 1999.

Mitchell, Stephen, and Marc Waelkens. *Pisidian Antioch: The Site and its Monuments.* London: Duckworth, 1998.

Moreau, A. Scott, Harold A. Netland, Charles E. Van Engen and David Burnett, eds. *Evangelical Dictionary of World Missions.* Grand Rapids: Baker, 2000.

Moreau, A. Scott, Gary Corwin and Gary B. McGee. *Introducing World Missions: A Biblical, Historical, and Practical Survey.* Grand Rapids: Baker Academic, 2003.

Mounce, William D. *Pastoral Epistles.* WBC 46. Nashville: Nelson, 2000.

Mowery, Robert L. "Paul and Caristanius at Pisidian Antioch." *Biblica* 87 (2006): 221-42.

Muggeridge, Malcolm. *Christ and the Media.* Grand Rapids: Eerdmans, 1977.

Munck, Johannes. *Paul and the Salvation of Mankind.* 1959. Atlanta: Knox, 1977.

Murphy-O'Connor, Jerome. *Paul: A Critical Life.* Oxford: Oxford University Press, 1996.

———. "Paul in Arabia." *CBQ* 55 (1993): 732-37.

———. *St. Paul's Corinth: Texts and Archaeology.* Wilmington: Glazier, 1983.

Murray, Oswyn, and Simon Price. *The Greek City: From Homer to Alexander.* Oxford: Clarendon, 1991.

Mutafian, Claude. *La Cilicie au carrefour des empires.* Paris: Belles Lettres, 1988.

Neff, David. "Stepping on Toes." *EMQ* 36 (2000): 238-42.

Nelson, Marlin L., ed. *Readings in Third World Missions: A Collection of Essential Documents.* South Pasadena, Calif.: William Carey Library, 1976.

Newton, Derek. *Deity and Diet: The Dilemma of Sacrificial Food at Corinth.* JSNTSS 169. Sheffield, U.K.: Sheffield Academic Press, 1998.

Nickelsburg, George W. E. "An ἔκτρωμα, Though Appointed from the Womb: Paul's Apostolic Self-Description in 1 Corinthians 15 and Galatians 1." *HThR* 79 (1986): 198-205.

Nickle, Keith Fullerton. *The Collection: A Study in Paul's Strategy*. Studies in Biblical Theology 48. London: SCM, 1966.

Niebuhr, Karl-Wilhelm. *Heidenapostel aus Israel. Die jüdische Identität des Paulus nach ihrer Darstellung in seinen Briefen*. WUNT 62. Tübingen: Mohr-Siebeck, 1992.

Nigdelis, Pantelis M. "Synagoge(n) und Gemeinde der Juden in Thessaloniki: Fragen aufgrund einer neuen jüdischen Grabinschrift der Kaiserzeit." *ZPE* 102 (1994): 297-306.

Nilsson, Martin P. *Geschichte der griechischen Religion*. 4th ed. 1992/1988. Handbuch der Altertumswissenschaft V. 2. München: Beck, 1941/1950.

Nobbs, Alanna. "Cyprus." In *The Book of Acts in Its Graeco-Roman Setting*, edited by D. W. J. Gill and C. Gempf, 279-89. The Book of Acts in Its First-Century Setting 2. Exeter, U.K.: Paternoster, 1994.

Noy, David, Alexander Panayotov, and Hanswulf Bloedhorn. *Inscriptiones Judaicae Orientis*. Vol. 1: *Eastern Europe*. TSAJ 101. Tübingen: Mohr-Siebeck, 2004.

O'Brien, Peter T. "The Church as Heavenly and Eschatological Entity." In *The Church in the Bible and the World*, edited by D. A. Carson, 88-119, 307-11. 1987. Reprint, Grand Rapids: Baker, 1993.

———. *Colossians, Philemon*. WBC 44. Waco, Tex.: Word, 1982.

———. *The Epistle to the Philippians. A Commentary on the Greek Text*. NIGTC. Grand Rapids: Eerdmans, 1991.

———. *Gospel and Mission in the Writings of Paul: An Exegetical and Theological Analysis*. Grand Rapids: Baker, 1995.

———. *Introductory Thanksgivings in the Letters of Paul*. NTSup 49. Leiden: Brill, 1977.

———. *The Letter to the Ephesians*. PNTC. Grand Rapids: Eerdmans, 1999.

———. "Mission, Witness, and the Coming of the Spirit." *BBR* 9 (1999): 203-14.

Oepke, Albrecht. *Die Missionspredigt des Apostels Paulus. Eine biblisch-theologische und religionsgeschichtliche Untersuchung*. Missionswissenschaftliche Forschungen 2. Leipzig: Hinrichs, 1920.

Ollrog, Wolf-Henning. *Paulus und seine Mitarbeiter*. WMANT 50. Neukirchen-Vluyn: Neukirchener Verlag, 1979.

Olson, C. Gordon. *What in the World Is God Doing? The Essentials of Global Missions: An Introductory Guide*. 5th ed. Cedar Knolls, N.J.: Global Gospel Publishers, 2003.

Osei-Bonsu, Joseph. "The Contextualization of Christianity: Some New Testament Antecedents." *Irish Biblical Studies* 12 (1990): 129-48.

Oswalt, John N. *The Book of Isaiah. Chapters 40—66.* NICOT. Grand Rapids: Eerdmans, 1986.

Ott, Craig. "Let the Buyer Beware." *EMQ* 29 (1993): 268-91.

Owens, Virginia Stem. *The Total Image, or, Selling Jesus in the Modern Age.* Grand Rapids: Eerdmans, 1980.

Padberg, Lutz E. von. *Mission und Christianisierung. Formen und Folgen bei Angelsachsen und Franken im 7. und 8.* Jahrhundert. Stuttgart: Steiner, 1995.

Padilla, René. "The Unity of the Church and the Homogeneous Unit Principle." *International Bulletin of Missionary Research* 6, no. 1 (1982): 23-30.

Pao, David W. *Acts and the Isaianic New Exodus.* WUNT 2.130. Tübingen: Mohr-Siebeck, 2000.

————. *Thanksgiving: An Investigation of a Pauline Theme.* NSBT. Downers Grove, Ill.: InterVarsity Press, 2002.

Parker, R. C. T. "What Are Sacred Laws?" In *The Law and the Courts in Ancient Greece*, edited by E. M. Harris and L. Rubinstein, 57-70. London: Duckworth, 2004.

Pascarella, Perry, and Mark A. Frohman. *The Purpose-Driven Organization: Unleashing the Power of Direction and Commitment.* San Francisco: Jossey-Bass, 1989.

Pate, Larry D. *From Every People: A Handbook of Two-Thirds World Missions with Directory.* Monrovia, Calif.: MARC, 1989.

Peace, Richard V. *Conversion in the New Testament: Paul and the Twelve.* Grand Rapids: Eerdmans, 1999.

Penner, Peter F., ed. *Theological Education as Mission.* Schwarzenfeld, Germany: Neufeld Verlag, 2005.

Penney, John M. *The Missionary Emphasis of Lukan Pneumatology.* JPTSup 12. Sheffield, U.K.: Academic Press, 1996.

Pesce, Mauro. *Le due fasi della predicazione di Paolo. Dall'evangelizzazione alla guida delle communità.* Studi biblici 22. Bologna: Dehoniane, 1994.

Pesch, Rudolf. *Die Apostelgeschichte.* EKK 5. Zürich: Benziger; Neukirchen-Vluyn: Neukirchener Verlag, 1986.

Peskett, Howard, and Vinoth Ramachandra. *The Message of Mission: The Glory of Christ in All Time and Space.* Downers Grove, Ill.: InterVarsity Press, 2003.

Peterson, David G. "Prayer in Paul's Writings." In *Teach Us to Pray: Prayer in the Bible and the World*, edited by D. A. Carson, 84-101, 325-28. Grand Rapids: Baker; Exeter, U.K.: Paternoster, 1990.

Peterson, David. *Engaging with God: A Biblical Theology of Worship*. Leicester, U.K.: Inter-Varsity Press, 1992.

Peterson, Erik. *Frühkirche, Judentum und Gnosis*. Studien und Untersuchungen. Rome: Herder, 1959.

Philostratus. *The Lives of the Sophists*. London: Heinemann, 1922.

Pichler, Josef. *Paulusrezeption und Paulusbild in der Apostelgeschichte 13,16-52*. IThS 50. Innsbruck: Tyrolia, 1997.

Pilhofer, Peter. *Philippi. Band I: Die erste christliche Gemeinde Europas. Band II: Katalog der Inschriften von Philippi*. WUNT 87.119. Tübingen: Mohr-Siebeck, 1995-2000.

Pilhofer, Susanne. *Romanisierung in Kilikien? Das Zeugnis der Inschriften*. Quellen und Forschungen zur Antiken Welt 46. München: Herbert Utz, 2006.

Pillai, C. A. Joachim. *Early Missionary Preaching: A Study of Luke's Report in Acts 13*. Hicksville, N.Y.: Exposition Press, 1979.

Plassart, André. *Inscriptions de la terrasse du temple et de la region nord du sanctuaire, Nos. 276 à 350. Les inscriptions du Temple du IVe siècle*. Fouilles de Delphes III: Épigraphie 4. Paris: Boccard, 1970.

Plummer, Robert L. *Paul's Understanding of the Church's Mission*. Paternoster Biblical Monographs. Bletchley, U.K.: Paternoster, 2006.

Porter, Stanley E., ed. *Handbook of Classical Rhetoric in the Hellenistic Period, 330 B.C.—A.D. 400*. Leiden: Brill, 2001.

Porter, Stanley. "Jesus and the Use of Greek in Galilee." In *Studying the Historical Jesus. Evaluations of the State of Current Research*, edited by B. Chilton and C. A. Evans, 123-54. NTTS 19. Leiden: Brill, 1994.

Powers, Bruce P., ed. *Christian Education Handbook*. Nashville: Broadman & Holman, 1996.

Praet, Danny. "Explaining the Christianization of the Roman Empire: Older Theories and Recent Developments." *Sacris Erudiri* 33 (1992-1993): 5-119.

Preston, Rebecca. "Roman Questions, Greek Answers: Plutarch and the Construction of Identity." In *Being Greek Under Rome: Cultural Identity, the Second Sophistic and the Development of Empire*, edited by S. Goldhill, 86-119. Cambridge: Cambridge University Press, 2001.

Price, Simon R. F. "Local Mythologies in the Greek East." In *Coinage and Identity in the Roman Provinces*, edited by C. Howgego, V. Heuchert and A. Burnett, 115-24. Oxford: Oxford University Press, 2004.

———. *Rituals and Power: The Roman Imperial Cult in Asia Minor*. Oxford: Oxford University Press, 1984.

Priest, Robert J., Thomas Campbell and Bradford A. Mullen. "Missiological Syncretism: The New Animistic Paradigm." In *Spiritual Power and Missions: Raising the Issues*, edited by E. Rommen, 143-68. Pasadena, Calif.: William Carey Library, 1995.

Prior, Michael. *Paul the Letter-Writer and the Second Letter to Timothy.* JSNTSup 23. Sheffield, U.K.: JSOT Press, 1989.

Pucci Ben Zeev, Miriam. *Jewish Rights in the Roman World: The Greek and Roman Documents Quoted by Josephus Flavius.* TSAJ 74. Tübingen: Mohr Siebeck, 1998.

Rainer, Thom S. *The Book of Church Growth: History, Theology, and Principles.* Nashville: Broadman, 1993.

Rajak, Tessa. "The Location of Cultures in Second Temple Palestine: The Evidence of Josephus." In *The Book of Acts in its Palestinian Setting*, edited by R. Bauckham, 1-14. The Book of Acts in Its First-Century Setting 4. Exeter, U.K.: Paternoster, 1995.

Ramsay, William M. *St. Paul the Traveller and the Roman Citizen.* London: Hodder & Stoughton, 1896.

Rapske, Brian. *The Book of Acts and Paul in Roman Custody.* The Book of Acts in Its First-Century Setting 3. Exeter, U.K.: Paternoster, 1994.

Reck, Reinhold. *Kommunikation und Gemeindeaufbau.* Stuttgart: Katholisches Bibelwerk, 1991.

Reed, Jonathan L. *Archaeology and the Galilean Jesus: A Re-Examination of the Evidence.* Harrisburg, Penn.: Trinity Press International, 2000.

Refoulé, François. ". . . et ainsi tout Israël sera sauvé." *Romains 11.25-32.* LD 117. Paris: Cerf, 1984.

Reinbold, Wolfgang. *Propaganda und Mission im ältesten Christentum. Eine Untersuchung zu den Modalitäten der Ausbreitung der frühen Kirche.* FRLANT 188. Göttingen: Vandenhoeck & Ruprecht, 2000.

Reinhardt, Wolfgang. "The Population Size of Jerusalem and the Numerical Growth of the Jerusalem Church." In *The Book of Acts in its Palestinian Setting*, edited by R. Bauckham, 237-65. The Book of Acts in Its First-Century Setting 4. Exeter, U.K.: Paternoster, 1995.

Richardson, John S. *The Romans in Spain.* Oxford: Blackwell, 1996.

Richardson, Peter. *Herod: King of the Jews and Friend of the Romans.* 1996. Minneapolis: Fortress, 1999.

Rickett, Daniel. *Making Your Partnership Work.* Enumclaw, Wash.: WinePress, 2002.

Riesner, Rainer. *Paul's Early Period: Chronology, Mission Strategy, Theology.*
Grand Rapids: Eerdmans, 1998.

Robertson, Noel. "The Religious Criterion in Greek Ethnicity." *American Journal of Ancient History* 1 (2002): 5-74.

Roloff, Jürgen. *Die Kirche im Neuen Testament.* Grundrisse zum Neuen Testament 10. Göttingen: Vandenhoeck & Ruprecht, 1993.

Romano, David G. "A Tale of Two Cities: Roman Colonies at Corinth." In *Romanization and the City: Creation, Transformations, and Failures,* edited by E. Fentress, 83-104. JRASup 38. Portsmouth: Journal of Roman Archaeology, 2000.

Rousselle, Aline. *Porneia: On Desire and the Body in Antiquity.* Oxford and New York: Blackwell, 1988.

Russell, Donald A. *Greek Declamation.* Cambridge: Cambridge University Press, 1983.

Salditt-Trappmann, Regina. *Tempel der ägyptischen Götter in Griechenland und an der Westküste Kleinasiens.* EPRO 15. Leiden: Brill, 1970.

Sanders, Guy D. R. "Urban Corinth: An Introduction." In *Urban Religion in Roman Corinth: Interdisciplinary Approaches,* edited by D. N. Schowalter and S. J. Friesen, pp. 11-24. HTS 53. Cambridge, Mass.: Harvard University Press, 2005.

Sanders, J. T. "Christians and Jews in the Roman Empire: A Conversation with Rodney Stark." *Sociological Analysis* 53 (1992): 433-45.

Sargeant, Kimon Howland. *Seeker Churches: Promoting Traditional Religion in a Nontraditional Way.* New Brunswick, N. J.: Rutgers University Press, 2000.

Schaller, Lyle E. *Church Marketing: Breaking Ground for the Harvest.* Ventura, Calif.: Regal Books, 1992.

———. *Small Congregation, Big Potential: Ministry in the Small Membership Church.* Nashville: Abingdon, 2003.

———. *The Very Large Church: New Rules for Leaders.* Nashville: Abingdon, 2000.

Schlatter, Adolf. *Paulus der Bote Jesu. Eine Deutung seiner Briefe an die Korinther.* 1934. Reprint, Stuttgart: Calwer, 1969.

Schnabel, Eckhard J. *Der erste Brief des Paulus an die Korinther.* Historisch-Theologische Auslegung. Wuppertal: R. Brockhaus, 2006.

———. *Early Christian Mission.* 2 vols. Downers Grove, Ill.: InterVarsity Press, 2004.

———. "How Paul Developed His Ethics." In *Understanding Paul's Ethics.*

Twentieth-Century Approaches, edited by B. S. Rosner, 267-97. Carlisle, U.K.: Paternoster, 1995.

Schnackenburg, Rudolf. *The Church in the New Testament.* London: Burns & Oates, 1968.

Schrage, Wolfgang. *Der erste Brief an die Korinther.* EKK VII. Zürich: Benziger; and Neukirchen-Vluyn: Neukirchener Verlag, 1991-2001.

Schreiner, Thomas R. *Paul, Apostle of God's Glory in Christ: A Pauline Theology.* Downers Grove, Ill.: InterVarsity Press, 2001.

Schrenk, Gottlob. "Der Römerbrief als Missionsdokument." In *Studien zu Paulus*, 81-106. AThANT 26. Zürich: Theologischer Verlag, 1954.

Schürer, Emil. *The History of the Jewish People in the Age of Christ (175 B.C. - A.D. 135).* Revised by G. Vermes, F. Millar, M. Black and M. Goodman. Edinburgh: T & T Clark, 1973-87.

Schwarz, Christian A. *Natural Church Development: A Guide to Eight Essential Qualities of Healthy Churches.* Carol Stream, Ill.: ChurchSmart Resources, 1996.

Scott, James M. *Paul and the Nations: The Old Testament and Early Jewish Background of Paul's Mission to the Nations with Special Reference to the Destination of Galatians.* 1995. WUNT 84. Tübingen: Mohr-Siebeck, 2002.

Segal, Alan F. *Paul the Convert: The Apostolate and Apostasy of Saul the Pharisee.* New Haven, Conn.: Yale University Press, 1990.

Sellin, Gerhard. *Der Streit um die Auferstehung der Toten. Eine religionsgeschichtliche und exegetische Untersuchung von 1 Korinther 15.* FRLANT 138. Göttingen: Vandenhoeck & Ruprecht, 1986.

Sharpe, Eric J. "Mission." In *A Dictionary of Comparative Religion*, edited by S. G. F. Brandon, 44. London: Weidenfeld & Nicolson, 1970.

Shawchuck, Norman, Philip Kotler, Bruce Wrenn and Gustave Rath. *Marketing for Congregations: Choosing to Serve People More Effectively.* Nashville: Abingdon, 1992.

Shear, T. Leslie. "Athens: From City-State to Provincial Town." *Hesperia* 50 (1981): 356-77.

Shelton, R. Larry. *Cross and Covenant: Interpreting the Atonement for 21st Century Mission.* Carlisle, U.K.: Paternoster, 2006.

Shenk, Wilbert R. "Mission Strategies." In *Toward the Twenty-First Century in Christian Mission: Essays in Honor of Gerald H. Anderson*, edited by J. M. Phillips and R. T. Coote, 218-34. Grand Rapids: Eerdmans, 1993.

Shillington, George. "Paul's Success in the Conversion of Gentiles: Dynamic Center in Cultural Diversity." *Direction* 20 (1991): 125-34.

Skarsaune, Oskar, "Jewish Believers in Jesus in Antiquity—Problems of Definition, Method, and Sources." In *Jewish Believers in Jesus: The Early Centuries*, edited by O. Skarsaune and R. Hvalvik, 3-21. Peabody, Mass.: Hendrickson, 2007.

Smith, Colin. "Keeping Christ Central in Preaching." In *Telling the Truth: Evangelizing Postmoderns*, edited by D. A. Carson, 111-22. Grand Rapids: Zondervan, 2000.

Sokolowski, Franciszek. *Lois sacrées de l'Asie Mineure*. Travaux et mémoires 9. Paris: Boccard, 1955.

———. *Lois sacrées des cités grecques*. Paris: Boccard, 1969.

———. *Lois sacrées des cités grecques*. With Supplément. Paris: Boccard, 1962.

Somnath, Sarah. "The Relevance of Cultural Distance Between Patients and Physicians to Racial Disparities in Health Care." *Journal of General Internal Medicine* 21, no. 2 (2006): 203-5.

Söding, Thomas. "Der Skopos der paulinischen Rechtfertigungslehre." *ZThK* 97 (2000): 404-33.

Søgaard, Viggo. *Media in Church and Mission: Communicating the Gospel*. Pasadena, Calif.: William Carey Library, 1993.

Spawforth, Antony J. S. "The Early Reception of the Imperial Cult in Athens: Problems and Ambiguities." In *The Romanization of Athens*, edited by Michael M. C. Hoff and S. I. Rotroff, 183-202. Oxbow Monograph 94. Oxford: Oxbow Books, 1997.

Spicq, Ceslas. *Les Épîtres pastorales*. Quatrième édition refondue. Éditions Bibliques. Paris: Gabalda, 1969.

Squarciapino, Maria Floriani. "The Synagogue at Ostia." *Archaeology* 16 (1963): 194-203.

Stambaugh, John E. *The Ancient Roman City*. Baltimore: Johns Hopkins University Press, 1988.

Stanley, Brian. *The Bible and the Flag: Protestant Missions and Imperialism in the Nineteenth and Twentieth Centuries*. Leicester, U.K.: Inter-Varsity Press, 1990.

Stark, Rodney. *The Rise of Christianity*. San Francisco: HarperCollins, 1997.

Stenschke, Christoph W. *Luke's Portrait of Gentiles Prior to Their Coming to Faith*. WUNT 2.108. Tübingen: Mohr-Siebeck, 1999.

Stephan, Eckhard. *Honoratioren, Griechen, Polisbürger. Kollektive Identitäten innerhalb der Oberschicht des kaiserzeitlichen Kleinasien*. Hypomnemata 143. Göttingen: Vandenhoeck & Ruprecht, 2002.

Stetzer, Ed. *Planting New Churches in a Postmodern Age*. Nashville: Broadman & Holman, 2003.

Stott, John. *Between Two Worlds: The Art of Preaching in the Twentieth Century*. Grand Rapids: Eerdmans, 1987.

Stuhlmacher, Peter. *Biblische Theologie des Neuen Testaments*. Göttingen: Vandenhoeck & Ruprecht, 1992/1999.

―――. *Paul's Letter to the Romans*. Louisville: Westminster, 1994.

Syme, Ronald. *Anatolica: Studies in Strabo*. Edited by A. Birley. Oxford: Clarendon, 1995.

Talbert, Richard J. A., ed. *Barrington Atlas of the Greek and Roman World*. Princeton, N.J.: Princeton University Press, 2000.

Taylor, Justin. *Les Actes des deux Apôtres*. *Études Biblique*. Paris: Lecoffre, 1990-2000.

Taylor, William David, ed. *Internationalizing Missionary Training: A Global Perspective*. Grand Rapids: Baker, 1991.

Telford, Tom, and Lois Shaw. *Missions in the Twenty-First Century: Getting the Church into the Game*. Wheaton: Shaw, 1998.

Theissen, Gerd. *The Social Setting of Pauline Christianity*. Philadelphia: Fortress, 1982.

Thielman, Frank. *The Law and the New Testament: The Question of Continuity*. New York: Crossroad, 1999.

―――. *Paul and the Law: A Contextual Approach*. Downers Grove, Ill.: InterVarsity Press, 1994.

Thiselton, Anthony C. *First Corinthians: A Shorter Exegetical and Pastoral Commentary*. Grand Rapids: Eerdmans, 2006.

―――. *The First Epistle to the Corinthians*. NIGTC. Grand Rapids: Eerdmans, 2000.

Thom, Johan Carl. *Cleanthes' Hymn to Zeus: Text, Translation, and Commentary*. Studien und Texte zu Antike und Christentum 33. Tübingen: Mohr Siebeck, 2005.

Thompson, Glen L. "In Darkest Lycaonia: Paul as Foreign Missionary at Lystra." Evangelical Theological Society Annual Meeting. San Diego, November 14, 2007.

Thompson, James. *Pastoral Ministry According to Paul: A Biblical Vision*. Grand Rapids: Baker Academic, 2006.

Thrall, Margaret E. *The Second Epistle to the Corinthians*. ICC. Edinburgh: T & T Clark, 1994/2000.

Todd, M. "Forum and Capitolium in the Early Empire." In *Roman Urban To-pography in Britain and the Western Empire*, edited by F. Grew and B. Hobley, 56-66. Proceedings of the Third Conference on Urban Archaeology. London: Council for British Archaeology, 1985.

Towner, Philip H. *The Goal of Our Instruction: The Structure of Theology and Ethics in the Pastoral Epistles.* JSNTSup 34. Sheffield, U.K.: JSOT Press, 1989.

Towner, Philip H. "Mission Practice and Theology under Construction (Acts 18—20)." In *Witness to the Gospel. The Theology of Acts*, edited by I. H. Marshall and D. Peterson, 417-36. Grand Rapids: Eerdmans, 1998.

Turner, Max M. B. "Mission and Meaning in Terms of 'Unity' in Ephesians." In *Mission and Meaning*, edited by A. Billington et al., 138-66. Carlisle, U.K.: Paternoster, 1995.

Ueding, Gert, ed. *Historisches Wörterbuch der Rhetorik.* Tübingen: Niemeyer, 1992-2011.

Unnik, Willem C. van. "Tarsus or Jerusalem: The City of Paul's Youth." In *Sparsa Collecta*, 259-320. NovT Suppl. 29. 1952. Reprint, Leiden: Brill, 1973.

Van Engen, Charles, *God's Missionary People: Rethinking the Purpose of the Local Church.* Grand Rapids: Baker, 1991.

Veit, W. F. "Argumentatio." In *Historisches Wörterbuch der Rhetorik.* Vol. 1. Edited by G. Ueding, 904-10. Tübingen: Niemeyer, 1992-2007.

Versnel, Hendrik S. *Ter unus: Isis, Dionysos, Hermes: Three Studies in Henotheism.* Inconsistencies in Greek and Roman Religion 1. Leiden: Brill, 1990.

Versnel, Hendrik Simon. *Triumphus: An Inquiry into the Origin, Development and Meaning of the Roman Triumph.* Leiden: Brill, 1970.

Verwer, George. *Out of the Comfort Zone.* Minneapolis: Bethany House, 2000.

Veyne, Paul. "The Roman Empire." in *A History of Private Life.* Vol.1: *From Pagan Rome to Byzantium*, edited by P. Veyne, 5-234. 1987. Reprint, Cambridge, Mass.: Harvard University Press, 2003.

Voss, Florian. *Das Wort vom Kreuz und die menschliche Vernunft. Eine Untersuchung zur Soteriologie des 1. Korintherbriefes.* FRLANT 199. Göttingen: Vandenhoeck & Ruprecht, 2002.

Wagner, C. Peter. *Church Growth and the Whole Gospel: A Biblical Mandate.* San Francisco: Harper & Row, 1987.

———. *Confronting the Powers: How the New Testament Church Experienced the Power of Strategic-Level Spiritual Warfare.* Ventura, Calif.: Regal Books, 1996.

Wagner, C. Peter, and Edward R. Dayton. "The People-Group Approach to World Evangelization." In *Unreached Peoples 1981*, 19-35. Elgin, Ill.: Cook, 1981.

Walbank, Mary E. H. "The Foundation and Planning of Early Roman Corinth." *JRA* 10 (1997): 95-130.

Wallace-Hadrill, Andrew. *Houses and Society in Pompeii and Herculaneum.* Princeton, N.J.: Princeton University Press, 1994.

Walls, Andrew F. *The Missionary Movement in Christian History: Studies in the Transmission of Faith.* Maryknoll, N.Y.: Orbis, 1996.

Walters, James C. "Egyptian Religions in Ephesos." In *Ephesos, Metropolos of Asia: An Interdisciplinary Approach to its Archaeology, Religion, and Culture,* edited by H. Koester, 281-309. HThS 41. Valley Forge, Penn.: Trinity Press International, 1995.

Wander, Bernd. "Die letzte Jerusalemreise des Paulus." In *Warum wollte Paulus nach Spanien? Ein forschungs- und motivgeschichtlicher Überblick,* edited by F. W. Horn, 175-95. BZNW 106. Berlin: De Gruyter, 2001.

———. *Gottesfürchtige und Sympathisanten. Studien zum heidnischen Umfeld von Diasporasynagogen.* WUNT 104. Tübingen: Mohr-Siebeck, 1998.

Warren, Rick. *The Purpose-Driven Church: Growth Without Compromising Your Message and Mission.* Grand Rapids: Zondervan, 1995.

Wedderburn, Alexander J. M. *Baptism and Resurrection: Studies in Pauline Theology Against Its Graeco-Roman Background.* WUNT 44. Tübingen: Mohr-Siebeck, 1987.

———. "Paul's Collection: Chronology and History." *NTS* 48 (2002): 95-110.

Welch, Robert H. *Church Administration: Creating Efficiency for Effective Ministry.* Nashville: Broadman & Holman, 2005.

Weld, Wayne C. *The World Directory of Theological Education by Extension.* Pasadena, Calif.: William Carey Library, 1973.

Wells, David F. *Above All Earthly Pow'rs: Christ in a Postmodern World.* Grand Rapids: Eerdmans, 2005.

———. *God the Evangelist: How the Holy Spirit Works to Bring Men and Women to Faith.* Grand Rapids: Eerdmans, 1987.

———. *No Place for Truth, or, Whatever Happened to Evangelical Theology?* Grand Rapids: Eerdmans, 1993.

Wenham, David. "Acts and the Pauline Corpus II: The Evidence of Parallels." In *The Book of Acts in Its Ancient Literary Setting,* edited by B. W. Winter and A. D. Clarke, 215-58. The Book of Acts in Its First-Century Setting 1. Exeter, U.K.: Paternoster, 1993.

———. *Paul: Follower of Jesus or Founder of Christianity?* Grand Rapids: Eerdmans, 1995.

Westerholm, Stephen. *Israel's Law and the Church's Faith: Paul and His Recent Interpreters*. Grand Rapids: Eerdmans, 1988.

White, Jerry. *The Church and the Parachurch: An Uneasy Marriage*. Portland, Ore.: Multnomah, 1983.

White, L. Michael. "Adolf Harnack and the 'Expansion' of Early Christianity: A Reappraisal of Social History." *Second Century* 5 (1985-86): 97-127.

———. "Finding the Ties that Bind: Issues from Social Description." *Semeia* 56 (1991): 3-22.

———. *The Social Origins of Christian Architecture*. HThS 42. Valley Forge, Penn.: Trinity Press International, 1996/1997.

———. "Synagogue and Society in Imperial Ostia: Archaeological and Epigraphic Evidence." In *Judaism and Christianity in First-Century Rome*, edited by K. P. Donfried and P. Richardson, 30-68. Grand Rapids: Eerdmans, 1998.

Wilckens, Ulrich. *Die Missionsreden der Apostelgeschichte. Form- und traditionsgeschichtliche Untersuchungen*. 3rd ed. WMANT 5. Neukirchen-Vluyn: Neukirchener Verlag, 1974.

Wiles, Gordon P. *Paul's Intercessory Prayers: The Significance of Paul's Intercessory Prayer Passages in the Letters of St. Paul*. SNTSMS 24. Cambridge: Cambridge University Press, 1974.

Williams, Charles K. "Roman Corinth as a Commercial Center." In *The Corinthia in the Roman Period*, edited by T. E. Gregory, 31-46. JRASup 8. Ann Arbor, Mich.: Journal of Roman Archaeology, 1993.

Williams, Raymond. *The Long Revolution*. London: Chatto & Windus, 1961.

Williamson, George. "Aspects of Identity." In *Coinage and Identity in the Roman Provinces*, edited by C. Howgego, V. Heuchert and A. Burnett, 19-27. Oxford: Oxford University Press, 2004.

Willmer, Wesley K., et al. *The Prospering Parachurch: Enlarging the Boundaries of God's Kingdom*. San Francisco: Jossey-Bass, 1998.

Wimber, John. *Power Evangelism: Signs and Wonders Today*. London: Hodder & Stoughton, 1985.

Winter, Bruce W. "Acts and the Pauline Corpus: I. Ancient Literary Parallels. III. Favorinus, Gellius and Philostratus." In *The Book of Acts in Its Ancient Literary Setting*, edited by B. W. Winter and A. D. Clarke, 196-205. The Book of Acts in Its First-Century Setting 1. Exeter, U.K.: Paternoster, 1993.

———. *After Paul Left Corinth: The Influence of Secular Ethics and Social Change*. Grand Rapids: Eerdmans, 2001.

————. "Civil Litigation in Secular Corinth and the Church: The Forensic Background to 1 Corinthians 6.1-8." In *Understanding Paul's Ethics. Twentieth-Century Approaches*, edited by B. S. Rosner, 85-103. 1991. Carlisle, U.K.: Paternoster, 1995.

————. "Dangers and Difficulties for the Pauline Missions." In *The Gospel to the Nations: Perspectives on Paul's Mission*, edited by P. Bolt and M. Thompson, 285-95. Leicester, U.K.: Inter-Varsity Press, 2000.

————. "In Public and in Private: Early Christian Interactions with Religious Pluralism." In *One God, One Lord in a World of Religious Pluralism*, edited by A. D. Clarke and B. W. Winter, 112-34. Cambridge: Tyndale House, 1991.

————. "On Introducing Gods to Athens: An Alternative Reading of Acts 17.18-20." *TynB* 47 (1996): 71-90.

————. *Philo and Paul Among the Sophists*. SNTSMS 96. Cambridge: Cambridge University Press, 1997.

————. *Seek the Welfare of the City: Christians as Benefactors and Citizens*. Carlisle, U.K.: Paternoster; Grand Rapids: Eerdmans, 1994.

————. "Theological and Ethical Responses to Religious Pluralism: 1 Corinthians 8—10." *TynB* 41 (1990): 209-26.

Winter, Ralph D. "The Highest Priority: Cross-Cultural Evangelism." In *Let the Earth Hear His Voice*. International Congress on World Evangelization, Lausanne, Switzerland. Official Reference Volume: Papers and Responses. Edited by J. D. Douglas, 213-41. Minneapolis: World Wide Publications, 1975.

————. "Momentum Building in Global Missions." *International Journal of Frontier Missions* 7 (1990): 49-59.

————. *Theological Education by Extension*. Pasadena, Calif.: William Carey Library, 1969.

————. "The Two Structures of God's Redemptive Mission." *Missiology* 2 (1974): 121-39.

Winter, Ralph, and Steven C. Hawthorne, eds. *Perspectives on the World Christian Movement. A Reader*. Rev. ed. Pasadena, Calif.: William Carey Library; Carlisle, U.K.: Paternoster, 1992.

Witherington, Ben. *The Acts of the Apostles: A Socio-Rhetorical Commentary*. Grand Rapids: Eerdmans, 1998.

————. *New Testament History: A Narrative Account*. Grand Rapids: Baker, 2001.

Witulski, Thomas. *Die Adressaten des Galaterbriefes. Untersuchungen zur Gemeinde von Antiochia ad Pisidiam*. FRLANT 193. Göttingen: Vandenhoeck & Ruprecht, 2000.

Wordelman, Amy L. "Cultural Divides and Dual Realities: A Greco-Roman Context for Acts 14." In *Contextualizing Acts: Lukan Narrative and Greco-Roman Discourse*. SBL Symposium 20. Edited by T. C. Penner and C. Vander Stichele, 205-32. Leiden: Brill, 2004.

Wright, Christopher J. H. *The Mission of God: Unlocking the Bible's Grand Narrative*. Downers Grove, Ill.: InterVarsity Press, 2006.

Wright, N. T. *The Climax of the Covenant: Christ and the Law in Pauline Theology*. Philadelphia: Fortress, 1992.

———. *The Resurrection of the Son of God*. Christian Origins and the Question of God 3. London: SPCK; Minneapolis: Fortress, 2003.

Zeigan, Holger. *Aposteltreffen in Jerusalem. Eine forschungsgeschichtliche Studie zu Galater 2,1-10 und den möglichen lukanischen Parallelen*. Arbeiten zur Bibel und ihrer Geschichte 18. Leipzig: Evangelische Verlagsanstalt, 2005.

Zweck, Dean. "The Exordium of the Areopagus Speech, Acts 17.22,23." *NTS* 35 (1989): 94-103.

Author Index

Abegg, Martin, 176
Adams, James, 323
Allen, Hubert J. B., 12
Allen, Roland, 11-14, 21, 282,
    284, 286-87, 420
Ameling, Walter, 69
Anderson, Gerald H., 30
Anderson, Graham, 156, 342
Anderson, Justice C., 421
Anderson, Leith, 432
Anthony, Michael J., 421
Arn, Winfield C., 381
Arnold, Clinton E., 457
Bachmann, Philipp, 46
Badenas, Robert, 218
Baker, Mark D., 399
Balch, David L., 171
Ball, Warwick, 321
Balz, Horst, 8, 288
Banks, Robert, 199, 232, 412
Barclay, John M. G., 326, 419
Barna, George, 432-33
Barrett, C. K., 43, 113, 177,
    202, 273-74, 278, 294,
    297, 314, 332
Bartels, Ulrike, 436
Barth, Karl, 447
Barth, Markus, 373
Bauckham, Richard J., 52, 56,
    60, 325
Baugh, Steven M., 43
Beale, Gregory K., 198, 419
Beard, Mary, 187
Beasley-Murray, George R.,
    26, 230,
Beasley-Murray, Paul, 196
Bechard, Dean Philip, 87,
    164, 307
Becker, Jürgen, 300, 306
Behm, Johannes, 226
Bertram, Georg, 225
Best, Ernest, 146, 149, 372
Bietenhard, Hans, 64, 231,
    288
Blanke, Helmut, 373
Blue, Bradley B., 303
Böhme, Hartmut, 319
Bonk, Jonathan J., 442
Bonner, Stanley F., 297
Bonnington, Mark, 51

Booth, Alan, 242
Bormann, Lukas, 92, 271
Bornkamm, Günther, 196
Borthwick, Paul, 394
Bosch, David J., 281, 394, 396
Bowers, W. Paul, 112, 197,
    281, 386
Bowersock, Glen Warren,
    157, 321, 342
Bowie, Ewan L., 342
Breytenbach, Cilliers, 83, 138,
    165, 167, 264
Brocke, Christoph vom, 96
Brown, Harold O. J., 447
Brown, Patricia Leigh, 426
Brown, Raymond E., 149
Brox, Norbert, 360
Bruce, F. F., 103-4, 106, 113,
    168, 172, 180, 187, 191-
    92, 194-95, 200, 240-41,
    243, 264, 267, 300, 308-9,
    315-16, 339, 342-43, 347,
    366-67, 393, 419, 421
Burchard, Christoph, 238
Burgoon, Michael, 402
Burkert, Walter, 86, 164
Burton-Christie, Douglas,
    447
Bush, Luis, 441
Buss, Matthäus F. J., 159-60
Cahill, Michael, 144
Caldwell, Kirbyjon, 433
Camp, Bruce K., 393
Camp, John McK. 100, 179
Campbell, Alastair, 150
Campbell, Douglas A., 264
Campbell, J. Brian, 313
Campbell, William S., 139,
    200
Caragounis, Chrys C., 26,
    145
Carson, Donald A., 174, 198-
    200, 235, 373, 419, 423
Casson, Lionel, 34
Chae, Daniel J.-S., 218, 306
Chester, Stephen J., 225, 229
Chew, Jim, 440
Christol, Michel, 264, 312
Clarke, Andrew D., 48, 104,
    131, 240, 242, 315, 343

Coenen, Lothar, 215
Cohen, Shaye J. D., 326
Collart, Paul, 92
Cook, Harold R., 387, 405,
    440
Corbeill, Anthony, 242
Cosgrove, Charles H., 329
Covington, Daryl, 428
Cranfield, C. E. B., 196, 212
Cribiore, Raffaella, 297
Cully, Kendig Brubaker, 421
Davids, Peter H., 368
Dayton, Edward R., 405
DeLaine, Janet, 293
Dickson, John P., 211, 248
Dodds, Eric R., 361, 364,
    367, 369
Downey, Glanville, 73
Downey, Steven, 441
Downs, Perry G., 421
Drew-Bear, Thomas, 264
DuBose, Francis M., 22-23
Dudley, Carl S., 432
Dueck, Daniela, 324
Dumais, Marcel, 174
Dunn, James D. G., 46, 65,
    199, 202, 205, 226, 230,
    259, 261, 267, 340, 407,
    412, 420
Elia, Olga, 298
Eliot, Thomas S., 319
Ellis, E. Earle, 117, 248
Engels, Donald, 104, 275
Epstein, David F., 242
Erdemgil, Selahattin, 301
Escobar, Samuel, 440
Evans, Craig A., 211, 438
Feldtkeller, Andreas, 72
Fendrich, Herbert, 250
Ferguson, Everett, 232, 412,
    422
Ferris, Robert W., 421
Fields, Doug, 428
Finley, Bob, 437-38
Fishwick, Duncan, 305
Fitzmyer, Joseph A., 43, 158
Flemming, Dean, 103, 171,
    174, 182, 318
Fore, William F., 415
Fotopoulos, John, 194

Fournier, Marianne, 164
Fraser, David A., 405
Freitag, Klaus, 324
French, David, 69, 264
Friedrich, G., 41, 210
Frier, Bruce W., 300
Friesen, Steven, 188, 294
Frohman, Mark A., 428
Funk, Robert W., 253
Furnish, Victor Paul, 192
Gadamer, Hans-Georg, 27
Garland, David E., 47, 349, 353
Garland, Robert, 100
Garnsey, Peter, 242
Gärtner, Bertil, 174
Gehring, Roger W., 199, 232, 303
Gempf, Conrad, 39, 86, 103-4, 113, 267, 303, 311, 314
Georgi, Dieter, 56, 249
Gerber, Vergil, 421
Geyer, Paul, 318
Gibson, Richard J., 174
Gill, David W. J., 86-87, 102, 112, 191, 240, 275, 303, 311, 314-16, 366
Gilliland, Dean S., 45, 60, 395, 400, 409, 443
Gleason, Maud W., 343
Goerner, H. Cornell, 405
Goldhill, Simon, 319, 321-22
Goodman, Martin, 22
Gore, Charles, 420
Grahame, Mark, 322
Gralfs, Bettine, 298
Green, Joel B., 399
Greenway, Roger S., 281
Griffin, Miriam T., 116
Gruen, Erich S., 329
Gruenler, Royce Gordon, 150
Guinness, Os, 410, 424, 427-8, 431, 433, 436, 453
Gutbrod, Walter, 216
Guthrie, Stan, 394, 441, 457
Haacker, Klaus, 183, 203, 215
Haas, Odo, 281
Hahn, F., 184
Hahn, Johan G., 415
Hall, Jonathan M., 324

Hansen, G. Walter, 161
Haraguchi, Takaaki, 249
Harnack, Adolf von, 11, 127, 360
Harris, Gerald, 192
Harris, Murray J., 102, 372, 390
Hartman, Lars, 231
Hasler, Victor, 225
Hawthorne, Gerald F., 231
Hays, Richard B., 38, 199, 376, 380
Heiligenthal, Roman, 249
Hellenkemper, Hansgerd, 41, 69
Hemer, Colin J., 39, 69, 107, 297
Hengel, Martin, 41, 43-45, 60-61, 63-64, 73, 77, 94, 185-86, 191, 261, 293
Henry, Carl F., 13, 448
Herrmann, Peter, 269
Hesselgrave, David J., 30-31, 37, 86, 174, 394
Hiebert, Eloise Meneses, 318, 413, 427
Hiebert, Paul G., 318, 413, 427
Hild, Friedrich, 41, 69
Hock, Ronald F., 298
Hoff, Michael C., 180
Hoffmann, Hilmar, 436
Hofius, Otfried, 65, 259
Hollander, Harm W., 47
Hölscher, Tonio, 293
Holtz, Traugott, 356
Horsley, Greg H. R., 111, 211
Hout, Gijsbert. E. van der, 47
Howell, Don N., 357, 400
Hurtado, Larry W., 128, 162, 191
Hvalvik, Reidar, 22, 44
Isaac, Benjamin H., 69, 160, 166, 216, 323, 457
Janne, Henri, 185
Jervell, Jacob, 72, 289
Jewett, Robert, 300
Jones, A. H. M., 282
Joubert, Stephan, 56, 443
Judge, Edwin A., 311
Kallestad, Walt, 433

Kammler, Hans-Christian, 354
Kane, J. Herbert, 29-30, 32, 386
Käsemann, Ernst, 340
Kasher, Aryeh, 61
Kelly, John M., 242
Kelly, John N. D., 225
Kennedy, George A., 342, 344
Kent, John Harvey, 243, 315
Keyes, Lawrence E., 440
Kilde, Jeanne Halgren, 436
Kim, Seyoon, 45, 201, 388, 419
Kinman, Brent Roger, 138
Kirchhoff, Renate, 192
Klauber, Martin, 440
Knibbe, Dieter, 331
Kofsky, Aryeh, 360
Köstenberger, Andreas J., 23, 124, 145, 218, 251
Kreitzer, Larry J., 191
Kruse, Colin G., 217
Kuck, David W., 133
Kuhli, H., 216
Kuhn, Karl Georg, 216
Kuper, Adam, 319
Lambert, Stephen D., 101-2
Lampe, Peter, 111
Lane Fox, Robin, 360, 362, 365-69
Lausberg, Heinrich, 344-5
Leonard, John S., 376
Levick, Barbara, 79, 81, 264-65, 311, 337
Levine, Lee I., 82, 268, 290, 292
Levinskaya, Irina, 185, 274-75
Liefeld, Walter L., 251
Lightfoot, J. B., 115, 225
Limbeck, Meinrad, 238-39
Lincoln, Andrew T., 146
Lingenfelter, Sherwood G., 449
Litfin, Duane, 190, 347, 350
Little, Christopher R., 317, 442-43
Llewelyn, Stephen R., 111, 211
Löhr, Hermut, 117

Longenecker, Richard N., 45, 48, 199, 225
Lowe, Chuck, 457
Luhmann, Niklas, 319
Lupieri, Edmondo, 447
Lupu, Eran, 100-101
MacMullen, Ramsay, 164, 322-33, 360-62, 365, 367-69
Magie, David, 262
Malherbe, Abraham J., 171, 244, 274, 311
Malphurs, Aubrey, 412
Manetsch, Scott M., 440
Marsden, George M., 448
Marshall, I. Howard, 26, 48, 108, 149, 161, 196, 199, 202-3, 206-7, 245, 247, 261, 267, 274, 276, 373, 420
Martin, Ralph P., 199, 420
May, Elmer C., 122
McDonald, James I. H., 419
McGavran, Donald Anderson, 381, 404-6, 409-10, 412
McGinn, Thomas A. J., 229
McIntosh, Gary L., 381, 406
McQuail, Denis, 402
McQuilkin, Robertson, 453
Meeks, Wayne A., 248, 298, 311, 314-15, 365
Merklein, Helmut, 226
Metcalf, Samuel F., 394
Meyer, Rudolf, 289
Meyers, Eric M., 438
Mihaila, Corin, 347
Millar, Fergus, 44, 321
Minear, Paul S., 412
Mitchell, Margaret M., 253
Mitchell, Stephen M., 81, 164, 262-65, 268, 293, 311
Moreau, A. Scott, 329, 386, 439, 443, 457
Mounce, William D., 150-51, 248, 314
Mowery, Robert L., 307, 312
Muggeridge, Malcolm, 415
Munck, Johannes, 308
Murray, Oswyn, 282
Mutafian, Claude, 41

Neff, David, 442
Nelson, Marlin L., 151, 440
Newton, Derek, 194
Nickelsburg, George W. E., 46
Nickle, Keith F., 56
Niebuhr, Karl-Wilhelm, 44
Nigdelis, Pantelis M., 326
Nilsson, Martin P., 305
Nobbs, Alanna, 311
Noy, David, 272, 274-75, 290
Nyquist, J., 409
O'Brien, Peter T., 2, 41, 97, 116, 124, 144-49, 175, 187, 197, 200, 204, 218, 233-36, 245-46, 251, 314, 373, 422, 437-38, 453
Oepke, Albrecht, 168, 231
Ollrog, Wolf-Henning, 248, 252
Olson, C. Gordon, 31
Oswalt, John N., 221
Ott, Craig, 441-42
Owens, Virginia Stem, 415
Padberg, Lutz E. von, 340-41
Padilla, René, 406
Pao, David W., 83, 175, 373
Parker, R. C. T., 101
Pascarella, Perry, 428
Pate, Larry D., 440
Peace, Richard V., 25, 225
Penner, Peter F., 338, 420
Penney, John M., 453
Pesce, Mauro, 127, 197
Pesch, Rudolf, 181
Peskett, Howard, 281
Peterson, David, 199
Peterson, David G., 15, 73, 162, 276
Pichler, Josef, 158
Pilhofer, Peter, 92, 270
Pilhofer, Susanne, 322
Pillai, C. A. Joachim, 161
Plassart, André, 106, 276
Plummer, Robert L., 200, 246, 248
Porter, Stanley E., 344, 438
Powers, Bruce P., 421, 456
Praet, Danny, 360, 369
Preston, Rebecca, 322
Price, Simon R. F., 187, 282-83

Priest, Robert J., 457
Prior, Michael, 77, 116
Pucci Ben Zeev, Miriam, 35, 106, 269, 326, 340, 362-63
Purcell, N., 284
Rad, Gerhard von, 216
Rajak, Tessa, 325-26
Ramachandra, Vinoth, 281
Ramsay, William M., 11, 88, 104, 164, 264, 285, 322, 360, 368-69
Rapske, Brian, 96, 115
Reck, Reinhold, 403
Reed, Jonathan L., 326
Refoulé, François, 218
Reinbold, Wolfgang, 22
Reinhardt, Wolfgang, 60
Rengstorf, K. H., 129
Richardson, John S., 118
Richardson, Peter, 274, 289
Rickett, Daniel, 443
Riesner, Rainer, 42, 69, 73, 97, 105, 106, 221, 261, 264, 276, 311
Robertson, Noel, 324, 453
Roloff, Jürgen, 412
Romano, David G., 275
Rommen, Edward, 86, 174, 456
Roozen, David A., 432
Rousselle, Aline, 229
Russell, Donald A., 342-43
Sanders, Guy D. R., 294
Sanders, J. T., 369
Sargeant, Kimon Howland, 435
Šašel Kos, Marjeta, 113
Schaller, Lyle E., 425-27, 434
Schlatter, Adolf, 133, 336
Schnabel, Eckhard J., 22, 31, 40, 47, 52, 60, 67, 71, 75, 79, 90, 92, 101, 104, 108-9, 113, 118, 123, 139, 174, 186, 199, 218-19, 248, 264-65, 267-70, 274-75, 278-79, 294, 311, 315, 326, 347, 352, 389, 391, 402-3, 438, 443
Schnackenburg, Rudolf, 199
Schneider, Gerhard, 46, 113, 282, 324

Schrage, Wolfgang, 255
Schreiner, Thomas R., 199,
    420
Schrenk, Gottlob, 139
Schürer, Emil, 61, 67, 69,
    105
Scott, James M., 222
Segal, Alan F., 45, 136, 310
Seitz, Manfred, 250
Sellin, Gerhard, 46
Sharpe, Eric J., 22
Shaw, Lois, 394
Shawchuck, Norman, 433
Shear, T. Leslie, 179
Shelton, R. Larry, 399
Shenk, Wilbert R., 30
Shillington, George, 359
Silva, Moisés, 419
Skarsaune, Oskar, 44
Smith, Colin, 423
Smith, Ebbie C., 456
Söding, Thomas, 201
Søgaard, Viggo, 401-2,
    413-15
Sokolowski, Franciszek,
    100-101
Solin, H., 42
Somnath, Sarah, 320
Spicq, Ceslas, 225
Squarciapino, Maria Floriani,
    289
Stahlmann, Ines, 229
Stambaugh, John E., 284
Stanley, Brian, 27
Stark, Rodney, 369-70
Steffen, Tom A., 389, 441
Stenschke, Christoph W., 77,
    164, 338
Stephan, Eckhard, 283, 323,
    325
Stetzer, Ed, 405
Stott, John, 415
Strange, James F., 438

Stuhlmacher, Peter, 203, 228
Swain, N., 323
Swain, Simon, 323
Syme, Ronald, 324
Talbert, Richard J. A., 89
Taylor, Hudson, 378
Taylor, Justin, 294
Taylor, William David, 389,
    440
Telford, Tom, 394
Theissen, Gerd, 311, 315
Thielman, Frank, 217
Thiselton, Anthony C., 131,
    308, 349
Thom, Johan Carl, 172, 405
Thompson, Glen L., 330
Thompson, James, 196
Thompson, M., 175, 187, 197,
    200, 251
Thompson, Michael B., 419
Thrall, Margaret E., 139, 252
Todd, M., 293
Tomlinson, Richard A., 293
Towner, Philip H., 150, 248,
    276
Turner, Max M. B., 148
Twelftree, Graham H., 368
Ueding, Gert, 345, 347
Unnik, Willem C. van, 43
Van Engen, Charles, 394
Veit, W. F., 345
Versnel, Hendrik Simon,
    100, 138
Verwer, George, 442
Veyne, Paul, 181, 228-29, 231
Voss, Florian, 354
Waelkens, Marc, 81, 164,
    265, 311
Wagner, C. Peter, 404-5, 409,
    454-56
Walbank, Mary E. H., 275
Walls, Andrew F., 394, 447,
    449

Walters, James C., 331
Warren, Rick, 157, 428
Wedderburn, Alexander
    J. M., 230, 443
Welch, Robert H., 427
Weld, Wayne C., 421
Wells, David F., 426, 431-33,
    435-63, 449-50, 453-54
Wenham, David, 48, 419
Westerholm, Stephen, 217
White, Jerry, 409
White, L. Michael, 289, 360,
    370
Wilckens, Ulrich, 127
Wiles, Gordon P., 199
Williams, Charles K., 275,
    294
Williams, J. F., 357
Williams, P. J., 104, 192
Williams, Raymond, 320,
Williamson, George, 43
Willmer, Wesley K., 409
Wimber, John, 454
Winter, Bruce W., 48, 103-4,
    106, 167, 171, 180, 186,
    190, 194, 200, 240-41,
    243, 293, 308-9, 315-26,
    339, 342-43, 347, 366-
    67, 393
Winter, Ralph D., 405, 410,
    421
Witherington, Ben, 40, 43,
    52, 104, 169, 176, 267,
    277, 438
Witulski, Thomas, 79
Wordelman, Amy L., 338
Wright, Christopher J. H.,
    21
Wright, N. T., 46-47, 218
Wu, Julie L., 420
Würthwein, Ernst, 226
Zeigan, Holger, 52
Zweck, Dean, 169

Subject Index

Aaron, 64, 384
abortion, 46
Abraham, 28, 33, 61, 64, 84,
  141-43, 148, 158, 160,
  166, 167n. 19, 202-3, 216,
  240, 331-32, 334, 378,
  413, 437-38, 457
accommodation, 137-38, 154,
  177, 181-82, 184, 339
Achaia, 21, 31-32, 40, 56, 58,
  89, 91, 98, 105, 108, 112-
  13, 120, 123, 127, 131,
  197, 223-24, 233, 244,
  250-52, 254, 272, 275,
  280, 282, 286-88, 313,
  315, 363, 407
Achaicus, 315
Achilles, 164
Adam, 142, 177-78, 192, 351
Adana, 69, 123n. 155
administration, 147, 189,
  268, 284, 286, 294, 323,
  331, 401
admonition, 126, 145, 194,
  236, 345
adoption, 26, 126, 148, 205,
  326, 336, 352
Adramyttium, 91, 188
Adriatic, 113, 271-72
adultery, 228, 242, 333
advertisements, 410, 434
Aegean, 91, 270
Aelius Aristides, 342, 350
Aeolis, 108-9
Aeschylus, 182
aesthetic, 192, 319, 351
affect, 278, 308
afflictions, 144, 418
affluence, 380, 442
Afranius Burrus, 117, 314
Africa, 14-15, 221, 330, 435n.
  108, 440
afterlife, 182, 367
agnostics, 449
agora (marketplace), 35, 86,
  100, 179-81, 258, 293-94,
  305-6, 335, 359
agriculture, 132, 168, 192,
  240
Agrippa I, 48, 114, 121

Agrippa II, 73, 280, 285, 313
Aigai, 69
Aigeus, 180
Ajax, 180
Akamas, 180
Akmonia, 270, 326
Alcmene, 164
Alexamenos, 351
Alexander, 123n. 159, 164,
  325
Alexandreia (Syria), 67, 70
Alexandria (Egypt), 98, 251,
  297
Alexandria (Syria), 68
Alexandria Troas (Asia), 91,
  92, 112, 123n. 158
alien (resident aliens), 94,
  96, 135, 148, 173, 190,
  200, 334, 337, 408, 446,
  447, 451
allegory, allegorical, 207, 345
altar, altars, 101-4, 169-70,
  176, 179, 183, 188, 239,
  329, 339-41, 361, 436,
  446
Alytarch, 301
Amaseia, 324
Amathus, 75, 262
ambassador(s), 149, 153, 306,
  358, 363, 372, 386, 403
ambiguity, 107, 368, 385, 400,
  455-56
ambition, 39, 411, 431
ambrosia, 186
Amorion, 108
Ampelites, 87
Amphilochos, 324
Amphipolis, 270-71
amphitheater, 64, 238
Ampliatus, 317
Ananias, 45, 280
anastasis, 101
Anatolia, 79, 264, 267, 269,
  325, 368
Anazarbus, 69, 123n. 155,
  325
ancestor(s), 42, 45, 94, 157-
  58, 160, 165, 170, 177-78,
  216, 271, 324, 329, 407
Anchises, 165

Ancyra, 282
Andeda, 263, 266
Andrew (apostle), 382
Anemurion, 69
angel(s), 126, 129, 206, 240,
  335, 456
anger, 206, 230
animals, 55, 111-12, 139,
  220, 312
Antaradus, 67
anthropology, 318-19, 321,
  442
Antidodos, 102
Antioch (Phrygia/Pisidia),
  31, 77, 79, 80-85, 87-89,
  90, 105, 157, 160-61, 163,
  165, 188, 223, 262-67,
  289, 307, 310-12, 364,
  369-70
Antioch (Syria), 30, 40, 47-
  48, 50-54, 57, 66-69, 70-
  75, 79, 89, 91, 98, 108-9,
  123, 186, 197, 223-24,
  244, 250, 252, 260-61,
  266-67, 279, 281, 288,
  328, 331,
  362, 376, 385-86, 391-93,
  406-8, 438,
  443
Antiocheia, 77, 79, 81-82,
  84, 370
Antiochia (ad Maeandrum),
  268-69
Antiochos (hero), 180
Antiochos II, 81
Antiochos III, 81
Antonius Felix. See Felix
Antony, 110, 270
Anubis, 180, 331
anxiety, 21, 197, 229, 231,
  276, 367
Apameia (Asia), 78, 80, 89,
  266-69
Apameia (Syria), 67, 123n.
  155
apartheid, 412
Aphaka, 67
Aphrodisias, 69, 327
Aphrodite, 102-3, 110, 166,
  180

Apis, 331
apocalyptic, 144, 147
apodeixis, 191, 344, 346, 353
Apollo, 35, 164, 166, 180-82,
    294-95, 321
Apollodoros, 102
Apollonia, 89, 113, 115, 263,
    266, 272
Apollonios, 210-11, 325
Apollos, 109, 131-33, 209,
    241, 251, 295, 402-3
apologia, 329
Apostles' Council, 52-56
apostleship, 27, 124, 126, 385
apotheosis, 11
Apphia, 251
Aqaba, 61, 64
Aquila, 105, 109, 111-12,
    250, 277, 298, 316
Arabia (Nabatea), 31-32,
    40, 47, 57-58, 60-61, 63-
    64, 71, 75, 121, 123, 222-
    24, 259, 287, 388, 392
Aradus, 67
Aramaic, 41, 44, 216, 328,
    330, 337, 391, 438
Aratos, 177
Aratus, 173, 180
Archaicus, 111
archisynagogos, 82, 106, 316,
    327
architect, architecture, 134-
    35, 321
Areopagus (council in
    Athens), 100-101, 103-
    4, 169-71, 174, 177-78,
    181-83, 296, 330, 338-39,
    341, 348, 362-63, 367
Ares, 110, 180
Aretas IV (king), 59-61, 63,
    288
argumentatio, 159, 164, 170,
    345
argumentation, 341, 408
Ariassos, 263, 266
Aristarchus, 111
aristocracy, 42n. 6, 84-85, 94,
    97, 105, 115, 275, 308,
    310-11, 366
Aristogeiton, 180
Aristotle, 191, 344, 346, 349,
    353

Arka, 67
Arles, 342
Armenia, 23, 220
arrogance, 131-32, 426-27
Arsinoe, 164
Artemis, 88, 110, 112, 166,
    180, 263, 283-84, 331,
    359
Artemis Boulaia, 180
Asclepius, 164, 166, 180
asiarchs, 43, 314, 325
Aspendos, 263
Asprokambos, 275
assize, 267-68
Assos, 188
astrologer, 75, 454
atheism, 427, 449
Athene, 179
Athens, 15, 35, 71, 79n. 72,
    98, 100-102, 104-5, 169,
    172, 174, 179-80, 181n.
    48, 183, 223-24, 251, 257,
    272-73, 174n. 38, 282,
    289, 294-95, 309-10, 328,
    330-31, 338-39, 341-42,
    348, 362
athletes, 88, 188, 263
atonement, 28, 33, 45, 126,
    142, 205, 217, 227, 278,
    353, 397, 399, 401
atrium, 292, 298, 300-301,
    303
Attaleia, 2623, 283
Attalos, 108, 181
Attica, 98
auctoritas, 346, 352
audience, 81, 83, 103, 143,
    159, 162-64, 170-71,
    173-74, 177, 182, 184,
    187, 191, 250, 258, 260,
    285, 295, 322, 338-39,
    341, 343-45, 347, 350,
    353-54, 356, 377, 396,
    399-400, 402, 414-16,
    425, 427, 445
auditorium, 297, 436
Augusta (Cilicia), 69-70
Augustus, 41, 75, 81-82, 85-
    86, 91, 98, 100, 102, 108,
    110, 129, 165, 188, 211,
    263-64, 270-72, 283, 295,
    307, 312, 337, 359, 362

Aurelius, 324, 327, 369
Auschwitz, 142
Baal, 321
Babbius, 295
Babel, 381
Baetica, 120
Baetocaece, 67
Baiae, 69
Balaneae, 67
Balbus, 172
banquets, 188, 194-95, 228,
    242-43, 301, 316, 377,
    446
baptism, 29, 77, 158, 227,
    230-31, 239, 411, 421,
    454
Barbalissos, 67
barbarians, 32, 36, 154, 207,
    307-8, 310, 322, 325,
    336-38, 412
Barcino, 120, 123n. 156
Barnabas, 35, 40, 47-48,
    51-54, 65-67, 69, 71-72,
    74-75, 77, 79, 81-83,
    85-89, 159, 163-65, 185n.
    55, 244, 250, 252, 260-62,
    265, 267, 285, 287-89,
    313, 368, 376-77, 385-87,
    392, 406-7
Barsabbas, 54
basilica, 64, 294-95, 297,
    301, 303
baths, 64, 88, 238, 268, 294,
    297, 323
Baucis, 87
beggars, 86, 100
behavior, 14, 22, 29, 49-50,
    128, 131, 136-38, 145,
    150-51, 154, 159, 181-
    82, 190-91, 193-96, 200,
    203, 205-7, 225, 228-31,
    236-40, 242-44, 247-48,
    258, 318-19, 331, 333-34,
    336, 342, 344, 348, 354-
    55, 359, 377, 379, 391,
    395, 444
beliefs, 65, 73, 145, 181-82,
    206, 208, 328, 333, 339,
    350, 363, 375, 403, 414-
    15, 451
bema, 290, 294
benefactor, benefaction, 100,

274n. 38, 290, 292, 312, 315
Bermion, 272
Bernice, 115
Beroea, 79n. 72, 91, 98, 105, 113, 198, 223-24, 251, 270, 272-74, 289, 310, 315, 369
Berytus, 67
bicultural, 329-30, 376, 391
bilingual, 323, 328, 330, 439
biography, 43, 139, 333, 388
bishop, 13, 120, 360
Bithynia, 7, 91, 108, 221-24, 270, 324, 360
blasphemy, 55, 83
Blaundos, 270
blood, 24, 55, 149, 179, 182, 195-96, 217, 369, 408
Boeotia, 98, 321
boldness, 116, 146, 149, 184, 215, 372
Bosporos, 271
Bostra, 64, 121n. 154
bouleuterion, 64, 288, 294
Bracara Augusta (Spain), 119
Brauronia, 180
bread, 193, 195-96, 229
brevitas, 345
bribe, 115
bridgehead, 184
bronze, 165, 181
brothels, 229
Brutus, 270
Byblos, 67
Byzantion, 272
Caesar, 81, 100, 105, 109, 165, 180-81, 211, 270-71, 275, 275n. 42, 283n. 59, 362
Caesaraugusta, 120, 123n. 156
Caesarea, 3, 48, 50, 53, 58, 65-67, 72, 81, 112, 115, 280, 313, 326n. 154, 359, 376, 438, 445
cajolery, 36, 131, 355
calendar, 102, 211, 239, 324, 333
Caligula, 73, 98, 121
Calpurnii, 263
Canaan, 157

candelabrum, 292
canon, 38, 118, 202, 375
Canon Muratori, 118
Capernaum, 25
Cappadocia, 41, 69, 222, 267, 324
captatio benevolentiae, 170, 345
Caria, 108, 267
Caristanii, 265, 312
Carthago, 120
Cassius, 102, 187, 270, 275n. 42
catechism, 421
causa, 346
Celsa (Spain), 119-20, 123n. 156
Celsus, 366n. 221, 370
Celtic, 219, 224
Cenchreae, 275, 277, 295
censure, 175, 339, 422
centurion, 72, 115
Cephas, 58, 65, 194, 201, 259, 406. *See also* Peter
Ceres, 337
Chaeronia, 321
Chalcedon, 270
Chaldeans, 162
Charalambos, 275
Charax, 67
charismata, 245
Chersonasos, 121
China, 11, 14, 330, 378, 401
Chios, 188
Chloe, 317
Chrestus, 186
Christiani, 72
christianoi, 185
chronology, 113, 274
Chrysippos, 172
Chrysostom, 69, 342, 343n. 182, 344
church growth, 424-36
church, local, 422-44
church planting, 152-53, 213, 223, 281, 284, 375, 379, 400, 404, 408-9, 424, 426, 431, 442, 448, 457. *See also* mission
church, seeker-driven, 431-36
Cicero, 42n. 9, 172n. 27, 191, 242n. 64, 268, 318, 344n.

185, 349, 350, 353
Cilicia, 3, 7, 31-32, 40-41, 43-44, 53, 57-58, 66-67, 69, 71, 74, 89, 108, 123, 197, 221-24, 252, 260, 281, 286-87, 324-5, 328
circumcision, 41, 50-53, 126, 137, 148, 163, 201-4, 205, 207, 216, 218, 226, 237, 239, 252, 288, 308, 328, 332-33, 359, 366, 397, 406, 408, 413, 445-46
Citians, 102-3
Claudius, 91, 98, 105, 107, 117, 180, 186, 268, 272, 277, 291, 311-12, 327, 362
Cleantes, 172-73
Clement, 117-18, 315
clients, 41, 73
cognitio, 107
cognomen, 42, 185, 327
coinage, 283
coins, 271-72, 274, 283, 337
colonists, 81, 91, 106, 223, 263, 270, 307, 315, 328
colony, colonies, 79, 81, 84-86, 91, 164, 263-64, 270-72, 274, 275n. 44, 293, 315-16, 322-23, 337, 363-64
Colossae, 111, 124, 144-45, 188, 198-99, 200, 206, 238, 251, 254, 268-69, 284, 317, 372
Come, 270
comedy, 353
communication, 15, 34, 81, 284, 287, 338, 348, 356, 360, 399, 401-3, 414-16, 418, 450
compassion, 207, 411
conclusio, 345
concubines, 64, 229
confession, 110, 142, 175, 186, 189, 204, 228, 341, 361, 375
conflict, 47, 364, 379-80, 431
confrontation, 182, 184, 188, 190, 201
conscience, 131, 150, 229
Constantinople, 272

consultation, 47-52, 58, 252, 392
consumer, 426-27, 434-36, 448, 450-51
contextualization, 174, 377, 380, 399, 448-49
contradiction, 51, 172, 174-75, 329, 350, 417
controversies, 207, 397-98
controversy, 52, 54, 324
conventions, 191, 196, 344
conversion, 29, 40, 44, 45-47, 53, 57-61, 63, 65, 72-73, 74, 94, 96, 113, 124-25, 127, 130, 137, 139-41, 147-48, 151, 154, 157, 202-3, 208, 218, 222, 224-29, 230-31, 259, 264, 267, 276, 285-87, 289, 303, 354, 382-83, 392, 404-5, 430, 454
converts, 4, 12-13, 28, 36-37, 59, 104-6, 110, 127, 190, 192, 199, 201, 208, 210, 231-32, 236, 238, 244, 250, 272-73, 288, 304, 311, 332-33, 359, 361, 363, 365, 384, 406-8, 410, 416-17, 419, 421, 449, 456
Corinth, 7, 31, 36, 57, 79n. 72, 98, 100, 105-9, 111-13, 118, 134-35, 190-91, 197-99, 214n. 8, 223-24, 233, 238, 240-43, 250-52, 254, 257, 260, 272-79, 282, 289, 294-95, 297, 304, 311, 313, 315-17, 328, 331, 343-44, 347-48, 354, 363-64, 366, 369-71, 373, 384, 386, 391, 393, 396, 406, 419
Cornelius, 53, 72, 366n. 221
corruption, 158, 162
Cos, 188
cosmology, 319, 339
Cotenna, 263
countryside, 219, 285-86, 306, 308
courage, 215, 256, 352, 355, 369, 372
courtesans, 229

courts, 73, 75, 215, 240, 242, 267, 290, 294-95, 454
covenant(s), 33, 143, 195, 204, 215-16, 218, 237, 334, 388, 390, 408, 422, 437
coworker(s), 66, 71, 74, 87-89, 94, 100, 111, 121, 133-34, 141, 144, 150, 154, 198-99, 224, 231, 233, 248-51, 251-55, 261, 271, 274, 287, 311, 316-17, 358, 368, 388, 393, 402, 417, 424
creation, 23, 167-68, 171, 177-78, 220, 339, 413
creator, 142, 167, 170-72, 177-78, 180-81, 183, 192, 195, 220, 226, 228-29, 334, 339, 352-53, 371
credentials, 353
credibility, 4, 152, 247-48, 346, 352, 354-56, 364
Crescens, 224
Crete, 3, 7, 112, 121, 123, 223, 250-51, 253, 281
Crispus, 105-6, 276, 304, 316
cross, 33, 45, 52, 142, 148, 150, 156, 163, 189, 192-93, 195, 202, 204, 206, 228, 237, 246, 270, 283, 317, 320, 329-30, 332-34, 347-49, 351-52, 383, 390-91, 394, 397-401, 403-4, 406n. 37, 407-8, 411, 412n. 47, 425, 427, 437n. 115, 438-40, 444, 446, 452
crucifixion, 28, 187, 192, 350-52, 382, 446
cult, 79, 85, 98, 102-3, 128, 168, 179-80, 181n. 48, 187-88, 211, 271-72, 301, 305, 322, 324, 340, 359, 362, 364-65, 397, 445
cultura, 318
culture, 27, 34, 36, 86n. 92, 88, 181, 238, 258, 306, 310, 317-23, 326, 328, 330-31, 336, 340, 359, 364, 389-92, 394, 399, 404, 411, 417, 423-24, 438-39, 444-50

curse, 83, 332, 350, 398, 411
customs, 41, 56, 96, 107, 184, 206, 242-43, 293, 305, 321, 326, 331, 334, 356, 363, 391, 446, 448, 451
Cyprus, 3, 7, 32, 40-41, 43, 47, 51-53, 58, 67, 71, 74-75, 77, 79, 82, 223-24, 250, 252, 261-64, 281, 287, 289, 311, 370, 376, 386, 392, 445
Cyrene, 71
Cyrus, 166
Dalisandos, 265
Dalmatia, 250, 253
Damaris, 105
Damascus, 30, 40, 44-45, 47, 57-61, 63-65, 67, 74, 98, 121n. 154, 123n. 155, 139-40, 153, 223-24, 257, 259, 267, 285, 287-88, 353, 369, 386, 388, 392, 451
dance, dancers, 88, 243, 263, 442
Daniel, 16, 166
Danube, 271
David, 124, 158-61, 187, 331
David, Son of, 187, 437
Davidic king, 129n. 5
declamations, 104, 157, 342-44, 346-48, 354
Delphi, 276, 322
Demeter, 179, 305
Demetrios, 112
demigods, 164
demons, 25, 28, 96, 456
Demosthenes, 229
Derbe, 79n. 72, 87-89, 105, 188, 223, 262-63, 265, 285, 316
Dertosa, 120
devil, 149, 247, 372, 389. See also Satan
diakonia, 254
diakonos, 132, 145, 249n. 78, 417
dialexis, 343
dialogue, 141, 176, 204, 288, 350

Diaspora, 166, 216, 290, 292-93, 326-29, 340, 363, 390, 438
didaskalos, 292
Dinar, 89
Diodorus, 117
Dionysia, 210
Dionysius, 104, 180, 303
disciples, 25-26, 28, 46n. 21, 58, 60, 65, 72, 85, 88, 109, 232, 248, 253, 265, 279, 379, 382-83, 387, 407, 421, 426, 438-39
discipleship, 383, 421, 428
divorce, 61, 238, 304, 378
doctors, 316, 434
doctrine, 33, 152, 183, 202, 208, 248, 361-62, 390, 431
Dorians, 109, 323
Doric, 294
Dorla, 87
Dorylaion, 91
drunkenness, 228, 230, 333, 389
Drusilla, 115
duoviri, 85, 294
Dyrrhachium, 113-15, 272
earthquake, 96, 262, 272
Easter, 382-83
eating, 55, 195, 330, 391, 407
economic, 14, 79, 100, 266, 268, 273, 275, 308, 355, 404, 441, 450
Edessa, 67, 272
edification, 235-36, 422-23
Edom, 61
education, 40, 43-44, 83, 88, 224, 241, 287, 297, 318, 328-29, 336, 348, 350, 370, 418
effectiveness, 50, 130-31, 133, 138, 152, 247, 250, 255, 346, 404-5, 411, 417, 426, 448, 453
egoism, 191, 195
Egypt, 103, 120, 157, 180, 228, 251, 309, 331, 343-44
ekklēsia, 233-34, 393, 412n. 50
elders, 48, 51-54, 57, 66, 69, 85, 121, 199, 247, 266, 370, 420n. 77
election, 159-60

Eleusinion, 180
Elijah, 62
elocutio, 345
eloquence, 344, 347
Elymas, 75, 77
emotion, 361, 365
emperor(s), 23, 34, 69, 81, 91, 102, 107, 115-17, 129, 165, 180-81, 186-88, 190, 211-12, 264, 268, 271, 277, 280, 305, 312-14, 343, 360, 362-65, 369, 397, 446
encouragement, 4, 106, 196, 243-44, 275-76, 411
endoxa, 347n. 189, 352
enmity, 230
enthymēmata, 346
entrepreneur, entrepreneurial, 427, 433 112
envoys, 23, 51, 221, 249, 253-54, 255, 300, 357, 402, 451
envy, 220, 230
Epaenetus, 317
Epaphras, 111, 198n. 88, 223, 238n. 57, 254, 284-85, 317
Epaphroditus, 97, 253-54, 368
Ephesus, 7, 31, 35, 40, 43, 50, 69, 79n. 72, 87-89, 98, 105, 107-12, 123, 144, 151, 185, 188, 197-99, 211, 223, 247, 250-52, 254, 260, 263, 267, 269, 277-79, 283-84, 289, 297, 301, 311, 314, 316-17, 328, 331, 359, 369-70, 422, 446
Epictetus, 268, 369
Epicureans, 100, 169, 174, 178-79, 182, 294-95, 331-32, 338-39, 361-62
Epicurus, 174, 179
epideictic, 348
epiphany, 361
Epirus, 100, 123n. 158
episkopos, 88
Epitegios (hero), 180
Erastus, 238, 315
Erechtheus, 180
eschatology, 54, 142
Essenes, 328, 350
Etenna, 262
ethics, 22, 37-38, 191, 194, 376, 419

ethnarch, 60, 288
ethnicity, 42, 318, 320, 324, 326, 329, 404
ethnos, ethnē, 48-49, 84, 109, 167, 218-20, 307, 323-26
ēthos, 346, 354
euangelion, 34, 210, 212, 214, 245
euangelistai, 245
euangelistēs, 249
Eudoxiopolis, 263, 266
Eumeneia, 270
Euodia, 251, 316
Eurysakes, 180
Eusanbatios, 327
Eusebius, 225n. 30, 359
evangelism, 30, 141, 143-44, 295, 375, 394, 400-401, 410, 413, 423, 429, 453-54, 456, 457
evangelists, 22, 151, 235, 245, 247, 249, 297, 402, 404, 416, 418, 423, 429, 432, 441, 453-54, 450, 455-56
evil, 110, 144, 149-50, 189, 193, 206, 220, 246-47, 372, 433, 435
exemplum, 346-47, 352
exhortation, 35, 151, 193, 195, 240, 247-48, 304
exile, 83, 117, 159, 242, 351, 446
exorcism, 110, 368
exordium, 170, 345
eyewitness, 345, 352, 368
Ezekiel, 268
Ezra, 59
faithfulness, 205, 230, 417-18, 425, 437, 444
famine, 47-48, 252, 443
Favorinus, 342-43
feasts, 359, 410
Felix (governor of Judea), 57, 73n. 64, 86, 115, 280, 313
festivals, 102, 104, 112, 188, 206, 232, 239, 271, 278, 314, 322, 328, 331, 333, 359, 438
Festus (governor of Judea), 115, 280, 313
finance, 12, 50, 57, 71, 97, 103, 191, 207, 242, 245, 298,

315, 366, 370, 377, 386, 414, 416, 420, 431, 441-43
fire, 132, 136, 209
fish, fishmongers, 100, 382
fishers, 28, 248, 383, 385-86, 389
Flaccus, 267-68
foolishness, 32, 156, 184, 189, 220, 349, 425, 452
foreign, 12, 23, 101-2, 182, 186, 305, 310, 401, 423, 438, 440-41
foreigner(s), 55-56, 154, 317, 326, 336-37
forgiveness, 126, 158-59, 161-63, 168, 199, 207, 215, 227, 234, 237, 239, 352, 388, 397
fornication, 193, 206, 230, 242-43
Fortunatus, 111, 315
freeborn, 307, 335, 393
freedmen, 105, 116, 120, 240, 271, 275, 300, 307, 314-17, 320, 335, 365, 409
freewoman, 203
friendship, 43, 363
Fronto, 312
funerals, 69, 102, 325, 327
future, 101, 147, 181, 194, 205-7, 278-79, 332-33, 350, 372, 386, 389, 424, 440, 449
Gades, 117, 280
Gaius Caligula. See Caligula
Gaius (of Corinth), 106, 111, 315
Gaius (of Derbe), 88
Gaius (of Macedonia), 16
Gaius Rabirius (proconsul), 268
Galatia, 3, 7, 21, 31-32, 40-41, 47, 51-53, 58, 67, 74-75, 77, 79, 85, 88-89, 108, 123, 126, 197, 200, 203, 223-24, 226, 250-52, 262-65, 268, 271, 278-79, 282, 286-88, 311, 317, 325, 332, 368, 376, 396, 408, 419
Galilee, 42, 49, 61, 158, 186, 213, 282, 285, 327, 386, 389, 438-39

Gallia, 224
Gallio (proconsul), 107, 276, 313, 363
Gamaliel, 44, 335, 354, 388
games, 239, 243, 268, 283, 294, 312, 314, 322
Gangites, 94, 270
gatekeepers, 402, 414
Gaul, 117, 120, 221, 224
gender, 36, 258, 306, 336, 393, 450
genealogies, 150
geography, 283, 324
Gerasa, 64
Germany, 120, 219-20, 436
gifts, 47, 71, 132-34, 152, 162, 200, 384-85, 423, 443
Gindaros, 67
Gischala, 42
globalization, 14, 440
glossolalia, 245, 378
gnostics, 447
godfearers, 161, 252, 293, 304, 310, 335, 406
gravestones, 182, 327
greed, 130-31, 206, 228, 256, 333, 355
greeting(s), 66, 111, 173, 233, 251, 279
guidance, 21, 30, 37, 75, 261, 277, 380, 386-87, 392
guild, 110, 112
guilt, 142, 204, 357, 403
gymnasium, 297, 322, 329
Hadad, 321
Hadrian, 343
Hadrianothera, 91, 342
Hagar, 64
hair, 277
Ham, 222
Harpocrates, 180, 331
harvest, 26, 168
hatred, 65, 369
Hauran, 61
healing, 86, 163, 165-66, 213, 338, 384, 455
health, 11, 428
Hebrew, 41-44, 59, 135, 167, 212, 216, 221n. 27, 225, 227, 268, 280, 328-31, 337, 339, 391, 438
hedonism, 191, 193-94

Hegra, 64
heir(s), 146, 148, 212, 290, 334
Hekate, 180
Hellenistic, 44, 65, 101, 133, 177n. 42, 282, 300, 321, 324n. 145, 326, 328-29, 340, 360-62, 364, 367, 391
Hephaistos, 100, 179-80
Hera, 180
Heracles, 180
herald, 117, 212-15
Hercules, 164
Hermes, 86-87, 163, 168, 180, 295, 337
Hermos, 269
Herod I, 61, 71, 73n. 66, 135, 274
Herod Antipas, 61, 63
Herod Philip, 283
Herodes Atticus, 157n. 3
Herodians, 73
Herodias, 61
heroes, 164, 166, 180, 283
Hestia, 180
Hierapolis, 67, 69, 111, 188, 198n. 88, 254, 268-69, 284
hierarchy, 188, 190, 283, 362, 370
Hippolytus, 222
Hispania (Spain), 120, 281
Hittites, 109
holiness, 124, 163, 218, 237, 243, 397, 447, 450, 453
Holy Spirit, 12-13, 30, 74, 126-27, 144-45, 148, 150, 203-5, 231, 240, 243, 245-46, 306, 353, 358, 371, 374, 385, 390, 392, 396-97, 400-404, 407-8, 411, 417-18, 423-24, 426, 430, 444, 447-48, 450-54, 456-57
Homer, 177n. 42
homily, 82
homogeneous people groups, 404-13
homologia, 228
homosexuality, 228-29, 238, 327, 333, 447
honor, 103, 109, 132, 139, 165, 179, 188, 220, 239, 254, 305, 309, 359, 373
hospitality, 87, 94, 389

host, 106, 331, 447
hostility, 111, 323n. 142, 350,
    399n. 25, 408
houses, 4, 35-36, 178, 188, 232,
    234, 239, 258, 287, 298,
    300-301, 303-5, 327
humiliation, 87
humility, 207, 348, 374, 411,
    417
humor, 436
hymn(s), 172, 232, 236, 341,
    420n. 75, 422
hyperbole, 98, 345
hypocrisy, 406-7
hypothesis, 112, 223, 364
Hyrcanus, 61
Iberia (Spain), 117
Iconium, 77, 79n. 72, 85, 88-
    89, 105, 188, 223, 262-63,
    265-66, 285, 289, 310,
    369, 454
ideology, 184, 188, 190, 319,
    364, 434
idolatry, 54-55, 178, 206, 230
idol(s), 97, 128, 164, 166-67,
    171-72, 176, 179-80, 180,
    182, 195, 226, 273, 330,
    335, 448, 458
Idumeans, 61
ignorance, 170-71, 173, 176,
    181-83, 227, 339
Ilerda, 120, 123n. 156
Ilici, 120
illness, 323, 368
Illyricum, 32, 39, 112-13, 115,
    123n. 158, 141, 210, 222,
    253, 279, 451
Ilyas, 263, 266
images, 164-65, 171, 179-80,
    183, 220, 340, 361, 412
imagination, 170, 179
imitation, 59, 127, 353, 358,
    447
Imma, 67
immigrants, 81, 322, 426, 438
immorality, 11, 203, 207, 228,
    240, 242, 333
immortal, 172, 174, 220, 351
imperialism, 27
imprisonment, 58, 96, 115-17,
    123, 223, 245, 253, 280,
    313-14, 374, 391, 401, 445

incarnation, 337n. 169, 364
incest, 55, 193, 241
India, 11, 330, 391, 440
integration, 225, 236-37, 241,
    438
integrity, 154, 201, 242
intelligibility, 16, 47, 245, 377,
    386
intentionality, 22-24, 26-27
Ionia, 108-9, 223, 283, 323-24
Irenaeus, 120
irony, 182n. 52, 345
Isaac, 69, 160, 166, 216, 457
Isaiah, 125, 175, 178, 212-13,
    221
Isauria, 41, 87
Ishmael, 61
Isis, 35, 103, 180, 331
Isocrates, 101, 191, 344, 350n.
    196
Israel, 28, 33, 41, 45, 57, 83-84,
    125, 142-43, 148, 157-58,
    160-63, 166-67, 169, 175-
    77, 179, 184, 190, 201,
    216-19, 221, 227-28, 232,
    234, 237, 293, 331-32, 341,
    375, 382, 384, 388, 397-98,
    403, 408, 413, 446, 457
Issos, 69
Isthmus, 105, 275
Italy, 224, 315, 322, 363
Iulia, 85-86, 94, 105, 270-71,
    275
Iullus, 312
Iunius, 107, 276, 313
Jacob, 125, 160, 166, 175, 216
Jaffa, 69
James, 16, 51, 53-54, 56-58,
    65, 126, 406
Japhet, 222-23
Jason, 105
Javan, 221, 223
jealousy, 83, 143, 230
Jeremiah, 125
Jerome, 42n. 10, 73n. 64, 219
Jerusalem, 30, 32, 39-40, 43-
    45, 47-54, 56-60, 63-67,
    69, 71-75, 77, 89, 108-9,
    112-13, 115-16, 120, 121n.
    154, 123, 125-27, 135, 141,
    158, 160, 187, 201, 204,
    210, 212, 216, 221-22, 224,

    227, 250, 252, 257, 259-61,
    267-68, 278-80, 285-86,
    288, 292, 326, 328-29, 331,
    354, 369-70, 374, 376, 385,
    391-92, 396-97, 407-8,
    410, 418, 438-39, 443-46,
    451, 454
Joppa, 454
Jordan, 63, 230
Joseph, 129n. 5, 166n. 17
Josephus, 61, 64, 67, 71, 81,
    101, 102, 107, 117, 135,
    201, 222, 268, 269, 274,
    325, 326, 362, 363
joy, 87, 127, 163, 167-68, 210-
    11, 230, 231n. 46, 254, 358,
    373, 411, 442, 444
Judah, 212, 216, 292
Judaizer, Judaizers, 201
Judas, 54
Judea, 28, 32, 44, 48-50, 58-59,
    64, 66, 69, 72-73, 107, 189,
    250, 280, 282, 285-86, 313,
    327, 438-39
judges, 157, 159, 400
Judith, 221
Jupiter, 139
Justin, 350
Kadoi, 91
Kanatha, 64
Karrhai, 67
Katabolos, 69
kēryx, 214
Kition, 75, 262
Knosos, 121, 123nn. 157-58
Kodylessos, 265
Koliakome, 325
Komama, 263, 266
Korykos, 69, 123n. 155, 327
Kotiaeion, 91
Kourion, 75, 262
Kremna, 263, 266
Krommyon, 275
Kydonia, 121, 123n. 157
Kypros, 61
Kyrrhos, 67, 123n. 155
landholding, 263
Laodicea, 67, 188, 198n. 88,
    254, 268-69, 283-84, 342,
    418, 422
Laranda, 265
lares, 165, 329

leadership, 48, 53, 74, 151, 191,
	208, 240, 247, 249, 261,
	384, 389, 397, 427
leatherworker, 297-98, 305,
	316
Lechaeum, 275, 295
Levites, 74, 384
Libya, 120
lifestyle, 191, 193-4, 206, 242-
	43, 309, 321, 328, 405, 448
linguistics, 184, 226, 324, 338-
	39, 341, 377, 398, 405,
	411, 439
liturgy, 292, 341, 416
Livia, 271
logic, 52, 341, 344, 350, 367,
	410, 417, 437-38, 446, 449
love, 24, 131, 143, 145, 147,
	150-51, 165-66, 180, 190,
	204, 207, 230, 234, 244,
	247, 306, 356, 369, 373,
	390, 404, 411, 417, 422-23,
	432, 434, 444, 448, 457
loyalty, 131, 154, 192, 240,
	325, 363
Lucius, 316. See Luke
Lucius Antonius, 269
Lucius Antonius (proquaestor),
	269
Lucius Castricus Regulus
	(Corinth), 243
Lucius (Christian), 315
Lucius Mummius (consul),
	105, 275
Lucius Sergius Paullus
	(Rome), 311
Lucius Vitellius (consul), 313
Lud, 221-22
lusts, 220, 395
Luther, 379
Lycaonia, 41, 86-87, 108, 250,
	262-63, 283, 285-86, 307,
	310, 330, 337, 368
Lycia, 7, 41, 77, 88, 108, 262,
	325
Lycurgus, 103
Lydda, 454
Lydia, 81, 94, 96, 105, 108,
	221-23, 267, 304, 316-17
Lykos, 111, 198n. 88, 223, 254,
	268, 284
Lyon, 120

Lyrba, 263
Lysinia, 263, 266
Lystra, 35, 77, 79n72, 85-89,
	105, 163-68, 223, 250-51,
	262-66, 285, 310, 330,
	337-38, 365, 368-69, 455
Macedonia, 3, 7, 21, 31-32, 40,
	56, 58, 71, 88-89, 91, 97-
	99, 100, 106, 108, 111-13,
	120, 123, 127, 164, 198,
	221, 223-24, 244, 250-52,
	270-74, 280-82, 286-87,
	290, 316, 392, 407
Madai, 223
Maeander, 79, 81, 111, 268,
	284
Maecenas, 102
magic, 110, 229, 289, 455
magistrates, 73, 81, 96, 102,
	104, 186n. 67, 215, 268,
	283, 287, 294, 305, 340,
	357
Magnesia, 81, 268-69, 327
Maiandros, 269
malaria, 263, 368
Mallos, 69, 123n. 155
Malta, 314, 338
marketing, 416, 433, 436, 442,
	451, 457n. 156
marketplace, 35, 100, 232, 258,
	273, 287, 294, 304, 416,
	427, 433. See also agora
marriage, 42, 61, 207, 211,
	430-31
martyrdom, 369, 427, 247
Mary, 251
Massalia, 224
mathētēs, 292
mature, 33, 144, 204-5, 236,
	370, 422
maturity, 145, 205, 373
Medes, 223
media, 223, 410, 416, 430, 436
megachurches, 413, 418, 425-
	27, 431-33, 435-36, 448
megacities, 14, 423
memoria, 345
memorize, 104, 157
Men (deity), 85-86, 325
Menophilus, 211
menorah, 292, 327
Mercurius, 337

Meshech, 221-22
Mesopotamia, 321
Messiah, 4, 28, 32-34, 36, 40,
	44, 49, 53-54, 58-59, 65,
	73, 82-83, 97, 106-10, 116,
	121, 126-27, 135-37, 142-
	45, 148, 153, 160-63, 184-
	88, 190-91, 196, 199, 201-
	4, 206, 208, 213-14, 216-
	18, 225-28, 232-35, 237,
	257, 260, 280, 288, 303,
	307, 320, 330, 332, 334-35,
	347-50, 353-57, 361, 364,
	371, 378, 380, 382-83, 386,
	388-89, 395-400, 403-4,
	406, 416-17, 420, 422, 425,
	429, 431, 437, 443-44, 446,
	448, 450-51, 457-58
metalworkers, 298
metaphor, 23, 112, 132, 134,
	138, 140, 153, 235, 345,
	369, 412
methods, 11-15, 21-22, 29-31,
	34, 36-38, 89, 131, 135,
	152, 197, 210, 256-57, 266,
	276, 279, 304, 347, 354-56,
	358, 375, 394, 401, 404-5,
	410, 413, 416-17, 428,
	430-32, 436, 453, 457
Miletus, 111, 188, 268-69,
	284, 368
military, 29, 79, 81, 86, 115,
	139, 263, 311, 313, 323
Minerva, 337
miracle(s), 86, 110, 129, 163,
	165, 173, 354, 365, 368,
	384, 403, 410, 451, 453-55
missiology, 405, 448
mission, missionary work
	application of the New
		Testament, 376-82
	call, 382-88
	church growth, 424-36
	church, local, 422-44
	church planting, 231-36,
		400-419, 424
	church, seeker-driven,
		431-36
	crosscultural mission,
		317-34
	and culture, 444-51
	definition of, 22-31

of the disciples, 26
of early church, 27-29
evangelism, 423
goals, 32-33
homogeneous people
    groups, 404-13
of Jesus, 24-24
methods, 29-31, 416-19,
    428-36
missionary task, 124-55
of Paul. *See* Paul
power of God, 401-4,
    451-58
proclamation/preaching,
    210-20, 394-400
sending, 392-94, 437-44
strategy, 29-31, 34-36,
    221-25, 256-373
success, 357-73
teaching, 236-48, 419-21
television, 413-16
training, 388-92
See also Paul
Mitylene, 188
Mizraim (Egypt), 222
Moab, 61
modalities, 72
Moesia, 91
money, 13, 96, 111, 249, 292,
    326, 355, 365, 389, 416,
    418, 425-26, 437n. 115,
    439, 441-42
monocultural, 376
monotheism, 128, 293, 362-63
Mopsuestia, 69, 123n. 155
Mordiaion, 89
mortality, 139, 164-65, 173,
    182, 444
mourning, 87, 213, 254
multicultural, 37, 423
music, 64, 166, 180, 188, 268,
    288, 436
musicians, 88, 263
Mysia, 91, 108, 221-23, 270,
    324
myth, mythological, 87, 150,
    164, 178, 186, 207-8, 283,
    303, 321, 352, 361, 365,
    370, 429, 455
Naaman, 230
Nabaioth, 61
Nabatea, 7, 59, 61, 63-64, 66,

222, 259-60, 288. *See also*
    Arabia
Narbo, 224
narratio, 159, 164, 345
narrative, 94, 178, 197, 262,
    273, 285, 324, 377, 379,
    395, 400, 406, 454
Nazareth, 25, 28, 33, 129, 160,
    163, 184, 213, 226, 228,
    335, 375, 398, 401, 445
Neapolis, 91, 265, 271
networks, 34, 120, 360, 370,
    421n. 83, 434
Nicaea, 270
Nicomedia, 270
Nigeria, 440
Nike, 180
Nikokratos, 102
Nikopolis, 67, 123n. 158
Noah, Noahic, 54-55, 222
Nysa, 268-69
Oceania, 440
Octavian, 270
odeion, 64, 268, 288, 343
offering(s), 142, 163, 166, 174,
    178-79, 239, 359, 365,
    399n. 25, 434, 450
office, 28, 117, 145, 263, 294,
    312, 316
officials, 35, 63-64, 73,
    83-84, 98, 110, 184, 211,
    259, 271, 280, 285, 287,
    310, 313-14, 325, 328,
    364
oikodomē, 235
Oineus, 180
Olba, 69
Olbasa, 263, 266
Olybrios, 325
Olympias, 164
Onesimus, 317
orator(s), 36, 101, 103-4, 106,
    131, 157, 191, 240, 258,
    309, 335, 338, 343-47,
    353-54, 356
Orontes, 67, 71, 74, 79
orthodox, 381, 422, 431, 435
Ostia, 7, 120, 289
Ovid, 87
paganism, 359, 364
paganus, 219-20
palla, 366

Palmyra, 67
Paltus (Syria), 67
Pamphylia, 7, 32, 41, 77, 88,
    108, 262-63, 266-67, 282,
    286, 324, 368
Pan, 180
Pandion, 180
Paphos, 75, 77, 79, 105, 223-
    24, 262-64, 281, 289, 310-
    11, 454
Pappa (Phrygia), 80, 265
Pappa Tiberia, 92
Pappa Tiberiopolis, 78
Pappas (deity), 86
parachurch, 409
paradigm(s), 38, 377-79, 383-
    84, 387-89, 391-96, 405,
    408, 411-12, 418-19, 424-
    25, 428, 432, 437, 456-57
parents, 41, 43, 207, 220, 300
parousia, 253
Parthenon, 180-81, 274
passion(s), 118, 206, 220, 229-
    30, 281, 346, 352, 395,
    403, 444
Patara, 188
pathos, 346, 352
patience, 207, 227, 230, 239,
    373, 381, 411, 444
patriarchs, 159, 290, 292
patron(s), 168, 179, 215, 241,
    253, 288, 325
Paul, apostle 40-47.
    in Antioch, 51-52
    apologetics, 201-8
    and the Apostles' Council,
        52-56
    in Caesarea, 115, 279-80
    call, 45-47
    church planting, 231-36
    cities, 259-86
    in civic settings, 169-84
    and the collection, 56-57
    conversion of Paul, 45-47
    conversion of unbelievers,
        225-31
    coworkers, 111, 248-55
    credibility, 354-56
    and crosscultural mission,
        317-34
    and culture, 190-96, 317-
        34

defense of the gospel,
201-8
establishing contact, 334-
41
and ethnic identity, 306-7
geographical strategy,
221-25
and Jerusalem, 47-58, 64-
66, 259
and local elites, 307-17
mission in Achaia, 98-107,
272-77
mission in Antioch
(Pisidia/Phrygia), 79-
85, 157-63, 262-65
mission in Antioch (Syria),
71-74, 260-61
mission in Arabia, 60-64,
259
mission in Asia (Roman
province), 89-90, 107-
12, 267-69, 277-79
mission in Athens, 100-
105, 169-84, 272-74
mission in Beroea, 98, 272
mission in Cilicia, 66-71,
260
mission in Corinth, 105-7,
274-77
mission on Crete, 121
mission on Cyprus, 74-77,
261-62
mission in Damascus, 58-
60, 259
mission in Derbe, 88, 265
mission in Ephesus, 108-
12, 277-79
mission in Galatia, 77-89
mission in Iconium, 85,
265
mission in Illyricum,
112-15
mission in Lystra, 85-88,
163-69, 265
mission in Macedonia, 91-
98, 270-72
mission in Perge, 88-89,
266
mission in Philippi, 91-87,
270-71
mission in Pontus/
Bithynia, 91, 270

mission in Spain, 116-21,
280-81
mission in Syria, 58-60,
66-74, 260
mission in Thessalonica,
97-98, 271
missionary goals, 32-33,
225-55
missionary message, 156-
208
missionary methods. See
missionary strategy
missionary strategy, 30-31,
34-36, 221-25, 256-
373
missionary success, 357-73
missionary task, 124-55
pastoral concern, 196-200
and Peter, 47-58
as pioneer missionary,
334-41
preaching in lecture halls,
297
preaching in marketplaces,
293-97
preaching in private
houses, 300-304
preaching in synagogues,
288-93
preaching in workshops,
297-99
preaching the gospel,
210-20
proclamation before
Gentiles, 163-69, 215-
20, 397-98
proclamation before Jews,
157-63, 215-18, 396-
97
proclamation of Jesus as
crucified Savior, 188-90
proclamation of Jesus as
Lord, 187-88
proclamation of Jesus as
Messiah, 184-87
and rhetoric, 341-54
and Roman provinces,
286-87
in Rome, 115-16, 280
and social class, 307-17
and Tarsus, 40-44, 260
teaching, 236-48

training new missionaries,
248-55
travels, 121-23
and villages, 285
See also the individual
geographical terms
Paullus. See Sergius Paullus
Pella, 64, 272
Peloponnes, 98
Pentecost, 16, 112n. 138, 121,
185, 410, 438
Pergamon, 88, 108, 111, 188,
263, 270, 305
Perge, 77, 79n. 72, 88-89, 188,
263, 265-66, 283
peroratio, 159, 170-71, 345
persecution, 44, 46-48, 51, 65,
71, 127, 139, 261, 266, 306,
358, 360, 365, 370, 374,
388, 451
Persians, 109, 166, 216
Persis, 251
perspicuitas, 345
persuasion, 191, 344, 454
persuasiveness, 341, 347, 380
Peter (apostle), 28, 30, 47-54,
57, 65, 72, 118, 121, 126,
185, 259, 267, 334, 376-77,
379, 382, 392, 406-7, 444-
46, 454
Petra, 62-64
Phanostratos, 103
Pharisees, 41, 52-53, 349n. 191
Philadelphia, 111, 188, 270
Philemon, 86, 111, 124, 317
Philip, 61, 283, 376, 454
Philippi, 79, 91, 94, 96-97, 105,
113, 116, 124, 127, 198-
99, 205, 223-24, 245, 250,
256, 270-72, 274, 282, 289,
304, 310, 314-16, 368-69,
386, 446
Philo, 46n. 22, 121, 177n. 39,
309, 329
Philodemos, 61
Philomelion, 108
philosopher(s), 36, 88, 100,
117, 133, 169, 172-75,
179-80, 263, 268, 294-95,
297, 305, 309-10, 319,
331, 338-39, 342-44, 346,
361-62

Philostratus, 69, 117n. 148,
    350n. 196
Philtatos, 88
Phoebe, 251, 315
Phoenicia, 261, 445
Phrygia, 79, 81, 84, 86, 91, 101,
    108, 168, 180, 262, 264,
    267, 279, 283, 286, 307,
    324-26
pilgrim, pilgrimage, 121, 329,
    425, 438, 447, 449
Pisidia, 41, 77, 79, 84, 88, 108,
    168, 262-64, 266-67, 286,
    307, 325
Platanoi, 67
plausibility, 263, 367, 391
pleasure, 194, 229, 242, 309,
    445
Pliny, 79n. 73, 117n. 148
Plutarch, 174, 179, 275n. 42,
    309, 321
poet(s), 88, 170, 173, 175,
    177n. 42, 178, 263, 331,
    347
Pogla, 263, 266
polemic, 55, 98, 180
Polemon, 342
Polyarchmos, 292
Polycharmos, 290, 292, 327
Polyrrhenia, 121
polytheism, 32, 87, 97, 106,
    130, 169, 176, 178, 184,
    226, 333, 359, 361-62,
    365, 455
Pompeii, 7, 229, 297-98, 322
Pompey, 41-42, 109, 331
Pontus, 7, 91, 224, 270, 324,
    360
Porcius Festus. See Festus
porneia, 55, 242
Posala, 265
Posidonius, 172
possessions, 79n. 74, 134, 216,
    231, 242, 327, 449
prayer, 74-75, 94, 146, 149,
    151, 166, 176, 200, 207,
    232, 238-40, 245, 266, 304,
    316, 341, 368, 371-72, 373,
    381, 386, 392, 415-16, 422,
    456-57
Priene, 211, 268-69
priest(s), 11, 14, 35, 58, 86, 98,

106, 188, 211, 239, 271-72,
    280, 283, 310, 312, 321,
    364, 384
Prisca, Priscilla, 105, 109, 111-
    12, 250-51, 277, 298, 316
probatio, 170, 345
procession(s), 102, 138-40,
    153, 188, 239, 241, 327,
    341, 359, 361
proofs, 159, 170, 191, 344-47,
    352
prophecy, 56, 160, 162, 166,
    213, 377, 384
prophet(s), 25, 75, 82, 116,
    124-25, 146, 148, 157-58,
    160, 175, 178, 202, 213,
    217, 235, 245, 249, 280,
    289, 331, 335, 384, 408,
    423, 446
propositio, 170
prostitution, 28, 55, 106, 228-
    29, 238, 282, 352 327, 333,
    446
Ptolemais, 67
punishment, 44, 75, 96, 110,
    274, 350-51, 399, 454
purification, 102, 137, 201-2,
    206, 218, 230-31, 237, 239,
    243, 292, 333, 345, 445
Put, 149, 221
Puteoli, 31
Pydna, 98
Qadesh, 64
Quartus, 118, 315
Quintilian, 191, 344, 346
reconciliation, 21, 127, 149,
    204, 215, 252, 352, 357-58,
    399, 403
redemption, 217, 234, 239,
    452-53
refutatio, 345
repentance, 72, 141, 158-59,
    182, 199, 227, 230, 285,
    374, 380, 400, 412, 417,
    422, 452, 454
Resafa, 67
reward, 132, 134, 154, 209, 212
rhetoric, 4, 36, 106, 191, 258,
    341-45, 347-50, 354, 400-
    401, 406, 425
rhetors, 297
Rhithymna, 121, 123n. 157

Rhoda, 120
Rhodes, 188
ridiculum, 353
righteousness, 117, 126, 134,
    142, 149, 156, 170, 176,
    199, 202, 204, 213, 217-18,
    243, 332, 358, 388, 403,
    452-53
rites, 101-2, 239, 319, 327,
    359, 361
ritual, 33, 51, 55, 188, 201, 217,
    231n. 45, 359
Roupheina, 327
sabbath, 56, 77, 82, 84, 94, 97,
    106, 110, 158, 206, 312,
    326, 328
sacrifice(s), 35, 86, 101-2, 104,
    140, 163-64, 166, 169, 171,
    174, 178-79, 181, 187, 189,
    195-96, 217, 239, 312, 333,
    336, 368, 397, 399
Saetabis, 119, 120
Sagalassos, 263
Saguntum, 120
Salamis, 75, 224, 262, 289, 310
Salome, 61
Samaria, Samaritans, 26, 376,
    454
Samos, 188
Samuel, 157, 160
Sarah, 203
Sarapis, 180, 331
Sardis, 111, 188, 270
Satan, 149-50, 198, 225,
    246-47
Saul, 42-45, 58, 60, 74, 157,
    159-60
scandal, scandalous, 190, 242,
    357, 400, 403-4, 453
Scodra, 113
Scythia, 307-8, 337
Scythopolis, 64
Sebaste, 69, 265, 267, 270
Sedasa, 87
seekers, 417, 422, 424-27, 429,
    431-36, 449
Selaima, 64
Seleucia, 67, 69, 75, 123n. 155
Seleukos I Nikator, 71, 79
Selge, 263
Sergii, 79, 264-65, 312
Sergius Paullus (governor), 43,

105, 262, 264, 289, 311, 370, 454
Set, 74
Shahba, 64
Sibidunda, 263, 266
Sidon, 67
Sikyon, 243
Silas, 54, 66, 89, 96-99, 100, 106, 198, 251, 272-74, 287
Sillyon, 263
silver, 110-11, 132, 136, 170, 179-80, 209
silversmiths, 112
Sinai, 64, 216, 227
sin(s), 28, 33, 45, 126-27, 130, 138, 141-43, 158-59, 160-63, 189, 193-94, 202-5, 215, 217-18, 227, 231, 237, 242, 352-53, 357-58, 400, 403, 411, 417, 424, 435, 446, 448, 452, 457
skandalon, 349-50
slaves, slavery, 28, 33, 42, 64, 94, 96, 116, 120, 136-37, 139, 142, 151-53, 184, 207, 229, 240, 247-49, 275, 300, 307-9, 316-17, 333-37, 351, 357, 365-67, 370-71, 378, 391, 393, 408-9, 411, 413, 418, 444, 451, 458
slogans, 428-29, 242-43
Smyrna, 69, 111, 188, 211, 270, 305, 327, 343
Soada, 64
Socrates, 100, 352
Soloi, 69, 177n. 42
Solomon, 177, 216
sorcery, 230, 310
Sozopolis, 89
Spain, 3, 7, 32, 39, 112-13, 116-18, 120-21, 123, 140-41, 204, 210, 221-24, 280-81, 286-87, 360, 386, 391
speech, 35, 53, 57, 100, 102-4, 131, 157n. 3, 165, 169-71, 173-75, 183, 192, 229, 256, 330, 338-39, 341-42, 343n. 182, 345-46, 348, 356, 367, 436, 452
Spirit. See Holy Spirit
statistics, 59, 121
statues, 73, 102, 109, 164, 179-

80, 188, 271, 274, 295, 312, 314, 331, 340, 359
status, 41, 43-44, 50, 77, 106, 129, 132, 137, 140, 153, 181, 191-92, 200, 203, 215, 217, 229, 232, 240-43, 253, 283, 292, 308-9, 311, 316, 318, 322, 340, 345, 350, 362, 365-66, 378, 393, 450
Stephanas, 106, 111, 254, 304
Stephen, 16, 44, 71, 261, 377, 444
Stobi, 290, 292
Stoics, 100, 169, 172-74, 177, 179, 182, 294-95, 361-62
Strabo, 79n. 74, 81, 97n. 109, 113, 117, 262n. 7, 267, 271, 275n. 42, 324
strategy, 12, 22, 29-31, 64, 141, 191-92, 209, 222-24, 257, 261-65, 270, 272-73, 276, 287, 304, 307, 313, 317, 340, 347, 349, 402, 353, 371, 375, 400-404, 408, 414, 416, 429-31, 435, 442, 457
subcultures, 318
success, 4, 31, 37, 50, 59, 64, 66, 83-84, 97, 111, 133-34, 146, 152-54, 279, 348, 355, 359-61, 364, 367-71, 381, 401, 404, 411, 416-18, 430, 436, 451, 453
Suetonius, 186
suffering, 60, 111, 144-45, 153, 231, 351, 372, 373n. 240, 383, 390, 427
Sukkot, 278
Sunday, 330, 421, 434
Syllaios, 61
symbols, 240, 292, 319, 327, 390-91
synagogue(s), 7, 25, 34-37, 44, 49, 58-59, 63, 65-66, 69, 71, 73, 75, 77, 81-85, 94, 97-98, 100, 106, 108-10, 128, 142, 157, 160-61, 163, 167, 185, 186, 213, 232-33, 239, 258, 270, 273-75, 276, 279, 287-90, 292-93, 303-5, 310, 316, 327-28, 330, 332, 354, 367, 377, 388,

391, 412, 445
Synaos, 91
syncretism, 96, 101, 362
Syntyche, 251, 316
Syria, 3, 7, 31-32, 40-41, 44, 53-54, 57-58, 61, 63, 66, 67n. 50, 69, 71, 73-75, 77, 79, 85, 87, 89, 107, 123, 186, 197, 222-24, 250, 252, 260-62, 267, 278, 279n. 52, 286-87, 328, 360, 363, 391, 445
Tacitus, 117n. 148, 121
tactics, 29, 71, 141, 340
Tarchunt, 86
Tarraco, 120, 123n. 156, 281
Tarshish, 221, 281
Tarsus, 40-41, 43-44, 65-67, 69, 72, 91, 101, 116, 123n. 155, 188, 221, 223-24, 260-61, 263, 265, 267, 281, 328-29, 331, 340, 391, 418, 438
Tartessos, 221
Taurus, 69, 260, 265n. 17
television, 413-16, 434
Temenouthyrai, 270
temple in Jerusalem, 187, 267, 329
temple(s), 14, 28, 33, 35, 54-55, 64, 71, 73, 81-82, 86, 88, 100, 102-4, 106, 110, 113, 135, 139, 160, 163, 165-66, 169, 171, 174, 178-81, 183, 187-89, 194-95, 200, 209, 215-16, 232, 235, 239-40, 243, 243, 263-64, 267, 280, 283-84, 294-95, 305, 312, 316, 327, 321, 329, 333, 337, 339-40, 348, 359, 361, 364, 377, 384, 397, 408, 425, 439, 445-46
tentmaker, 106n. 127, 277, 297, 383
Termessos, 263
Tertius, 315
Tertullian, 73n. 64, 369
thanksgiving, 373
Thargelion, 331
theater, 35, 64, 82, 88, 238, 268, 288, 297, 315
Theseus, 180

Thessalonica, 79n. 72, 91, 97-98, 105, 127-28, 197-99, 223-24, 233, 244, 251, 254, 270-72, 274, 282, 289, 310, 315-16, 327, 358, 363, 367-69, 373, 395

Thessaly, 98

Thetis, 164

Thracia, 94, 324

Thyatira, 88, 94, 111, 188, 263, 270

Tiber, 311

Tiberius, 41, 71, 98, 180, 290, 327

Timothy, 3, 87, 99, 100, 106, 111, 117, 150-51, 198-99, 207-8, 214n. 8, 224, 247, 250-54, 272-74, 287, 358, 368, 388, 390

Titius, 106

Titus, 3, 48, 69, 121, 150-51, 198-99, 207-8, 250, 252-54, 390

Tlos, 88, 263

toga, 139, 240, 242, 295

tolerance, 240, 360, 362

Torah, 44-45, 51, 126, 137, 202-3, 237, 290, 292, 304, 327-28, 331, 335, 352, 361, 383, 388, 446

Tragurium, 113

Tralles, 268-69

transformation, 29, 200, 206, 225, 229-30, 349, 383, 403, 412, 423, 430, 432, 448, 454

translation(s), 40, 43, 59, 61, 81, 185, 210, 212, 219-20, 268, 378, 421

travels, 32, 121, 123, 139, 197, 248, 274, 315, 354-55, 384, 423

tribe, tribal, 41-42, 61, 81, 102-3, 125, 157, 216, 220, 323, 326, 384

trickery, 130, 256, 355

triclinium, 290, 292, 298

Tripolis, 67, 268-69

triumphalism, 11, 427

Troas (region in Asia), 108, 198, 270, 335

Trophimus, 111, 368

Troy, 324

Tryphaena, 251

Trypho, 350

Tryphosa, 251

Tubal, 221-22

Turronius, 327

Tychasios, 325

Tyche, 166, 295, 337

Tychicus, 111, 198, 250

Tymandos, 263, 266

Tyrannus, 110, 279, 297

Tyre, 67

Ulfilas, 220

unbelievers, 22, 133, 151, 208, 238, 244, 298, 304, 369, 377, 386, 400, 405, 409, 430, 449

uncircumcised, 48, 52, 57, 308, 361, 366, 408

unity, 12, 38, 50, 133, 137, 149, 154, 235-36, 310, 360, 406, 408-12, 422, 426, 443

values, 139, 184, 191, 196, 205, 230, 237-38, 240, 283, 318-20, 327, 334, 390-91, 396, 411-12

velato, 295, 316, 366

venatio, 312

Venus, 165, 228, 295

Vespasian, 41, 275n. 44

Vetissus, 79, 264

Via Egnatia, 113, 271-73, 282

vice(s), 206, 228, 241, 333, 353

Vitellius, 313

weak, weakness, 63, 136, 143, 153, 190, 195, 226, 254, 256, 284, 306-8, 342, 348, 413-14, 416, 425, 430, 452

wealth, wealthy, 71, 84, 88, 210, 240, 269, 308-9, 315-17, 320, 365, 370, 394, 418, 427, 448

Whitefield, George, 297

wisdom, 30, 33, 131, 144-46, 148, 156, 173, 177, 179, 184, 189, 191-92, 206, 208, 236, 239-40, 256-57, 335, 342, 347, 349-54, 371, 373, 379-82, 432, 452

witness, 45, 117, 130, 148-49, 151, 154, 163, 167-68, 183, 217, 247, 254, 256, 280, 355, 380, 383, 446, 457

workshop(s), 30, 35, 106, 258, 287, 295, 297-98, 304-5, 335

worldview, 175, 196, 318, 391

worship, 28, 54-55, 87, 94, 101-2, 106-7, 128-30, 147-48, 165-70, 175, 178-80, 196, 200, 206, 216, 232, 234, 239-40, 264, 269, 271, 300, 304, 312, 327, 330-31, 333, 337, 340, 362-64, 380, 395, 398, 406-7, 412, 415-16, 420, 425-26, 428-29, 457-58

Zenon, 172

Zephyrion, 69

Zeugma, 67

Zeus, 35, 86-87, 96, 163-65, 168, 172-73, 179-80, 283, 310, 321, 324, 337

Zion, 148, 212-13, 221, 443

Scripture Index

OLD TESTAMENT

Genesis
1:1, *166*
1:26-27, *177*
2:7, *177*
3, *450*
6:2, *128*
8:21, *139*
10, *222*
10:22, *222*
11, *381*
12:1-3, *147*
12:3, *201*
15:6, *201, 332*
25:13, *61*
28:9, *61*
35:16-20, *46*
36:3, *61*

Exodus
20:3, *164*
20:10, *56*
29:18, *139*
29:25, *139*
29:41, *139*
32:25-29, *384*

Leviticus
1:9, *139*
1:13, *139*
1:17, *139*
2:2, *139*
2:9, *139*
2:12, *139*
3:5, *139*
3:11, *139*
3:16, *139*
17—18, *55, 56*
17:7, *165*
17:13, *55*
17:14, *55*
18:10, *55*
18:12, *55*

Numbers
6:1-21, *277*
12:12, *46*
18, *384*
20:22, *64*

Deuteronomy
5:14, *56*
5:26, *165*
10:8-9, *384*
18:5, *384*
21:22-23, *83*
21:23, *332, 350*
32:8, *128, 175*

Joshua
3:10, *165*

1 Samuel
17:26, *165*
17:36, *165*

2 Samuel
7:12, *160*
7:12-13, *160*
7:14, *128, 160*
7:15-16, *160*

1 Kings
16:2, *165*
16:13, *165*

2 Kings
5:14, *230*
19:4, *165*
19:16, *165*

1 Chronicles
1:29, *61*

Nehemiah
1:3-4, *261*

Esther
8:17, *200*

Job
1:6, *128*
2:1, *128*
3:16, *46*
37:2, *165*

Psalms
2:7, *128*
29:1, *128*
35:10, *166*
40:9, *212*
41:2, *166*
50:12-13, *178*
83:3, *166*
89:6, *128*
89:26-27, *128*
145:18, *176*

Ecclesiastes
6:3, *46*

Isaiah
37:4, *165*
37:17, *165*
40:9, *212*
40:9-11, *212*
40:18-19, *180*
41:27, *212*
42:5, *178*
44:9-20, *180*
45:15, *174*
45:15-24, *180*
45:18-19, *175*
45:18-25, *174*
45:20-21, *175*
45:22-23, *175*
46:5-7, *180*
49:4, *46*
49:5-6, *124*
49:6, *83, 221*
52:7, *212*
55:3, *158, 160, 161*
58:6, *25*
60:6, *212*
61:1, *212*
61:1-2, *25, 213*
61:1-3, *213*
66:1-2, *178*
66:18, *221*
66:19, *221, 222*

Jeremiah
1:5, *124*
2:13, *166*
12:16, *56*
17:13, *166*
24:6, *235*
31:4, *235*
33:7, *235*
46:9, *221*

Ezekiel
27:10, *221*
27:18, *269*
30:5, *221*

Daniel
1, *128*
3:25, *128*
4:1, *165*
5:23, *165*

Hosea
13:13, *46*

Amos
9:11-12, *54, 56*

Nahum
1:15, *212*
2:1, *212*

Habakkuk
1:5, *159, 161*

Zechariah
2:11, *56*

APOCRYPHA

Bel and the Dragon
5, *166*
5-6, *165*
24-25, *165*

Judith
2:23, *221*

2 Maccabees
7:33, *165*
15:4, *165*

3 Maccabees
2:6, *216*
2:10, *216*
6:32, *216*
7:16, *216*
7:23, *216*

Tobit
13:1-3, *165*

Wisdom of Solomon
13, *180*
13:5-6, *176*

NEW TESTAMENT

Matthew
3:9, *227*
3:10, *227*
4:19, *383, 386, 392*
5:13-16, *386*

9:38, *26*
10, *389*
10:1, *28*
10:1-15, *386*
10:5, *26*
10:5-8, *28*
10:16, *26*
11:2-6, *213*
12:38-39, *349*
16:1-4, *349*
18:20, *233*
22:37-40, *428, 429*
28:18-20, *392*
28:19, *28*
28:19-20, *232, 421,*
428, 429
28:20, *383*

Mark
1:4-5, *227*
1:15, *213*
1:17, *28, 248, 382*
3:6, *73*
3:13-15, *248*
3:14, *26*
6, *389*
6:7, *26*
7:26, *220*
8:11-13, *349*
8:27-30, *382*
8:31-33, *383*
10:2-12, *378*
12:13, *73*

Luke
2:37, *261*
4:18-19, *25, 213*
4:21, *213*
4:43, *25*
9, *389*
9:1-5, *28*
9:2, *26*
10:1, *26*
10:2, *26*
10:9, *227*
10:13, *227*
11:16, *349*
11:32, *227*
13:3-5, *227*

John
1:1-3, *23*
1:3, *24*
1:6-9, *24*

1:9-14, *24*
1:35-42, *382*
1:41, *184, 382*
2:18-22, *349*
3:16-17, *24*
4:25, *184*
6:30, *349*
6:38, *24*
7:18, *25*
8:29, *25*
12:49, *25*
13:20, *253*
17:14-16, *447*
17:17-18, *447*
20:21, *25*

Acts
1, *30*
1:8, *28, 281*
1:25, *28*
2, *438*
2—12, *30*
2:5, *439*
2:9, *286*
2:10, *286*
2:11, *121*
2:38, *227*
2:41, *59*
3:17, *227*
3:19, *227*
4—5, *445*
4:4, *59*
4:36, *74, 261*
5:15-16, *455*
5:31, *227*
6—7, *445*
6:7, *289*
6:9, *65, 69, 286, 328*
8:3, *44*
8:4, *262*
8:5-8, *455*
8:12, *455*
8:22, *227*
9:1-2, *31*
9:1-21, *45*
9:2-3, *44*
9:3, *45*
9:10, *31*
9:11, *41*
9:15, *28*
9:15-16, *45, 385,*
386, 392

9:19-20, *267*
9:19-21, *259*
9:19-22, *59*
9:19-25, *257*
9:20, *59, 288*
9:22, *59, 288*
9:23-25, *59, 60, 61,*
259, 288
9:26, *267*
9:26-29, *58, 259*
9:26-30, *65, 257*
9:27, *47, 74, 372*
9:27-30, *47*
9:28, *47, 65*
9:29, *65, 260*
9:29-30, *260*
9:30, *66, 260, 267*
9:31, *285*
9:34-35, *455*
9:40-42, *455*
10—11, *445*
10:1-48, *72*
11:1, *72, 285*
11:1-18, *72*
11:18, *72, 227*
11:19, *261, 446*
11:19-26, *72*
11:20, *71*
11:20-21, *72*
11:20-24, *260*
11:21-24, *72*
11:22, *72, 261, 385*
11:22-24, *74*
11:24, *288, 289*
11:25-26, *69, 260,*
267
11:26, *72, 73, 288*
11:26-30, *260*
11:27-30, *48, 58, 75,*
443
11:29, *285*
11:30, *48*
12:1-4, *48*
12:25, *75*
13, *161, 376*
13—14, *40, 77, 197*
13—19, *445*
13—28, *31*
13:1, *249, 260*
13:1-2, *244*
13:1-4, *386, 392*
13:2, *75, 261, 392*

13:2-3, *74*
13:3, *108, 261, 392*
13:4, *392*
13:4-12, *43*
13:4-12, *75*
13:5, *75, 289, 310*
13:6, *75, 262*
13:6-7, *289, 310*
13:6-12, *75, 264*
13:7, *104, 289*
13:12, *77, 104, 264,*
311, 455
13:13, *262, 286*
13:13-14, *77, 311*
13:14, *79, 81, 286,*
289, 310
13:14-50, *156*
13:14-52, *79*
13:14—14:23, *77,*
262
13:15, *84*
13:16, *84, 158, 310*
13:16-41, *81, 156,*
158, 289
13:17, *159*
13:22-23, *159*
13:23, *159*
13:24, *227*
13:24-25, *159*
13:26, *84, 158, 310*
13:26-37, *158*
13:27-29, *159*
13:30-31, *161*
13:32-37, *161*
13:38, *158*
13:38-39, *160, 161*
13:38-41, *158*
13:40-41, *161*
13:41, *161*
13:42, *88*
13:42-43, *310*
13:43, *82, 84, 264*
13:44, *82, 84, 312*
13:45, *83, 88, 289*
13:46, *83, 372*
13:47, *83*
13:48, *84, 231, 264,*
310
13:48-49, *83, 84*
13:49, *264*
13:50, *84, 265, 312*
13:50-51, *313*

13:52, *231*
14, *35, 262, 338*
14:1, *289, 310*
14:1-7, *85*
14:1-28, *281*
14:3, *372, 455*
14:4, *249, 455*
14:5, *219*
14:6, *286*
14:6-7, *285*
14:6-20, *251*
14:7, *86, 310*
14:7-20, *85, 164*
14:8-10, *86*
14:8-18, *156, 330*
14:8-19, *368*
14:8-20, *87, 164,*
    267, 307
14:11, *286, 330, 337,*
    455
14:11-13, *86*
14:13, *35, 337*
14:13-17, *310*
14:14, *87, 249*
14:15, *163, 164, 165,*
    166, 397
14:15-17, *87, 162,*
    330
14:15-18, *163, 338*
14:16, *166*
14:17, *167*
14:18, *163, 330*
14:20, *455*
14:20-21, *88, 265*
14:21, *77, 265*
14:21-23, *85, 87,*
    197, 266
14:22-23, *85*
14:23, *77, 261*
14:24, *286*
14:24-25, *88*
14:24-26, *266*
14:25, *265, 266*
14:26-28, *89*
15, *52, 445*
15:1, *52*
15:1-29, *58*
15:1-35, *89*
15:2, *48, 52*
15:3, *54*
15:4, *48, 53*
15:5, *52, 53*

15:6, *48, 53*
15:7, *53*
15:7-11, *53, 407*
15:8, *53*
15:9, *53*
15:11, *53*
15:12, *53, 54*
15:14-21, *54*
15:19, *219*
15:20, *56*
15:22, *48, 54*
15:23, *48, 54, 66,*
    219, 286
15:23-29, *54*
15:24-27, *54*
15:27, *54*
15:28-29, *54*
15:29, *55, 56*
15:30-40, *66*
15:32, *249*
15:36, *66*
15:36—18:22, *40*
15:38, *286*
15:39, *262*
15:41, *66, 67, 89,*
    286
16, *223*
16:1, *89*
16:1-3, *87, 251*
16:1-4, *388*
16:1-5, *197*
16:2-5, *89*
16:4, *48*
16:6, *89, 222, 223,*
    267, 269, 270,
    277, 286, 392
16:6-8, *90*
16:7, *90, 270*
16:7-8, *223*
16:8, *90*
16:9, *286*
16:9-10, *92, 270,*
    286, 385, 392
16:10, *286*
16:12, *286*
16:12-13, *289*
16:12-40, *92*
16:13, *89, 92, 270*
16:13-15, *310*
16:14, *89, 94, 104*
16:14-15, *304, 316*
16:17, *94*

16:19, *94*
16:20-21, *305*
16:25-34, *96*
16:29-31, *310*
16:32, *89*
16:32-34, *304*
16:34, *231*
16:35-36, *96*
16:37, *96, 287*
16:38-39, *96*
16:40, *96, 108*
17, *102, 103, 104,*
    169, 266
17:1, *289*
17:1-9, *96*
17:2, *108, 310*
17:4, *97, 310, 315*
17:5-7, *36*
17:5-9, *97*
17:6, *97, 104*
17:6-7, *305*
17:7, *363*
17:10, *97, 108, 272,*
    289, 310, 358
17:10-11, *272*
17:10-14, *98*
17:12, *98, 310, 315*
17:14, *98, 108, 198,*
    251, 274, 358
17:14-15, *97, 98,*
    273
17:15, *251, 273, 274,*
    358
17:15-16, *99, 257*
17:16, *273*
17:16-19, *311*
17:16-20, *103*
17:16-34, *156, 273,*
    338
17:17, *99, 273, 289,*
    294
17:18, *99, 100, 338*
17:18-19, *297*
17:19, *89*
17:22, *175*
17:22-23, *169*
17:22-31, *104, 168,*
    169, 341, 361
17:23, *99, 103, 168,*
    174, 339
17:24, *172*
17:24-26, *103*

17:24-29, *170*
17:26, *175*
17:30, *180, 181, 227,*
    339
17:30-31, *170, 229,*
    367, 398
17:31, *339*
17:32, *362*
17:32-34, *311*
17:34, *104*
18—20, *276*
18:1, *257, 274, 289*
18:1-3, *383*
18:1-5, *105*
18:2, *104, 134, 278*
18:2-3, *316*
18:2-4, *274*
18:3, *298*
18:4, *289, 311*
18:4-8, *275*
18:5, *97, 257, 274,*
    286, 383
18:6, *276*
18:6-7, *105*
18:8, *104, 105, 276,*
    304, 316
18:9, *89, 276*
18:9-10, *106, 276*
18:9-11, *257*
18:10, *106*
18:11, *104, 134, 275,*
    276
18:12, *134, 286*
18:12-13, *36*
18:12-16, *313*
18:13, *106, 363*
18:14-16, *107*
18:18, *104, 108, 275,*
    277, 286
18:18-22, *107*
18:18-23, *107*
18:19, *108, 289*
18:20, *108*
18:21, *107, 108, 278*
18:22, *58, 279*
18:22-23, *277, 279*
18:23, *87, 107, 197,*
    286
18:23—21:16, *40*
18:25-26, *108*
18:26, *108*
18:27, *108, 286*

19, *223*
19:1, *279*
19:2-9, *279*
19:4, *227*
19:7, *59*
19:8, *109, 184, 289,
    372*
19:8-10, *311*
19:9, *109, 297*
19:9-10, *109*
19:10, *110, 279, 286*
19:11, *109*
19:13, *214*
19:13-16, *110*
19:17, *110, 311*
19:18-19, *110*
19:20, *109*
19:21, *111, 280, 286*
19:21-41, *111*
19:22, *250, 286, 315*
19:23-40, *111*
19:26, *286, 289*
19:27, *286*
19:29, *88, 110, 249,
    286, 316*
19:30-31, *35*
19:31, *286, 314*
20:1, *112, 286*
20:1-3, *111*
20:2, *112*
20:3, *286*
20:4, *88, 110, 286,
    316*
20:15, *110*
20:16, *286*
20:17-38, *110*
20:18, *286*
20:18-24, *374*
20:20, *198*
20:21, *227*
20:25, *214*
20:27, *198*
20:31, *110*
20:36-38, *108*
21—26, *113*
21:3, *286*
21:15-17, *58*
21:17-18, *57*
21:18, *48*
21:20, *59*
21:27, *286*
21:27—22:23, *113*

21:39, *40, 69, 286*
22—28, *446*
22:3, *40, 43, 286,
    388*
22:5, *44*
22:6, *45*
22:6-21, *45*
22:12-16, *46*
22:14-15, *45, 385,
    386, 392*
22:15, *383*
22:17-18, *112*
23:23—26:32, *113*
23:34, *286*
24:1, *280*
24:1-27, *280*
24:5, *73*
24:17, *57*
24:19, *286*
24:23, *113*
24:24-25, *113*
24:26, *113*
24:26-27, *113*
25:1—26:32, *280*
25:2-7, *280*
25:13, *280*
25:22, *249*
25:23, *114*
26:1, *280*
26:9, *73*
26:12, *44*
26:12-18, *45*
26:13, *45*
26:16-18, *28, 385,
    386, 392*
26:18, *225, 227*
26:19-20, *285*
26:20, *227*
26:28, *73*
27, *286*
27:1—28:16, *114*
27:2, *110, 286*
27:5, *286*
28:2-4, *338*
28:7, *314*
28:8-9, *338*
28:10, *338*
28:13-14, *31*
28:14-15, *31*
28:16, *114, 313*
28:17, *280*
28:17-28, *280*

28:17-31, *114*
28:20, *115*
28:23, *114, 115, 280*
28:24, *280*
28:24-25, *115*
28:30-31, *115, 313*
28:31, *184, 214*

Romans
1—3, *140*
1—11, *419*
1:1, *32, 210, 214,
    249, 418, 437*
1:1-2, *438*
1:1-5, *203*
1:1-6, *123*
1:1-17, *437*
1:3-4, *203, 438*
1:3-5, *156*
1:5, *28, 437, 438*
1:7, *383*
1:9, *214, 437*
1:11-15, *280*
1:14, *32, 36, 153,
    336, 412*
1:14-16, *308*
1:15, *437*
1:16, *32, 140, 215,
    216, 259, 438*
1:16-17, *155, 438*
1:18, *217, 220*
1:18-20, *220*
1:18-32, *141, 341*
1:18—3:20, *203,
    217, 450*
1:21-22, *220*
1:23, *173, 220*
1:24-27, *220, 238*
1:25, *420*
1:29-31, *220*
1:32, *220*
2, *216, 286*
2:4, *227*
2:9, *216*
2:9-10, *140, 215*
2:10, *216*
2:17, *216*
2:22, *340*
2:25-29, *216*
2:28, *216*
2:29, *216*
3:1, *216*

3:9, *215, 216, 217*
3:21, *57*
3:21-25, *217*
3:21-26, *156, 398*
3:21-31, *141, 203*
3:21—5:21, *217, 450*
3:23, *36*
3:24-26, *129*
3:25-26, *203*
3:29, *216*
4, *203, 333*
4:1, *413*
4:1-25, *141*
4:9-12, *216*
4:11, *142*
4:12, *413*
4:16, *413*
4:16-17, *438*
4:25, *203, 398*
5:1-2, *156*
5:1-11, *204*
5:1-21, *141*
5:6, *185*
5:6-11, *398*
5:8, *185*
5:11-21, *204*
5:12-21, *141*
6, *204*
6—8, *419*
6:1—8:39, *142*
6:3-4, *156, 185*
6:9, *185*
6:17, *203*
6:17-19, *156*
7, *204*
7:4-6, *156*
7:12, *217*
8:1-4, *156*
8:1-17, *204*
8:3, *141, 203, 398*
8:10, *185*
8:11, *185*
8:14-17, *235*
8:15, *235*
8:17, *147*
8:18, *231*
8:18-39, *204*
8:22, *231*
8:29, *413*
8:31-39, *231*
8:32, *156*
8:32-35, *398*

8:34, *185*
9—11, *140, 204, 215*
9:1-3, *259*
9:1—11:32, *142*
9:2, *218*
9:4-5, *216*
9:5, *185, 420*
9:7, *413*
9:24, *216*
10, *218*
10:2, *218*
10:3, *218*
10:4, *218*
10:6, *185*
10:7, *185*
10:9, *203, 228*
10:9-10, *420*
10:12, *215, 216, 413*
10:14-15, *142*
10:14-17, *152*
10:16, *153*
10:18, *153*
11:1, *41, 218, 413*
11:11-15, *142*
11:11-24, *195*
11:26, *218*
11:33-36, *420*
12—15, *204, 419*
12:1-2, *195, 248, 333*
12:1—15:29, *142*
12:2, *238*
12:4-5, *235, 413*
12:7, *419*
12:9-10, *142*
12:19-21, *142*
12:21, *143*
13:8-9, *203*
13:11, *153*
14—15, *333*
14:1, *413*
14:9, *185, 398*
14:10, *413*
14:13, *413*
14:15, *185*
14:17, *203*
14:21, *413*
15:2, *413*
15:3, *185*
15:14-15, *203*
15:14-21, *56, 225, 408, 443*
15:14-29, *386*

15:16, *139, 214, 249, 306*
15:17-24, *39*
15:18, *151, 152, 185*
15:18-19, *452*
15:19, *32, 112, 140, 214, 221, 222, 279*
15:20, *185*
15:21, *249*
15:22-24, *222*
15:22-29, *391*
15:23, *280*
15:23-24, *33, 203*
15:23-28, *281*
15:23-29, *118*
15:24, *117, 140, 280, 287, 337*
15:24-28, *112*
15:25-28, *280*
15:26, *287*
15:26-27, *57*
15:27, *57, 219*
15:28, *140, 280, 287, 337*
15:28-29, *222*
15:30-31, *203, 280*
15:30-33, *373*
15:31, *57*
16:1-2, *251, 315*
16:2, *315*
16:3, *249, 251*
16:3-4, *111*
16:3-5, *316*
16:4, *250*
16:5, *286, 317*
16:6, *249, 251*
16:7, *249, 251*
16:8, *317*
16:9, *249*
16:12, *249, 251*
16:16, *233*
16:21, *249, 315*
16:22, *315*
16:23, *105, 238, 249, 315*
16:25-27, *156, 420*
16:26, *143*

1 Corinthians
1—4, *130, 190, 347, 400*
1—6, *131, 240, 315*

1:1, *249*
1:2, *233, 383*
1:10, *411, 426*
1:10-17, *132*
1:11, *317*
1:13, *132, 185, 413*
1:13-17, *231*
1:14, *110, 315, 316*
1:16, *304*
1:17, *185, 210, 231, 347*
1:17-18, *132, 188*
1:17—2:5, *398*
1:18-23, *357, 403*
1:18-24, *155*
1:18-25, *228*
1:18-31, *129, 380*
1:18—2:5, *33, 156, 349, 371, 379, 396, 397, 453*
1:18—3:20, *398*
1:18—4:21, *190*
1:22, *216*
1:22-23, *349*
1:22-24, *183*
1:23, *32, 134, 151, 185, 191, 214, 216*
1:24, *151, 216, 349*
1:26, *105*
1:26-28, *284*
1:26-29, *308*
1:26-30, *228*
2:1, *190, 214, 342, 347*
2:1-2, *335*
2:1-5, *36, 105, 151, 190, 208, 241, 257, 342, 344*
2:2, *32, 104, 132, 134, 151, 185, 188, 191, 266, 344, 348, 351*
2:4, *227, 353, 371*
2:4-5, *191*
2:5, *250, 354*
2:14, *357, 403*
3, *192*
3:1-4, *132*
3:1-23, *417*
3:3, *241*
3:5, *131, 132, 151, 152, 249*

3:5-8, *241*
3:5-9, *192, 241, 403, 417*
3:5-15, *130, 131*
3:5-17, *209*
3:5—4:5, *133*
3:5—6:9, *251*
3:6, *132, 152*
3:6-7, *132, 151*
3:7, *132*
3:8, *132, 133, 153, 250*
3:9, *132, 151, 249, 250*
3:10, *37, 132, 133, 152*
3:10-15, *396, 399*
3:11, *134, 151*
3:12-14, *135*
3:12-15, *134, 137, 153*
3:15, *135*
3:16, *420*
3:16-17, *235*
3:18, *105*
3:19, *357, 403*
3:21-22, *241*
3:23, *185*
4:1, *241, 249*
4:1-2, *249*
4:8-13, *241*
4:11-12, *355*
4:15, *241, 413*
4:17, *237, 254, 413*
4:19, *278*
4:20, *127*
5, *192*
5:1, *242*
5:1-13, *192, 242*
5:2, *241, 420*
5:6, *241*
5:8, *192*
5:11, *333*
6, *194, 446*
6:1-8, *242*
6:1-11, *105, 194, 316*
6:2, *242, 420*
6:3, *420*
6:5, *242*
6:5-8, *413*
6:8-10, *243*
6:9, *420*
6:9-10, *127, 333*

6:9-11, *228*
6:11, *243*
6:12, *242*
6:12-18, *105*
6:12-19, *238*
6:12-20, *192*
6:13, *242*
6:15, *413, 420*
6:16, *420*
6:19, *420*
7:16, *238, 245, 304*
7:17, *237*
7:17-24, *366*
7:19, *216*
7:20-24, *317*
8—10, *241, 446*
8:1—11:1, *194, 243*
8:4-6, *187*
8:6, *194, 364, 406*
8:9, *316*
8:10, *106, 243*
8:11, *185, 194, 398*
8:11-13, *413*
8:13, *243*
9, *336, 377*
9:1, *45*
9:2, *28*
9:5, *49, 244*
9:6-18, *355*
9:7, *249*
9:10, *152*
9:12, *194, 287*
9:13, *420*
9:14, *214*
9:16, *210, 260*
9:17, *133*
9:18, *133, 210*
9:19, *135, 136, 137,*
    152, 153, 287, 336
9:19-20, *49*
9:19-23, *135, 215, 391*
9:20, *136, 137, 216*
9:20-21, *287*
9:20-22, *136, 310*
9:20-23, *306*
9:21, *136*
9:22, *136, 137, 153,*
    309, 336, 379, 449
9:23, *137, 153, 208,*
    309, 450
9:24, *133, 420*
9:25, *133*

9:27, *214*
10, *35*
10:4, *185*
10:7-8, *243*
10:16, *194*
10:16-17, *413*
10:21, *187*
10:23, *242*
10:23-33, *243*
10:25-26, *238*
10:32, *216*
11, *240, 316*
11:1, *243*
11:3, *185*
11:4, *106, 240, 316*
11:17-34, *195*
11:21-22, *106*
11:23-25, *398*
11:26, *214*
12, *384*
12:2, *219*
12:3, *420*
12:4-5, *384*
12:12, *185*
12:12-13, *408*
12:12-17, *235*
12:12-26, *426*
12:13, *216, 308, 317*
12:28, *384*
12:28-29, *244, 419*
12:29-30, *384*
14, *377*
14:3-5, *235, 422*
14:6, *419*
14:12, *235, 422*
14:17, *235, 422*
14:23-24, *238, 244,*
    386
14:23-25, *304*
14:26, *235, 422*
15, *46*
15:1, *210*
15:1-2, *152*
15:1-5, *33*
15:1-11, *396*
15:1-58, *193, 367*
15:2, *151, 210*
15:3, *129, 188*
15:3-4, *156*
15:3-5, *185, 398, 420*
15:5-8, *352*
15:5-11, *46*

15:8, *45*
15:8-11, *46*
15:11, *152, 214*
15:12, *185, 214*
15:12-17, *185*
15:20, *185*
15:23, *185*
15:32, *111*
15:50, *127*
15:58, *250, 413*
16:1, *286*
16:1-4, *112, 280, 408*
16:5, *57, 286*
16:7, *278*
16:8, *111*
16:8-9, *110, 279*
16:10, *110*
16:10-11, *250, 253*
16:12, *249, 251*
16:15, *105, 254, 286,*
    304
16:16, *254*
16:17, *110, 255, 315*
16:19, *110, 250, 279,*
    286, 316

2 Corinthians
1:1, *233, 249, 286*
1:3-11, *420*
1:7, *413*
1:8, *286*
1:11, *371*
1:15-16, *57*
1:16, *286*
1:19, *128, 185, 214,*
    250
2, *138*
2:1, *197*
2:4, *252*
2:12, *112, 197, 214,*
    335
2:13, *112, 197, 198,*
    249, 252, 286
2:14, *138, 139*
2:14-16, *137, 152, 369*
2:17, *355*
3:1, *152, 390, 418*
3:1-3, *355*
3:5-6, *390*
3:6, *249*
3:12, *372*
3:16, *226*

4:4, *214*
4:5, *185, 214*
4:5-6, *183*
4:7, *152*
4:7-15, *152*
4:8, *445*
4:10-12, *445*
5:6-8, *129*
5:12, *152*
5:14—6:2, *398*
5:16, *185*
5:18-21, *357, 358, 403*
5:18—6:2, *386*
5:20, *152, 306*
5:21, *129*
6:4, *249, 418*
6:5, *250, 355*
6:16, *413*
6:16-18, *235*
7:5, *286*
7:6-7, *198, 252, 254*
7:9, *227*
7:10, *227*
7:13-14, *252*
7:13-15, *198*
7:15, *254*
8—9, *280*
8:1, *286*
8:1-15, *56, 408, 443*
8:4, *413*
8:6, *198, 252*
8:10, *252*
8:16, *252*
8:16-17, *198, 252*
8:18, *252*
8:22, *252*
8:23, *198, 245, 249,*
    252, 255, 413
9:1-5, *56, 408, 443*
9:2, *286*
9:4, *286*
9:13, *214*
10:1, *348*
10:7, *185*
10:7—11:33, *355*
10:10-11, *348*
10:12, *418*
10:14, *214*
10:15, *250*
10:16, *210*
10:18, *418*
11:4, *214, 356*

11:6, *348*
11:7, *210*
11:9, *274, 286*
11:22, *215, 413*
11:22-23, *41*
11:23, *250*
11:23-33, *111*
11:24, *216, 293*
11:24-25, *44*
11:25, *306*
11:26, *306*
11:27, *250*
11:28, *196*
11:31, *420*
11:32, *40, 59, 222, 259, 288*
11:32-33, *60, 257*
12:2, *261*
12:7, *368*
12:10, *306*
12:17-18, *252*
12:18, *198, 252*
12:21, *227*
13:3, *152*
13:5, *185*
13:13, *413*
13:14, *306*

Galatians
1, *46, 65, 124, 259*
1—4, *419*
1:1, *27, 124, 125, 202*
1:1-5, *398*
1:2, *286*
1:3-4, *156*
1:4, *129, 188*
1:5, *420*
1:6-9, *33, 125, 202*
1:6-10, *399*
1:7, *214*
1:8, *210*
1:9, *210*
1:9-10, *378*
1:10, *355*
1:11, *210*
1:11—2:10, *125, 202*
1:14, *41*
1:15-16, *27, 28, 40, 124, 383, 392*
1:15-17, *60, 61, 257, 259*
1:15-24, *58*

1:16, *47, 63, 210, 213*
1:16-17, *40*
1:17, *59, 60, 222, 259, 392*
1:18, *65, 259, 267*
1:18-19, *47, 65*
1:21, *260, 286*
1:21-24, *40, 66, 69*
1:22-23, *44*
1:23, *210, 213*
2, *50*
2:1-10, *48, 49*
2:2, *48, 50, 214*
2:3, *252*
2:5, *125, 202, 207*
2:6, *50*
2:7, *50, 125, 216, 225*
2:7-9, *48, 51*
2:8, *28, 50, 216*
2:9, *50, 126, 216*
2:10, *56, 408, 443*
2:11-14, *49, 51, 406*
2:12, *51, 216, 219*
2:13, *216*
2:14, *51, 125, 200, 202, 207, 216, 219*
2:15, *216, 219*
2:15-21, *407*
2:15—3:18, *125, 202*
2:16, *125, 156, 202, 228*
2:18, *407*
2:19, *185*
2:19-21, *398*
2:20, *128, 129, 185, 188*
2:21, *185*
3—4, *333*
3:1, *125, 129, 156, 185, 398*
3:1-2, *208*
3:2, *240*
3:6-9, *332*
3:8, *202, 219*
3:8-9, *202*
3:10-14, *398*
3:13, *156, 185*
3:13-14, *332*
3:14, *240*
3:19—4:7, *125, 202*
3:25, *202*
3:25-29, *334*

3:27-29, *413*
3:28, *141, 216, 307, 317, 451*
3:29, *185*
4:1-7, *235*
4:4, *202*
4:4-5, *26*
4:5-6, *202*
4:6, *235*
4:8-20, *126, 202*
4:9, *226*
4:10, *239*
4:13, *210, 264, 368*
4:14, *185, 335*
4:19, *185*
4:21-31, *202*
5—6, *419*
5:1—6:16, *126, 203*
5:2-3, *239*
5:11, *214*
5:19-24, *230*
5:22-26, *444*
5:24, *185*
6:6, *419, 420*
6:12-13, *239*
6:14, *129*
6:15, *413*
6:16, *413*

Ephesians
1:3-14, *156, 420*
1:9-10, *148*
1:13, *147, 214*
1:15-16, *373*
1:15-23, *373*
1:22-23, *234*
2, *185*
2:1, *450*
2:1-10, *156*
2:4-6, *234*
2:11, *219*
2:11-13, *147*
2:11-22, *408, 409, 426*
2:13, *147, 214*
2:14-15, *147*
2:14-16, *420*
2:15, *147*
2:17, *210*
2:18, *147*
2:19-20, *147*
2:20-22, *235*
3, *146*

3:1, *219*
3:1-13, *145, 153*
3:2, *146*
3:3, *146*
3:3-4, *147*
3:3-6, *146*
3:4, *185*
3:7, *146*
3:8, *146, 210, 214*
3:9, *147*
3:14-21, *373*
3:17, *185*
3:21, *420*
4:1-6, *412*
4:7, *235*
4:11, *235, 245, 249, 419, 422, 423*
4:11-16, *235, 422*
4:12, *185, 236, 245*
4:12-13, *422*
4:13, *128, 236*
4:15, *185*
5:2, *185*
5:5, *127*
5:8, *156*
5:14, *420*
5:18-20, *236*
5:19-20, *422*
5:22-33, *235*
5:22—6:9, *413*
6:5-8, *317*
6:10-17, *372*
6:10-18, *457*
6:10-20, *148, 246*
6:15, *149, 214, 246*
6:17, *149, 246*
6:19-20, *372*
6:21, *249, 251*

Philippians
1, *45*
1:1, *249, 254*
1:3-8, *373*
1:5, *96, 245, 386, 413*
1:9-10, *458*
1:9-11, *373*
1:12, *245, 386*
1:13, *115, 313*
1:14, *245*
1:14-18, *244*
1:15, *185, 214*
1:17, *185, 214*

1:18, *185, 214*
1:19, *245, 386*
1:20, *372*
2:1, *413*
2:1-5, *411*
2:1-11, *348*
2:2, *426*
2:5, *426*
2:5-8, *444*
2:5-11, *129*
2:6-11, *398, 420*
2:14-16, *200*
2:16, *398*
2:19-24, *198*
2:22, *413*
2:25, *245, 249, 255*
2:25-30, *96*
2:26-27, *368*
2:29, *254*
2:30, *245, 255*
3:3-4, *204*
3:3-17, *45*
3:5, *41, 216*
3:5-6, *41*
3:14, *205*
3:15, *205, 426*
3:17-21, *204*
4:1, *413*
4:2-3, *249, 251, 254, 316*
4:3, *251, 315*
4:10-20, *96*
4:14, *274*
4:15, *286*
4:15-16, *245, 386*
4:20, *420*
4:22, *115, 314*

Colossians
1, *144*
1:1, *249*
1:3-6, *373*
1:3-8, *110*
1:4, *144*
1:6, *373*
1:7, *223, 249, 255, 284*
1:7-8, *254*
1:9-10, *373*
1:9-12, *381*
1:9-14, *239, 373*
1:12-14, *234*

1:13-14, *156*
1:15-20, *420*
1:18, *234*
1:20, *398*
1:21-22, *156*
1:23, *143, 144, 152, 214*
1:24, *143, 152*
1:24-29, *143*
1:24—2:5, *373*
1:25, *144, 152*
1:25-29, *33*
1:27, *185, 214, 240*
1:28, *144, 152, 214*
1:29, *144, 152*
2, *333*
2:1, *254*
2:2-3, *205*
2:3, *240*
2:5-7, *205*
2:8, *379*
2:8-15, *205*
2:13-14, *398*
2:16, *239*
2:16-18, *205*
2:16-23, *240*
2:17, *205*
2:19, *205*
2:20-23, *205*
3:1, *185*
3:1-4, *205*
3:3, *185*
3:5, *206*
3:8, *206*
3:10-11, *206*
3:11, *216, 307, 308, 317, 337*
3:12-17, *206*
3:16, *236, 254, 422*
3:18—4:1, *206, 413*
3:22, *317*
4:2-4, *206*
4:3, *185*
4:3-4, *372*
4:6, *206*
4:7, *110, 249*
4:7-9, *198*
4:9, *249, 317*
4:10, *249*
4:10-11, *249*
4:11, *127, 216*
4:12, *249, 254, 285*

4:12-13, *255, 285*
4:13, *110, 284*
4:14, *316*
4:16, *254*

1 Thessalonians
1:1, *233, 250, 395*
1:3, *250*
1:4, *413*
1:4-10, *127*
1:4—3:10, *355*
1:5, *227*
1:5-6, *129, 231, 357, 358*
1:7, *286*
1:8, *129, 244, 286*
1:9, *97, 127, 129, 173, 226, 335, 395, 398*
1:9-10, *33, 127, 156, 168, 201, 357, 367*
1:10, *395, 396*
2:1-12, *256*
2:2, *214, 372*
2:3-8, *36, 130, 355*
2:4, *355*
2:5, *355*
2:6, *355*
2:7, *249*
2:8, *214*
2:9, *214, 250*
2:9-12, *396*
2:11, *413*
2:11-12, *201*
2:12, *127*
2:13, *129, 357, 358, 403*
2:14, *216*
2:14-16, *395*
2:15-16, *395*
2:17-18, *197*
3:1-5, *251, 274, 358*
3:1-6, *250*
3:1-8, *198*
3:2, *214, 249, 395*
3:5, *97, 250*
3:6, *210, 214, 251*
3:11-13, *373*
3:12, *244*
4:1-8, *396*
4:3-8, *395*
4:4, *383*
4:6, *413*

4:8, *357*
4:9, *251*
4:10, *286*
4:13, *251*
4:13-17, *396*
4:13-18, *153*
4:14, *396*
4:14-17, *396*
4:15—5:10, *395*
5:1, *251*
5:9, *395*
5:9-10, *188, 201, 396*
5:10, *398*
5:11, *235, 422*
5:12-13, *254*
5:16-24, *357*
5:25, *371*
5:26-27, *233*

2 Thessalonians
1:1, *250*
1:8, *214*
1:11, *357*
2:13, *357*
2:15, *420*
3:1, *372*
3:6, *420*
3:6-11, *254*
3:8, *250*

1 Timothy
1:3, *250, 286*
1:4, *149*
1:5, *149*
1:11, *173*
1:11-16, *150*
1:11-17, *150*
1:15-17, *207*
1:17, *420*
2:1-4, *150*
2:1-6, *247*
2:4-6, *206*
2:7, *206, 214*
2:8-15, *150, 413*
2:11-15, *206*
2:15, *206*
3, *389*
3:1-13, *207*
3:2, *388, 419*
3:2-7, *389*
3:7, *247*
3:15, *235*
3:16, *206, 214, 420*

4:3, *206*
4:9-10, *247*
4:10, *206*
4:11, *421*
4:13-16, *198*
5:6, *207*
5:11, *207*
5:17, *250, 420*
5:17-18, *420*
5:23, *206, 368*
6:1-2, *413*
6:2, *421*
6:3-5, *206*
6:5-10, *207*
6:13, *398*
6:16, *420*

2 Timothy
1:6-8, *390*
1:11, *214*
1:13-14, *207, 390*
1:16-17, *116*
2:2, *207, 227, 390*
2:3, *249*
2:6, *249*

2:8-13, *207*
2:14-16, *206*
2:18, *206*
2:22, *207*
2:23, *206*
2:24, *249*
3:1-5, *207*
3:10, *207*
3:13, *206*
3:14-17, *207*
3:16, *420*
4, *150, 247*
4:3-4, *207*
4:4, *206*
4:5, *150, 247, 249*
4:8, *133*
4:10, *224, 250, 253, 286*
4:11, *116*
4:12, *251*
4:16, *116*
4:17, *314*
4:18, *420*
4:20, *315, 368*

Titus
1, *389*
1:4-5, *253*
1:5, *121, 250, 281*
1:5-9, *207*
1:6-7, *207*
1:7, *249*
1:9, *390*
1:10, *206, 216*
1:11, *207*
1:14, *206*
1:15, *206*
1:16, *207*
2:1, *207, 421*
2:1-10, *413*
2:3, *421*
2:3-5, *150, 247*
2:9-10, *150, 248*
2:11, *206*
3:3-8, *207*
3:9, *206*
3:12, *251*
3:13, *251*

Philemon
1, *249*
1-2, *110*
1:24, *249*
2, *249, 251*
10, *317*
13, *255*
17, *249, 413*
23, *110, 249*

Hebrews
6:3, *278*

James
4:15, *278*

1 Peter
1:1, *334, 447*
2:11, *334, 447*
4:16, *73*
5:12, *250*

Revelation
2—3, *446*
2:1-7, *422*
3:14-20, *418*
3:14-22, *422*